Oil Paintings in Public Ownership in South Yorkshire

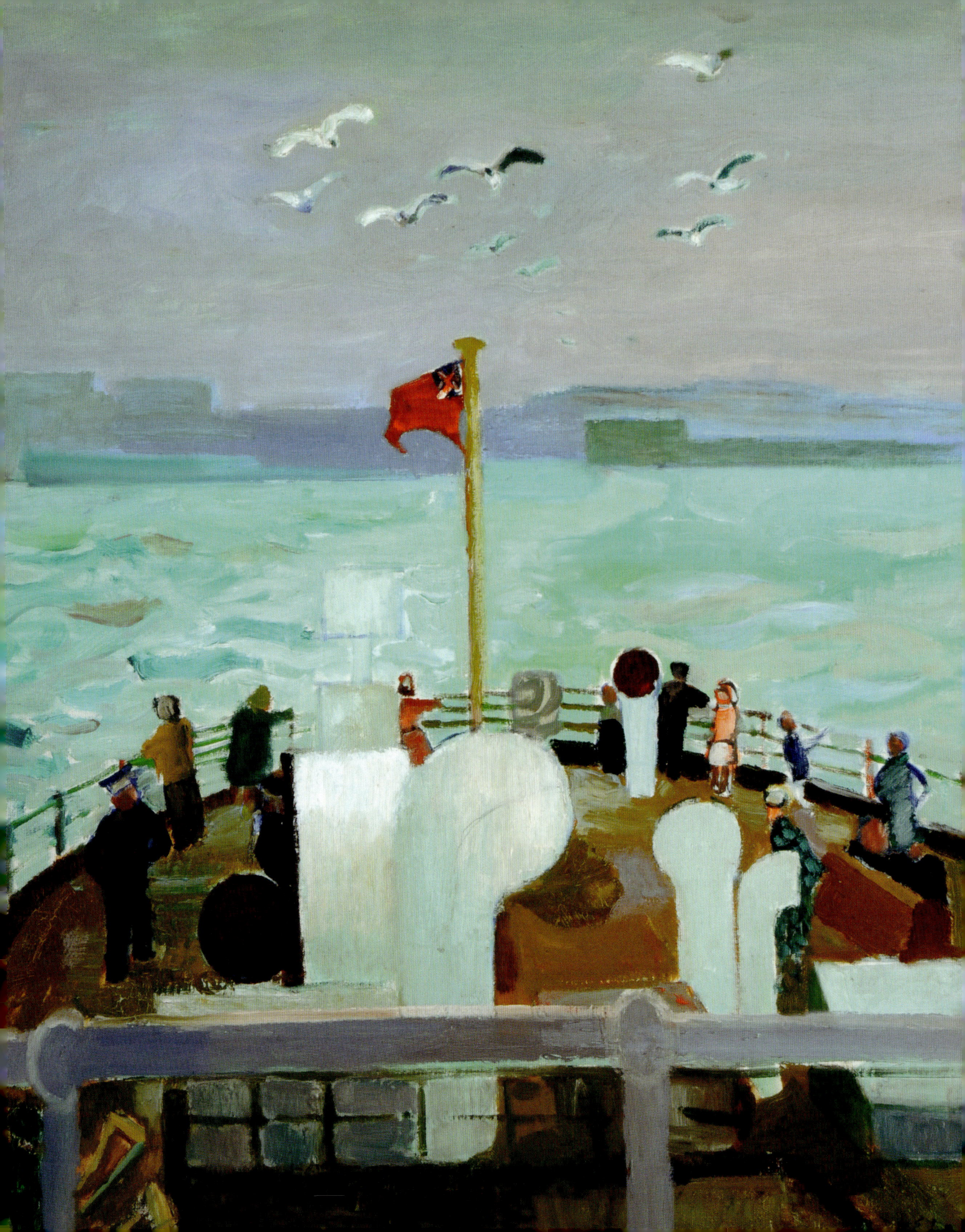

The *Oil Paintings in Public Ownership* series of catalogues is an extraordinary work in progress. Published by The Public Catalogue Foundation, it is the result of the determined efforts of a small team of administrative staff, researchers and photographers spread across the United Kingdom.

Our national collection of oil paintings in public ownership is probably one of the finest anywhere in the world. It is held not just by our museums and galleries but is also to be found in hospitals, universities and other civic buildings throughout the United Kingdom. A large proportion of these paintings are not on display and many have never before been reproduced.

This series of books for the first time allows the public to see an entire photographic record of these works – a collection likely to number some 200,000 in total. In doing so, these volumes provide a unique insight into our nation's artistic and cultural history.

As Patron of The Public Catalogue Foundation, my visits to collections across the country have highlighted to me not only the desire of curators to publicise their paintings, but also the limited resources at their disposal. The Foundation's work goes a long way towards helping to create access to these collections, while at the same time giving the British public the opportunity to see and enjoy *all* the paintings that they own.

I wish The Public Catalogue Foundation every success in its continuing endeavours.

Camilla

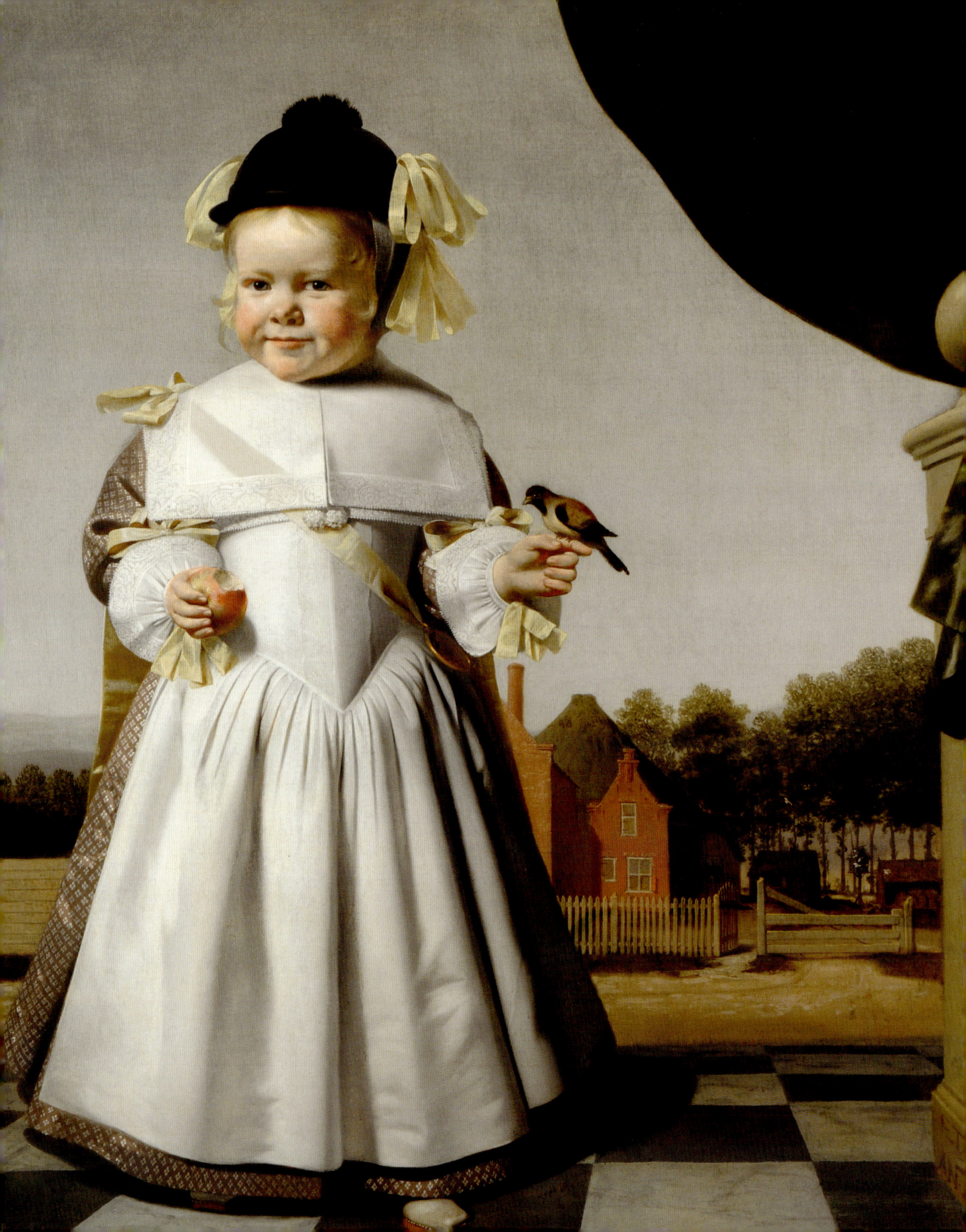

Oil Paintings in Public Ownership in South Yorkshire

Coordinators: Dr Camilla Stewart & Hazel Buchan-Cameron
Photographer: Norman Taylor

The Public Catalogue Foundation
Patron
HRH The Duchess of Cornwall

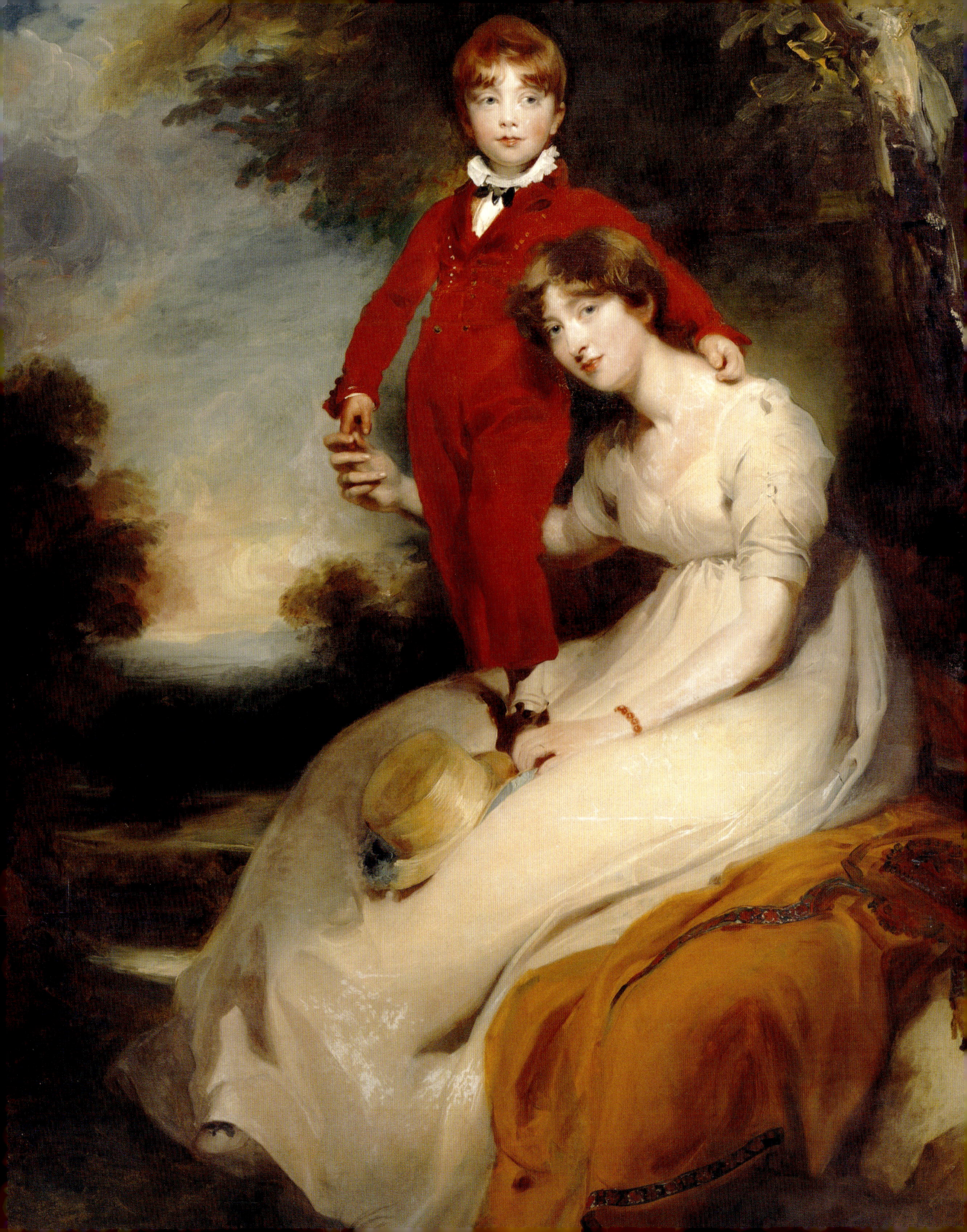

Contents

Facing page: Lawrence, Thomas, 1769–1830, *Mrs Charles Thellusso, née Sabine Robarts (1775–1814), and Her Son, Charles Thellusson (1797–1856)* (detail), c.1804, English Heritage, Brodsworth Hall, (p. 38)

Image opposite HRH The Duchess of Cornwall's statement: La Dell, Edwin, 1914–1970, *Leaving Boulogne, France* (detail), c.1960, Rotherham Museum & Art Gallery, (p. 129)
Image opposite title page: Everdingen, Cesar Boetius van, c.1606–1678, *Boy Holding an Apple* (detail), 1664, Barnsley Museum and Heritage Service, (p. 51)

[i] Barnsley Central Library, The Cooper Gallery and Barnsley Museum and Heritage Service are administered by Barnsley Metropolitan Borough Council

[ii] Doncaster Mansion House and Doncaster Museum Service are administered by Doncaster Metropolitan Borough Council

[iii] Rawmarsh Community Library, Rotherham Museum & Art Gallery, Rotherham Town Hall and Swinton Community Library are under the ownership of Rotherham Metropolitan Borough Council

Foreword

This is something of a valedictory – not to the Foundation (or to myself) but to the Foreword.

We are, God willing, nearing the end of the project. By the end of this year, the photography and related data will have been collected and within a few months of that, the last catalogue should have been sent off to the printers. We will have published some 40 catalogues over the 18 months period. At which point, if we follow our original concept, the Foundation will wind down to a small group of Trustees responsible for selling the catalogues and donating the proceeds to galleries to restore and rehang paintings. Our work will have been done.

In the beginning, the Foreword in each catalogue tended to record the journey the Foundation had taken to create it. Each county in its turn became the target of an awareness campaign and a fundraising effort, often led by a Lord Lieutenant. When a catalogue appeared, a launch, often at some wonderful venue lent for the occasion by a supporter (Highgrove, Chatsworth, Newby – to name a few highlights) celebrated its birth and thanked all those who had helped make it possible. All this was necessary because the Foundation was new and unknown, its programme viewed widely as unattainable, and the collections it covered viewed too often as being of little or no interest, merit or value.

All that has changed. Whilst not a household name, the Foundation is now a known-entity and the value of its work is recognised. More importantly, and driven largely by the Your Paintings programme, data collection (and publishing it all on the Your Paintings website) has had to be greatly accelerated and its funding, therefore, has been sought centrally from the larger funding trusts, rather than from individuals in the relevant counties. Now, only the county volumes hark back to our original, artisanal approach but with much less money to be raised our labours generate little local interest.

We are more efficient. The price for it has been a loss of a sense of community; of local communities coming to recognise that their galleries lay at their heart and so rallying in their support. It is a high price. We need to think about that.

Meantime, I do not think that 40 forewords from me over the next 18 months will achieve much in that (or any) direction. So they will appear from now on a less regular basis.

Fred Hohler, Founder

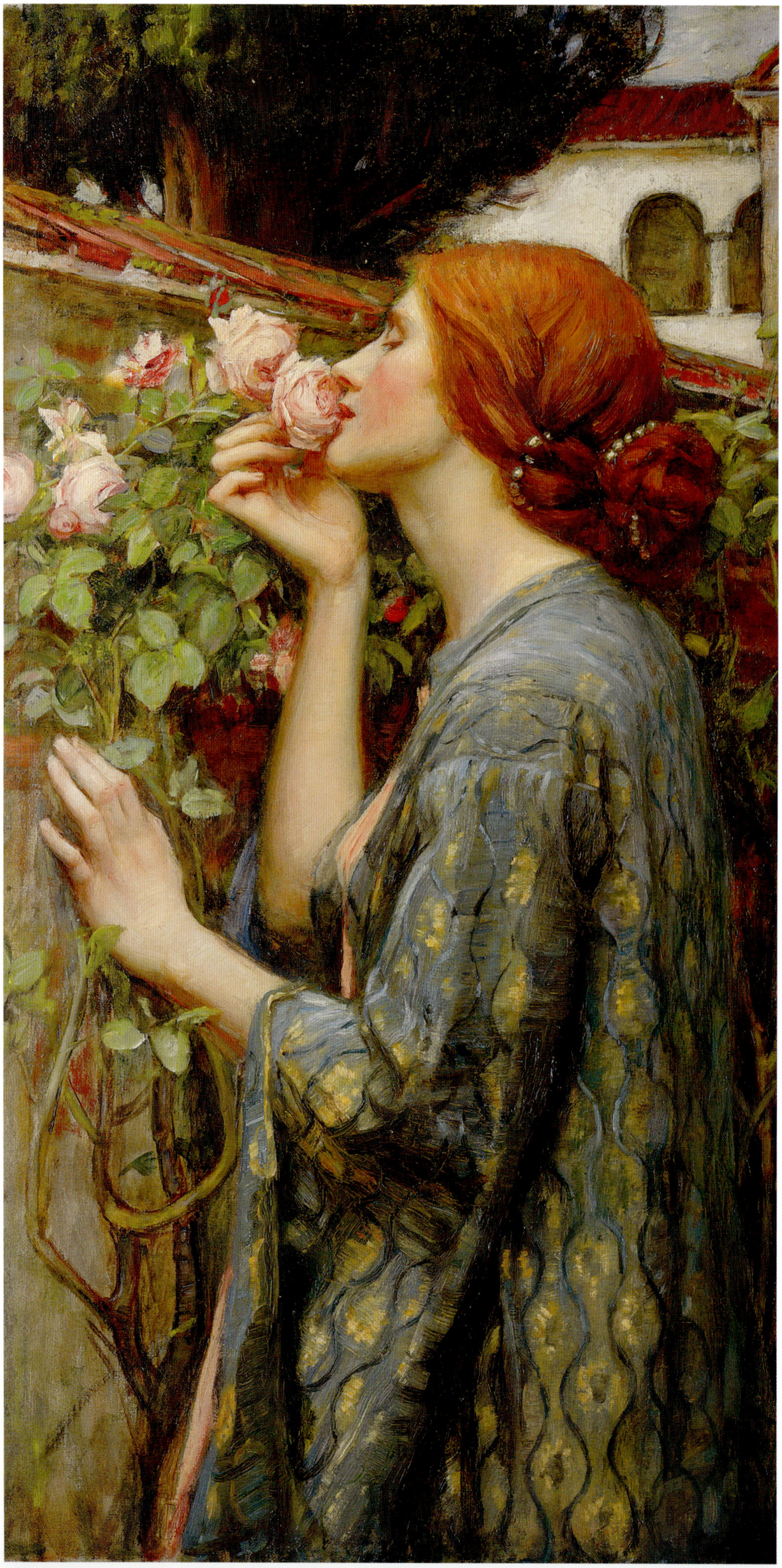

The Public Catalogue Foundation: People Involved

Trustees & Advisors

Staff

Catalogue Scope and Organisation

Medium and Support

The principal focus of this series is oil paintings. However, tempera and acrylic are also included as well as mixed media, where oil is the predominant constituent. Paintings on all forms of support (e.g. canvas, panel, etc.) are included as long as the support is portable. The principal exclusions are miniatures, hatchments or other purely heraldic paintings and wall paintings *in situ*.

Public Ownership

Public ownership has been taken to mean any paintings that are directly owned by the public purse, made accessible to the public by means of public subsidy or generally perceived to be in public ownership. The term 'public' refers to both central government and local government. Paintings held by national museums, local authority museums, English Heritage and independent museums, where there is at least some form of public subsidy, are included. Paintings held in civic buildings such as local government offices, town halls, guildhalls, public libraries, universities, hospitals, crematoria, fire stations and police stations are also included.

Geographical Boundaries of Catalogues

The geographical boundary of each county is the 'ceremonial county' boundary. This county definition includes all unitary authorities. Counties that have a particularly large number of paintings are divided between two or more catalogues on a geographical basis.

Criteria for Inclusion

As long as paintings meet the requirements above, all paintings are included irrespective of their condition and perceived quality. However, painting reproductions can only be included with the agreement of the participating collections and, where appropriate, the relevant copyright owner. It is rare that a collection forbids the inclusion of its paintings. Where this is the case and it is possible to obtain a list of paintings, this list is given in the Paintings Without Reproductions section. Where copyright consent is refused, the paintings are also listed in the Paintings Without Reproductions section. All paintings in collections' stacks and stores are included, as well as those on display. Paintings which have been lent to other institutions, whether for short-term exhibition or long-term loan, are listed under the owner collection. In addition, paintings on long-term loan are also included under the borrowing institution when they are likely to remain there for at least another five years from the date of publication of this catalogue. Information relating to owners and borrowers is listed in the Further Information section.

Layout

Collections are grouped together under their home town. These locations are listed in alphabetical order. In some cases collections that are spread over a number of locations are included under a single owner collection. A number of collections, principally the larger ones, are preceded by curatorial forewords. Within each collection paintings are listed in order of artist surname. Where there is more than one painting by the same artist, the paintings are listed chronologically, according to their execution date.

The few paintings that are not accompanied by photographs are listed in the Paintings Without Reproductions section.

There is additional reference material in the Further Information section at the back of the catalogue. This gives the full names of artists, titles and media if it has not been possible to include these in full in the main section. It also provides acquisition credit lines and information about loans in and out, as well as copyright and photographic credits for each painting. Finally, there is an index of artists' surnames.

Key to Painting Information

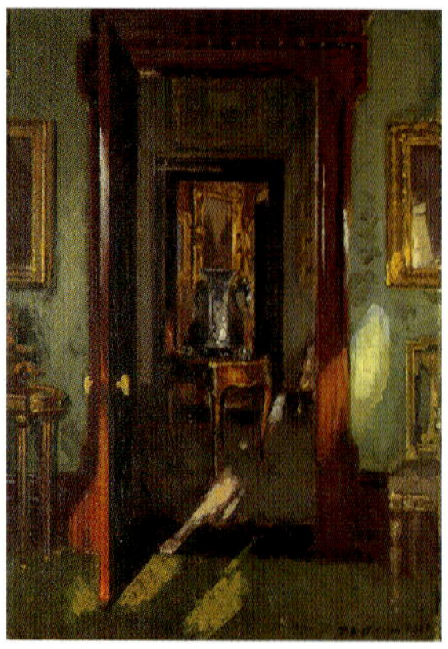

Almost all paintings are reproduced in the catalogue. Where this is not the case they are listed in the Paintings Without Reproductions section. Where paintings are missing or have been stolen, the best possible photograph on record has been reproduced. In some cases this may be black and white. Paintings that have been stolen are highlighted with a red border. Some paintings are shown with conservation tissue attached to parts of the painting surface.

Adam, Patrick William 1854–1929
Interior, Rutland Lodge: Vista through Open Doors 1920
oil on canvas 67.3 × 45.7
LEEAG.PA.1925.0671.LACF

Artist name This is shown with the surname first. Where the artist is listed on the Getty Union List of Artist Names (ULAN), ULAN's preferred presentation of the name is given. In a number of cases the name may not be a firm attribution and this is made clear. Where the artist name is not known, a school may be given instead. Where the school is not known, the painter name is listed as *unknown artist*. If the artist name is too long for the space, as much of the name is given as possible followed by (...). This indicates the full name is given at the rear of the catalogue in the Further Information section.

Painting title A painting title followed by *(?)* indicates that the title is in doubt. Where the alternative title to the painting is considered to be better known than the original, the alternative title is given in parentheses. Where the collection has not given a painting a title, the publisher does so instead and marks this with an asterisk. If the title is too long for the space, as much of the title is given as possible followed by *(...)* and the full title is given in the Further Information section.

Execution date In some cases the precise year of execution may not be known for certain. Instead an approximate date will be given or no date at all.

Artist dates Where known, the years of birth and death of the artist are given. In some cases one or both dates may not be known with certainty, and this is marked. No date indicates that even an approximate date is not known. Where only the period in which the artist was active is known, these dates are given and preceded with the word *active*.

Medium and support Where the precise material used in the support is known, this is given.

Dimensions All measurements refer to the unframed painting and are given in cm with up to one decimal point. In all cases the height is shown before the width. An (E) indicates where a painting has not been measured and its size has been calculated by sight only. If the painting is circular, the single dimension is the diameter. If the painting is oval, the dimensions are height and width.

Collection inventory number In the case of paintings owned by museums, this number will always be the accession number. In all other cases it will be a unique inventory number of the owner institution. (P) indicates that a painting is a private loan. Details can be found in the Further Information section. Accession numbers preceded by 'PCF' indicate that the collection did not have an accession number at the time of catalogue production and therefore the number given has been temporarily allocated by The Public Catalogue Foundation. The symbol indicates that the reproduction is based on a Bridgeman Art Library transparency (go to www.bridgemanart.com) or that Bridgeman administers the copyright for that artist.

Facing page: Brangwyn, Frank, 1867–1956, *Old Man at Assisi* (detail), Doncaster Museum Service, (p. 78)

THE PAINTINGS

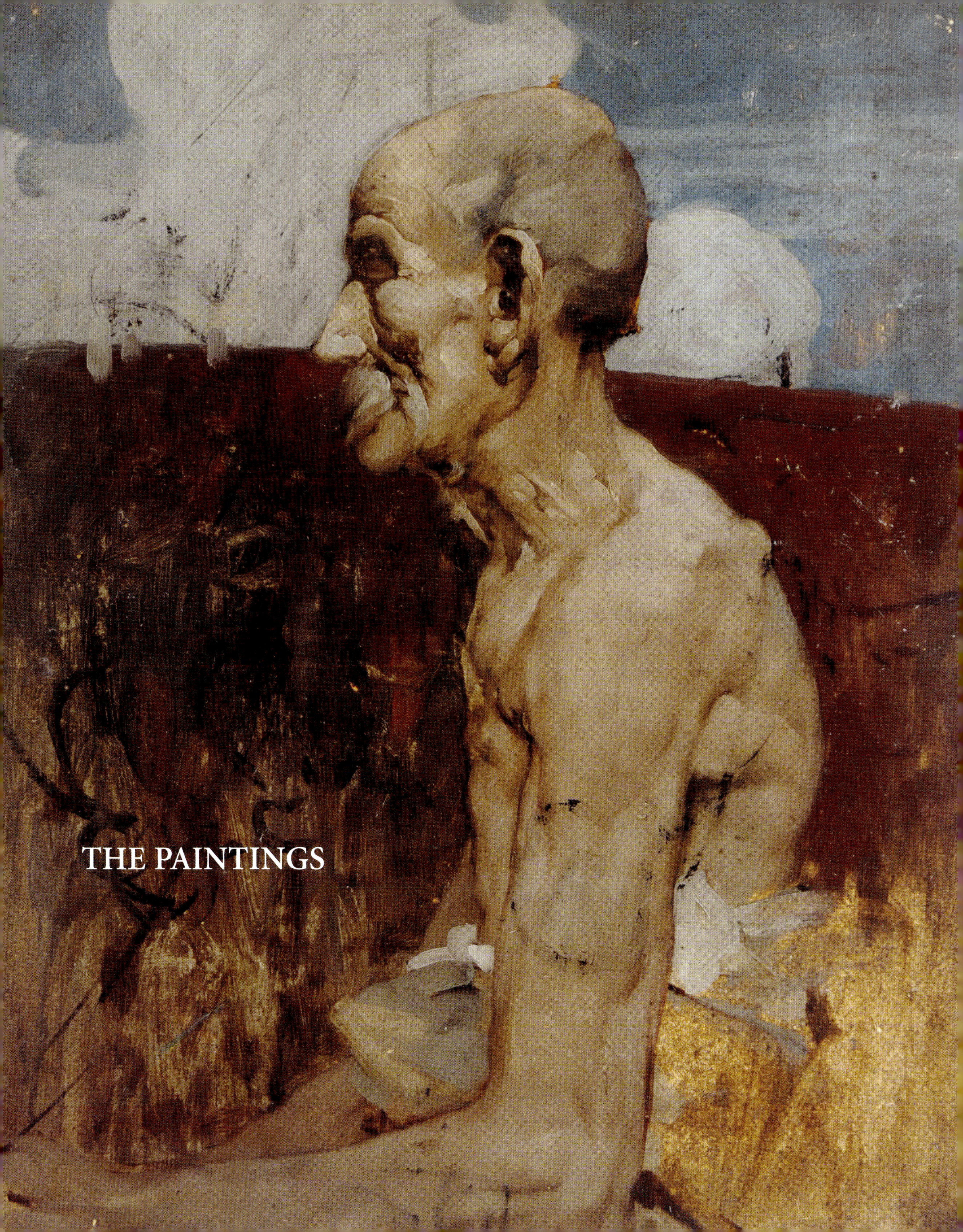

Barnsley Central Library

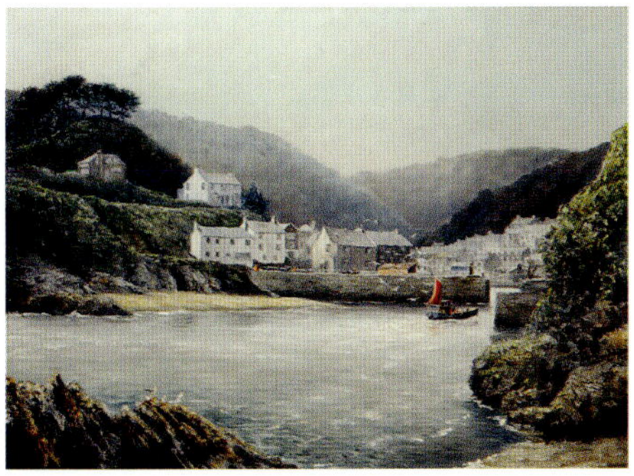

Burden, Samuel b.1932
Fishermen's Cottages, Polperro, Cornwall
oil on board 47 x 61
27

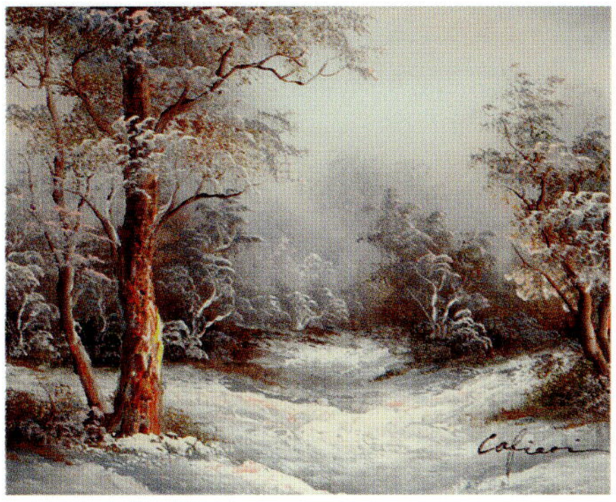

Cafieri, Irene
Winter Woodland
oil on board 20 x 25.5
611

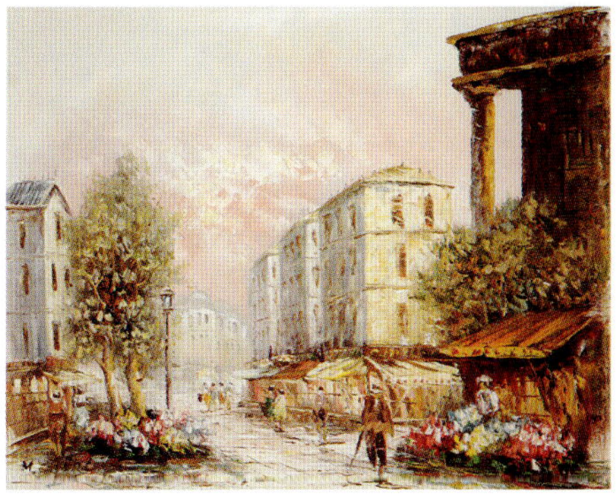

Church, M.
Parisian Street Scene
oil on canvas 45.5 x 56
567

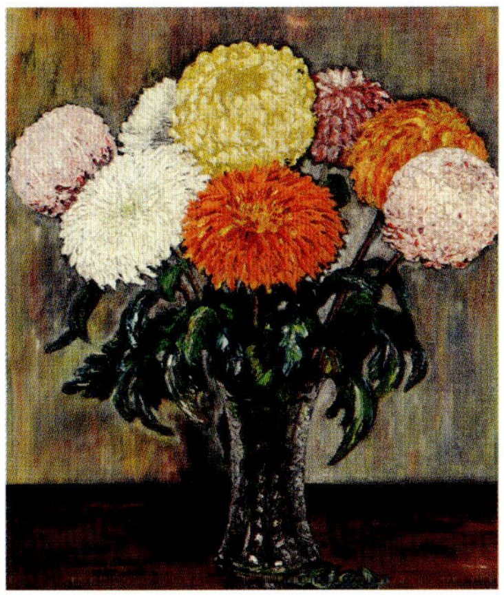

Slack, Muriel
Still Life 1967
acrylic on board 58 x 50
481

Barnsley College

Barnsley College is a large tertiary college, formed in September 1990 from a merger between three local colleges (the College of Technology, the College of Art and Design and the Sixth Form College) plus the sixth forms from the schools in the Barnsley area.

Barnsley College is the major provider of Further Education in the Barnsley Borough with approximately 3,500 full-time and 2,800 part-time students studying on both vocational and academic programmes.

With a wide range of courses from basic education to high-level professional qualifications, Barnsley College offers students the opportunity to train for a career, improve job prospects, qualify for university or simply learn a new skill.

The College has an excellent range of facilities, learning resource centres and student support services with dedicated teaching staff who are committed to helping students achieve their aims.

Rachael Ward, Marketing Team Leader

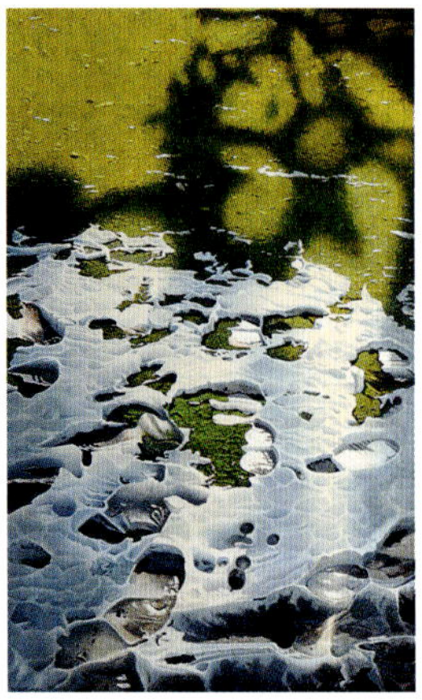

Evans, Peter
Footprints at Bretton Hall, West Yorkshire 1998
acrylic on board 100 x 60
9654

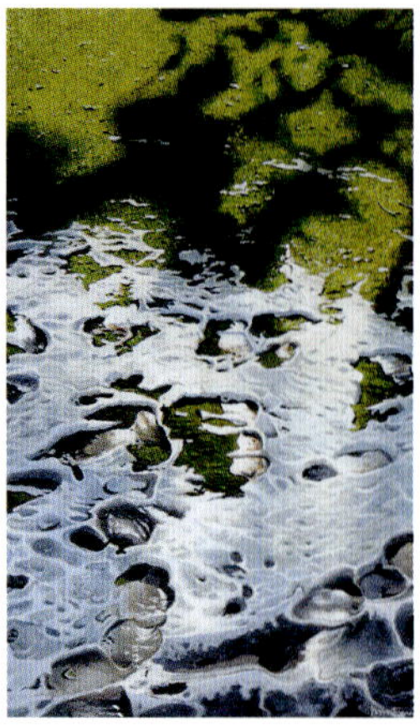

Evans, Peter
Footprints at Bretton Hall, West Yorkshire 1998
acrylic on board 37 x 22
9655

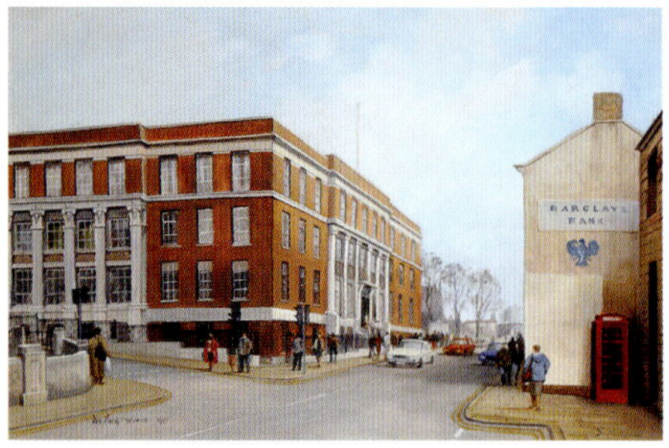

Mickelthwaite, Don b.1936
Church Street Site, Barnsley, South Yorkshire 1997
oil on canvas 50 x 75
9454

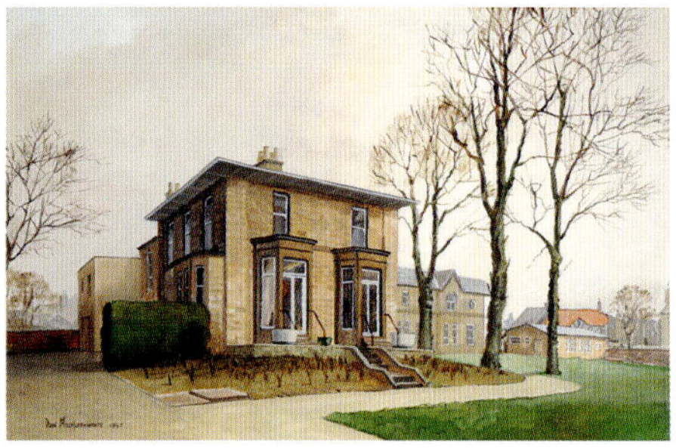

Mickelthwaite, Don b.1936
Fairfield House, Barnsley, South Yorkshire 1997
oil on canvas 50 x 75
9453

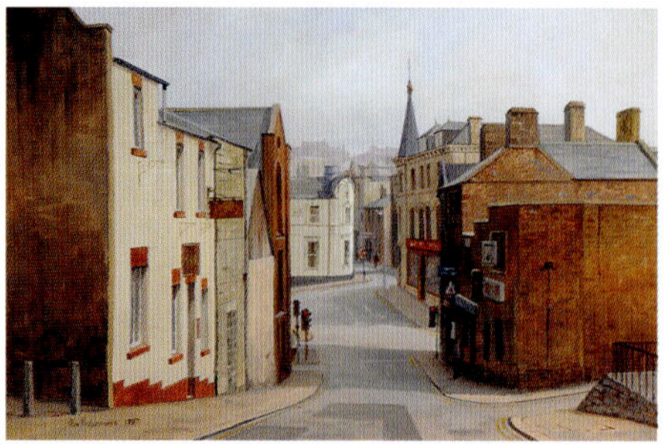

Mickelthwaite, Don b.1936
Graham's Orchard, Barnsley, South Yorkshire 1997
oil on canvas 50 x 75
9459

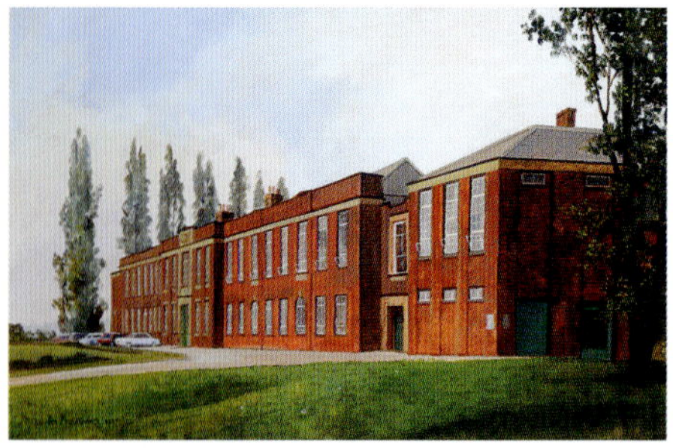

Mickelthwaite, Don b.1936
Honeywell Site, Barnsley, South Yorkshire 1997
oil on canvas 50 x 75
9452

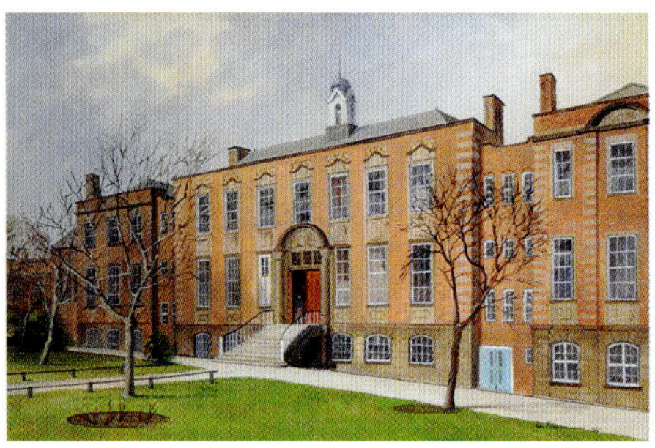

Mickelthwaite, Don b.1936
Huddersfield Road Site, Barnsley, South Yorkshire 1997
oil on canvas 50 x 75
9450

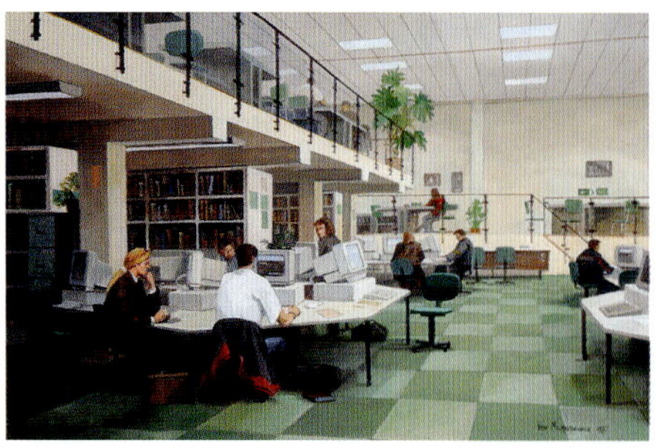

Mickelthwaite, Don b.1936
Old Mill Lane Learning Centre, Barnsley, South Yorkshire 1997
oil on canvas 50 x 75
9451

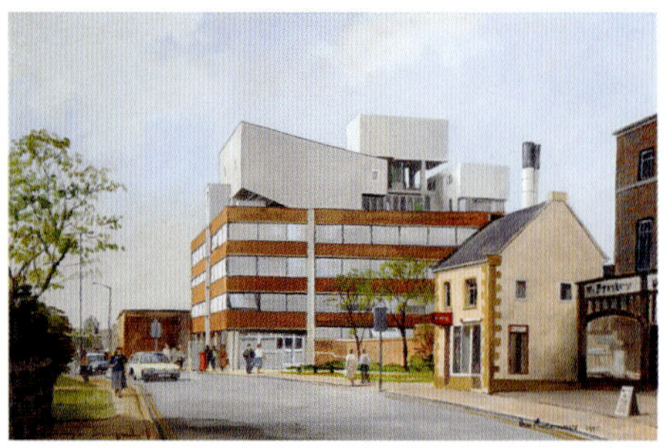

Mickelthwaite, Don b.1936
Old Mill Lane Site, Barnsley, South Yorkshire 1997
oil on canvas 50 x 75
9455

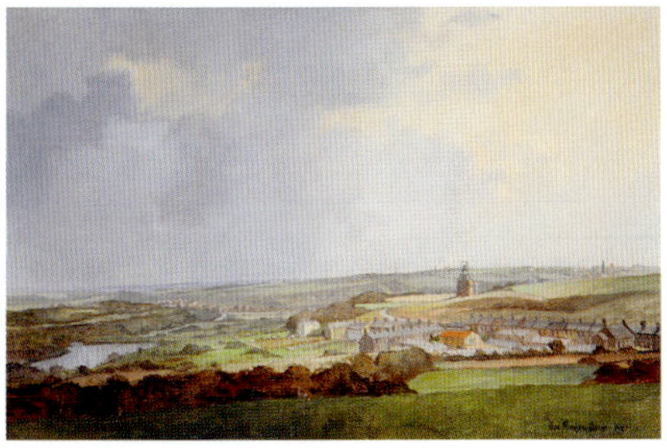

Mickelthwaite, Don b.1936
South East Barnsley Landscape, South Yorkshire 1997
oil on canvas 50 x 75
9458

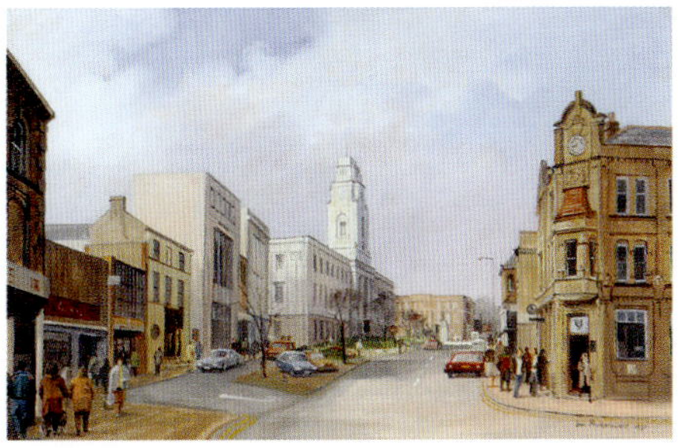

Mickelthwaite, Don b.1936
Town Hall, Barnsley, South Yorkshire 1997
oil on canvas 50 x 75
9456

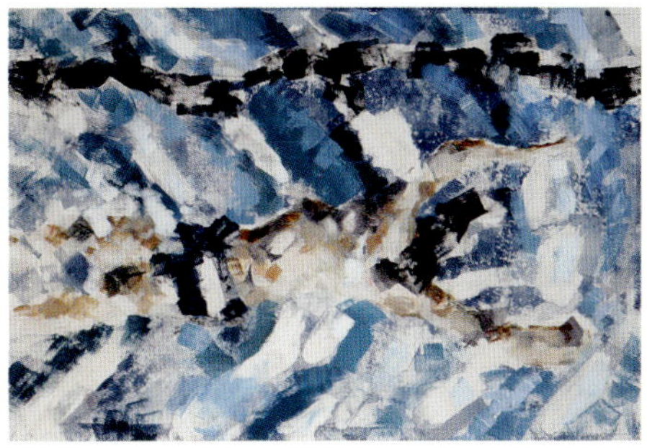

unknown artist
Swimmer c.2005
acrylic on board 38 x 58
PCF1

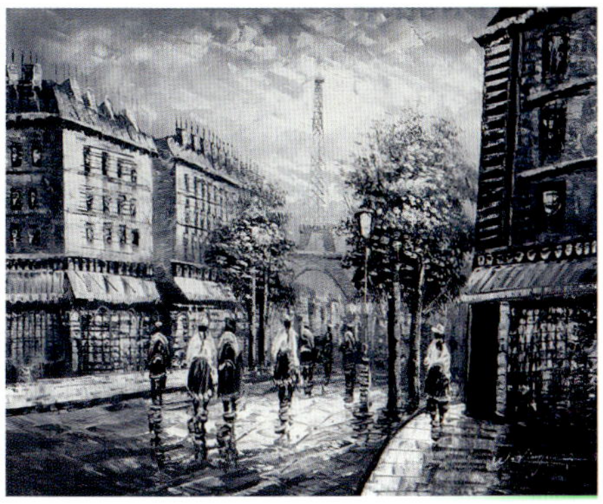

Virginio, W.
Parisian Street Scene c.2003
oil on canvas 50 x 60
PCF3

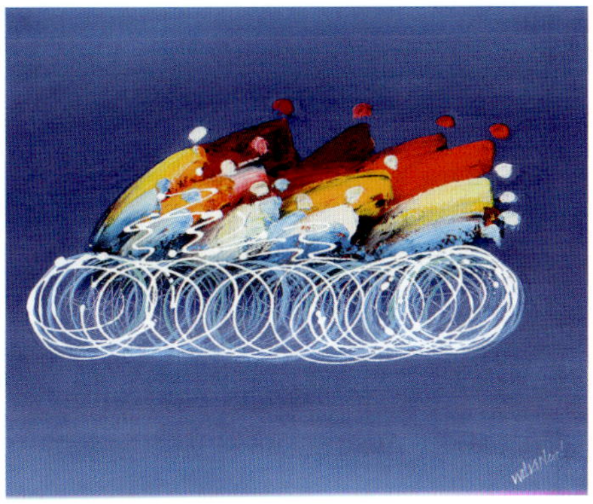

Wilkinson
Tour de France c.2003
oil on canvas 51 x 61
PCF2

Barnsley Hospital NHS Foundation Trust

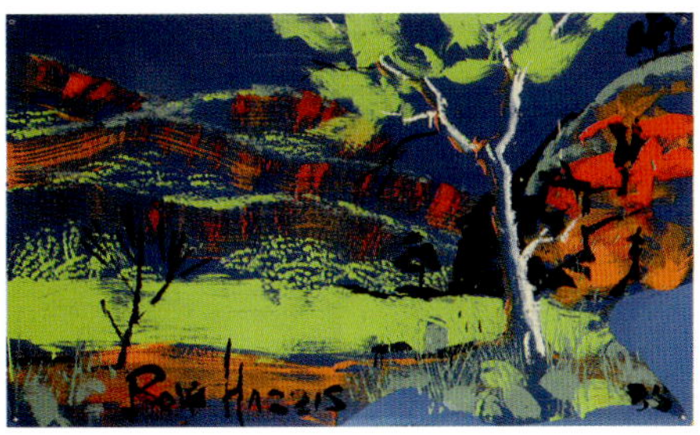

Harris, Rolf b.1930
River Don near Doncaster, South Yorkshire 1985
oil on hardboard 89 x 147
PCF2

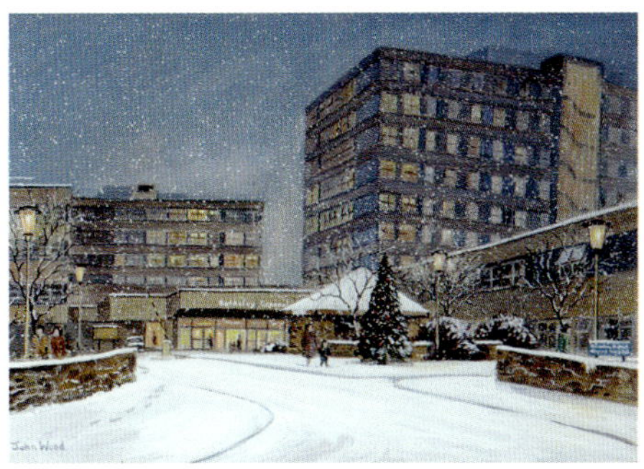

Wood, John
Barnsley General Hospital, South Yorkshire
acrylic on canvas 24 x 31
PCF1

South Yorkshire Police

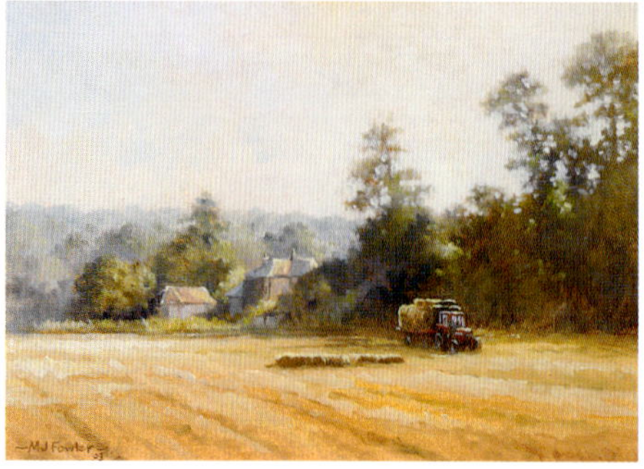

Fowler, Michael John b.1957
Evening Harvest, Sandbeck, South Yorkshire
oil on canvas 40 x 50
PCF2

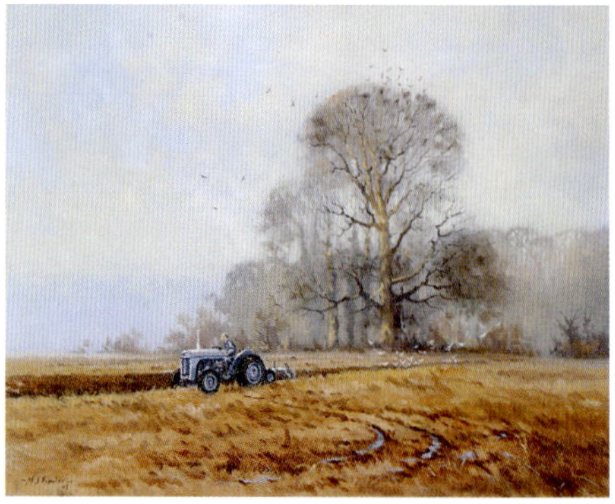

Fowler, Michael John b.1957
Tractor Ploughing a Field
oil on canvas 54 x 64
PCF1

The Cooper Gallery

The Collection at The Cooper Gallery in Barnsley represents a passion for art and a belief in sharing remarkable works freely with the public. Bequests by a small group of local benefactors throughout the twentieth century have brought together a very personal collection of works by British and Continental artists. These paintings give us an absorbing insight into collecting, fashions and the private tastes of people central to Barnsley's cultural heritage.

The Collection began with the vision of Samuel Joshua Cooper, the son of a prominent local linen manufacturer and mine owner. With the economic and social success of the Cooper family, Samuel had the opportunity to explore his much loved world of art, take the Grand Tour in the 1850s, and gather together a collection of paintings, sculpture and furniture.

It was Samuel Joshua Cooper who bought the Archbishop Holgate Grammar School, Barnsley in 1912 with the idea of turning it into a public art gallery to display his collection. Samuel Joshua Cooper sadly died in 1913, a year before the gallery opened. He left the building and collections to the people of Barnsley, administered by the Trustees of The Cooper Gallery. Today, the collections are managed by Barnsley Metropolitan Borough Council on behalf of the Trustees.

The Gallery and Collection continued to develop throughout the twentieth century. In 1930 an extension to the Gallery was added by the Fox family, who were local hotel owners and brewers. In 1934 they also donated a collection of oil paintings to the Trustees of the Cooper Gallery. A series of bequests were made by Sir Michael Sadler, son of a local GP, through the National Art Collections Fund.

In 1939, at the outbreak of the Second World War, the Gallery became an annexe for the nearby Beckett's Hospital and the collections were moved elsewhere for safety. The building was re-opened to the public in 1957.
In 1978 the Addy Bequest was made, consisting of eighteenth- and nineteenth-century oils and watercolours.

The oil paintings in the Collection are varied and lively. Mostly from the Continent, they present appealing groups and fascinating contrasts. The grand view of *The Doge's Palace, Venice* by Louis Désirée Thienon and the homely and personal *Dans la taverne* by Adolphe René Lefevre are two examples of this. The collection of watercolours and oils by Eugène Isabey features seascapes including the awe-inspiring *Hurricane before Saint-Malo, France*. The dramatic *Cardinal Valeane and the Cage of Torture* by Jean-Léon Gérome is a world away from the serene Impressionist views of Italy by Alberto Pasini and Rubens Santoro.

It is a Collection that draws people back again and again, to discover more in the same painting, or to find a new experience.

Natalie Murray, Collections Manager

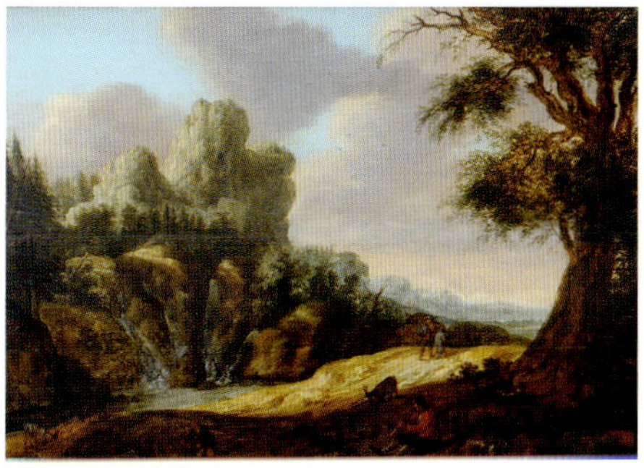

Asch, Pieter Jansz. van (attributed to) 1603–1678
A Mountainous Landscape with Goats 1627–1678
oil on panel 58.5 x 79.5
CP/TR 140

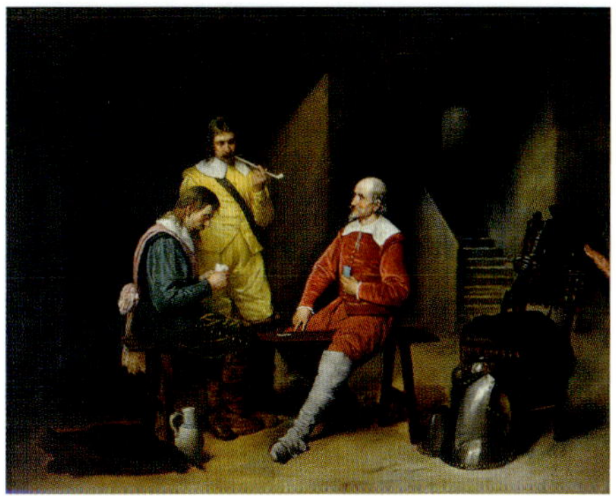

Aznar y García, Francisco 1831–1911
Guard Room 1850–1900
oil on canvas 37 x 45.5
CP/TR 318

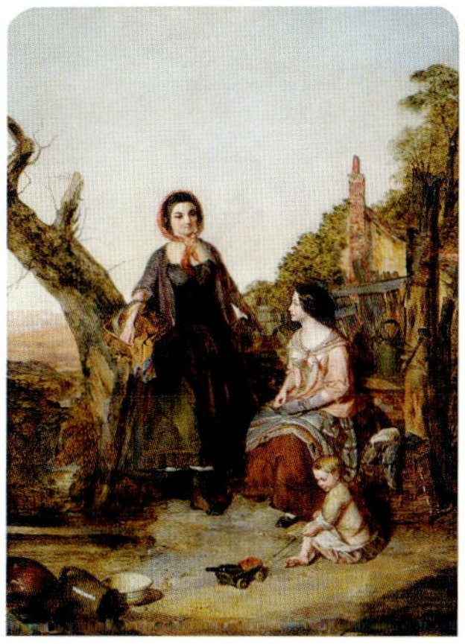

Baldwin, Samuel 1818–1891
Village Gossips
oil on canvas 90 x 65
CP/TR 215

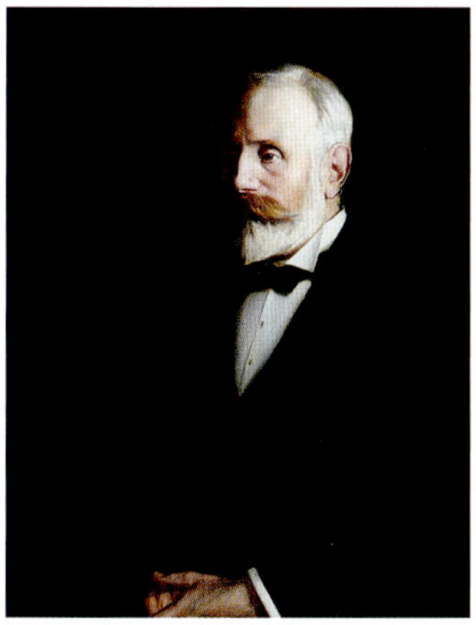

Balfour, James Lawson 1870–1966
Portrait of an Elderly Man
oil on canvas 91.5 x 71
CP/TR 311

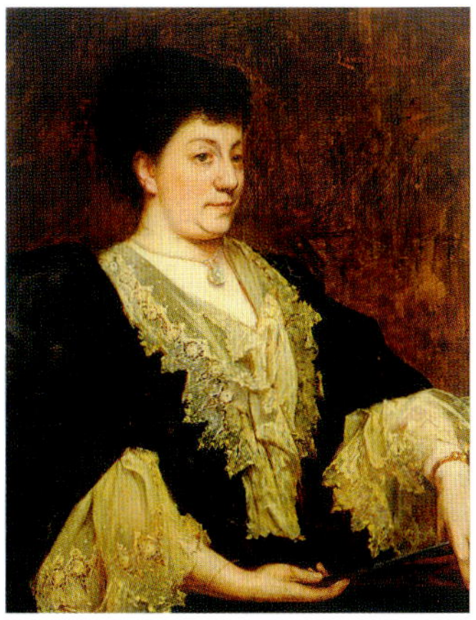

Balfour, James Lawson 1870–1966
Portrait of an Elderly Woman
oil on canvas 91.5 x 71
CP/TR 312

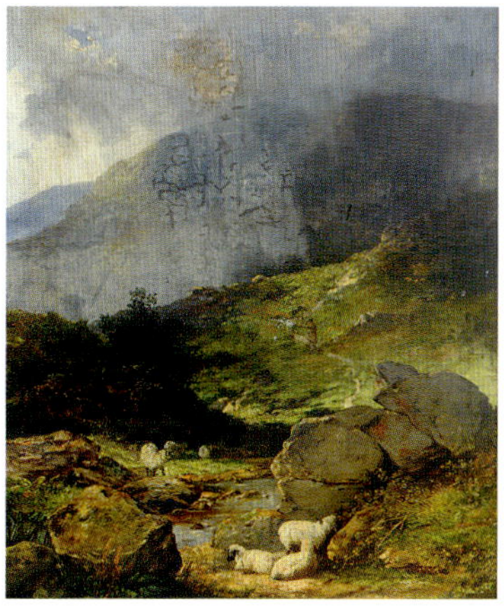

Banks, John Joseph
Yorkshire Moorland, near Whitby
oil on canvas 61 x 50
CP/TR 314

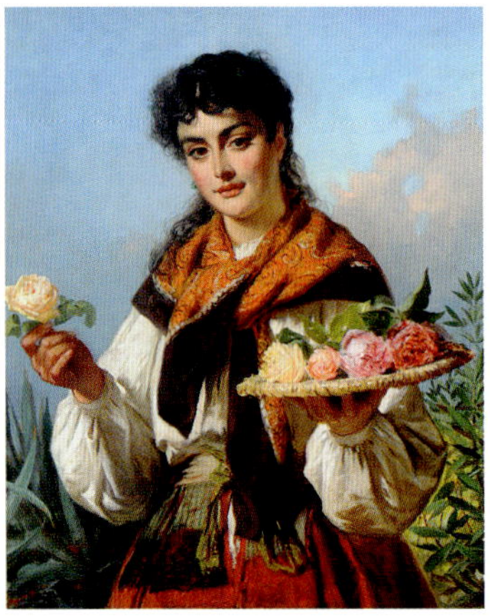

Barnes, Edward Charles 1830–1890
The Flower Girl
oil on canvas 53 x 43
CP/TR 202

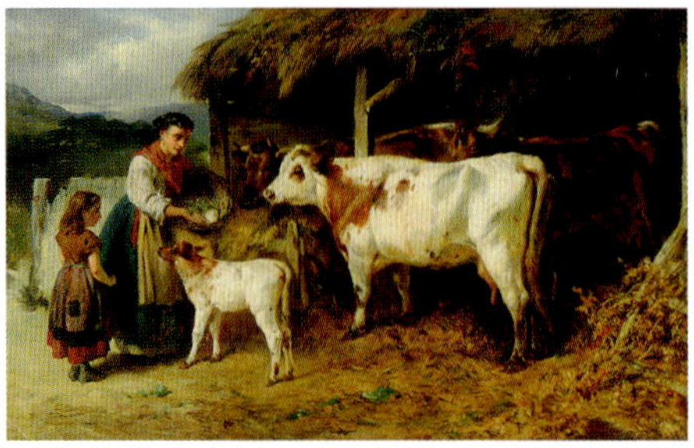

Barnes, Edward Charles, 1830–1890 &
Weekes, Henry I 1807–1877
Cattle and Figures
oil on canvas 66 x 102
CP/TR 258

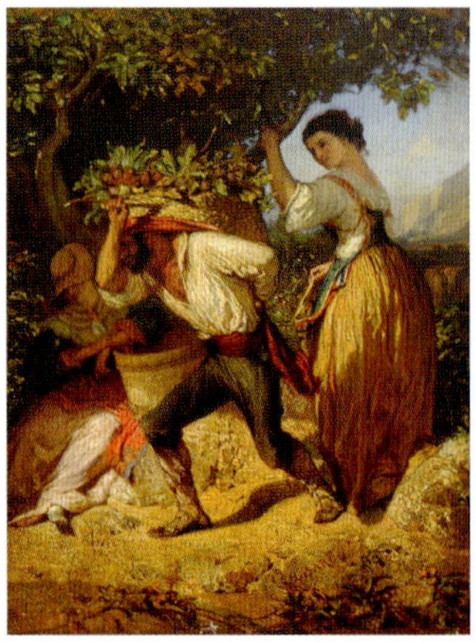

Baron, Henri Charles Antoine 1816–1885
Gathering Fruit 1860–1885
oil on panel 34 x 26
CP/TR 158

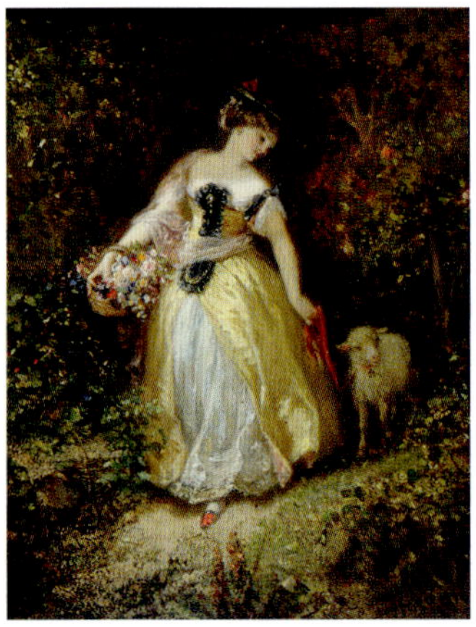

Baron, Henri Charles Antoine 1816–1885
Girl with a Lamb 1860–1885
oil on panel 22 x 18
CP/TR 221

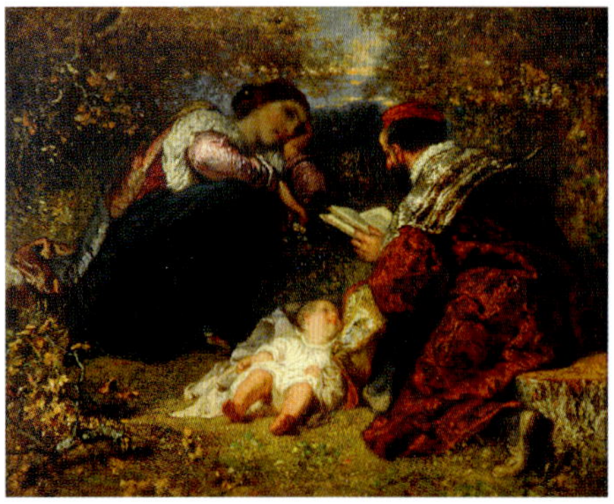

Baron, Henri Charles Antoine 1816–1885
La lecture dans la campagne 1860–1885
oil on panel 21.5 x 27.5
CP/TR 117

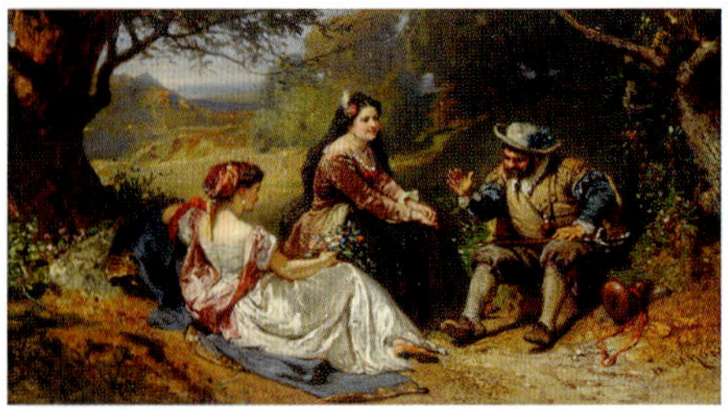

Baron, Henri Charles Antoine 1816–1885
Sancho Panza Recounting His Adventure
1860–1885
oil on panel 18.5 x 32.5
CP/TR 118

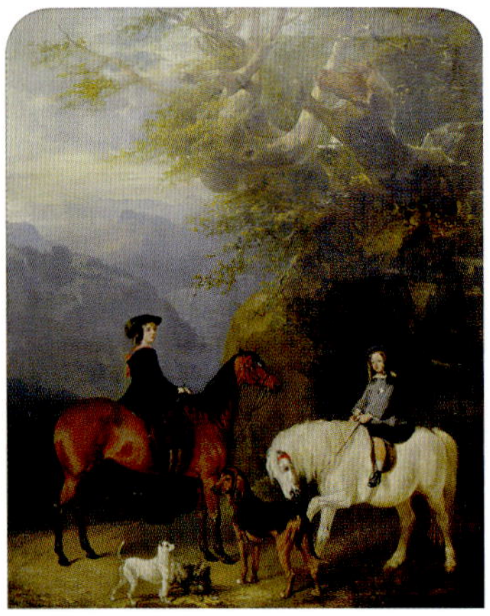

Barraud, Henry (circle of) 1811–1874
A Woman and a Girl Riding in a Mountainous Landscape
oil on canvas 143 x 111
CP/TR 264

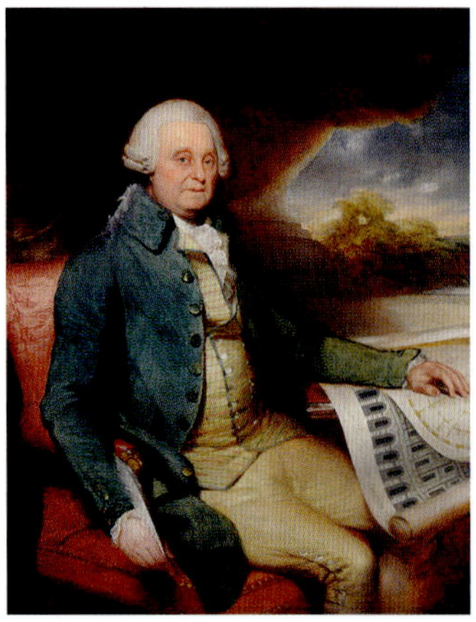

Beechey, William (studio of) 1753–1839
The Architect John Carr of York (1723–1807)
oil on panel 53 x 40.5
CP/TR 182

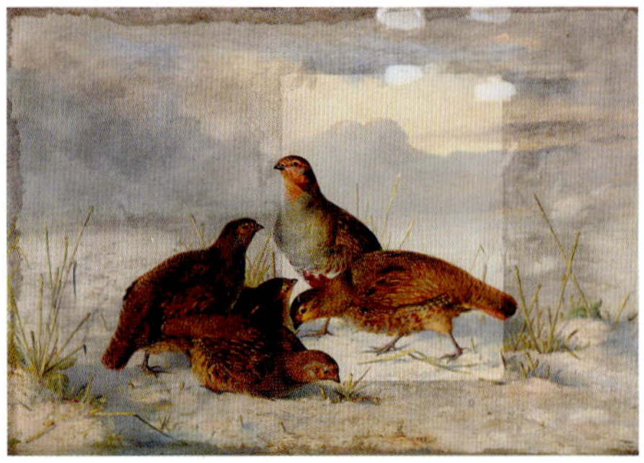

Bell, John Christopher 1823–1881
Patridges in the Snow
oil on canvas 56 x 76.5
CP/TR 278

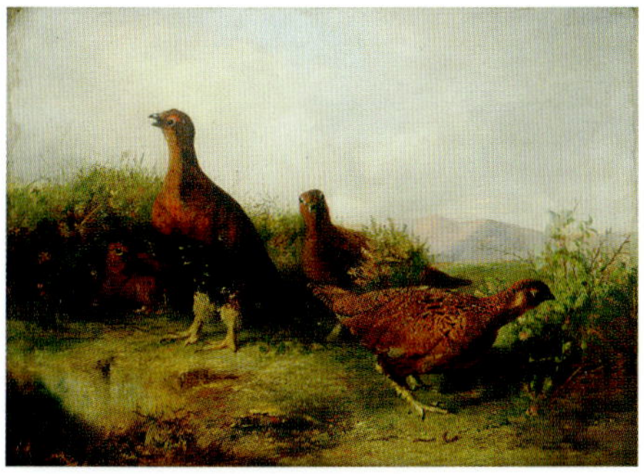

Bell, John Christopher 1823–1881
Red Grouse
oil on canvas 56 x 76.5
CP/TR 211

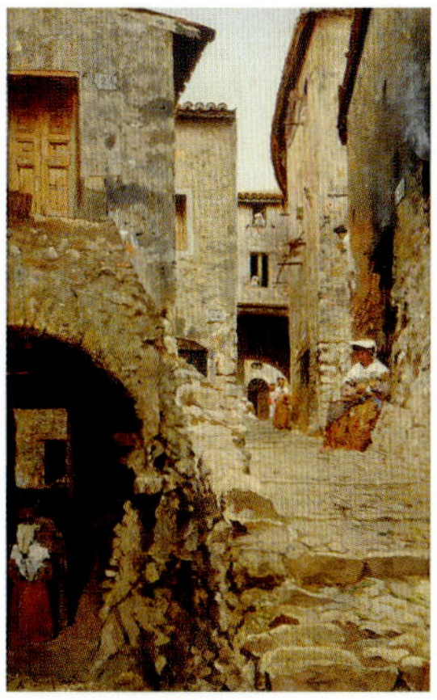

Bompiani, Augusto 1852–1930
Rocca di Papa, Rome 1880–1900
oil on panel 41 x 26
CP/TR 243

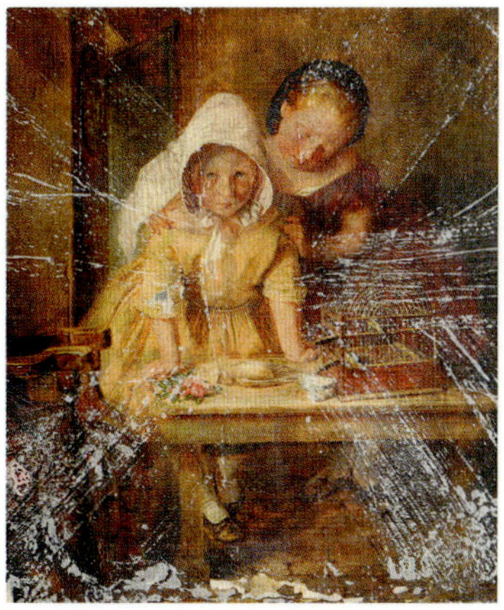

Bowman, Thomas Stanton 1845–after 1886
Rustic Grief
oil on canvas 35 x 30
CP/TR 330

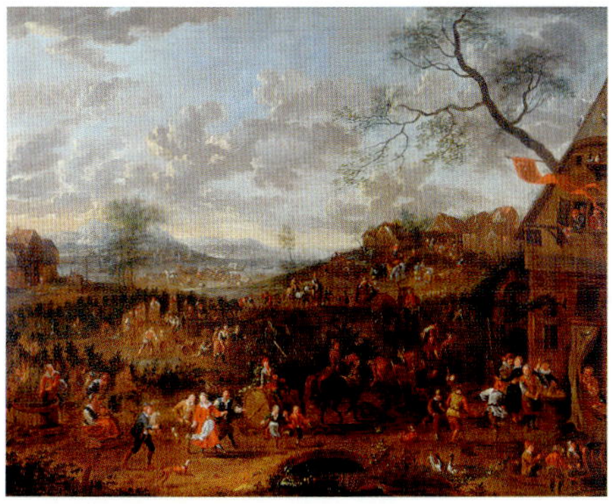

Bredael, Peeter van (school of) 1629–1719
The Vintage, Figures Celebrating the Wine Harvest 1700–1725
oil on canvas 57.5 x 68.5
CP/TR 220

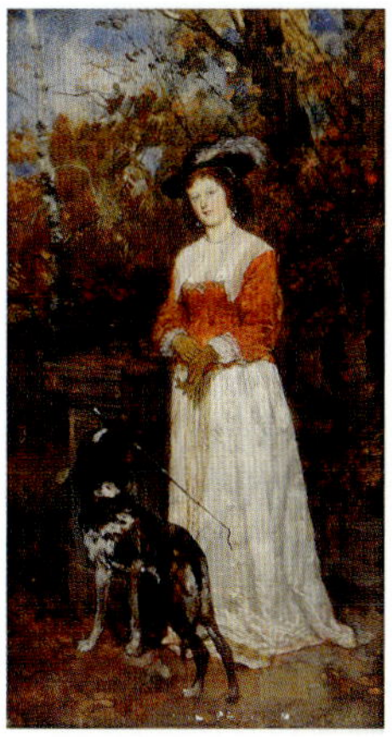

Breling, Heinrich 1849–1914
Lady with a Dog 1870–1890
oil on panel 18 x 9.5
CP/TR 234

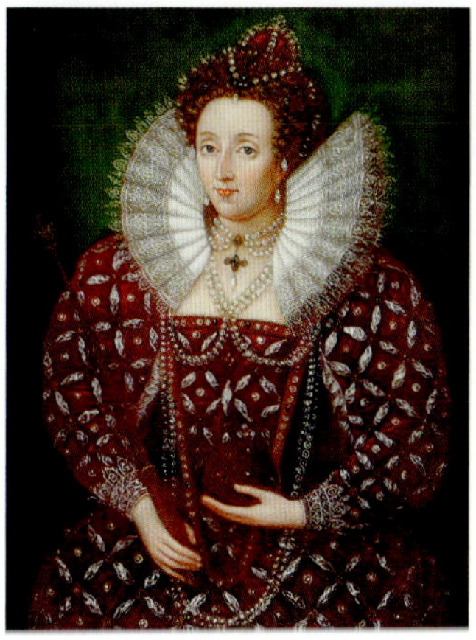

British (English) School 17th C
Elizabeth I (1533–1603)
oil on panel 23.5 x 17.5
CP/TR 185

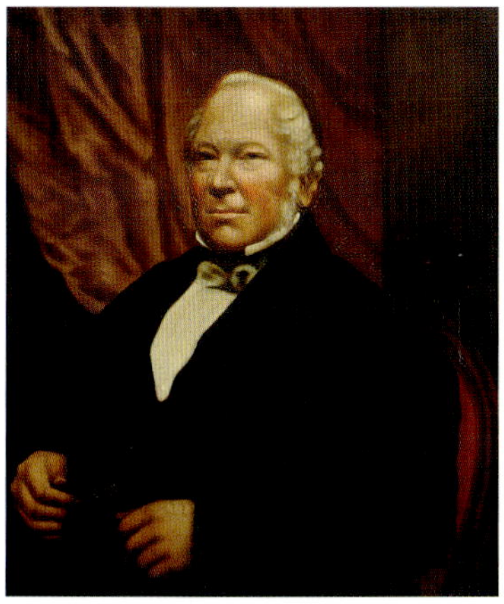

British (English) School 19th C
Portrait of a Gentleman
oil on canvas 75 x 63
CP/TR 343

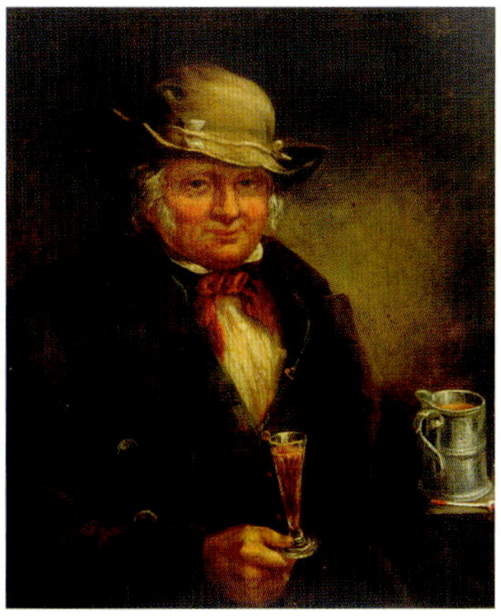

British (English) School 19th C
The Drinker
oil on canvas 30.5 x 25.5
CP/TR 370

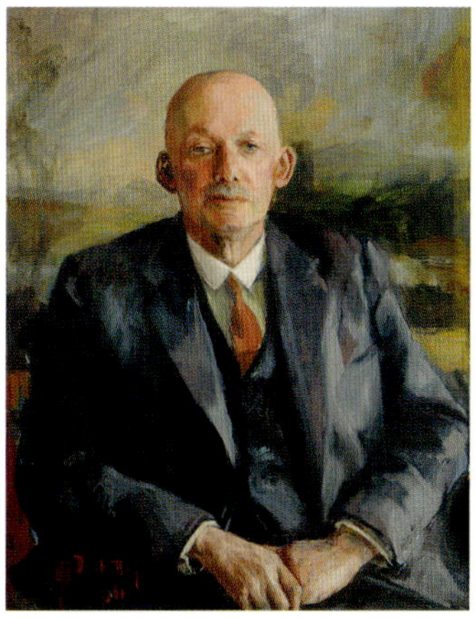

British (English) School mid-20th C
Colonel Rowland Addy (d.1963)
oil on canvas 91.5 x 71
CP/TR 394

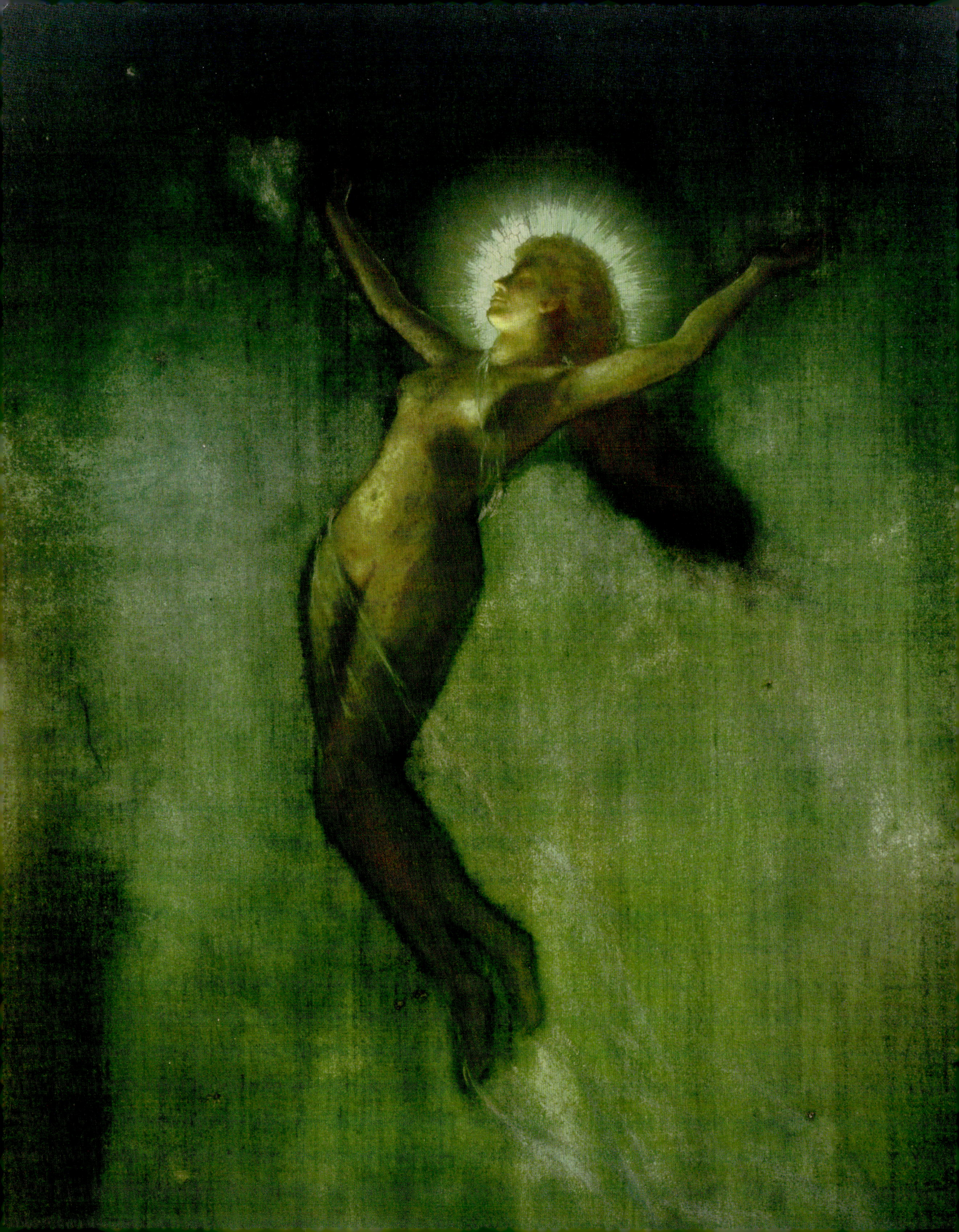

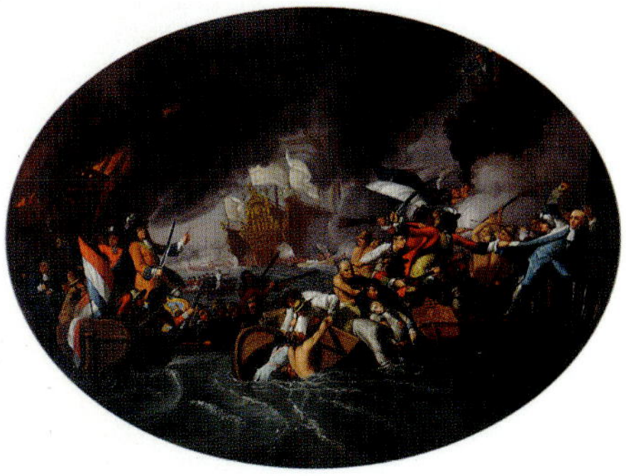

British School 18th C
A Naval Engagement
oil on copper panel 48 x 63.5
CP/TR 125

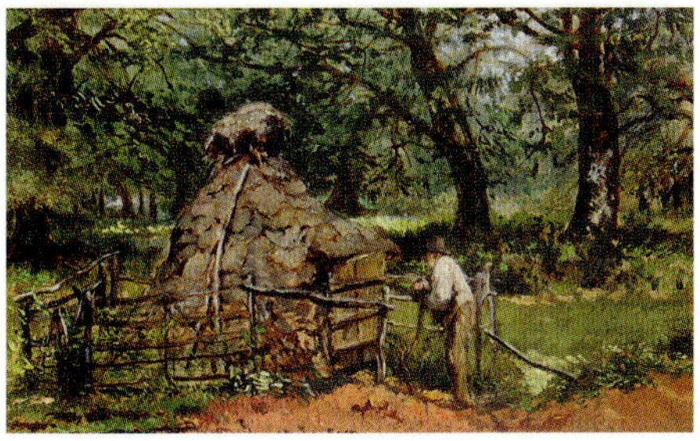

Buchser, Frank (attributed to) 1828–1890
Charcoal Burners' Hut in the New Forest
oil on board & card 14.5 x 23.5
CP/TR 268

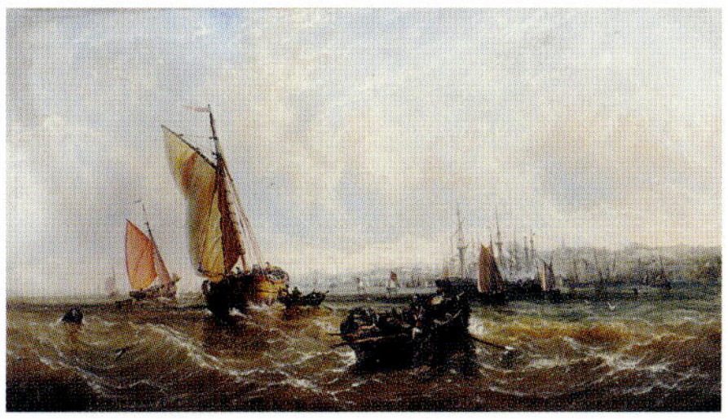

Callow, John 1822–1878
On the Mersey
oil on canvas 61 x 106
CP/TR 277

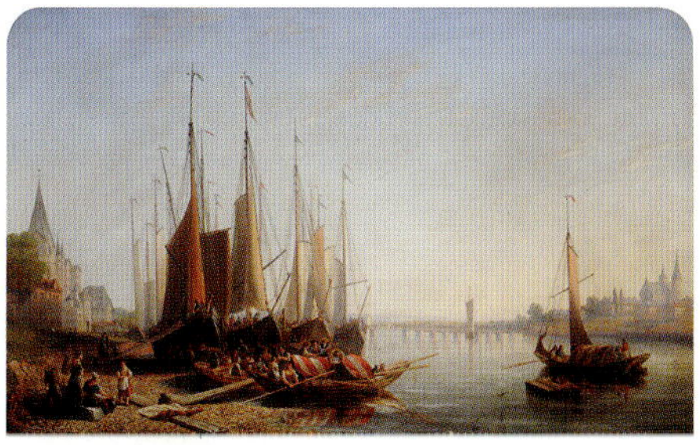

Carmichael, John Wilson 1799–1868
A German River Scene
oil on canvas 48 x 80.5
CP/TR 226

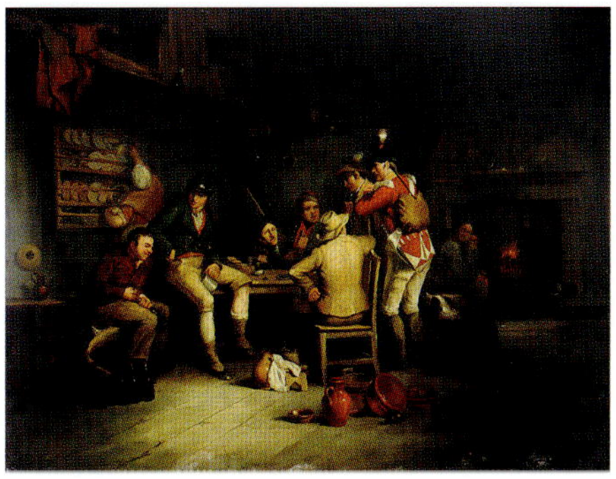

Carse, Alexander (attributed to)
c.1770–1843
Tavern Scene with a Soldier
oil on canvas 71.5 x 91.5
CP/TR 294

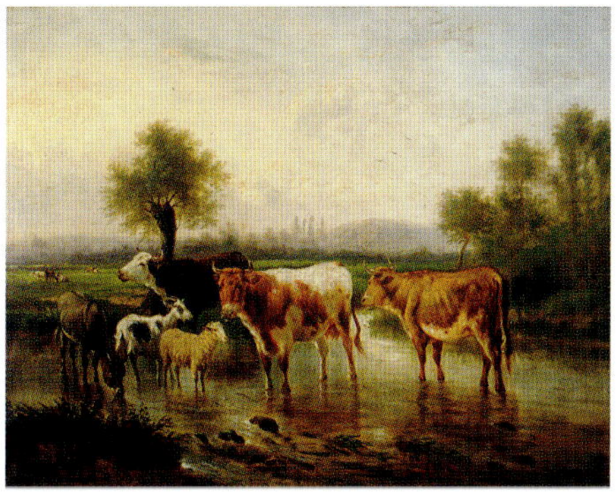

Cartier, Karl (attributed to) 1855–1925
Cattle
oil on canvas 72 x 90
CP/TR 213

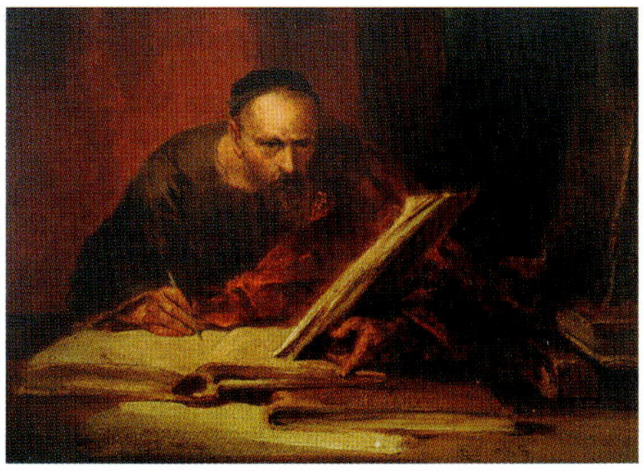

Cattermole, George 1800–1868
The Scribe
oil on millboard 28.5 x 39
CP/TR 223

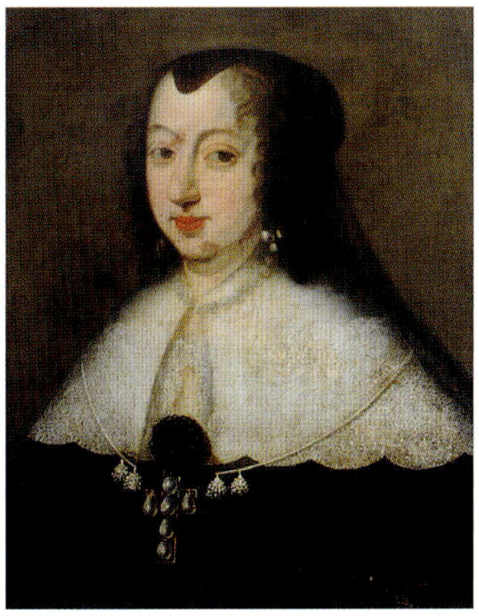

Champaigne, Philippe de (style of)
1602–1674
Anne of Austria (1601–1666) 1643–1660
oil on canvas 59 x 47
CP/TR 130

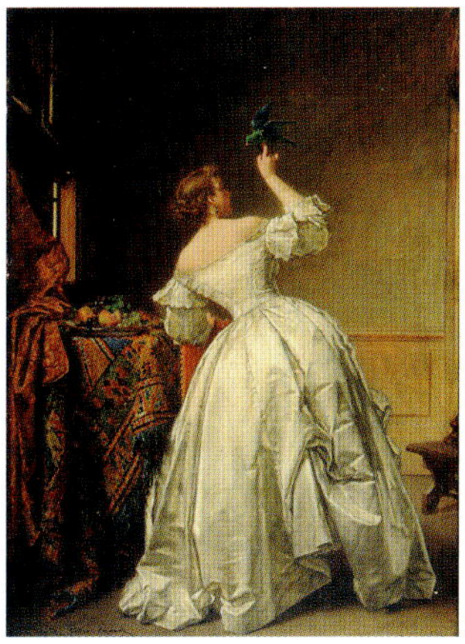

Chavet, Victor Joseph 1822–1906
The Blonde 1863
oil on panel 20.5 x 14.5
CP/TR 232

Facing page: Moore, Ernest, 1865–1940, *Evening Star* (detail), The Cooper Gallery, (p. 23)

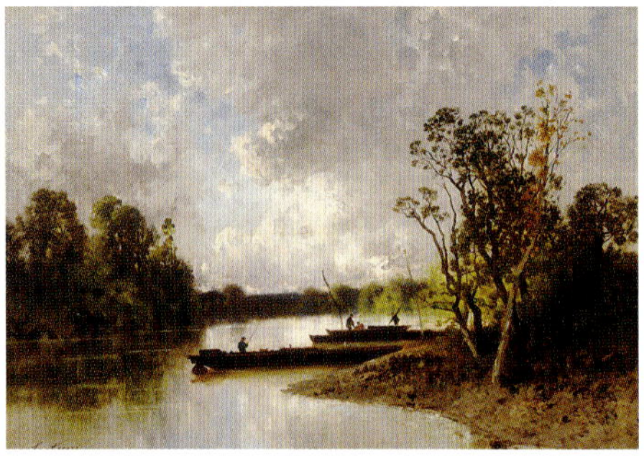

Cicéri, Eugène 1813–1890
A Bavarian Lake with Fishing Boats 1877
oil on panel 31.5 x 46
CP/TR 156

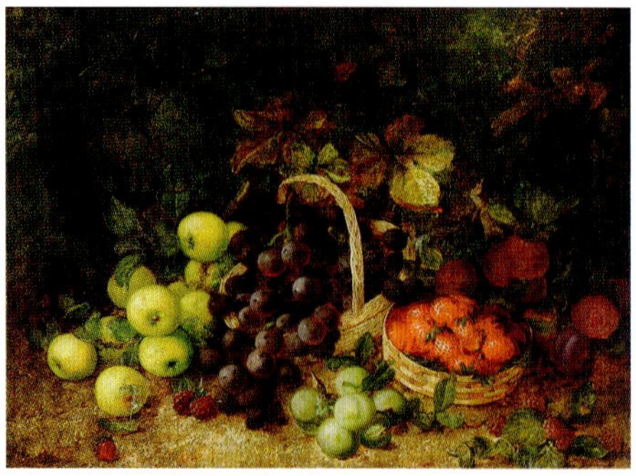

Clare, George c.1830–c.1900
Still Life of Various Fruit
oil on canvas 45 x 61
CP/TR 255

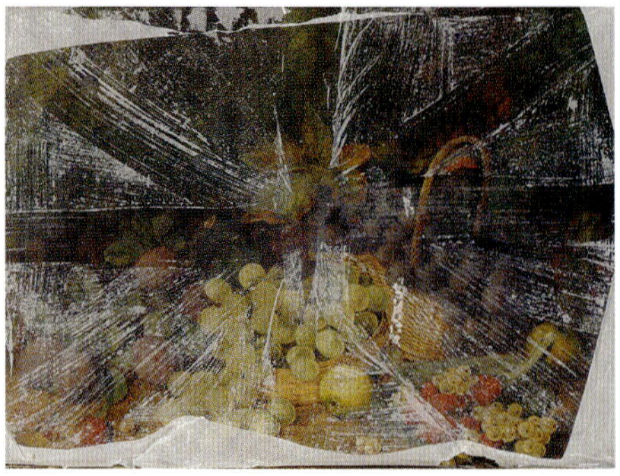

Clare, George c.1830–c.1900
Still Life with Fruit
oil on canvas 46 x 61
CP/TR 391

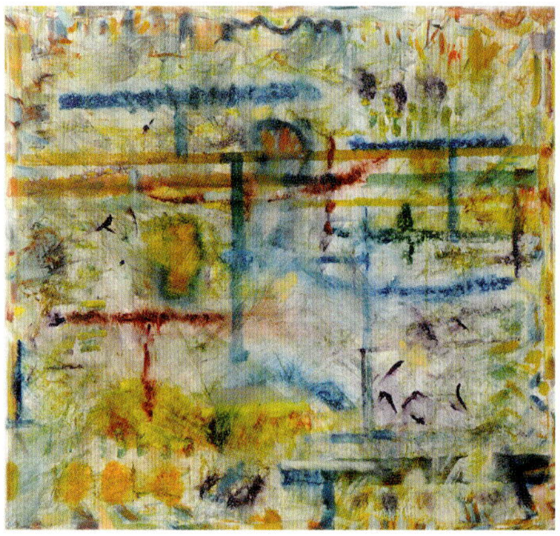

Clough, Prunella 1919–1999
Enclosed Landscape
oil on canvas 123 x 128
CLS.7

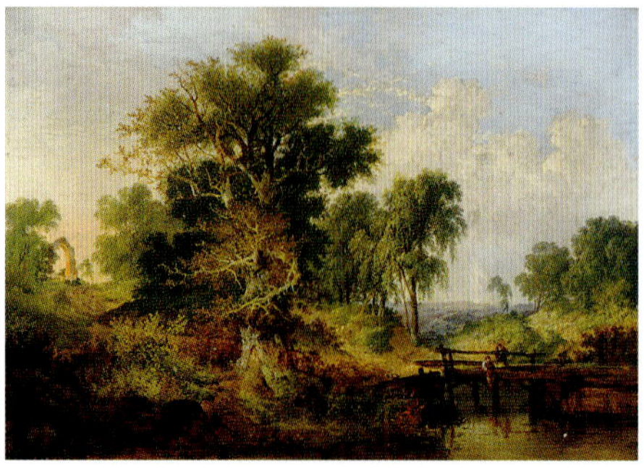

Colkett, Samuel David 1806–1863
A River Landscape with Figures on a Bridge
oil on canvas 56 x 78
CP/TR 210

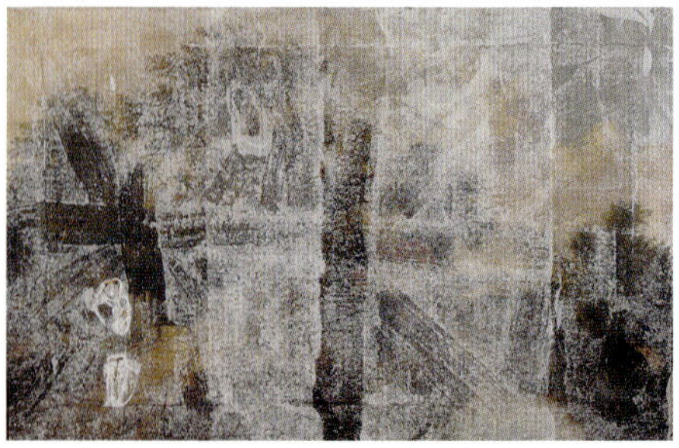

Colkett, Samuel David 1806–1863
The Old Mill Stream
oil on canvas 61 x 91
CP/TR 315

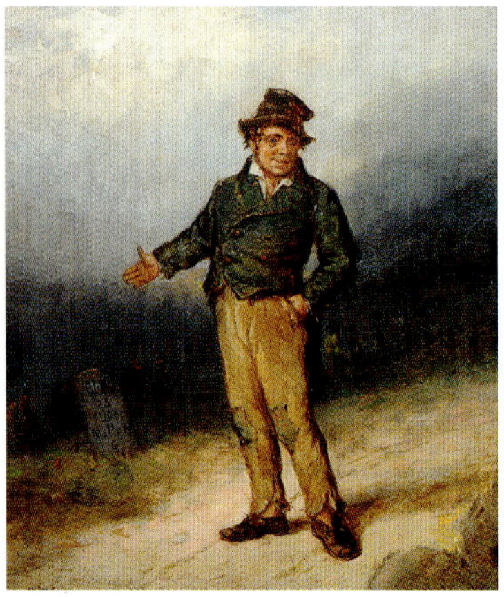

Cook, Charles Henry c.1830–1905
An Irish Character
oil on canvas 35 x 30
CP/TR 200

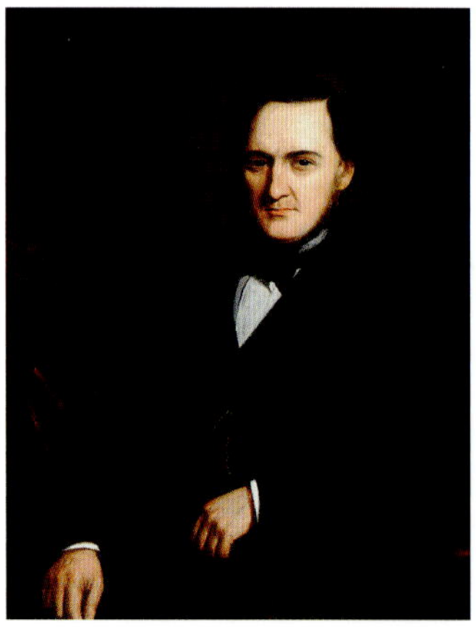

Cook, Charles Henry c.1830–1905
Mr James Fox (d.1885)
oil on canvas 91.5 x 71
CP/TR 216

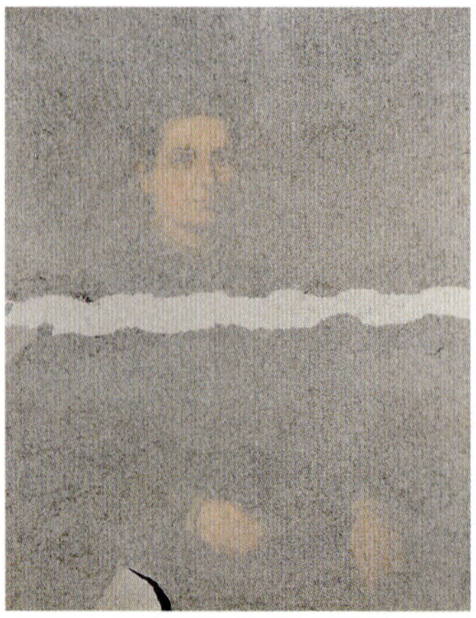

Cook, Charles Henry c.1830–1905
Mrs James Fox
oil on canvas 91.5 x 71
CP/TR 214

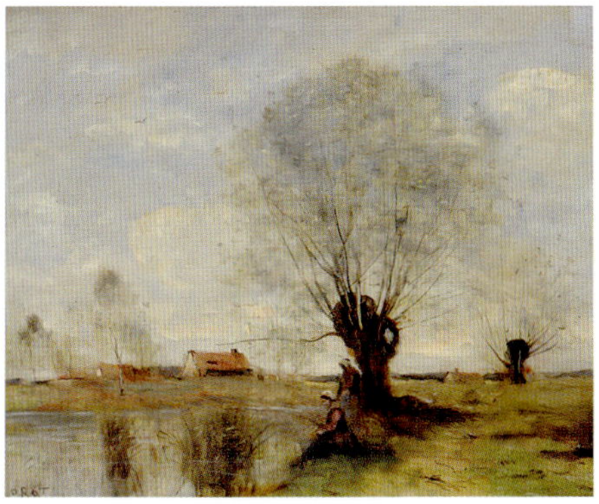

Corot, Jean-Baptiste-Camille (style of)
1796–1875
Women Fishing 1860–1875
oil on canvas 37.5 x 45
CP/TR 153

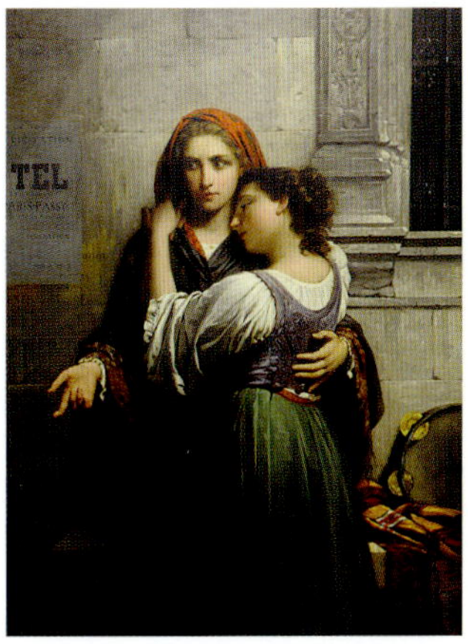

Cot, Pierre Auguste 1837–1883
The Beggar Girls
oil on canvas 146 x 106
CP/TR 265

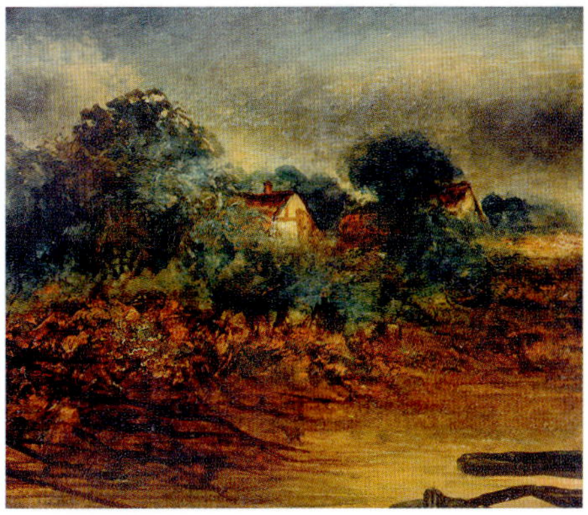

Cox, David the elder (circle of) 1783–1859
River Landscape
oil on canvas 20 x 23
CP/TR 254

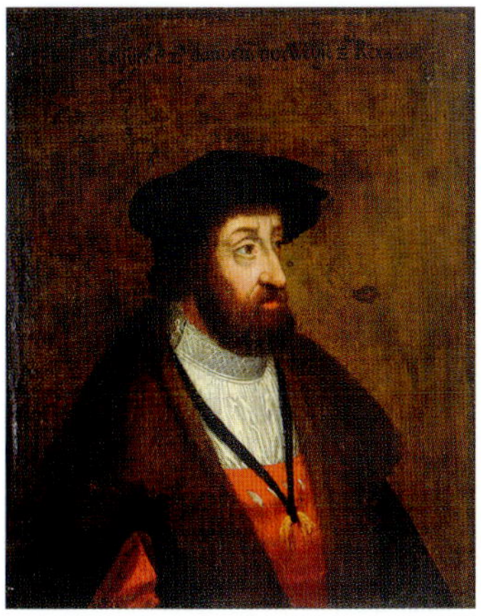

Cranach, Lucas the elder (after) 1472–1553
Christian II of Denmark (1481–1559)
1550–1600
oil on canvas & panel 27 x 21.5
CP/TR 253

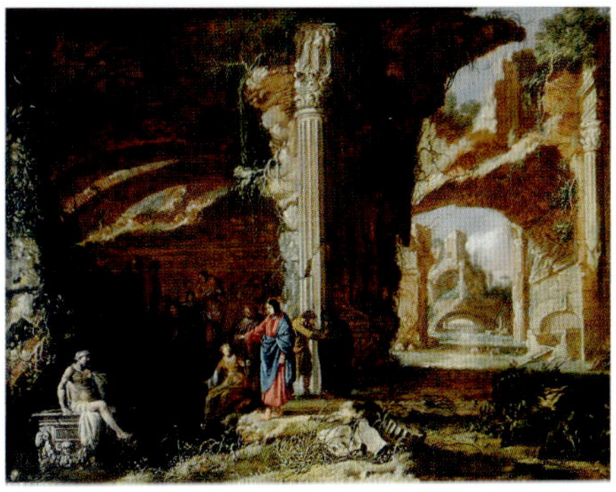

Cuylenborch, Abraham van (attributed to)
c.1610–1658
The Raising of Lazarus 1630–1658
oil on panel 41 x 53.5
CP/TR 147

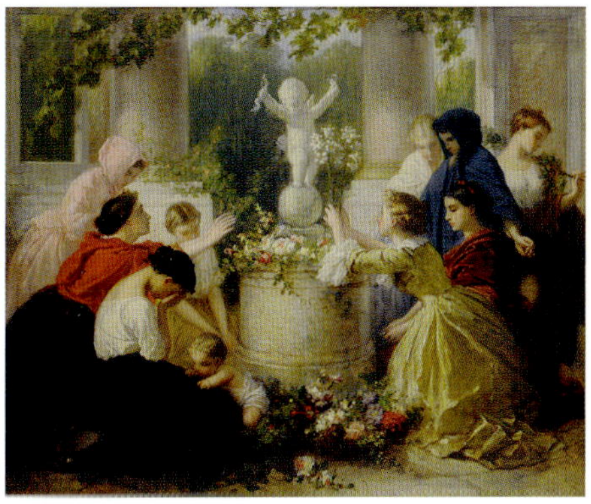

De Beaumont, Gustave 1851–1922
A Sacrifice to Cupid
oil on canvas 79 x 95
CP/TR 217

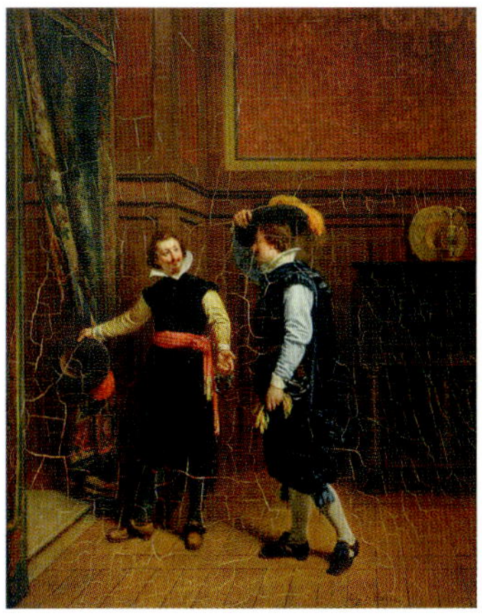

De Bergue, Tony-François 1820–1893
Il fait la politesse 1840–1860
oil on panel 40 x 32
CP/TR 219

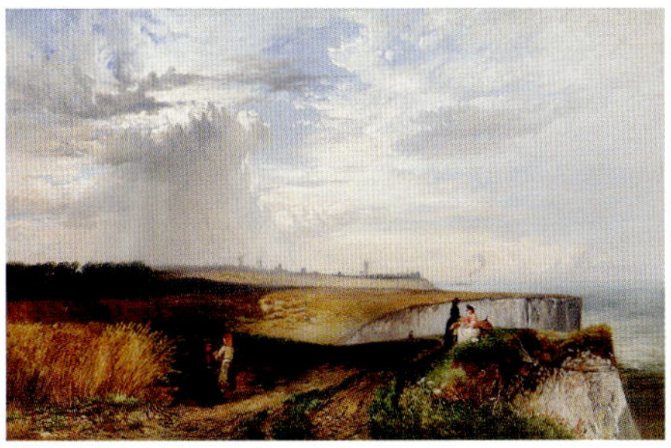

De Fleury, James Vivien de 1847–1902
Coast Scene, Margate, Kent 1860
oil on canvas 51 x 76
CP/TR 209

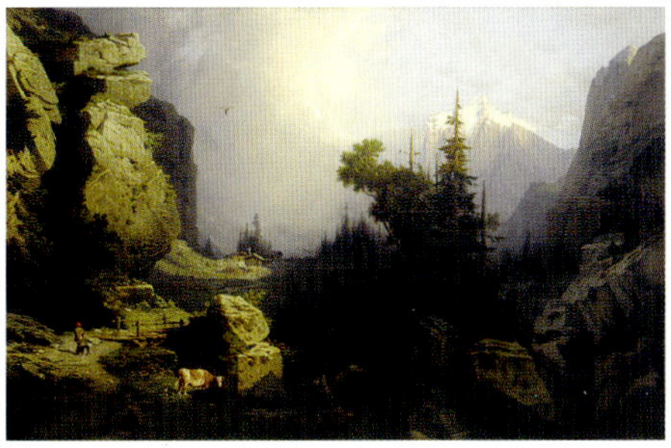

De Fontenay, Léonard Alexis Daligé
1813–1892
In the Grindelwald, Switzerland 1861
oil on canvas 110 x 166
CP/TR 113

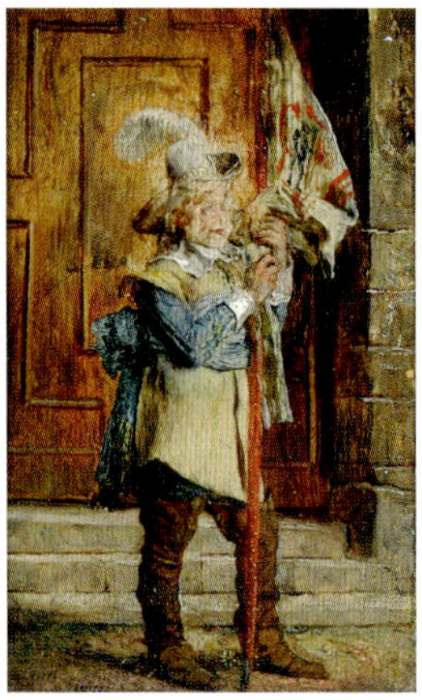

De Léon y Escosura, Ignacio 1834–1901
The Standard Bearer 1874
oil on panel 9 x 6
CP/TR 233

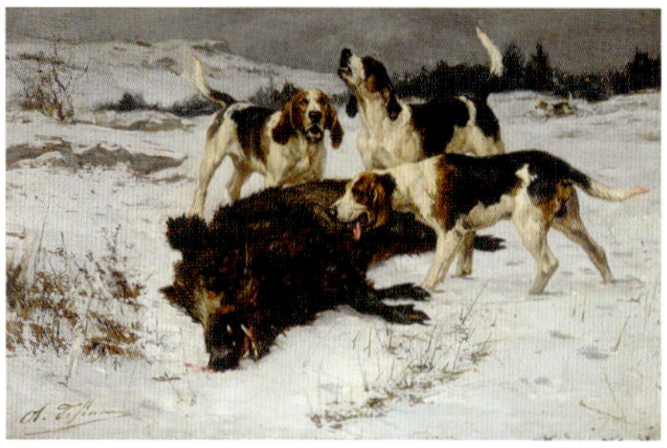

de Penne, Charles Olivier 1831–1897
Hounds with a Boar 1860–1897
oil on panel 28 x 42
CP/TR 242

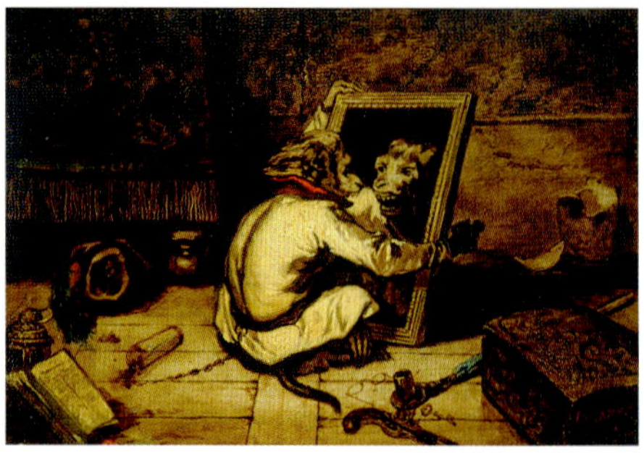

Decamps, Alexandre-Gabriel (attributed to)
1803–1860
Le singe au miroir (The Monkey and the Mirror)
oil on canvas 25.5 x 37
CP/TR 149

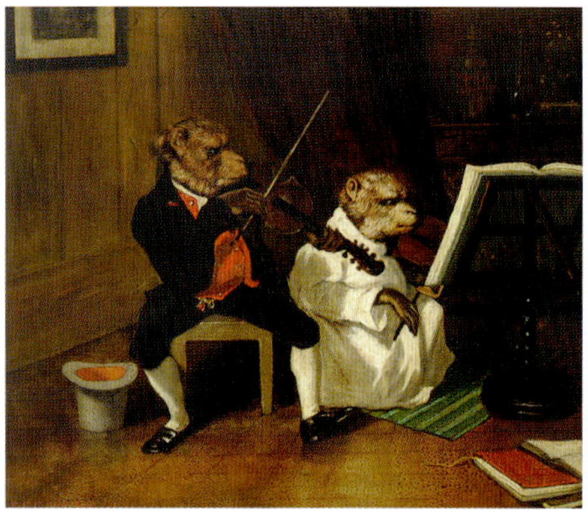

Decamps, Alexandre-Gabriel (attributed to)
1803–1860
Monkey Musicians 1838–1839
oil on panel 41 x 48.5
CP/TR 191

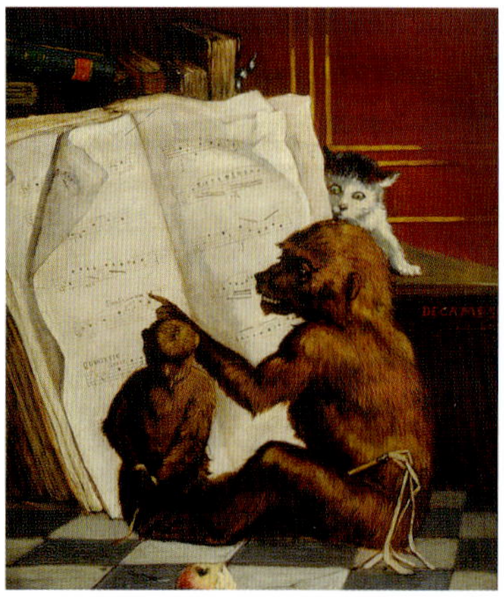

Decamps, Alexandre-Gabriel (attributed to)
1803–1860
Monkey's Music Lesson 1840
oil on wood & panel 51 x 43
CP/TR 138

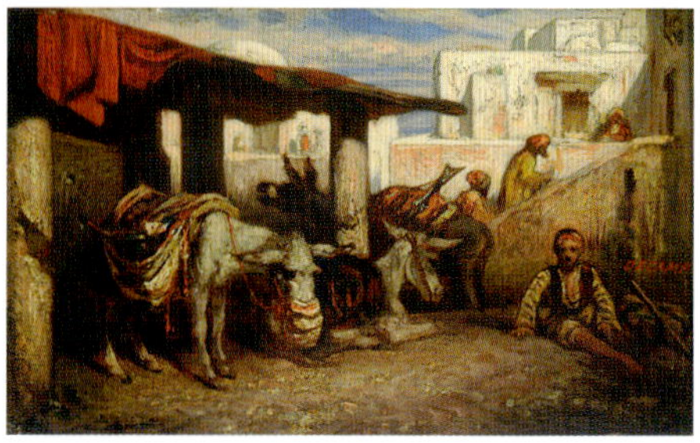

Decamps, Alexandre-Gabriel (attributed to)
1803–1860
An Arab Boy with Donkeys
oil on panel 10.5 x 17.2
CP/TR 120

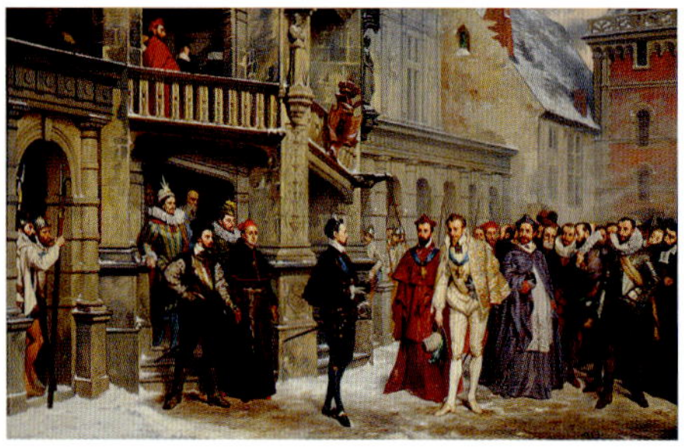

Delechaux, Marcelin 1821–1902
The Meeting 1850–1902
oil on canvas 64 x 99
CP/TR 261

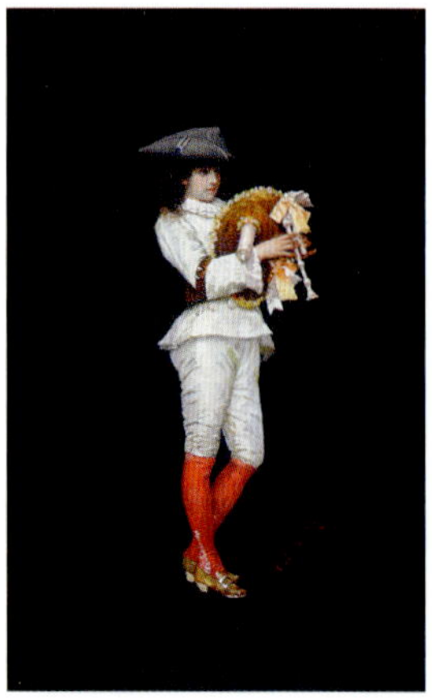

Delort, Charles Edouard 1841–1895
Girl with Bagpipes 1875–1895
oil on panel 31 x 20
CP/TR 119

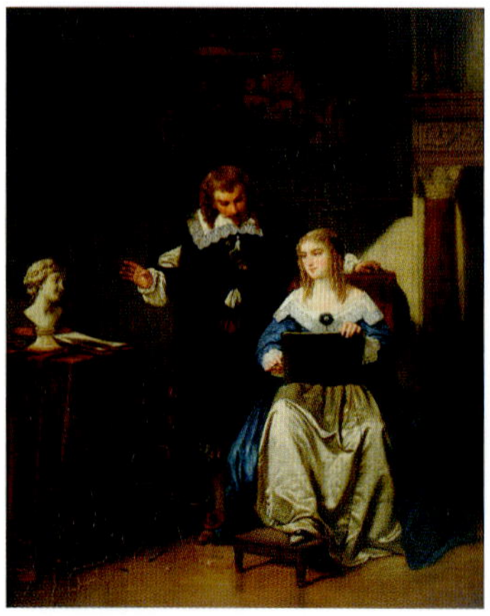

Devedeux, Louis 1820–1874
The Drawing Lesson
oil on panel 40 x 30
CP/TR 205

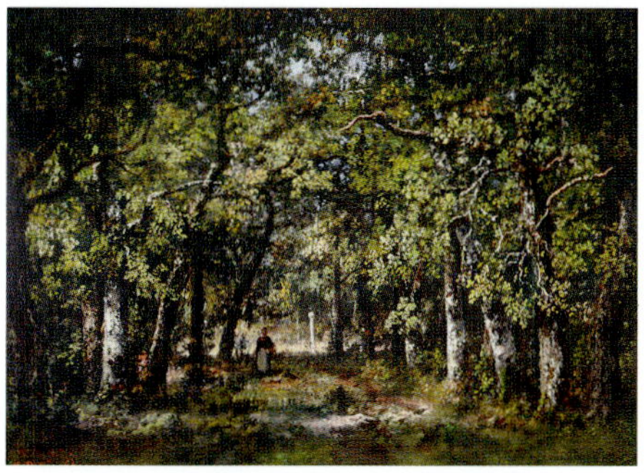

Diaz de la Peña, Narcisse Virgile 1808–1876
Bas Breau, par le carrefour de Clair-Bois en la forêt de Fontainebleau, France 1864
oil on panel 30.5 x 40.5
CP/TR 141

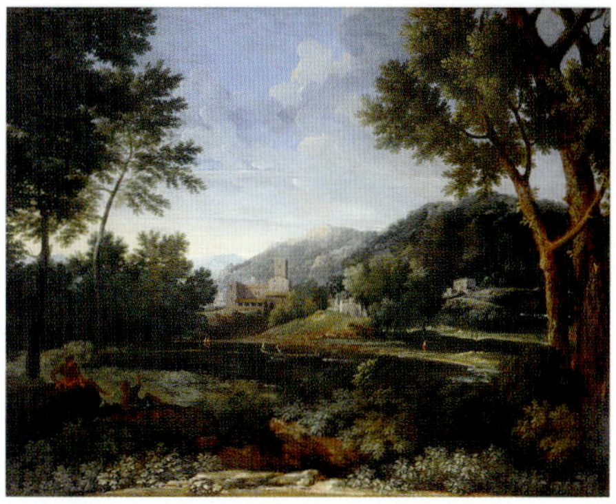

Dughet, Gaspard 1615–1675
An Italianate River Landscape 1655–1659
oil on canvas 96.5 x 122
CP/TR 372

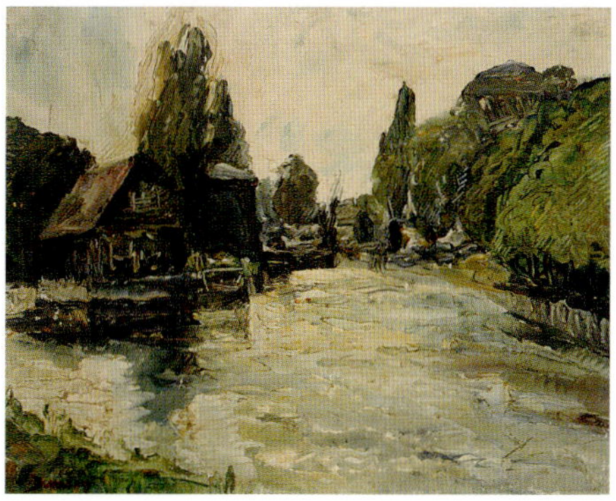

Dunlop, Ronald Ossory 1894–1973
The Weir
oil on canvas 39.5 x 49
CP/TR 77

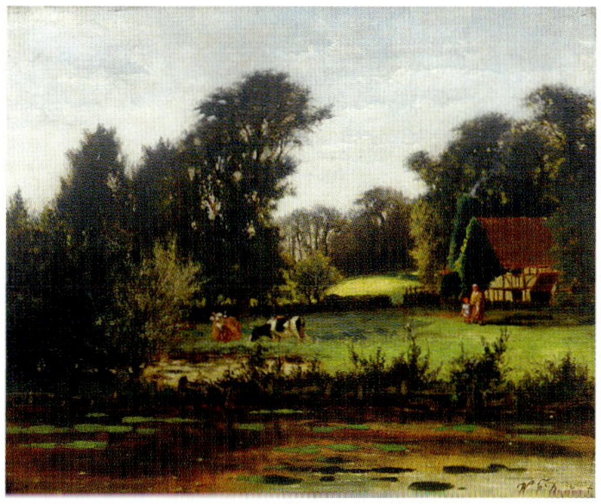

Dupont, William Frederick active 19th C
River Scene with Cattle
oil on canvas 51 x 61
CP/TR 284

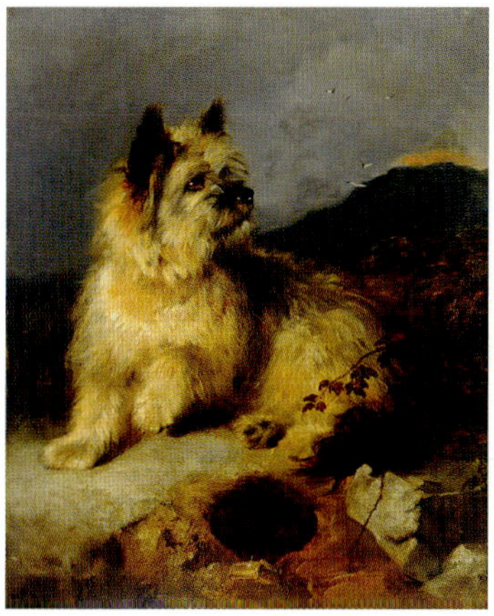

Earl, George (attributed to) 1824–1908
A Terrier by a Rabbit Hole
oil on canvas 67.5 x 54.5
CP/TR 366

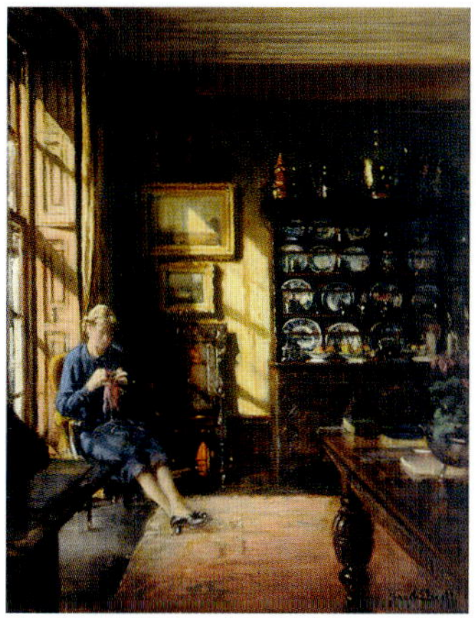

Elwell, Frederick William 1870–1958
Winter Sunshine
oil on canvas 51 x 40
CP/TR 371

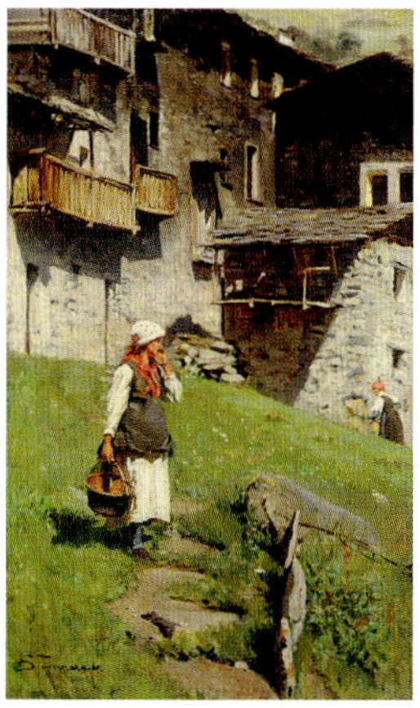

Fornara, Sallustro 1852–1922
The Call to Breakfast
oil on canvas 76 x 47
CP/TR 225

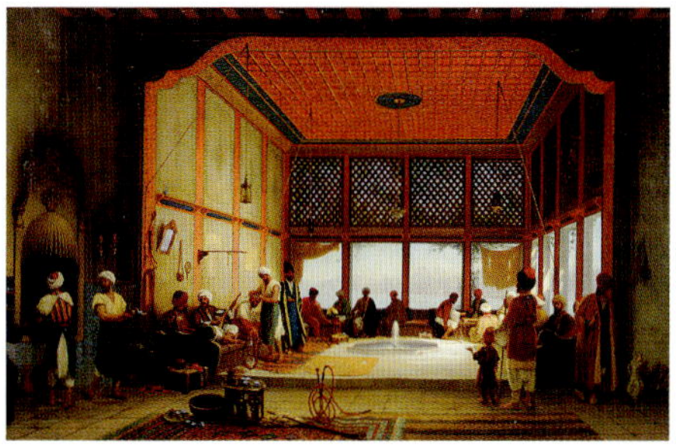

Frère, Charles Théodore 1814–1888
Café de Galata, Constantinople 1878–1882
oil on canvas 83 x 129
CP/TR 276

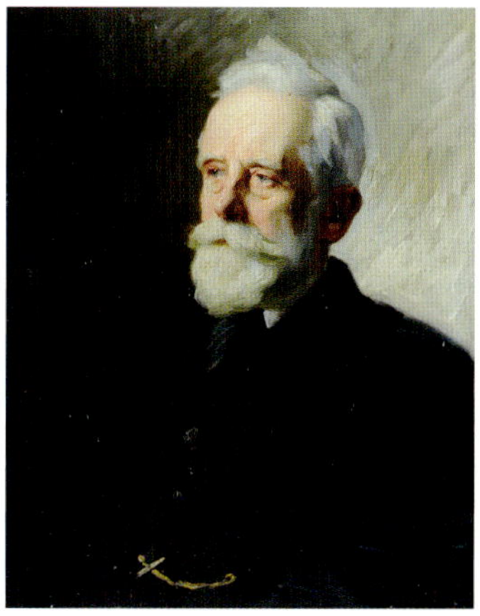

Furse, Charles Wellington 1868–1904
Dr M. T. Sadler, MD
oil on canvas 70 x 56
CP/TR 309

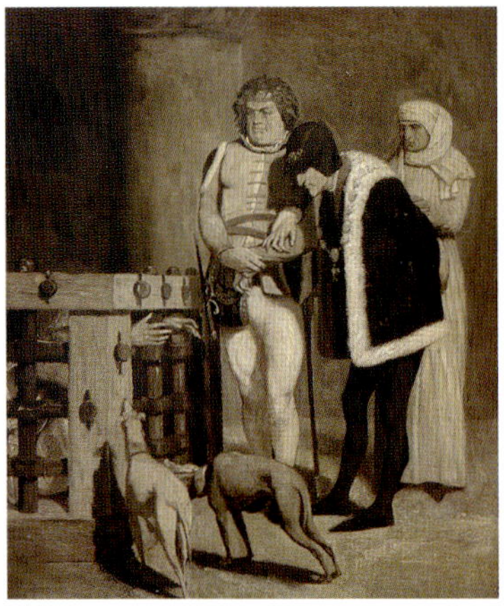

Gérome, Jean-Léon 1824–1904
Cardinal Valeane and the Cage of Torture
oil on canvas 45 x 37
CP/TR 192

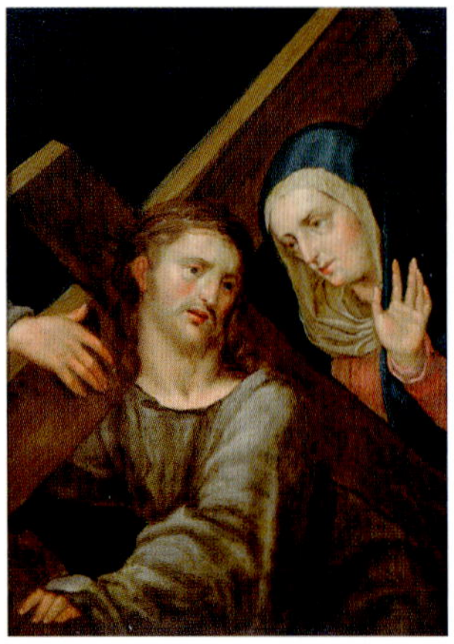

González, Bartolomé (attributed to)
1564–1627
Christ Bearing the Cross with the Virgin Mary
oil on copper panel 29.5 x 21
CP/TR 252

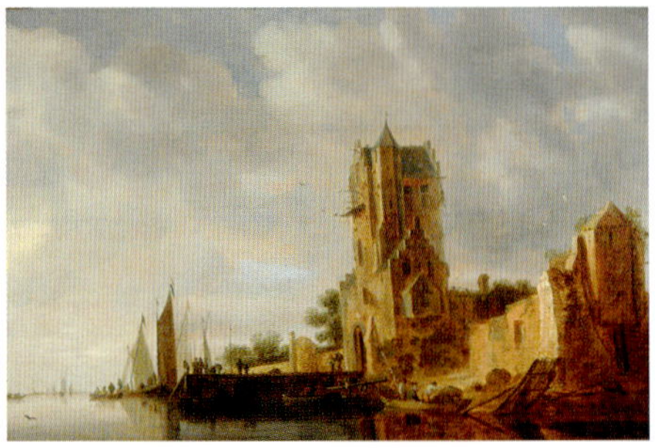

Goyen, Jan van 1596–1656
River Scene with a Tower
oil on panel 40 x 58
CP/TR 131

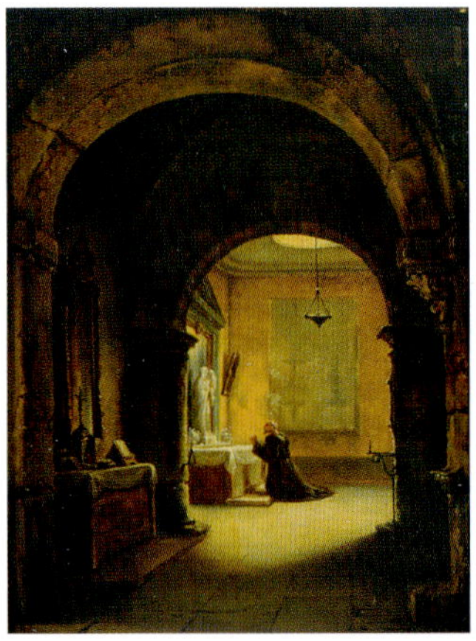

Granet, François-Marius 1775–1849
A Chapel in a Monastery 1797–1849
oil on canvas 31.5 x 23.5
CP/TR 151

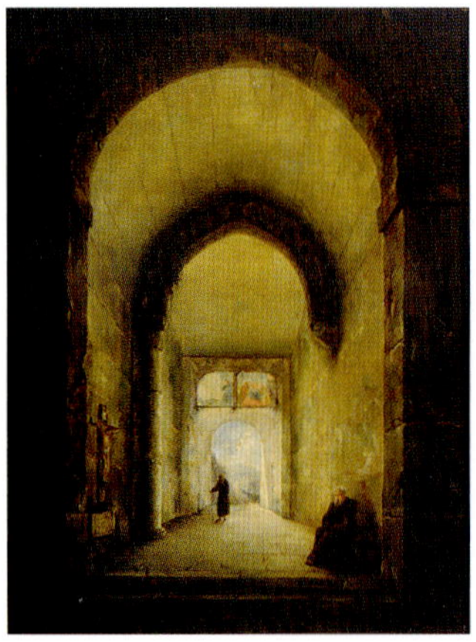

Granet, François-Marius (attributed to)
1775–1849
In the Cloisters 1797–1849
oil on canvas 32 x 23.5
CP/TR 148

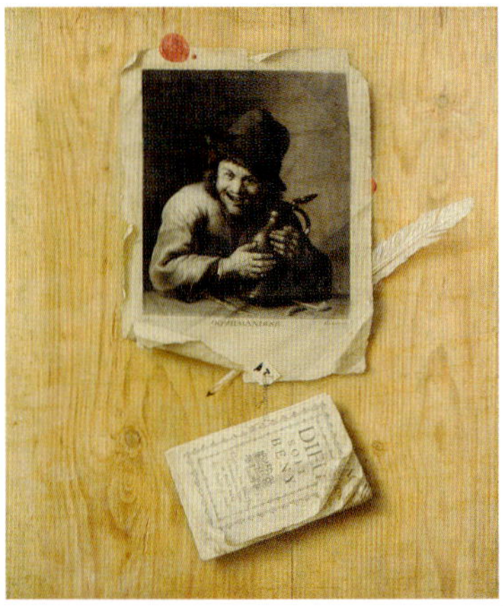

Grésely, Gabriel Gaspard 1712–1756
Gourmandise (Trompe l'Oeil)
oil on canvas 58.5 x 48.5
CP/TR 136

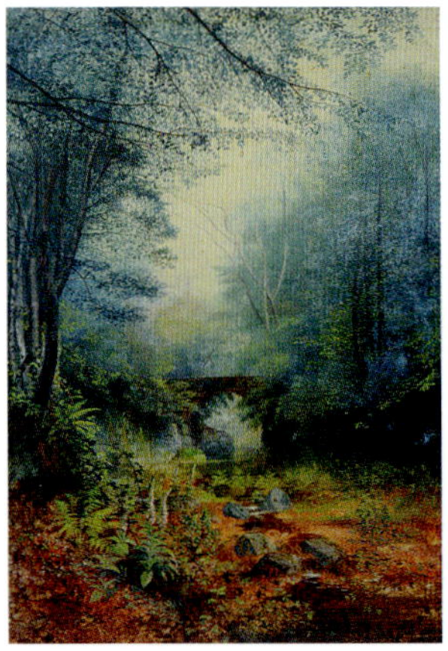

Grimshaw, John Atkinson 1836–1893
A Wooded Valley
oil on millboard 40.5 x 35.5
CP/TR 177

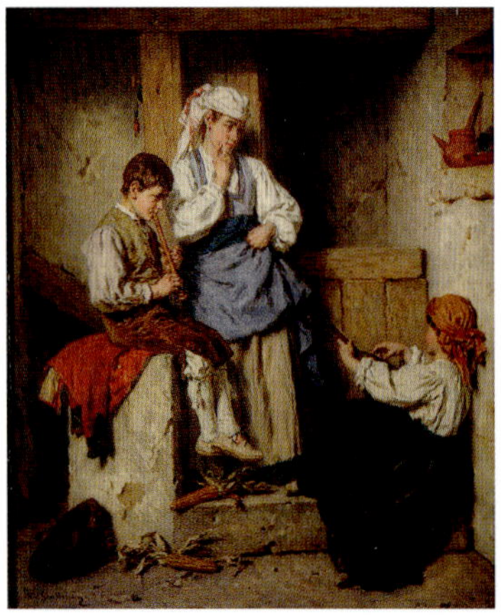

Guillemin, Alexandre Marie 1817–1880
In the Pyrenees
oil on panel 46 x 30.5
CP/TR 319

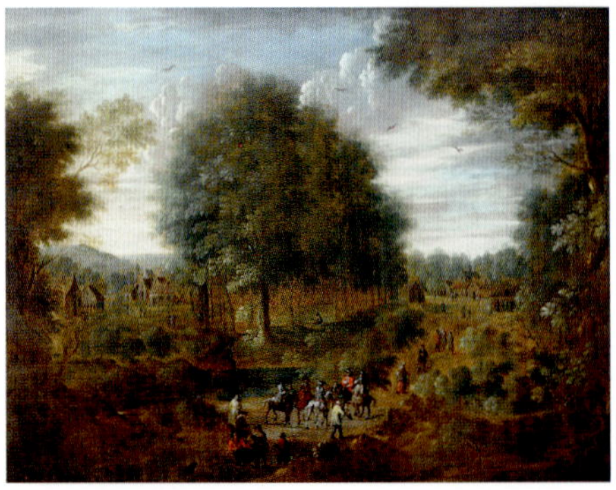

Gysels, Peeter (attributed to) 1621–1691
A Village Scene
oil on canvas 66 x 85
CP/TR 135

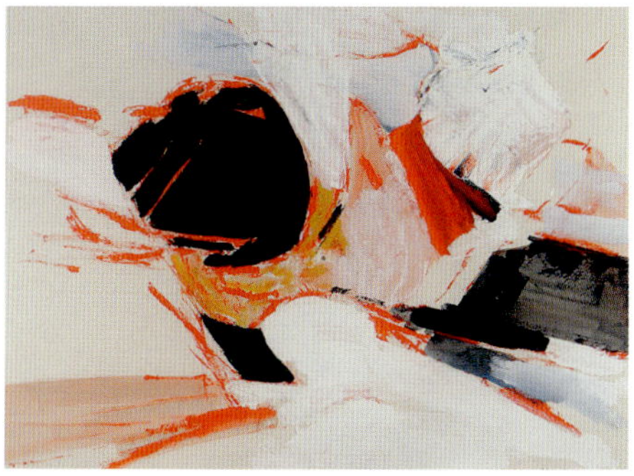

Heath, Adrian 1920–1992
Composition 1960
oil on canvas 72.5 x 93
CLS.1

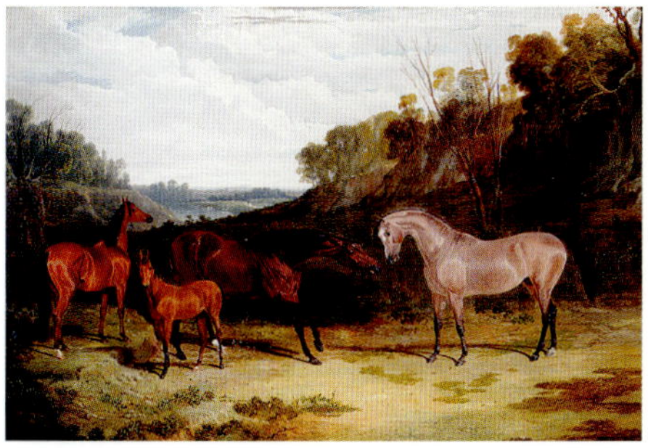

Herring, John Frederick I 1795–1865
Horses in a Landscape
oil on canvas 71 x 106
CP/TR 293

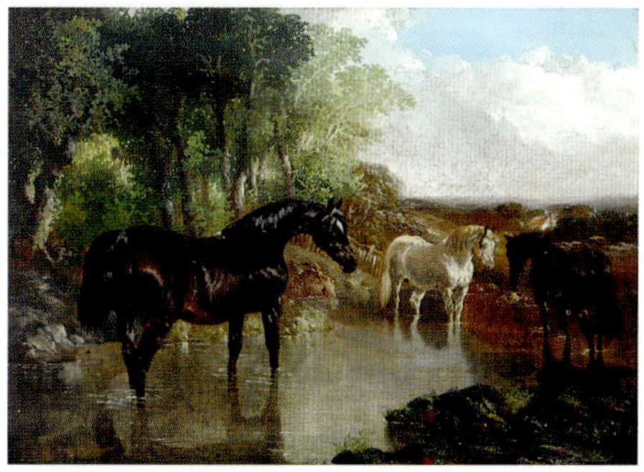

Herring, John Frederick I 1795–1865
The Brood Mare
oil on canvas 44 x 60
CP/TR 222

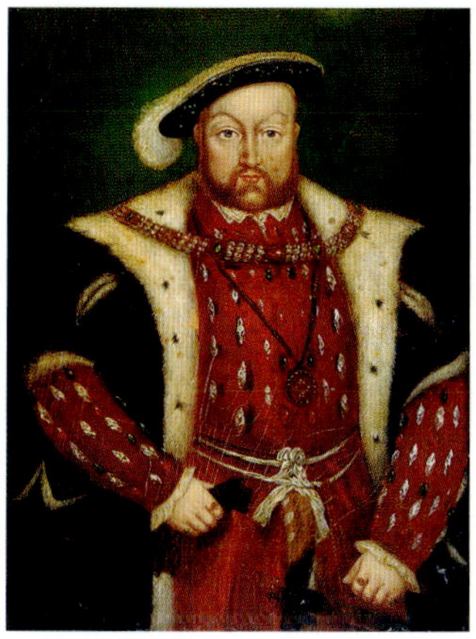

Holbein, Hans the Younger (after)
1497/1498–1543
Henry VIII (1491–1547) 17th C
oil on panel 23.5 x 17.5
CP/TR 170

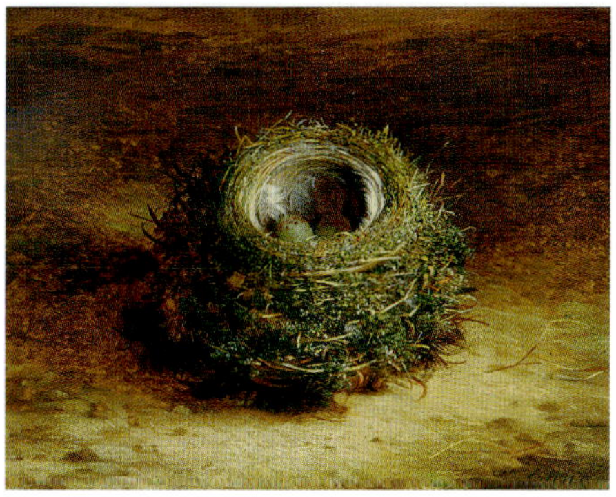

Hold, Abel 1815–1896
A Bird's Nest
oil on canvas 20 x 26
CP/TR 325

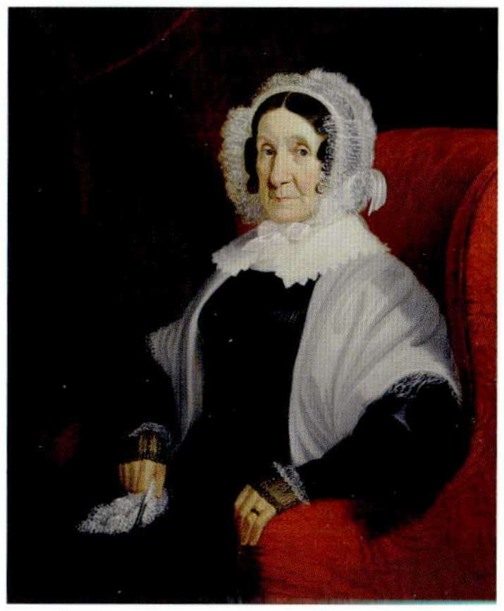

Hold, Abel 1815–1896
Mrs Tyas
oil on canvas 90 x 75
CP/TR 397

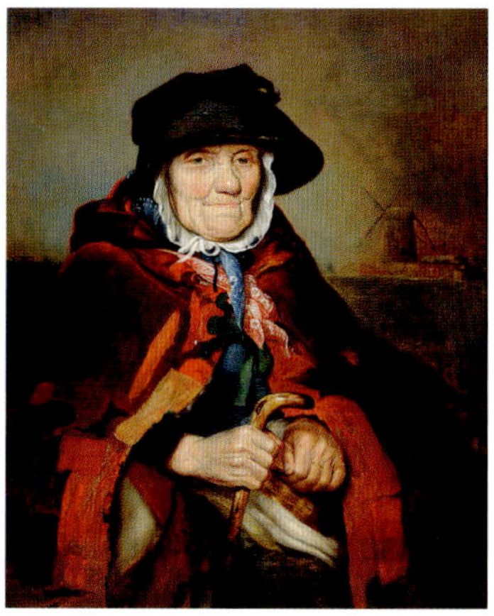

Hold, Abel 1815–1896
Peggy Airey (1759–1848)
oil on canvas 79 x 63.5
CP/TR 296

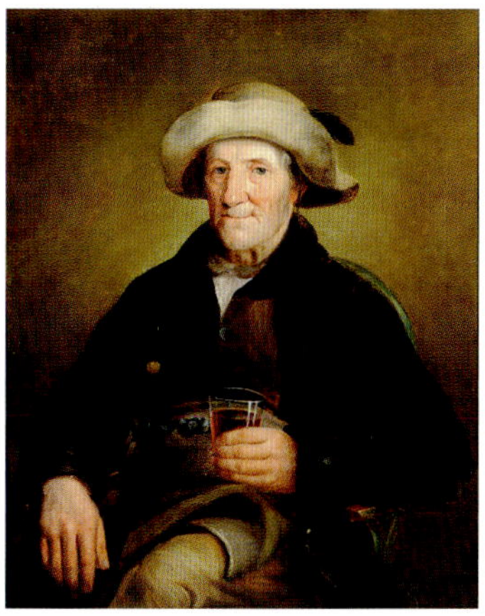

Hold, Abel 1815–1896
Watter Joe
oil on canvas 78.5 x 63.5
CP/TR 297

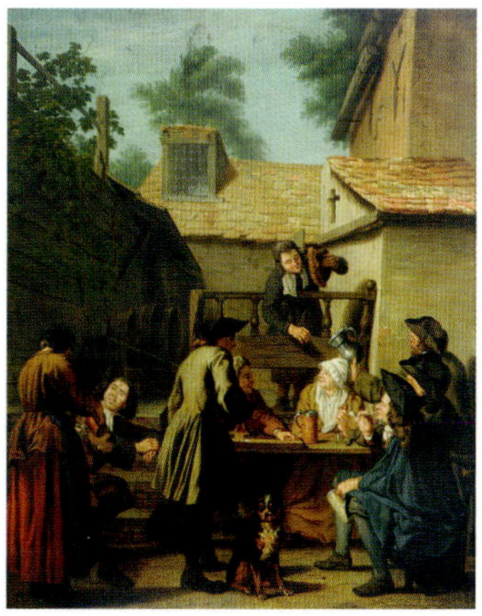

Horemans, Jan Josef the younger
1714–1790
A Tavern Scene
oil on woven material 56 x 46
CP/TR 132

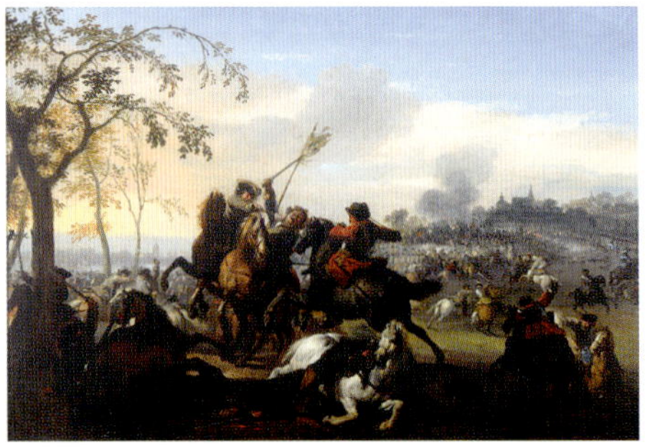

Huchtenburgh, Jan van 1647–1733
A Country Skirmish 1711
oil on panel & canvas 27 x 39
CP/TR 133

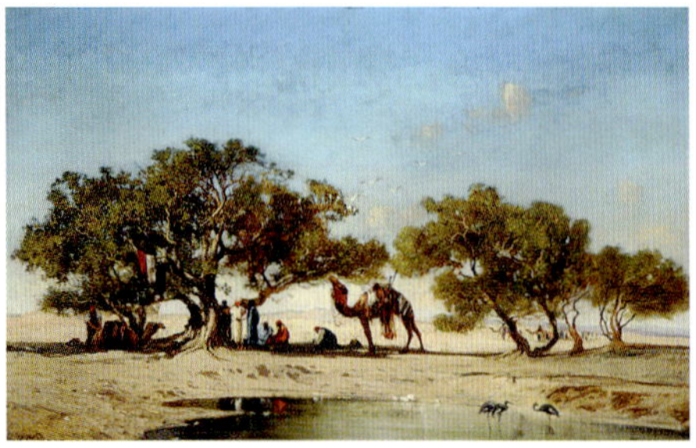

Huguet, Victor Pierre 1835–1902
An Eastern Scene with Camels and Figures Resting in the Shade under Trees 1860
oil on canvas 55 x 87
CP/TR 257

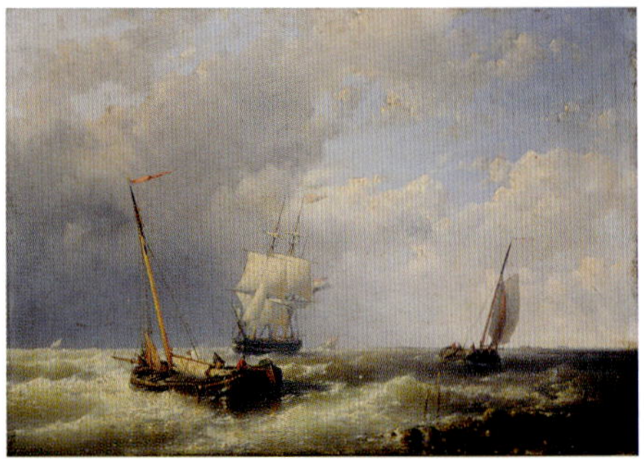

Hulk, Abraham I 1813–1897
Shipping off a Dutch Coast
oil on panel 31 x 44
CP/TR 327

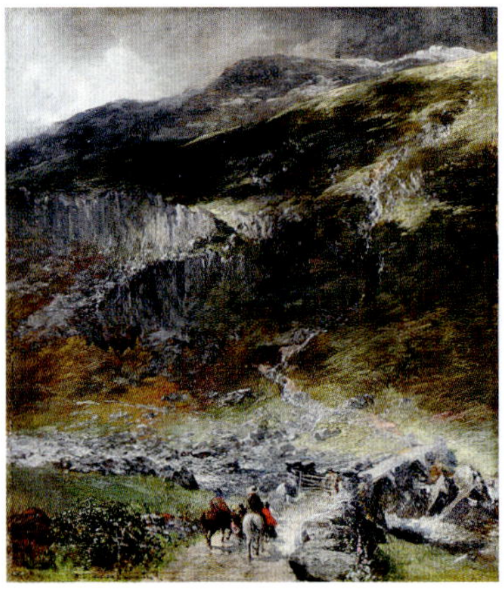

Hunt, Alfred William 1830–1896
Shadow of the Clouds
oil on canvas 42 x 35
CP/TR 160

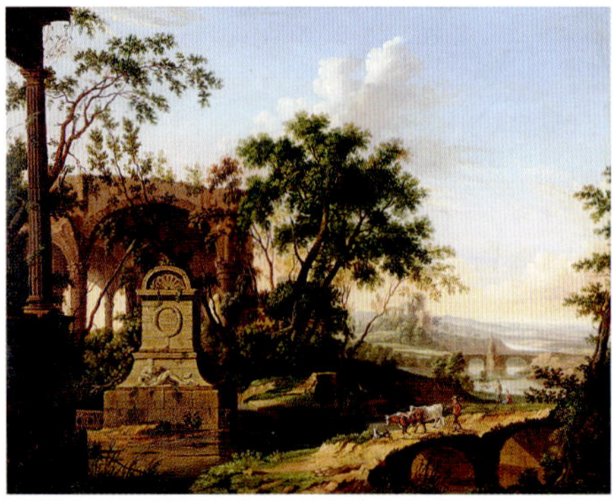

Huysmans, Jan Baptist (circle of) 1654–1716
Italianate Landscape with Classical Ruins 1680–1716
oil on canvas 35 x 42
CP/TR 144

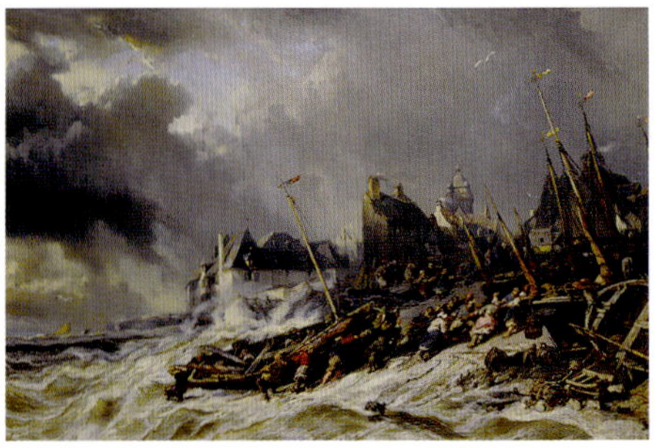

Isabey, Eugène 1803–1886
Hurricane before Saint-Malo, France 1860
oil on canvas 107 x 156
CP/TR 228

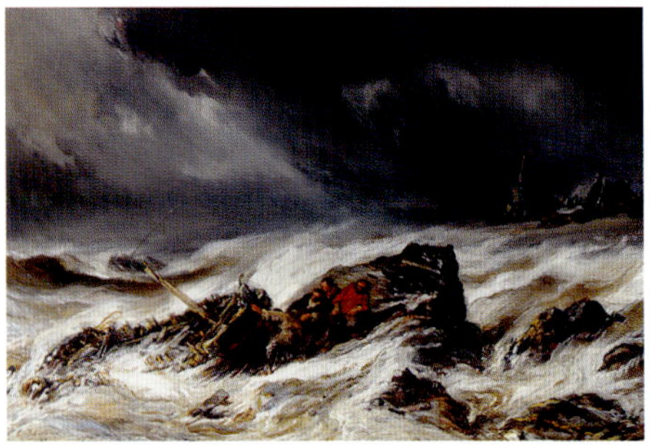

Isabey, Eugène 1803–1886
The Wreck 1860
oil on canvas 35 x 52
CP/TR 194

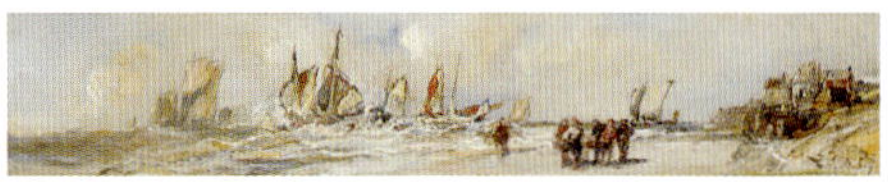

Isabey, Eugène 1803–1886
Boats Leaving Shore 1860–1870
oil on panel 11.5 x 54
CP/TR 183

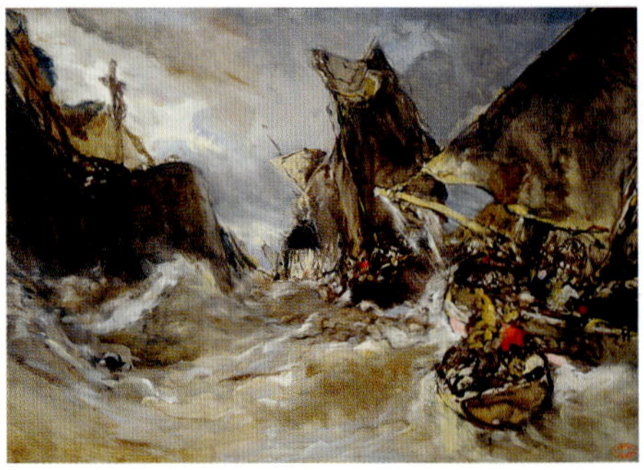

Isabey, Eugène 1803–1886
The Entrance into Port 1860–1870
oil on canvas 50 x 75
CP/TR 285

Facing page: Wright, John Michael, 1617–1694, *Henry Howard (1628–1684), 6th Duke of Norfolk* (detail), Barnsley Museum and Heritage Service, (p. 62)

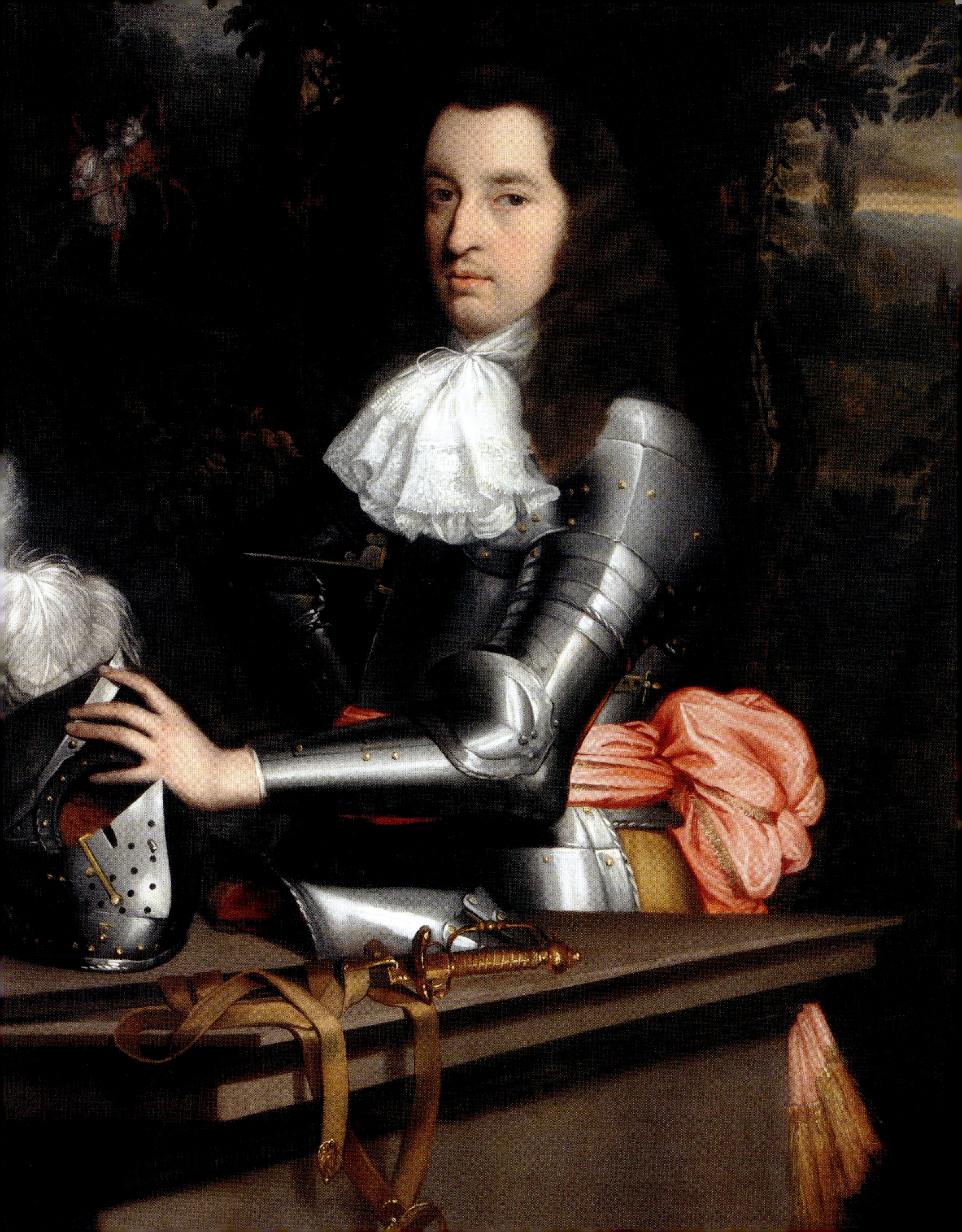

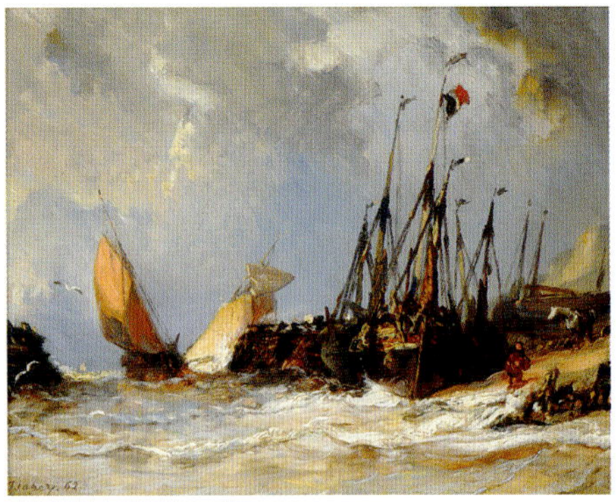

Isabey, Eugène 1803–1886
Fishing Boats on a Beach 1862
oil on panel 18.5 x 23.5
CP/TR 179

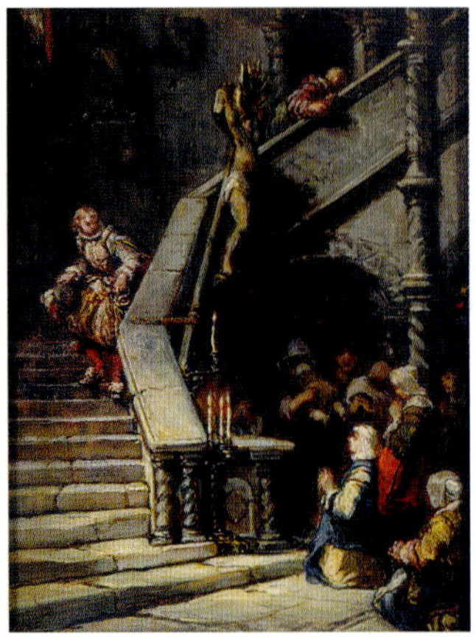

Isabey, Eugène 1803–1886
Good Friday in the Middle Ages 1862
oil on panel 32 x 23.5
CP/TR 189

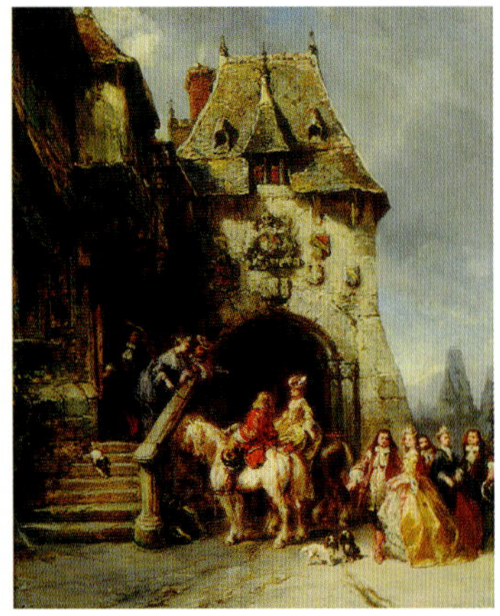

Isabey, Eugène 1803–1886
Une visite au château 1862
oil on panel 55 x 45
CP/TR 240

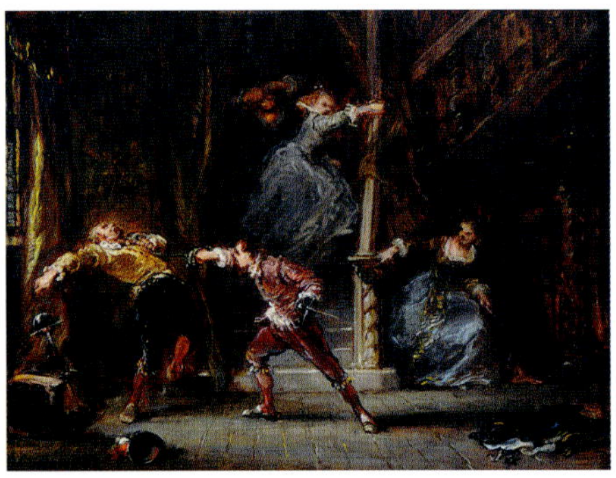

Isabey, Eugène 1803–1886
The Duel
oil on panel 21.5 x 34.5
CP/TR 184

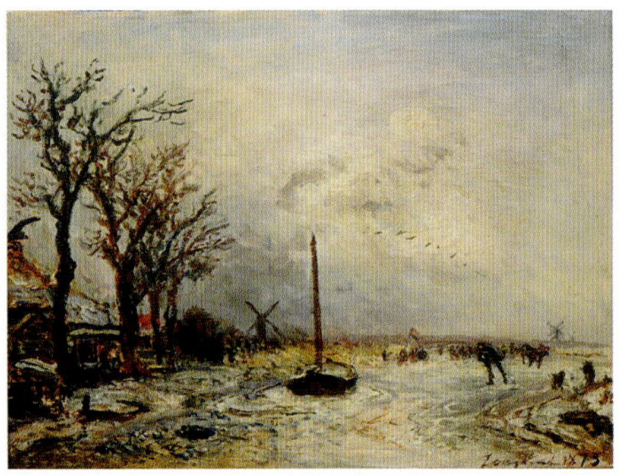

Jongkind, Johan Barthold 1819–1891
Coast Scene with Windmills 1873
oil on canvas 23 x 30.5
CP/TR 143

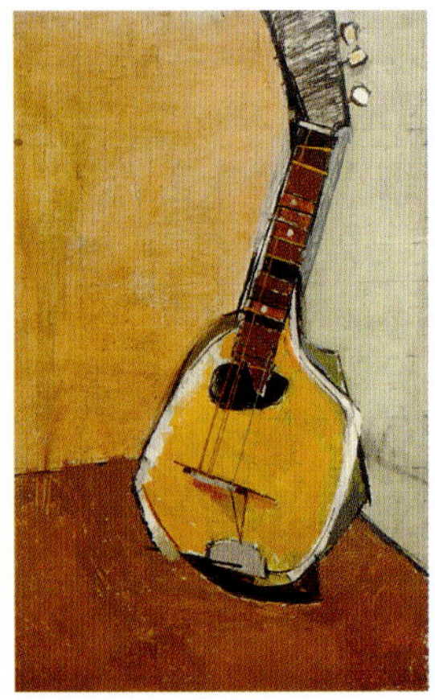

Kenning, N. W. active 20th C
Mandolin
oil on hardboard 76.5 x 48.5
CP/TR 128

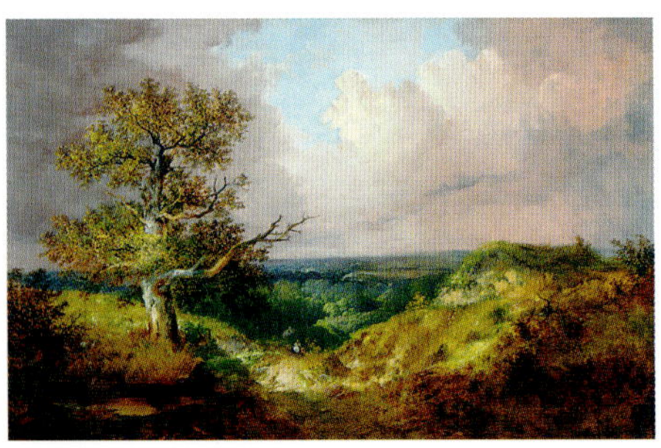

Ladbrooke, John Berney 1803–1879
A Passing Storm
oil on canvas 51 x 76
CP/TR 262

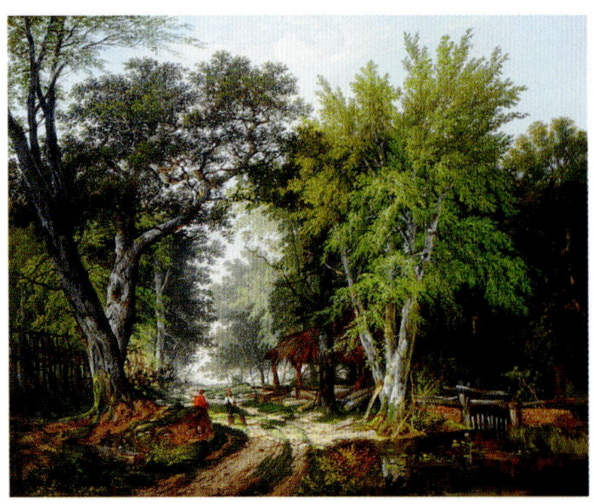

Ladbrooke, John Berney 1803–1879
Spring Morning in the Park
oil on canvas 63.5 x 76
CP/TR 114

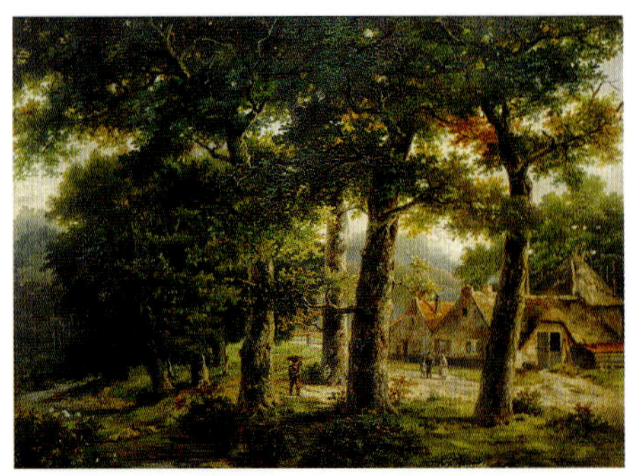

Ladbrooke, John Berney 1803–1879
Wooded Landscape with a Farm
oil on canvas 60 x 80
CP/TR 212

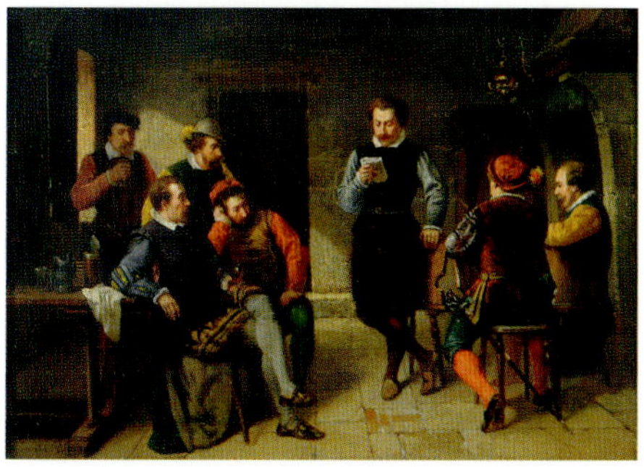

Lefevre, Adolphe René 1834–1868
Dans la taverne 1860–1868
oil on panel 16.5 x 21.5
CP/TR 116

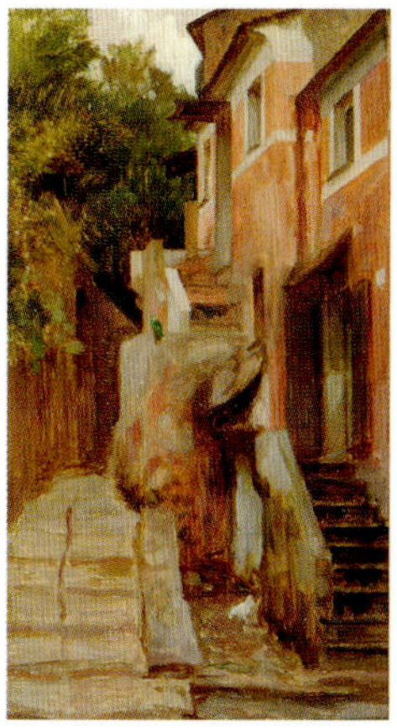

Leighton, Frederic 1830–1896
A Street in Lerici, Italy
oil on panel 18.5 x 10
CP/TR 238

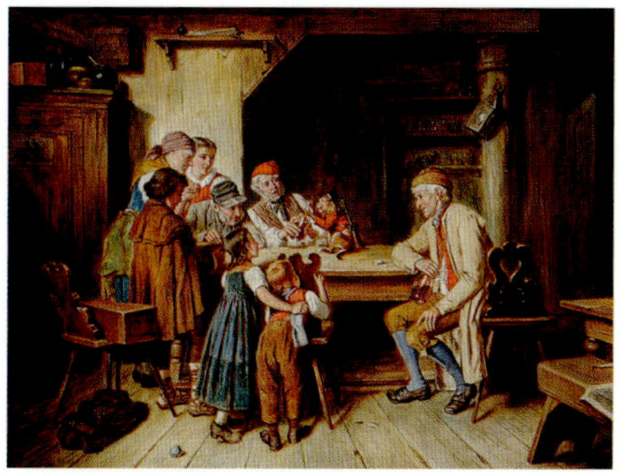

Lejin, M. W. active 19th C
The Performing Monkey
oil on canvas 71 x 91.5
CP/TR 280

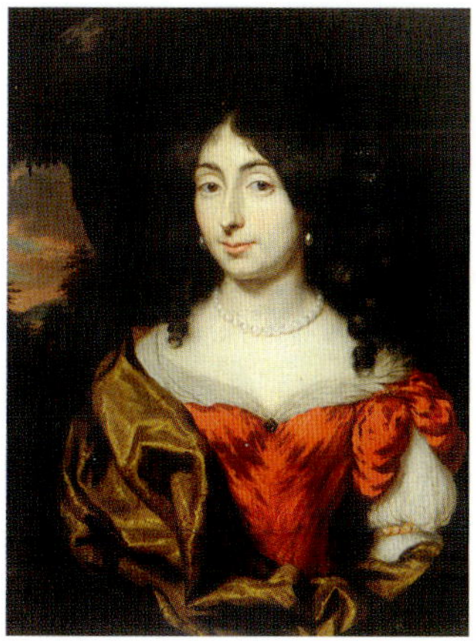

Lely, Peter (follower of) 1618–1680
Louise Renée de Penancoët de Querouaille (1649–1734), Duchess of Portsmouth 17th C
oil on canvas 40 x 30.5
CP/TR 155

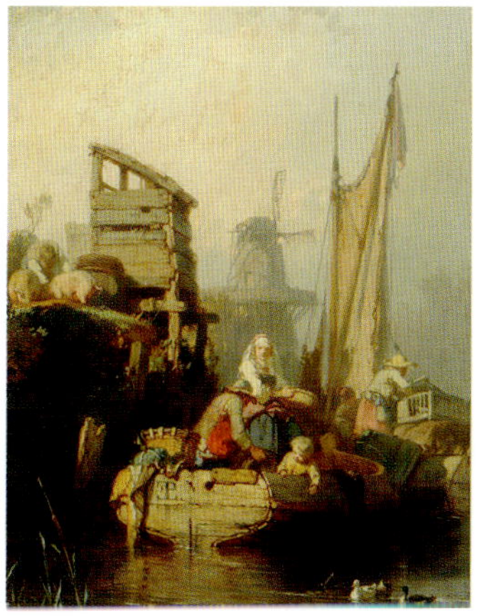

Lepoittevin, Eugène Modeste Edmond 1806–1870
A River Landscape
oil on canvas 39 x 32
CP/TR 188

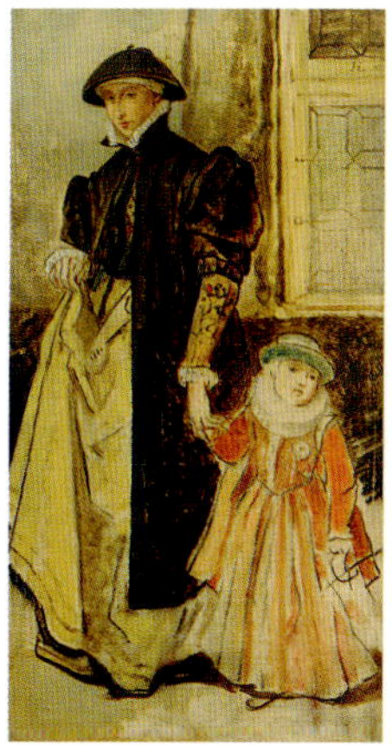

Leys, Hendrik (attributed to) 1815–1869
Mary of Burgundy (1457–1482) 1855
oil on panel 50 x 27
CP/TR 162

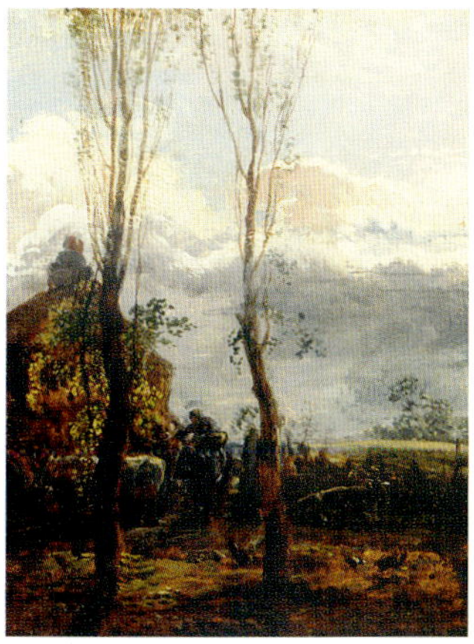

Linnell, John 1792–1882
Evening
oil on panel 14 x 11
CP/TR 187

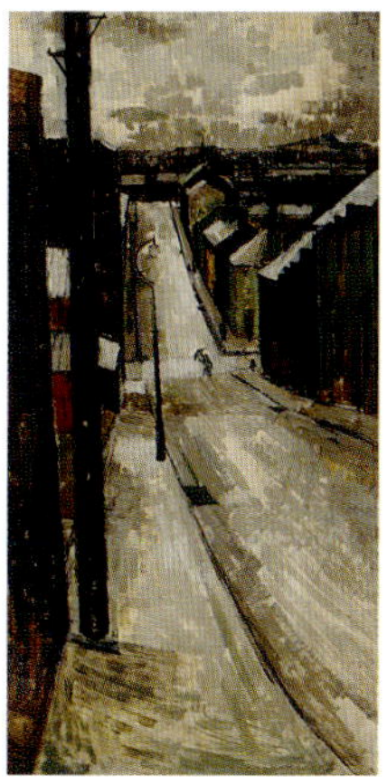

Long, John Kenneth 1924–2006
Fitzwilliam Street, Barnsley, South Yorkshire
oil & acrylic on hardboard 122 x 60
CP/TR 352

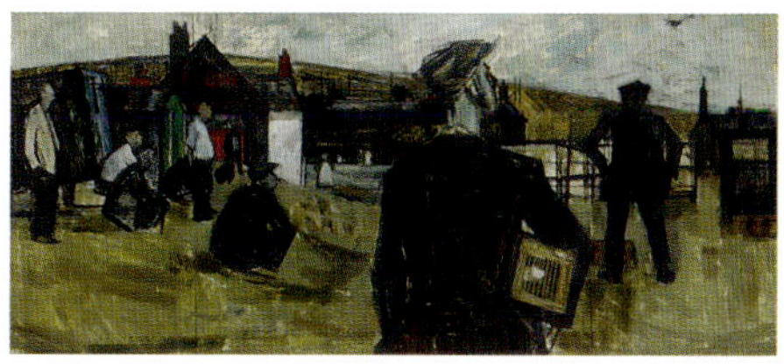

Long, John Kenneth 1924–2006
Pigeon Flying at the Red Lion, Worsbrough, South Yorkshire
oil & acrylic on hardboard 56 x 122
CP/TR 350

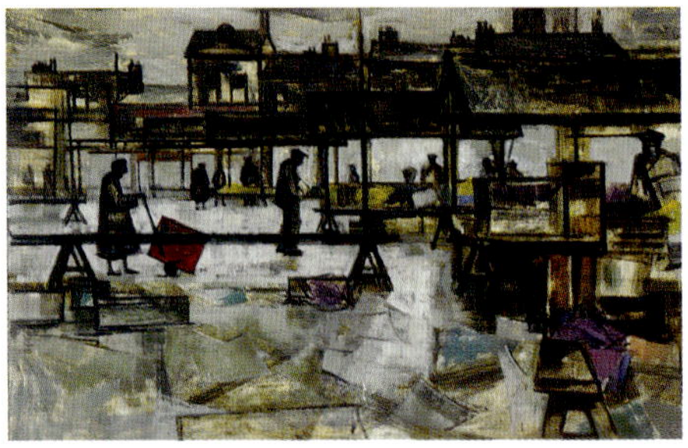

Long, John Kenneth 1924–2006
Winter Market
oil on canvas 61 x 91.5
CP/TR 351

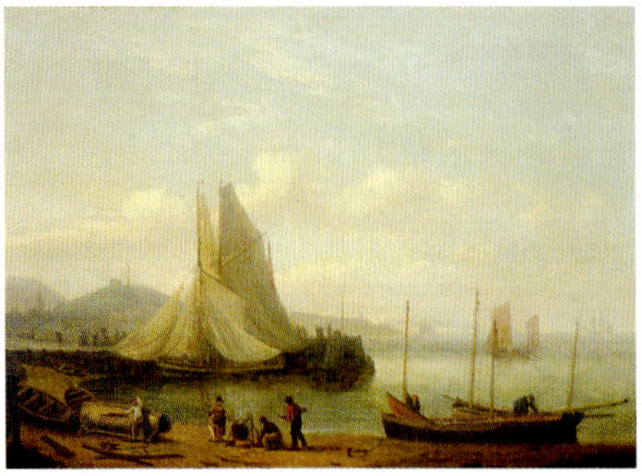

Luny, Thomas (attributed to) 1759–1837
Fisherfolk Repairing Boats on a Beach
oil on canvas 40 x 56
CP/TR 368

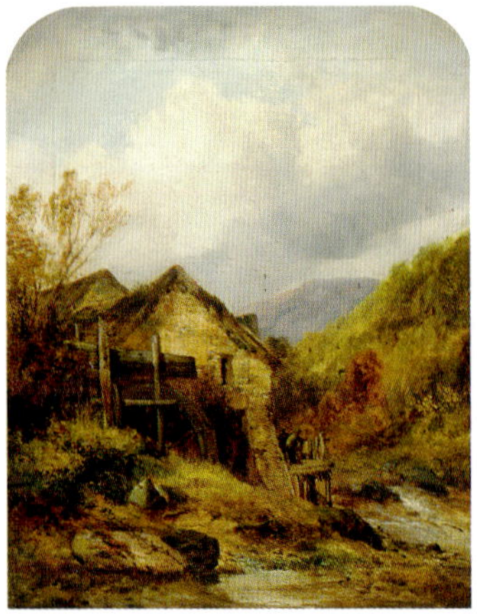

Mander, William Henry (circle of)
1850–1922
Autumn
oil on canvas 44 x 34.5
CP/TR 279

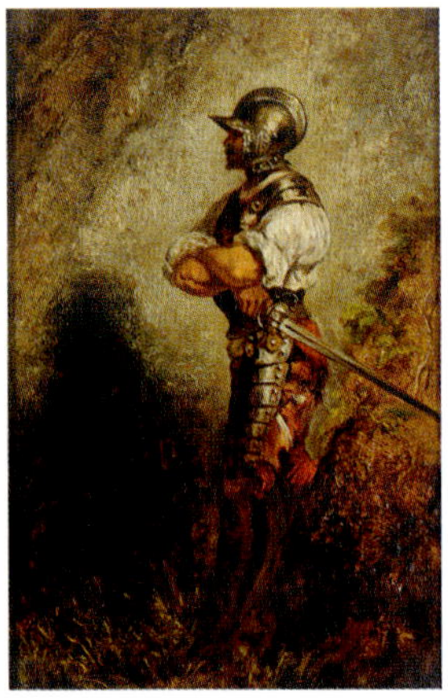

Martini, Salvatore 1823–1882
On Guard
oil on panel 27.5 x 18
CP/TR 275

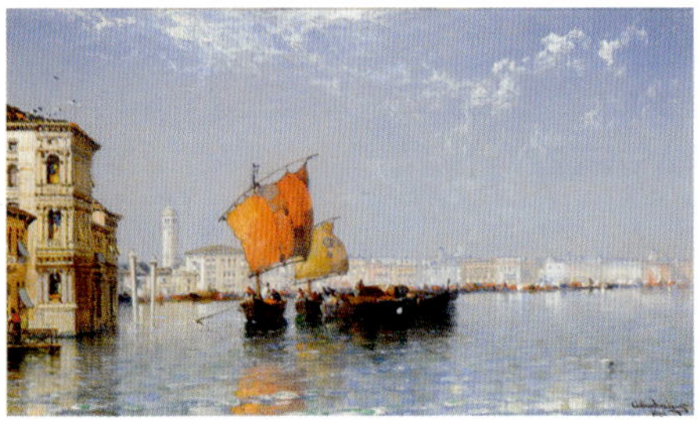

Meadows, Arthur Joseph 1843–1907
Palazzo Rezzonico, Venice
oil on canvas 30.5 x 51
CP/TR 110

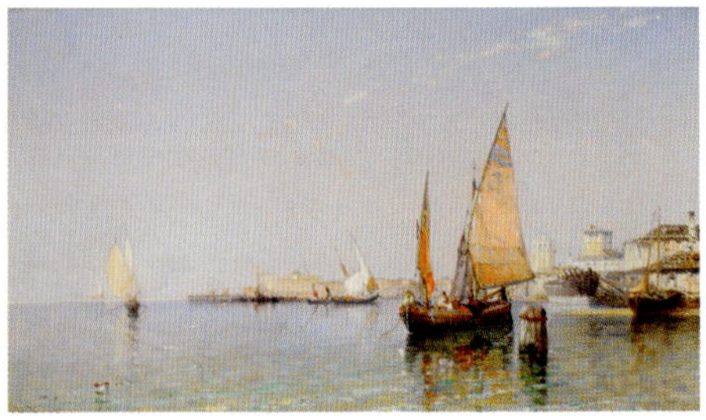

Meadows, Arthur Joseph 1843–1907
San Nicolò, Venice
oil on canvas 30.5 x 51
CP/TR 108

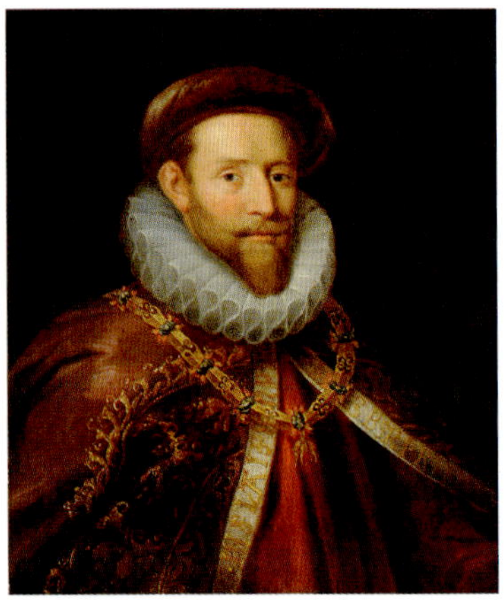

Miereveld, Michiel Jansz. van (circle of)
1567–1641
Portrait of a Gentleman Wearing the Order of the Golden Fleece 1590–1640
oil on canvas 73.5 x 61
CP/TR 231

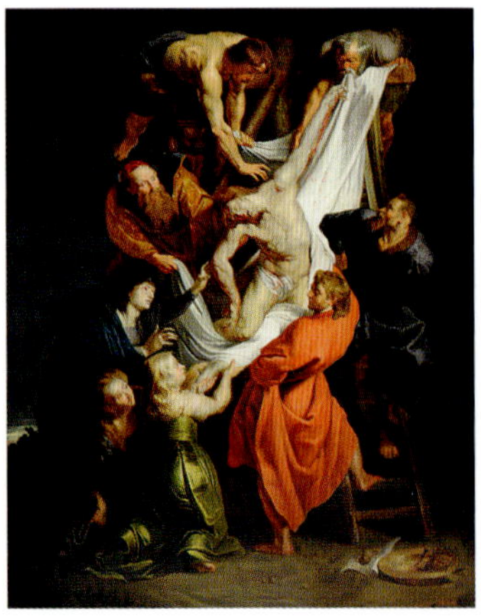

Mols, John Henry active 1880–c.1890
The Descent from the Cross (copy after Peter Paul Rubens)
oil on canvas 127 x 94.5
CP/TR 260

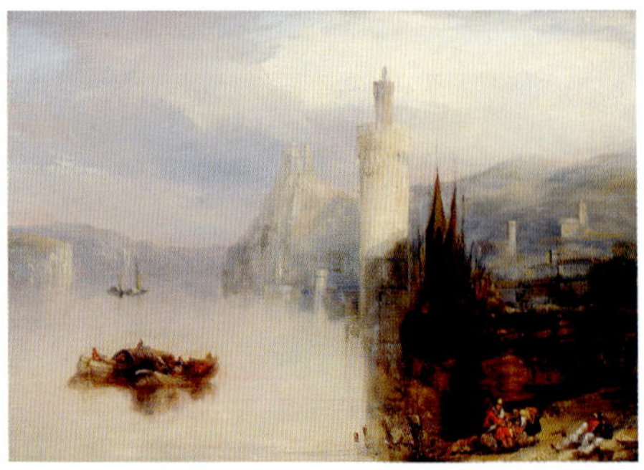

Moltino, Francis (attributed to) 1818–1872
Oberweisel on the Rhine, Germany
oil on canvas 40 x 56
CP/TR 369

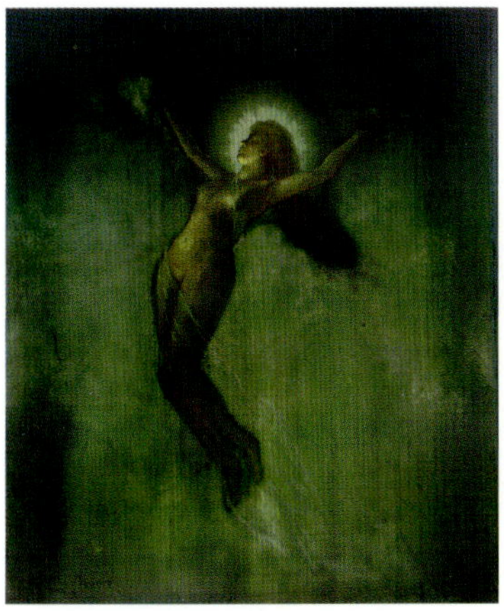

Moore, Ernest 1865–1940
Evening Star
oil on canvas 56 x 48
CP/TR 308

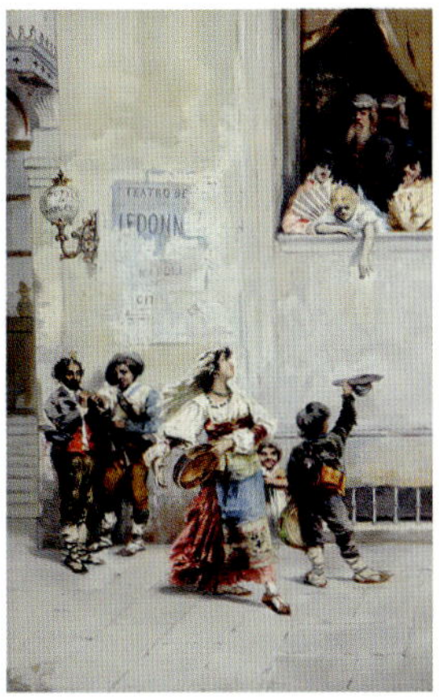

Moore, Madeline b.1869
Dancing Children (after Giacomo Mantegazza)
oil on canvas 40 x 25.5
CP/TR 246

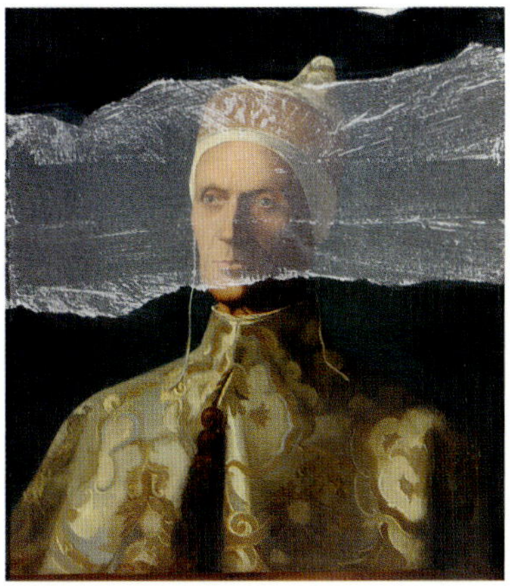

Moore, Madeline b.1869
Doge Loredan (1436–1521) (after Giovanni Bellini)
oil on canvas 54 x 45
CP/TR 204

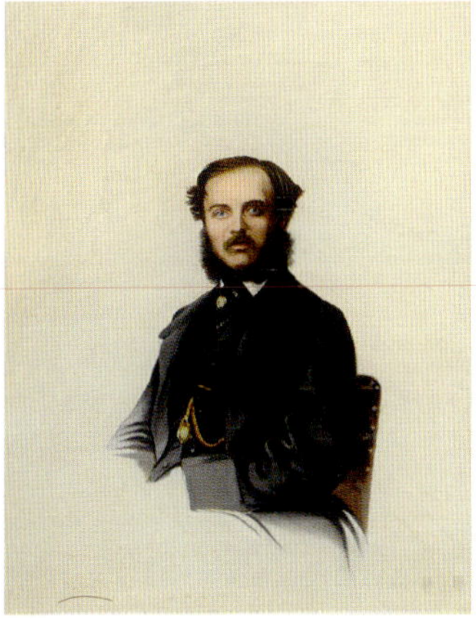

Moore, Madeline b.1869
Samuel Joshua Cooper (1830–1913)
oil on panel 24 x 18
CP/TR 251

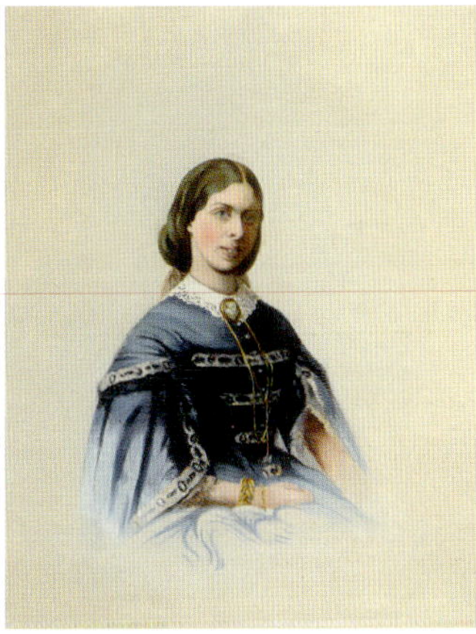

Moore, Madeline b.1869
Mrs Fanny Cooper
oil on panel 23 x 18
CP/TR 195

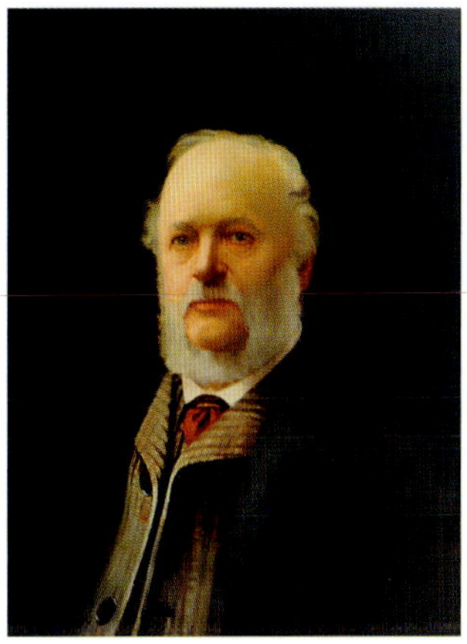

Moore, Madeline b.1869
Samuel Joshua Cooper (1830–1913)
oil on canvas 61 x 46
CP/TR 244

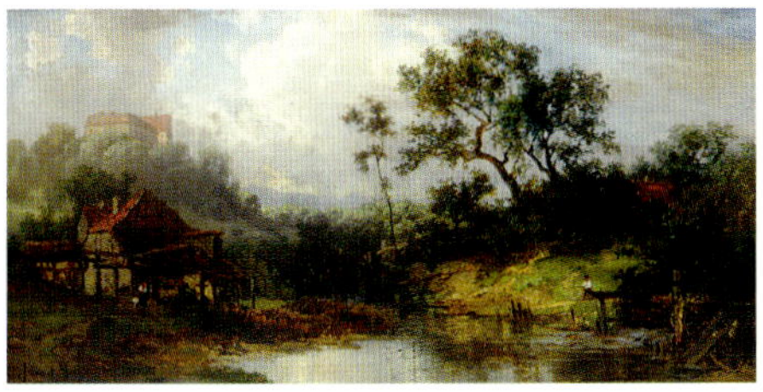

Morgenstern, Carl Ernst 1847–1928
Landscape with Peasants by a Pond 1875
oil on panel 22.5 x 45
CP/TR 239

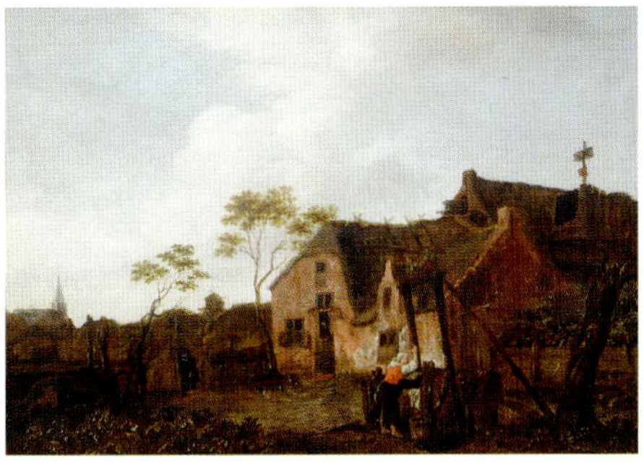

Murant, Emanuel 1622–1700
Woman at a Village Well
oil on panel 37 x 52.5
CP/TR 139

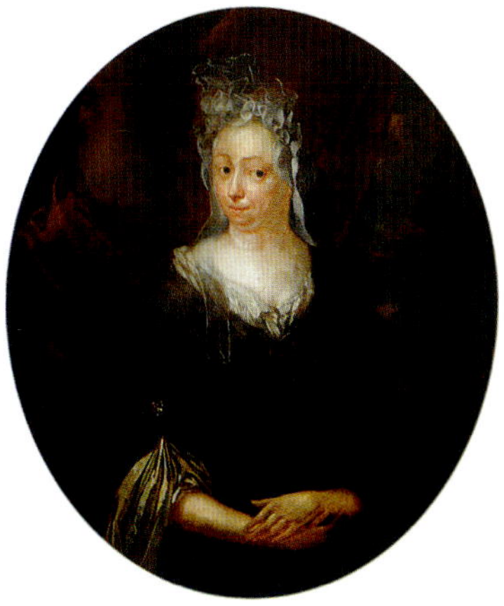

Netscher, Caspar (circle of) 1639–1684
Sarah Jennings (1660–1744), Duchess of Marlborough
oil on canvas 50 x 41
CP/TR 123

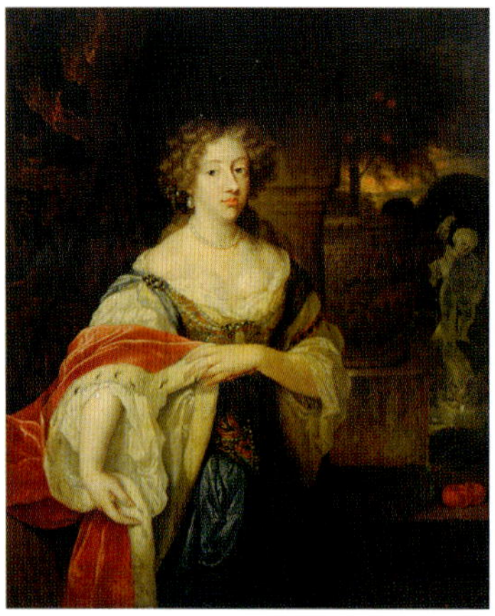

Netscher, Caspar (follower of) 1639–1684
Portrait of a Lady 1660–1680
oil on canvas 38.5 x 31
CP/TR 198

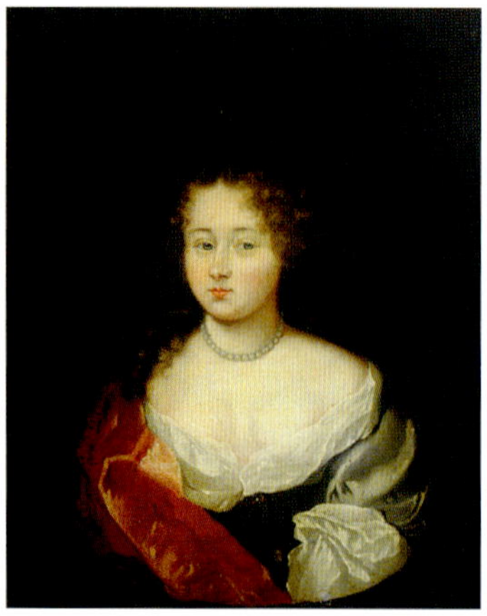

Netscher, Caspar (follower of) 1639–1684
Portrait of a Lady 1680–1700
oil on canvas 38 x 31
CP/TR 145

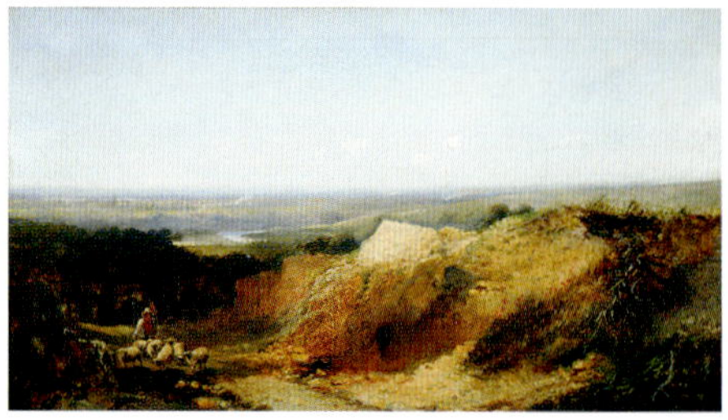

Niemann, Edmund John 1813–1876
Sandpits near London
oil on canvas 35.5 x 61
CP/TR 115

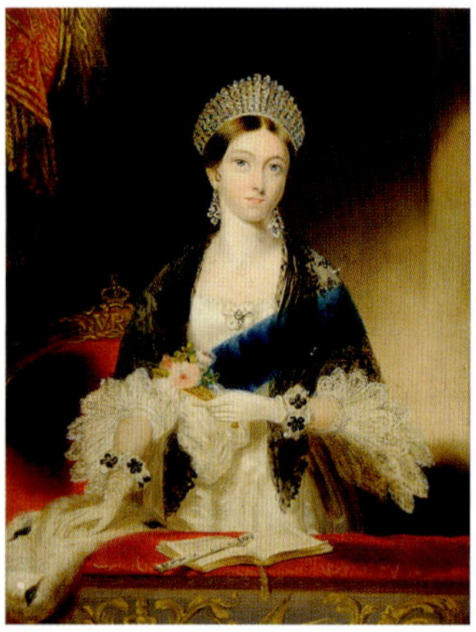

Parris, Edmund Thomas 1793–1873
The Young Queen Victoria (1819–1901)
oil on millboard 32.5 x 25
CP/TR 331

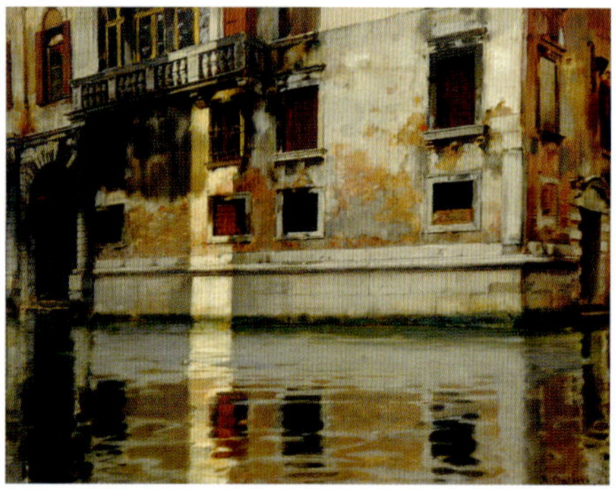

Pasini, Alberto 1826–1899
The Grimani Palace, Venice 1885
oil on canvas 33 x 42
CP/TR 321

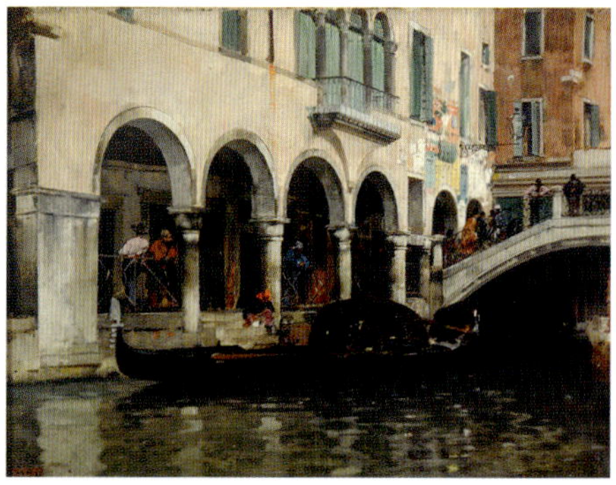

Pasini, Alberto 1826–1899
The Bridge of the Apostles, Venice 1885–1886
oil on canvas 28 x 36
CP/TR 218

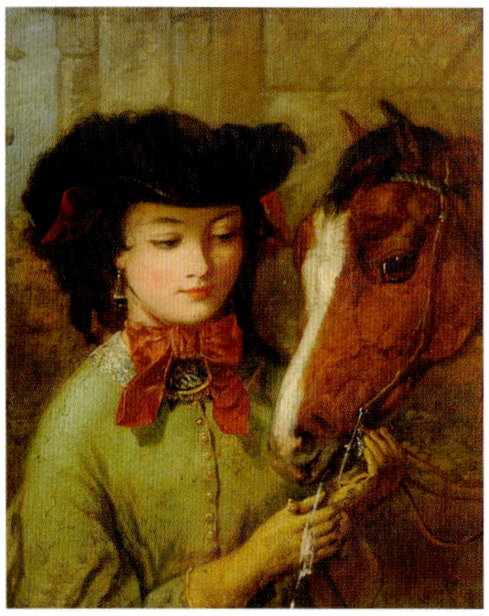

Pasmore, John Frederick 1820–1881
The Best of Friends
oil on canvas 58 x 48
CP/TR 316

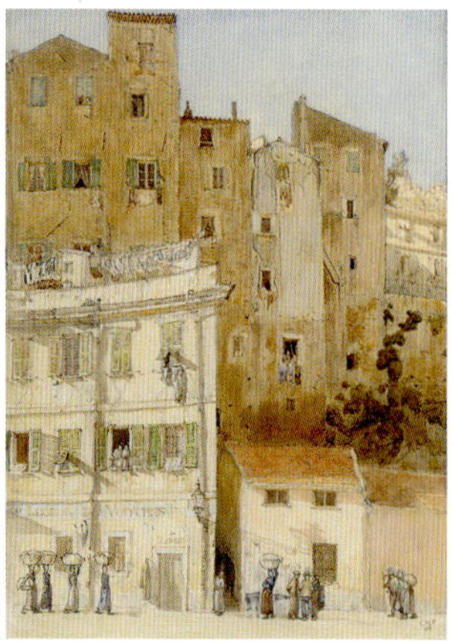

Pearce, Charles Maresco 1874–1964
A Street in Menton, France
oil on canvas 38 x 27
CP/TR57

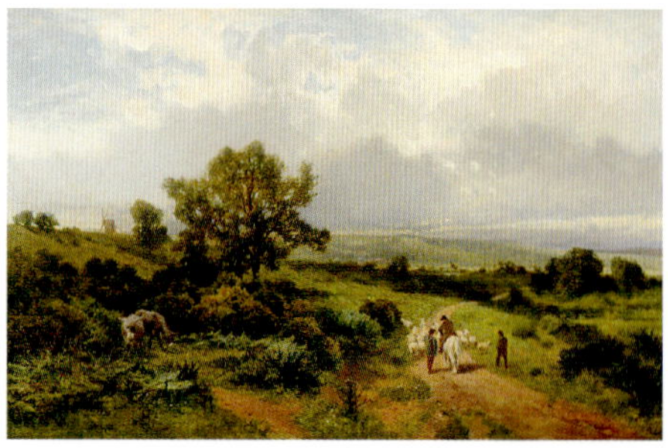

Peel, James 1811–1906
Wooded Landscape with Figures and Sheep
oil on canvas 48 x 74
CP/TR 301

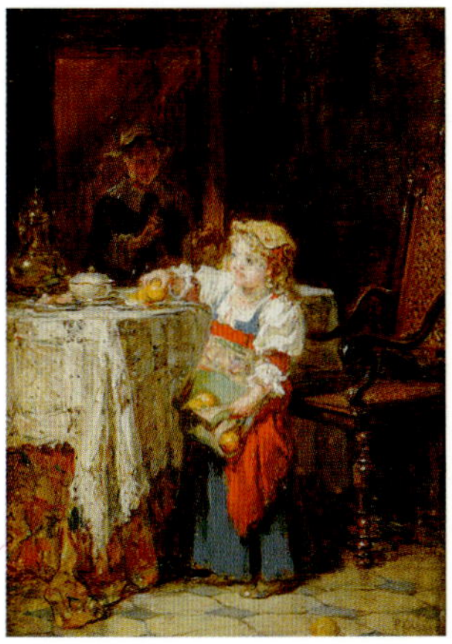

Plassan, Antoine Emile 1817–1903
Child with Fruit 1870–1890
oil on panel 21 x 15
CP/TR 235

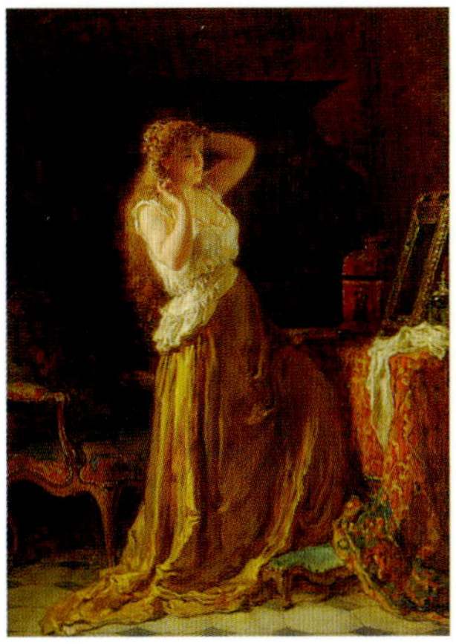

Plassan, Antoine Emile 1817–1903
The Toilet 1870–1890
oil on panel 21 x 15
CP/TR 250

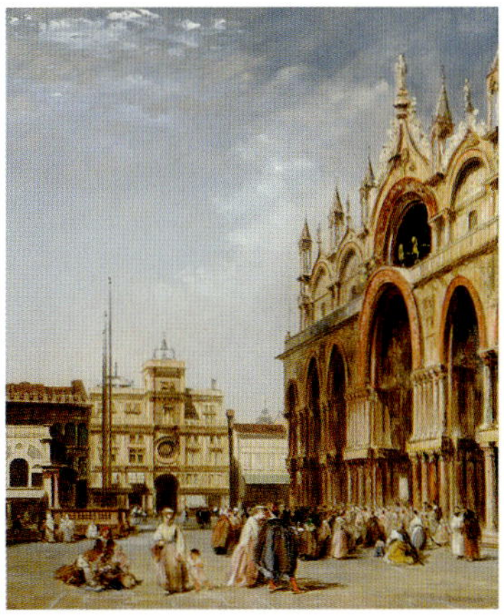

Pritchett, Edward active c.1828–1879
Piazza San Marco, Venice
oil on canvas 58.5 x 48
CP/TR 365

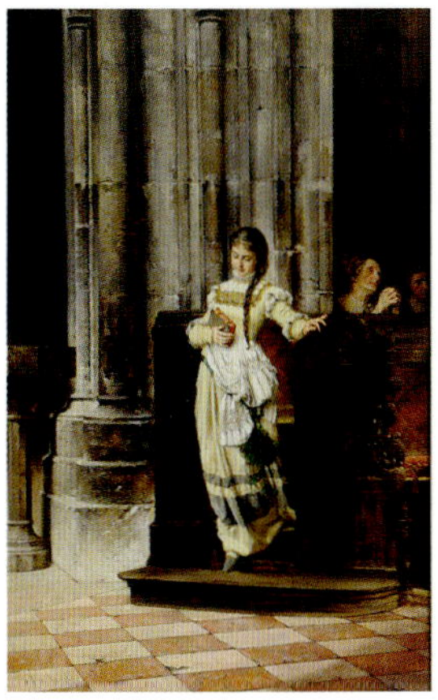

Probst, Carl 1854–1924
Leaving the Pew 1877
oil on panel 62 x 39
CP/TR 286

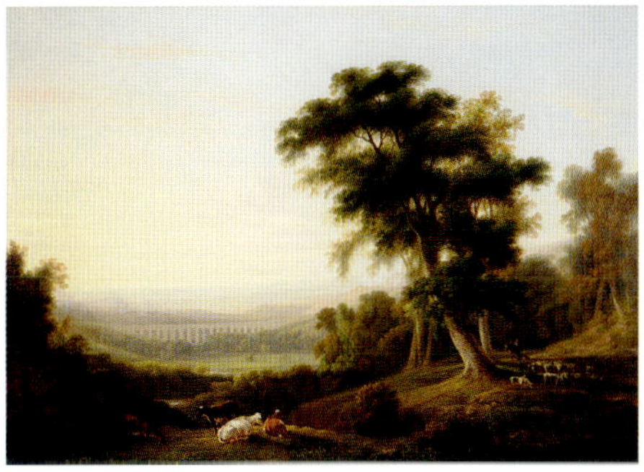

Rhodes, Joseph 1782–1854
Extensive Landscape with a Viaduct
oil on canvas 71 x 96
CP/TR 283

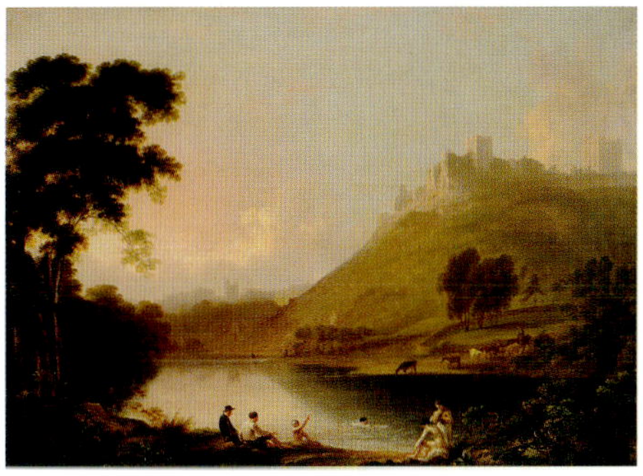

Rhodes, Joseph 1782–1854
Richmond Castle, Yorkshire
oil on canvas 71 x 96.5
CP/TR 282

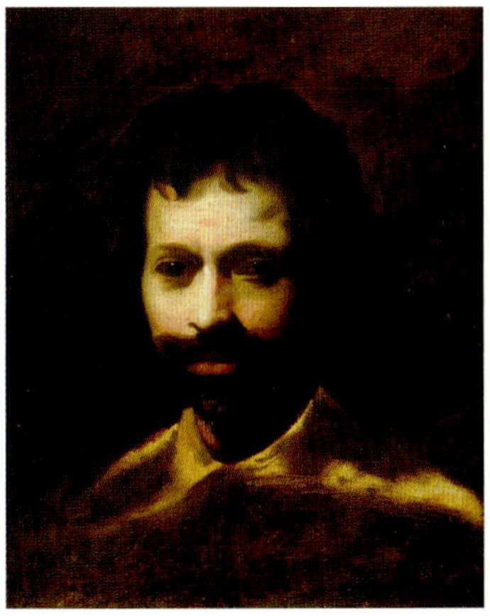

Ribera, Jusepe de (after) 1591–1652
Portrait of a Gentleman 1630–1640
oil on canvas 46 x 37
CP/TR 196

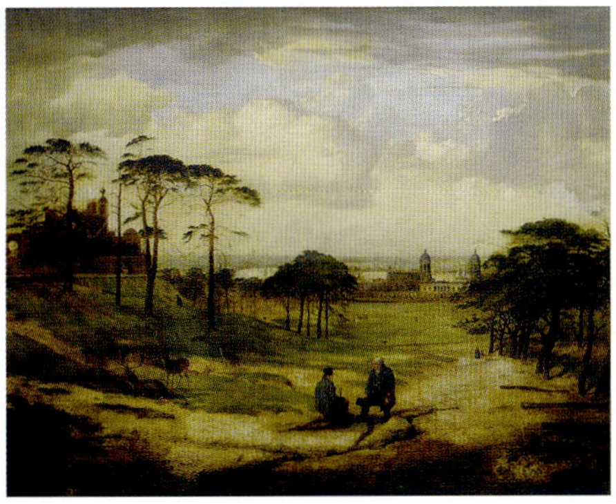

Ritchie, John active 1855–1897 & **Mote, George William** 1832–1909
Greenwich Park, London 1897
oil on canvas 101 x 123
CP/TR 299

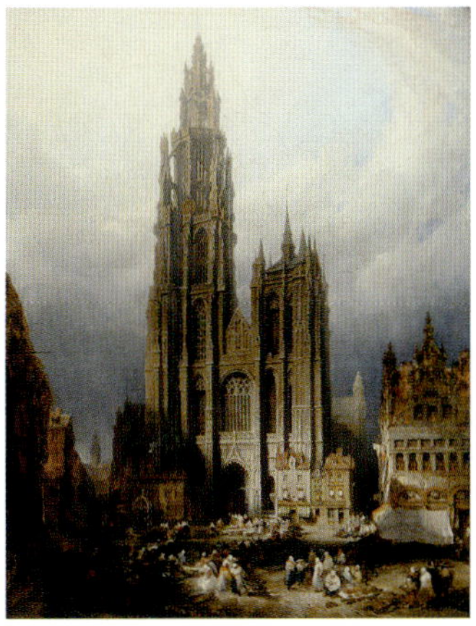

Roberts, David 1796–1864
Antwerp Cathedral, Belgium
oil on canvas 91 x 71
CP/TR 288

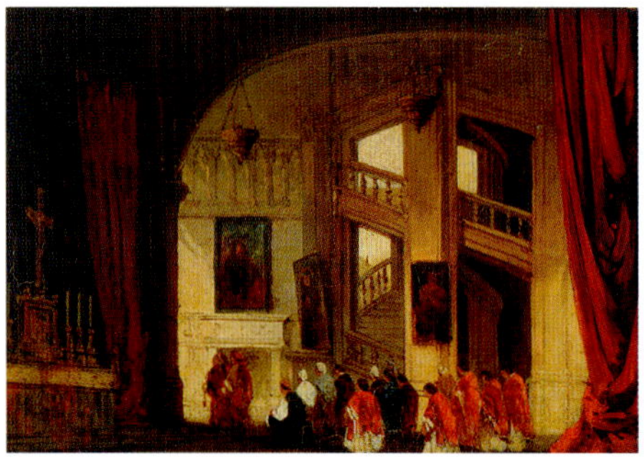

Roberts, David 1796–1864
The Château at Chambord, France
oil on panel 24 x 35
CP/TR 159

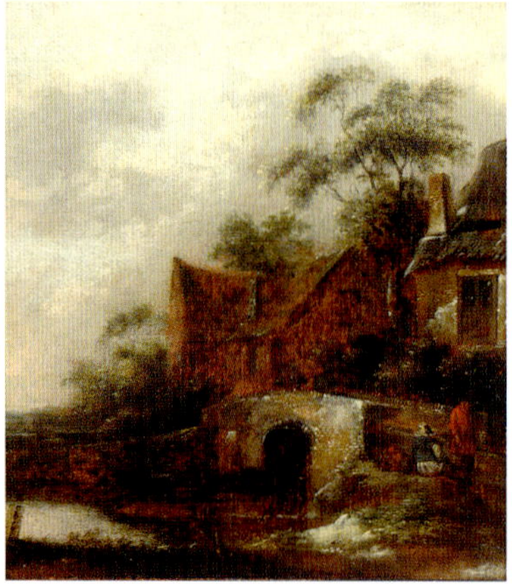

Rombouts, Salomon c.1652–c.1702
A River Scene with Figures
oil on panel 27 x 23.5
CP/TR 190

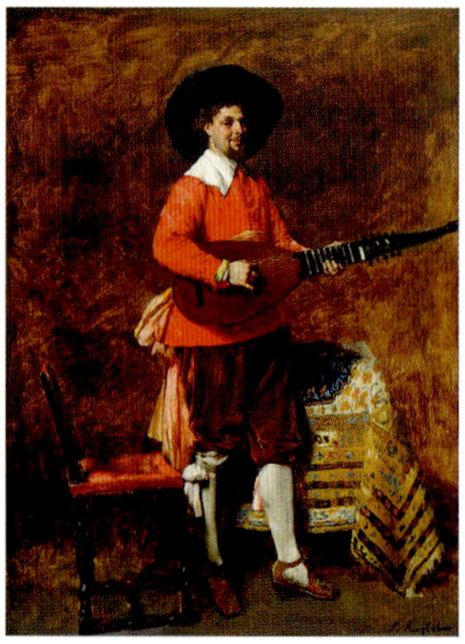

Roybet, Ferdinand 1840–1920
Man with a Guitar 1864–1879
oil on panel 60 x 45
CP/TR 229

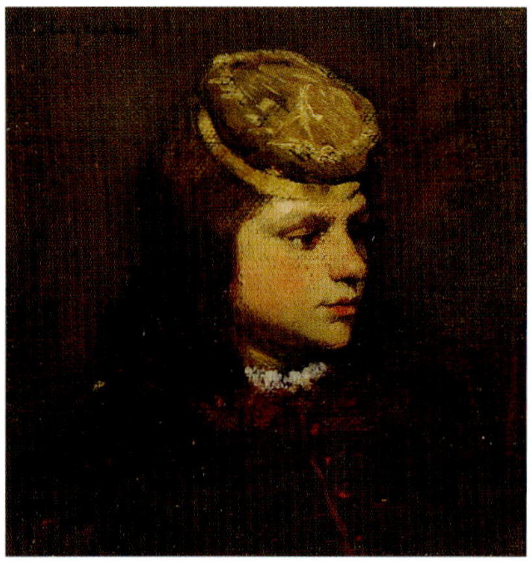

Roybet, Ferdinand 1840–1920
Head of a Boy 1864–1900
oil on canvas 15 x 14
CP/TR 230

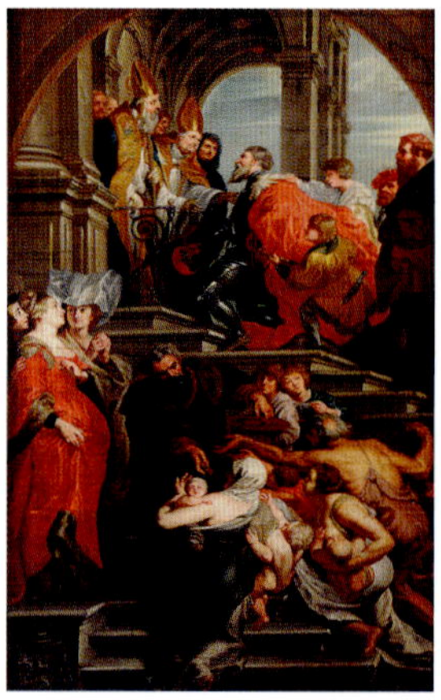

Rubens, Peter Paul (school of) 1577–1640
The Reception of St Bavo, the Patron Saint of Ghent 1670–1700
oil on canvas 86.5 x 51
CP/TR 259

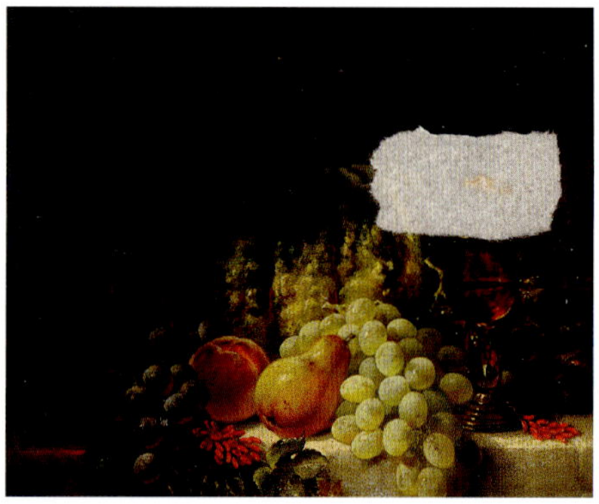

Rumley, Elizabeth active 1851–1876
Fruit
oil on canvas 40.5 x 48
CP/TR 197

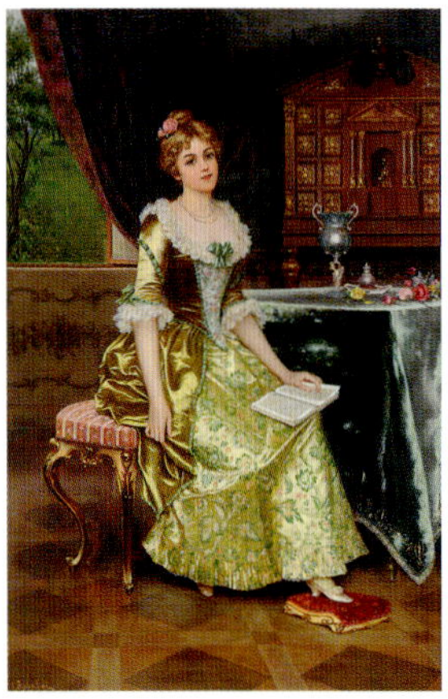

Sabatini, I. active late 19th C–early 20th C
A Lady Holding a Book
oil on canvas 96.5 x 61
CP/TR 300

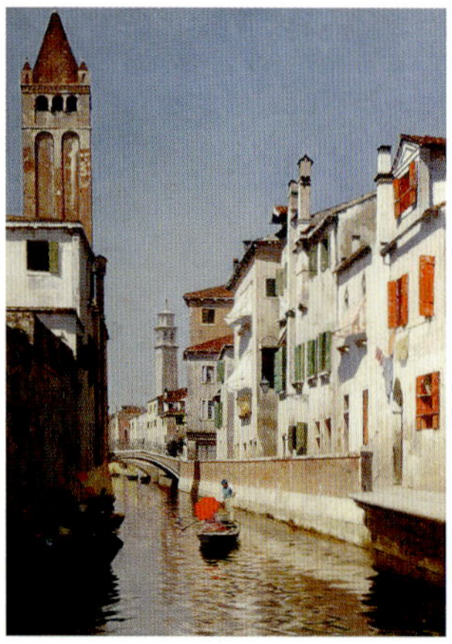

Santoro, Rubens 1859–1942
A Canal Scene, Venice 1890–1900
oil on panel 32.5 x 23.5
CP/TR 227

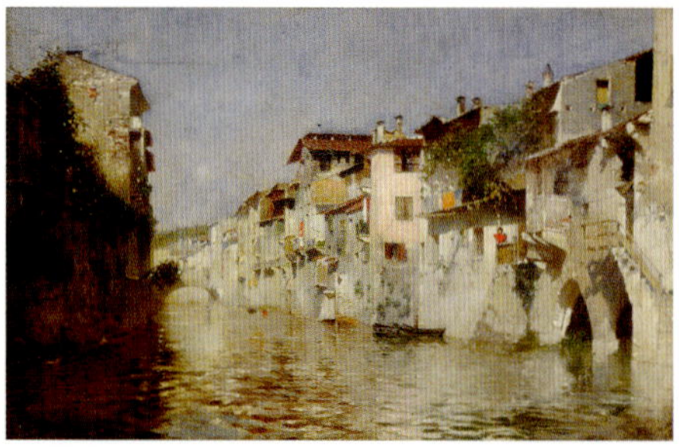

Santoro, Rubens 1859–1942
Verona, Italy 1890–1900
oil on canvas 25.5 x 38
CP/TR 317

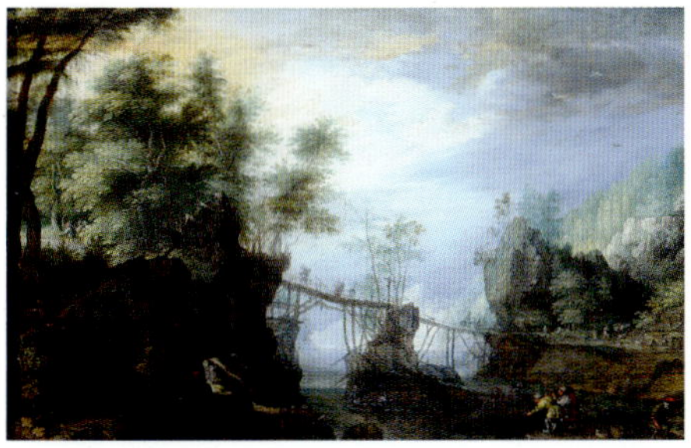

Savery, Roelandt (attributed to) 1576–1639
Wooded Landscape with a Bridge 1605–1615
oil on panel 28 x 42
CP/TR 137

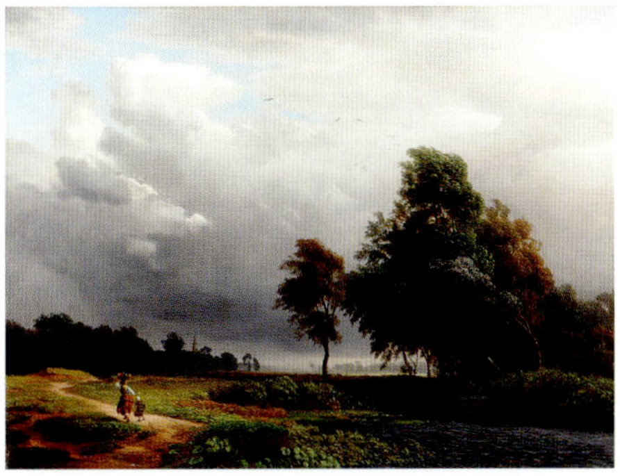

Schirmer, Johann Wilhelm 1807–1863
A Windy Day 1830–1863
oil on canvas 47 x 61.5
CP/TR 224

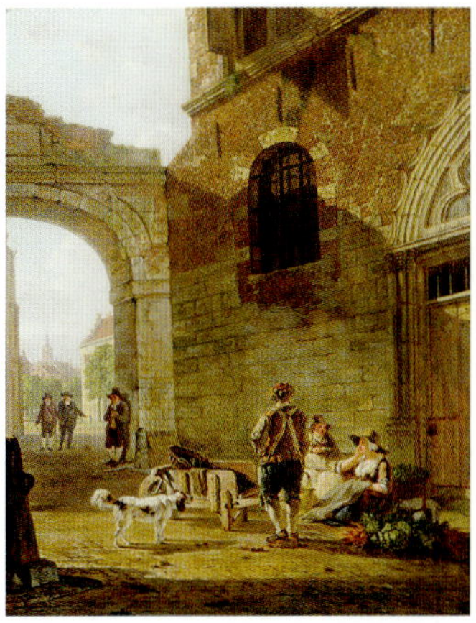

Schoenmakers, Johannes Pietersz. 1755–1842
The Oyster Seller in Town 1780–1815
oil on panel 61 x 48
CP/TR 134

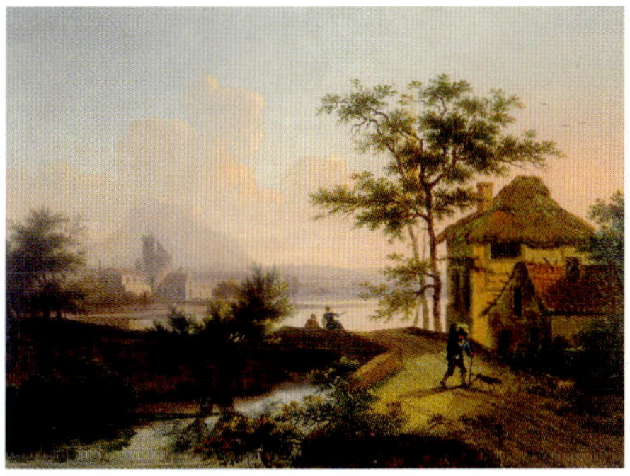

Schoevaerdts, Mathys (circle of)
c.1665–1723
A Landscape with Peasants on a Bridge
1685–1695
oil on panel 30.5 x 40.5
CP/TR 146

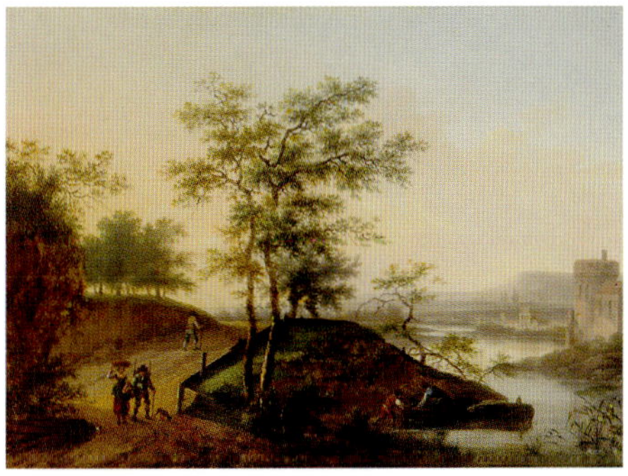

Schoevaerdts, Mathys (circle of)
c.1665–1723
River Landscape with Peasants on a Path
c.1700
oil on panel 30.5 x 40.5
CP/TR 154

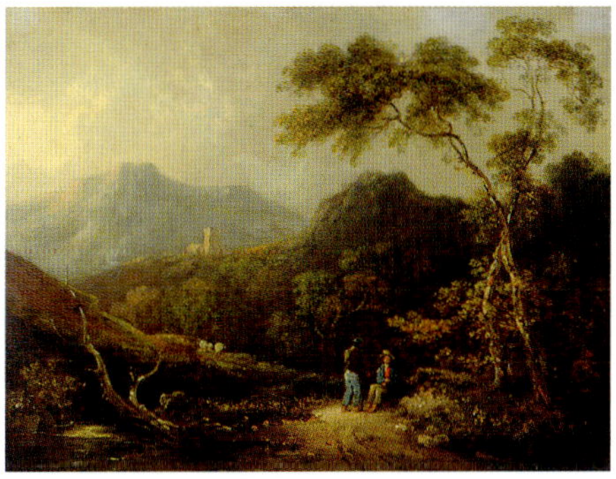

Schwanfelder, Charles Henry 1774–1837
Landscape with Figures
oil on panel 22.5 x 29.5
CP/TR 161

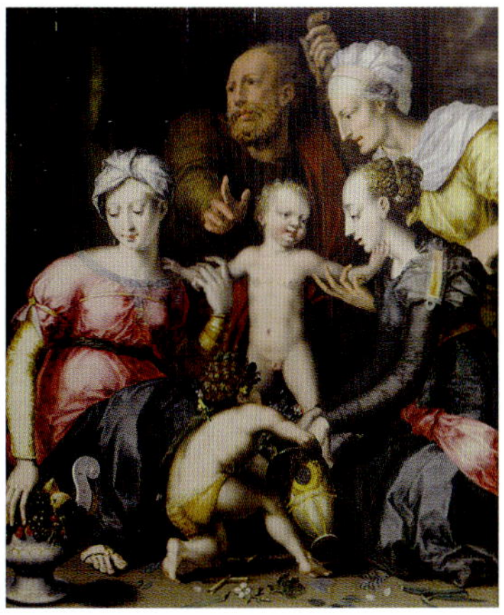

Sellaer, Vincent c.1500–c.1589
The Holy Family with Saints Elizabeth, Catherine and John the Baptist 1550–1575
oil on panel 135 x 111
CP/TR 295

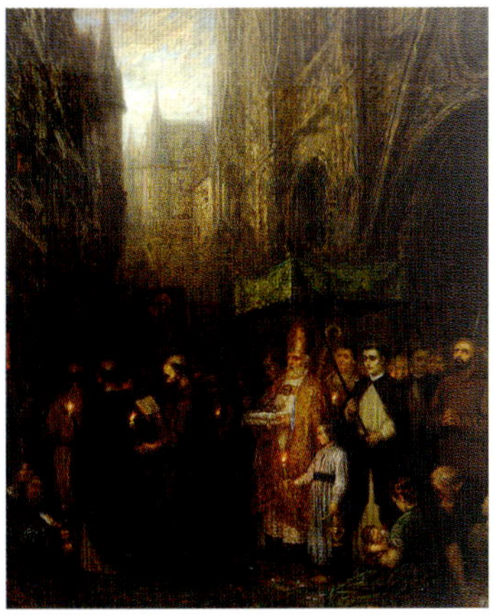

Serres, Antony 1828–1898
La procession de la couronne d'épines
1860–1890
oil on canvas 72 x 58.5
CP/TR 241

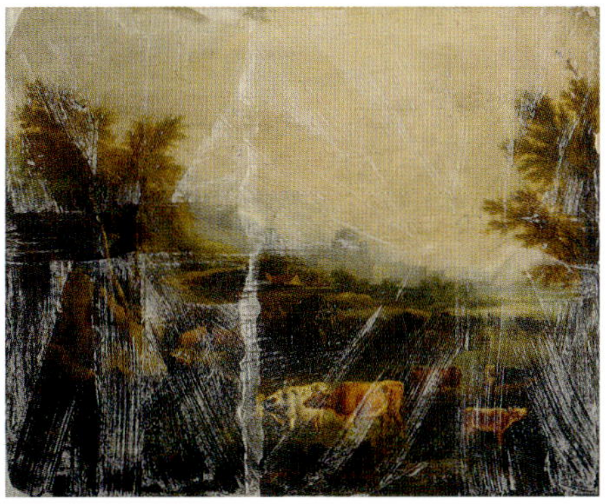

Shayer, Charles Waller (circle of) 1826–1914
& **Shayer, Henry Thring (circle of)** 1825–1894
Landscape with Cattle
oil on canvas 63 x 76.5
CP/TR 208

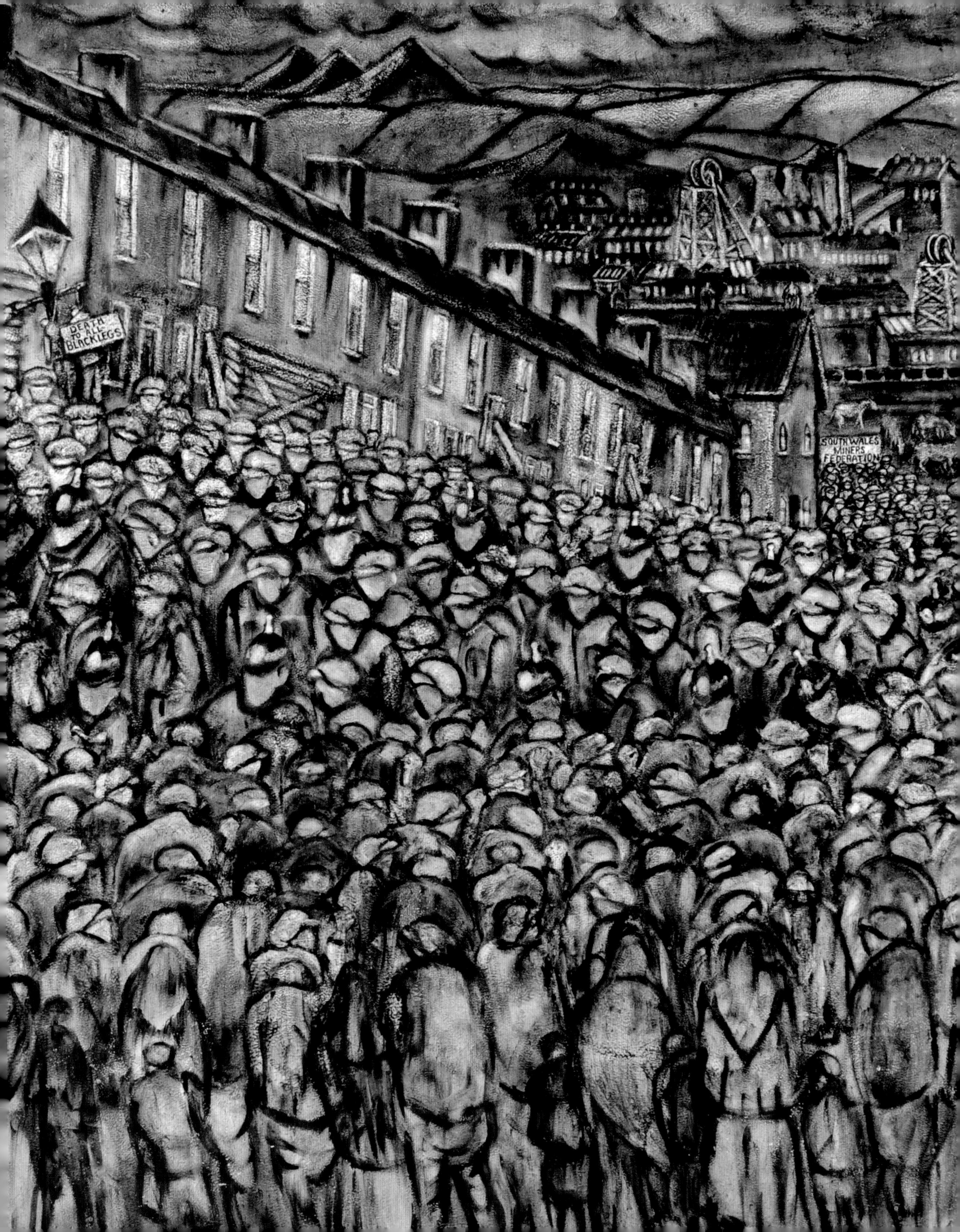
DEATH TO ALL BLACKLEGS
SOUTH WALES MINERS FEDERATION

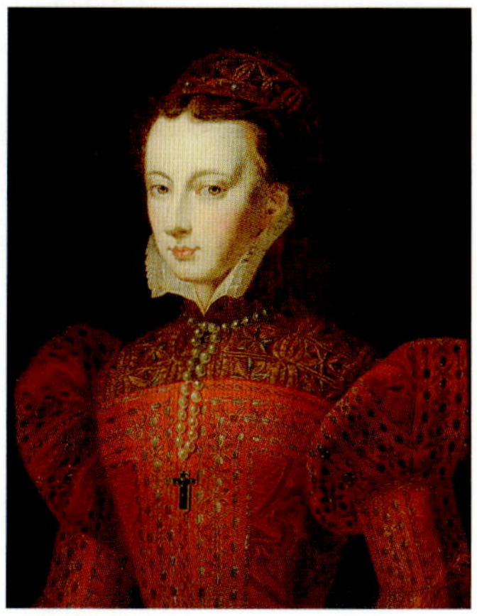

Somer, Paulus van I (attributed to) 1576–1621
Portrait of an Unknown Lady
oil on canvas 63 x 51
CP/TR 245

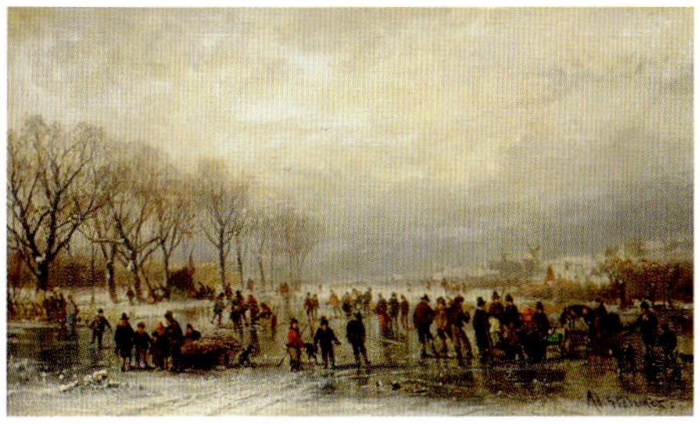

Stademann, Adolf 1824–1895
A Frozen River Scene 1870–1895
oil on canvas 33.5 x 56
CP/TR 201

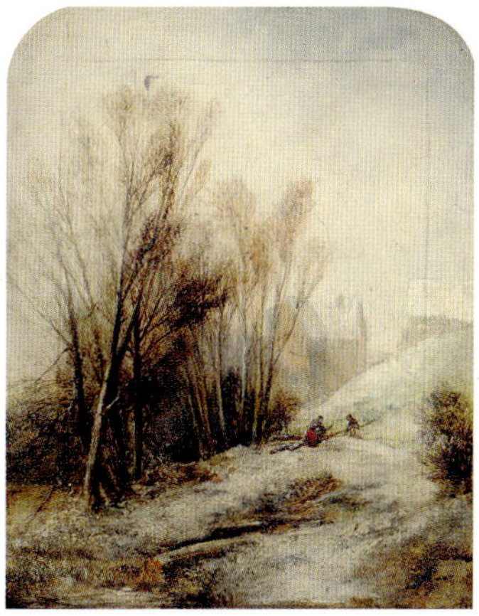

Stubbs, Ralph (attributed to) 1824–1879
A Winter Landscape
oil on canvas 44 x 34.5
CP/TR 180

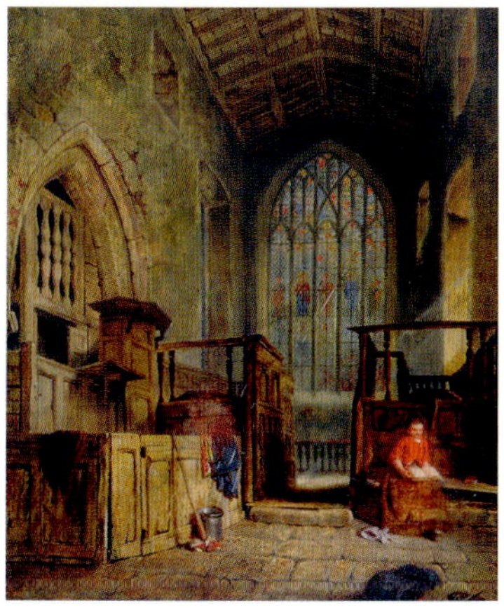

Swarbreck, Samuel Dukinfield c.1799–1863
A Church Interior with a Woman Reading
oil on millboard 30.5 x 25.5
CP/TR 178

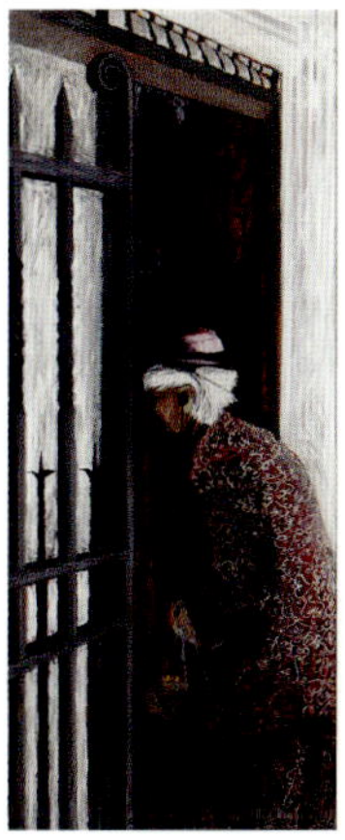

Swift, Richard b.1918
Winter
oil on hardboard 128 x 52
CP/TR 127

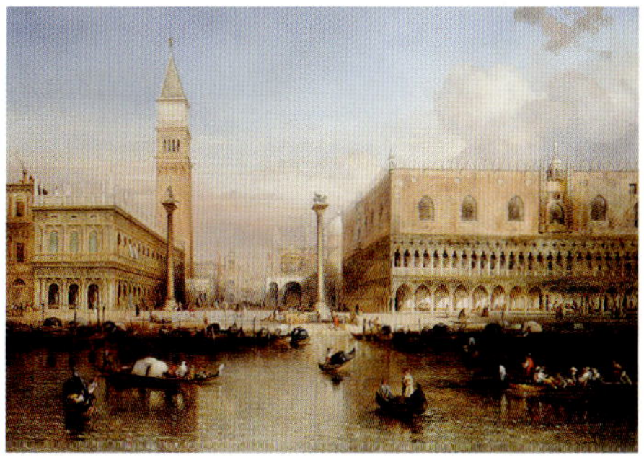

Thienon, Louis Désirée 1812–after 1884
The Doge's Palace, Venice 1848
oil on canvas 104 x 146
CP/TR 109

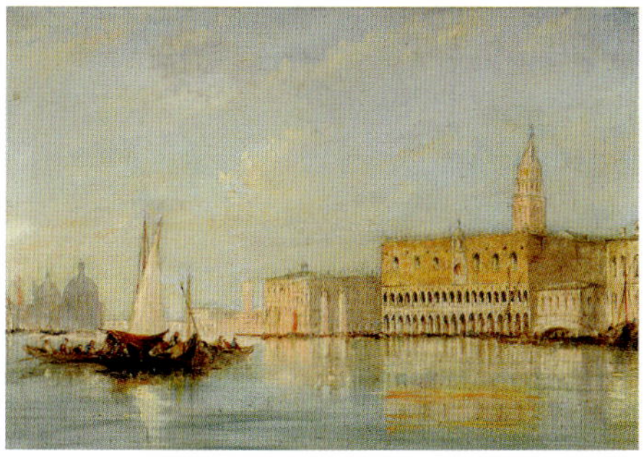

Tinkler, W. A.
The Doge's Palace, Venice c.1839
oil on panel 30 x 43
CP/TR 342

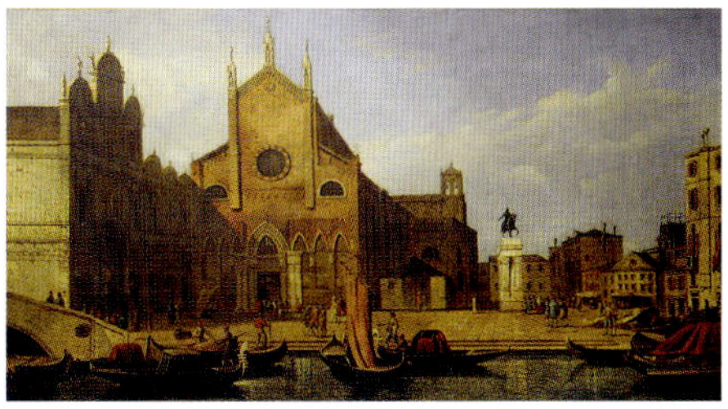

Tironi, Francesco (follower of) c.1745–1797
The Colleoni Monument, Venice 1770–1797
oil on canvas 60 x 104
CP/TR 150

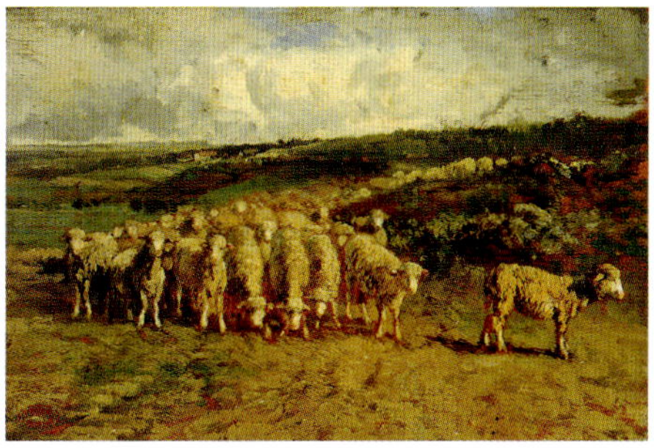

Troyon, Constant 1810–1865
A Flock of Sheep 1840–1865
oil on panel 24 x 36
CP/TR 152

Facing page: Evans, Nicholas, 1907–2004, *Trouble in the Twenties* (detail), 1978, Doncaster Museum Service, (p. 84)

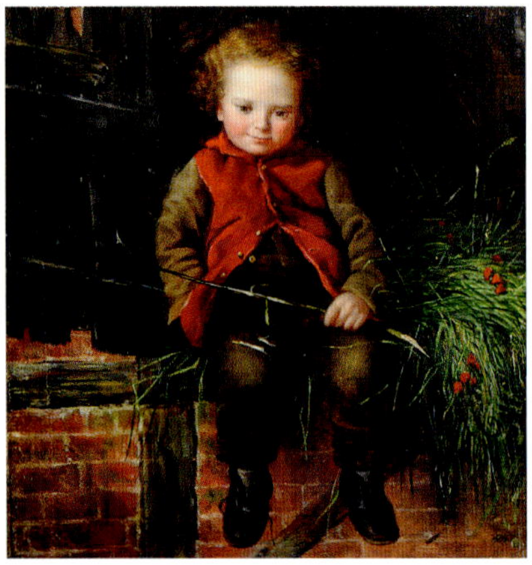

Turck, Eliza 1832–after 1901
The Berkshire Boy
oil on panel 19.5 x 18.5
CP/TR 333

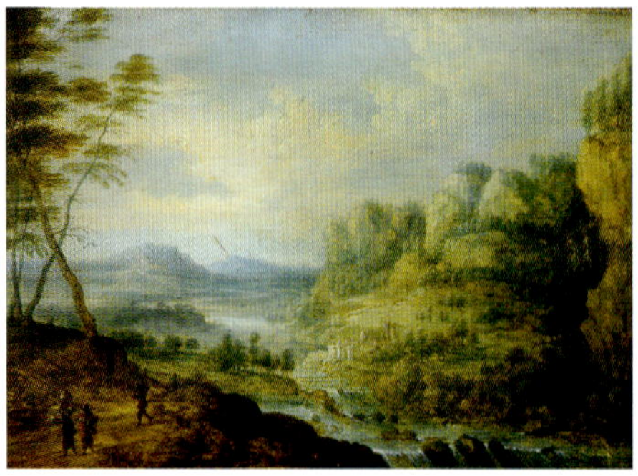

Uden, Lucas van 1595–1672
A River Scene
oil on panel 21.5 x 29.5
CP/TR 157

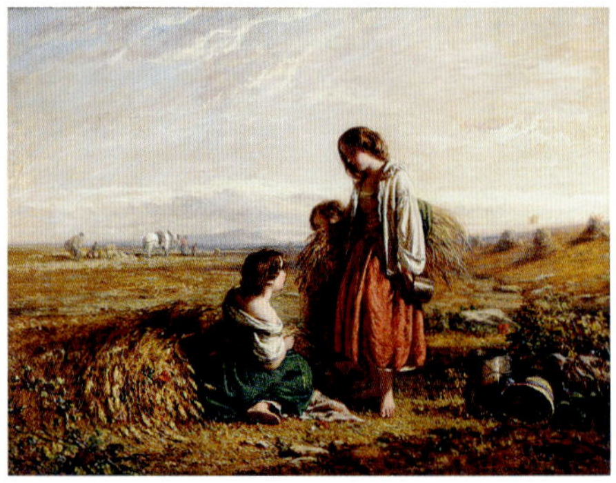

Underhill, William active 1848–1871
Children in a Hayfield
oil on canvas 70 x 90
CP/TR 281

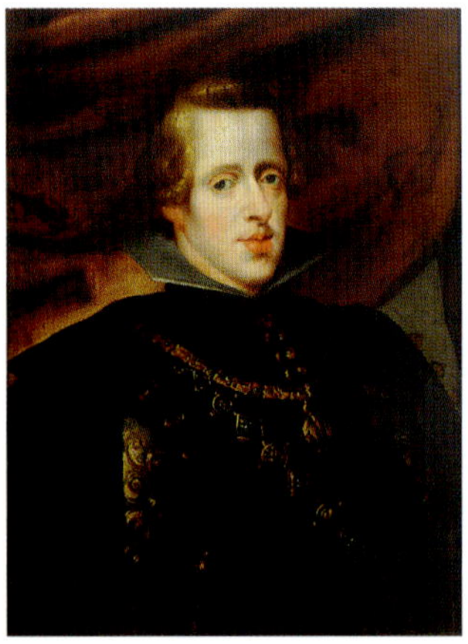

Velázquez, Diego (after) 1599–1660
Philip IV of Spain (1605–1665)
oil on canvas 72 x 53
CP/TR 298

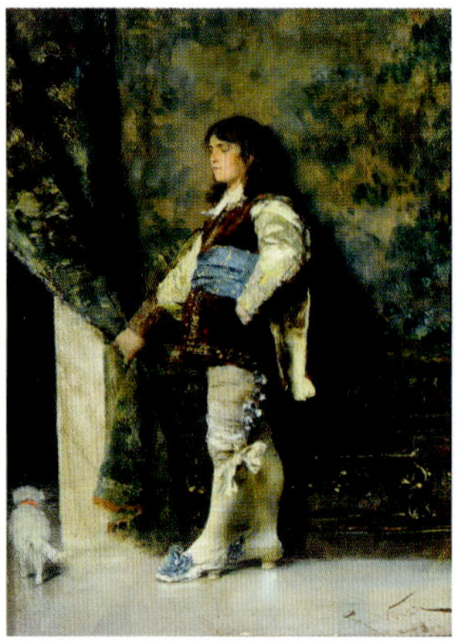

Vinea, Francesco 1845–1902
Page at a Window
oil on canvas 30.5 x 22
CP/TR 199

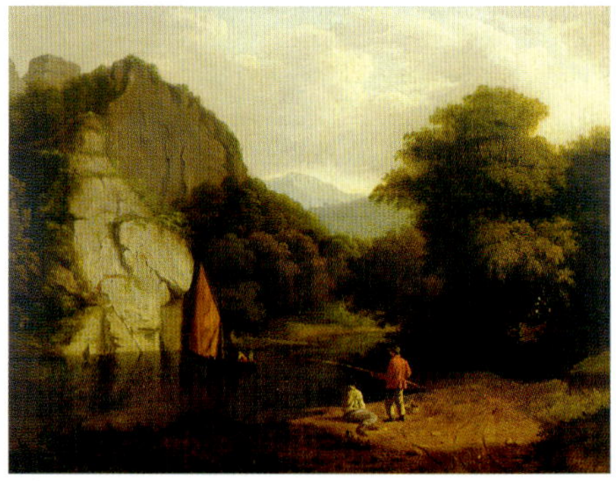

Viney, James active 19th C
Hilly River Landscape with Boys Fishing
oil on canvas 58 x 75
CP/TR 367

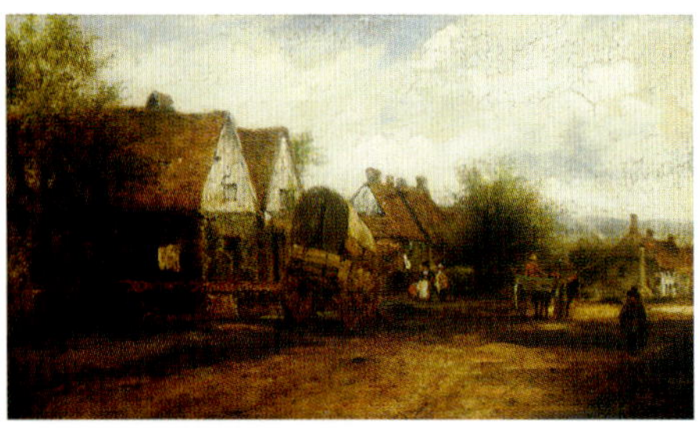

Watts, Frederick William 1800–1870
A Village Scene with Figures
oil on canvas 30.5 x 51
CP/TR 122

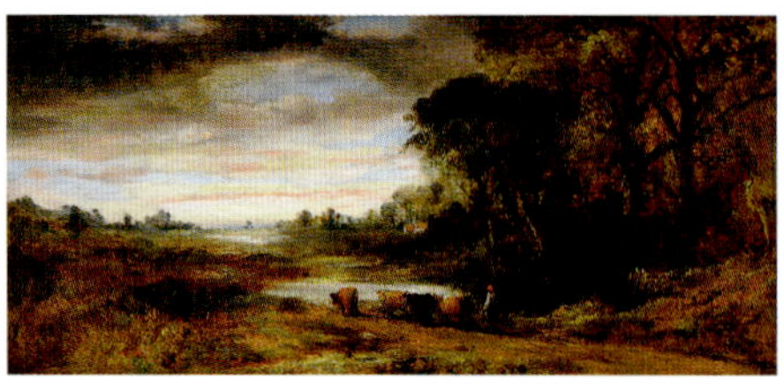

Watts, Frederick William 1800–1870
Landscape with Cattle
oil on canvas 28 x 59
CP/TR 124

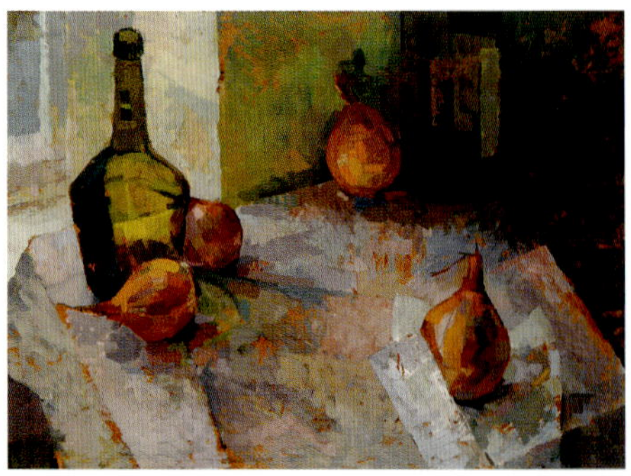

Whittaker, Malcolm b.1937
Still Life
oil on hardboard 51 x 68.5
CP/TR 126

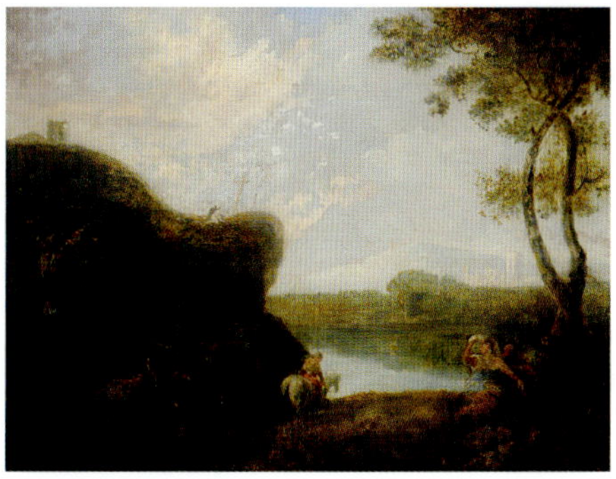

Wilson, Richard (after) 1712/1713–1782
The White Monk
oil on canvas 54 x 69
CP/TR 310

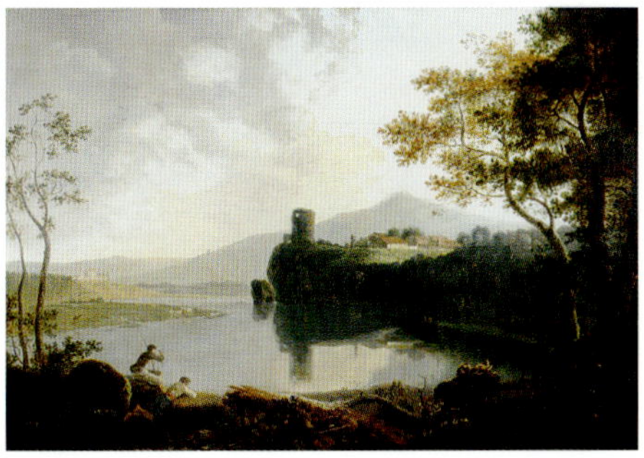

Wilson, Richard (attributed to) 1712/1713–1782
Dolbadern Castle and Llanberis Lake, Wales
oil on canvas 91.5 x 129.5
CP/TR 373

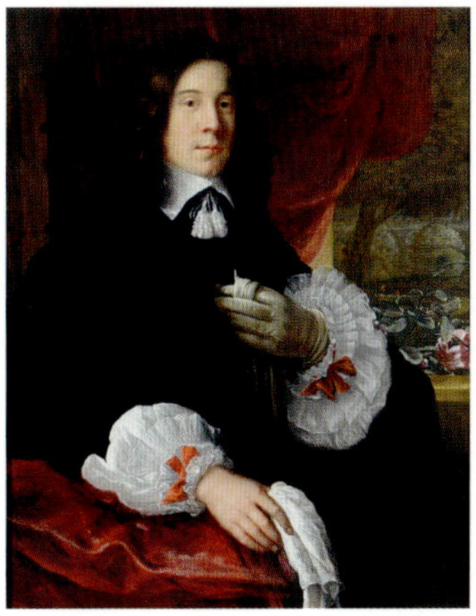

Wright, John Michael (school of) 1617–1694
Portrait of a Gentleman 1650–1656
oil on canvas 88 x 69
CP/TR 142

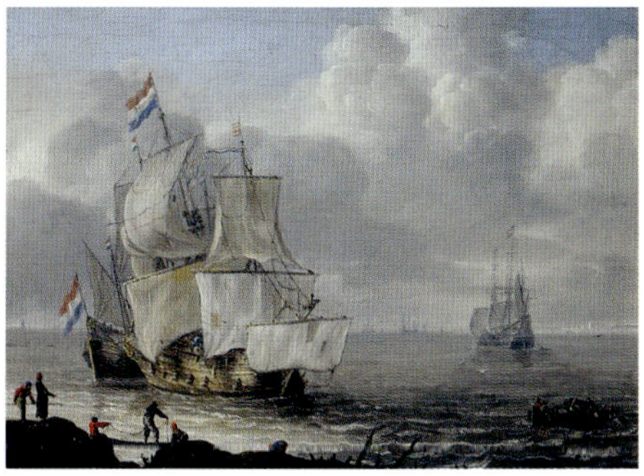

Zeeman, Reinier c.1623–c.1668
Shipping in an Estuary 1655–1667
oil on canvas 20.5 x 28
CP/TR 129

English Heritage, Brodsworth Hall

In 1990 English Heritage acquired Brodsworth Hall, a Victorian country house which had survived with many of its contents and surrounding gardens. Since opening to the public in 1995, Brodsworth has also become known for English Heritage's approach of conserving its interiors with all their layers of history, rather than restoring them.

Brodsworth Hall was built from 1861 to 1863 for Charles Sabine Augustus Thellusson, who had inherited an estate and substantial fortune through the celebrated will of his great grandfather. Thellusson's main purchase of works of art for his new Italianate house was of contemporary, principally Italian, sculpture which was placed throughout its spacious hallways. The paintings which were already in his possession, from both his own and his wife's family, were deployed with few additions in the main rooms. Over the years a few further paintings were acquired by members of the family, and there have also been some significant losses from the house. The range of the resulting picture collection is typical of a country house: old masters, family portraits, and paintings reflecting the sporting and leisure interests of the family. There are also a number of amateur works and unfinished sketches by members of the family, including children and others.

Amongst the paintings inherited from the Thellusson family are two of Brodsworth's most impressive portraits, *Madame Isaac de Thellusson, née Sarah le Boullenger* (1700–1770) by Nicolas de Largillière, and Thomas Lawrence's double portrait of *Mrs Charles Thellusson, née Sabine Robarts (1775–1814), and Her Son, Charles Thellusson (1797–1856)*. Other portraits by Margaret Sarah Carpenter, George Francis Joseph and James Ward came from the Theobald family, through Georgiana Theobald, wife of Charles Sabine Augustus Thellusson. The main portraits were hung in the dining room together with a small group of Dutch paintings which had once been in the extensive collection of Georgiana's father, William Theobald. Brodsworth also has a number of sporting paintings assembled by William and his father, John Theobald, who had owned a successful racing stud at Stockwell in the early nineteenth century. Foremost among these are the outstanding horse portraits by James Ward, and works by James Barenger, Harry Hall and John Frederick Herring I.

Most, but not all, of Brodsworth's contents and paintings were purchased from Mrs Pamela Williams, great-granddaughter of Charles Sabine Thellusson, by the National Heritage Memorial Fund in 1990, and minor pieces were included by her in the gift of 'the remaining contents of the hall'. A number of paintings and objects were retained by the Williams family in 1990, some being lent to English Heritage. English Heritage has had mixed success in acquiring these, purchasing *Travellers Passing through a Village* attributed to Frans de Momper and the Flemish School paintings of the four seasons.

Caroline Carr-Whitworth, Curator

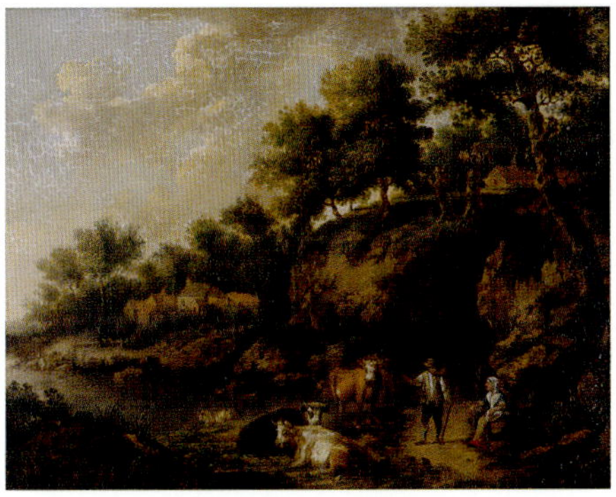

Antonissen, Henricus Josephus 1737–1794
Landscape with a Cowherd 1777
oil on oak panel 35.8 x 44.5
90006989

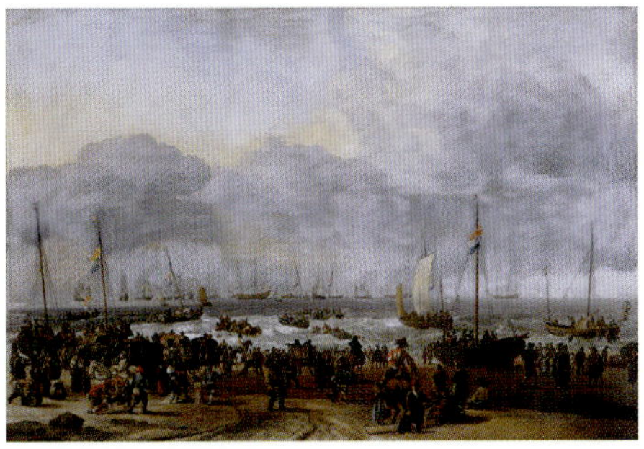

Backhuysen, Ludolf I 1630–1708 &
Dubbels, Hendrik Jacobsz. 1620/1621–1676
An Embarkation Scene c.1660
oil on canvas 79 x 115
90009225

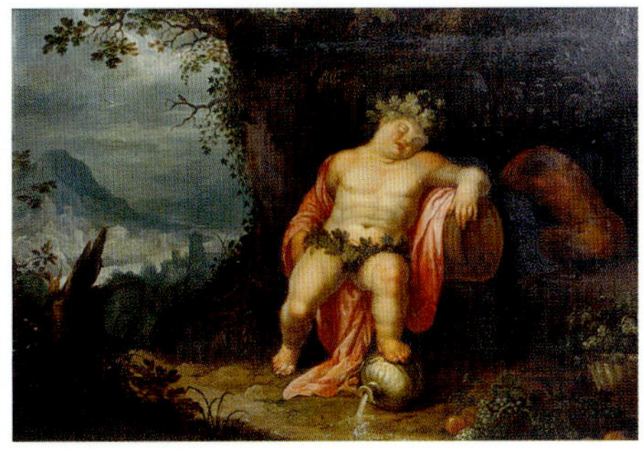

Balen, Hendrik van I (follower of)
1575–1632
Bacchus Asleep 1660–1690
oil on wood 29 x 40.5
90009741

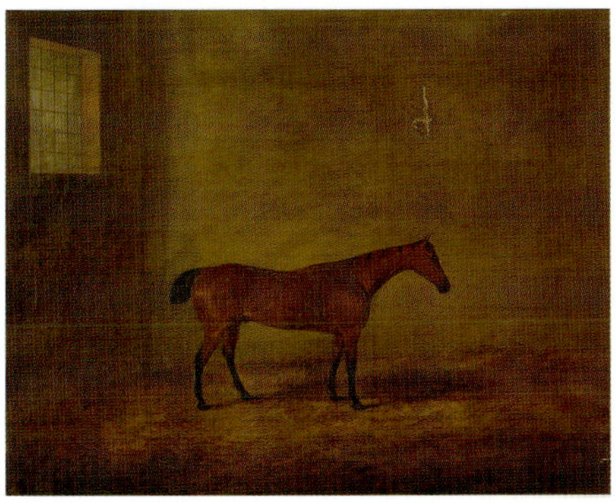

Barenger, James 1780–after 1831
Bay Stallion in a Stable c.1810–1830
oil on canvas 49 x 59.5
90004074

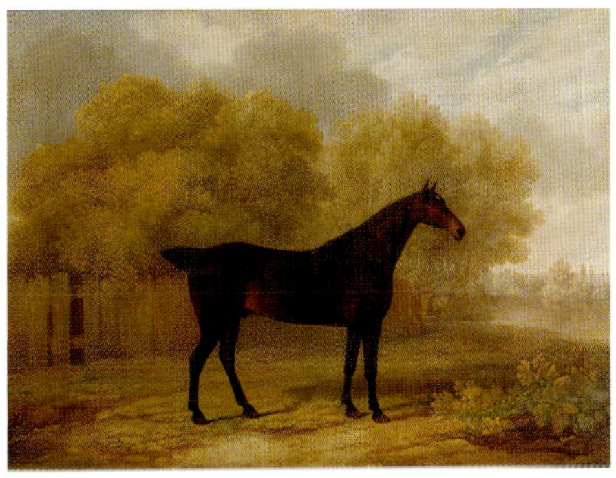

Barenger, James 1780–after 1831
Dark Bay Stallion 1812
oil on canvas 70 x 89
90009354

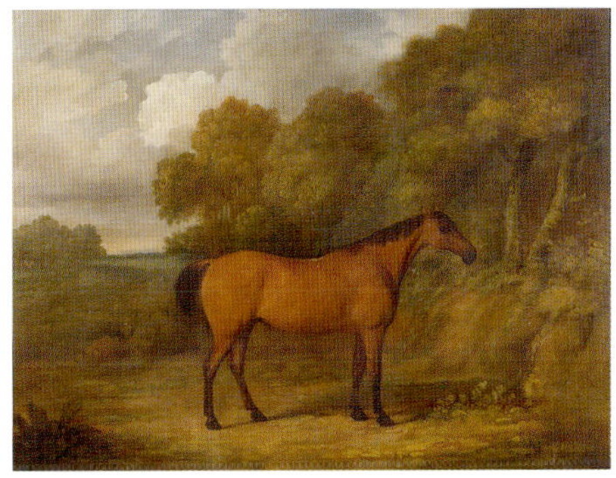

Barenger, James 1780–after 1831
Bay Cob c.1812
oil on canvas 70 x 89
90003040

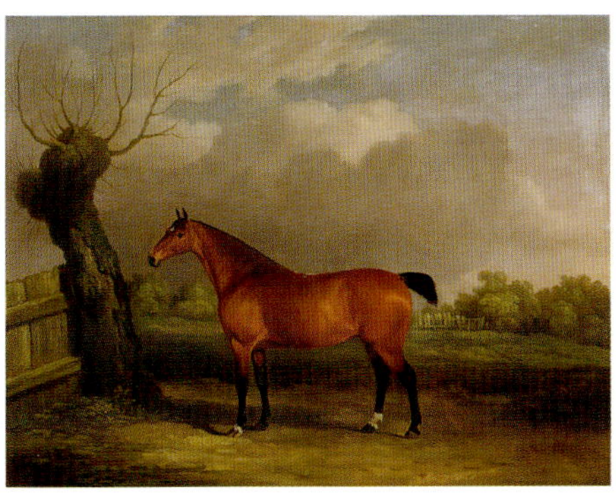

Barenger, James 1780–after 1831
Light Bay Mare c.1812
oil on canvas 70 x 90
90009352

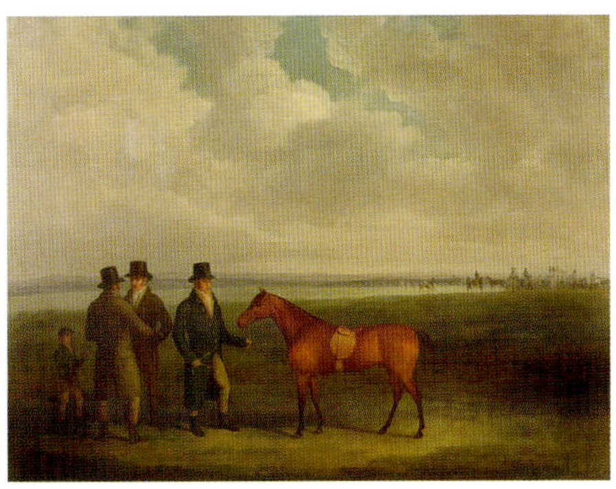

Barenger, James 1780–after 1831
Racehorse with Trainers c.1812
oil on canvas 70 x 89
90003041

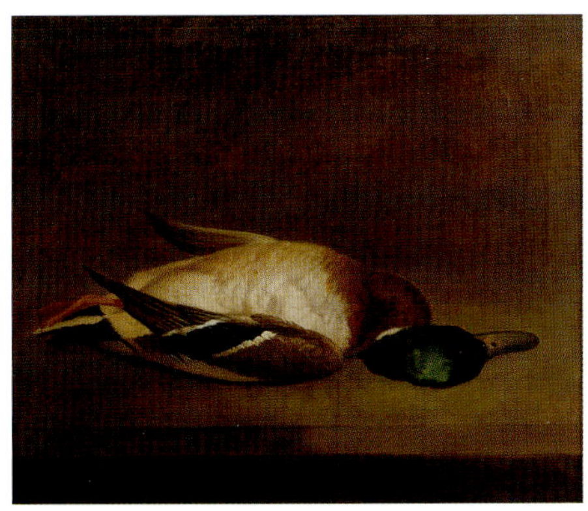

Barenger, James 1780–after 1831
Still Life with a Mallard 1824
oil on canvas 42 x 49
90004075

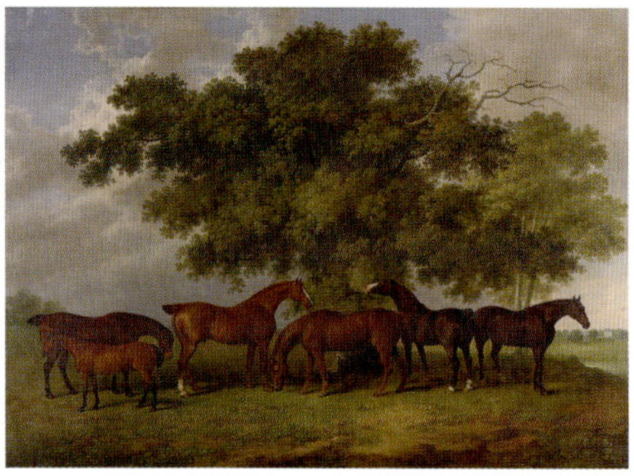

Barenger, James 1780–after 1831
The Theobald Stud 1825
oil on canvas 147.5 x 182
90009356

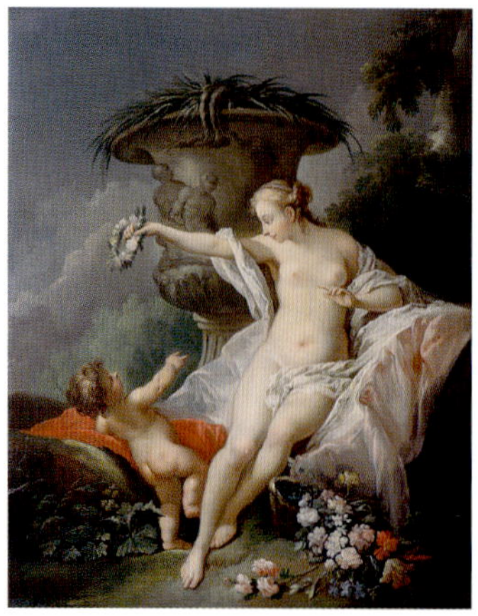

Boucher, François (after) 1703–1770
Venus and Cupid 1750–1775
oil on walnut panel 37.3 x 28.9
90009802

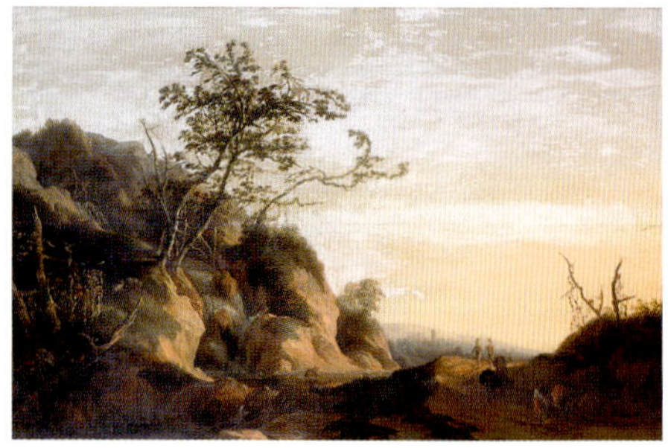

Camphuysen, Jochem Govertz. (attributed to) 1601–1659
Travellers in a Landscape c.1640
oil on wood 57 x 85.6
90009720

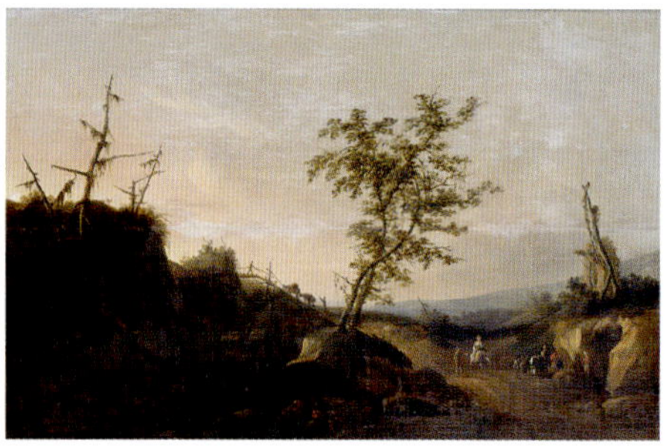

Camphuysen, Jochem Govertz. (attributed to) 1601–1659
Travellers in a Landscape c.1640
oil on wood 56.5 x 85
90009721

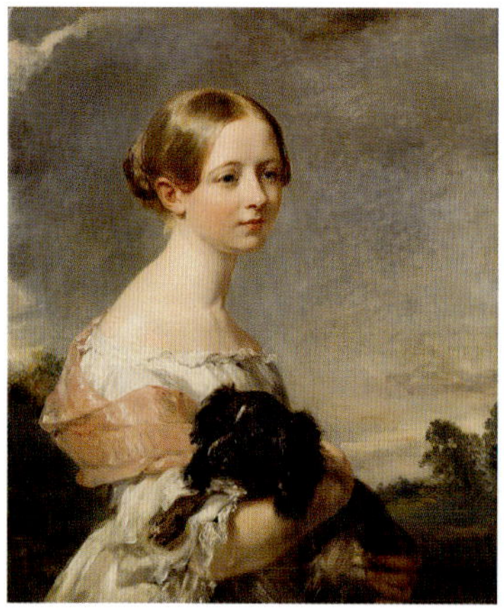

Carpenter, Margaret Sarah 1793–1872
Miss Theobald (probably Frances Jane, 1825–1841) 1840
oil on canvas 76 x 61
90009147

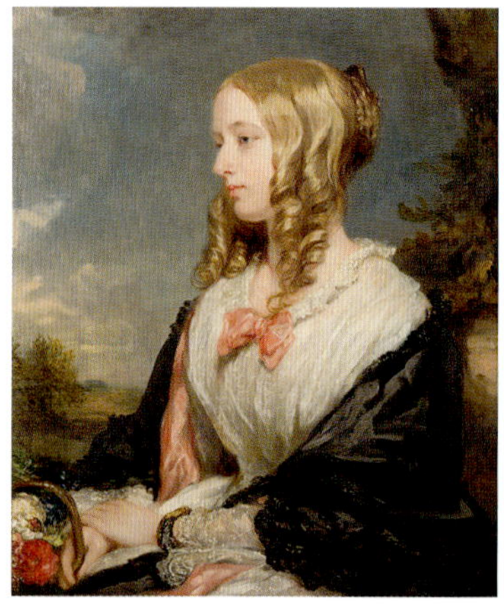

Carpenter, Margaret Sarah 1793–1872
Mrs Charles Sabine Thellusson, née Georgiana Theobald (1828–1883) 1850
oil on canvas 76 x 61
90009142

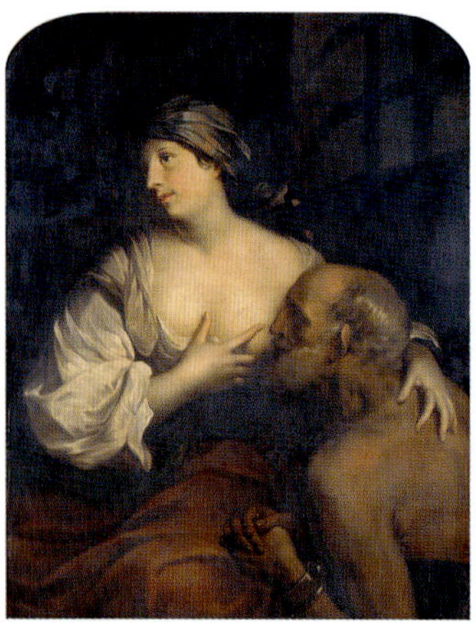

Cignani, Carlo (after) 1628–1719
Roman Charity: Cimon and Pero c.1801–1806
oil on canvas 118.1 x 89.4
90009718

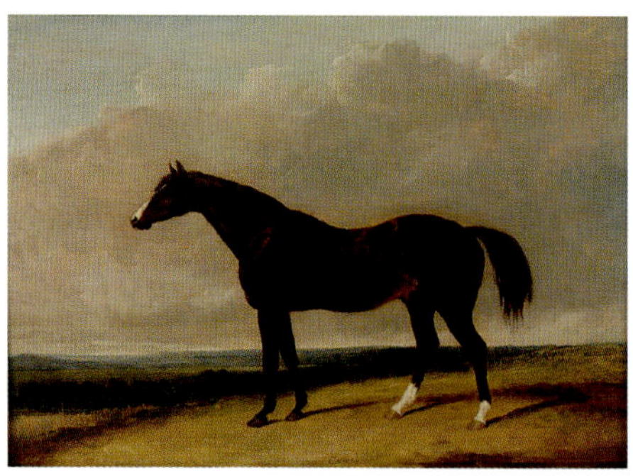

Cooper, Abraham 1787–1868
The Racehorse, 'Camel' c.1825–1845
oil on wood 29 x 38.5
90004076

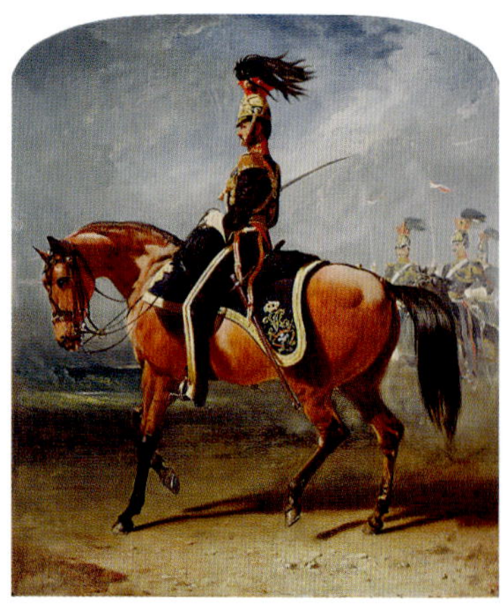

Corbould, Alfred (attributed to) c.1821–1874
Charles Sabine Augustus Thellusson (1822–1885), as Captain, 12th Royal Lancers 1848
oil on canvas 74.5 x 64.5
90009749

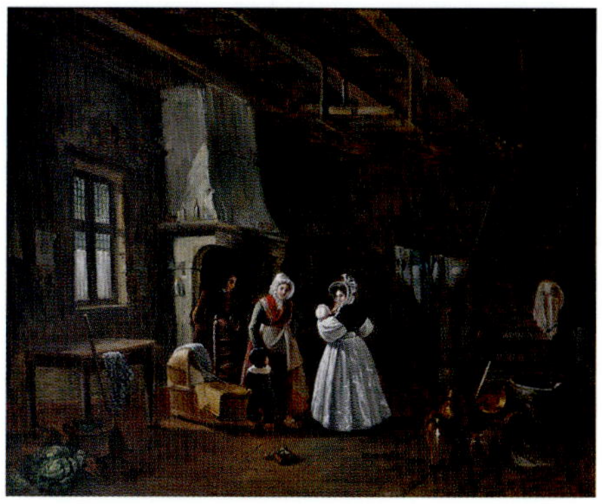

Donny, Désiré 1798–1861
Interior with Figures 1833
oil on canvas 40.8 x 48.9
90006988

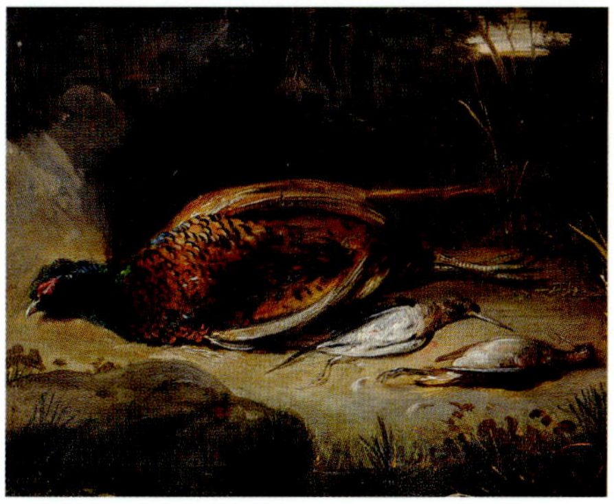

Elmer, Stephen (style of) c.1714–1796
Still Life with a Pheasant c.1775–1825
oil on wood 17 x 20.5
90009740

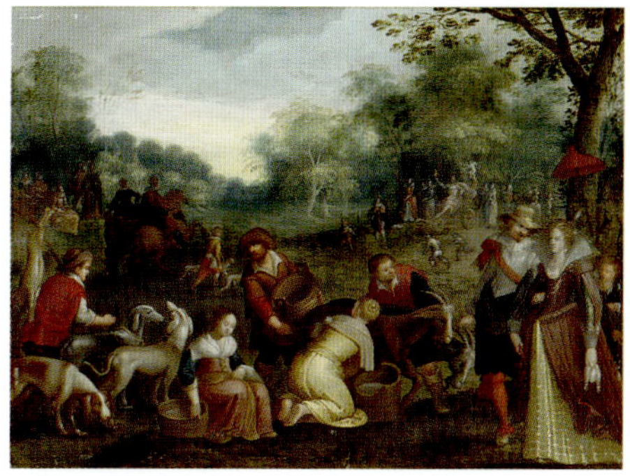

Flemish School
The Four Seasons: Spring 1600–1625
oil on copper 28.9 x 38.4
90011694

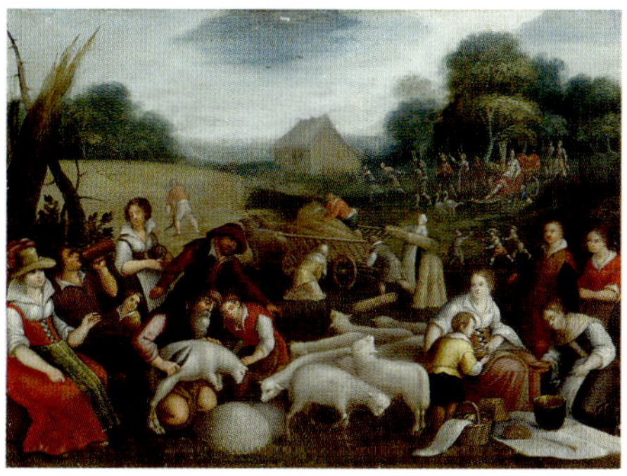

Flemish School
The Four Seasons: Summer 1600–1625
oil on copper 28.9 x 38.4
90011695

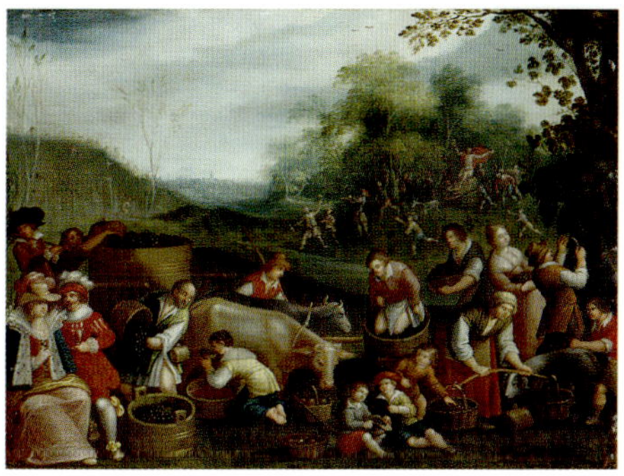

Flemish School
The Four Seasons: Autumn 1600–1625
oil on copper 28.9 x 38.4
90011696

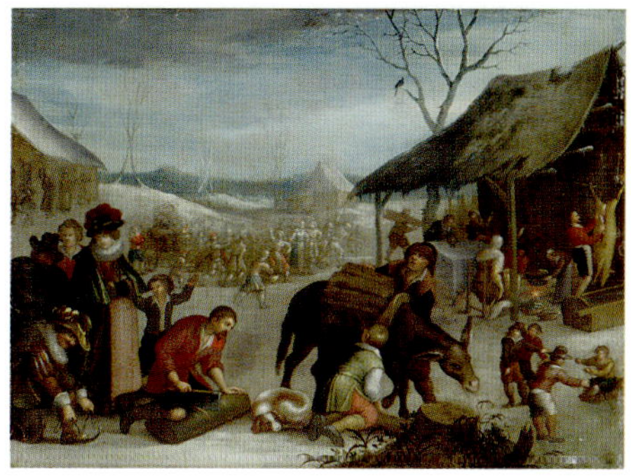

Flemish School
The Four Seasons: Winter 1600–1625
oil on copper 28.9 x 38.4
90011697

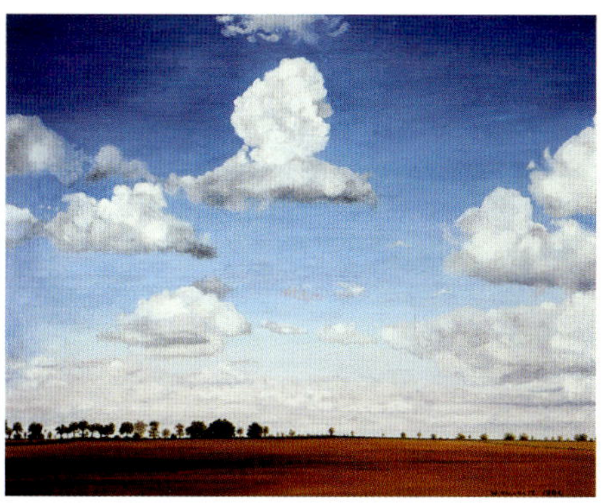

Halgate, W.
Fenland, Cambridgeshire 1981
acrylic on canvas 43 x 52.5
90007435

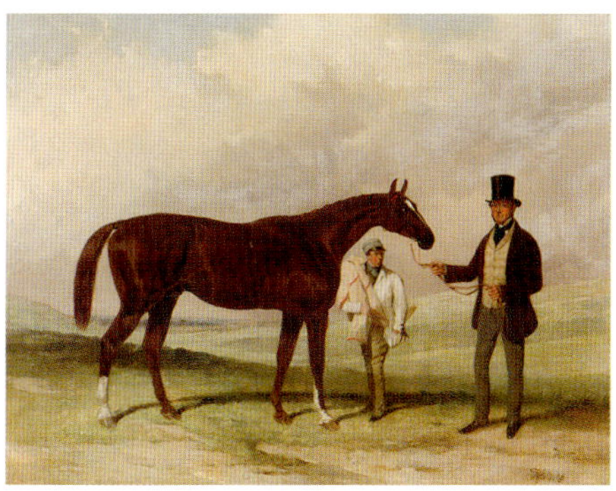

Hall, Harry 1814–1896
'Rataplan' 1855
oil on canvas 102 x 127
90009351

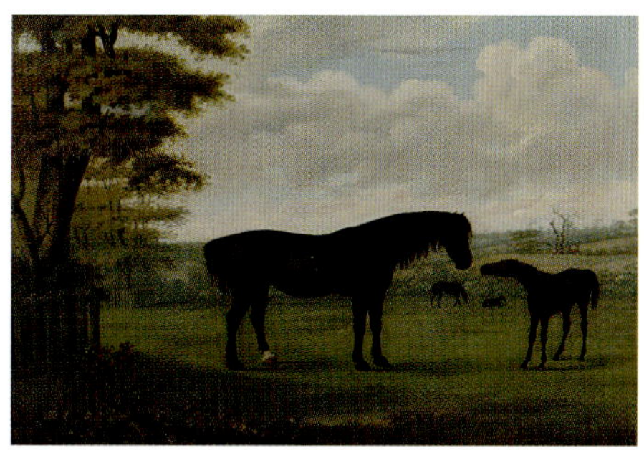

Hardman, John active 1799–1846
Horses in a Landscape 1799
oil on canvas 47.5 x 67
90008598

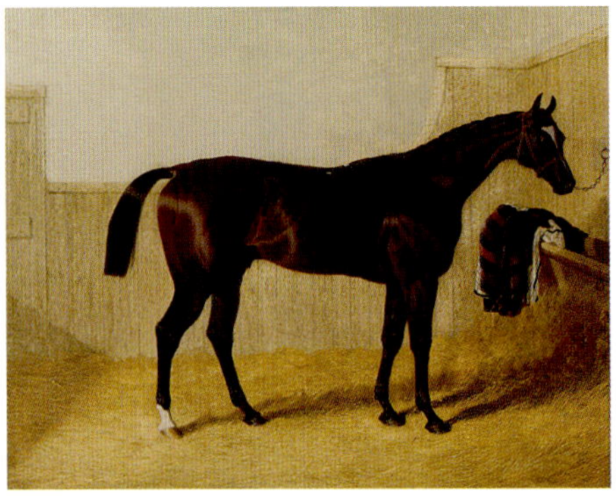

Herring, John Frederick I 1795–1865
Bay Stallion 1836
oil on canvas 34.5 x 43
90003664

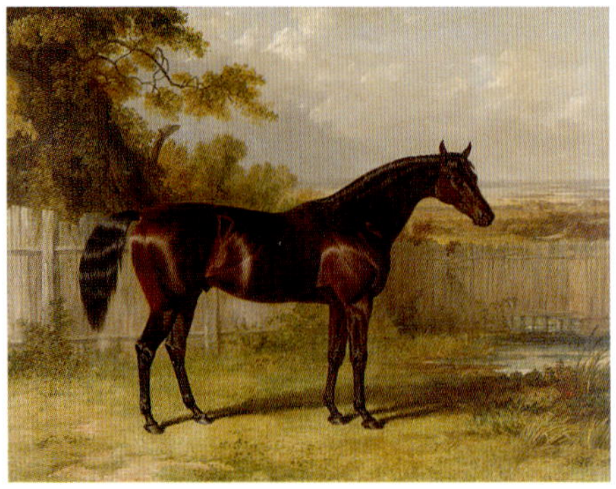

Herring, John Frederick I 1795–1865
'Rockingham' c.1838
oil on canvas 102 x 127
90009343

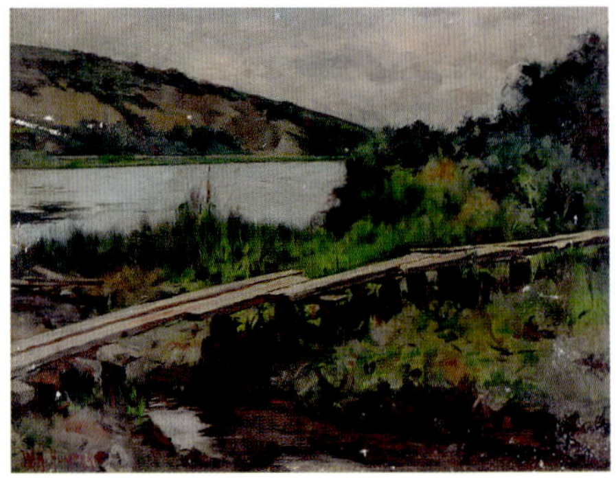

Humphris, William Henry 1850–c.1916
Bridge and Lakeside
oil on canvas 35 x 46
90007276

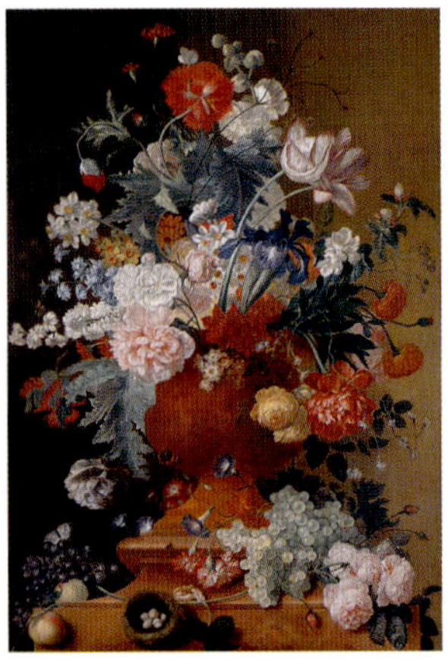

Huysum, Jan van (after) 1682–1749
Flowers in a Terracotta Vase with Fruit and a Bird's Nest 1869–1930
oil on canvas 132 x 89
90003583

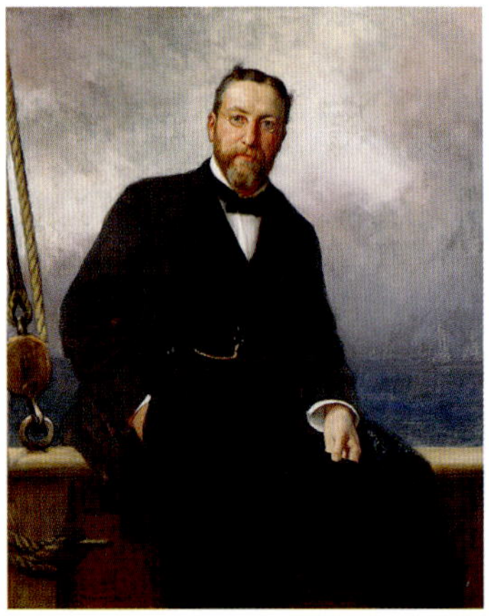

Jacomb-Hood, George Percy 1857–1929
Peter Thellusson (1850–1899), on Board the Yacht, 'Albion' c.1894
oil on canvas 128 x 102
90009336

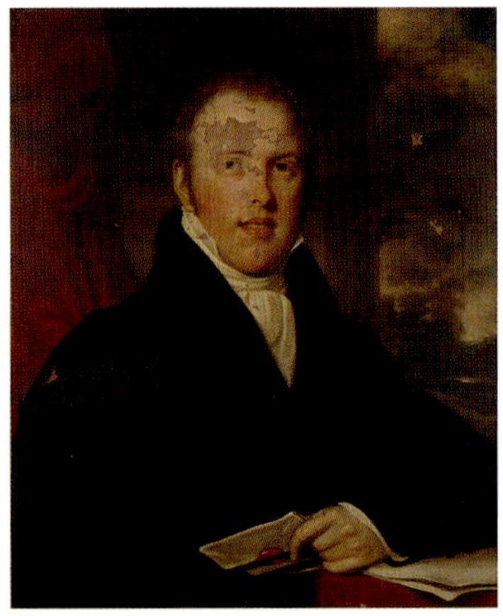

Joseph, George Francis 1764–1846
Head and Shoulders of a Man (probably William Theobald, 1795–1850) c.1815
oil on canvas 83 x 69
90008128

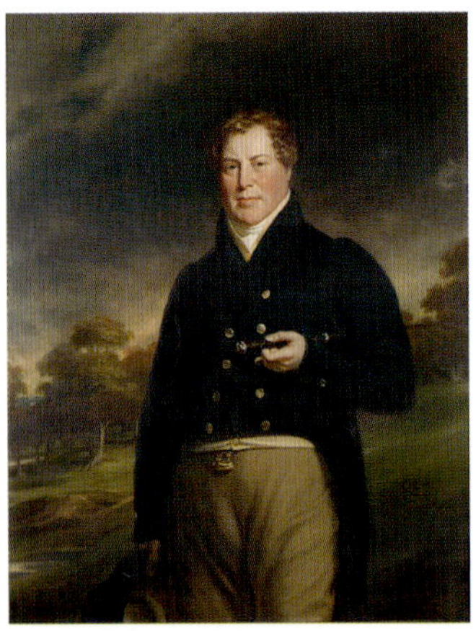

Joseph, George Francis 1764–1846
John Theobald (1766–1849) c.1815
oil on canvas 153 x 107
90009229

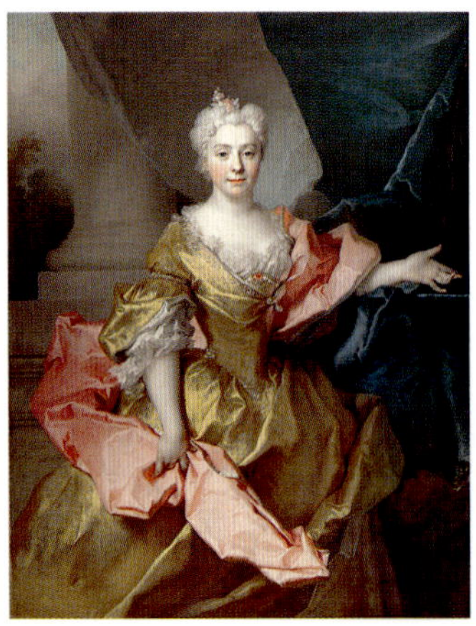

Largillière, Nicolas de 1656–1746
Madame Isaac de Thellusson, née Sarah le Boullenger (1700–1770) 1725
oil on canvas 137.5 x 104
90006927

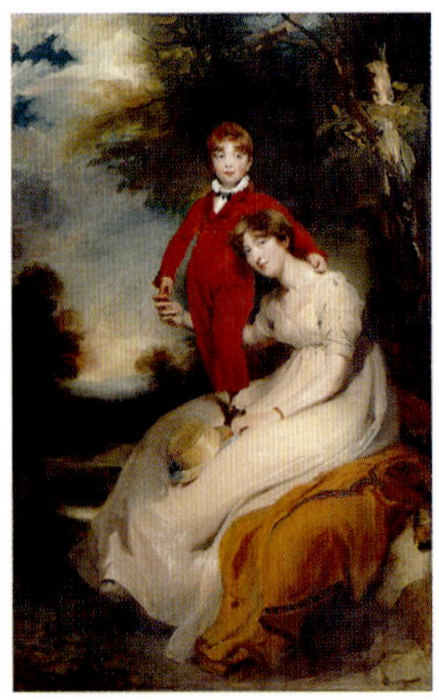

Lawrence, Thomas 1769–1830
Mrs Charles Thellusson, née Sabine Robarts (1775–1814), and Her Son, Charles Thellusson (1797–1856) c.1804
oil on canvas 240 x 146
90009300

Facing page: Roberts, David, 1796–1864, *Antwerp Cathedral, Belgium* (detail), The Cooper Gallery, (p. 25)

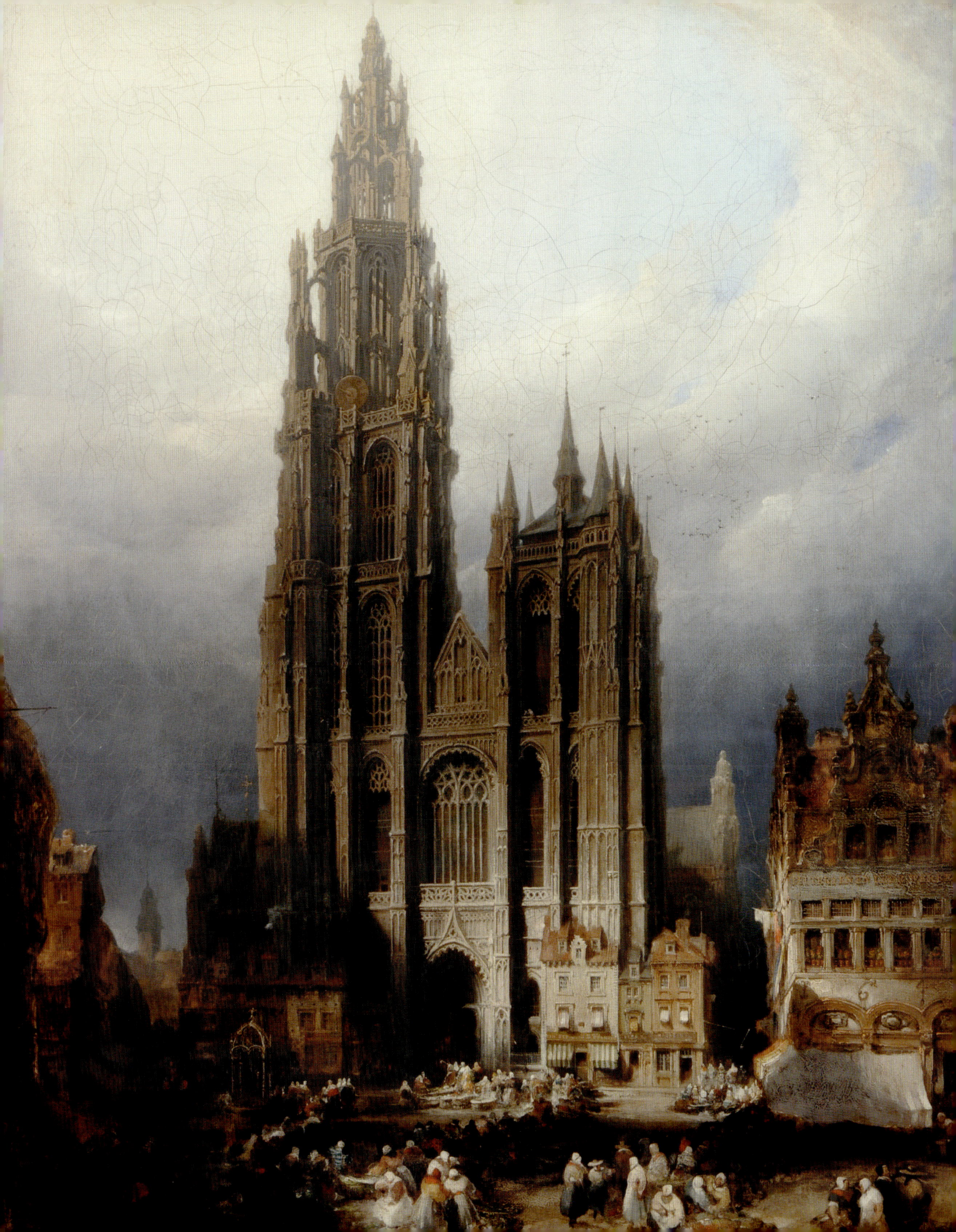

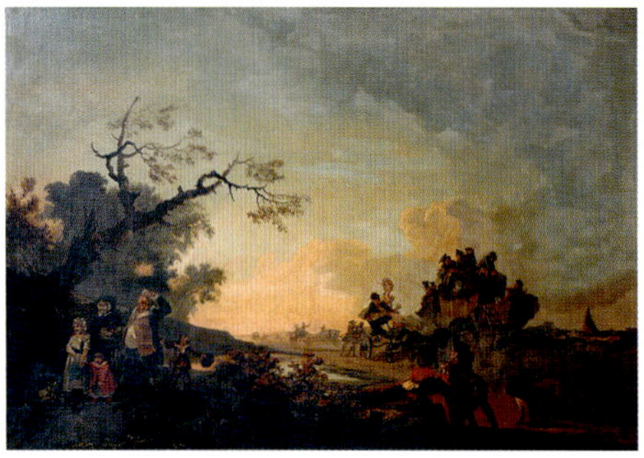

Loutherbourg, Philip James de (after) 1740–1812
A Summer's Evening with a View of a Public Road 1786–1793
polygraphic oil painting on canvas 86.5 x 123
90003038

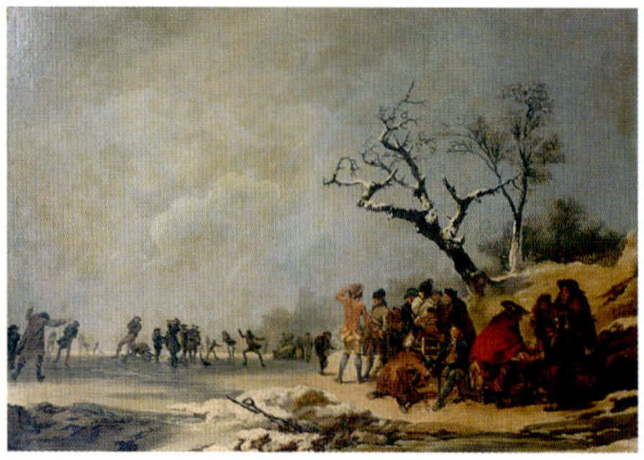

Loutherbourg, Philip James de (after) 1740–1812
A Winter Morning with a Party Skating 1786–1793
polygraphic oil painting on canvas 86.5 x 123
90003039

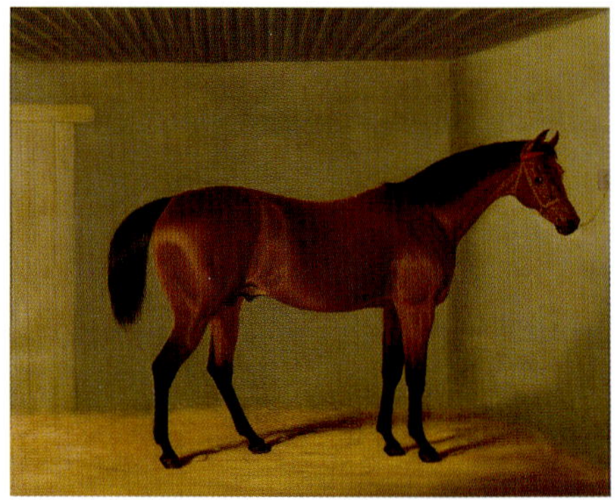

Marshall, William active c.1800–1840
Bay Stallion in a Stable
oil on canvas 49 x 59.5
90003997

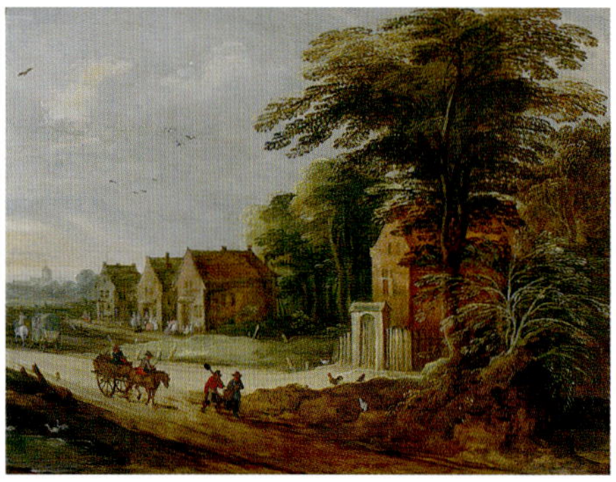

Momper, Frans de (attributed to) 1603–1660
Travellers Passing through a Village 1620–1659
oil on wood 58.4 x 73.7
90018143

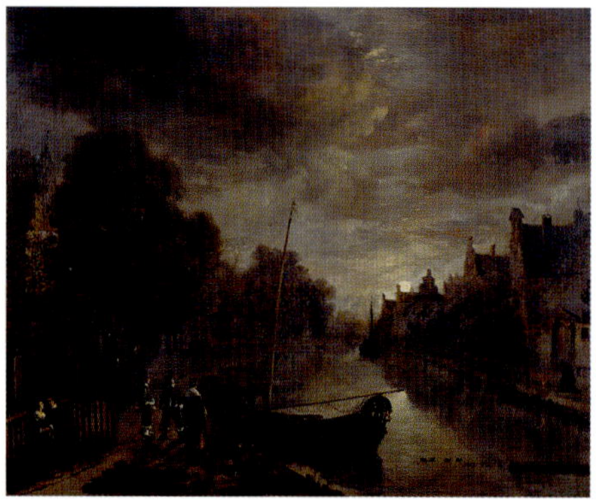

Neer, Aert van der 1603–1677
A Canal in a Dutch Town by Moonlight 1645–1655
oil on canvas 63.5 x 77
90009217

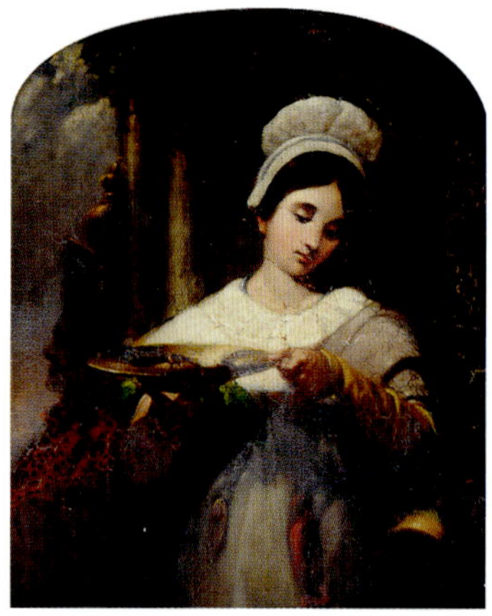

Opie, John (style of) 1761–1807 or **Wheatley, Francis (style of)** 1747–1801
Girl Holding a Silver Salver 19th C
oil on canvas 91 x 70
90007733

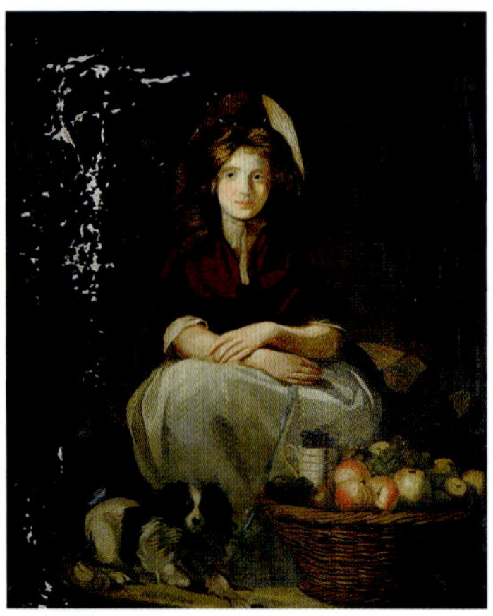

Opie, John (style of) 1761–1807 or **Wheatley, Francis (style of)** 1747–1801
Girl with a Dog and Fruit
oil on canvas 125 x 99
90007754

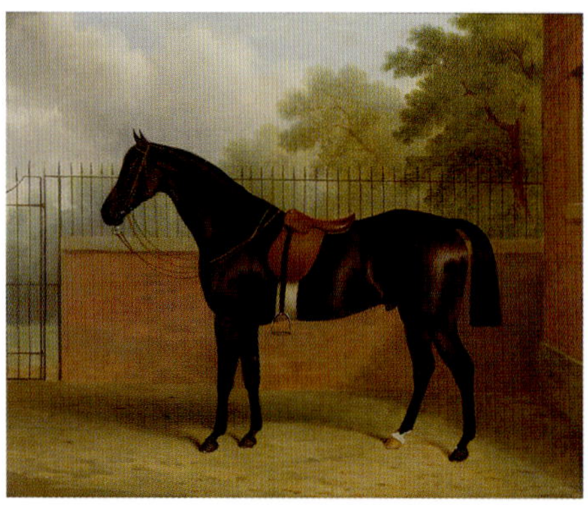

Paul, John active 1867–1886
Bay Stallion 1874
oil on canvas 48 x 59.5
90003663

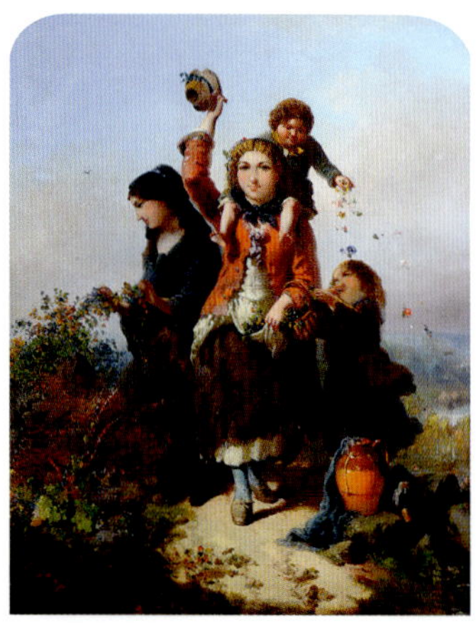

Perry, William J. active 1861–1871
Blackberrying 1861
oil on canvas 142 x 109
90009692

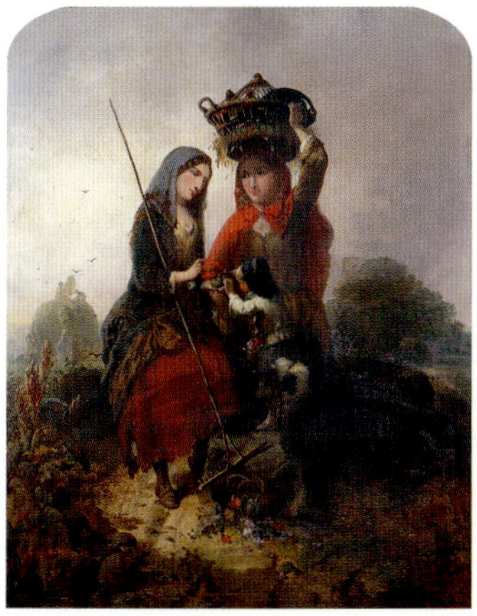

Perry, William J. active 1861–1871
The Bird's Nest 1861
oil on canvas 142 x 109
90009691

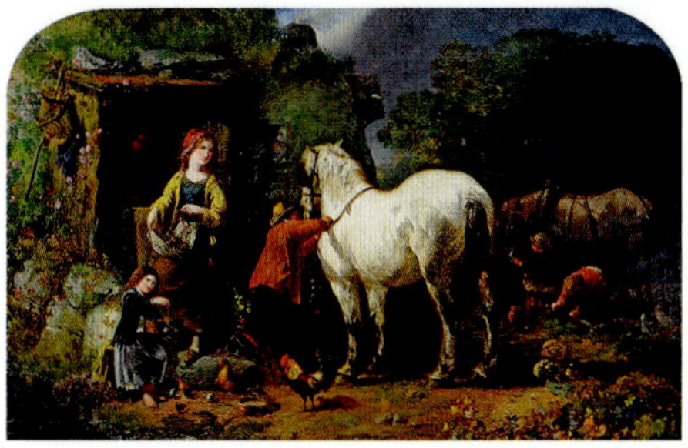

Perry, William J. active 1861–1871
The Old Carthorse 1861
oil on canvas 114 x 178
90009693

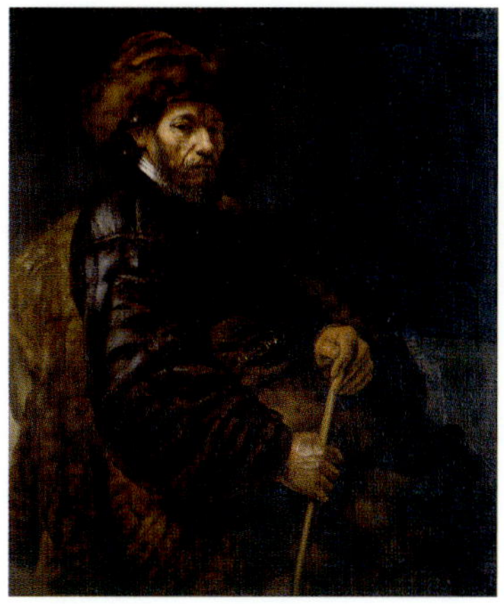

Rembrandt van Rijn (after) 1606–1669
A Seated Man with a Stick c.1800–1850
oil on canvas 55.3 x 46.1
90006943

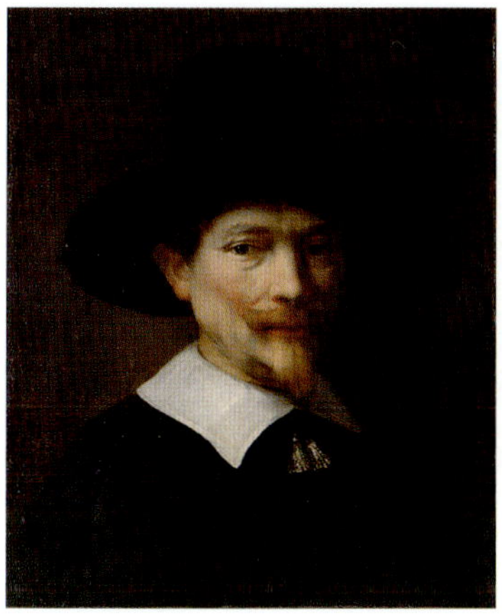

Rembrandt van Rijn (after) 1606–1669
Portrait of a Man c.1836–1885
oil on canvas 54.9 x 45.1
90006922

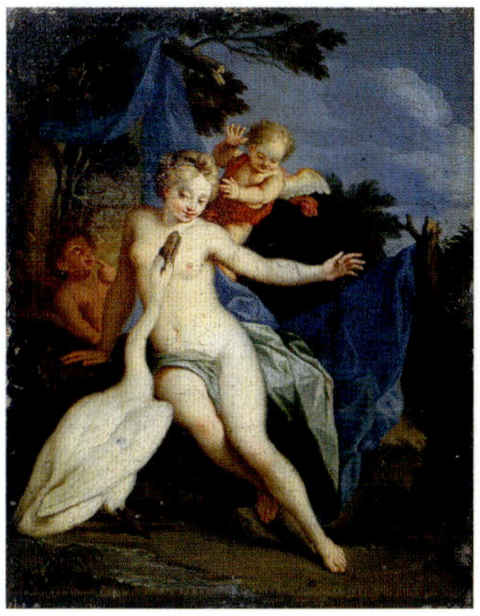

Rocca, Michele (attributed to) 1675–1751
Leda and the Swan 1700–1730
oil on canvas 20.6 x 16.2
90003584

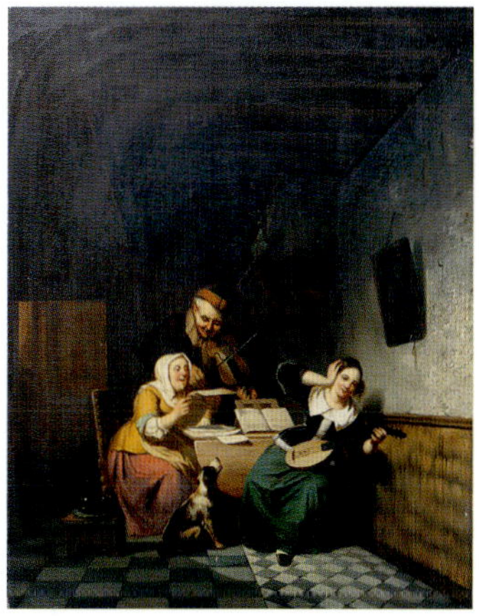

Schumann, Wilhelm active 1830–1844
A Music Party c.1840
oil on mahogany panel 52 x 45
90006947

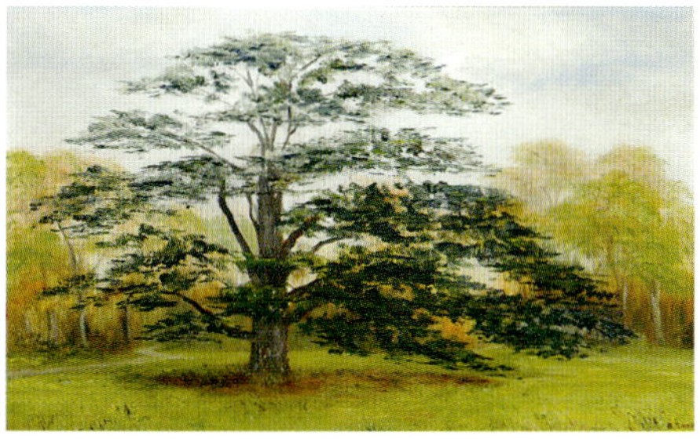

Short, Betty active c.1960–1988
The Old Cedar Tree at Brodsworth Hall
oil on board 25 x 40
90008704

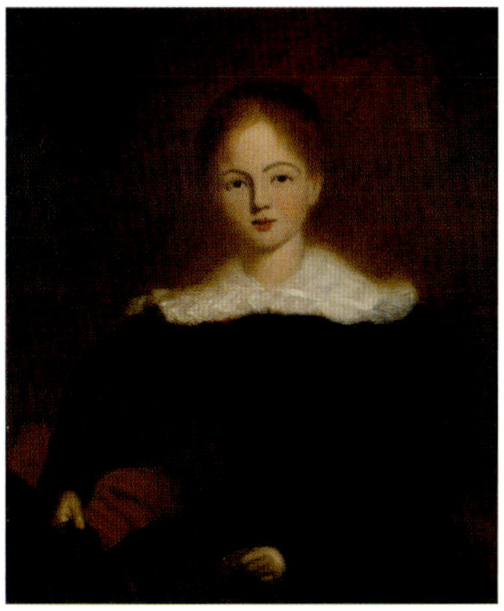

Solomons, Joel
John Theobald (b.1827), Aged 8½ Years 1836
oil on wood 30 x 24.5
90006923

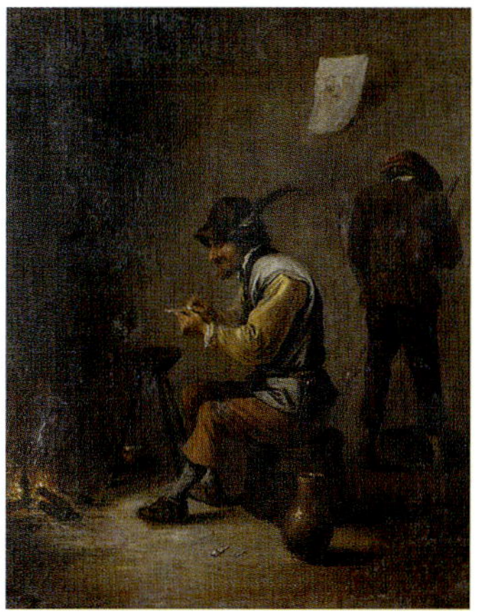

Teniers, David II (after) 1610–1690
Peasants in an Interior
oil on canvas 40.9 x 32.6
90009800

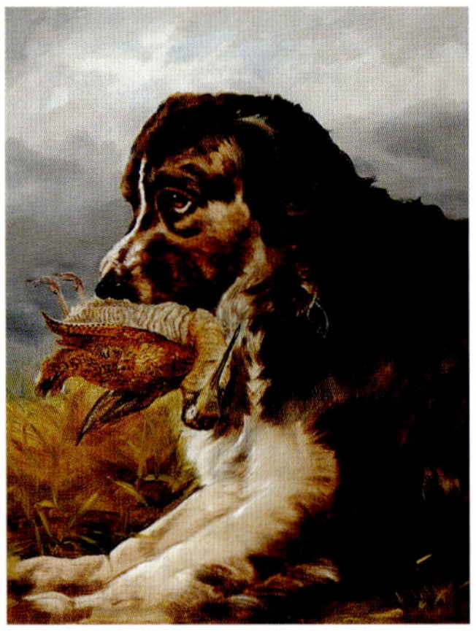

Thellusson, Aline 1856–1880
St Bernard with Game c.1870–1880
oil on canvas 67.5 x 49
90009747

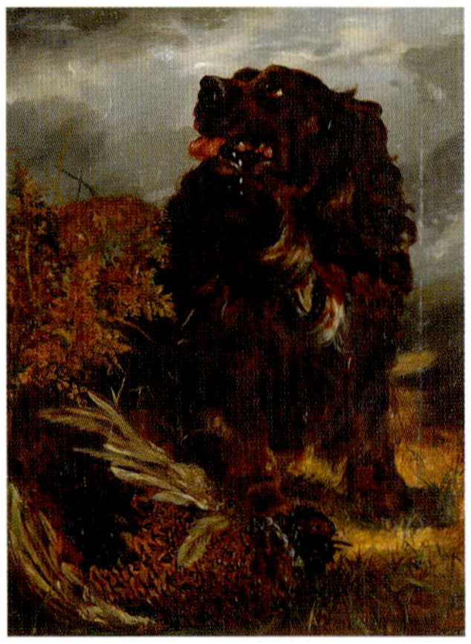

Thellusson, Aline 1856–1880
Spaniel with a Pheasant c.1870–1880
oil on canvas 67 x 49
90009748

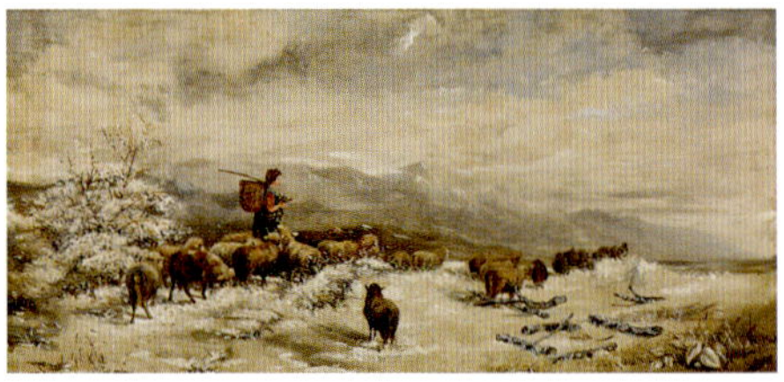

Thellusson, Aline 1856–1880
Winter Scene with a Shepherd and Sheep 1877
oil on canvas 44 x 92.5
90003995

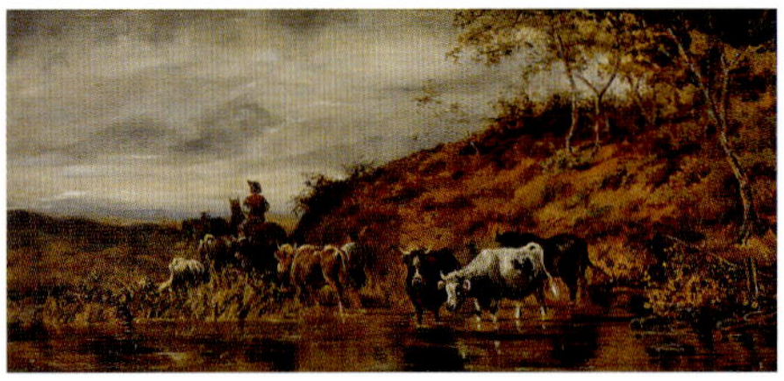

Thellusson, Aline 1856–1880
Cattle Crossing a River with a Drover c.1877
oil on canvas 44 x 92
90003996

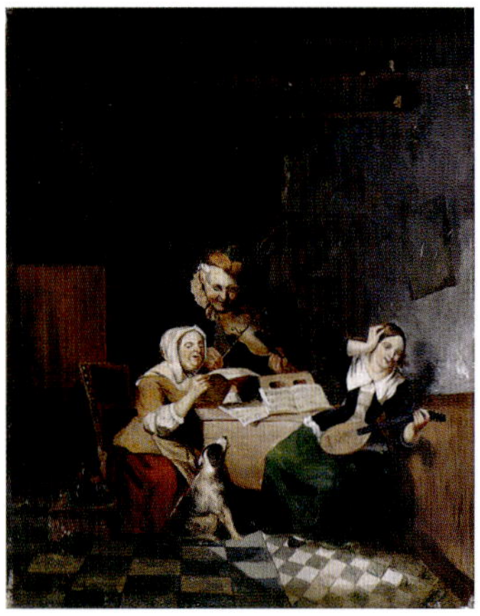

Thellusson, Aline (attributed to) 1856–1880
A Music Party (after Wilhelm Schumann) 1870–1880
oil on canvas 46 x 36
90006948

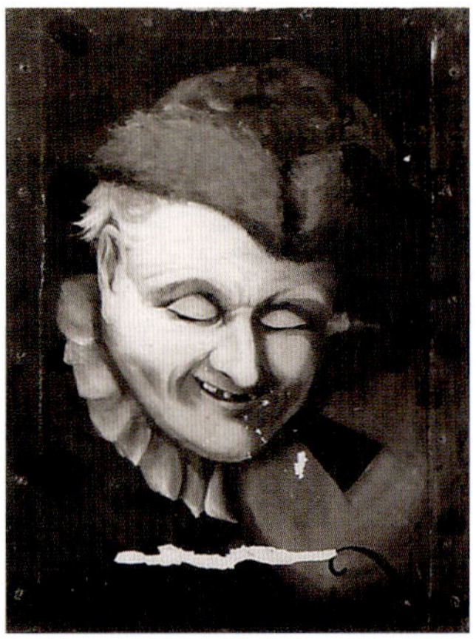

Thellusson, Aline (attributed to) 1856–1880
Man Playing a Violin (copy of a detail from 'A Music Party' by Wilhelm Schumann) c.1870–1880
oil on canvas 43 x 35
90015831

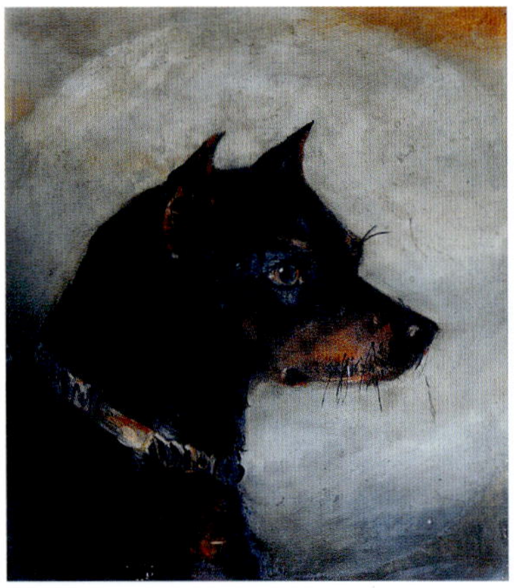

Thellusson, Aline (attributed to) 1856–1880
A Black Dog c.1870–1880
oil on canvas 28.5 x 24.5
90009742

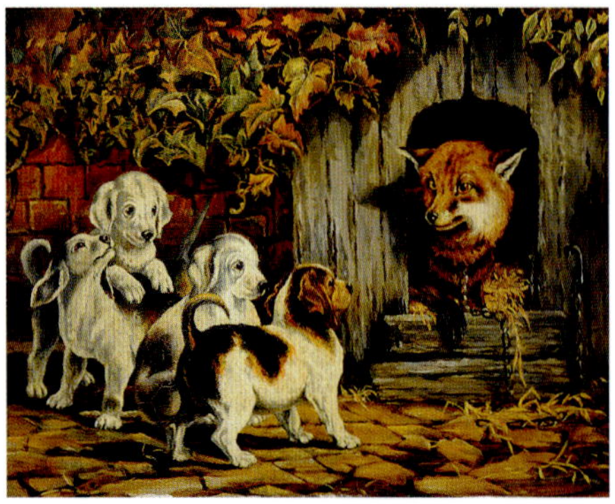

Thellusson, Aline (attributed to) 1856–1880
A Fox in a Kennel with Puppies c.1870–1880
oil on board 59 x 73.5
90008140

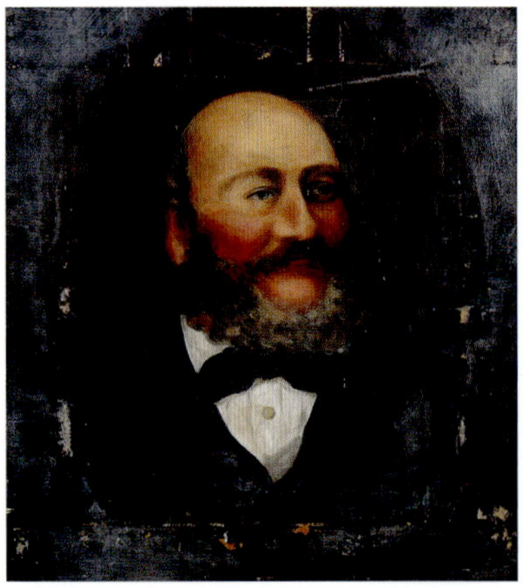

Thellusson, Aline (attributed to) 1856–1880
Charles Sabine Augustus Thellusson (c.1822-1885) c.1870–1880
oil on canvas 41 x 35.5
90009770

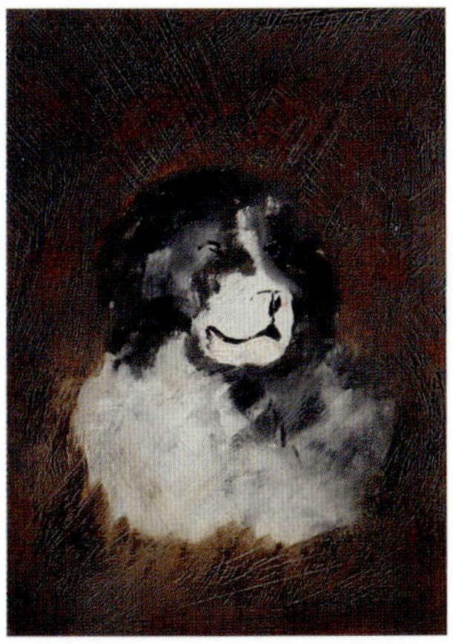

Thellusson, Aline (attributed to) 1856–1880
Sketch of a Dog's Head c.1870–1880
oil on milled board 35.5 x 25
90003700

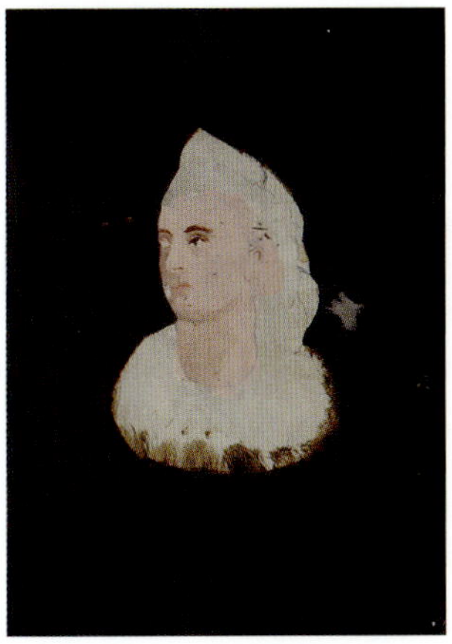

Thellusson, Aline (attributed to) 1856–1880
Sketch of a Female Head c.1870–1880
oil on milled board 23 x 16
90003697

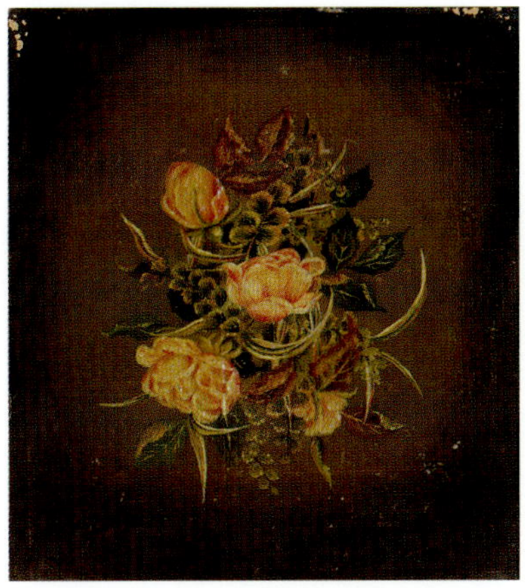

Thellusson, Aline (attributed to) 1856–1880
Still Life: Flowers (recto) c.1870–1880
oil on board 35.5 x 30.5
90003698

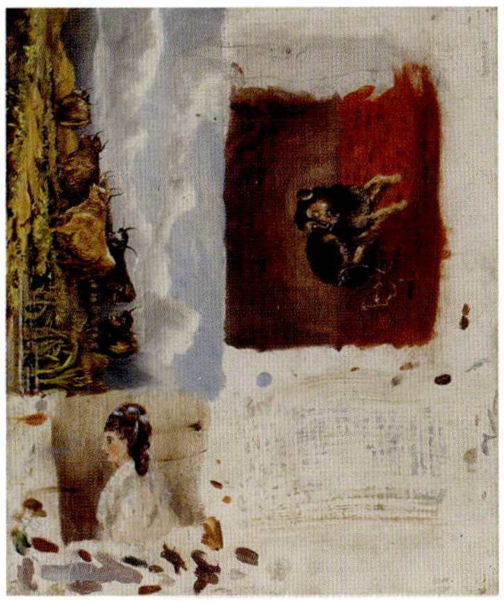

Thellusson, Aline (attributed to) 1856–1880
Sketch of Cows and Horses (verso)
oil on board 35.5 x 30.5
90003698verso

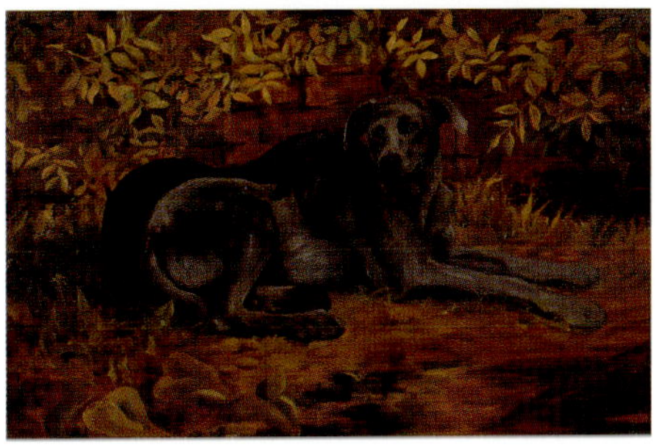

Thellusson, Aline (attributed to) 1856–1880
Two Dogs, 'Juliet' and 'Faust' c.1870–1880
oil on canvas 60 x 90
90004078

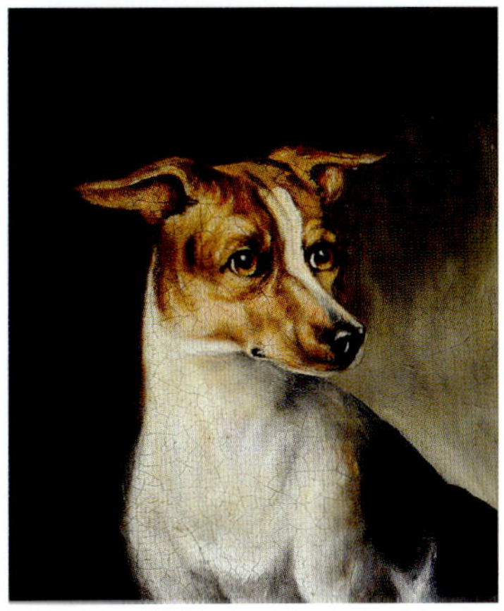

Thellusson, Aline (attributed to) 1856–1880
White Dog with Brown Markings c.1870–1880
oil on panel 37 x 29.5
90009743

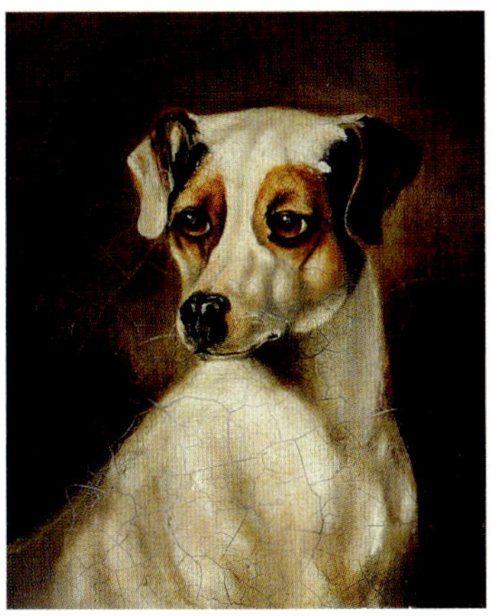

Thellusson, Aline (attributed to) 1856–1880
White Dog with Brown Markings c.1870–1880
oil on canvas 38 x 28
90009744

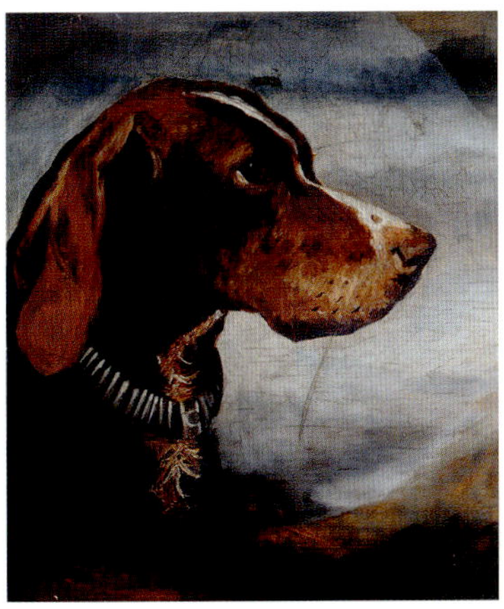

Thellusson, Aline (attributed to) 1856–1880
or **Thellusson, Herbert** 1854–1903
A Brown Dog with a Collar c.1870–1880
oil on canvas 29 x 24
90009745

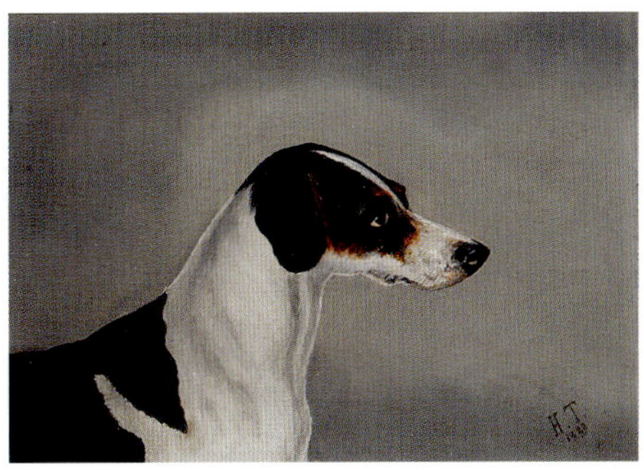

Thellusson, Herbert 1854–1903
A Dog 1888
oil on canvas 15.5 x 20.5
90003665

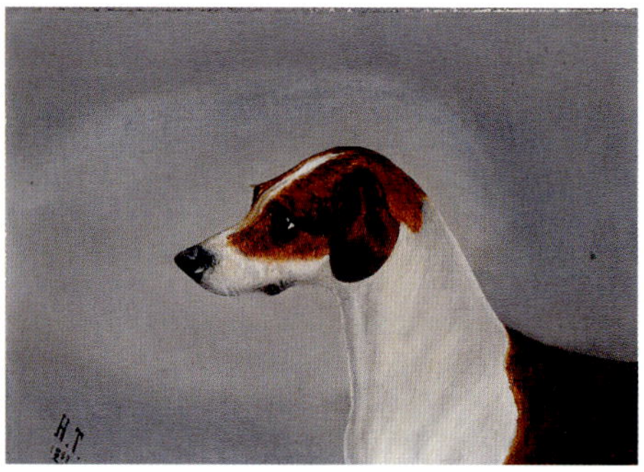

Thellusson, Herbert 1854–1903
A Dog 1888
oil on canvas 15.4 x 20.5
90003666

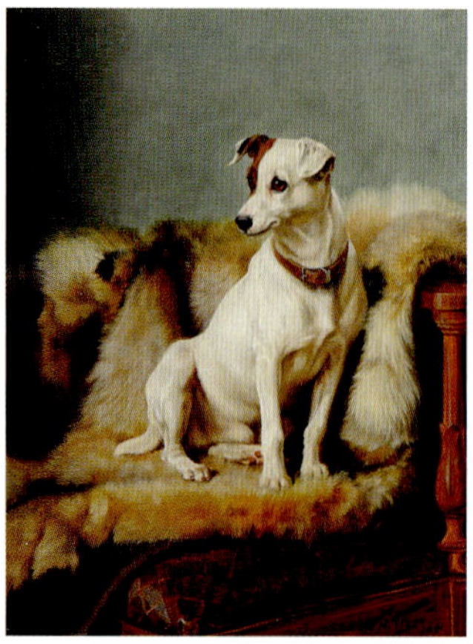

Trood, William Henry Hamilton 1848–1899
'Coup' 1891
oil on canvas 62.5 x 47
90009788

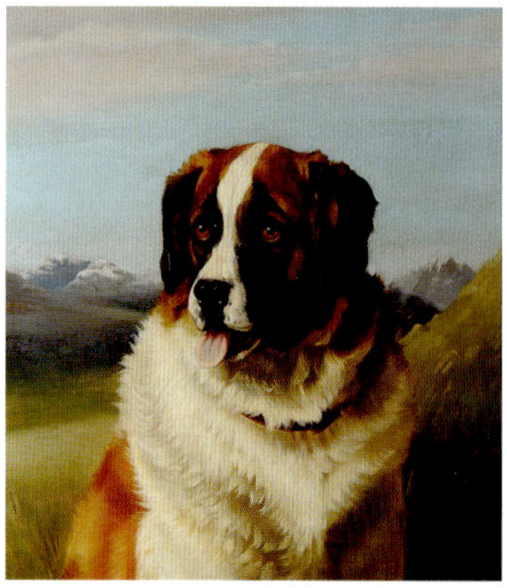

Trood, William Henry Hamilton 1848–1899
St Bernard Dog 1891
oil on canvas 67.5 x 59.5
90009768

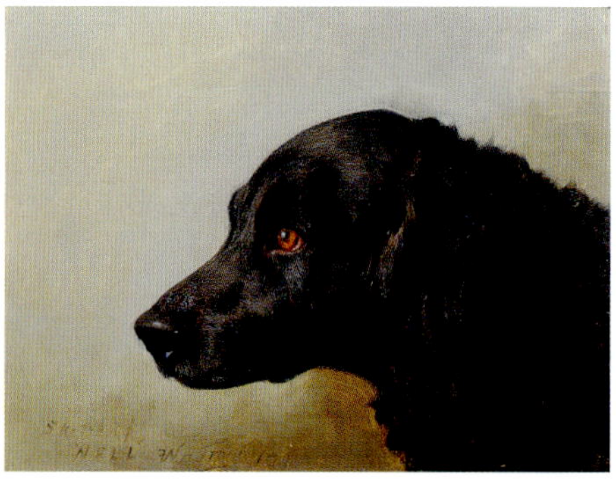

Trood, William Henry Hamilton 1848–1899
Sketch of 'Nell' 1891
oil on canvas 17 x 22
90009767

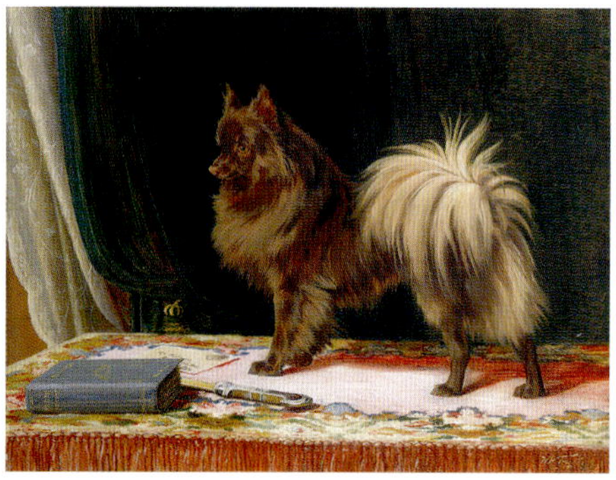

Trood, William Henry Hamilton 1848–1899
'Prairie Prince' 1897
oil on canvas 33 x 46
90009801

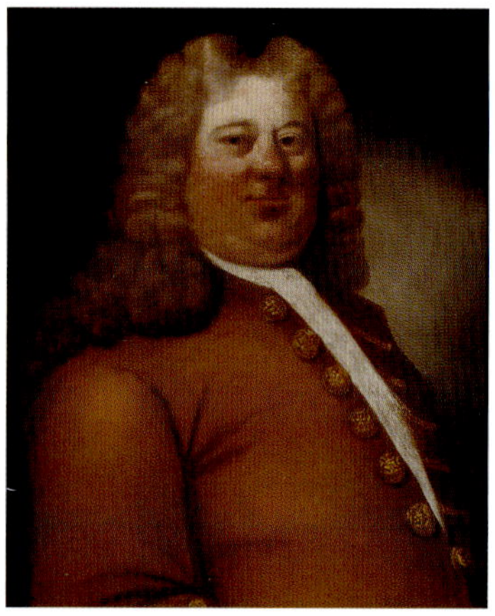

unknown artist
Sir Nicholas Watts (1675–1726), of Shanks House, Cucklington, Somerset c.1720
oil on canvas 73.5 x 61
90004077

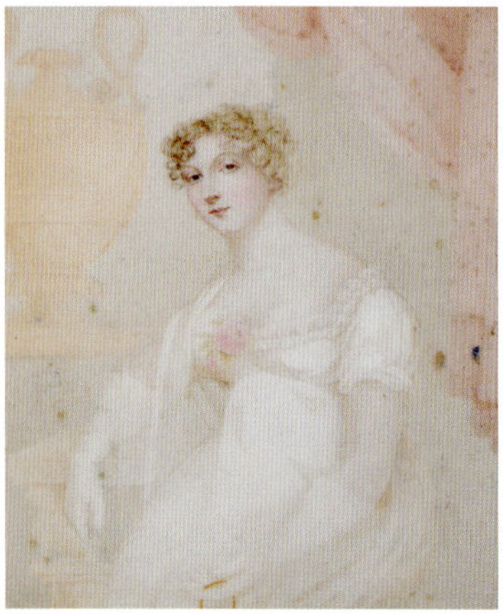

unknown artist
Portrait of an Unknown Lady c.1780–1820
oil on canvas 11 x 9.5
90007328

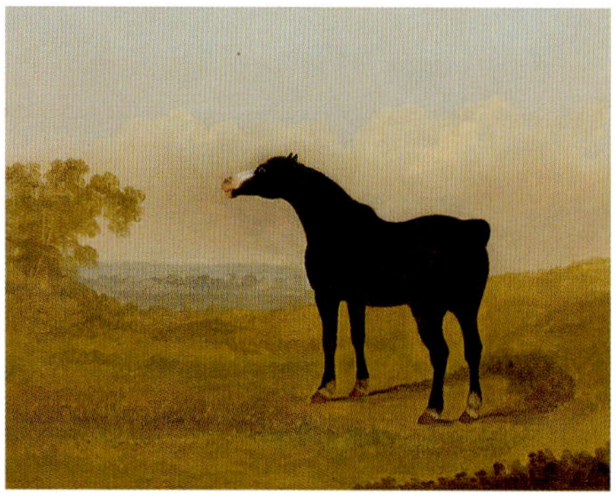

unknown artist
Horse in a Landscape c.1800–1830
oil on canvas 34.5 x 43.8
90004080

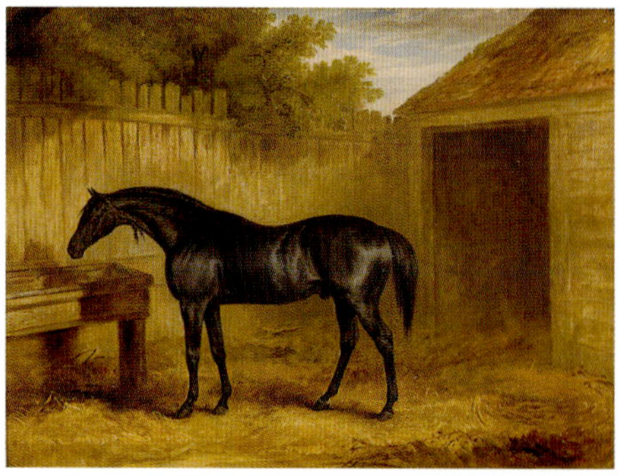

unknown artist
Black Stallion Outside a Stable c.1810–1850
oil on canvas 71 x 92
90009338

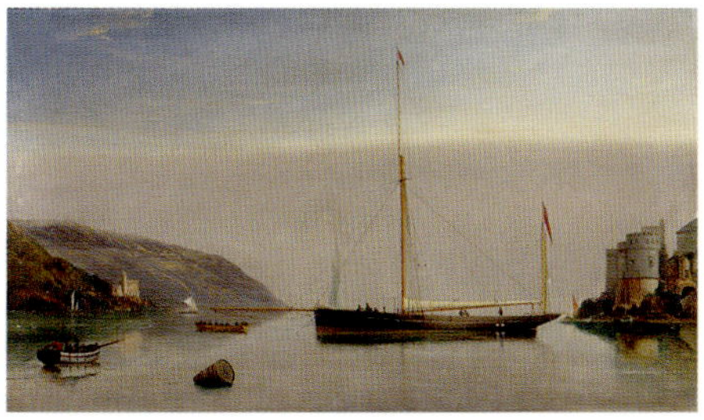

unknown artist
The Yacht, 'Tartar', in Harbour at Dartmouth, Devon 1850–1900
oil on canvas 44 x 76
90004079

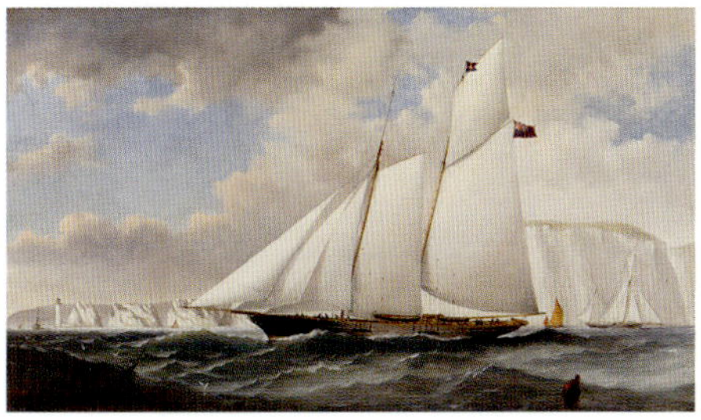

unknown artist
The Yacht, 'Rosalind' c.1850–1900
oil on canvas 63 x 94.5
90007679

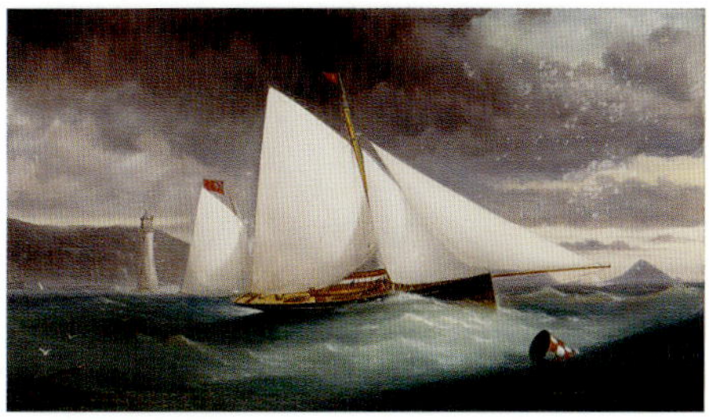

unknown artist
The Yacht, 'Tartar' c.1850–1900
oil on canvas 44 x 76
90007699

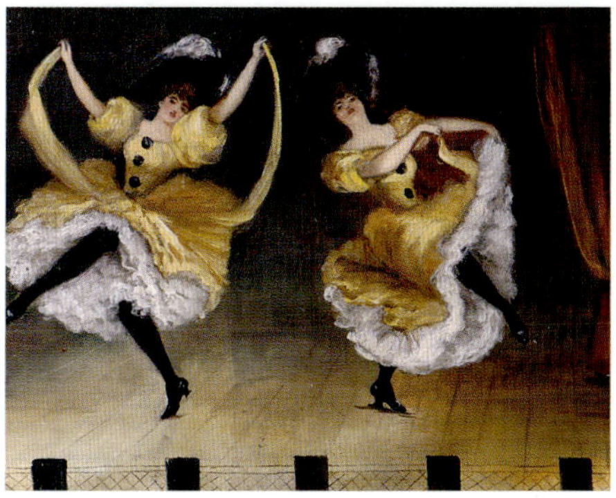

unknown artist
Can-Can Dancers c.1890–1900
oil on canvas 21.5 x 26.5
90003662

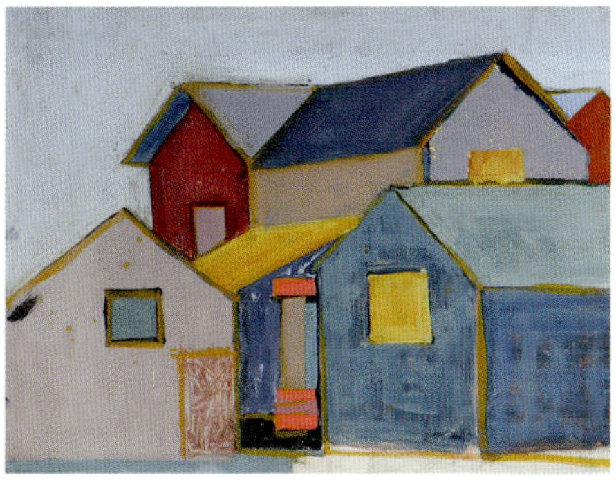

unknown artist 20th C
Houses
oil on hardboard 35.7 x 46
90016731

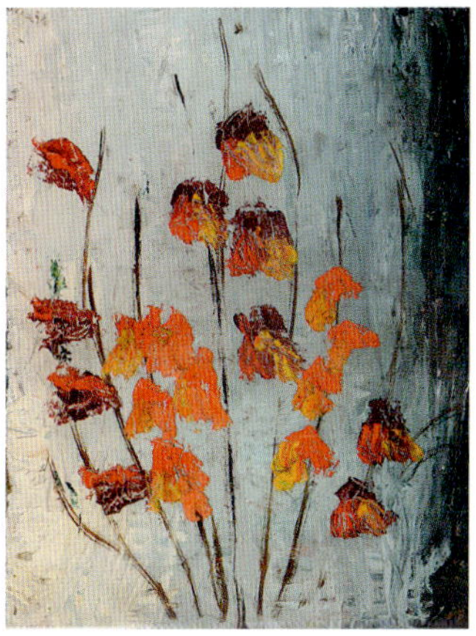

unknown artist 20th C
Red and Orange Flowers
oil on canvas 40 x 30
90016732

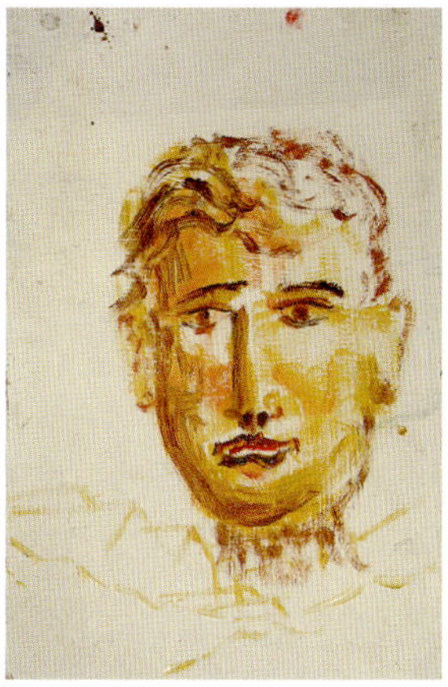

unknown artist 20th C
Sketch of a Male Head
oil on hardboard 40.5 x 27
90016730

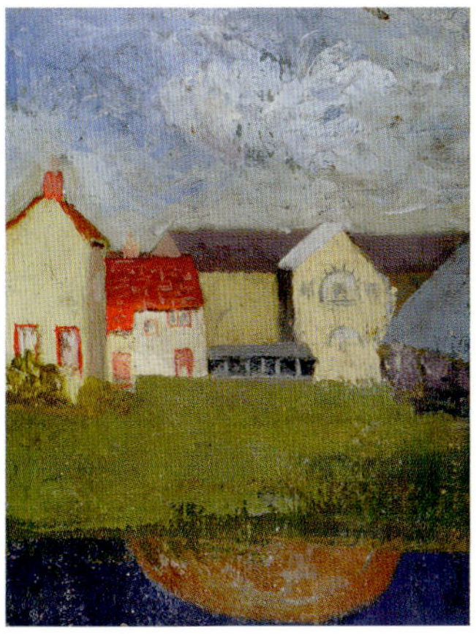

unknown artist 20th C
Village Scene
oil on canvas laid on board 41 x 30.5
90016736

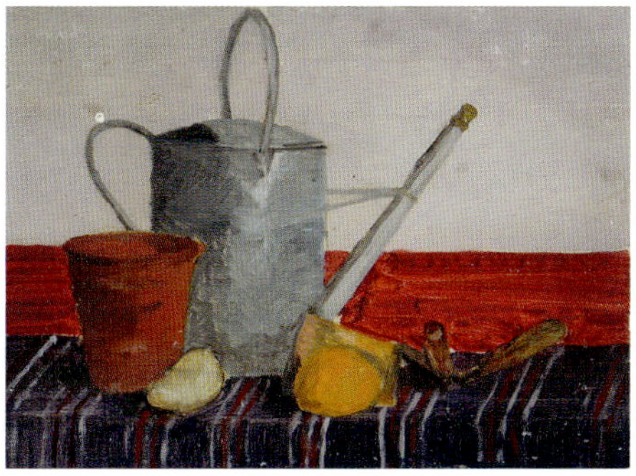

unknown artist 20th C
Watering Can and Objects
oil on canvas 30 x 40.5
90016734

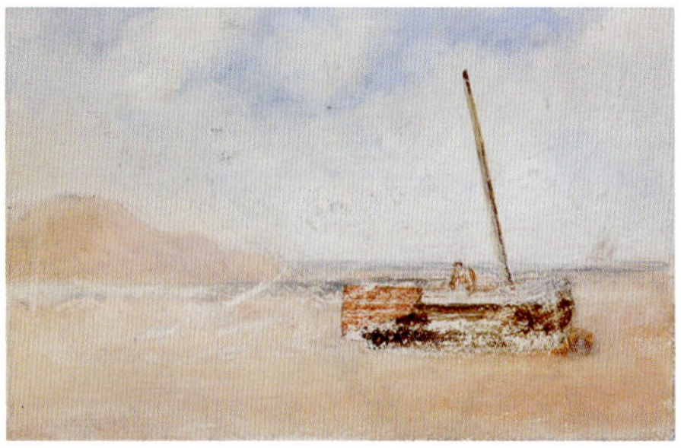

unknown artist
Boat on the Shore
oil on milled board 15 x 22
90003699

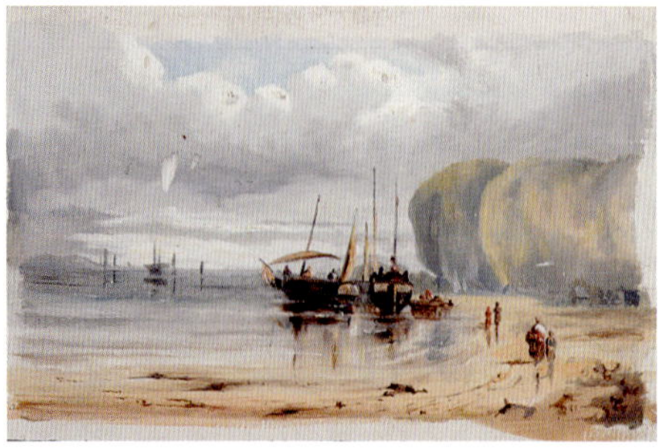

unknown artist
Coastal Scene
oil on milled board 18 x 26.5
90003768

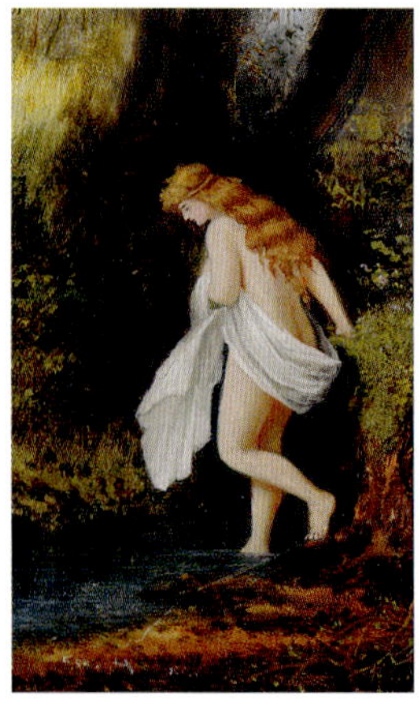

unknown artist
Nymph Bathing
oil on board 25 x 15
90007911

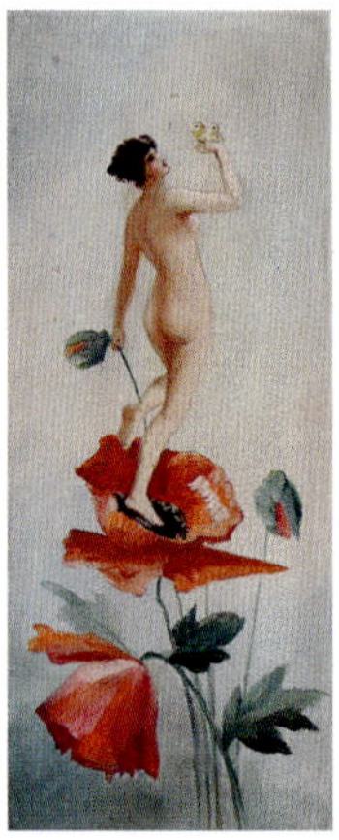

unknown artist
Nymph on a Poppy
oil on card 30 x 13
90007909

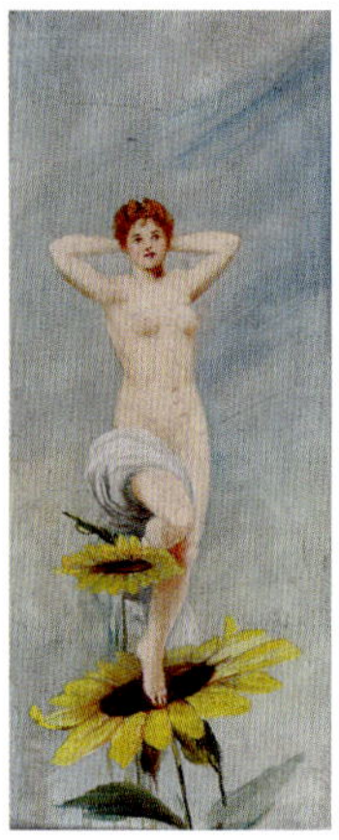

unknown artist
Nymph Posing on Daisies
oil on board 30.5 x 14
90007910

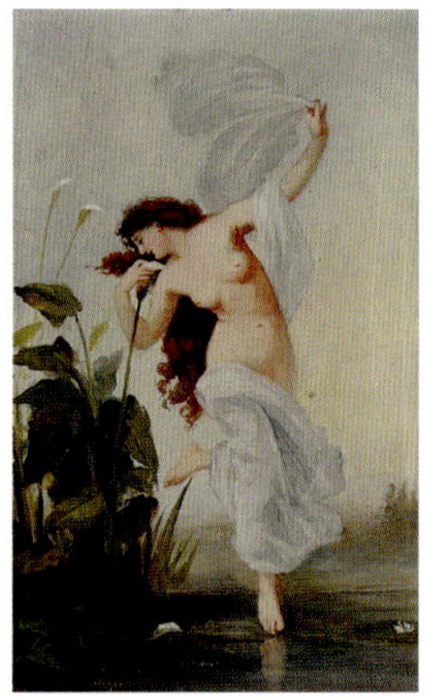

unknown artist
Nymph with Lillies
oil on board 26 x 16
90007912

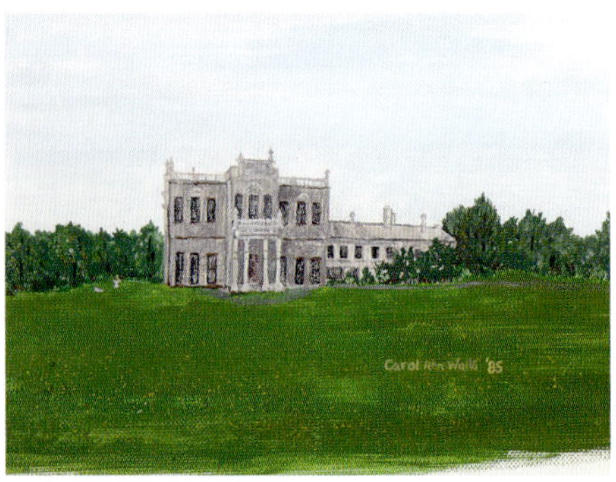

Walls, Carol Ann
Brodsworth Hall 1985
oil on card 19 x 24
90008488

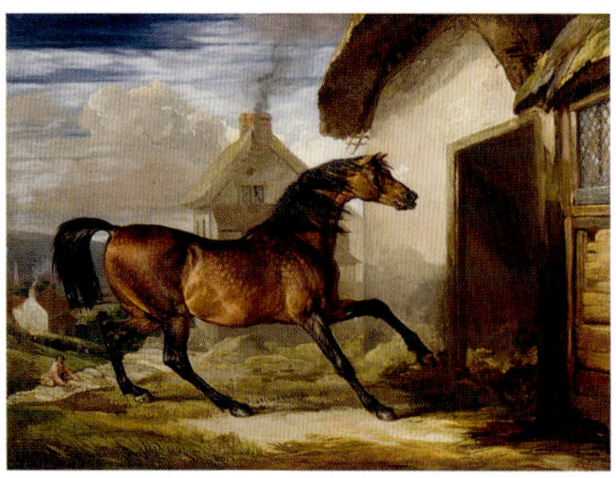

Ward, James 1769–1859
'Walton' 1812
oil on canvas 112 x 147.5
90009353

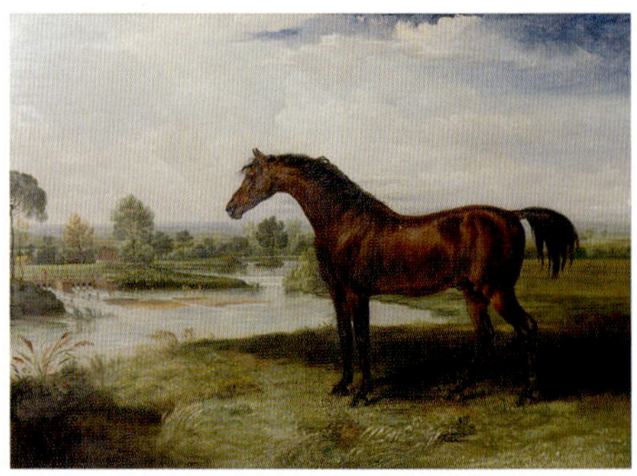

Ward, James 1769–1859
'Haphazard' 1820
oil on canvas 80.5 x 110.5
90009355

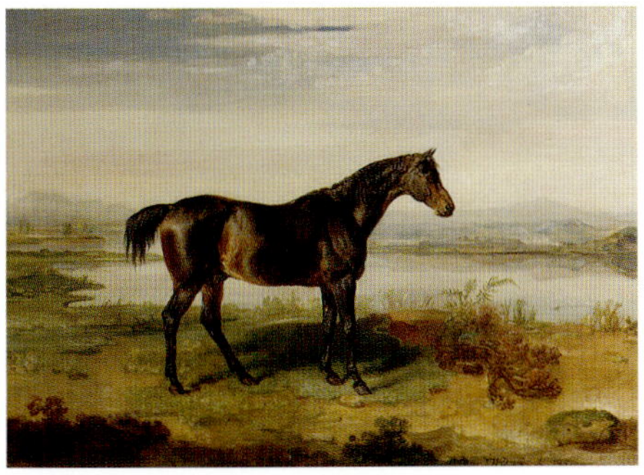

Ward, James 1769–1859
'Dr Syntax' 1821
oil on canvas 76 x 102
90009357

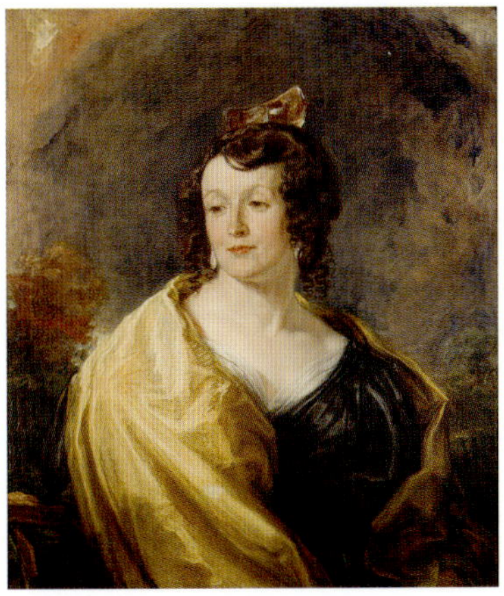

Ward, James 1769–1859
Mrs William Theobald, née Sarah Cooke (1795–1867) 1832
oil on canvas 75 x 62
90006944

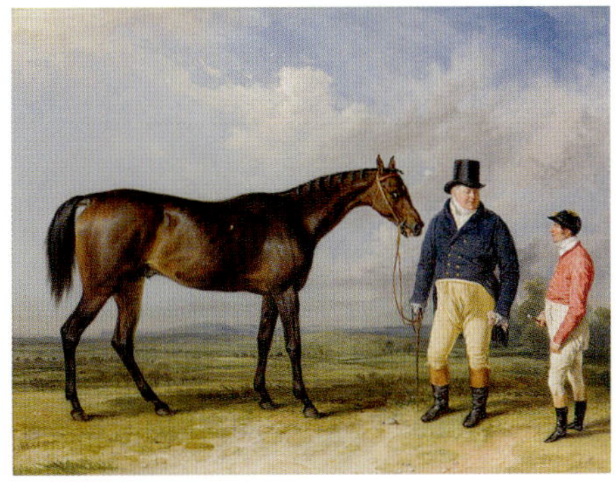

Ward, James 1769–1859
'Rockingham', with His Owner, John Theobald, and Jockey, Jem Robinson 1835
oil on canvas 76 x 102
90009342

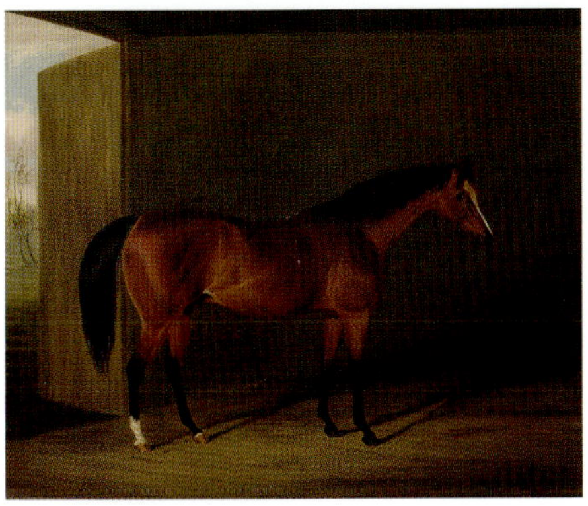

Webb, William 1780–1846
Bay Stallion in a Stable c.1830
oil on canvas 62 x 74
90009358

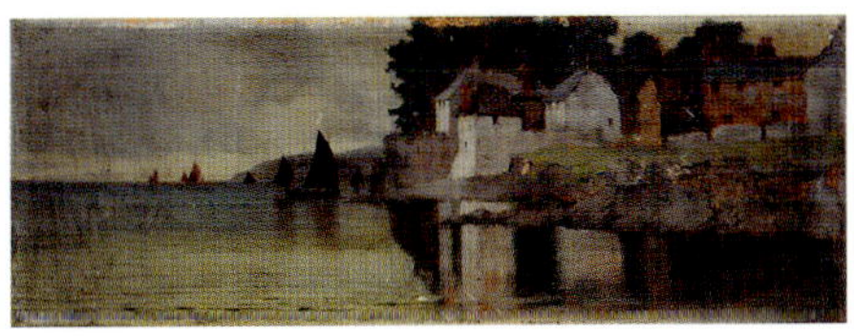

West, Reginald Cecil b.1865
Cornwall c.1880–1920
oil on wood panel 15 x 40
90007275

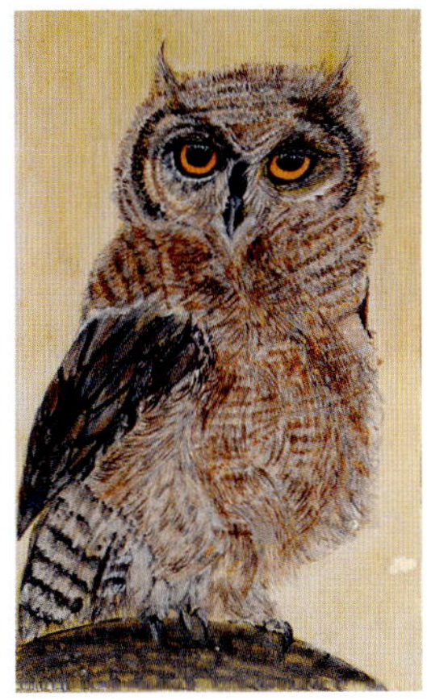

Williams, R. active c.1960–1988
Tawny Owl
oil on card 30.5 x 20.5
90007950

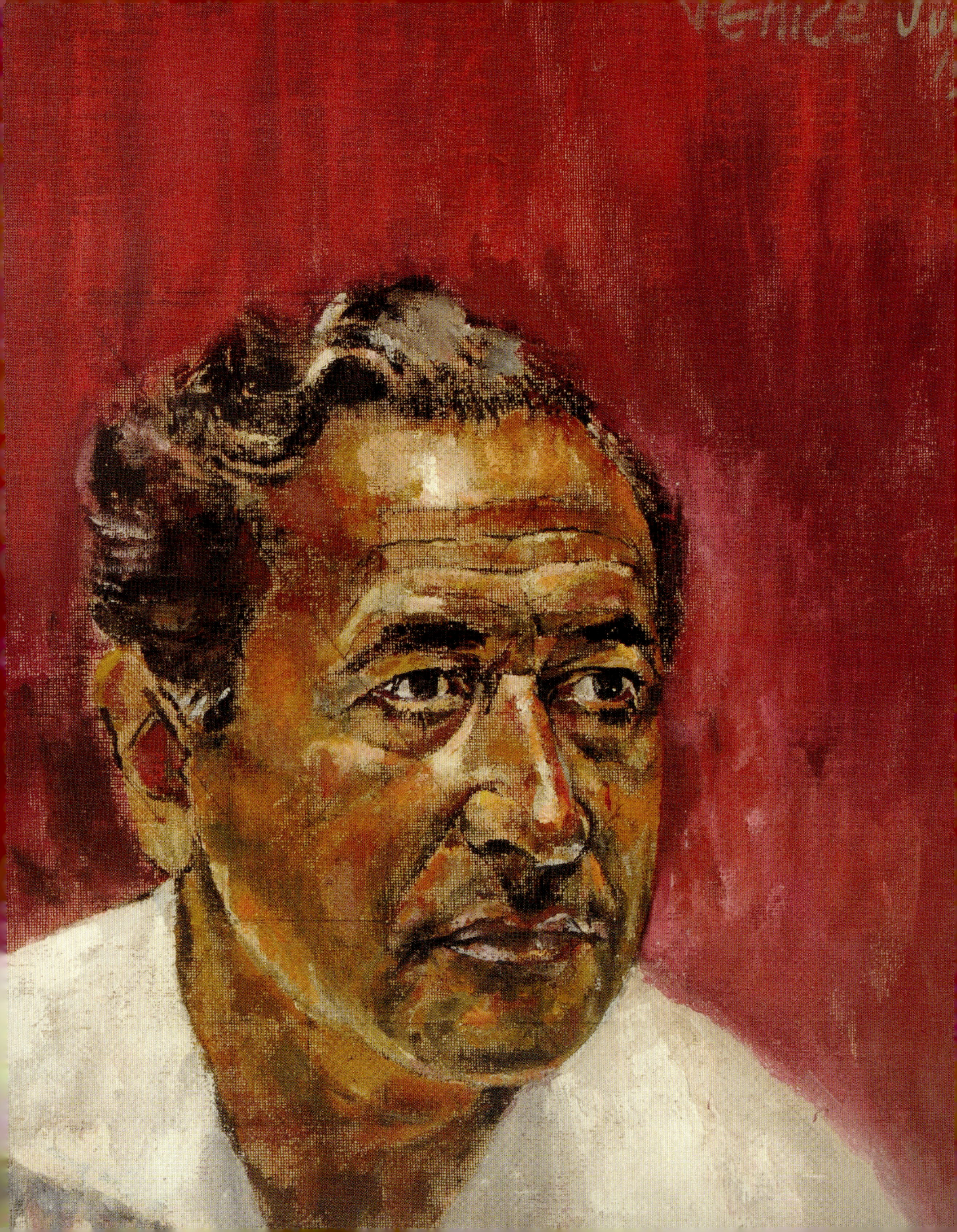
Venice

Barnsley Museum and Heritage Service

The centre for our Service's fine art collections is the picturesque Cannon Hall Museum, Park and Gardens. Viewing the paintings at the Museum will leave a visitor delighted and surprised. Among the stars of the show are works by Canaletto, John Constable and the circle of Aelbert Cuyp, with a background cast consisting of more Dutch and Flemish Masters, English portraiture and an attractive group of works by the local Hold family. The quality and variety of paintings, virtually all of which are on display, are a real find for those exploring the historic rooms and display galleries at the Museum.

After hundreds of years as a family home and working estate, Cannon Hall was purchased by Barnsley Corporation in 1951. The decision was made to open the estate to the public, turning the Hall into a Museum and giving access to the gardens and landscaped park. The Hall was empty when purchased and the early curators had the enviable task of furnishing the new Museum and laying the foundations of a stunning fine and decorative arts collection. Astute purchases were made at auction and through antique dealers, and in time the Collection grew to encompass 120 oil paintings.

The Collection includes striking individual works, but the centrepiece is a group of over 50 works which came to the Museum as a later acquisition. These paintings were collected by wealthy local businessman William Harvey in the nineteenth century and include the seventeenth- and eighteenth-century Dutch and Flemish Collection. Harvey made his fortune in the linen industry and was a benefactor of the town. His wealth allowed him to become a collector of art and this passion led him to encourage others towards the same. On his death he left £1,000 to establish a school of art in Barnsley, the forerunner of today's Barnsley College.

In 1917 William Harvey's nephew left the Collection to the nation and in the same year the National Loan Collection Trust was founded. The Harvey Collection was the first administered by the Trust and toured the British Commonwealth. Finally in 2003 it was bequeathed with the assistance of the National Art Collections Fund, on a permanent basis, to Cannon Hall Museum.

We owe thanks to many individuals and organisations who have supported the Museum and the collections, but perhaps none so much as the Friends of Cannon Hall. Through their work, we have been able to fund painting acquisitions and conservation. They have contributed much needed time and resources towards exhibitions and collections management. Through their efforts, we have also been supported by The Pilgrim Trust, helping us to breathe new life into the collections and enter a new era of increasing access through exhibitions, loans, activities, web resources and publications.

We are delighted to be a part of The Public Catalogue Foundation project, and anticipate it allowing more people to enjoy and discover these paintings.

Natalie Murray, Collections Manager

Facing page: Sutherland, Graham Vivian, 1903–1980, *Arthur Jeffress (1904–1961)* (detail), 1953, Doncaster Museum Service, (p. 102)

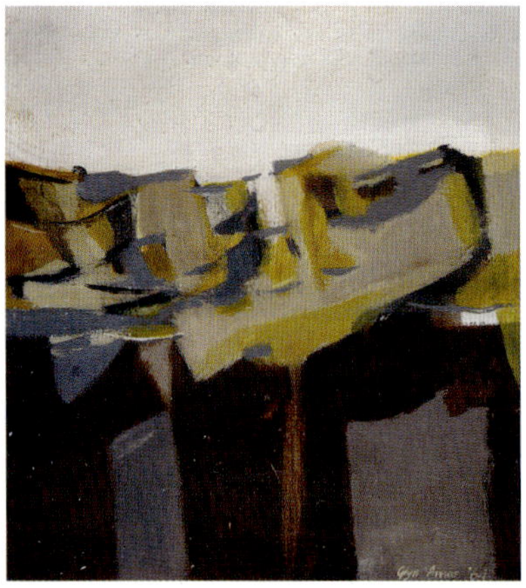

Amos, Glynn
Abstract Landscape 1964
oil on canvas 49.3 x 45
TEMP.CH.0018

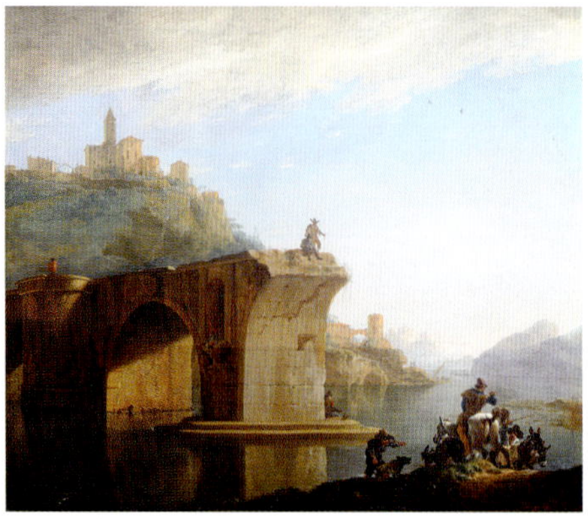

Asselyn, Jan after 1610–1652
Landscape with a Bridge in the Italian Countryside 1640–1652
oil on canvas 41.5 x 47.7
A.1904

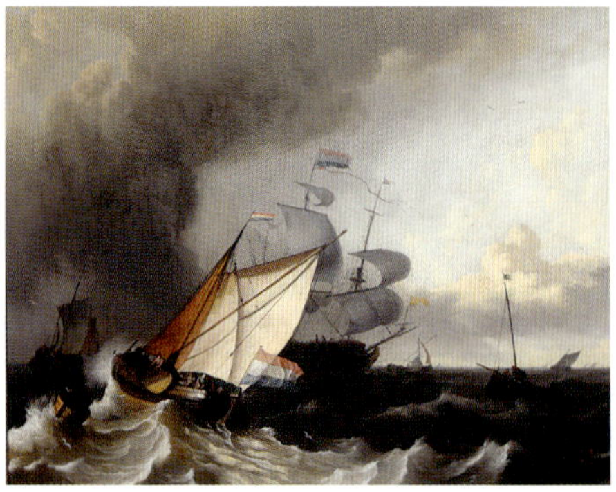

Backhuysen, Ludolf I 1630–1708
Shipping: A Fresh Breeze
oil on canvas 60.7 x 79
A.1905

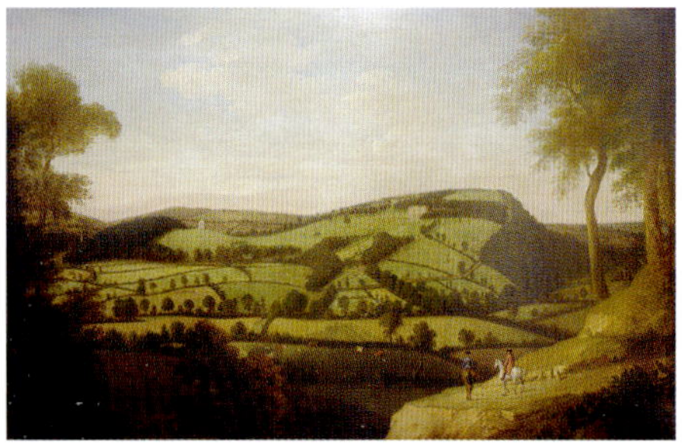

Bardwell, Thomas (attributed to) 1704–1767
Wentworth Castle Estate, Barnsley, South Yorkshire c.1751–1752
oil on canvas 119.5 x 180.5
RLI.0015.001 (P)

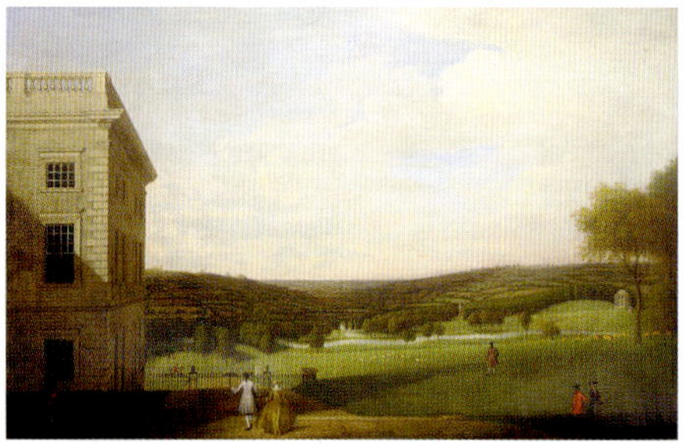

Bardwell, Thomas (attributed to) 1704–1767
Wentworth Castle Estate, Barnsley, South Yorkshire c.1751–1752
oil on canvas 119.5 x 180.5
RLI.0015.002 (P)

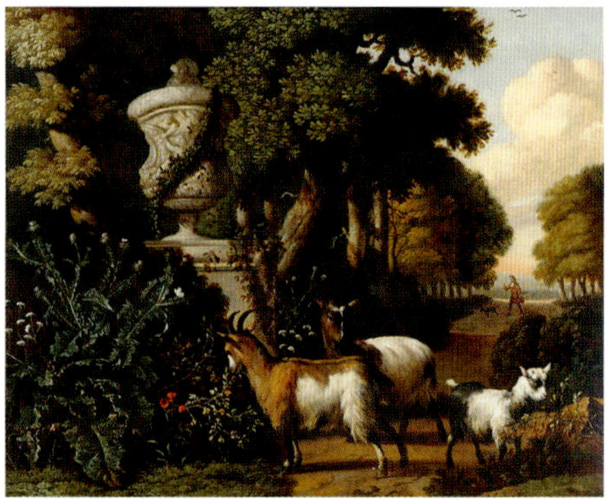

Begeyn, Abraham 1637/1638–1697
Landscape with Goats 1665–1697
oil on canvas 61.8 x 75
A.1906

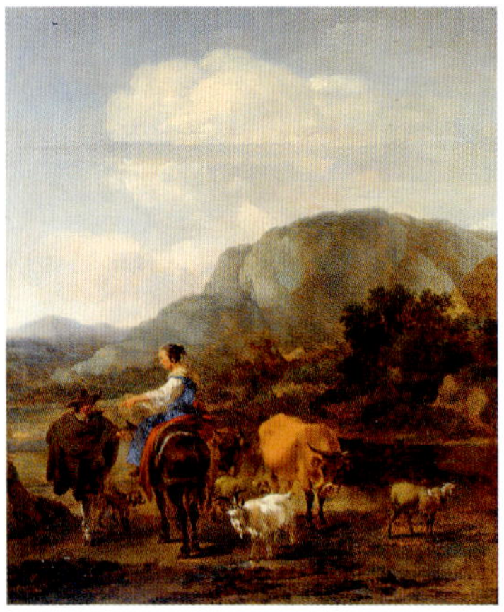

Berchem, Nicolaes 1620–1683
Italianate Landscape with Peasants Fording a Brook 1654
oil on board 44.5 x 36.5
A.1907

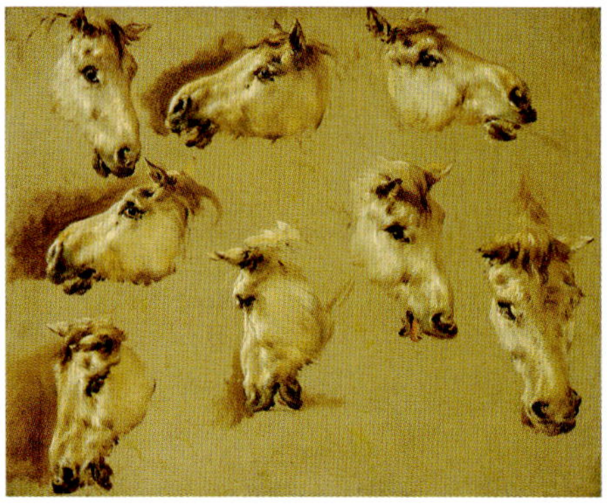

Berchem, Nicolaes 1620–1683
Studies of a Horse's Head
oil on canvas 29 x 36.2
A.1908

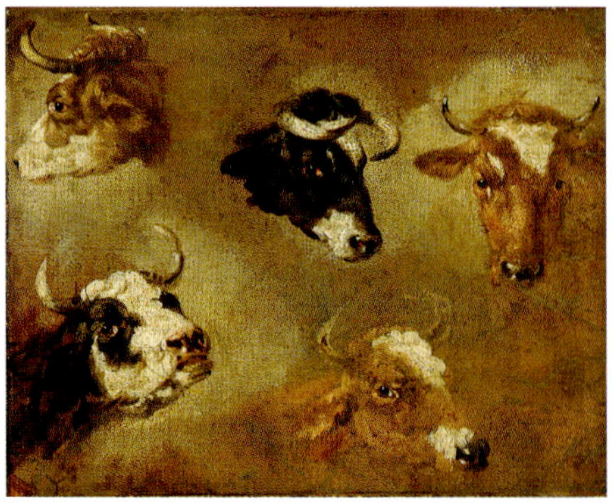

Berchem, Nicolaes 1620–1683
Studies of Cows' Heads
oil on canvas 23.4 x 28.5
A.1909

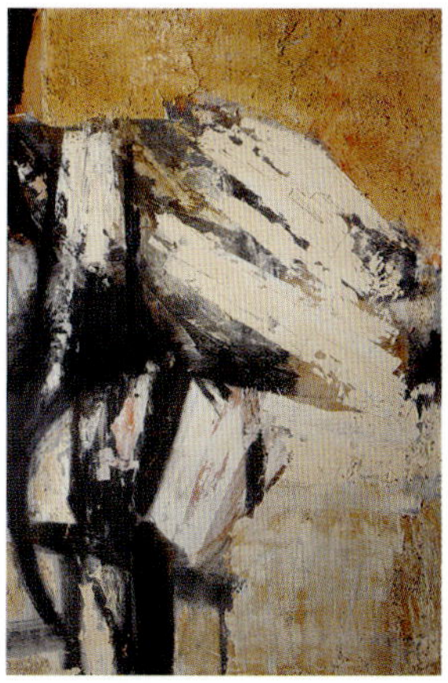

Blow, Sandra 1925–2006
Creation
oil on board 182 x 121
A.104

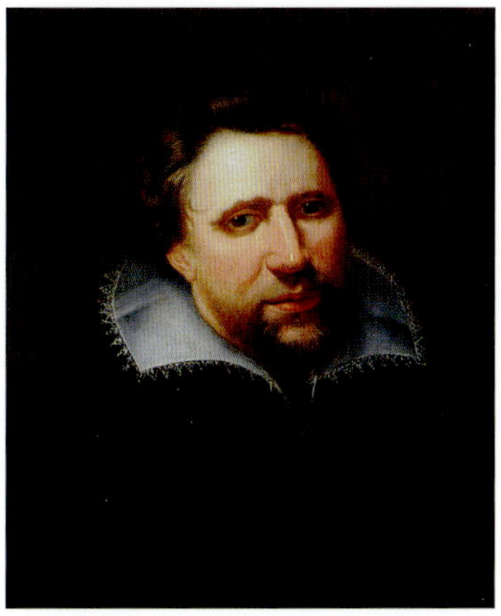

Blyenberch, Abraham van (after) 1575–1624
Ben Jonson 17th C–18th C
oil on canvas 55.3 x 45.4
A.2177

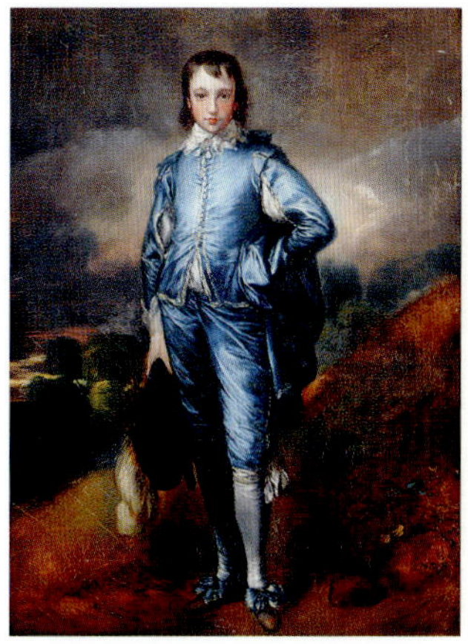

Bone, Henry 1755–1834
Blue Boy (copy after Thomas Gainsborough)
oil on canvas 51.2 x 37.3
A.1910

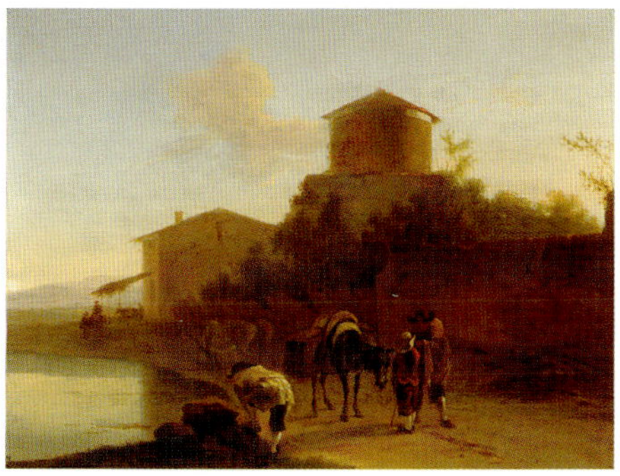

Both, Andries Dirksz. 1611/1612–1641 & **Both, Jan** c.1618–1652
Landscape with a Tower and Figures by a Lake 1639–1641
oil on panel 30.3 x 38.5
A.1911

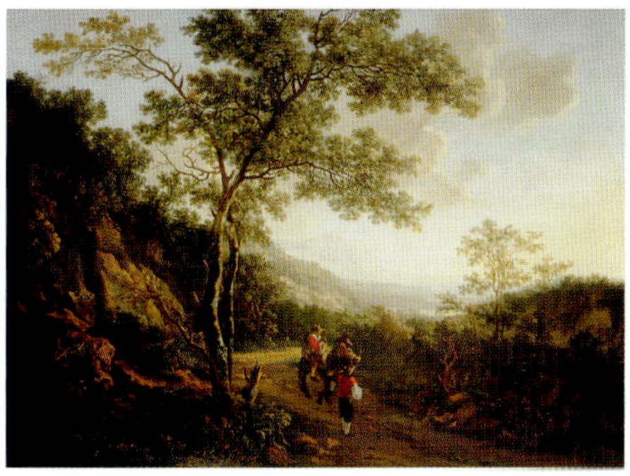

Both, Andries Dirksz. 1611/1612–1641 & **Both, Jan** c.1618–1652
Landscape with Figures, Evening 1640–1650
oil on canvas 91.5 x 116.8
A.1912

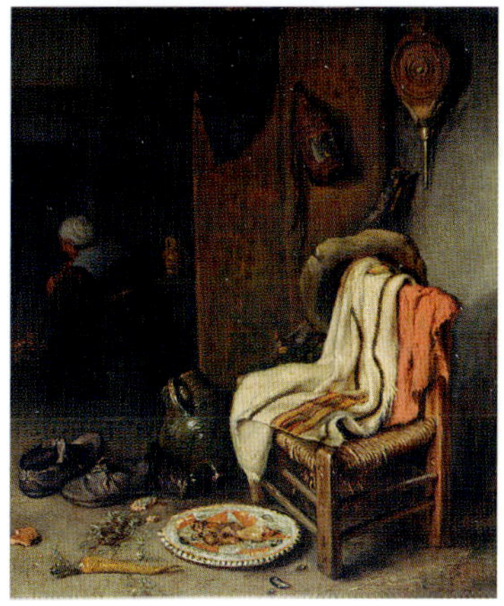

Boursse, Esaias 1631–1672
Domestic Interior with Still Life
oil on panel 27.5 x 22.5
A.1913

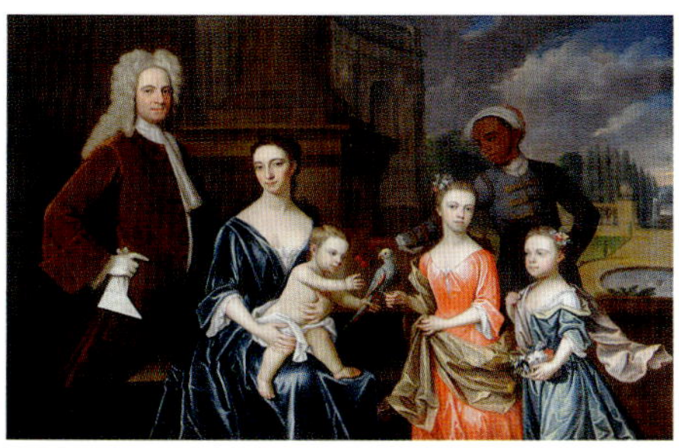

British (English) School
Philip Stanhope (1673–1726), 3rd Earl of Chesterfield, with His Wife, Lady Elizabeth Savile, Children and Nubian Slave c.1695
oil on canvas 100 x 125.5
A.44

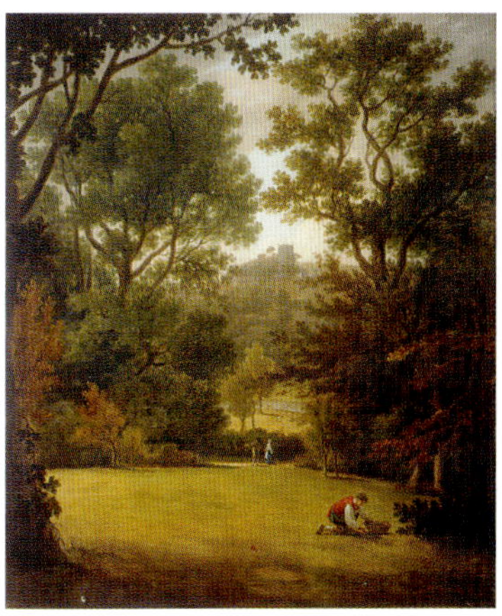

British (English) School mid-18th C
Cawthorne Church, South Yorkshire, from the Park
oil on canvas 100 x 80
A.42

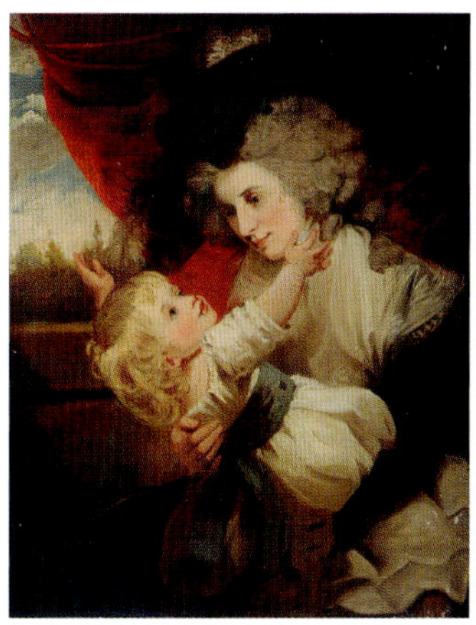

British (English) School
Mary Winifred Pulleine (1763–after 1787), and Her Son 1784
oil on canvas 90 x 69.3
RLI.0034.002 (P)

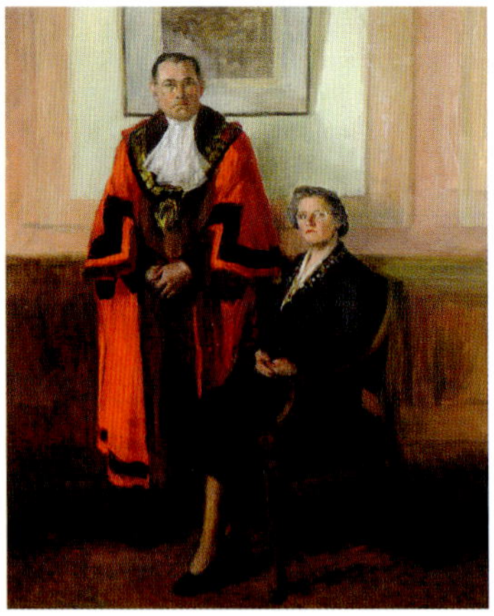

Bury, Brenda b.1932
Alderman A. E. McVie, JP and Mrs McVie 1955
oil on canvas 125 x 99.5
A.8

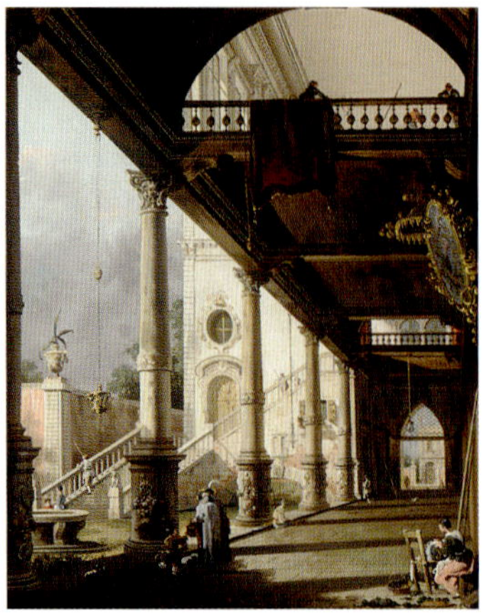

Canaletto 1697–1768
Capriccio: A Colonnade Opening onto the Courtyard of a Palace
oil on canvas 56 x 42
A.1914

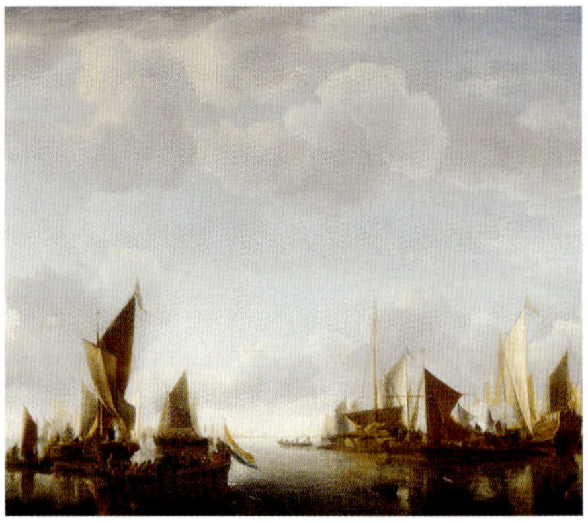

Cappelle, Jan van de (after) c.1624–1679
River Scene with Ships Becalmed 1645–1655
oil on canvas 46.2 x 52
A.1915

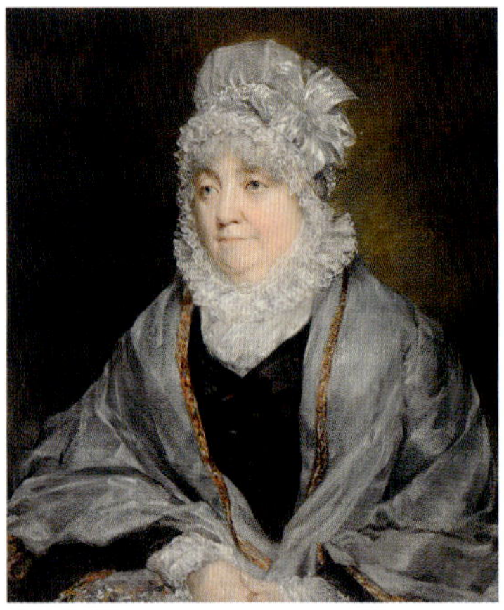

Constable, John 1776–1837
Mrs Tuder 1818
oil on canvas 73.5 x 60.8
A.66

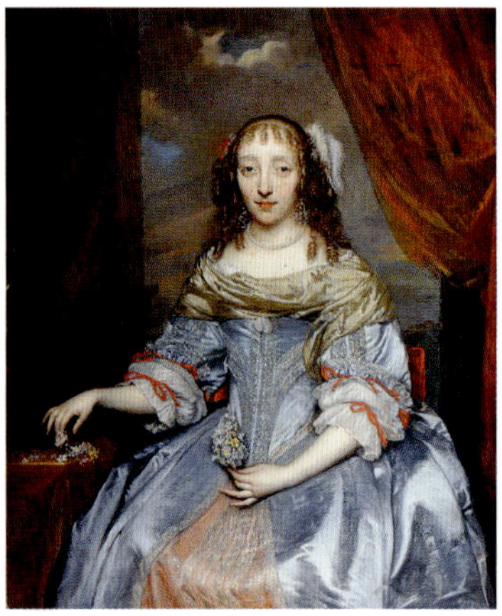

Coques, Gonzales c.1614–1684
Portrait of a Lady in a Blue Satin Dress 1640–1684
oil on canvas 34.5 x 28
A.1917

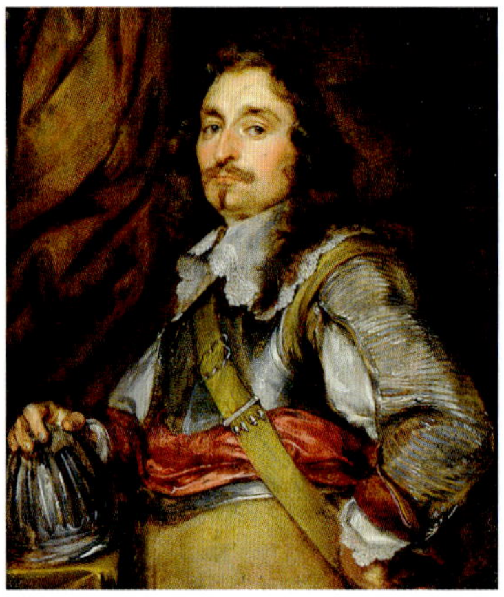

Coques, Gonzales c.1614–1684
Portrait of an Officer in Armour 1640–1684
oil on canvas 15.5 x 13.8
A.1916

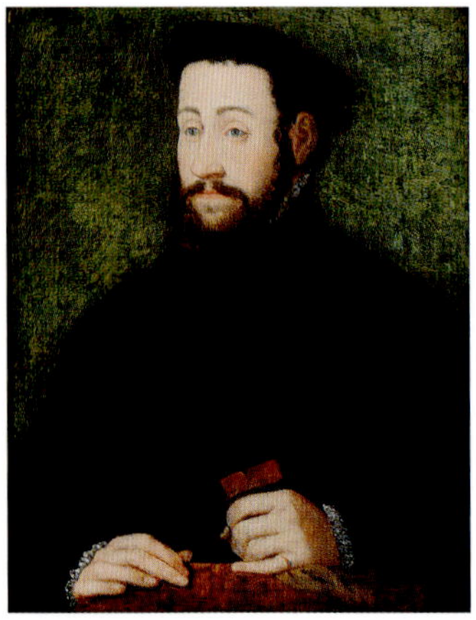

Corneille de Lyon, Claude (attributed to) 1510–c.1574
Sir John Cheke (1514–1557)
oil on board 21.5 x 16.5
A.1619

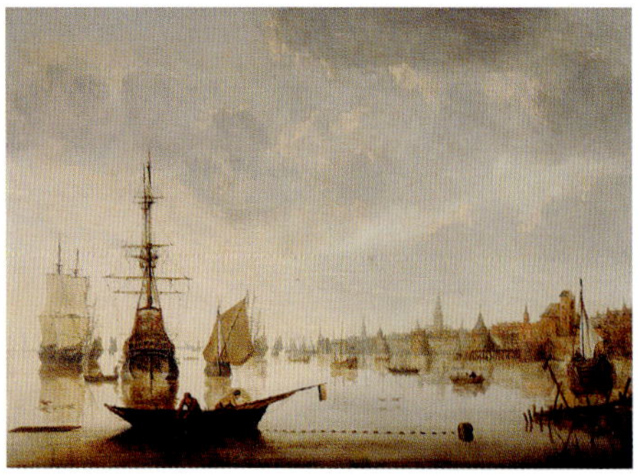

Cuyp, Aelbert (circle of) 1620–1691
River Scene with Town and Shipping 1635–1645
oil on canvas 39.3 x 52.3
A.1918

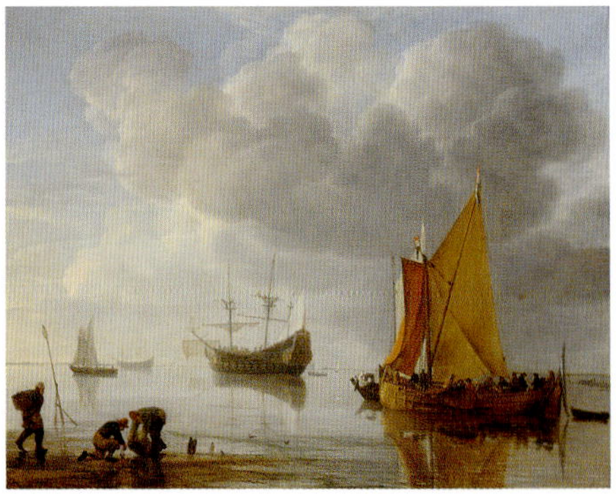

Dubbels, Hendrik Jacobsz. 1620/1621–1676
Calm 1655–1658
oil on canvas 48.5 x 64.3
A.1954

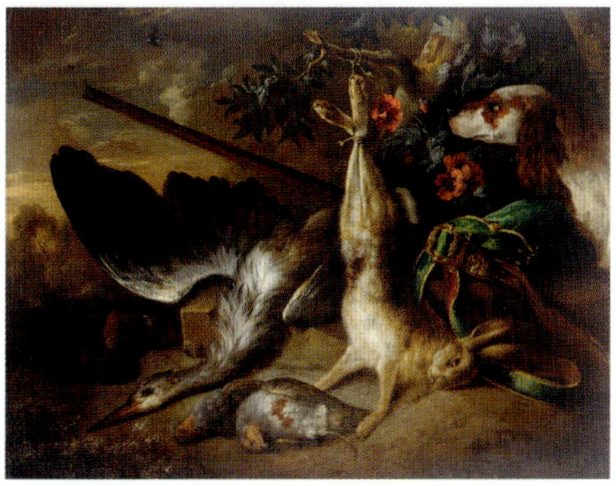

Dutch School 17th C
Still Life with Dead Game
oil on canvas 99 x 125
A.41

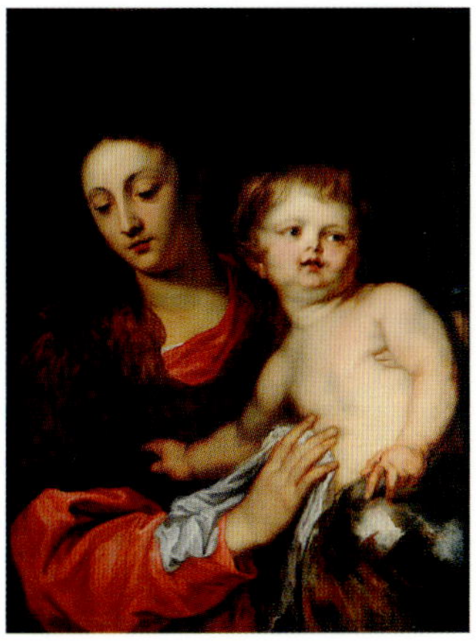

Dyck, Anthony van (style of) 1599–1641
Virgin and Child 18th C
oil on canvas 83.5 x 62.5
A.1919

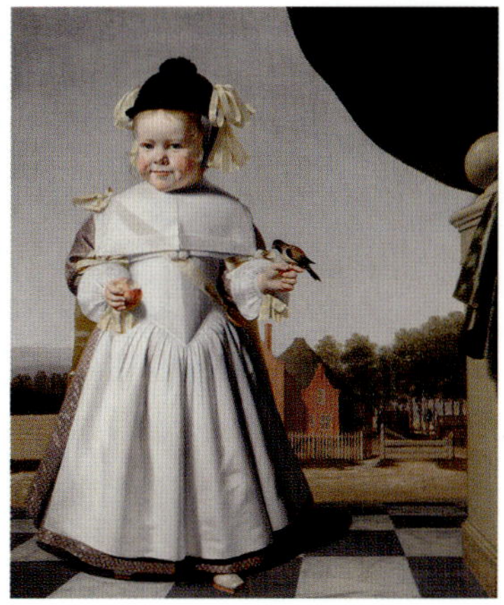

Everdingen, Cesar Boetius van c.1606–1678
Boy Holding an Apple 1664
oil on canvas 97.8 x 81.2
A.1920

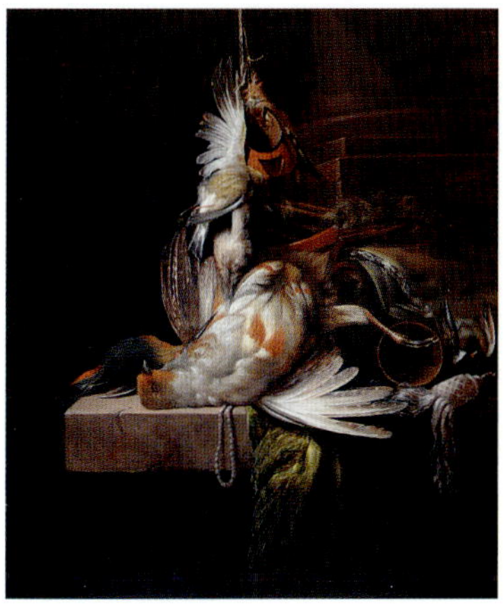

Ferguson, William Gowe
c.1632/1633–c.1695
Still Life 1679
oil on canvas 59.2 x 50
A.64

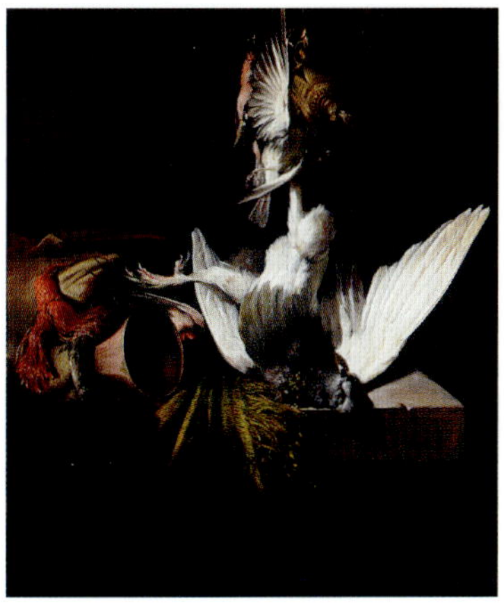

Ferguson, William Gowe
c.1632/1633–c.1695
Still Life 1679
oil on canvas 59.5 x 50
A.65

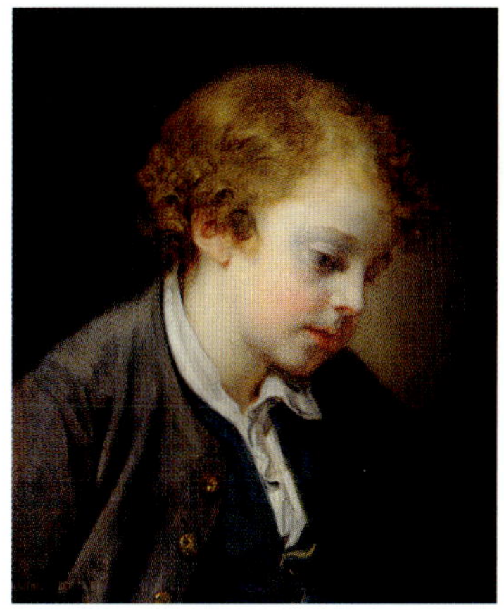

Greuze, Jean-Baptiste 1725–1805
L'écolier 1755–1759
oil on canvas 40.7 x 33
A.1922

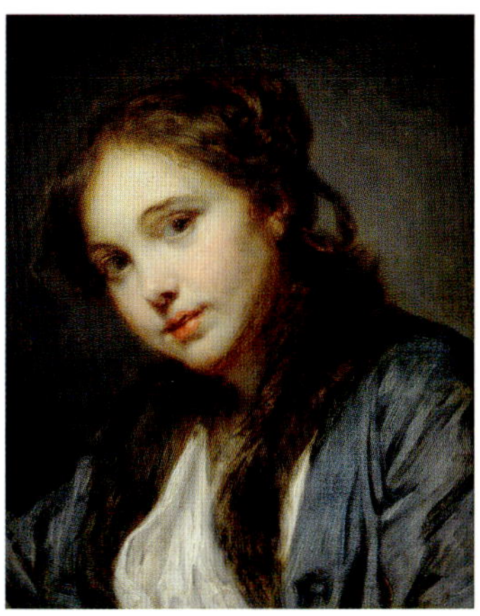

Greuze, Jean-Baptiste 1725–1805
La polonaise 1760–1765
oil on canvas 39.5 x 31.5
A.1921

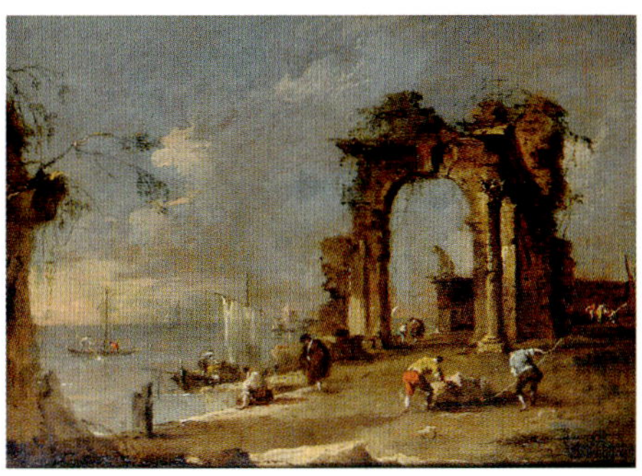

Guardi, Francesco 1712–1793
Capriccio with a Ruined Archway by the Banks of a Lagoon
oil on canvas 18.5 x 26.2
A.1923

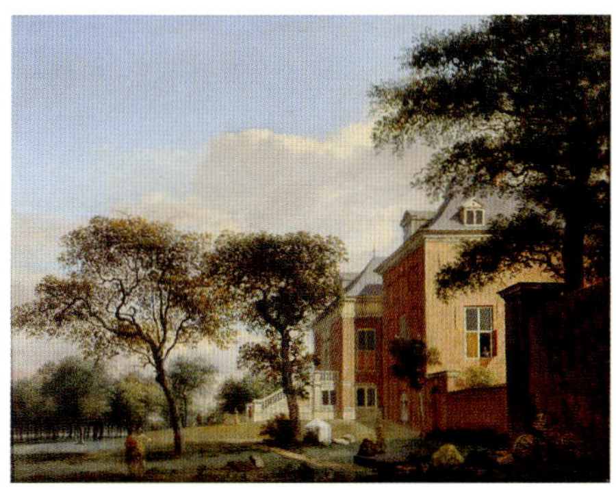

Heyden, Jan van der 1637–1712
The House in the Wood, The Hague, The Netherlands (Huis ten Bosch) 1665–1675
oil on canvas & panel 29.4 x 37.2
A.1924

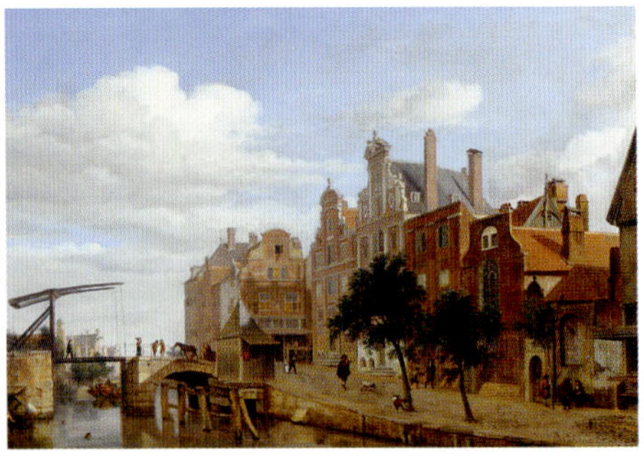

Heyden, Jan van der 1637–1712
View in Amsterdam, The Netherlands
1665–1675
oil on panel 36.2 x 50.5
A.1925

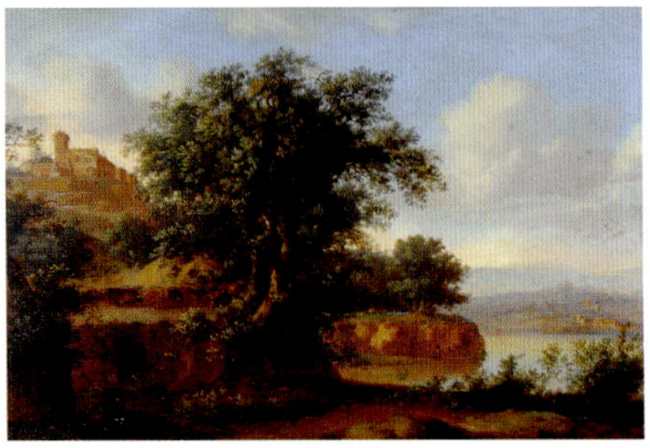

Heyden, Jan van der 1637–1712
The House on the Hill
oil on copper 11.3 x 17.2
A.1926

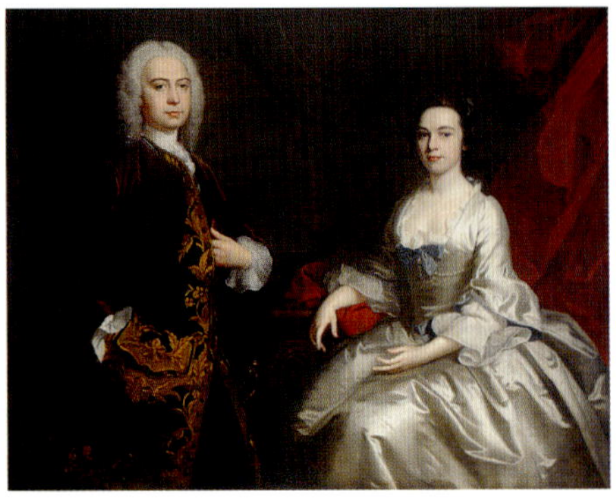

Highmore, Joseph 1692–1780
Sir Willoughby Aston and His Wife
oil on canvas 125 x 155.5
A.67

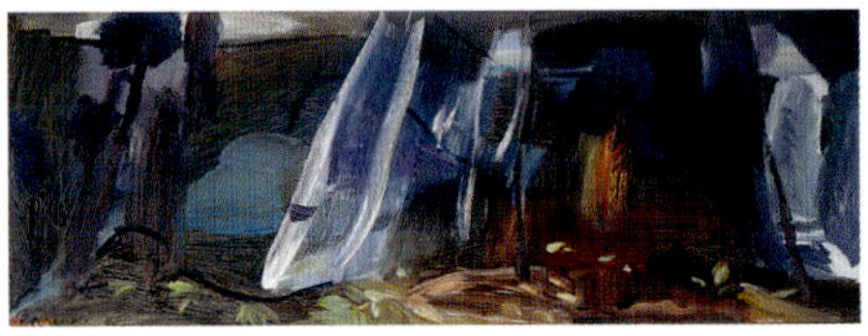

Hitchens, Ivon 1893–1979
Dark West Wood
oil on canvas 41 x 108
A.88

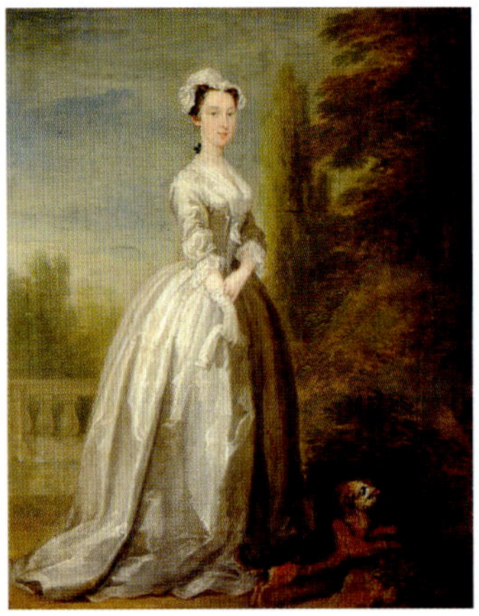

Hogarth, William 1697–1764
Portrait of a Lady
oil on canvas 44.5 x 34.2
A.1927

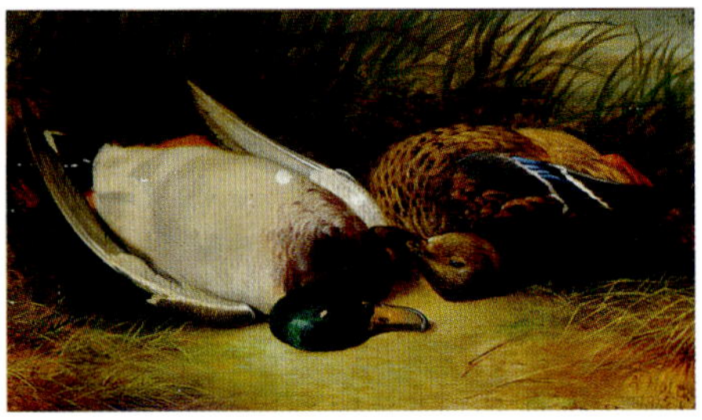

Hold, Abel 1815–1896
Still Life 1855
oil on board 34.7 x 60
A.117

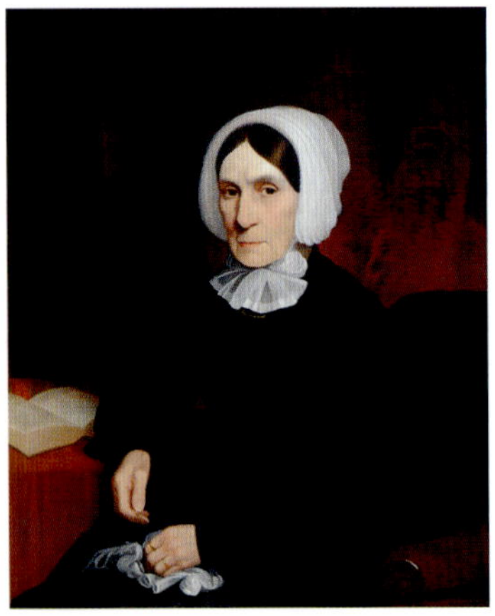

Hold, Abel 1815–1896
Mrs Elizabeth Spencer Stanhope (1795–1873)
1873
oil on canvas 89.8 x 72.3
A.2151

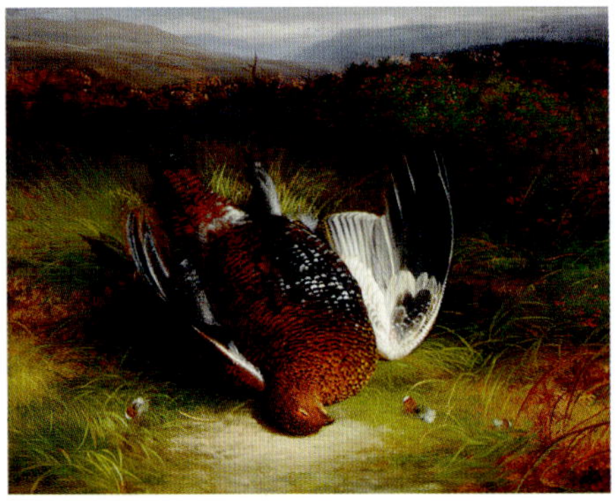

Hold, Abel 1815–1896
Dead Game 1880
oil on canvas 42 x 52.2
A.716

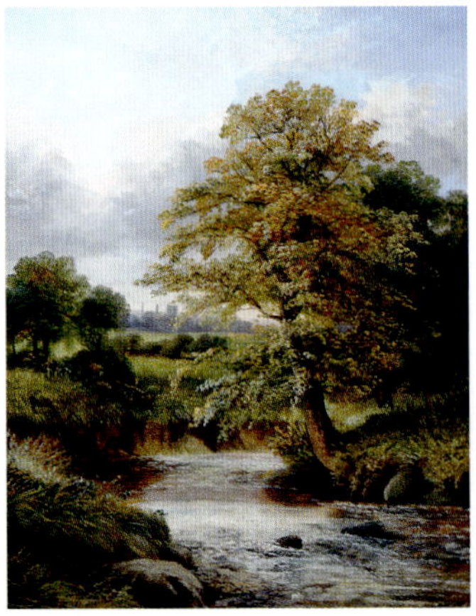

Hold, Abel 1815–1896
A Wooded River Landscape
oil on canvas 44.2 x 33.8
A.2162.001

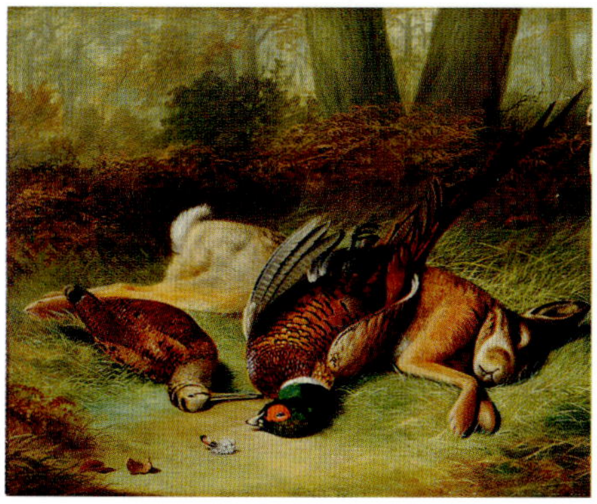

Hold, Abel 1815–1896
Still Life
oil on canvas 62.3 x 75.4
A.116

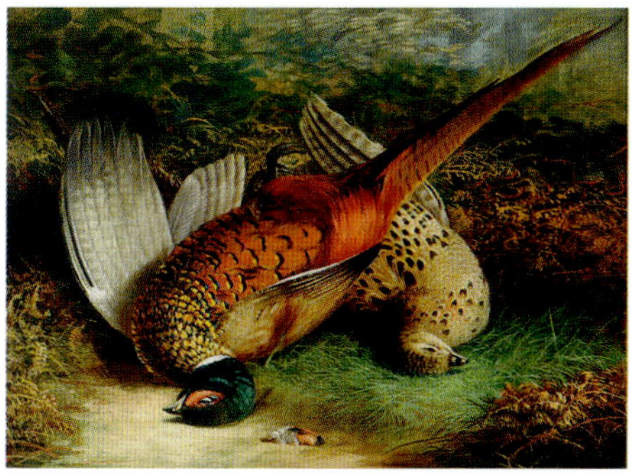

Hold, Abel 1815–1896
Still Life
oil on canvas 44.3 x 60
A.118

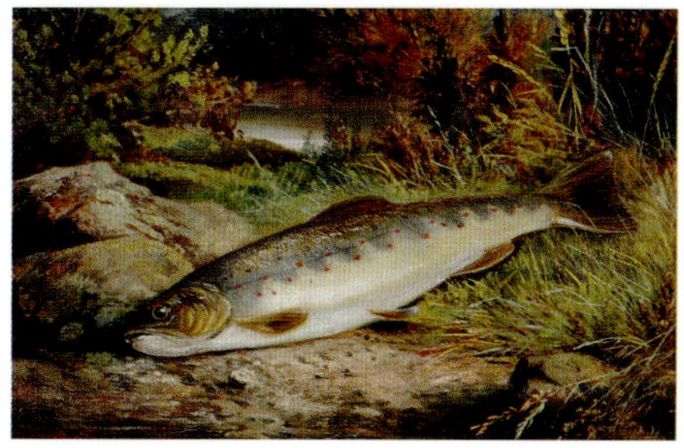

Hold, Benjamin 1858–1917
Fish on a Grassy Riverbank 1886
oil on canvas 18.6 x 29.1
A.2162.002

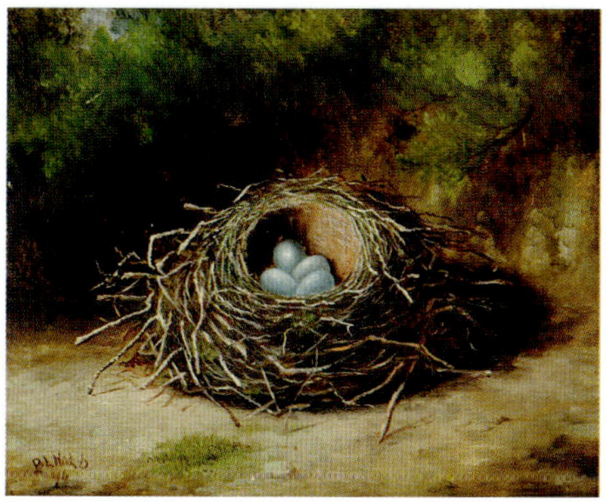

Hold, Benjamin 1858–1917
Still Life 1896
oil on canvas 24.5 x 30
A.112.001

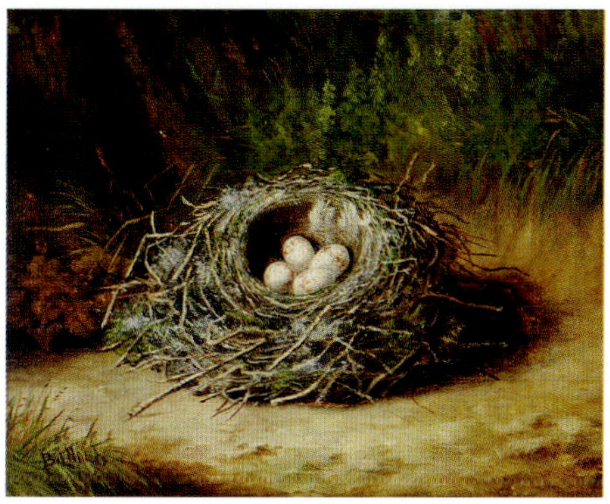

Hold, Benjamin 1858–1917
Still Life 1896
oil on canvas 24.5 x 30
A.112.002

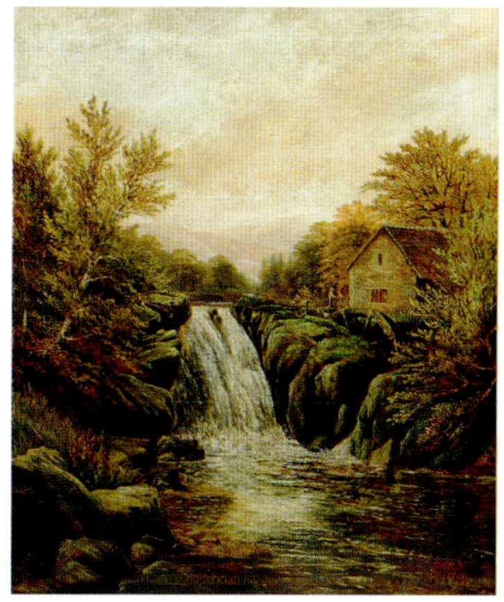

Hold, Benjamin 1858–1917
Saw Mill at Cawthorne, South Yorkshire 1898
oil on canvas 75.5 x 62.5
A.115

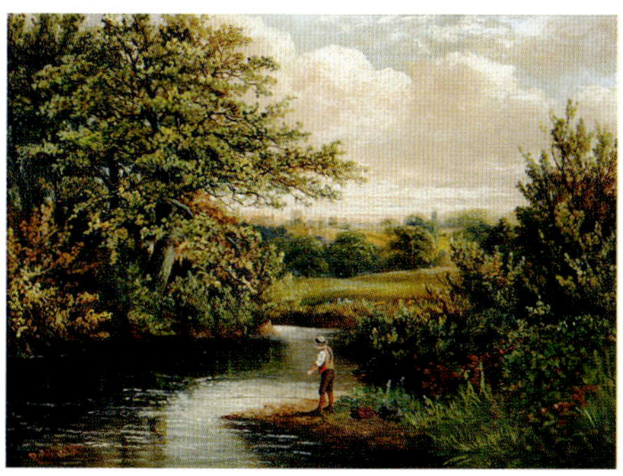

Hold, Benjamin 1858–1917
A Boy Fishing in a Wooded River Landscape
oil on canvas 29 x 38.3
A.2166.001

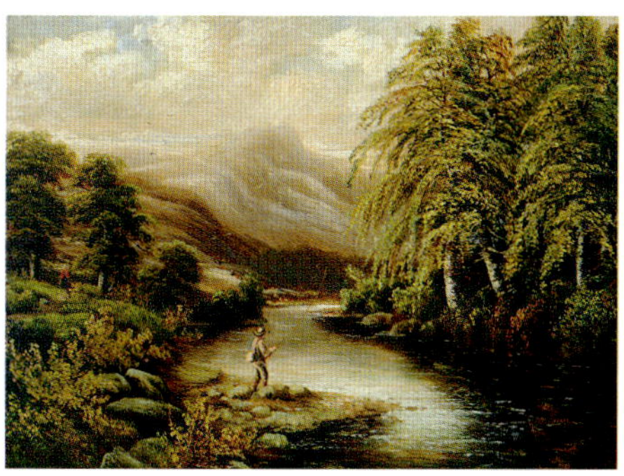

Hold, Benjamin 1858–1917
Fishing in the Highlands
oil on canvas 29 x 39
A.2166.002

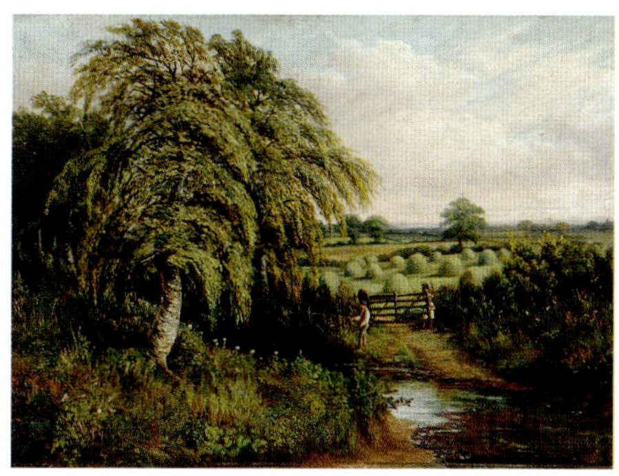

Hold, Benjamin 1858–1917
Landscape of Cawthorne Village, South Yorkshire
oil on canvas 44.2 x 59.7
A.113

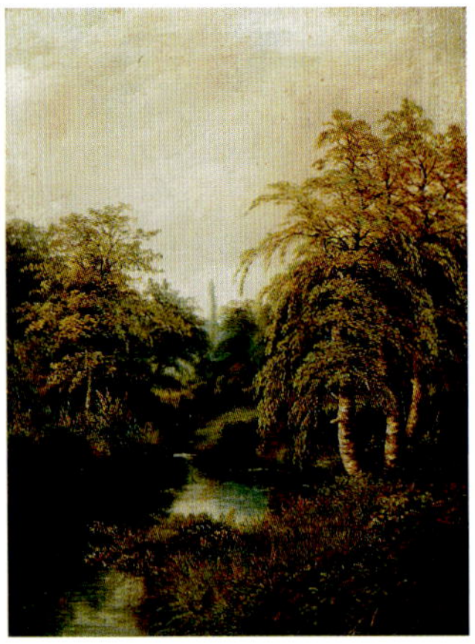

Hold, Benjamin 1858–1917
Landscape of Cawthorne Village, South Yorkshire
oil on canvas 60 x 44.2
A.114

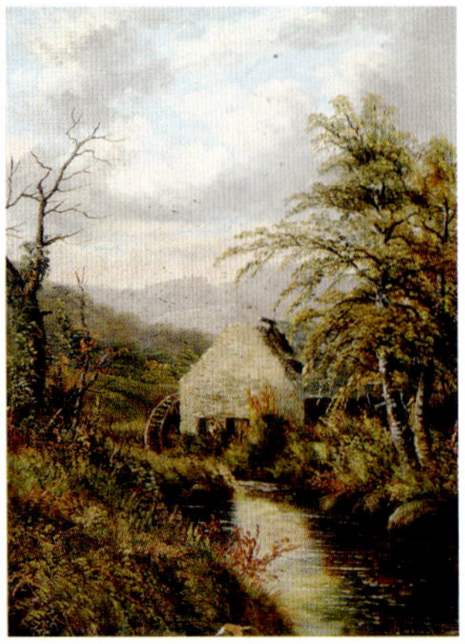

Hold, Benjamin 1858–1917
View of Saw Mill at Cawthorne, South Yorkshire
oil on canvas 33.3 x 24.3
A.111

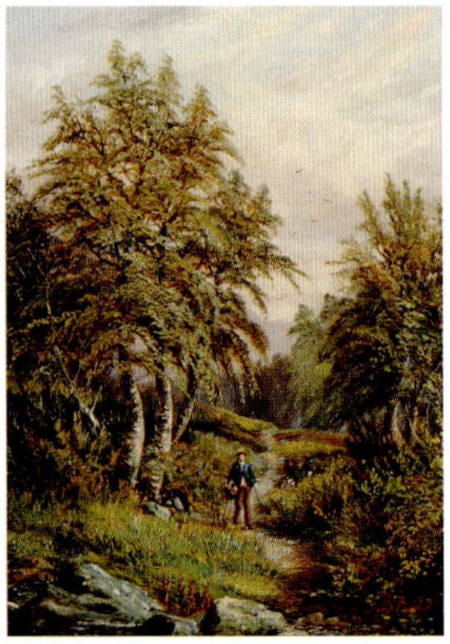

Hold, Benjamin 1858–1917
Wooded Scene with Figures
oil on canvas 34 x 24
A.1524

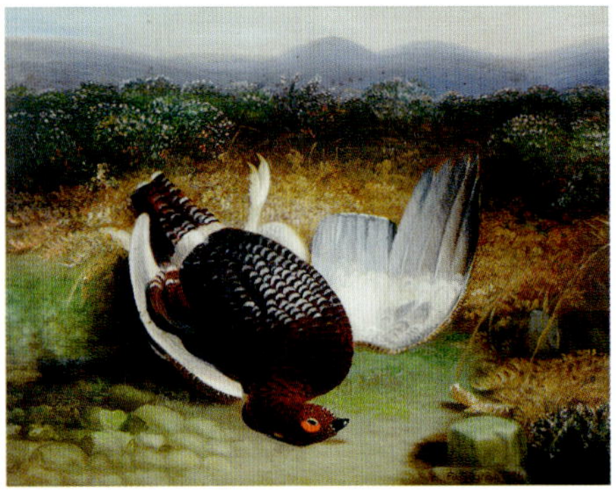

Hold, Florence 1860–after 1913
Dead Bird 1896
oil on canvas 47.2 x 52.3
A.2165.001

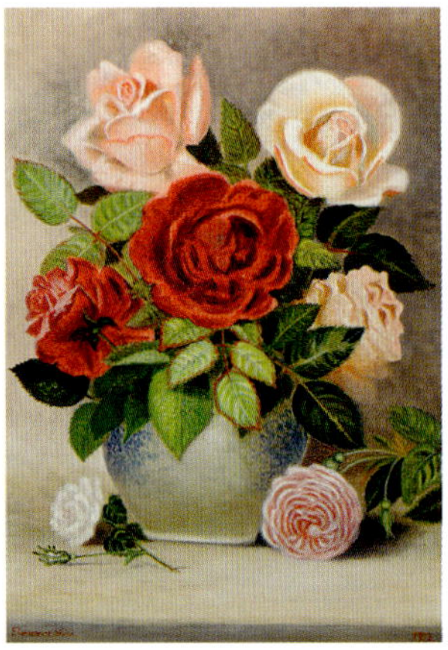

Hold, Florence 1860–after 1913
Flowers in a Vase 1913
oil on canvas 49.9 x 34.5
A.2165.002

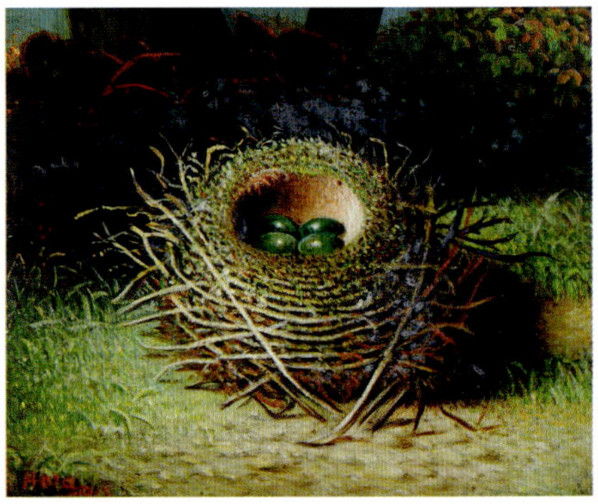

Hold, Florence (attributed to)
1860–after 1913
Bird's Nest with Eggs
oil on canvas 24 x 29
A.2165.005

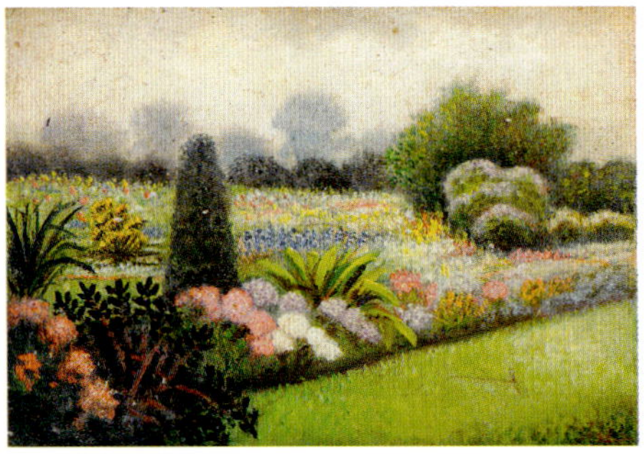

Hold, Florence (attributed to)
1860–after 1913
Garden View
oil on canvas 12.6 x 17.7
A.2165.006

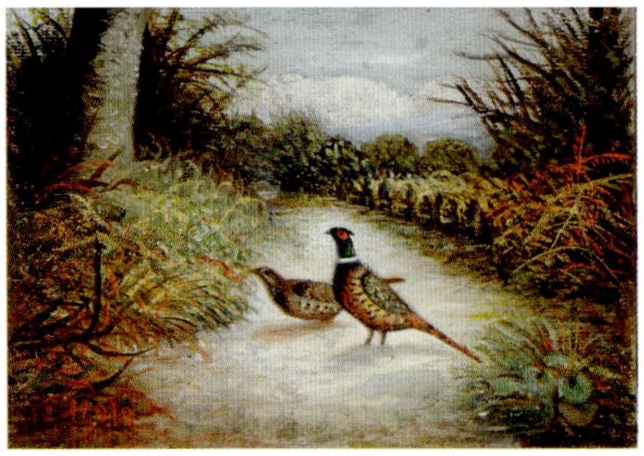

Hold, Florence (attributed to)
1860–after 1913
Landscape with a River
oil on canvas 12.5 x 17.5
A.2165.004

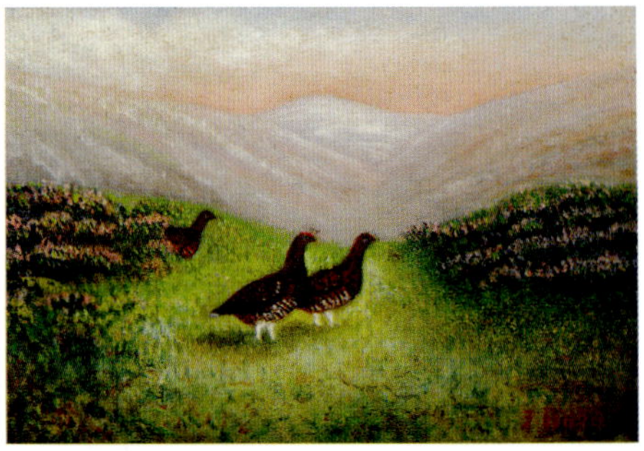

Hold, Florence (attributed to)
1860–after 1913
Landscape with Birds
oil on canvas 12 x 16.3
A.2165.003

Facing page: Largillière, Nicolas de, 1656–1746, *Madame Isaac de Thellusson, née Sarah le Boullenger (1700–1770)* (detail), 1725, English Heritage, Brodsworth Hall, (p. 36)

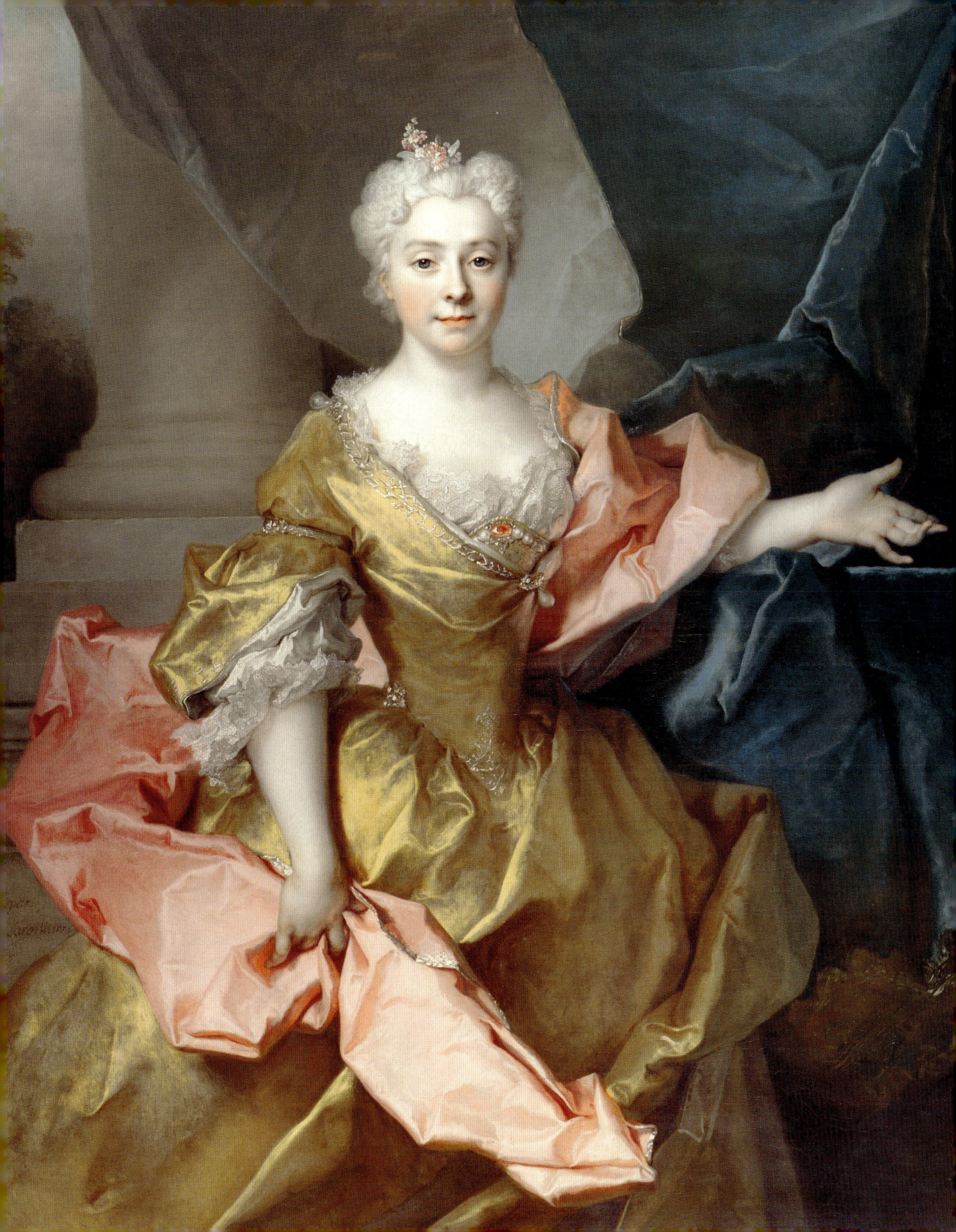

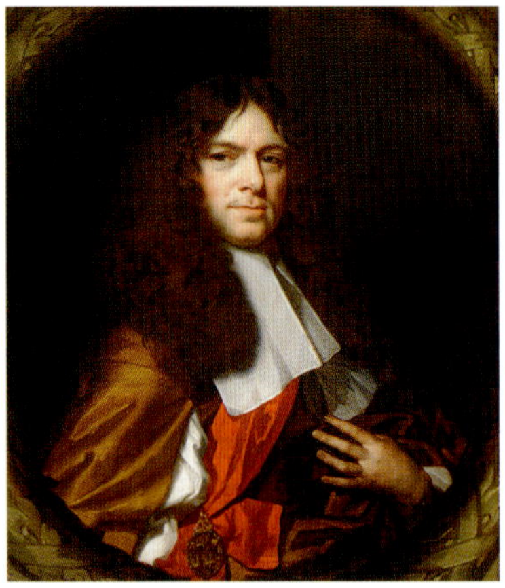

Huysmans, Jacob (attributed to)
c.1633–1696
Portrait of a Man (possibly Sir Thomas Wendy) 1688–1690
oil on canvas 77 x 63 (E)
A.80

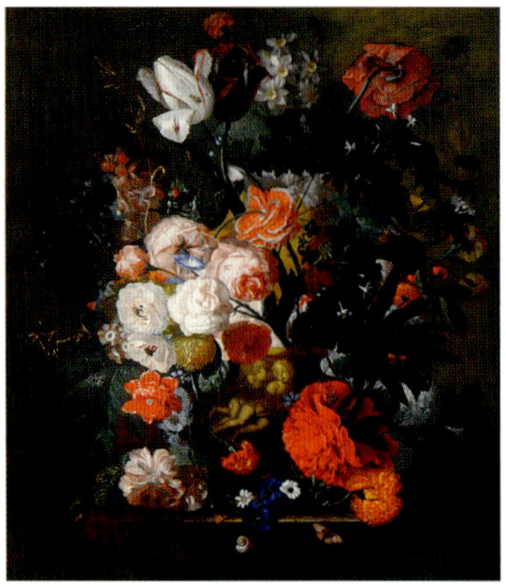

Huysum, Jan van 1682–1749
Flower Piece 1715–1720
oil on canvas 91.2 x 72
A.1928

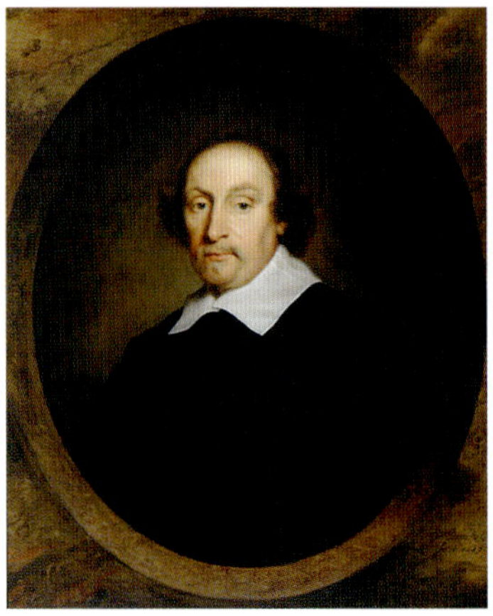

Janssens van Ceulen, Cornelis 1593–1661
Portrait of a Man 1649
oil on canvas 82.5 x 67.5
A.1929

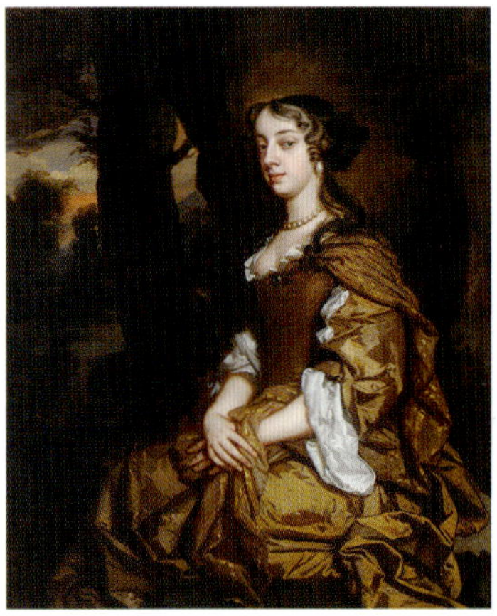

Lely, Peter (attributed to) 1618–1680
Lady Houblon 1670–1680
oil on canvas 125.5 x 99.5
A.16

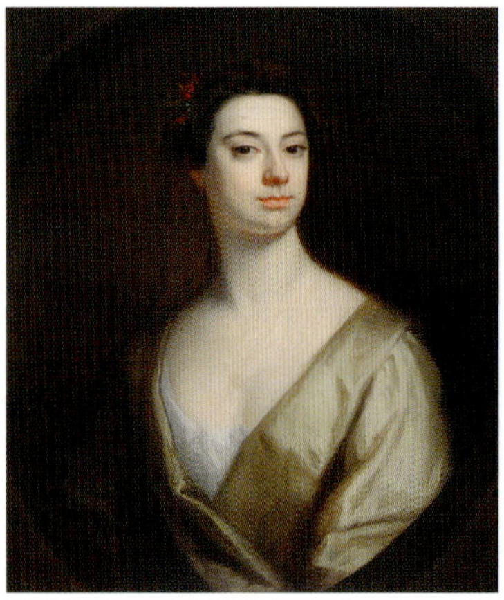

Lely, Peter (school of) 1618–1680
Portrait of a Lady
oil on canvas 103.7 x 81 (E)
A.2047

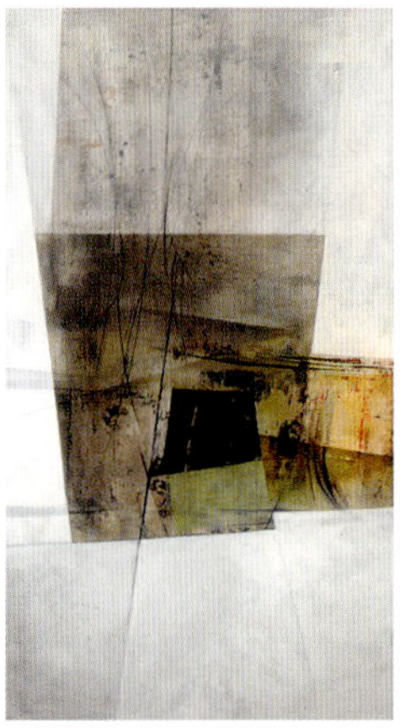

MacKenzie, Alexander 1923–2001
Gothic 1961
oil on hardboard 122 x 60.5
A.101

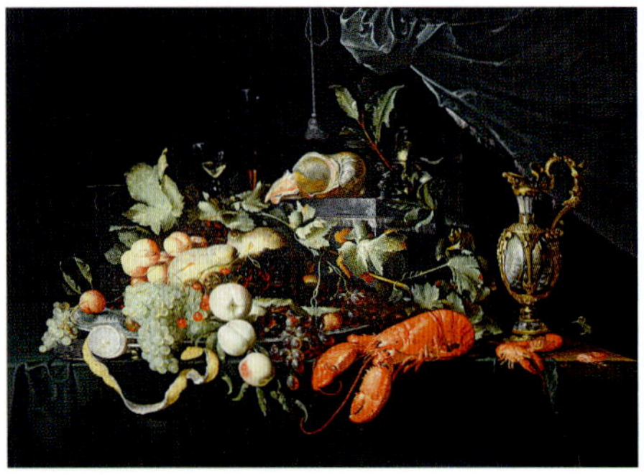

Marrel, Jacob 1614–1681
Fruit and Lobster 1649
oil on canvas 99.5 x 133
A.1930

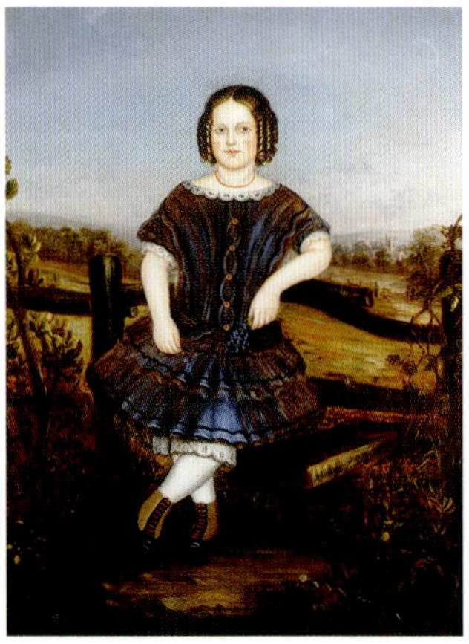

Mellor, James
Portrait of a Girl 1860
oil on canvas 142 x 107.3
A.1523

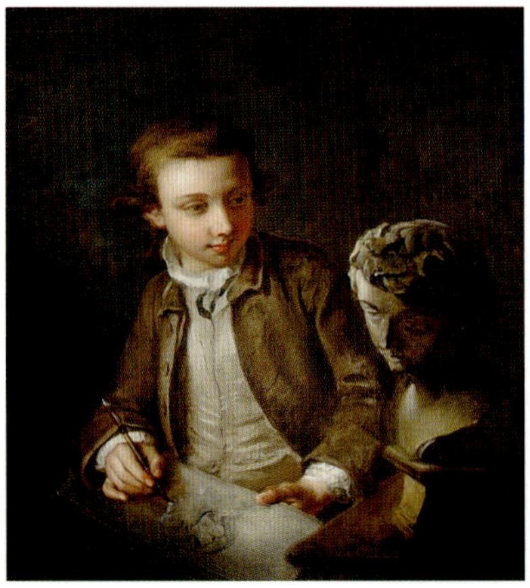

Mercier, Philippe 1689–1760
A Boy Drawing from the Antique 1739–1751
oil on canvas 75.5 x 61.8 (E)
A.82

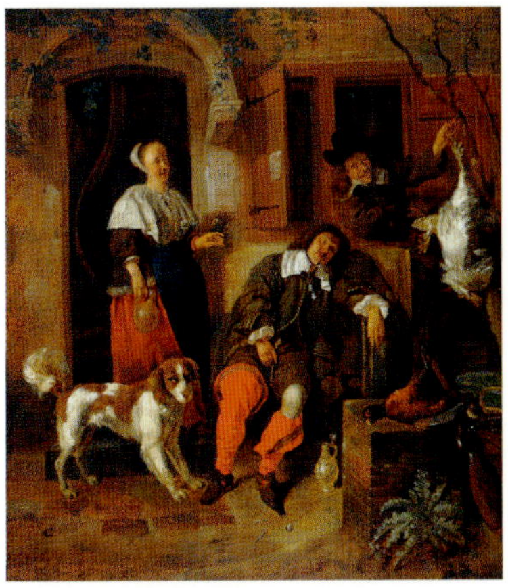

Metsu, Gabriel (after) 1629–1667
The Weary Sportsman late 17th C/early 18th C
oil on canvas 42.3 x 37
A.1932

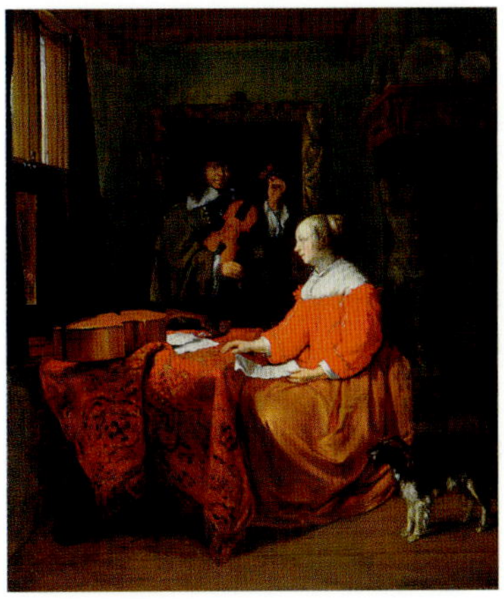

Metsu, Gabriel (studio of) 1629–1667
The Music Lesson 1655–1665
oil on canvas 43 x 36
A.1931

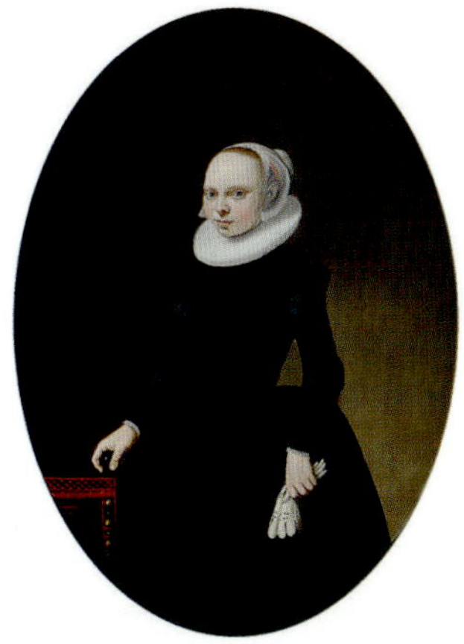

Miereveld, Pieter van (attributed to) 1596–1623 & **Miereveld, Michiel Jansz. van (attributed to)** 1567–1641
Portrait of a Girl, Aged 19 1600–1630
oil on board 31.5 x 24
A.1618

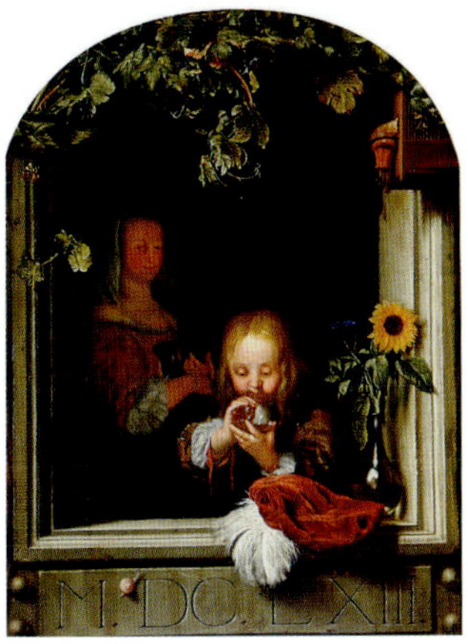

Mieris, Frans van the elder (studio of) 1635–1681
Boy Blowing Bubbles 1663–1680
oil on panel 25.5 x 19.3
A.1933

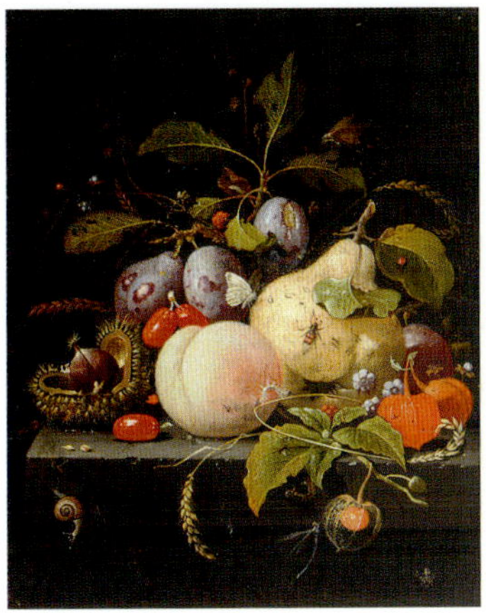

Mignon, Abraham (after) 1640–c.1679
Fruit and Insects 1675–1725
oil on canvas 33 x 26
A.1934

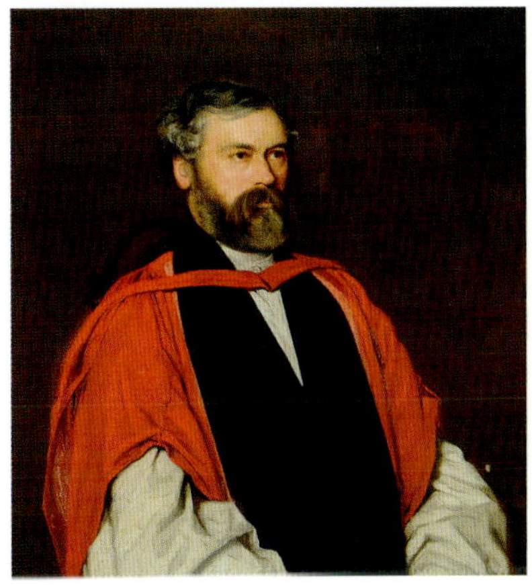

Moore, Ernest 1865–1940
Reverend John Sharp Lawson (?), MA, LLD, FRHS, Vicar of St George's, Barnsley, South Yorkshire 1891
oil on canvas 125 x 110
TEMP.CH.0009

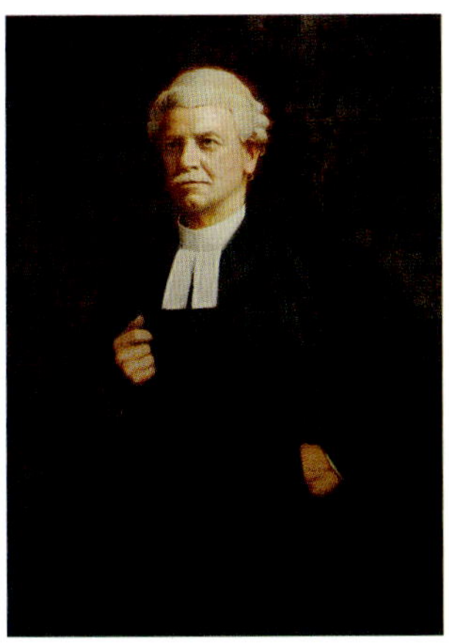

Moore, Ernest 1865–1940
Henry Horsfield (1879–1912), Town Clerk 1932
oil on canvas 130.7 x 98.2
TEMP.CH.0012

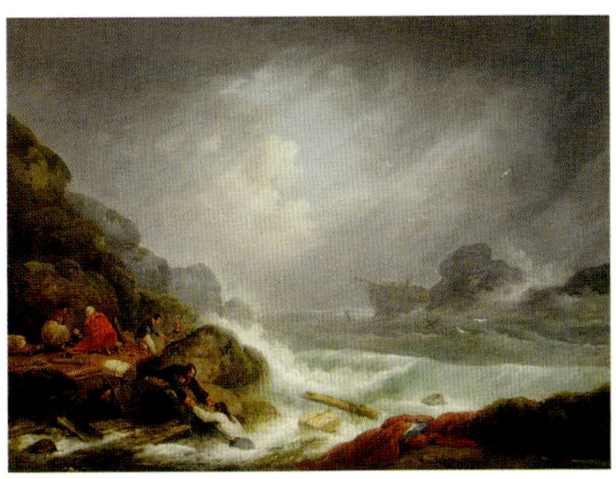

Morland, George 1763–1804
Shipwreck off a Rocky Coast
oil on canvas 69.5 x 90 (E)
A.87

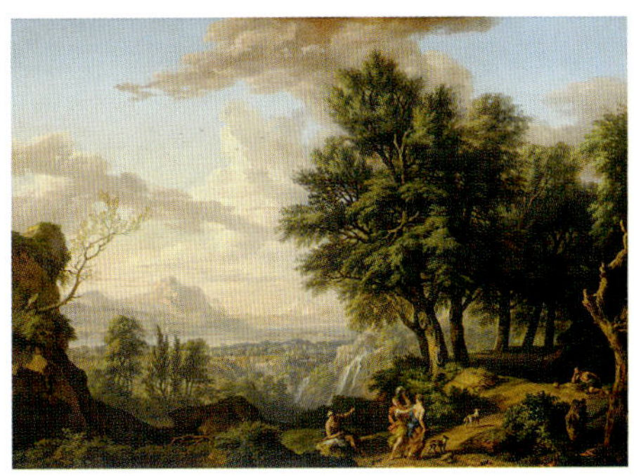

Moucheron, Isaac de 1667–1744
An Italian Landscape in the Region of Tivoli with Classical Figures 1725
oil on canvas 49.5 x 66.5
A.1936

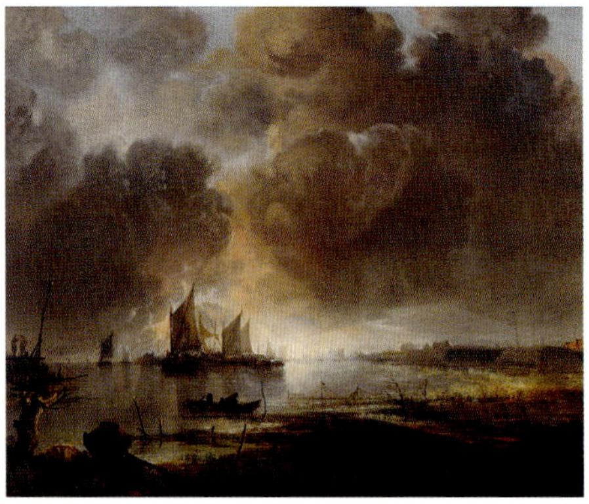

Neer, Aert van der 1603–1677
Coast Scene with a Fishing Boat
oil on canvas 36.3 x 42.3
A.1938

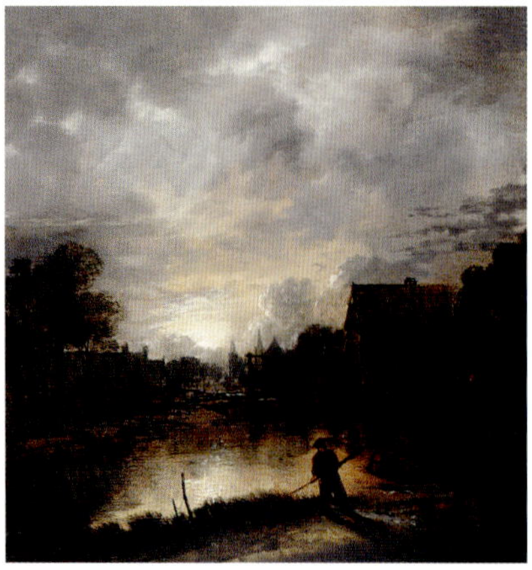

Neer, Aert van der 1603–1677
River Landscape in the Evening with Moonlight and a Watermill
oil on panel 302 x 285
A.1937

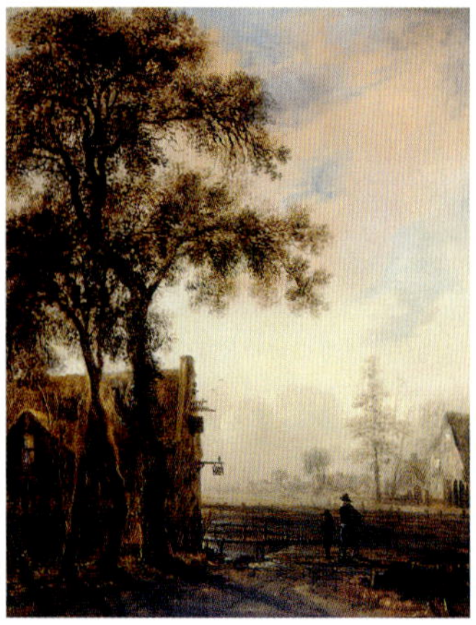

Neer, Aert van der 1603–1677
Village Landscape at Dusk
oil on panel 326 x 247
A.1939

Netscher, Caspar 1639–1684
Portrait of a Lady 1665–1668
oil on canvas 23.2 x 18
A.1941

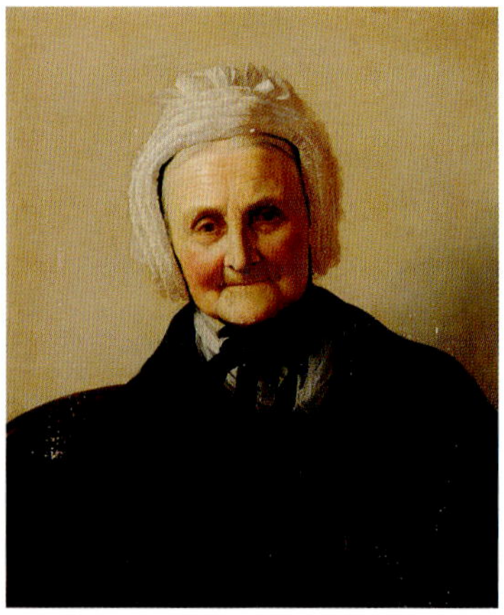

Nowell, Arthur Trevethin 1862–1940
Mrs A. Tyne 1883
oil on canvas 49.5 x 42
A.701

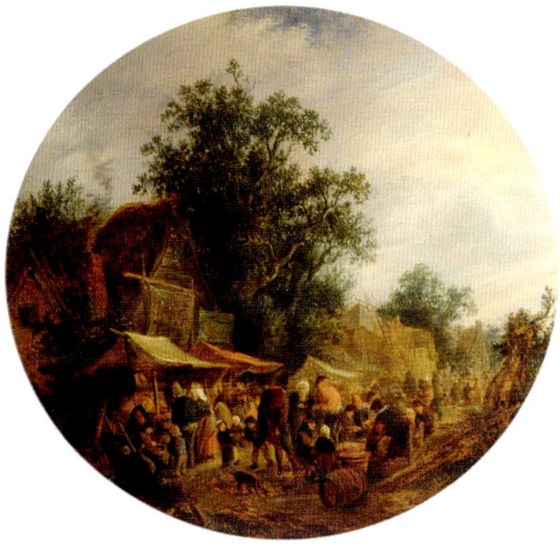

Ostade, Adriaen van 1610–1685
A Village Fair 1647–1648
oil on panel 24
A.1944

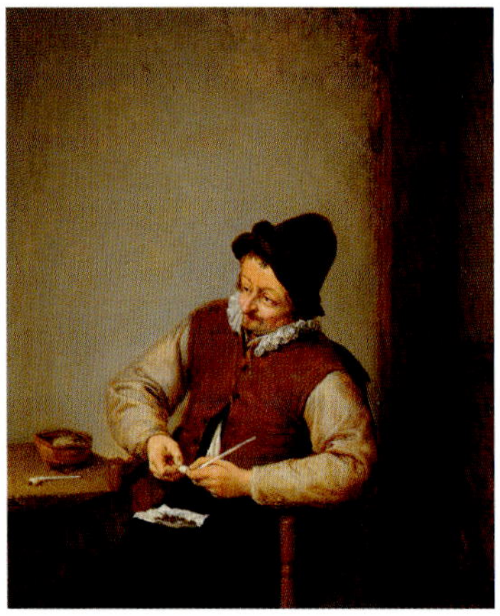

Ostade, Adriaen van 1610–1685
A Peasant Filling His Pipe 1660–1669
oil on panel 27.5 x 22.2
A.1942

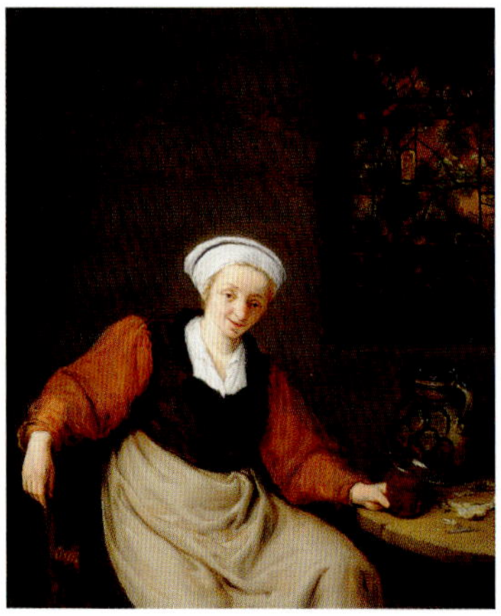

Ostade, Adriaen van 1610–1685
A Woman Drinking 1660–1669
oil on canvas 28 x 22
A.1943

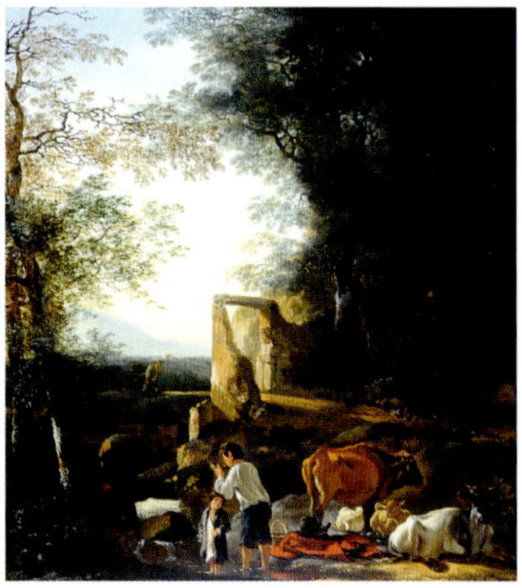

Pynacker, Adam c.1620–1673
Landscape with Cattle and Figures 1650–1653
oil on copper 27.3 x 24.5
A.1945

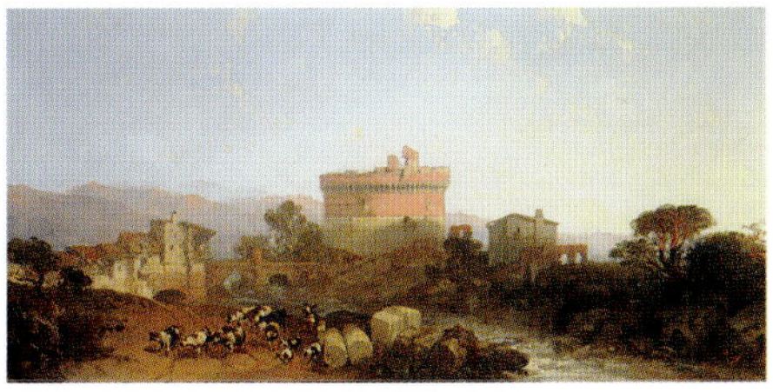

Roberts, David 1796–1864
The Mausoleum of Plautus Lucanus
oil on canvas 45 x 89.5
A.75

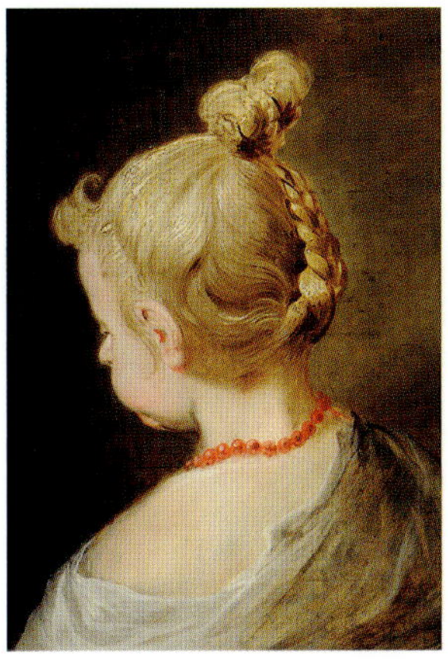

Rubens, Peter Paul (style of) 1577–1640
Sketch of One of the Artist's Daughters 18th C
oil on canvas 45.5 x 32.3
A.1946

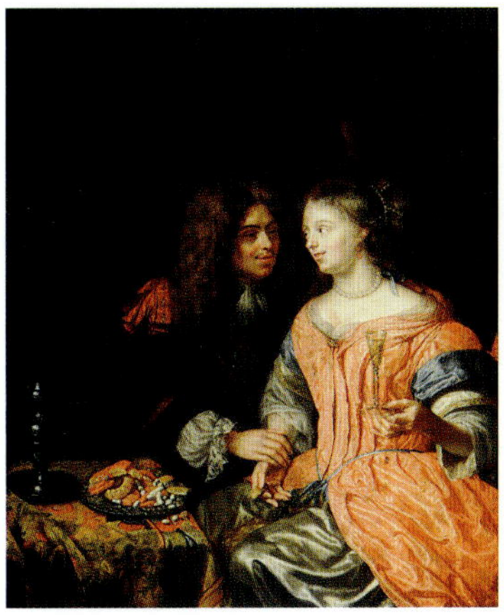

Schalcken, Godfried 1643–1706
Man and Woman with a Wine Glass
1675–1676
oil on canvas 29.2 x 23.8
A.1940

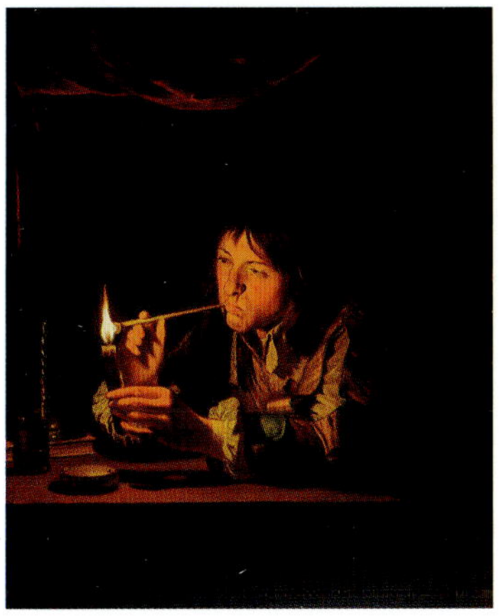

Schalcken, Godfried (after) 1643–1706
Candlelight: Youth Lighting a Pipe
oil on canvas 20.5 x 16.2
A.1948

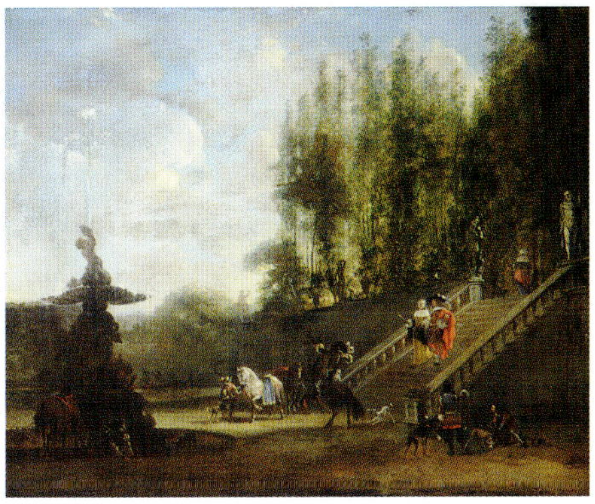

Schellinks, Willem 1627–1678
The Departure for the Chase 1646–1678
oil on canvas 45.2 x 53.5
A.1947

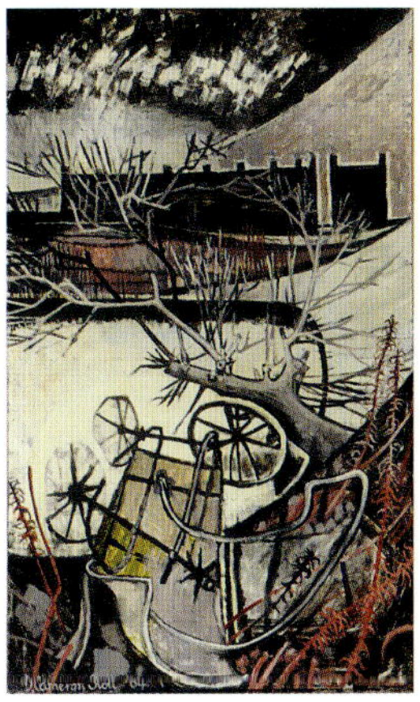

Stott, David Cameron b.1938
Quarry Pond 1964
oil on board 152.5 x 91.2
A.202

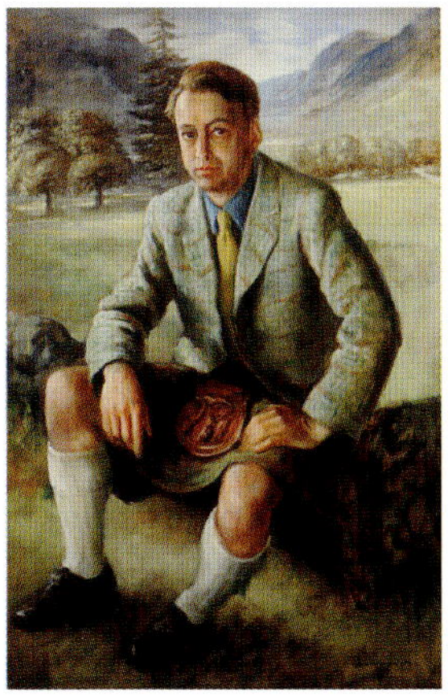

Sutherland, Alan b.1931
Simon Fraser (1924–2004) 1972
oil on canvas 151 x 99.5
RLI.0035.006 (P)

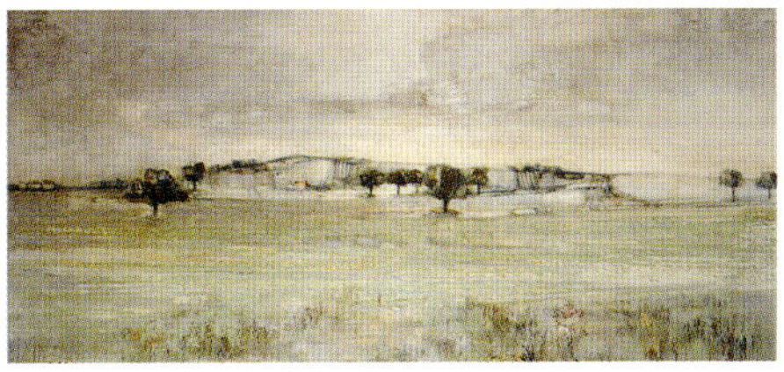

Taylor, James Spence b.1921
Paysage (Landscape)
oil on plyboard 57.7 x 117.7
A.72

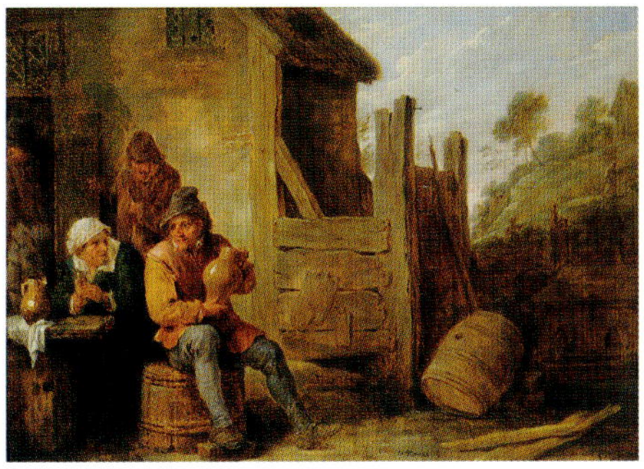

Teniers, David II 1610–1690
Exterior of an Inn: Peasants Drinking
1665–1675
oil on panel 18.4 x 25.5
A.1950

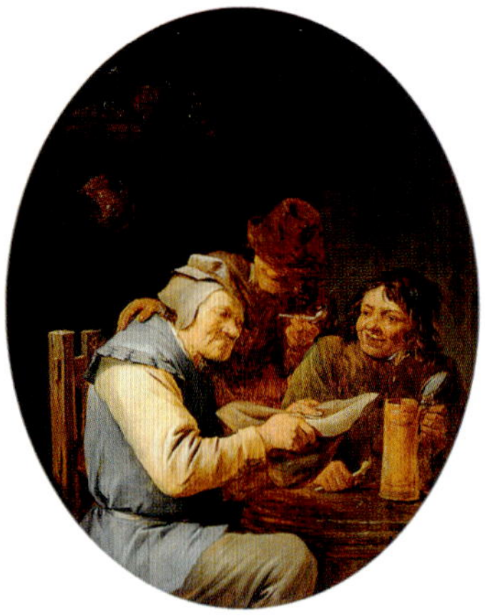

Teniers, David II 1610–1690
Hustle Cap 1670–1679
oil on panel 32 x 23.5
A.1949

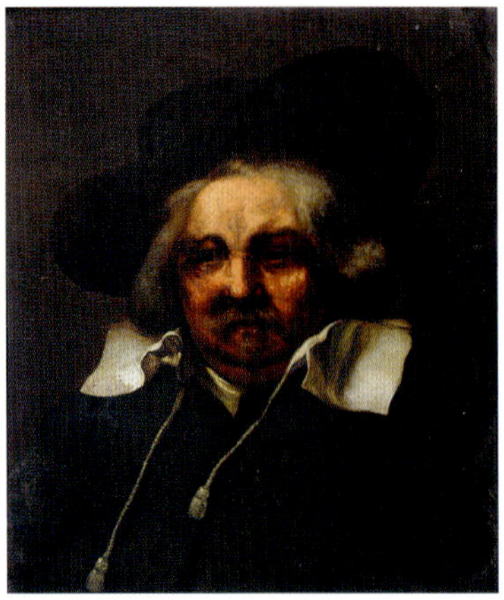

unknown artist 17th C
Portrait of an Unknown Gentleman
oil on canvas 60 x 49.5
TEMP.CH.0037

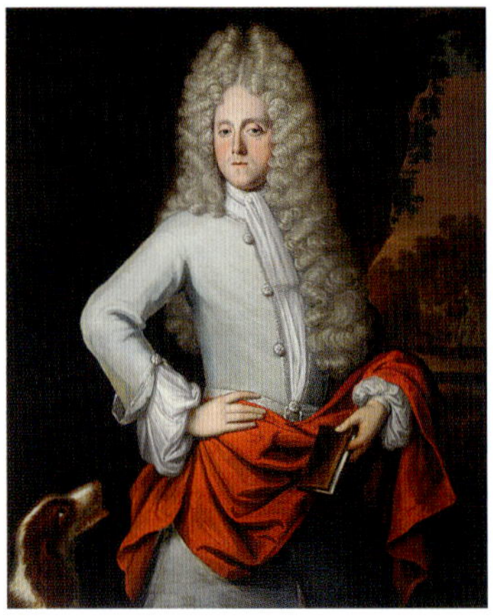

unknown artist
Sir Willliam Lowther (1663–1729), 1st Bt 1712
oil on canvas 125.2 x 99.5
RLI.0034.003 (P)

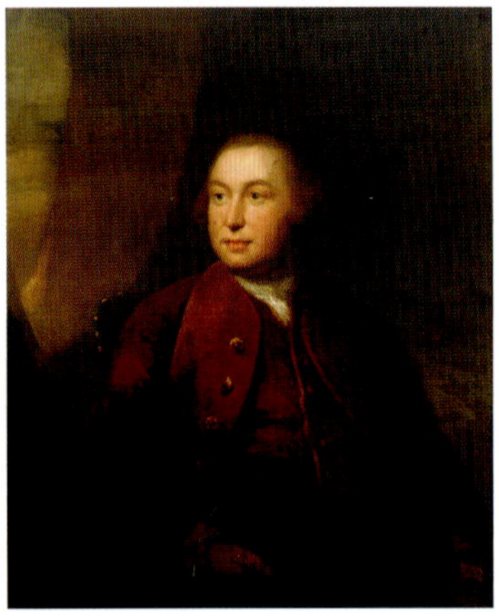

unknown artist
John Spencer 1719
oil on canvas 103 x 83 (E)
RLI.0034.004 (P)

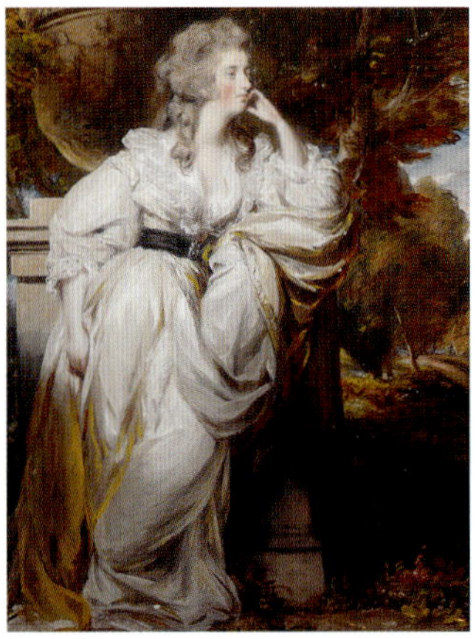

unknown artist
Adelaide Augusta Wilhelmina Dutton, Wife of Sir Henry Hunloke 1781
oil on canvas 130 x 80 (E)
RLI.0035.005 (P)

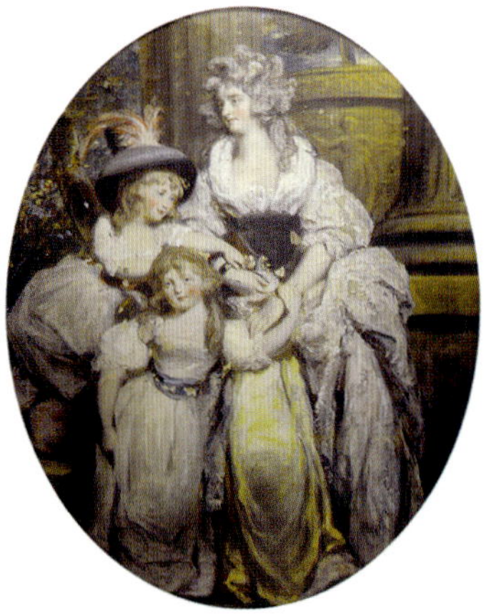

unknown artist
The Coke Sisters 1781
oil on canvas 104 x 80
RLI.0025 (P)

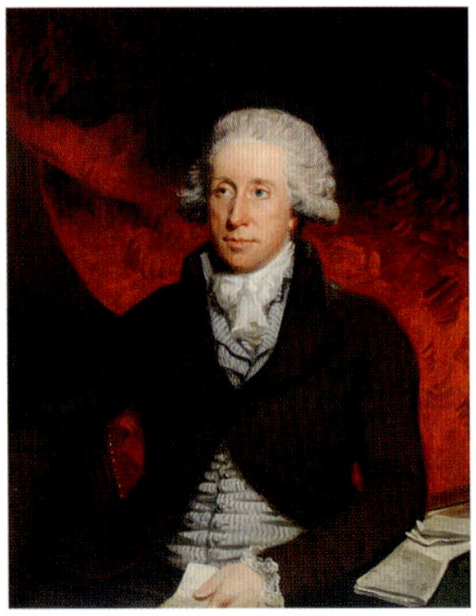

unknown artist
Walter Spencer Stanhope (1749–1822) 1784
oil on canvas 119.5 x 68.7
RLI.0034.001 (P)

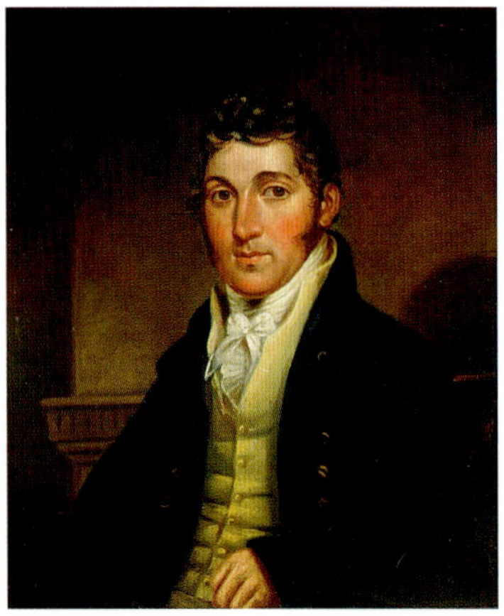

unknown artist late 18th C/early 19th C
Portrait of an Unknown Gentleman
oil on board 35 x 29.2
TEMP.CH.0016

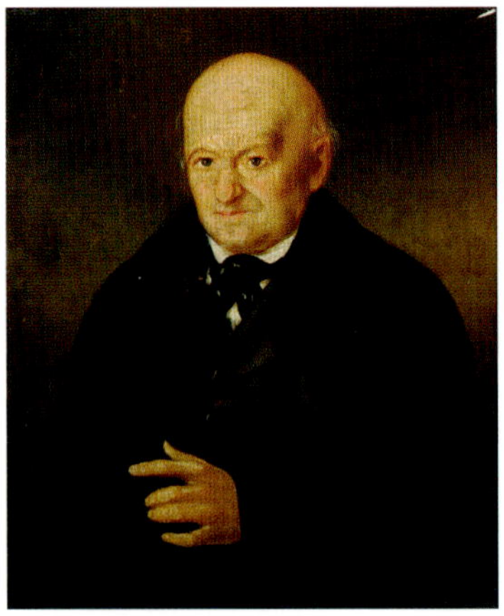

unknown artist
Robert McLintock c.1850
oil on canvas 73.8 x 61
A.920

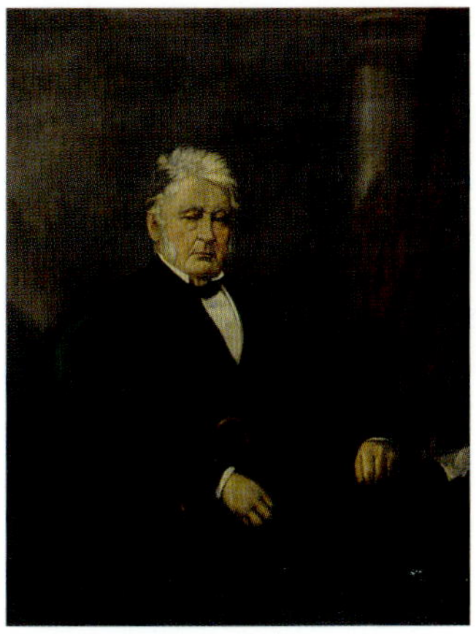

unknown artist 19th C
John S. Beckett, Founder of the Beckett Hospital
oil on canvas 51.2 x 39
TEMP.CH.0006

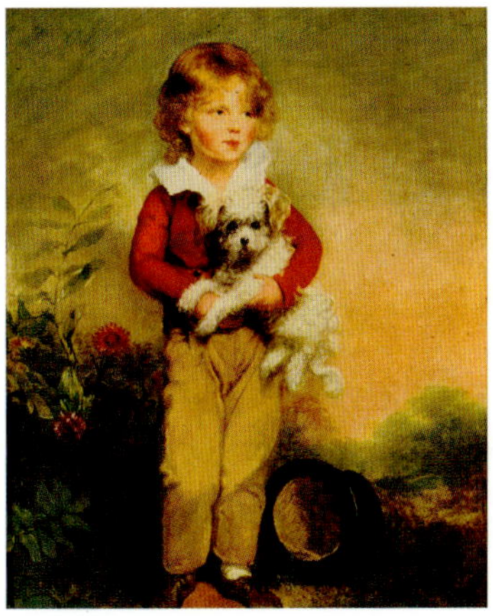

unknown artist 19th C
Portrait of a Child with a Dog
oil on board 15 x 12.5
TEMP.CH.0097

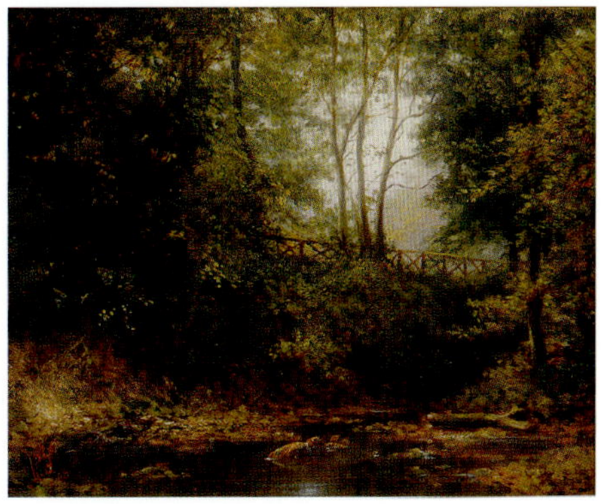

unknown artist 19th C
Rockley Woods, South Yorkshire
oil on canvas 24 x 29
TEMP.CH.0011

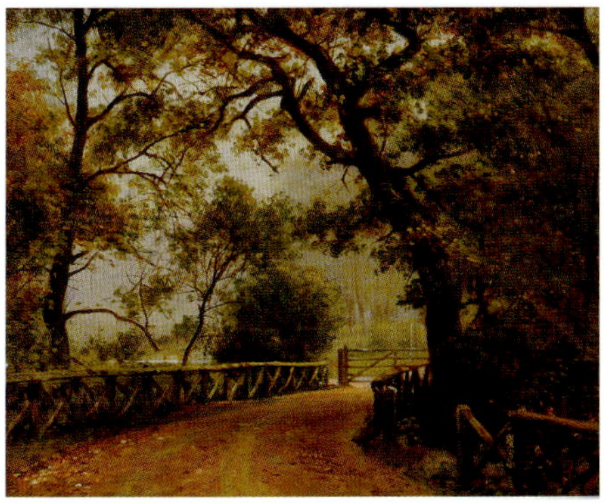

unknown artist
Wooded Landscape
oil on canvas 23.5 x 29
TEMP.CH.0020

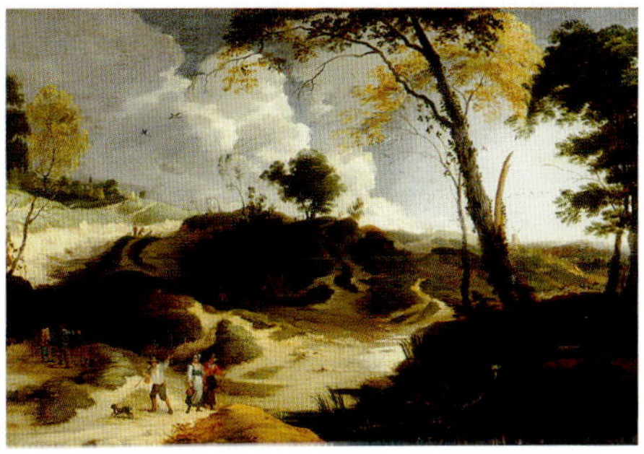

Vadder, Lodewijk de (style of) 1605–1655
Landscape with Figures and Haymakers
1650–1655
oil on canvas 68.5 x 99.5
A.1951

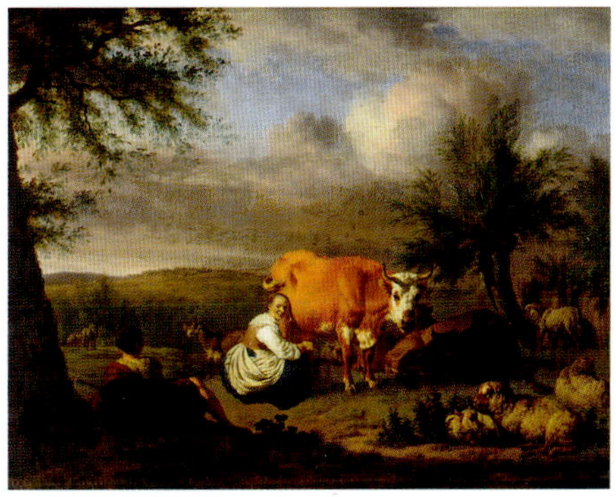

Velde, Adriaen van de 1636–1672
Landscape: Woman Milking a Cow c.1669
oil on canvas 31.2 x 39.8
A.1952

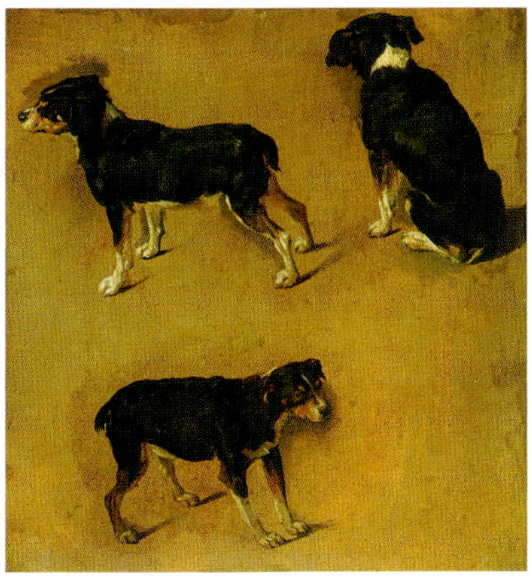

Velde, Adriaen van de 1636–1672
Studies of a Dog
oil on paper on wood 21.1 x 19
A.1953

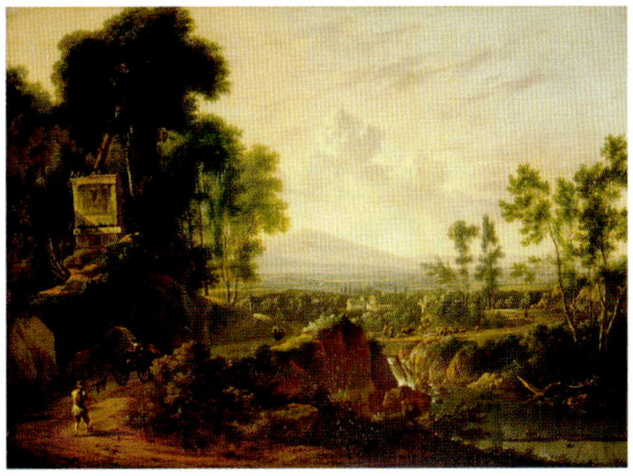

Velde, Adriaen van de 1636–1672 &
Moucheron, Frederick de 1633–1686
Landscape with a Shrine
oil on canvas 87.6 x 118.5
A.1935

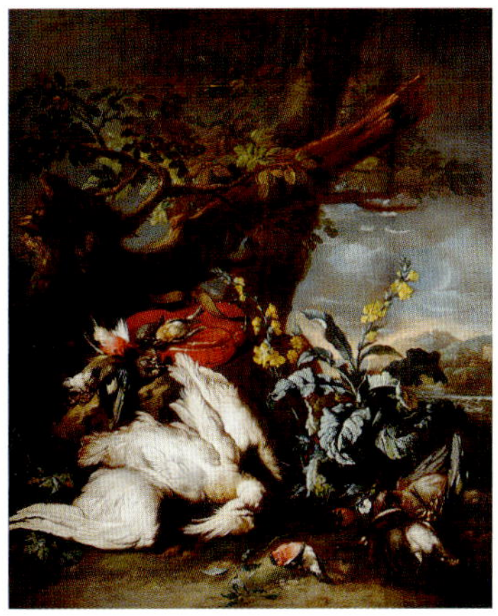

Von Tamm, Franz Werner 1658–1724
Dead Birds 1705–1715
oil on canvas 136.8 x 113
A.1955

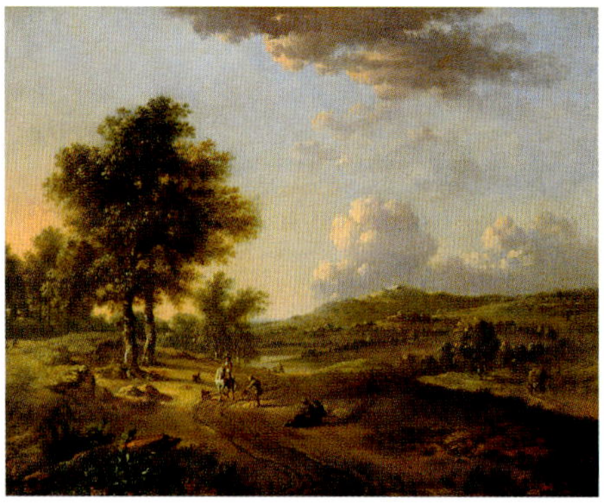

Wijnants, Jan c.1635–1684
Landscape: The Mendicant
oil on canvas 33.5 x 40.3
A.1956

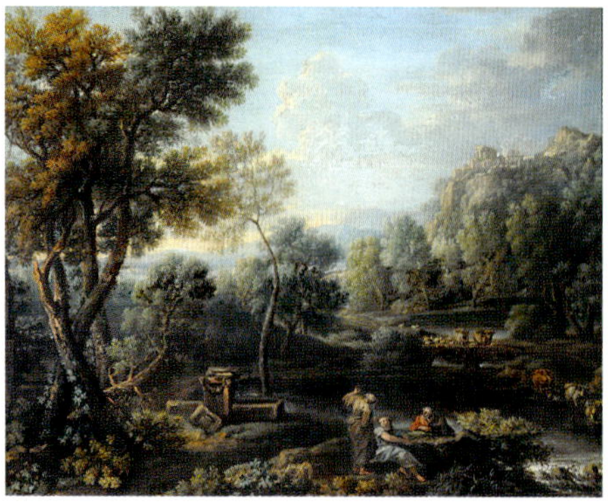

Wootton, John c.1682–1764
Landscape with Cattle c.1720
oil on canvas 60.4 x 72.8
A.109

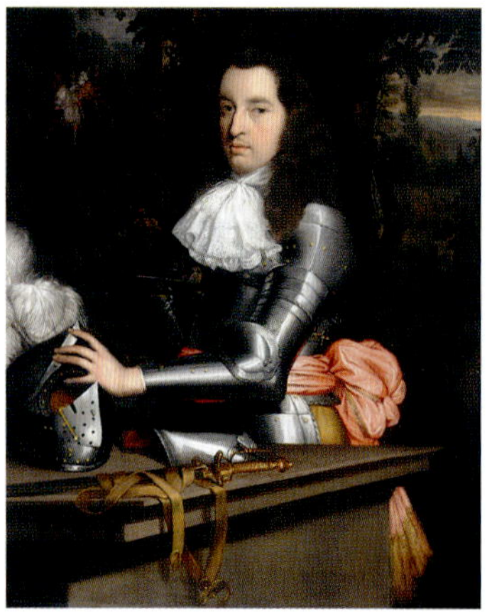

Wright, John Michael 1617–1694
Henry Howard (1628–1684), 6th Duke of Norfolk
oil on canvas 125.5 x 100
A.43

Cawthorne Victoria Jubilee Museum Trust

As its name indicates, the foundation stone of the Museum was laid in 1887, the year of Queen Victoria's Golden Jubilee. It was purpose-built by the Spencer Stanhopes of Cannon Hall to house the collections of members of the Museum Society which had been set up in 1884 by the second phase Pre-Raphaelite artist, John Roddam Spencer Stanhope, who was the Society's President. It became a repository for ethnographic items brought back from their travels by the Spencer Stanhope family, plus fossils (some contributed by John Ruskin), butterflies, moths and Victoriana. To this day it continues to be a treasure house of village life.

The Museum's paintings are chiefly by one family, the Holds (Abel, Benjamin and Tom), and depict local landscapes, dead game and portraits of servants on the Spencer Stanhope estate. Of the three, Abel (the father of Tom and Ben) had the greater reputation. He lived at Cawthorne from 1852 to 1896, exhibited 16 times at the Royal Academy and was proud of the fact that he never had a painting refused for exhibition there.

Barry Jackson, Museum Trustee and President of the Cawthorne Victoria Jubilee Museum Society

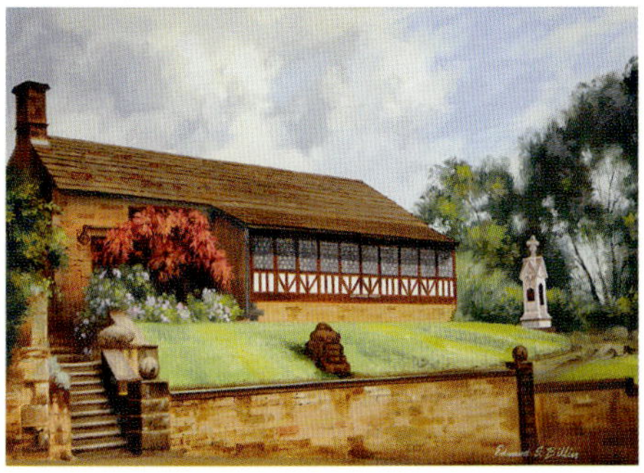

Billin, Edward Stanley 1911–1994
Cawthorne Museum 1970s
oil on board 49.5 x 75
T100

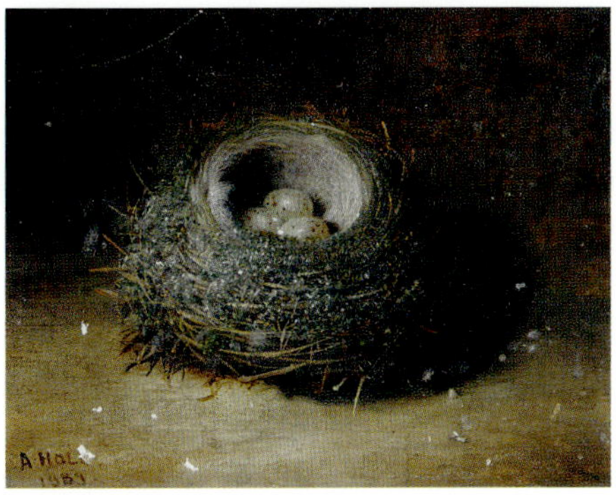

Hold, Abel 1815–1896
Nest with Three Eggs 1889
oil on canvas 19 x 24
1981.808

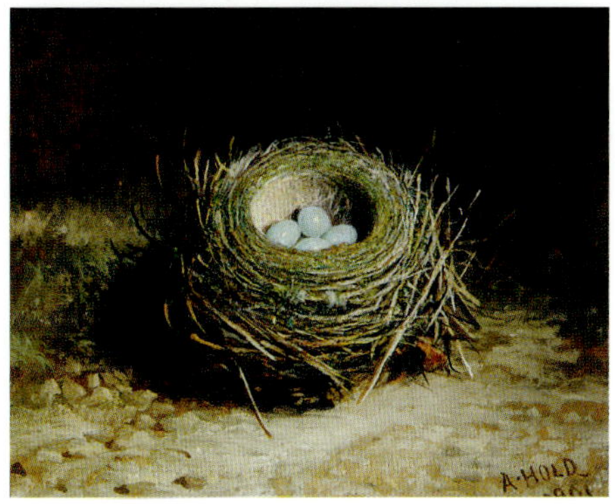

Hold, Abel 1815–1896
Nest with Four Eggs 1891
oil on canvas 25 x 31
1981.801

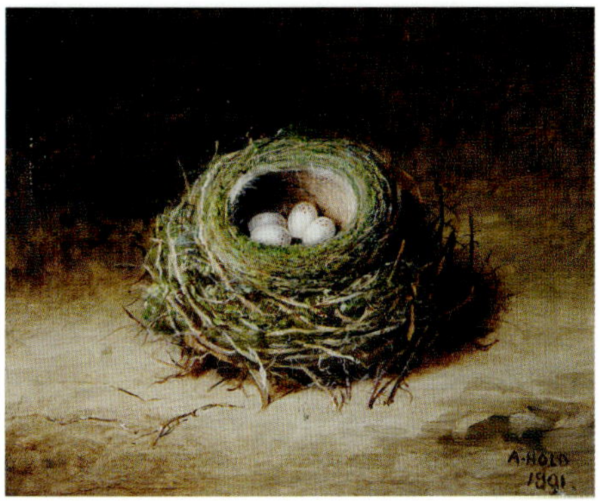

Hold, Abel 1815–1896
Nest with Four Eggs 1891
oil on canvas 24 x 29
1981.807

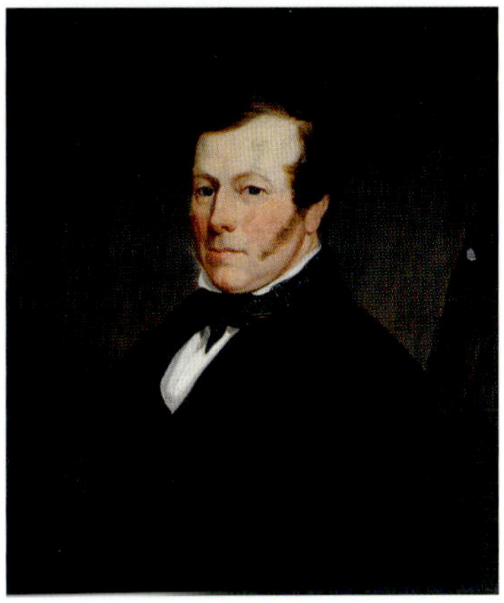

Hold, Abel 1815–1896
Elkanah Clegg (1803–1872), Woodman for the Spencer Stanhope Family
oil on canvas 75.5 x 63
1981.803

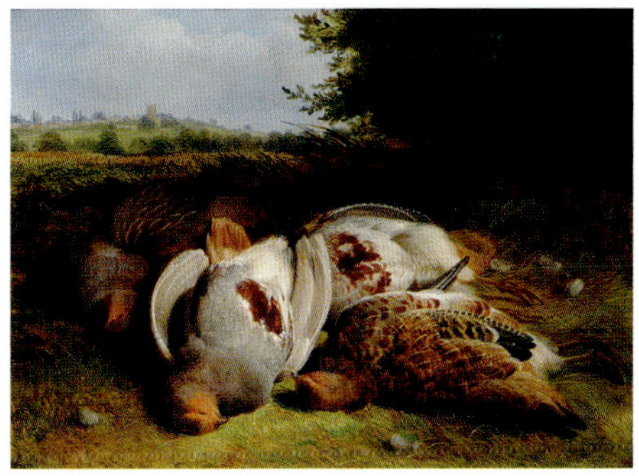

Hold, Abel 1815–1896
Four Partridge
oil on board 45 x 60
2000.2

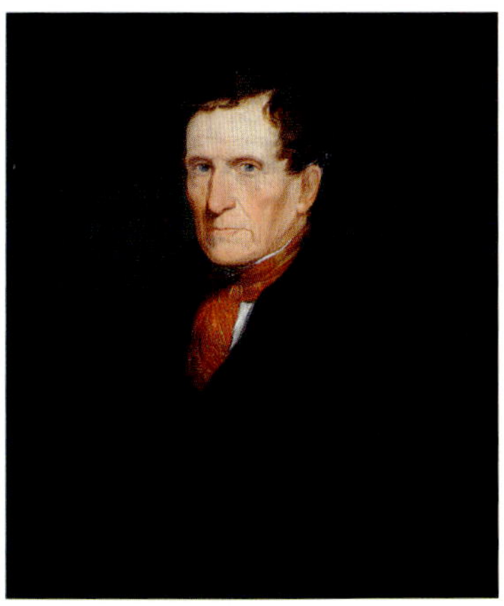

Hold, Abel 1815–1896
Jonas Beaumont (1783–1857), Estate Carpenter for the Spencer Stanhope Family
oil on canvas 72 x 59
1981.805

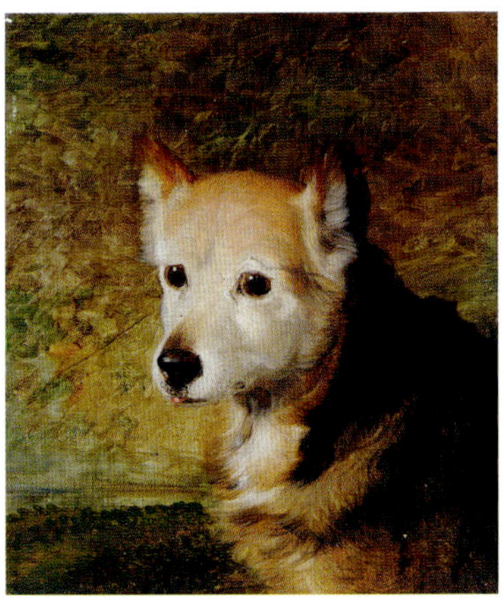

Hold, Abel 1815–1896
'Lady'
oil on canvas 29 x 24
1981.8

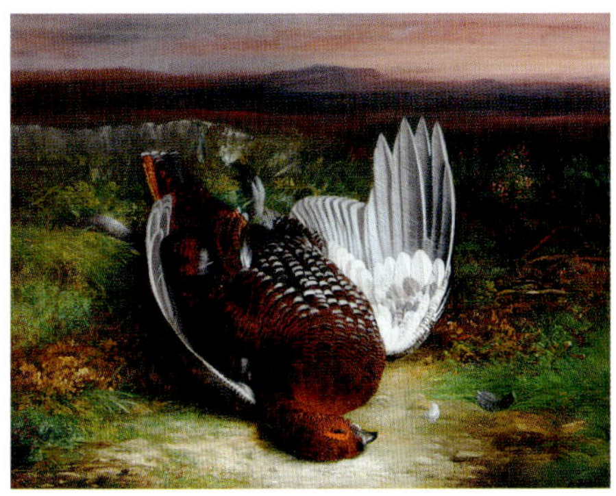

Hold, Abel 1815–1896
Red Cock Grouse
oil on canvas 40 x 50
2000.4

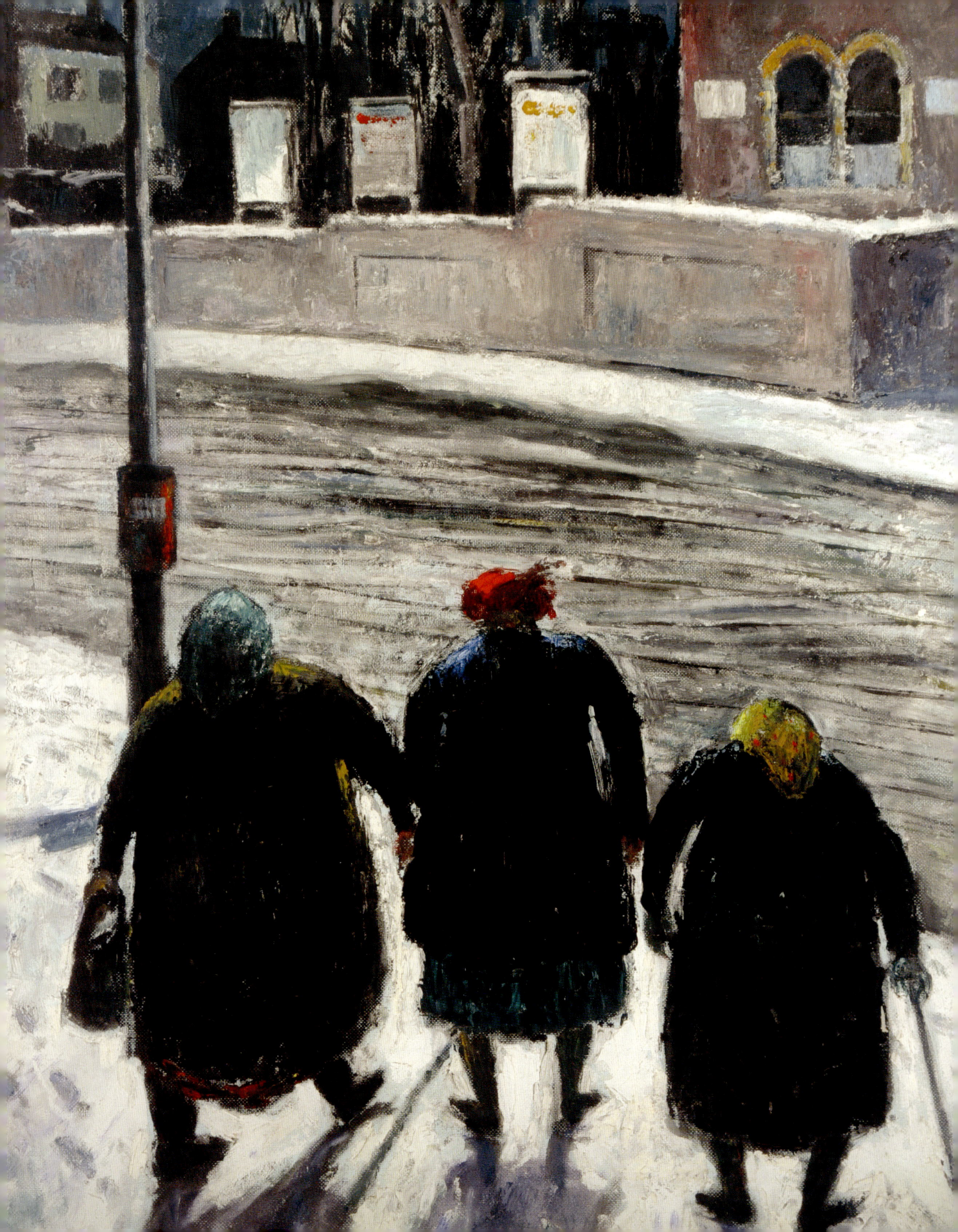

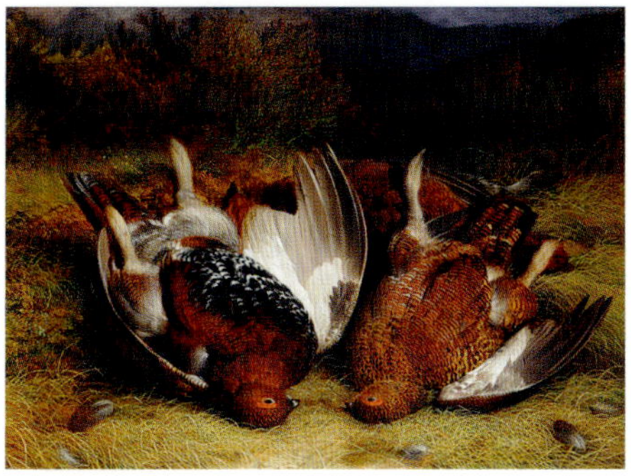

Hold, Abel 1815–1896
Three Red Grouse
oil on board 45 x 60
2000.1

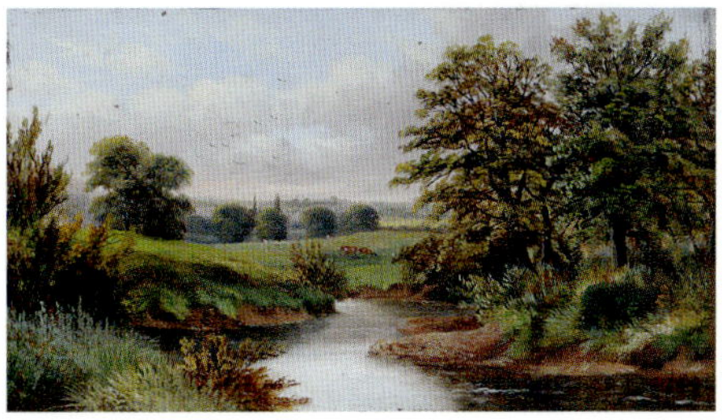

Hold, Benjamin 1858–1917
Canon Hall Park River Landscape, South Yorkshire
oil on canvas 22 x 37
1981.811

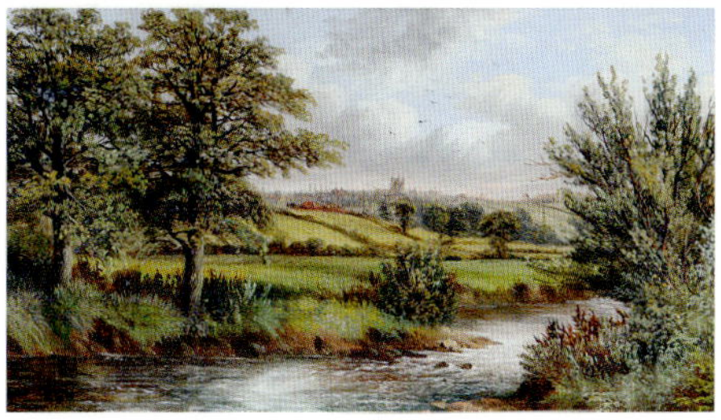

Hold, Benjamin 1858–1917
Canon Hall Park River Meadow with Church, South Yorkshire
oil on canvas 22 x 37
1981.802

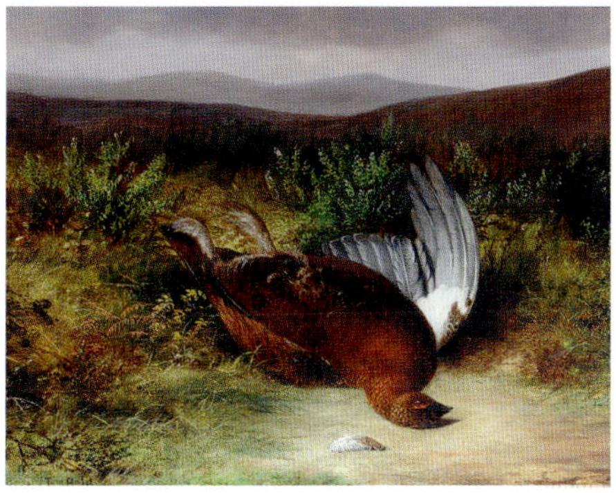

Hold, Tom 1843–1902
Red Grouse
oil on canvas 43 x 62.5
2000.3

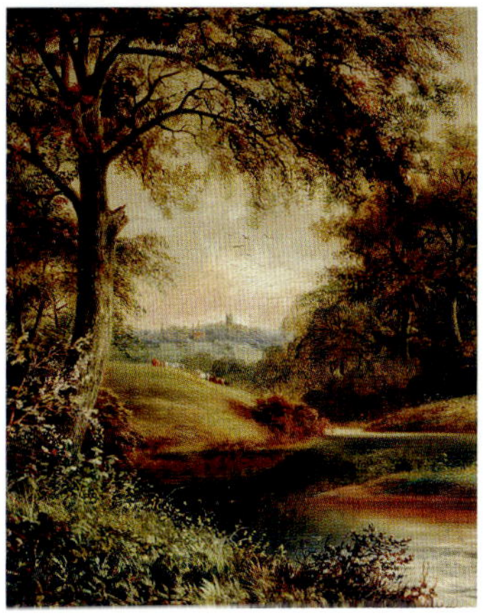

Hold, Tom 1843–1902
River Landscape with Church
oil on canvas 59 x 47
1981.804

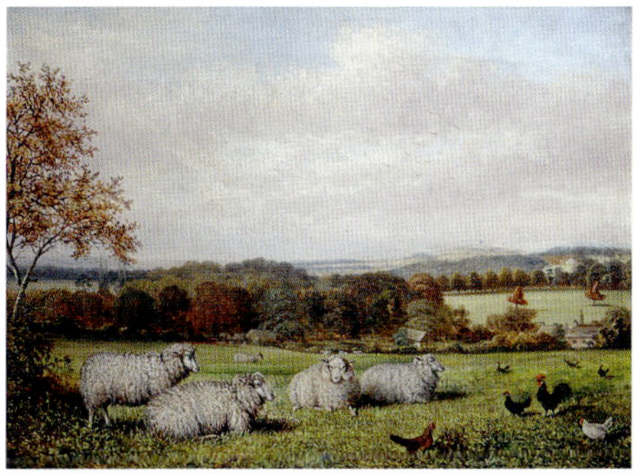

Hold, Tom 1843–1902
View of Canon Hall Park, South Yorkshire
oil on canvas 45 x 60
1981.806

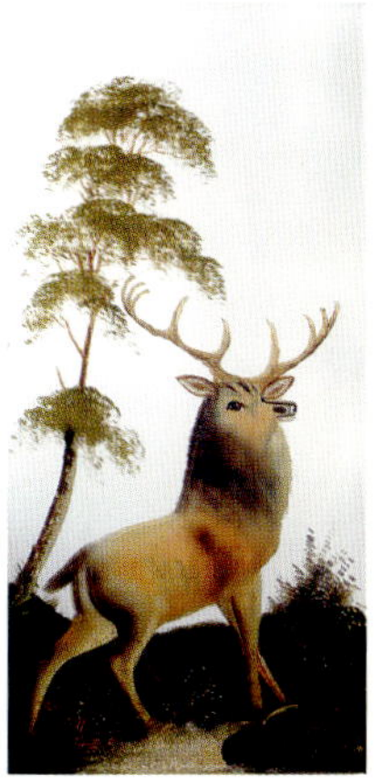

unknown artist
Red Deer Stag
oil on mirror 60 x 30
T102

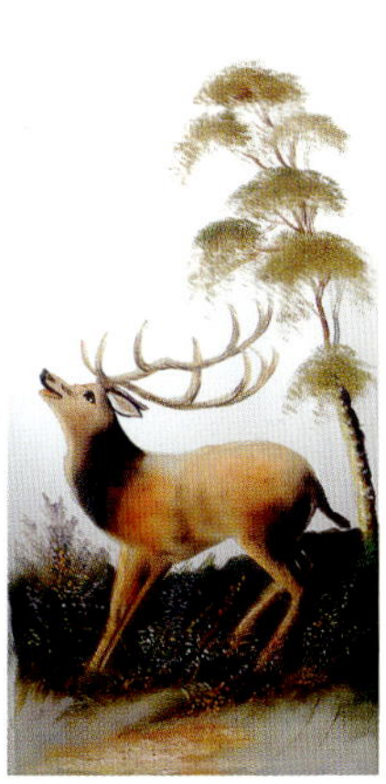

unknown artist
Young Red Deer Stag
oil on mirror 60 x 30
T103

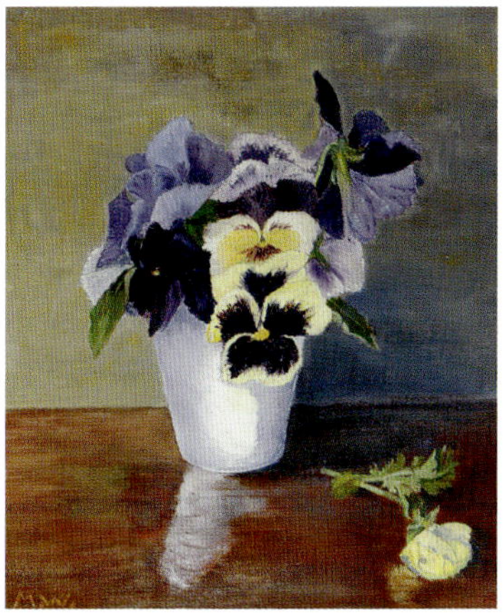

M. W.
Pansies
oil on board 30 x 25
T101

Facing page: Levy, Emmanuel, 1900–1986, *Snow in the North* (detail), Doncaster Museum Service, (p. 90)

The Regimental Museum of the 13th/18th Royal Hussars (QMO) and the Light Dragoons

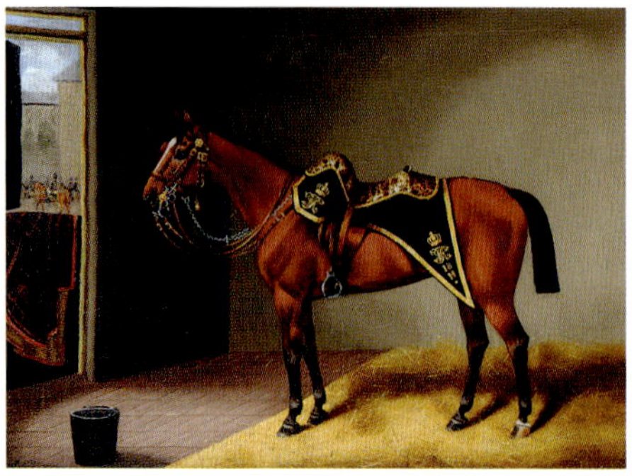

Hall, Harry 1814–1896
18th Hussar Charger 'Hussar' 1878
oil on canvas 57 x 73
1318H.LD.214

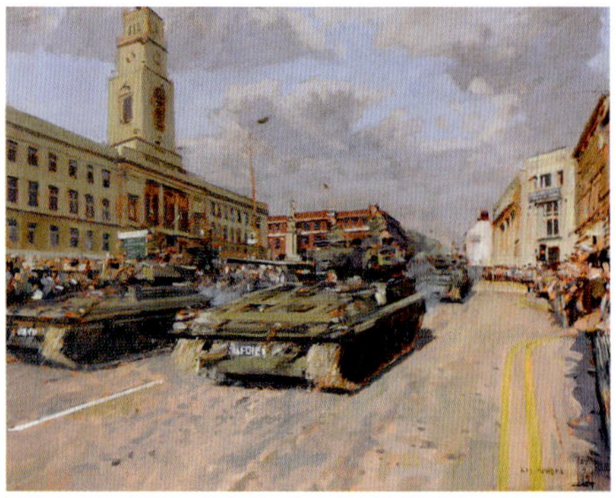

Howard, Ken b.1932
The Regiment Drives Past Barnsley Town Hall Following the Freedom Parade of 1979 1979
oil on canvas 70 x 77 (E)
13184.LD.530

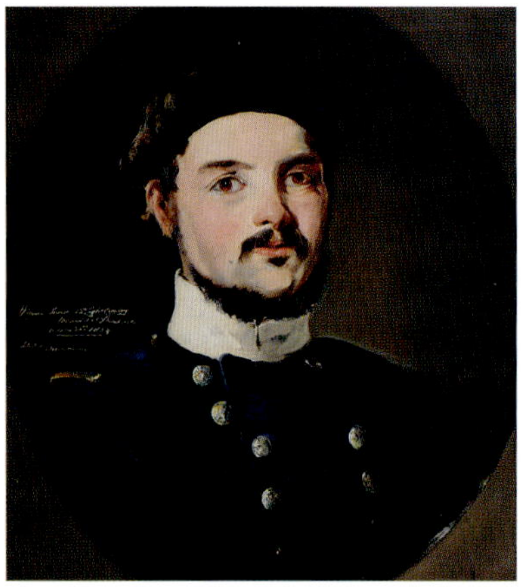

Kitodily Williams, J.
Private William Sewell (1830–1910), 13th Light Dragoons c.1855
oil on canvas 56 x 49
13184.LD470

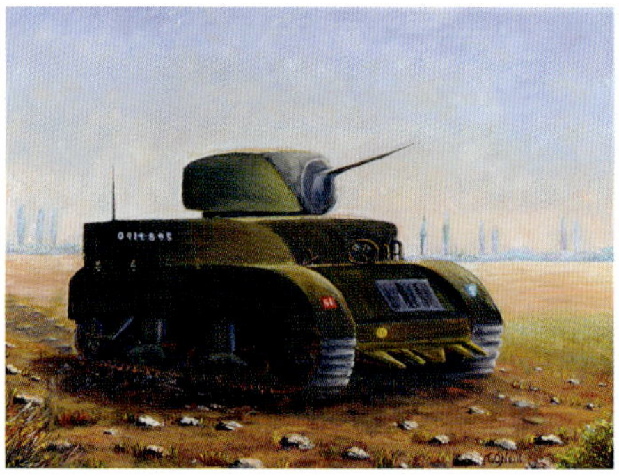

O'Neill, Tessa
Stuart Tank 'Honey'
oil on canvas 35 x 44.5
1318H.LD.531

Doncaster College: The Hub

Doncaster College is the largest provider of Further Education in South Yorkshire, with more than 22,000 people enrolled on 1,100 full- and part-time courses in 2008. These include A Level, degree, postgraduate and professional qualifications and apprenticeships. The main campus, The Hub, is a brand new purpose-built educational facility, which opened in 2006 in the centre of Doncaster. The Hub has a sister campus, known as The University Centre, set in 126 acres of idyllic countryside some six miles from Doncaster at High Melton.

The paintings in this volume are all situated in The Hub, on Doncaster's waterfront. They were commissioned by the College from students following a variety of courses as part of a special project to decorate the new building. Many are collaborations between several individuals. Large, bold and abstract, they are a striking complement to the airy, contemporary design of The Hub itself.

Camilla Stewart, South Yorkshire Coordinator for The Public Catalogue Foundation

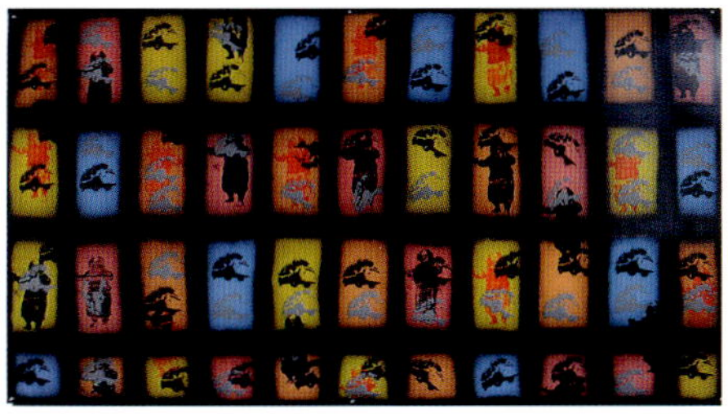

Arbones, Nathan
Sumo Sanderson 2009
acrylic spray & emulsion on steel 125 x 250 (E)
PCF10

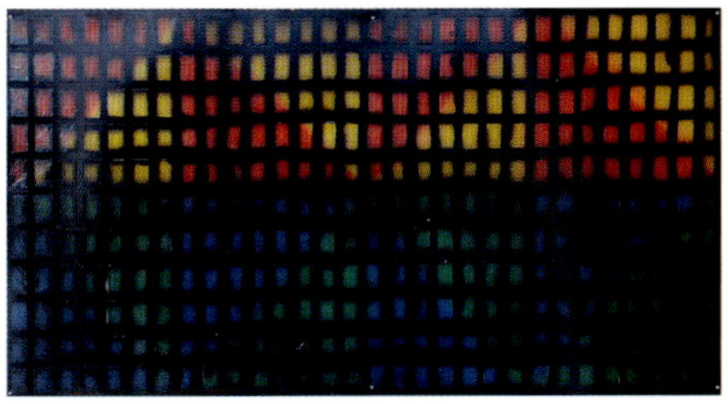

Falding, Jill; Blackhouse, Emma & Elwood, Paula
Black and Red Grid 2009
acrylic spray & emulsion on steel 125 x 250 (E)
PCF4

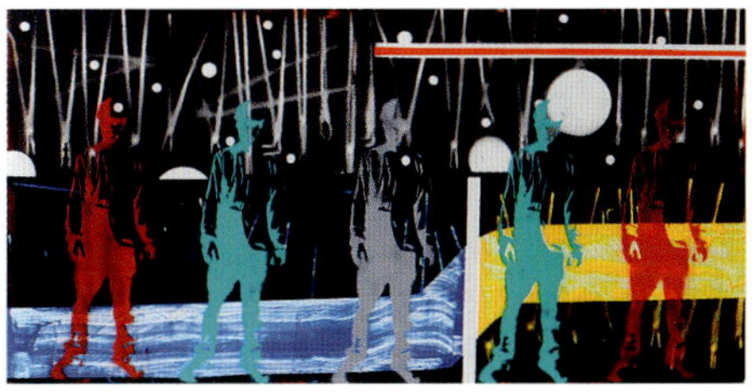

Kendal, Victoria; Ogden, Adam & Wright, Ann
Five Coal Miners 2009
acrylic spray & emulsion on steel 125 x 250 (E)
PCF1

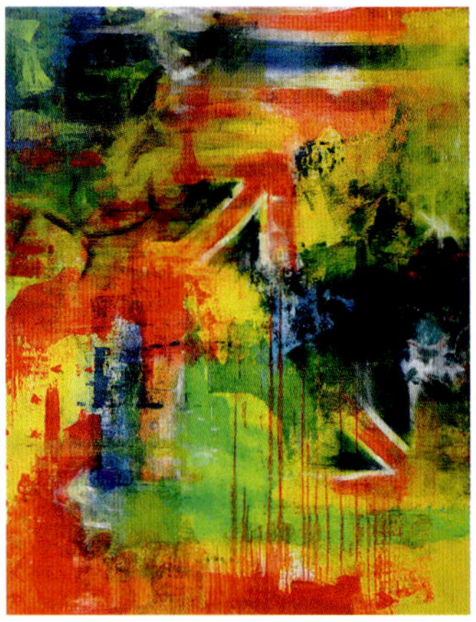

Langton, Adam
Flag 2006
acrylic on canvas board 158 x 122
PCF12

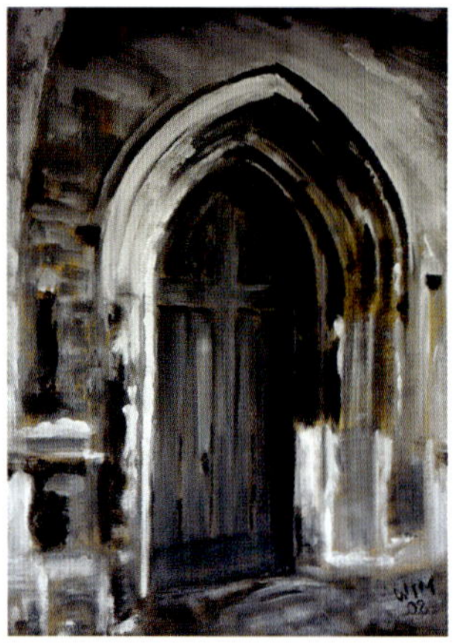

Moreman, Wendy
Christ Church Doorway, Doncaster, South Yorkshire 2008
acrylic on board 120 x 84
PCF7

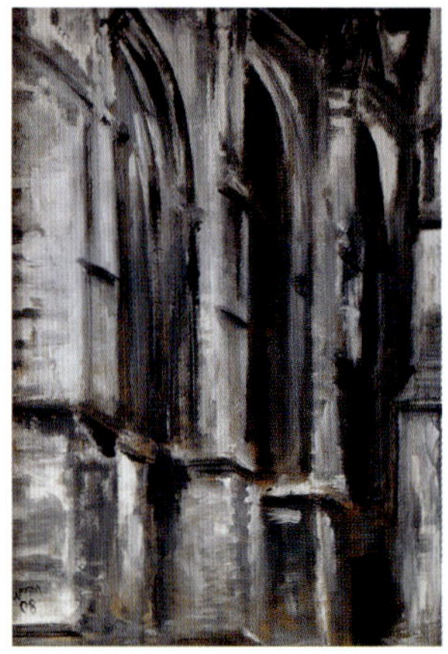

Moreman, Wendy
Minster Walls 2008
acrylic on board 120 x 82.5
PCF8

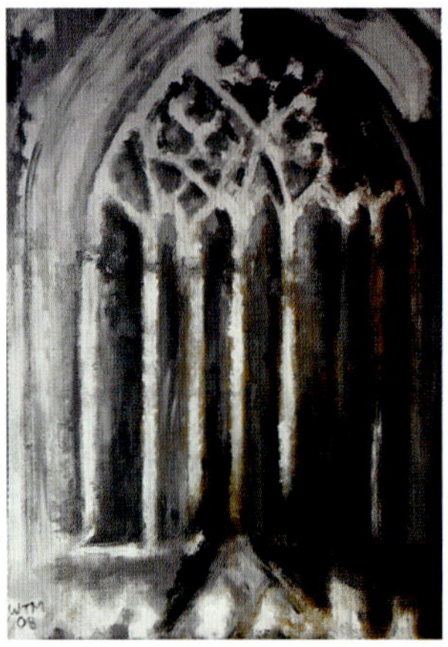

Moreman, Wendy
St George's Church Window, Doncaster, South Yorkshire 2008
acrylic on board 120 x 82.5
PCF13

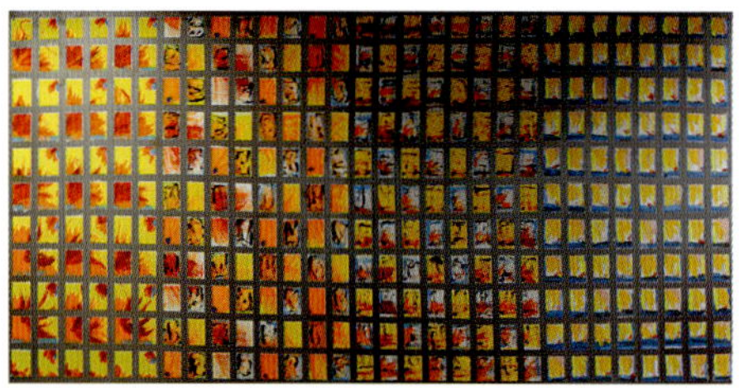

Smith, Penny & Pick, Madeleine
Orange and Lemon Colour Grid 2009
acrylic spray & emulsion on steel
125 x 250 (E)
PCF2

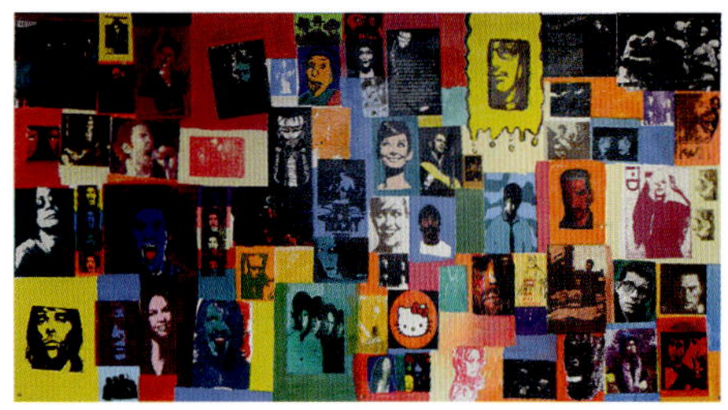

Students of the First Diploma in Art and Design
Famous Faces 2009
acrylic on steel 125 x 250 (E)
PCF9

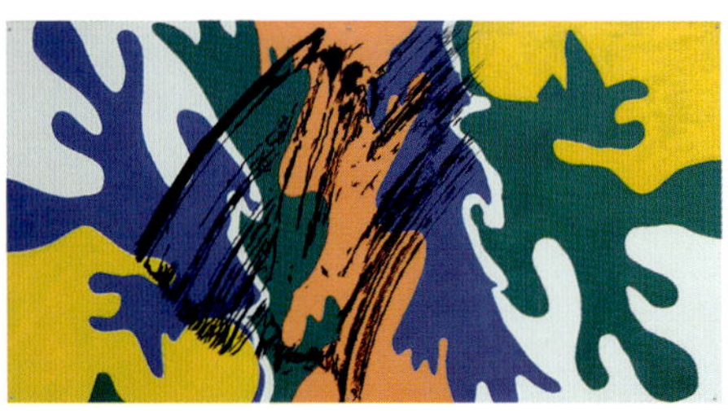

Students on the Foundation Course at Doncaster College
Beach Abstract 2009
acrylic spray & emulsion on steel 125 x 250 (E)
PCF5

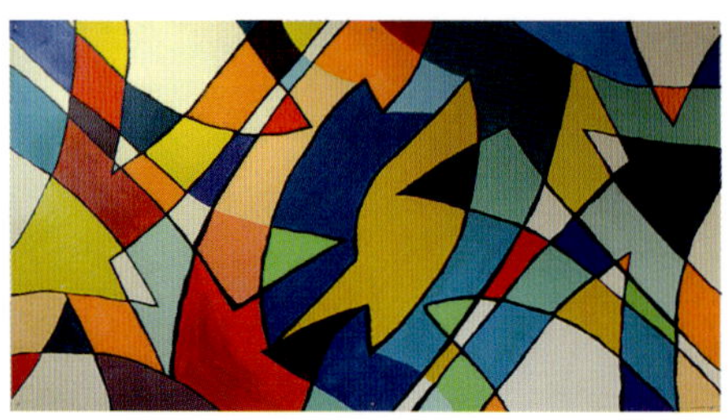

Students on the Foundation Course at Doncaster College
Geometric Abstract 2009
acrylic spray & emulsion on steel 125 x 250 (E)
PCF6

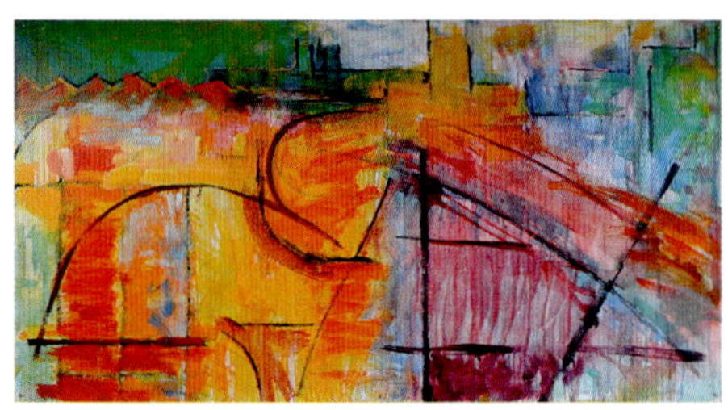

Ward, Rob; Pollit, Belinda & Leigh, Jerry
Town View Abstract 2009
acrylic spray & emulsion on steel 125 x 250 (E)
PCF11

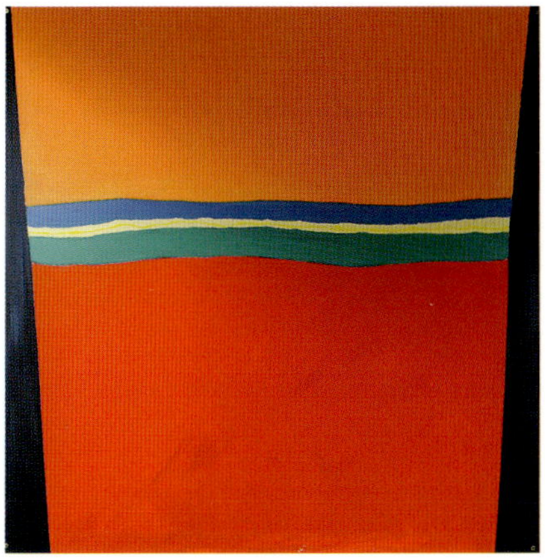

Webb, Julie
Australian Abstract 2009
acrylic on board 122 x 122
PCF3

Doncaster Deaf Trust

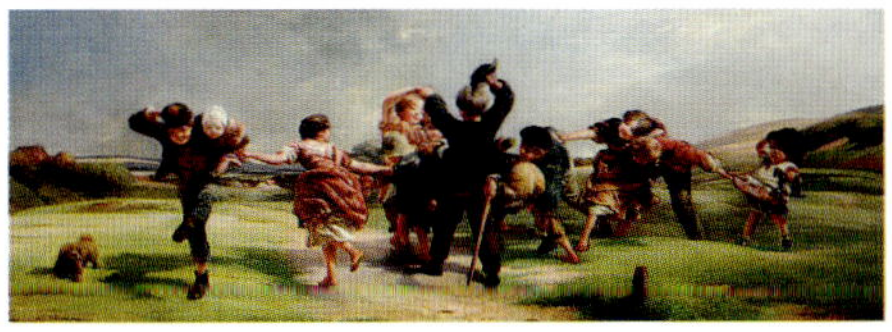

Gavin, Robert 1827–1883
Threading the Needle
oil on canvas 61 x 170
PCF3

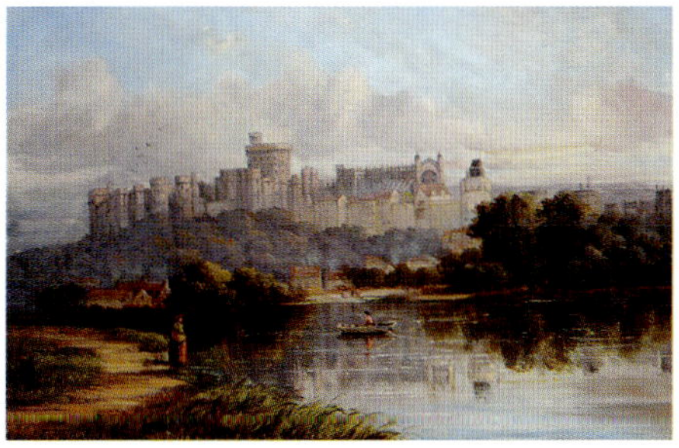

Hughes, John Joseph 1820–1909
Windsor Castle, Berkshire
oil on canvas 49 x 74
PCF2

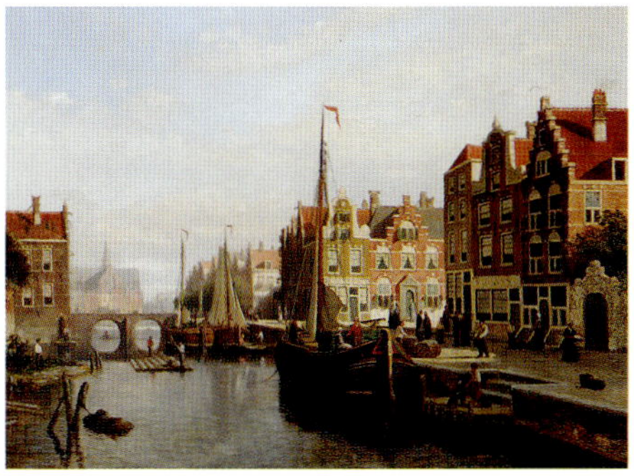

Hulk, Johannes Frederik 1829–1911
Amsterdam Canal Scene, The Netherlands
oil on canvas 75 x 100
PCF4

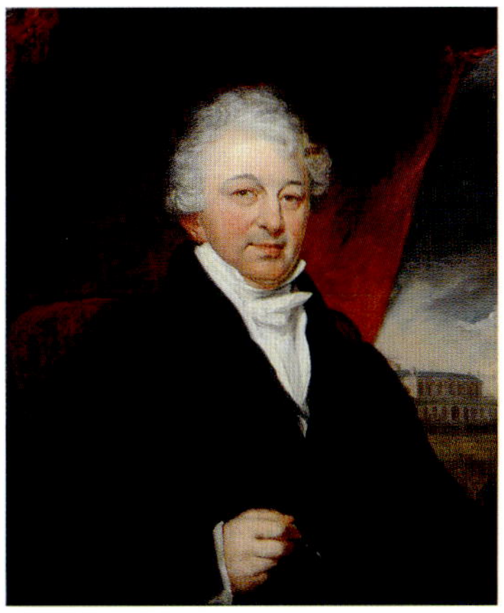

unknown artist mid-19th C
Reverend William Carr-Fenton (1784–1855)
oil on canvas 74 x 61.5
PCF1

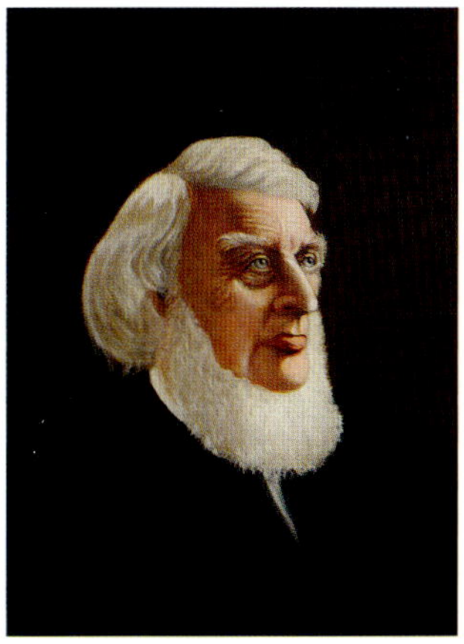

unknown artist
Portrait of Unknown Gentleman
oil on canvas 55 x 40
PCF5

Doncaster Magistrates' Court

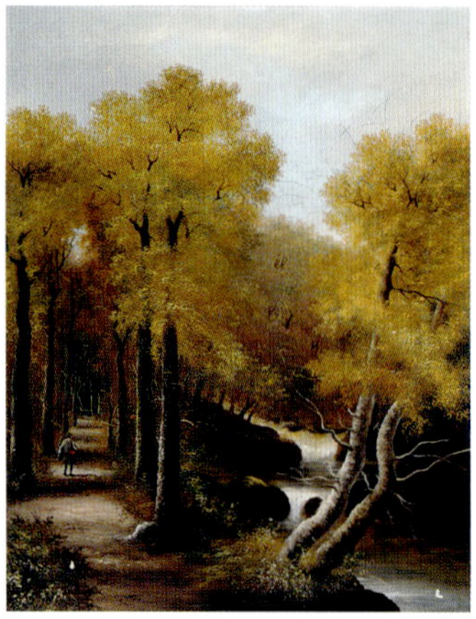

Marshall, M.
A Path through the Woodlands, Cleeve near Cheltenham, Gloucestershire
oil on canvas 90 x 70
PCF1

Doncaster Mansion House

Doncaster's iconic building, the Mansion House, was started in 1745 and completed in 1748. It was designed by James Paine and is the centrepiece of the town's main thoroughfare, the High Street, and the heart of civic life.

The Mansion House was the residence of the Mayor of Doncaster from 1750 to 1922 and as such was finished in a manner which reflected the importance, dignity and tradition of the office of the First Citizen of the Borough.

Although there have been minor changes to the Palladian design, the existing interior features have been retained. Within the impressive rooms many treasured artworks are displayed. The paintings have been acquired over a period of 200 years, representing a myriad of styles, as well as magnificently illustrating changes in local and national society and culture.

The portraits and landscapes capture the town's rich history and its sporting, theatrical and industrial core. It is thought that a number of paintings were originally commissioned specifically for the Mansion House; they are certainly uniquely showcased within this Grade I listed building. The portraits are a legacy from noble and distant times, when Doncaster played host to royalty and distinguished members of society.

The Mansion House and its art is the 'jewel in the crown' of Doncaster and a visitor can only be awed and impressed by the sense of pride and privilege that these impressive surroundings inspire.

The Collection is a vital reflection of the heritage that belongs to the people of Doncaster and must be carefully preserved and maintained to ensure that future generations can delight in viewing a pictorial representation of a window in time.

Paolo Marelli, Mansion House Officer

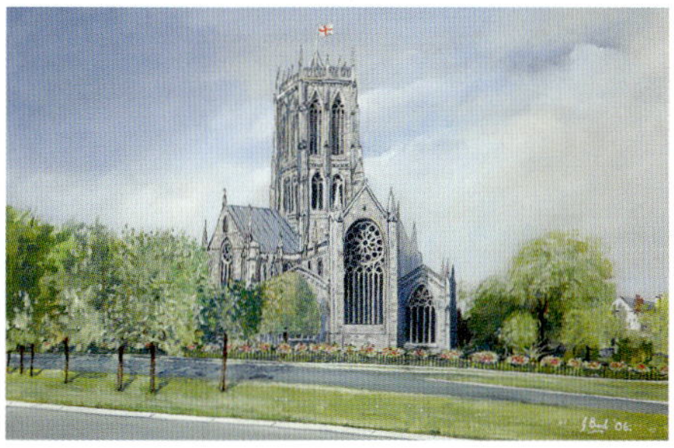

Bird, John b.1948
St George's Church, Doncaster, South Yorkshire 2006
oil on canvas 48.5 x 74.3
PCF23

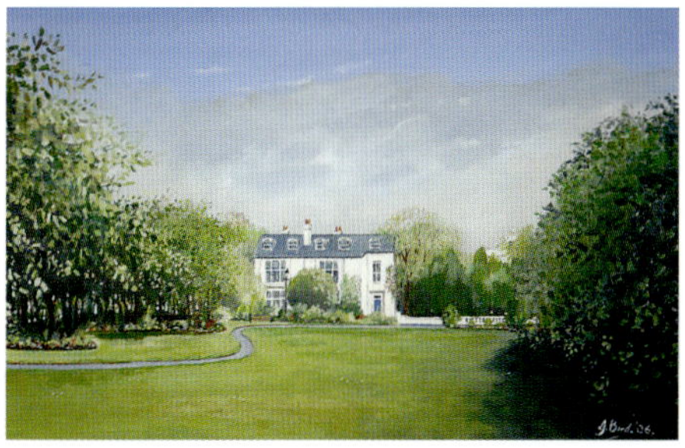

Bird, John b.1948
White House 2006
oil on canvas 48.5 x 74.3
PCF24

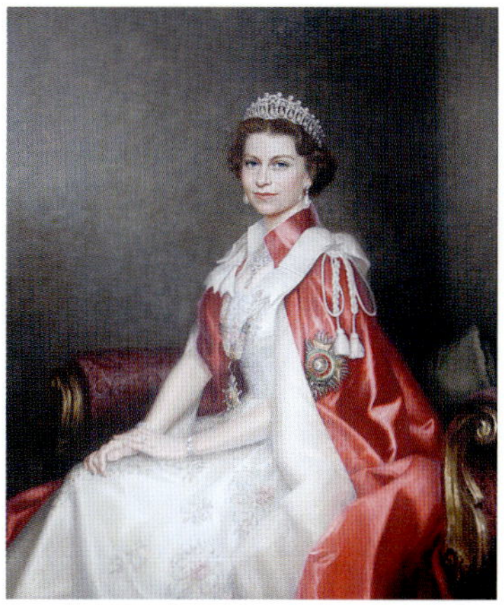

Boden, Leonard 1911–1999
Elizabeth II (b.1926)
oil on canvas 127 x 100
PCF13

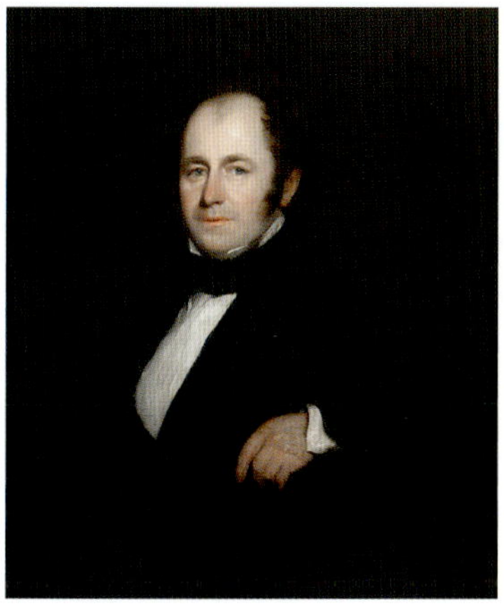

British (English) School
Fredrick Fisher, Mayor of Doncaster 1848
oil on canvas 76 x 63.5
PCF2

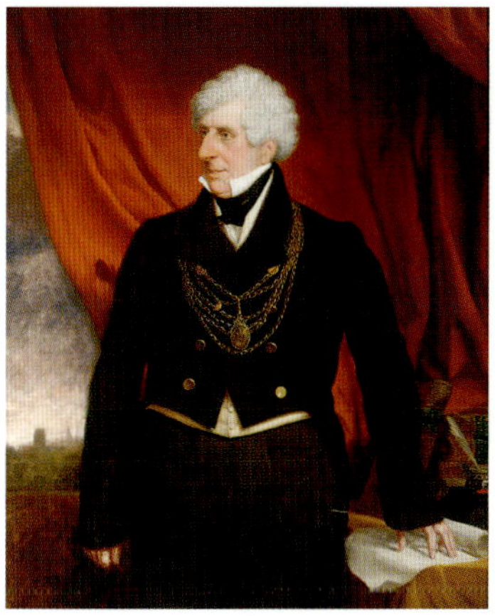

British (English) School early 19th C
Sir William Bryan Cooke (1782–1851), Mayor of Doncaster (1835–1836)
oil on canvas 143 x 112
PCF16

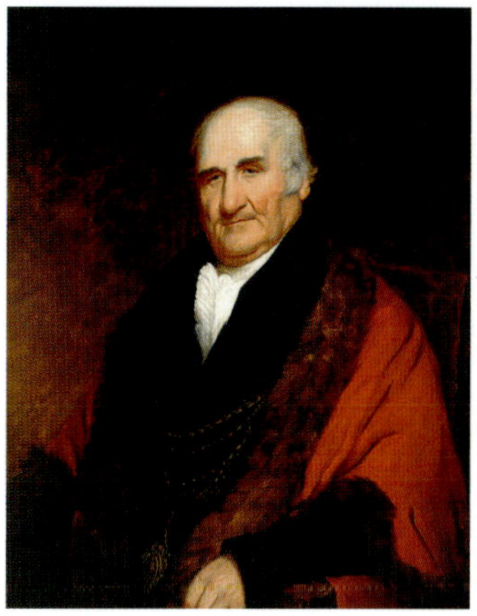

British (English) School 19th C
Joseph Lockwood, Esq.
oil on canvas 91.5 x 71
PCF14

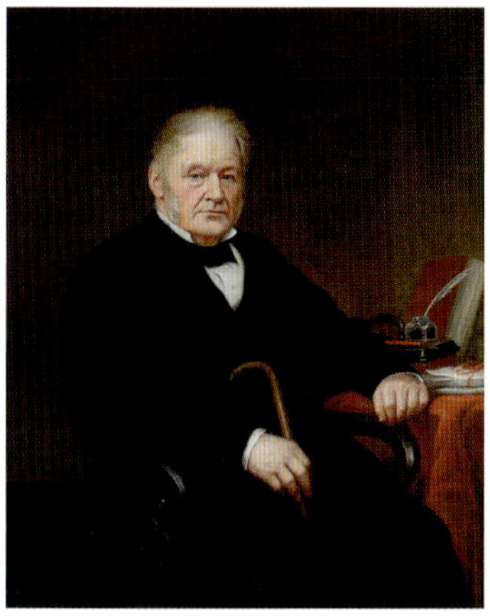

British (English) School 19th C
Sir Edmund Beckett (1787–1874), MP for The West Riding (1841–1859)
oil on canvas 127 x 102
PCF18

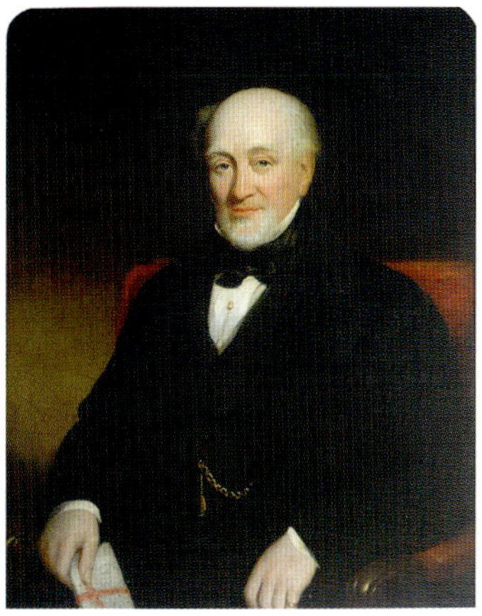

British (English) School 19th C
Thomas Blackwell Mason
oil on canvas 91.5 x 71
PCF22

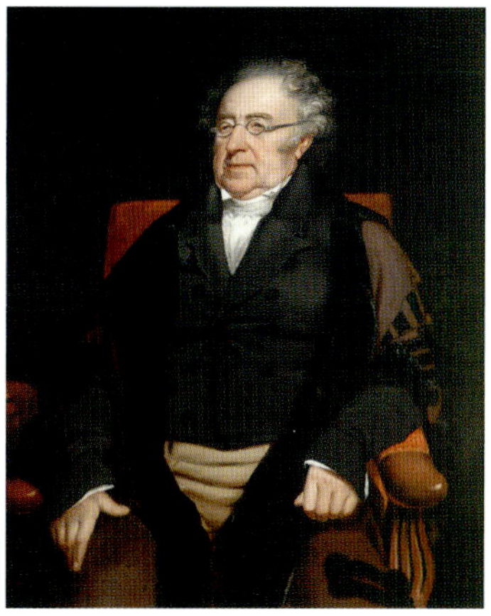

British (English) School
late 19th C/early 20th C
Portrait of a Seated Gentleman
oil on canvas 91.5 x 71
PCF15

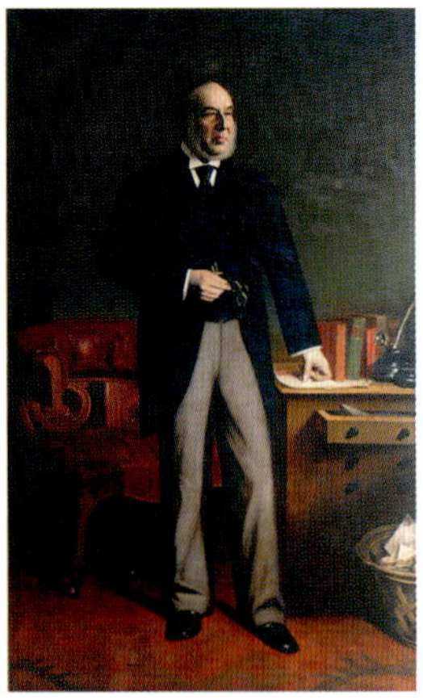

British (English) School
late 19th C/early 20th C
Robert Stockil, Esq., JP
oil on canvas 222 x 132
PCF10

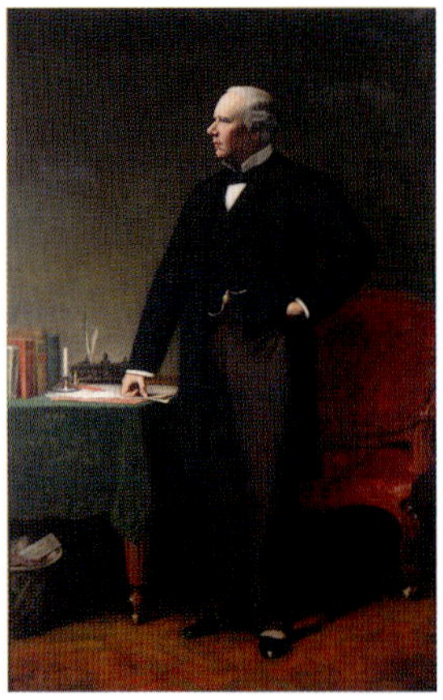

British (English) School
late 19th C/early 20th C
Sir Frank Lockwood (1846–1897)
oil on canvas 222 x 132
PCF8

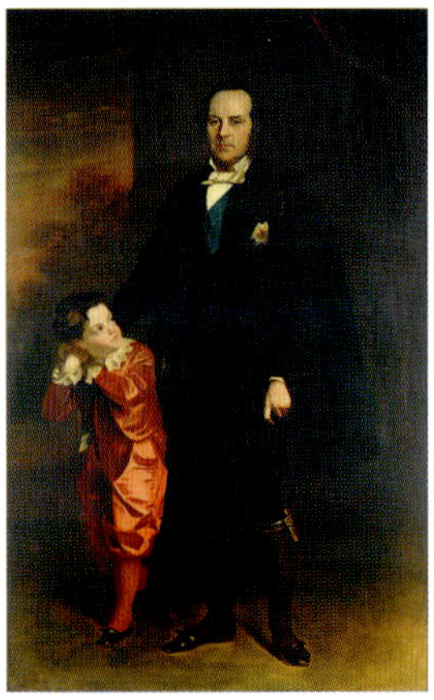

British (English) School
late 19th C/early 20th C
The Right Honourable William Thomas Spencer Wentworth-Fitzwilliam (1815–1902) (...)
oil on canvas 220 x 127
PCF7

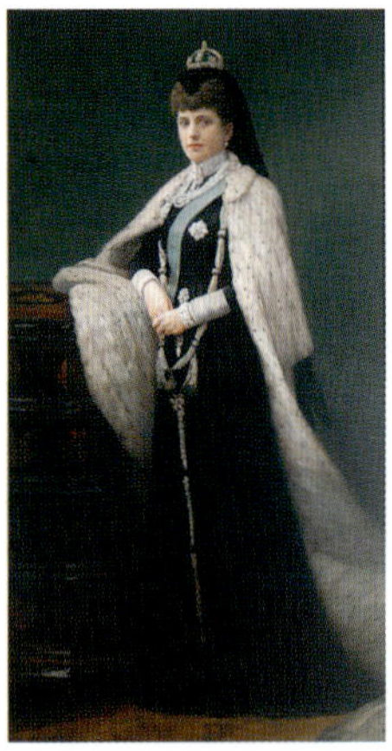

British (English) School 20th C
Queen Alexandra (1844–1925)
oil on canvas 230 x 101.5
PCF12

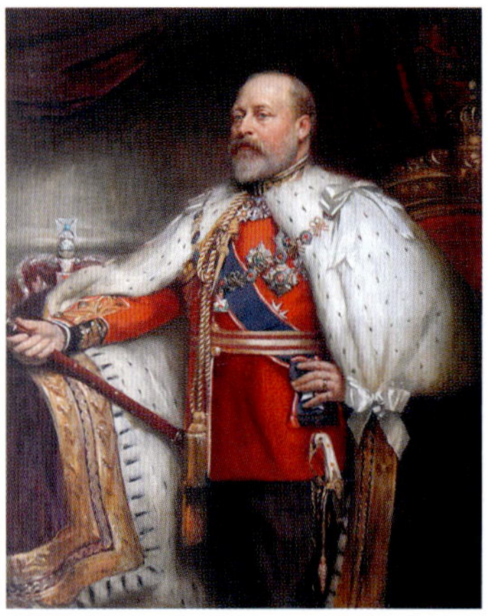

Calkin, Lance 1859–1936
Edward VII (1841–1910)
oil on canvas 141 x 111
PCF11

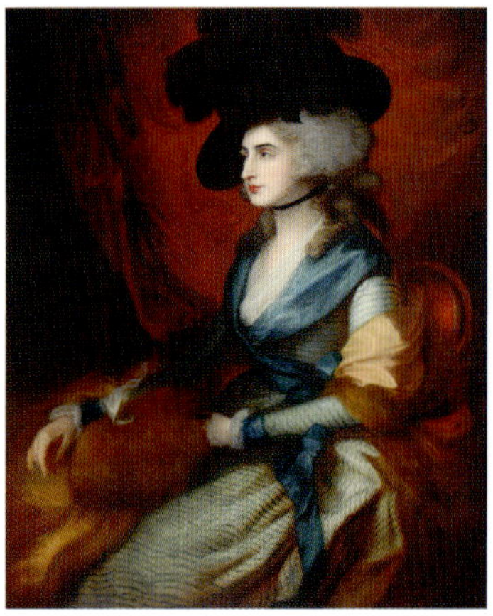

Gainsborough, Thomas (copy of)
1727–1788
Sarah Siddons late 19th C/early 20th C
oil on canvas 127 x 101.5
PCF21

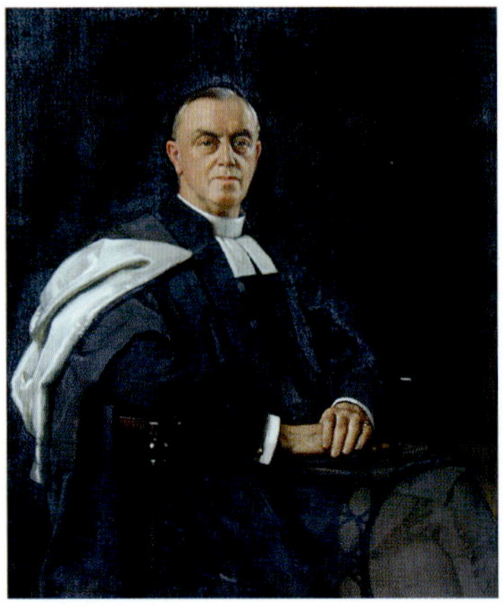

Jack, Richard 1866–1952
George Sandford, MA, Archdeacon of Doncaster 1927
oil on canvas 127 x 101.5
PCF19

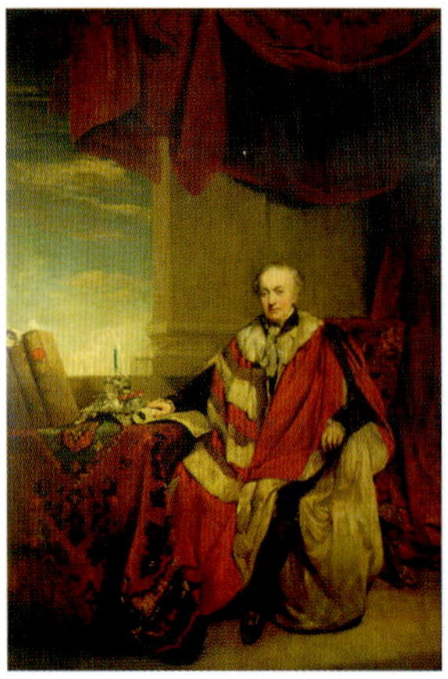

Jackson
The Right Honourable William Thomas Spencer Wentworth-Fitzwilliam (1815–1902), 6th Earl Fitzwilliam 1864
oil on canvas 320 x 180
PCF3

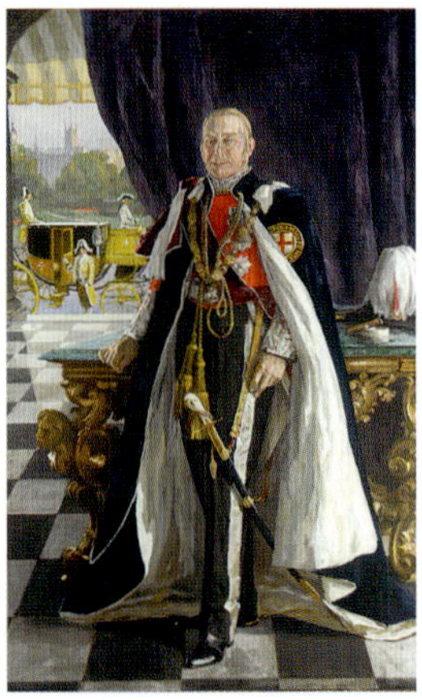

Lavery, John 1856–1941
The Right Honourable Earl of Lonsdale, KG, GCUO
oil on canvas 229 x 137
PCF6

Facing page: Mignon, Abraham (after), 1640–c.1679, *Fruit and Insects* (detail), 1675–1725, Barnsley Museum and Heritage Service, (p. 57)

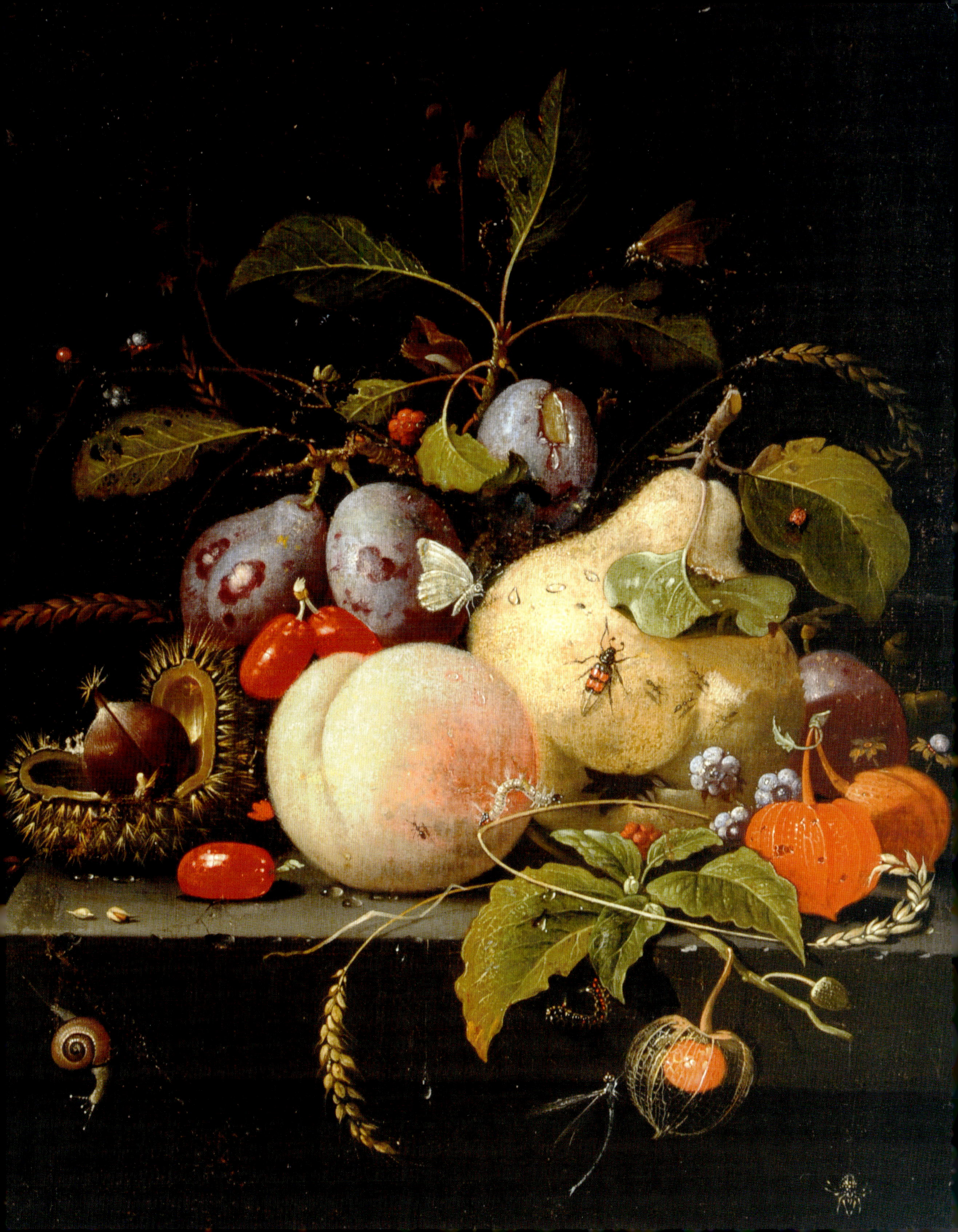

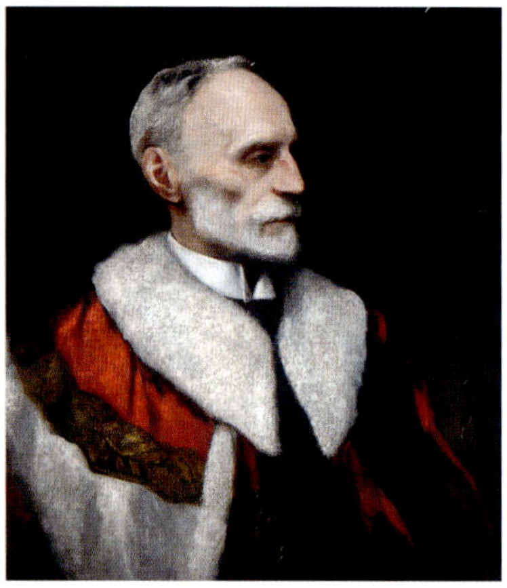

L'Hôpital, René le Brun Comte de 1877–1929
Charles Lindley Wood (1839–1934), Viscount Halifax
oil on canvas 76 x 63.5
PCF20

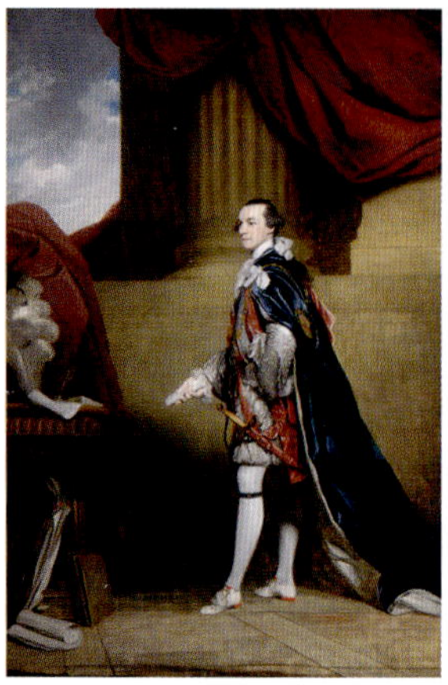

Phillips, Thomas 1770–1845
The Most Honourable Charles Watton-Wentworth (1730–1782), 2nd Marquess of Rockingham 1805
oil on canvas 320 x 180 (E)
PCF5

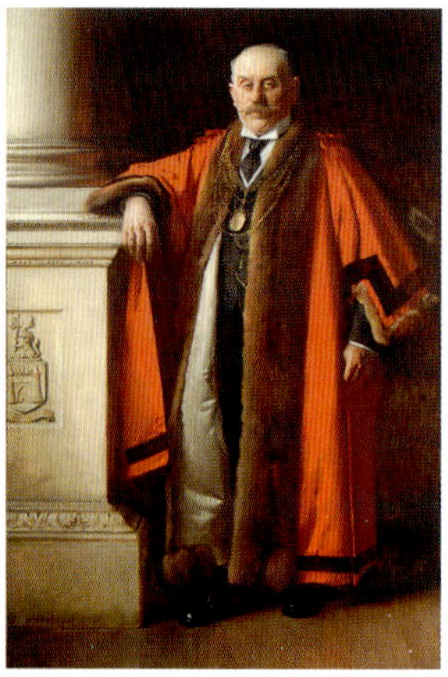

Priest, Alfred 1874–1929
Alderman George Thomas Tuby (1857–1932), Mayor of Doncaster (1921–1922)
oil on canvas 195 x 122
PCF17

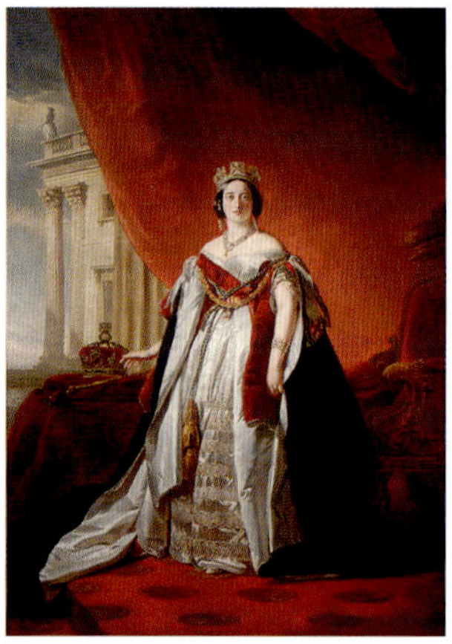

Winterhalter, Franz Xaver 1805–1873
Queen Victoria (1819–1901) 1864
oil on canvas 320 x 180 (E)
PCF4

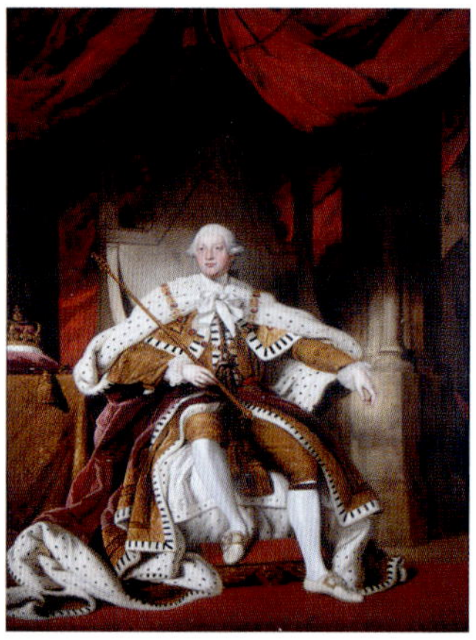

Woodforde, Samuel 1763–1817
George III (1738–1820) 1804
oil on canvas 274 x 182
PCF9

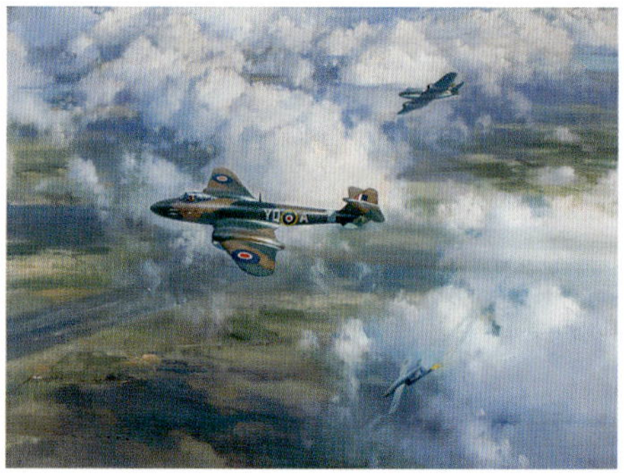

Wootton, Frank 1911–1998
616 AAE Squadron, Manston, Kent 1954
oil on canvas 76 x 101
PCF1

Doncaster Museum Service

The beginnings of what was to become Doncaster Museum Service can be traced back to 1900 when the Doncaster Scientific Society was granted space to display specimens and objects at the Guildhall in the town. The Collection grew rapidly and in 1908 Doncaster Corporation offered Beechfield, a Victorian townhouse in the Waterdale area of Doncaster, as a venue for a museum. That same year a request was made to the Corporation by Doncaster Art Club for there to be an art gallery in the town. The request was granted, and in 1909 an art gallery was opened on the first floor at Beechfield House. The following year saw the opening of the museum on the ground floor, creating Doncaster Museum & Art Gallery.

The museum and art gallery remained at Beechfield until its closure in 1962. Two years later our new purpose-built museum and art gallery was opened on Chequer Road. Our sister museum, Cusworth Hall, which displays our social history collection, was opened in 1967 and, like Doncaster Museum & Art Gallery, came under the control of Doncaster Metropolitan Borough Council in 1974 following a restructure of local government. In 1987 an extension was added to the museum and art gallery on Chequer Road, which houses the Regimental Museum of the King's Own Yorkshire Light Infantry.

To date, the Fine Art collection numbers around 2,000 works, the majority of which are works of art on paper, including a fine collection of prints and drawings by twentieth-century British artists. There are around 300 works of art in oil, acrylic and tempera, and our Collection is completed by a small group of sculptures, including works by Henri Gaudier-Brzeska (1891–1915) and Jacob Epstein (1880–1959).

The Fine Art Collection is currently displayed across three sites. The largest part is at Doncaster Museum & Art Gallery, with other works shown at Cusworth Hall Museum. At any one time a few works from the Collection are also on loan to the Mansion House in Doncaster.

The Collection has been built up over the years through a mixture of purchases, bequests and donations. Like most museums and galleries in this country we are also indebted to the Art Fund and more recently the Heritage Lottery Fund for their assistance with a number of purchases. The Contemporary Art Society also continues to be a generous benefactor.

Highlights of the Collection include, from the middle of the eighteenth century, three portraits by Joseph Wright of Derby (1734–1797). The portraits, which are still in their original frames, depict William Brooke, an Alderman of Doncaster, his daughter Elizabeth and her husband William Pigot. The pictures, which were painted at the beginning of Wright's career, reflect Doncaster's position in the eighteenth century as a centre of entertainment and culture, focused on the town's racecourse and Mansion House.

From the nineteenth century we have a group of works by the celebrated painter of horses, John Frederick Herring (1795–1865). Herring spent the early years of his life in London, but, so the story goes, one day while looking out of his window he saw a stage coach bound for Doncaster. On the spur of the moment he decided to come north to make his fortune. Originally trained as a coach painter and sign-writer he soon turned his hand to painting horses and painted 33 consecutive winners of the St Leger horse race. He also painted

21 winners of the Derby. Perhaps the finest example of his work in the Collection is *Finish of the 1827 Gold Cup* which depicts horses and riders straining to reach the line.

Highlights from later in the nineteenth century include a number of works by artists associated with the Newlyn School in Cornwall. These include *The Mariner's Sunday School* by William Holt Yates Titcomb (1858–1930), which shows the Primitive Methodist chapel in St Ives with an old mariner reading from the Bible to a young boy. Another picture by an artist associated with the Newlyn School is the wonderfully atmospheric marine painting *Cloudy Moonlight* by Albert Julius Olsson (1864–1942). Olsson was a keen sailor himself and regularly went out sketching in his boat to record different weather effects.

Into the twentieth century we have a group of paintings by artists who are as well known as teachers as they are as painters. These include two oils by Rodney Joseph Burn (1899–1984), who was a respected teacher of drawing at Camberwell School of Art in London; *From Camer Wood, Scotland* an impressionistic landscape by Sir Roger de Grey (1918–1995), a long-time President of the Royal Academy, and the enchanting painting *Child's Wonderment* by Carel Victor Morlais Weight (1908–1997) who was Professor of Painting at the Royal College of Art.

Doncaster Museum Service continues to take opportunities to acquire works that enhance our collection. Worthy of mention is one of our most recent purchases, which again we were able to acquire through the help of a number of grant giving bodies. The painting in question is *Giants Refreshed: Pacifics in the Doncaster Locomotive Works* by Terence Tenison Cuneo (1907–1996). The picture, which depicts two Pacific Class locomotives receiving their final coat of paint at the Locomotive Works in Doncaster, is not only a magnificent work of art in its own right, but a powerful reminder to the visitor to Doncaster Museum & Art Gallery of the importance of the railways to the social and industrial heritage of Doncaster.

It is wonderful for Doncaster Museum Service to be included in this publication, providing members of the general public the opportunity to see the range of different works in its Collection, many of which for reasons of space, or occasionally condition, are kept in storage.

Neil McGregor, Museums Officer (Art and Exhibitions)

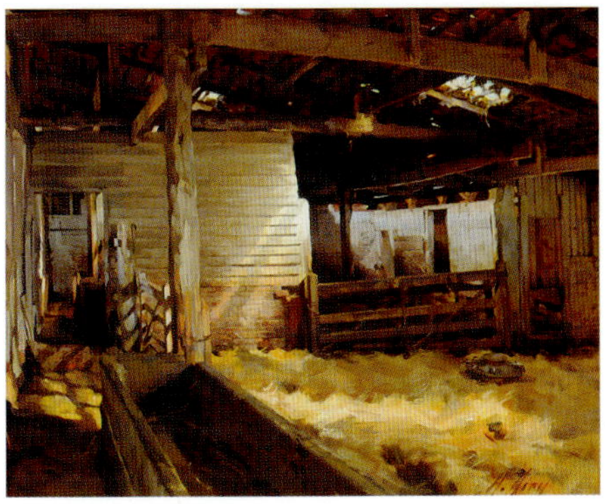

Airy, Anna 1882–1964
Morning Sunlight c.1926
oil on canvas 61 x 74
DONMG : 41.27

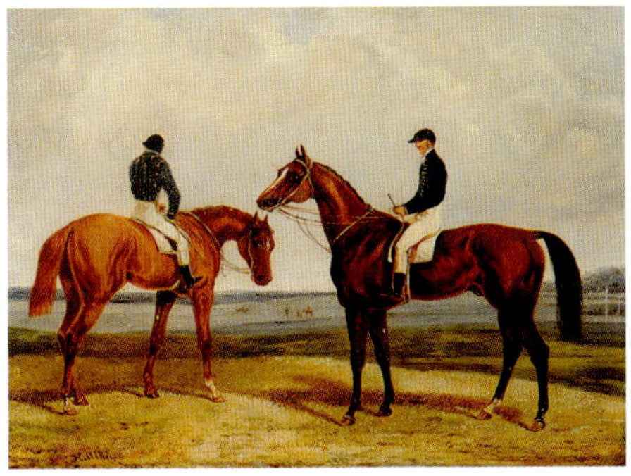

Alken, Samuel Henry 1810–1894
'Sittingbourne' with S. Rogers II and 'West Australian' with F. Butler, Winner of the 1853 Derby c.1853
oil on canvas 30 x 40
DONMG : 1994.10

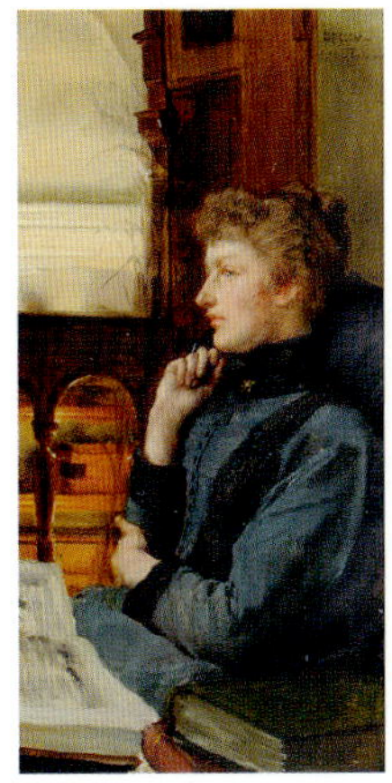

Alma-Tadema, Lawrence 1836–1912
Reverie: Far Away Thoughts 1874
oil on board 25 x 13
DONMG : 982.86

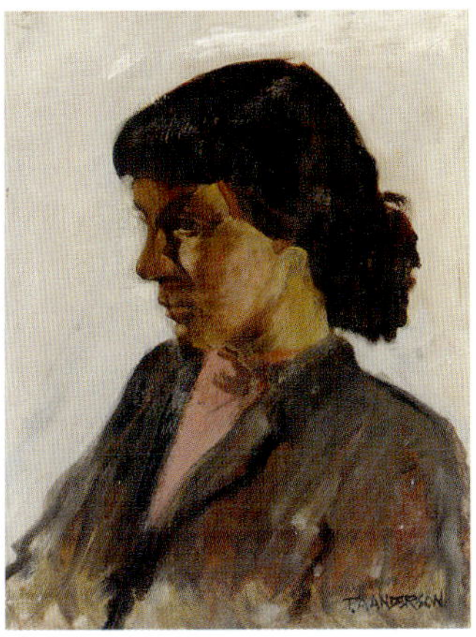

Anderson, Thomas Alexander
active 1929–1973
Miss Joan Hamilton c.1940
oil on canvas 168 x 71
DONMG : 1997.18

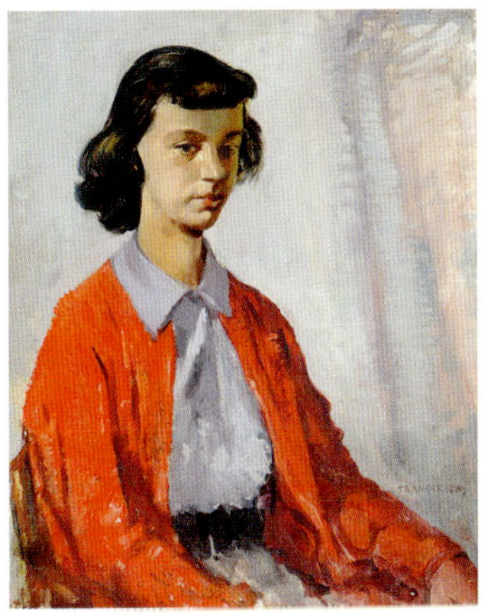

Anderson, Thomas Alexander
active 1929–1973
Portrait of an Unknown Woman c.1940
oil on canvas 46 x 35
DONMG : 1997.19

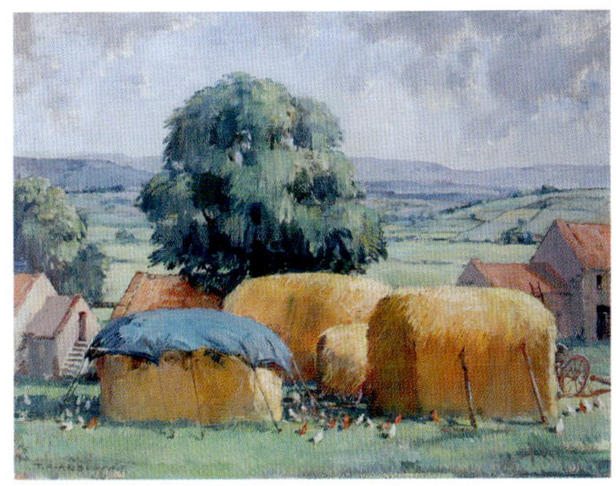

Anderson, Thomas Alexander
active 1929–1973
The Blue Tarpaulin
oil on panel 43 x 56
DONMG : 545.69

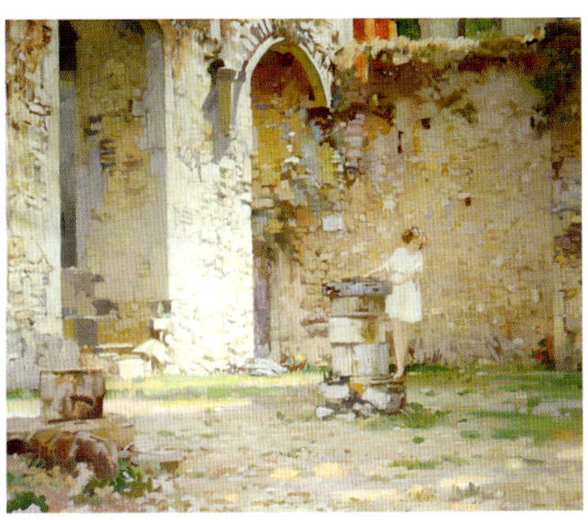

Appleyard, Frederick 1874–1963
Old Walls
oil on canvas 62 x 75
DONMG : 60.30

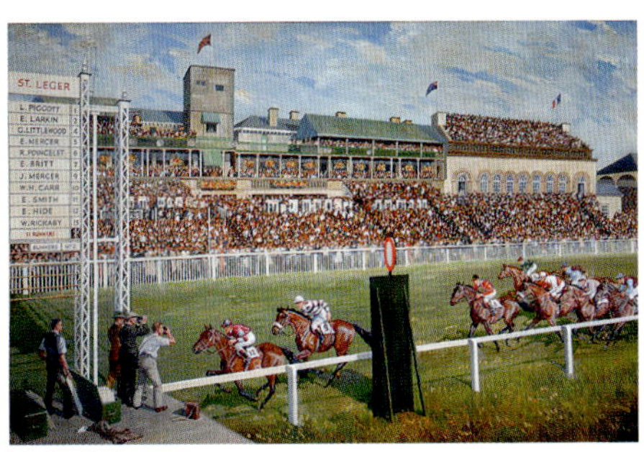

Appleyard, Joseph 1908–1960
The Finish of the 1959 St Leger Stakes 1960
oil on canvas 100 x 151 (E)
DONMG : 388.60

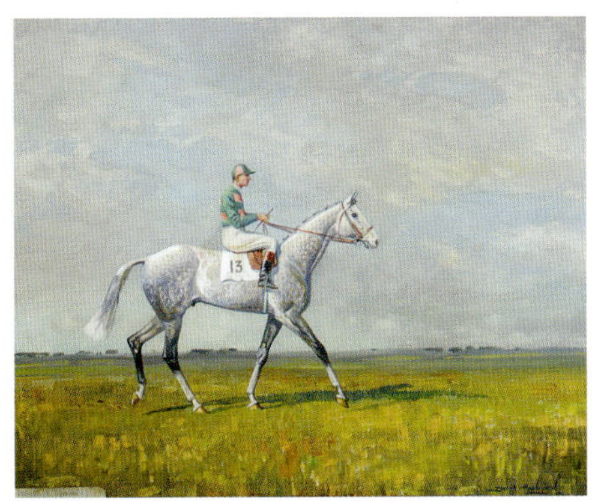

Appleyard, Joseph 1908–1960
'Airborne'
oil on canvas 47 x 56.5
DONMG : 395.60

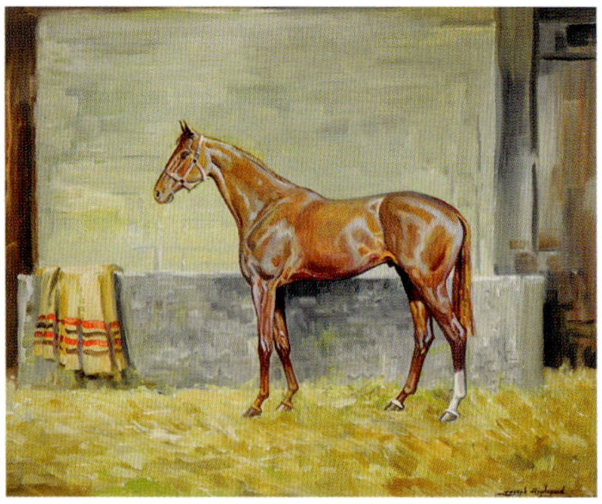

Appleyard, Joseph 1908–1960
'Ballymoss'
oil on canvas 46.5 x 56
DONMG : 398.60

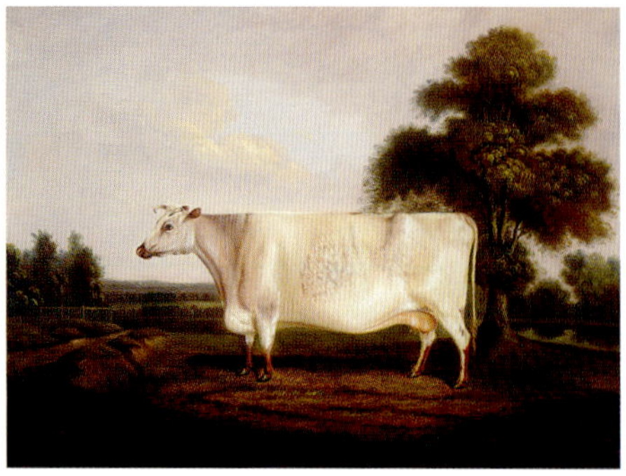

Bailey, George 1796–1822
'Lavinia'
oil on canvas 59.5 x 79
DONMG : 857.81

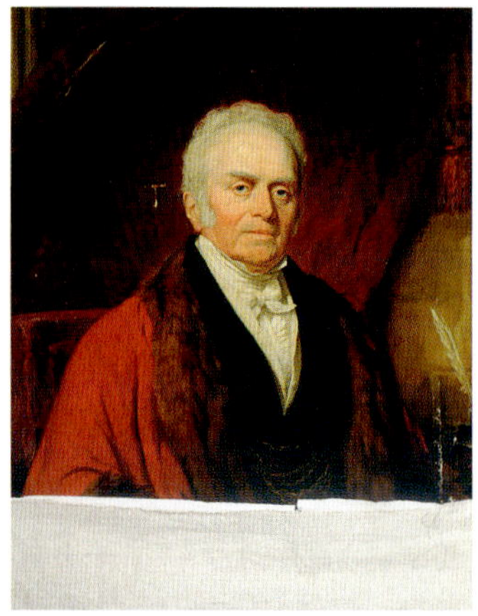

Beetham, William 1774–1853
William Sheardown (1797–1877) early 19th C
oil on canvas 88 x 72
DONMG : 794.77

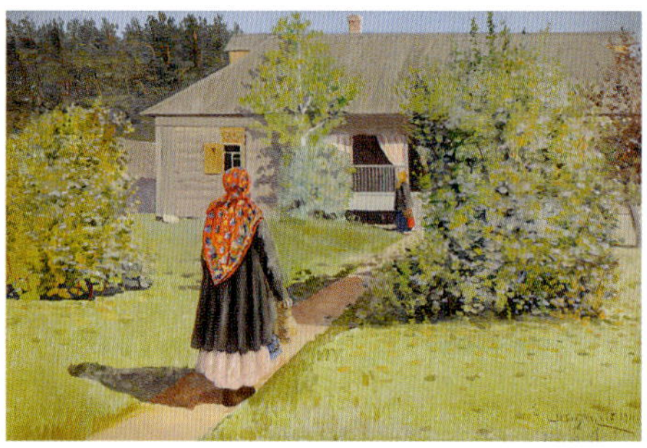

Belaevsky, Mikhael Nicolaevich
active 1893–1930
A Russian Summer House 1911
oil on canvas 67 x 98
DONMG : 550.69

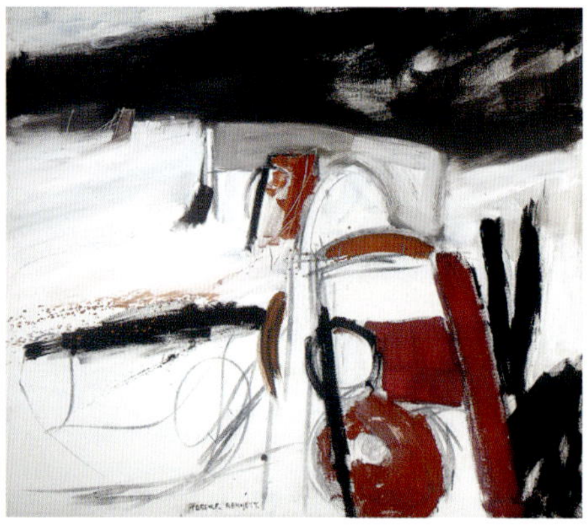

Bennett, Terence b.1935
Warmsworth Hall, South Yorkshire
oil on canvas 128 x 145
PCF11

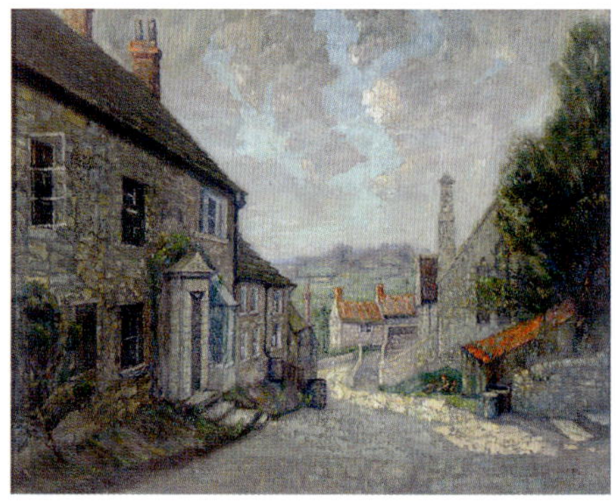

Bingham, Henry 1876–1954
Hooton Pagnell, Doncaster, South Yorkshire
oil on canvas 44 x 53.5
DONMG : 417.61

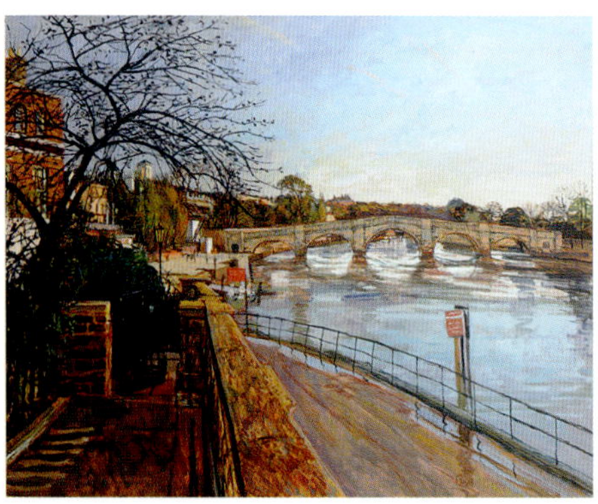

Bowyer, William b.1926
Richmond Bridge, Surrey 1982
oil on canvas 102 x 122
DONMG : 954.84

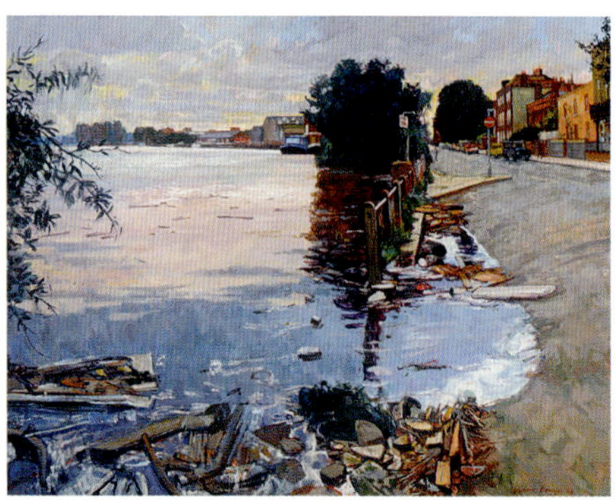

Bowyer, William b.1926
Ebb Tide, the Thames at Chiswick, London
1984
oil on canvas 101.4 x 127
DONMG : 1008.88

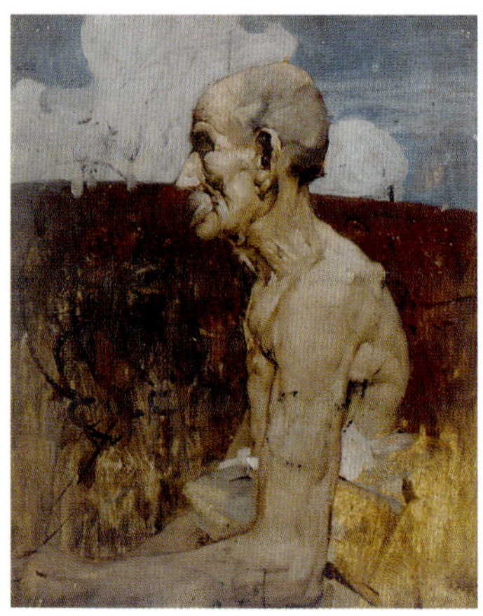

Brangwyn, Frank 1867–1956
Old Man at Assisi
oil on canvas 61 x 47.5
DONMG : 437.62

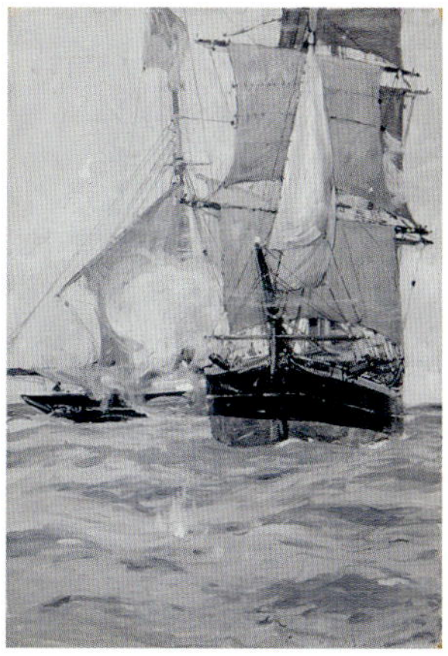

Brangwyn, Frank 1867–1956
Sailing Ships at Sea
oil on board 52 x 36
DONMG : 438.62

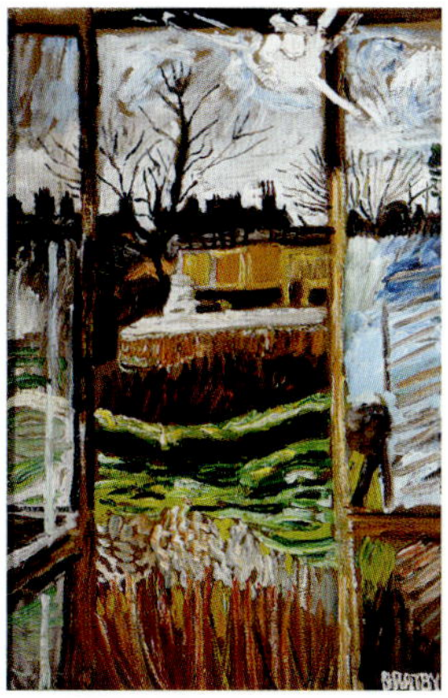

Bratby, John Randall 1928–1992
November Sun from Revolving Studio c.1979
oil on canvas 81 x 53
DONMG : 820.79

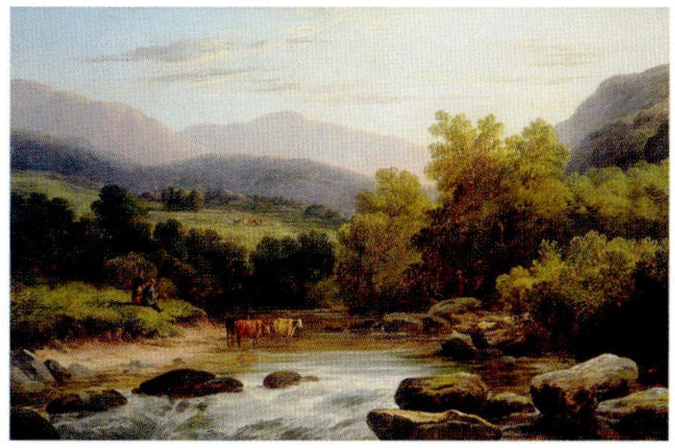

Bridgehouse, Robert 1818–1881
River Scene, North Wales
oil on canvas 61 x 91
DONMG : 514.64

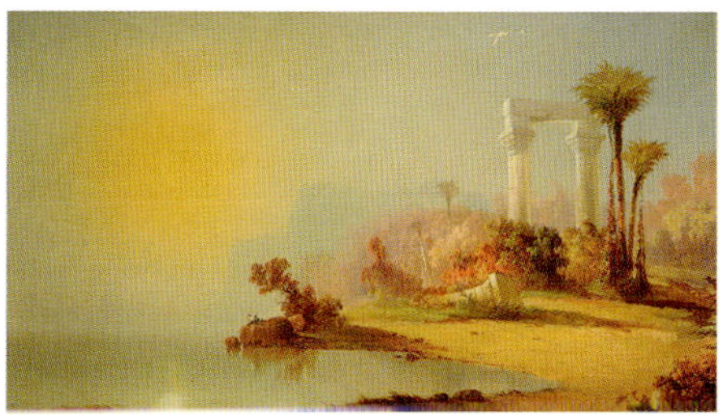

Brieau, P. D. active 19th C
The Nile
oil on canvas 76 x 126
DONMG : 78.33

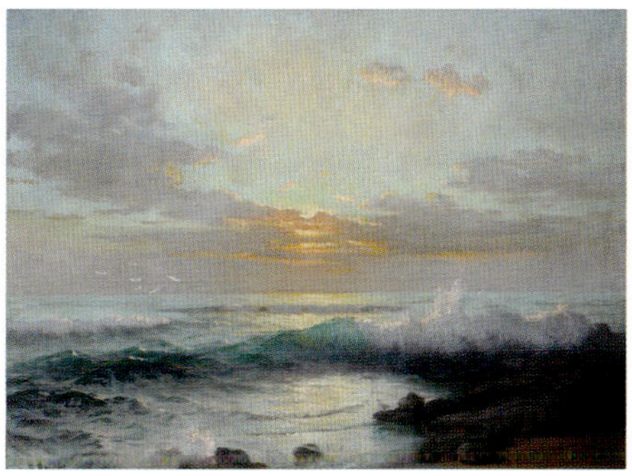

Bright, Beatrice 1861–1940
Breakers on the Shore
oil on canvas 67.5 x 90.5
DONMG : 128.40

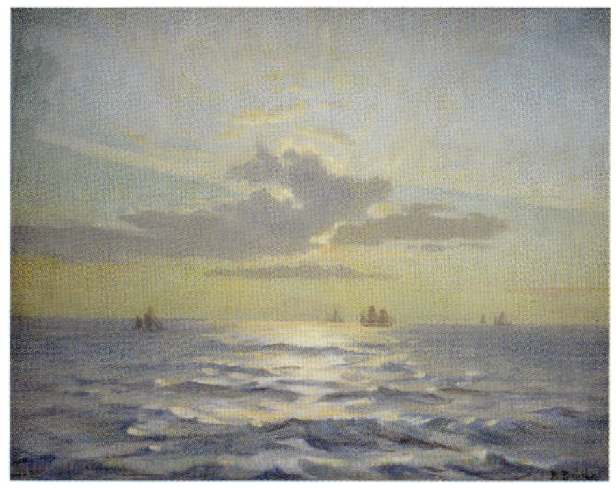

Bright, Beatrice 1861–1940
Seascape
oil on canvas 39.5 x 49.5
DONMG : 129.40

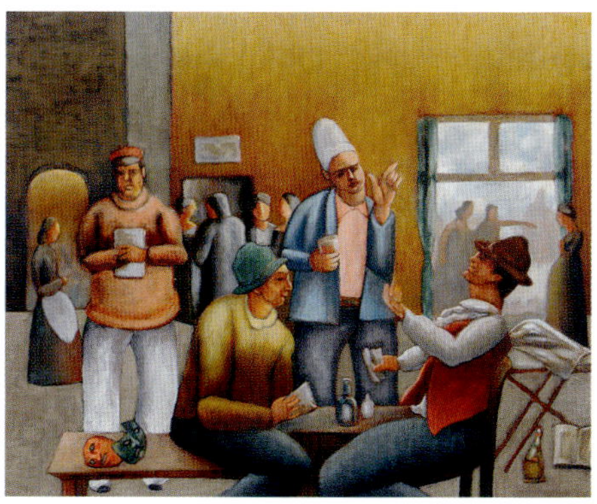

Brodzky, Horace 1885–1969
The Rehearsal 1960
oil on canvas 49 x 60
DONMG : 888.82

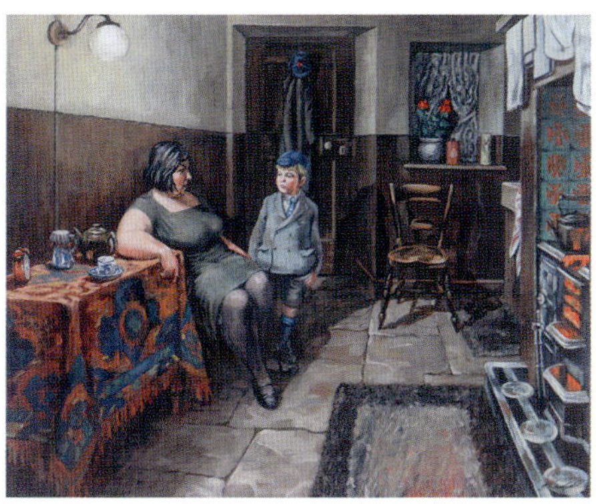

Brumfitt, George Edward 1917–1993
Hilda's Warning: 'Mind you're in by half-past seven, it's bath night' c.1950
oil on canvas 63.5 x 76
DONMG : 947.84

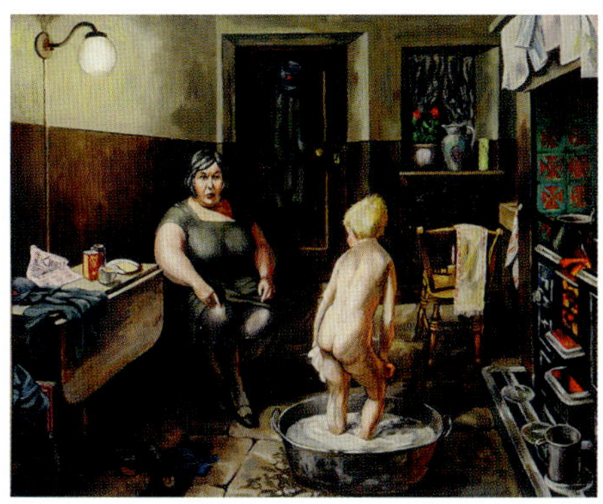

Brumfitt, George Edward 1917–1993
Cheeking Hilda c.1950
oil on canvas 64 x 76
DONMG : 948.84

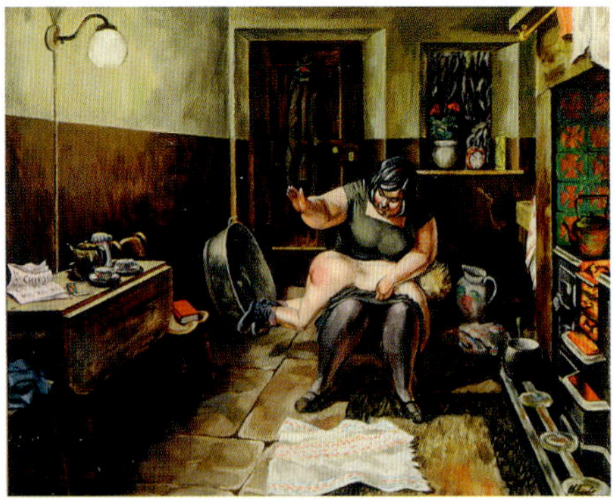

Brumfitt, George Edward 1917–1993
'You were having your way but I was having mine and I always won', Hilda to Me c.1950
oil on canvas 63.5 x 76
DONMG : 949.84

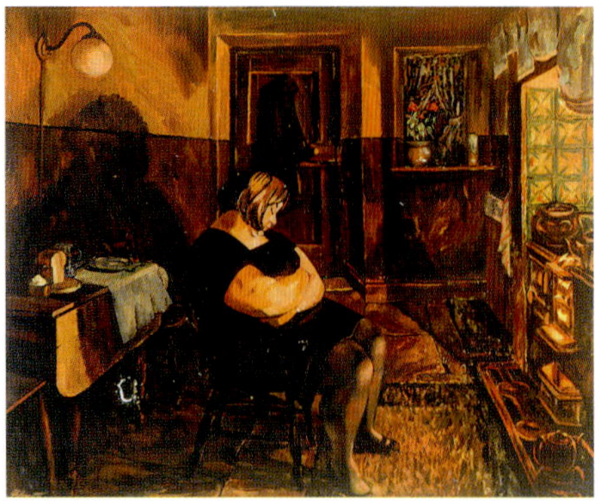

Brumfitt, George Edward 1917–1993
Aunty Hilda Waiting for Harry to Come Off Late Turn c.1950
oil on canvas 63.5 x 76
DONMG : 950.84

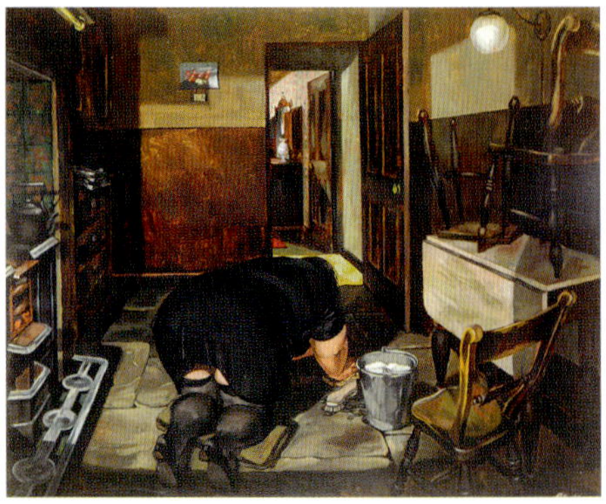

Brumfitt, George Edward 1917–1993
Hilda Fettling the Kitchen Floor c.1950
oil on canvas 64 x 76
DONMG : 951.84

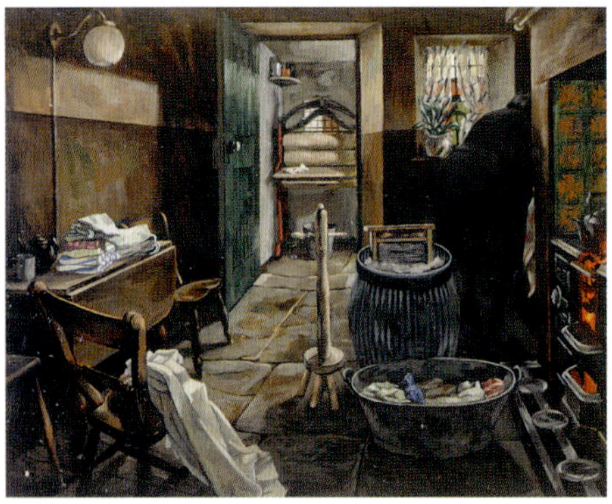

Brumfitt, George Edward 1917–1993
Aunty Hilda Washing c.1950
oil on canvas 63.5 x 76
DONMG : 952.84

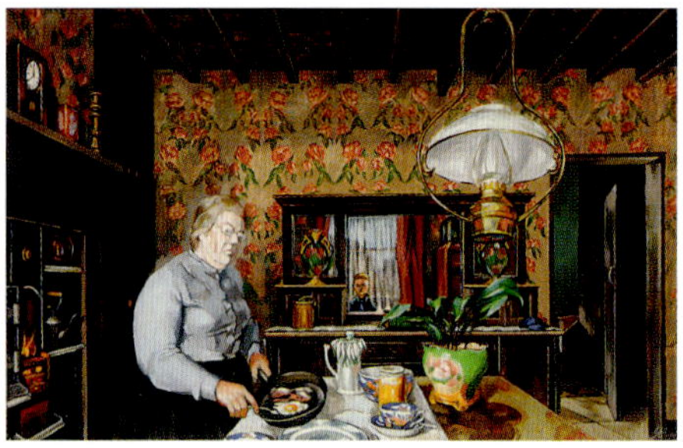

Brumfitt, George Edward 1917–1993
Things Past c.1950
oil on canvas 51 x 76
DONMG : 953.84

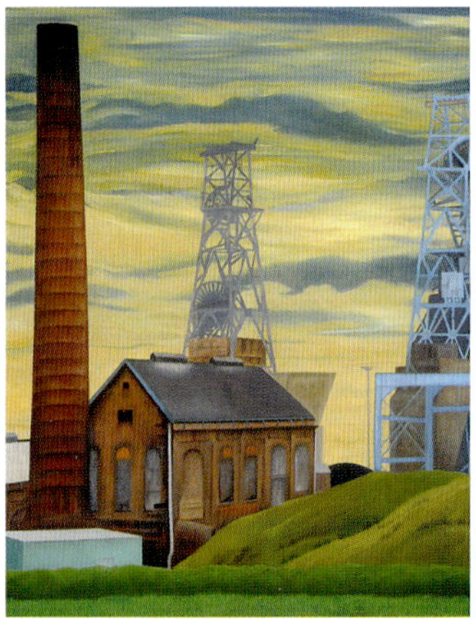

Buckle, Janet b.1945
The Sleeping Giant, Rossington, South Yorkshire 1996
oil on board 123 x 92.8
DONMG : 1997.39

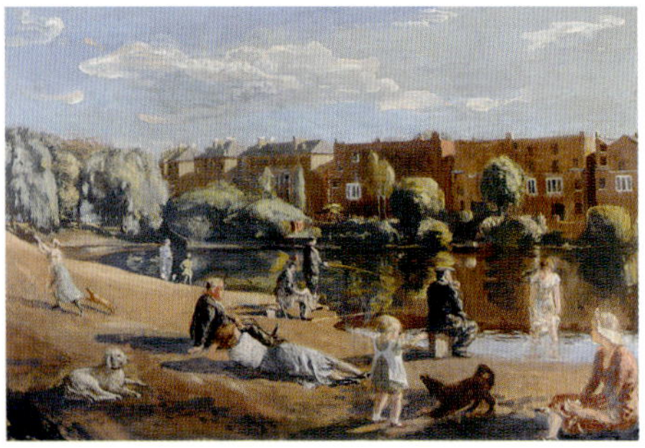

Burn, Rodney Joseph 1899–1984
Bank Holiday, Hampstead Heath, London
oil on canvas 81.5 x 116
DONMG : 806.78

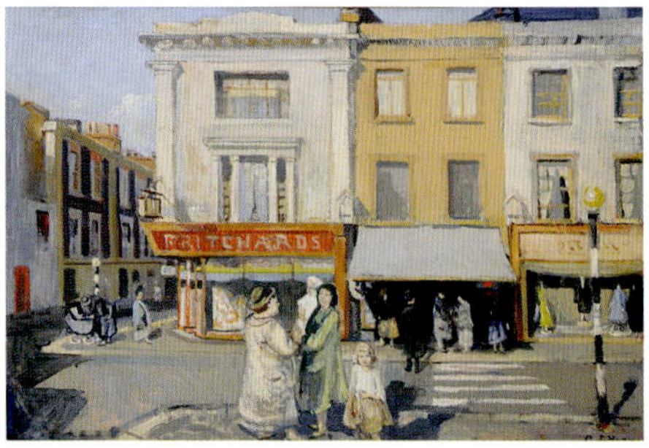

Burn, Rodney Joseph 1899–1984
King's Road, Chelsea, London
oil on panel 76 x 111
DONMG : 960.85

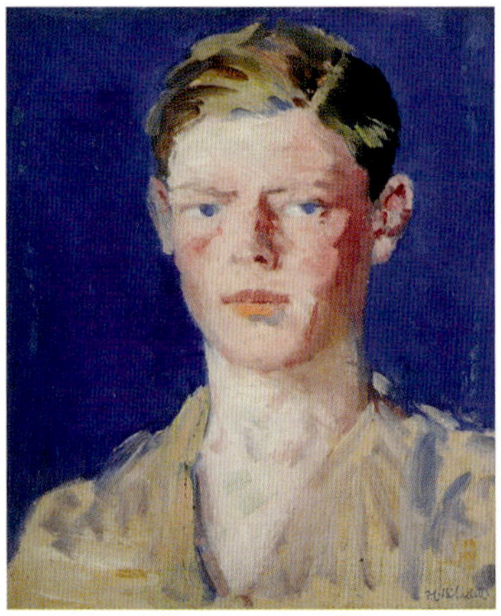

Cadell, Francis Campbell Boileau 1883–1937
Portrait of a Young Man
oil on canvas 56 x 35
DONMG : 1001.87

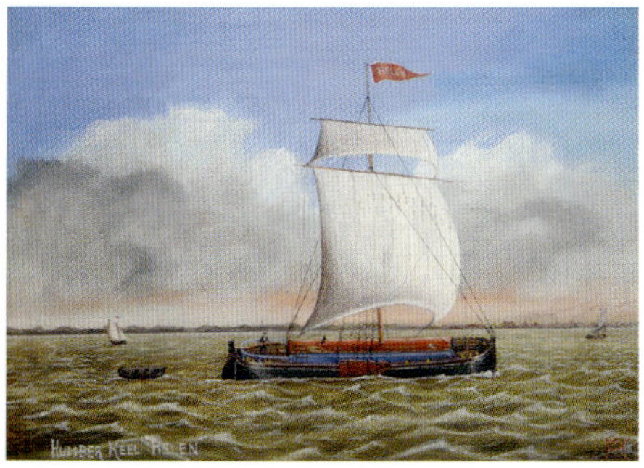

Chappell, Reuben 1870–1940
Humber Keel, 'Helen'
oil on canvas 31 x 44
PCF16

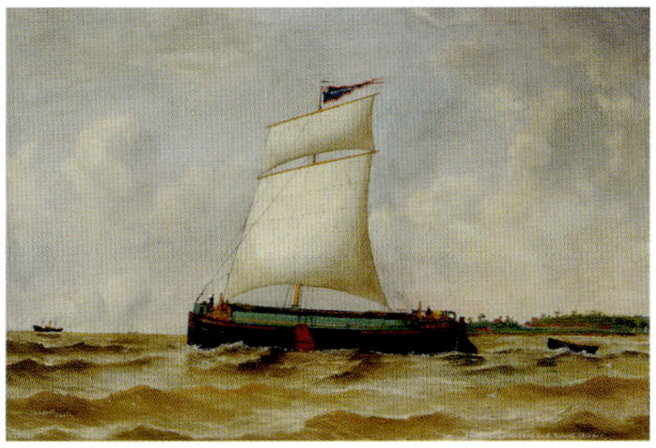

Chappell, Reuben 1870–1940
'William and Mary'
oil on canvas 50 x 75
DONMG : Chappell

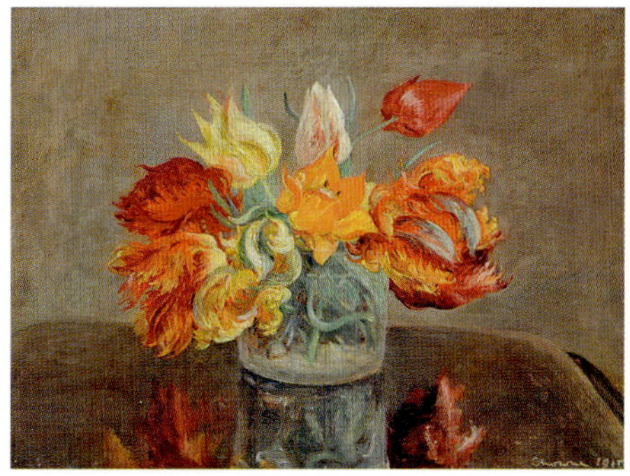

Chowne, Gerard 1875–1917
Flower Study
oil on canvas 29 x 40
DONMG : 476.63

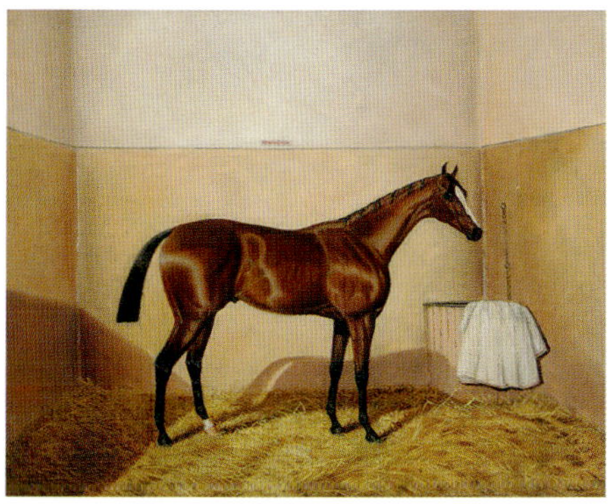

Clark, A.
'Flying Fox' 1899
oil on canvas 48.5 x 58.5
DONMG : 468.63

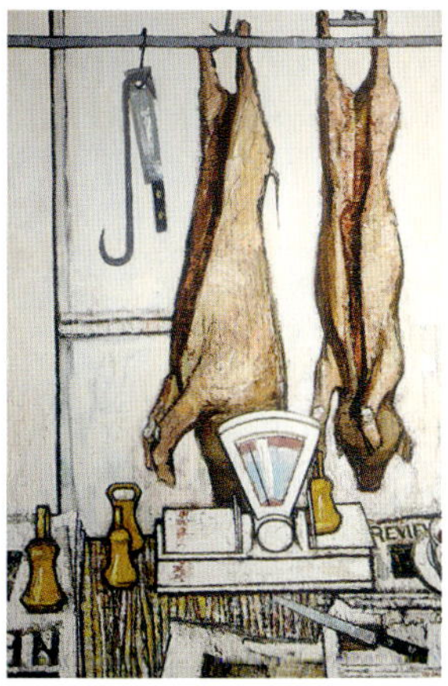

Coker, Peter 1926–2004
Butcher's Shop No.2 1955
oil on board 181 x 119.5
DONMG : 781.77

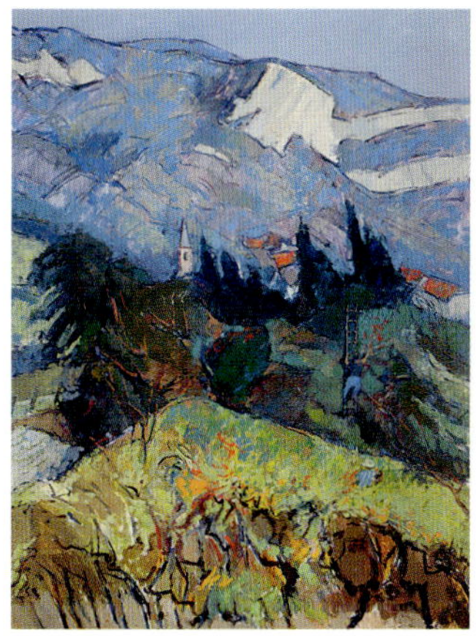

Coker, Peter 1926–2004
Picking Pears at Mouthier, France 1974
oil on canvas 122 x 91.5
DONMG : 2001.13.1

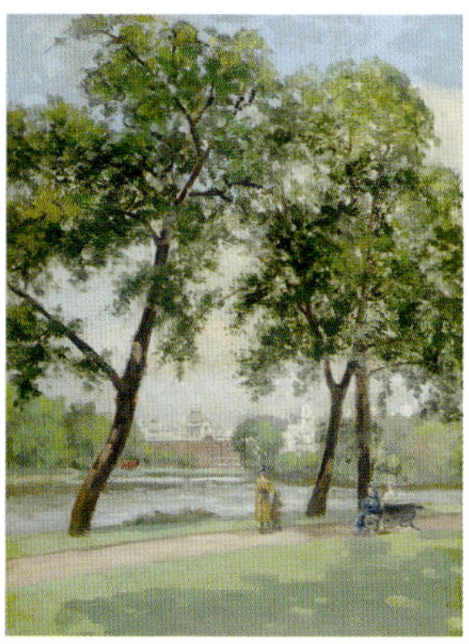

Craft, Percy Robert 1856–1934
A Glimpse of the Horseguards
oil on canvas 32 x 23.5
DONMG : 88.35

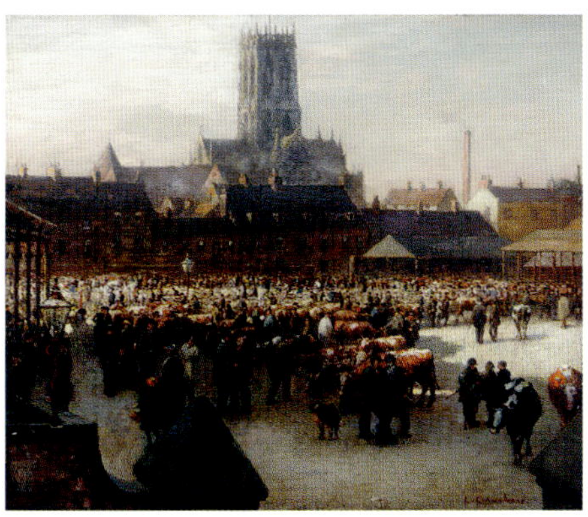

Crawshaw, Lionel Townsend 1864–1949
Cattle Market, Doncaster, South Yorkshire
c.1900
oil on canvas 85 x 100
DONMG : 16.16

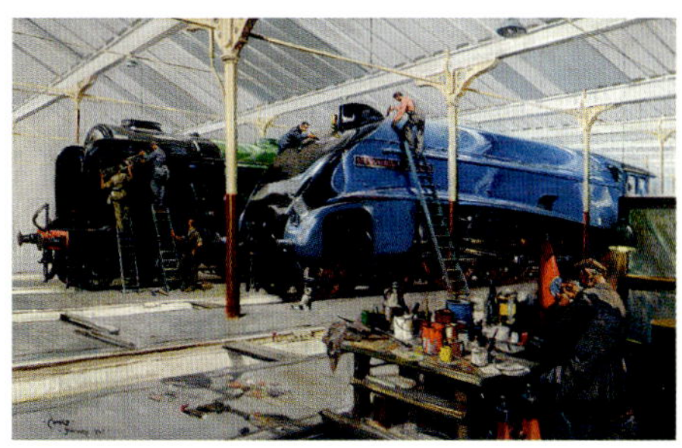

Cuneo, Terence Tenison 1907–1996
Giants Refreshed: Pacifics in the Doncaster Locomotive Works 1947
oil on canvas 78 x 122
DONMG : 2008.59

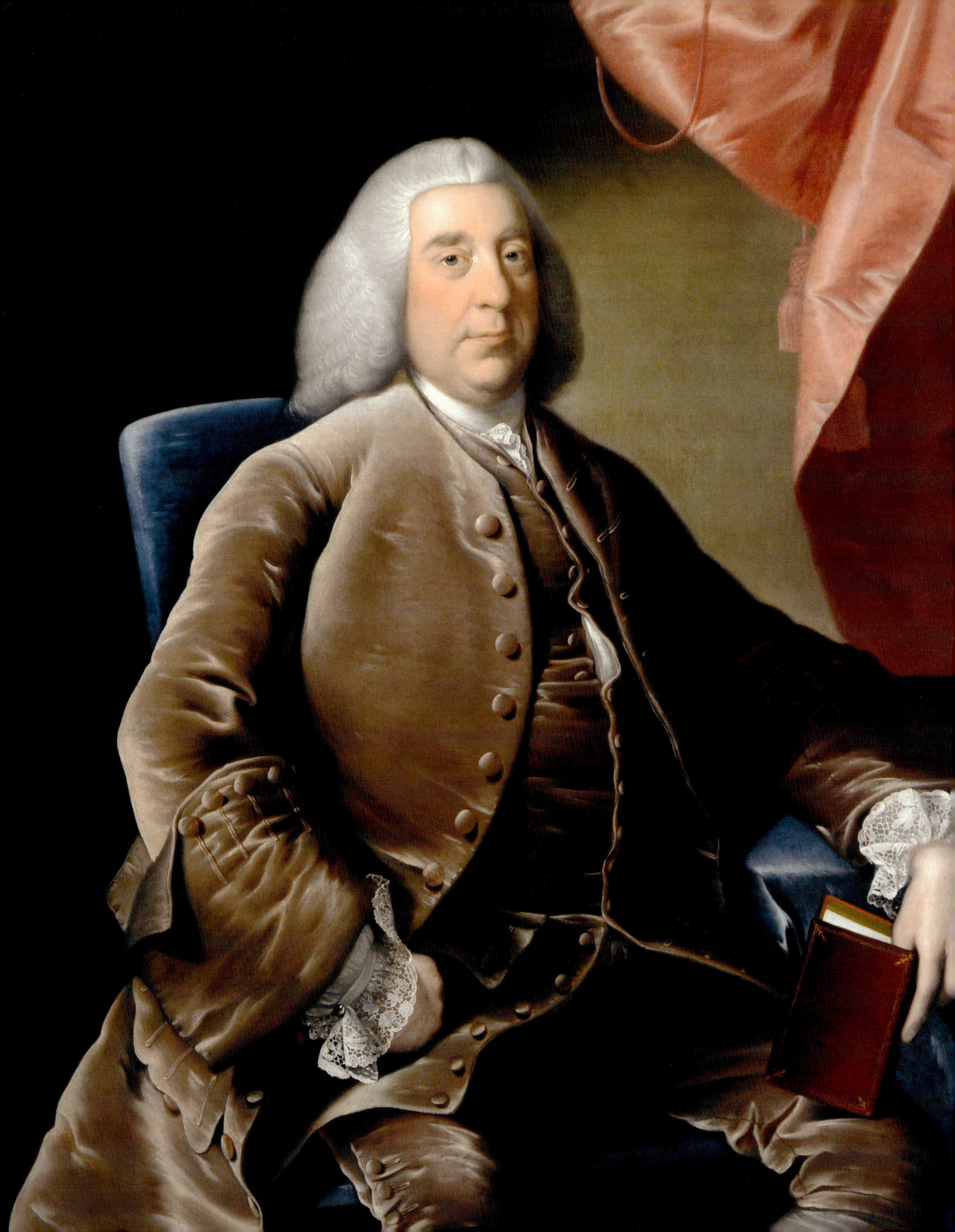

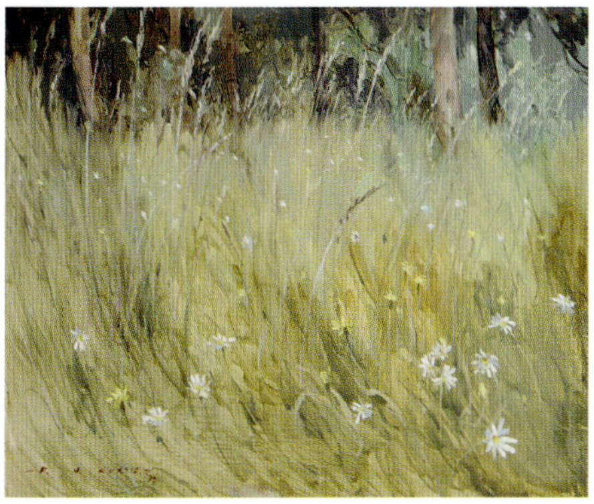

Curtis, David Jan b.1948
Long Grass 1979
oil on canvas 50 x 60
DONMG : 2005.13

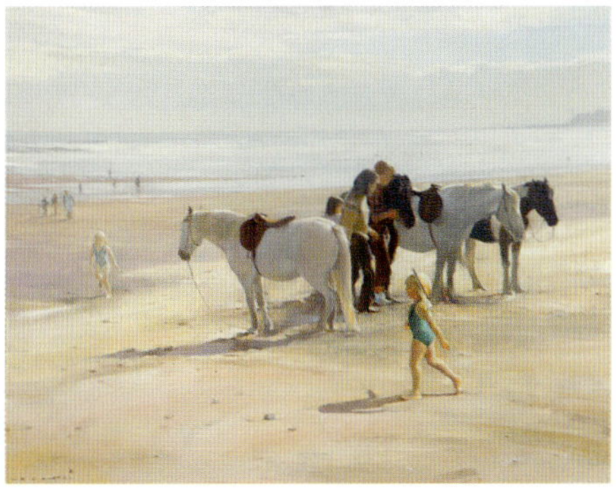

Curtis, David Jan b.1948
Rebecca, Low Tide, Sandsend, Whitby, North Yorkshire 1989
oil on canvas 60 x 75
DONMG : 1016.90

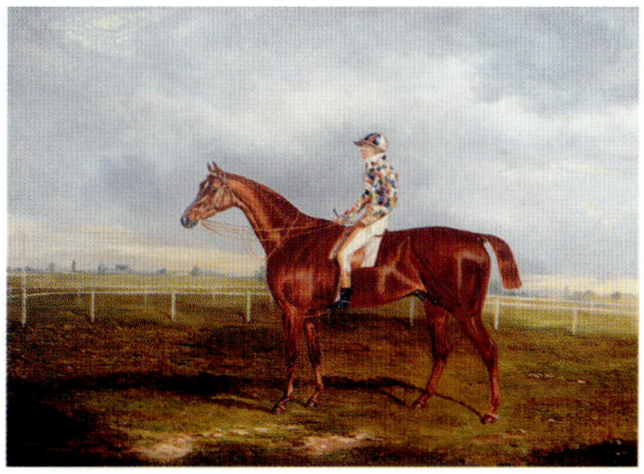

Dalby, David 1794–1836
'Barefoot' 1828
oil on canvas 54 x 75
DONMG : 819.79

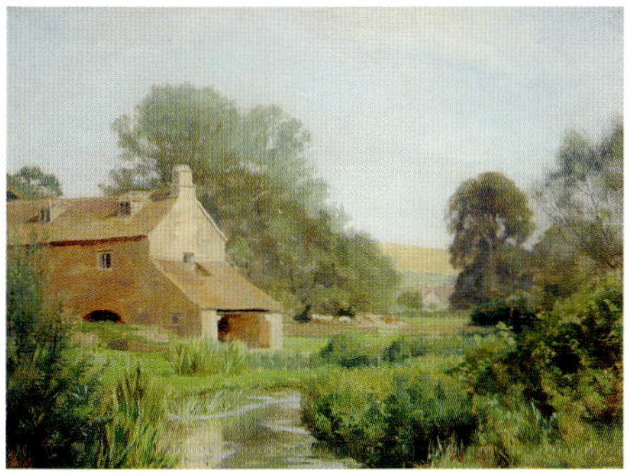

Davis, Joseph Barnard 1861–1943
Chedworth, Gloucestershire
oil on canvas 45 x 59
DONMG : 141.43

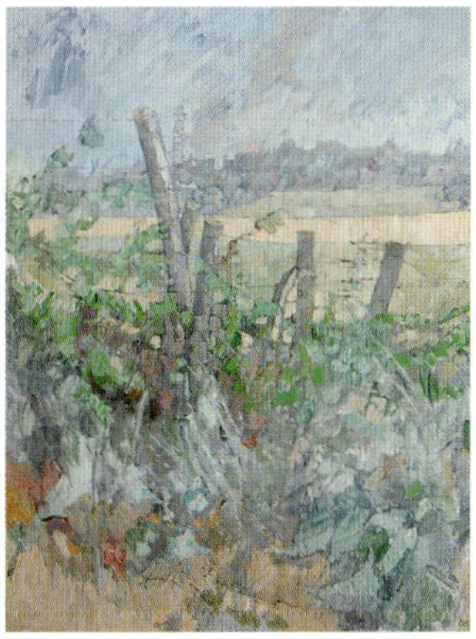

de Grey, Roger 1918–1995
From Camer Wood, Scotland
oil on canvas 120 x 90
DONMG : 805.78

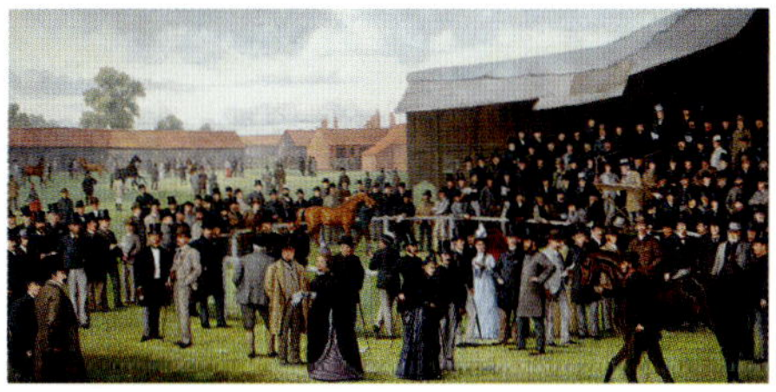

Dickinson, Lowes Cato 1819–1908
Yearling Sale at Doncaster, South Yorkshire c.1885
oil on canvas 127 x 256
DONMG : 656.75

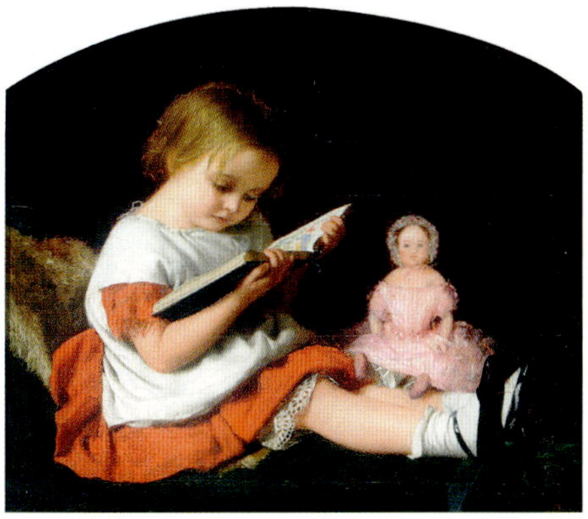

Dobson, William Charles Thomas 1817–1898
Fairy Tales
oil on canvas 46.5 x 53.5
DONMG : 776.77

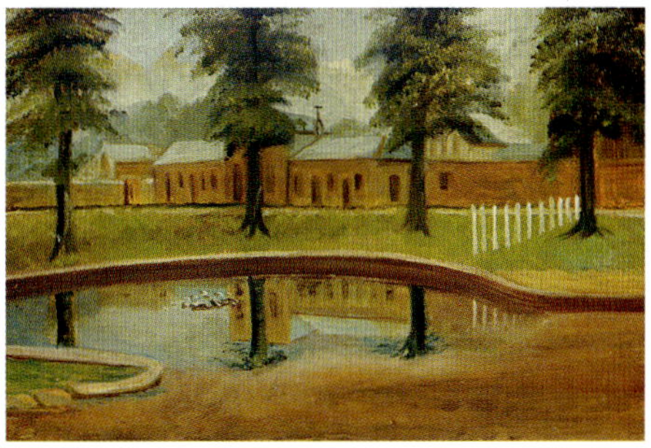

Donald, Richard Watson Phillip 1865–1937
The Horseshoe Pond c.1900
oil on panel 15 x 22.3
DONMG : 517.64

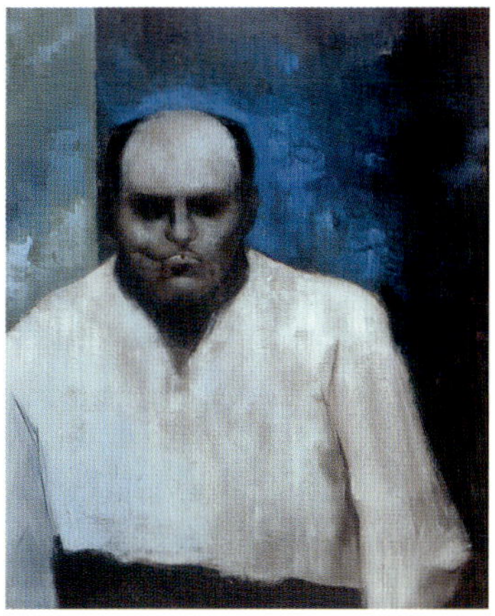

Drury, Paul 1903–1987
Man's Head in Blue c.1963
oil on canvas 71 x 59
DONMG : 473.63

Facing page: Wright, Joseph of Derby, 1734–1797, *William Brooke (1694–1763)* (detail), 1760, Doncaster Museum Service, (p. 110)

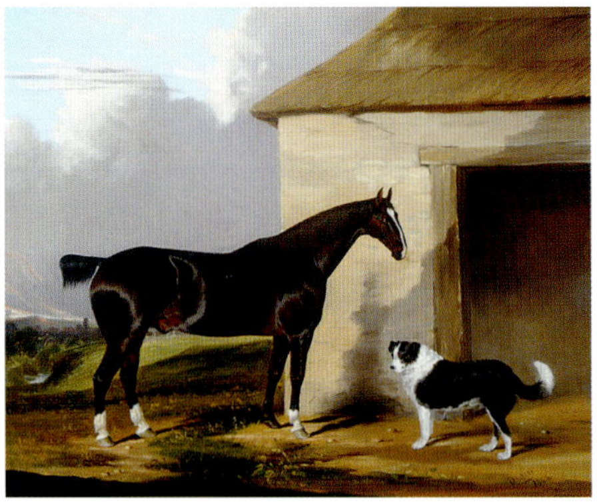

Dunn, Joseph 1806–1860
'Sportsman' 1844
oil on canvas 63 x 75
DONMG : 921.83

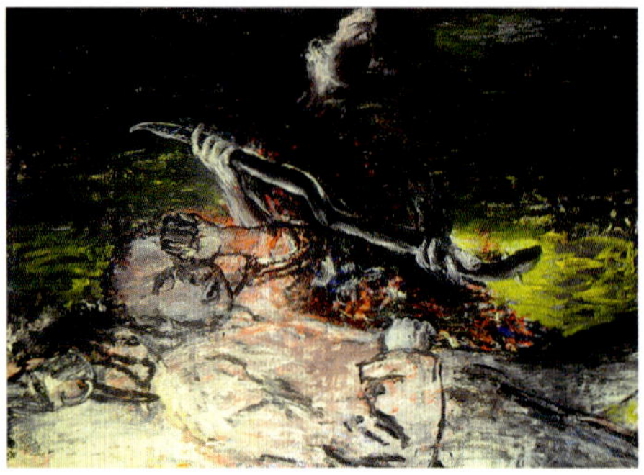

Edmondson, Simon b.1955
The Night c.1986
oil on canvas 150 x 203
DONMG : 987.86

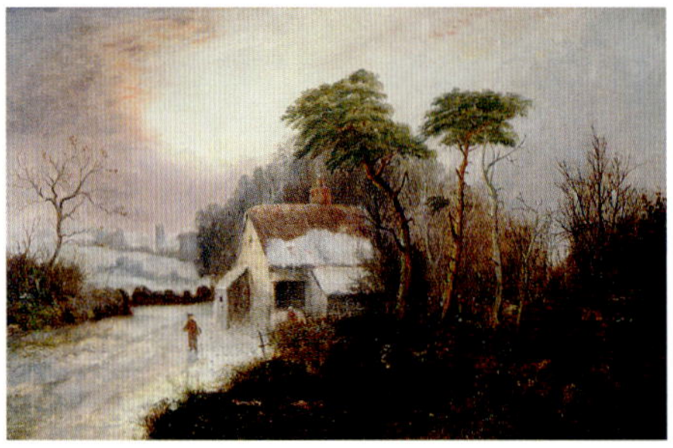

Edwards, J. G.
Evening Scene
oil on canvas 49.5 x 75
DONMG : 655.75

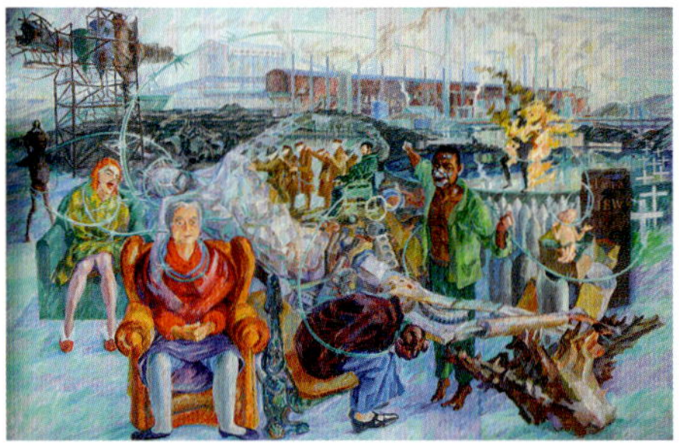

Etheridge, Peter d.1998
Pietà c.1980
acrylic on panel 152.5 x 230
DONMG : 1997.42

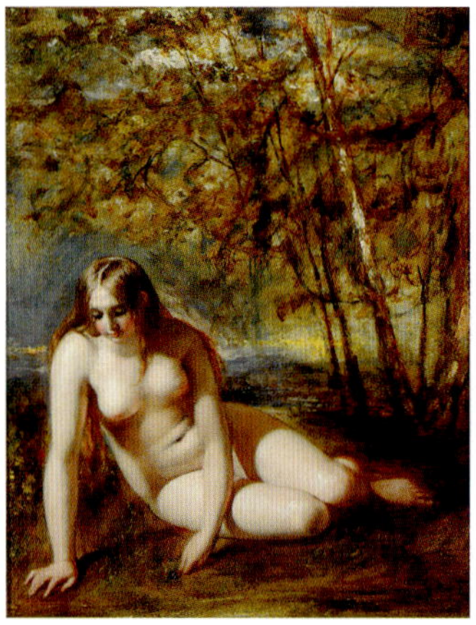

Etty, William 1787–1849
Eve at the Fountain
oil on board 65 x 49
DONMG : 221.49

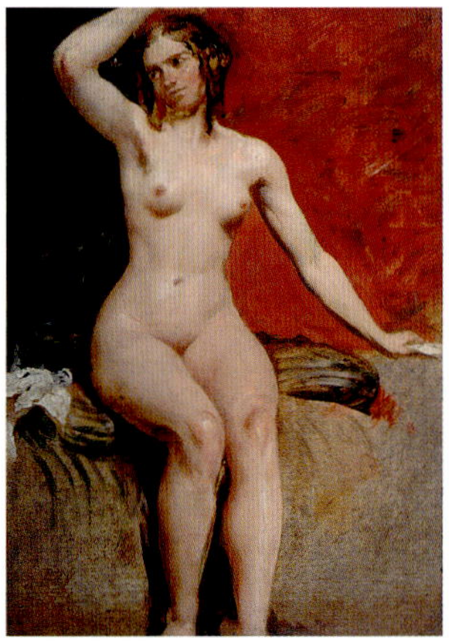

Etty, William 1787–1849
Nude
oil on canvas 51 x 36
DONMG : 264.55

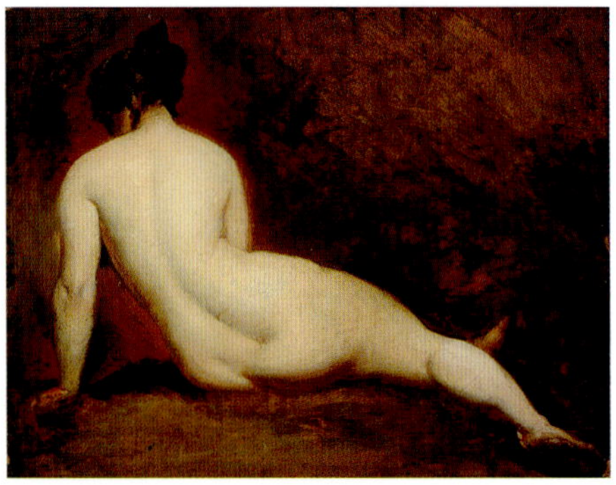

Etty, William 1787–1849
Nude Study
oil on canvas 38.5 x 48
DONMG : 13.14

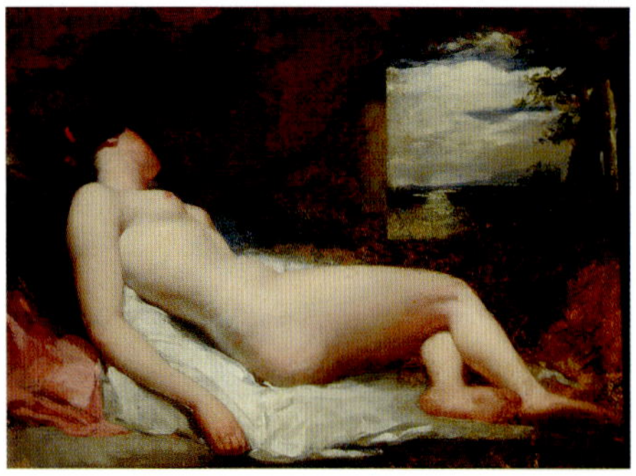

Etty, William 1787–1849
Reclining Nude
oil on board 36 x 47
DONMG : 241.53

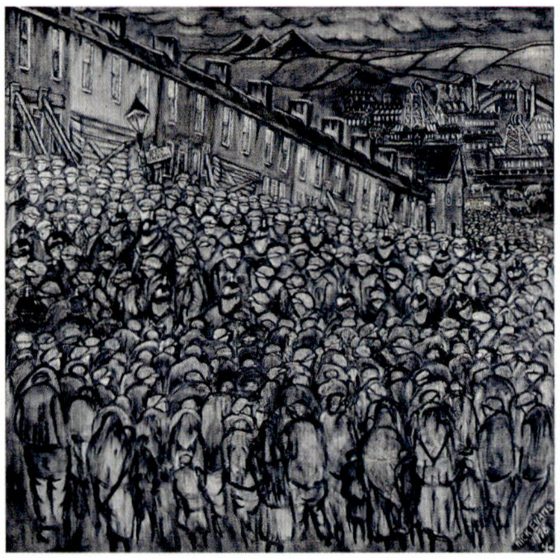

Evans, Nicholas 1907–2004
Trouble in the Twenties 1978
oil on board 123 x 123
DONMG : 822.79

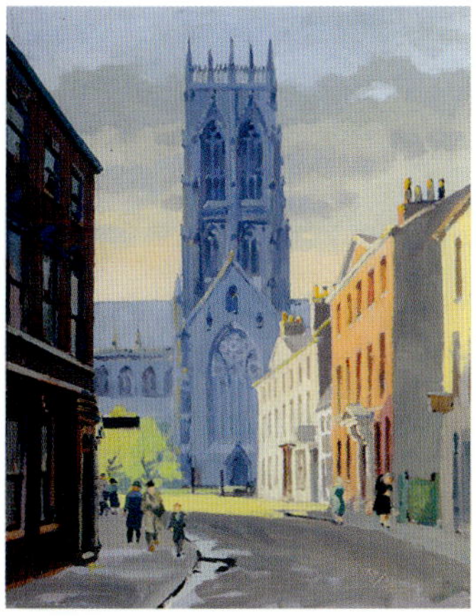

Fish, Harry 1894–1971
St George's Gate, Doncaster, South Yorkshire 1959
oil on canvas 48 x 38
DONMG : 478.63

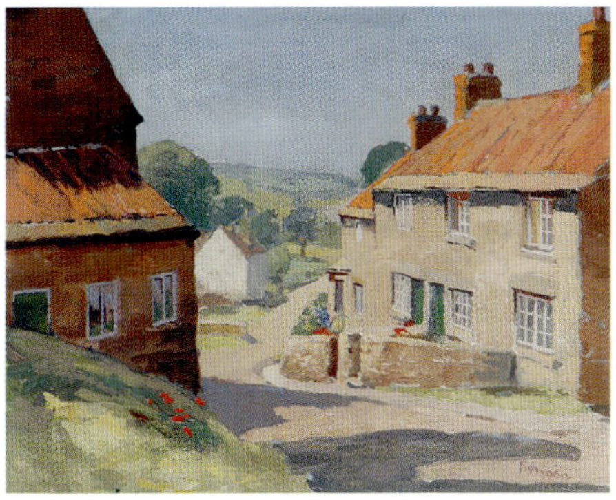

Fish, Harry 1894–1971
Hooton Pagnell, South Yorkshire 1960
oil on canvas 39.5 x 49 (E)
DONMG : 402.61

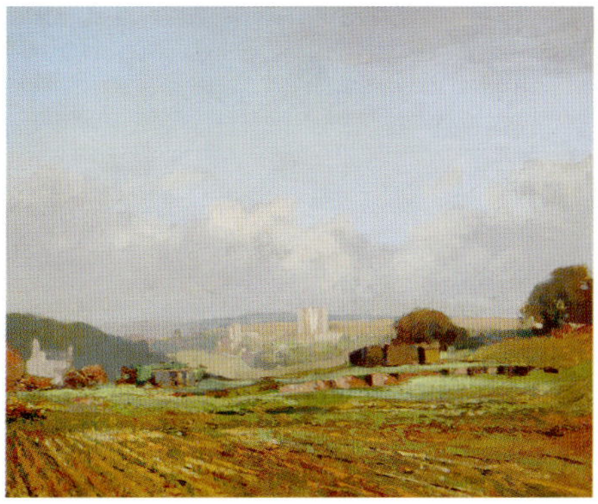

Fish, Harry 1894–1971
Conisbrough, South Yorkshire
oil on canvas 63 x 76
DONMG : 965.86

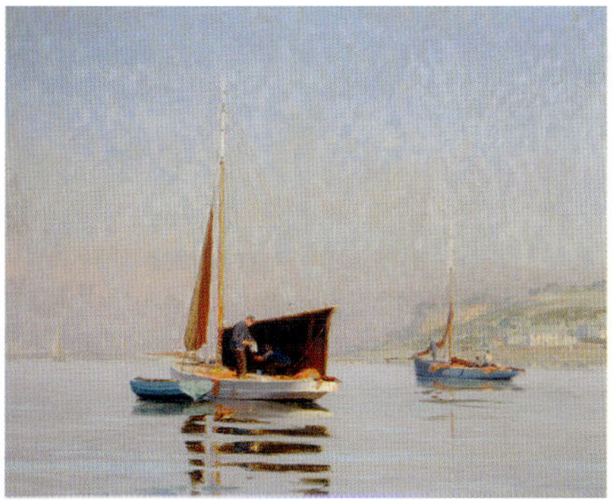

Gilchrist, Philip Thomson 1865–1956
Tarring the Main Sail 1934
oil on canvas 63 x 75.5
DONMG : 98.36

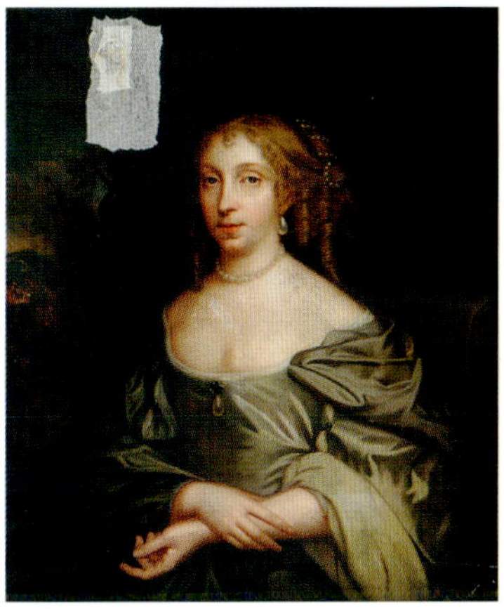

Glasgow, Alexander c.1840–1894
Lady Cooke
oil on canvas 92 x 77
PCF8

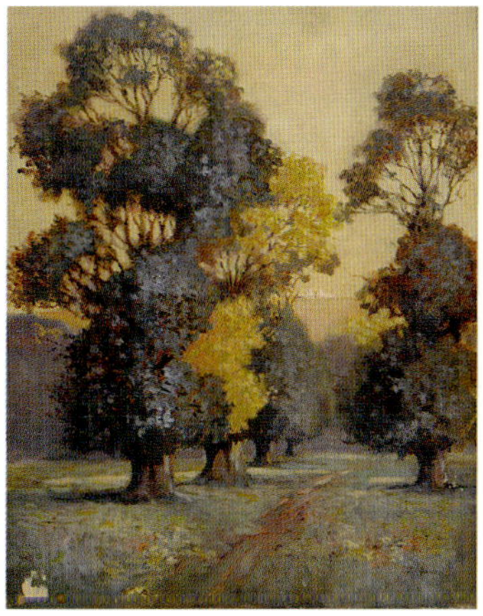

Glass, Frederick James 1881–1930
Stratford Park
oil on canvas 46 x 36
DONMG : 773.77

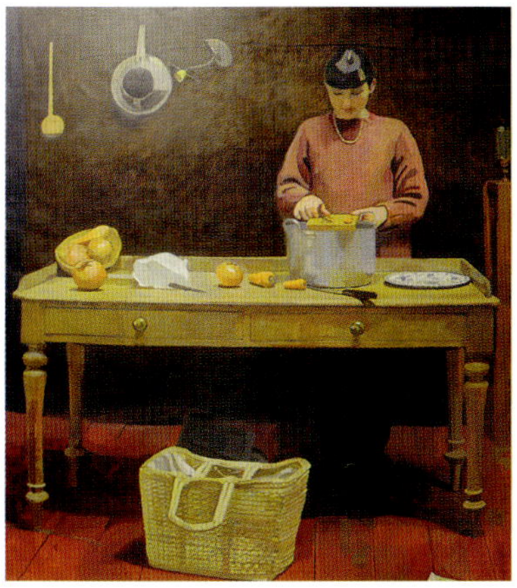

Gopal-Chowdhury, Paul b.1949
Preparing a Meal 1981
oil on canvas 213.5 x 183
DONMG : 919.83

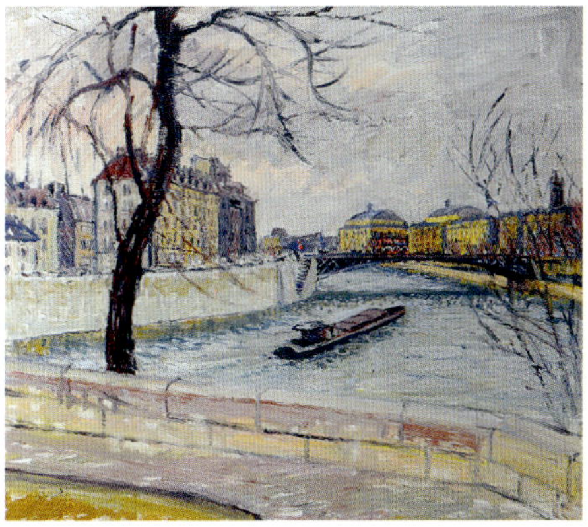

Gore, Frederick John Pym 1913–2009
New Year's Day, Paris 1976
oil on canvas 81 x 91
DONMG : 807.78

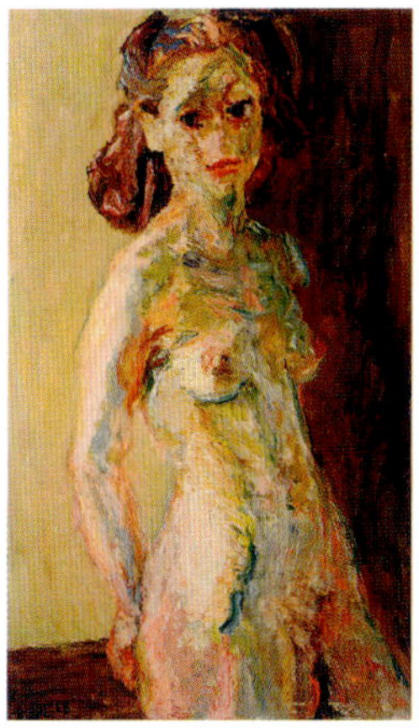

Gotlib, Henryk 1890–1966
Nude c.1950
oil on canvas 82.5 x 48
DONMG : 518.65

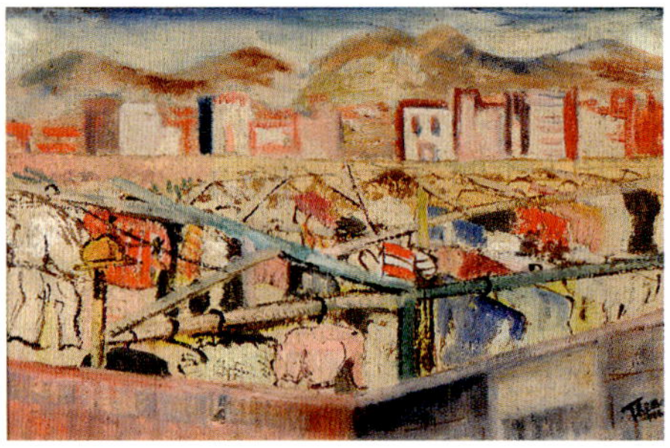

Haberfield, Théa
Paisagem (Landscape) c.1949
oil on canvas 35 x 52.5
DONMG : 231.49

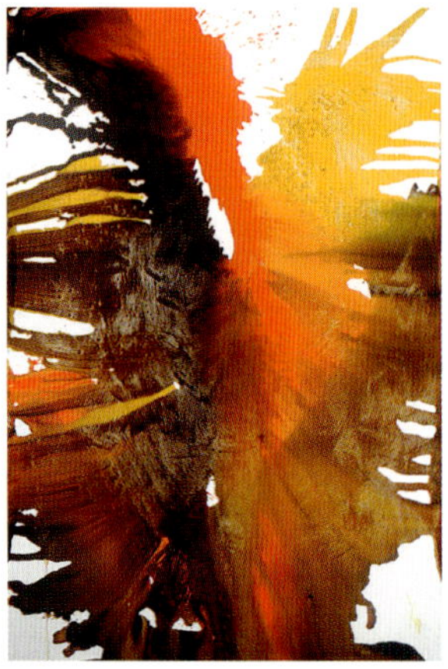

Haddock, Edwin Aldridge 1921–1996
Spartacus
oil on board 181 x 120
DONMG : 530.68

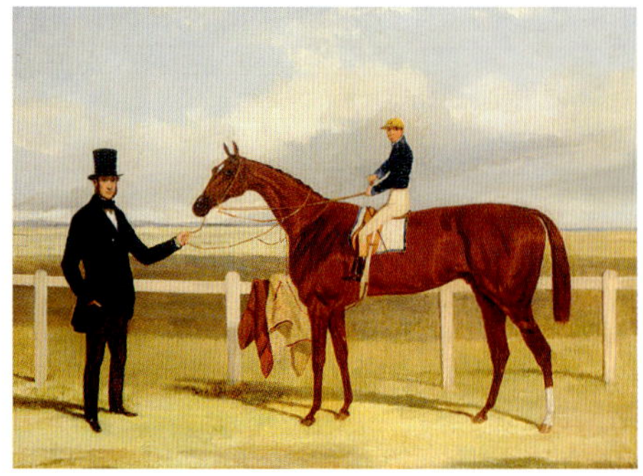

Hall, Harry 1814–1896
'Hungerford' 1828
oil on canvas 58.5 x 76
DONMG : 809.78

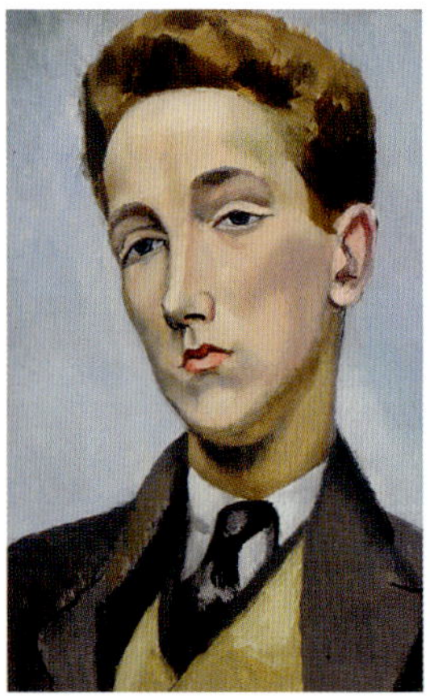

Hamnett, Nina 1890–1956
Rupert Doone (1903–1923), Dancer 1922–1923
oil on canvas 45 x 29
DONMG : 490.63

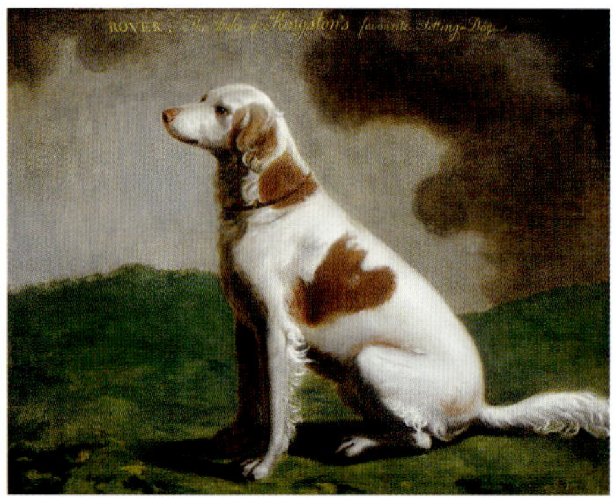

Haugh, George 1756–1827
'Rover', the Duke of Kingston's Favourite Setting Dog 1776
oil on canvas 100 x 125
DONMG : 1025.91

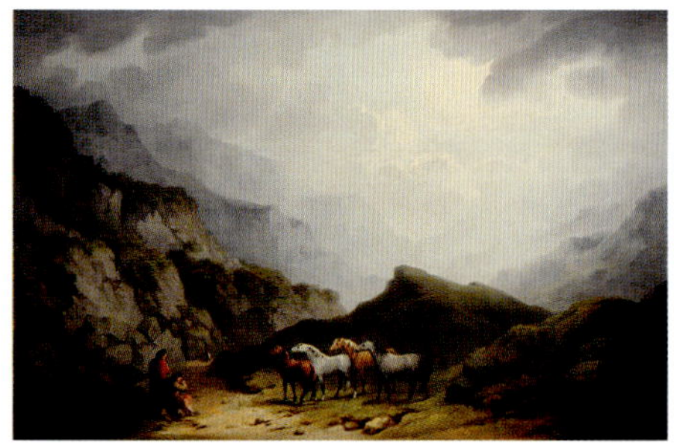

Haugh, George 1756–1827
View up Glen Kinglass, West Highlands, Scotland 1807
oil on canvas 60 x 90
DONMG : 1021.91

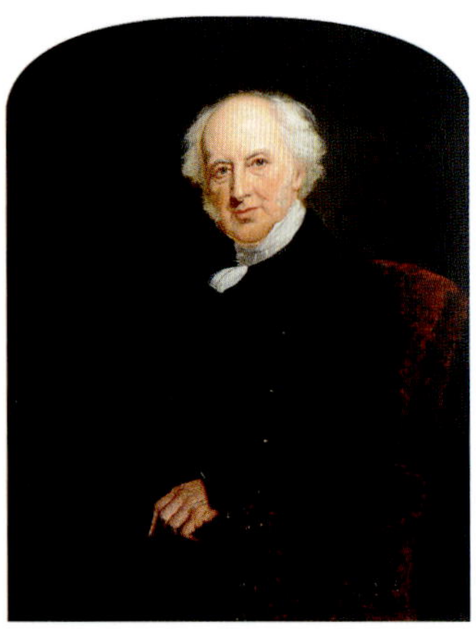

Havell, Edmund the younger 1819–1894
Reverend A. B. Wrightson (1793–1878)
oil on canvas 90 x 69
DONMG : 827.80

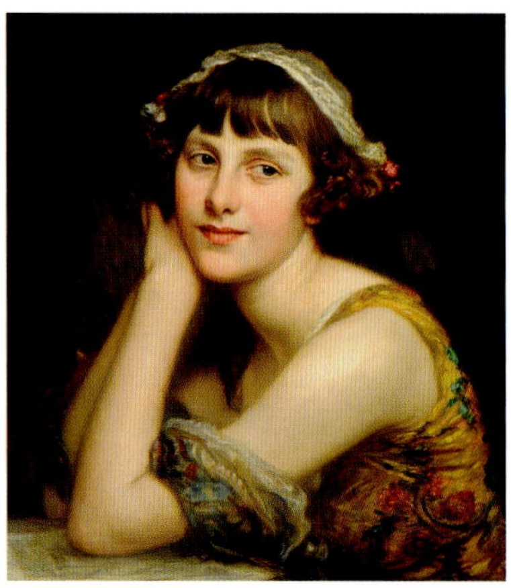

Hay, Peter Alexander 1866–1952
Romance
oil on canvas 50 x 43
DONMG : 51.29

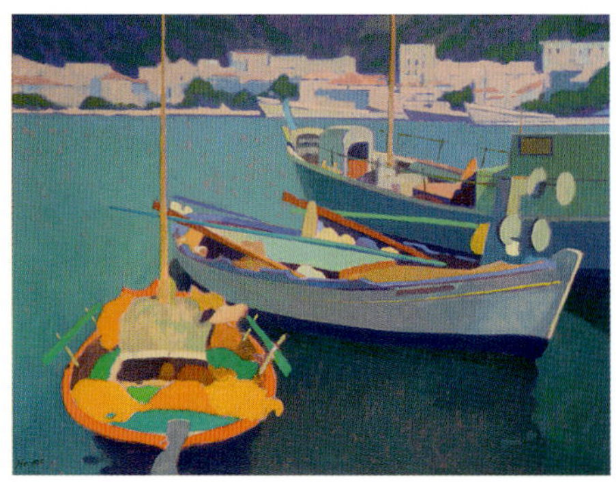

Hayes, Colin Graham Frederick 1919–2003
Samos, Greece
acrylic on canvas 70 x 90
DONMG : 1017.90

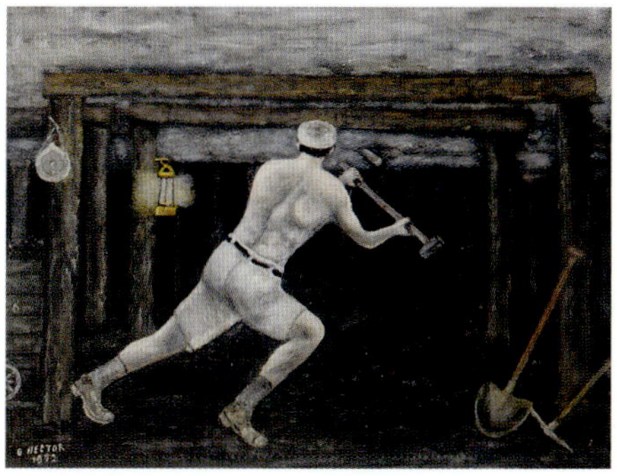

Hector, George active 1972–2006
Miner Working Underground 1972
oil on board 50 x 65
DONMG : 1999.33

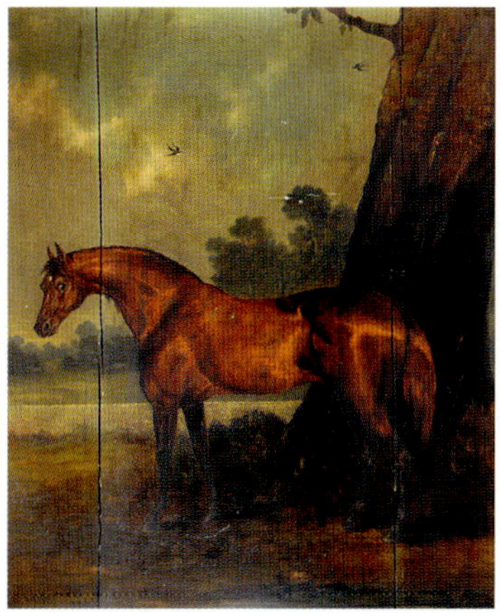

Hepworth, C. H.
Horse 1865
oil on board 102 x 84
DONMG : 715.75

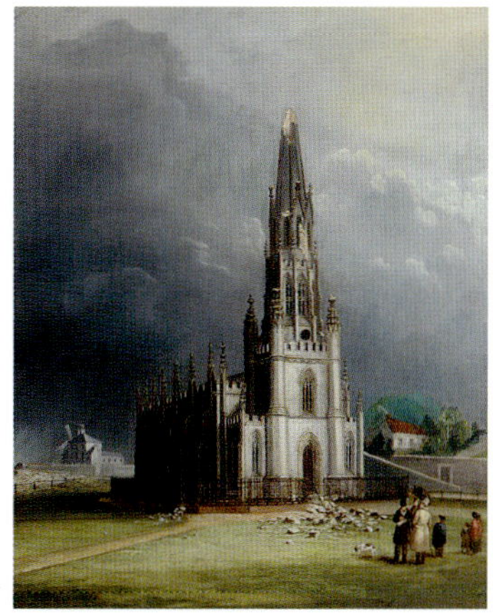

Hepworth, John
Christ Church, Doncaster, South Yorkshire, Struck by Lighting 1836
oil on canvas 72 x 59
DONMG : 448.63

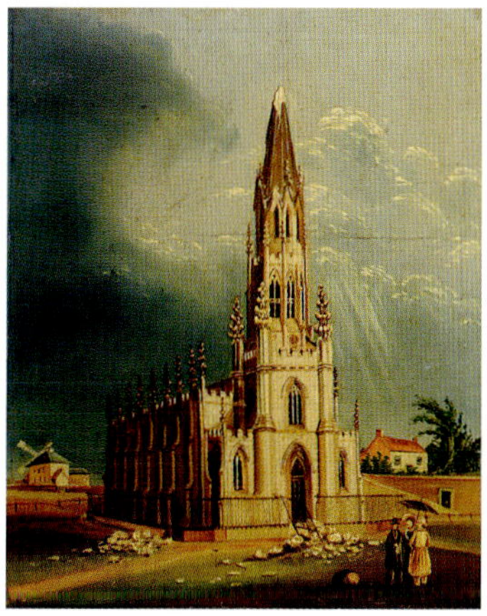

Hepworth, John
Christ Church, Doncaster, South Yorkshire, from the West, Showing the Spire Struck by Lightning, 1836 c.1836
oil on canvas 38.5 x 30.5
DONMG : 661.75

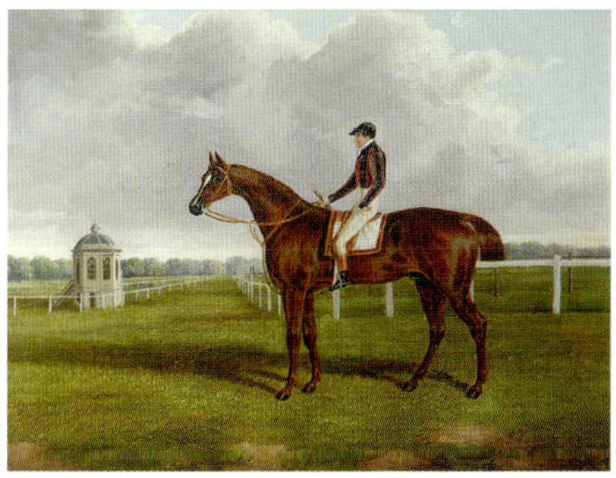

Herring, John Frederick I 1795–1865
'St Patrick' 1820
oil on canvas 35 x 45 (E)
DONMG : 442.62

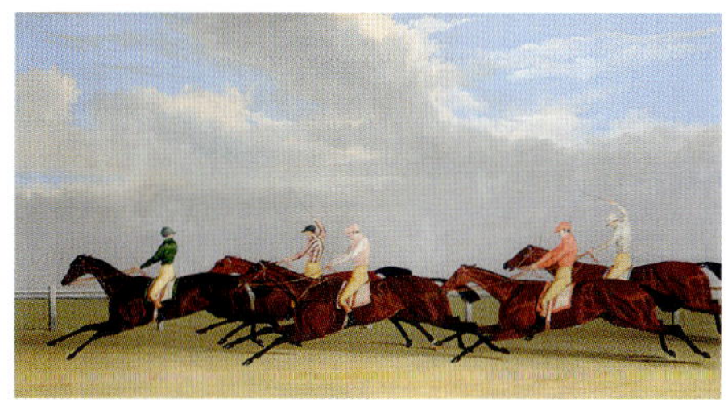

Herring, John Frederick I 1795–1865
Finish of the 1827 Gold Cup 1827
oil on canvas 49 x 89.5
DONMG : 447.63

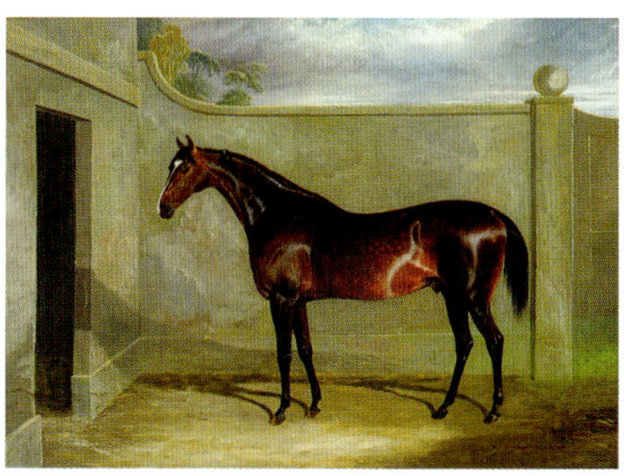

Herring, John Frederick I 1795–1865
'Filho da puta' 1828
oil on canvas 60 x 76
DONMG : 392.60

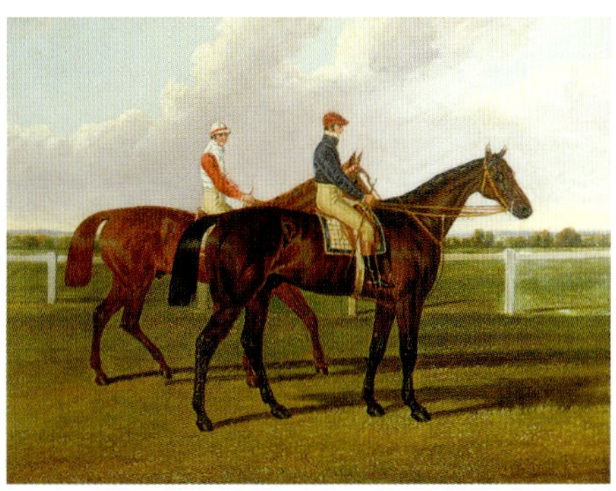

Herring, John Frederick I 1795–1865
'Charles XII' and 'Euclid'
oil on canvas 33 x 44
DONMG : 444.62

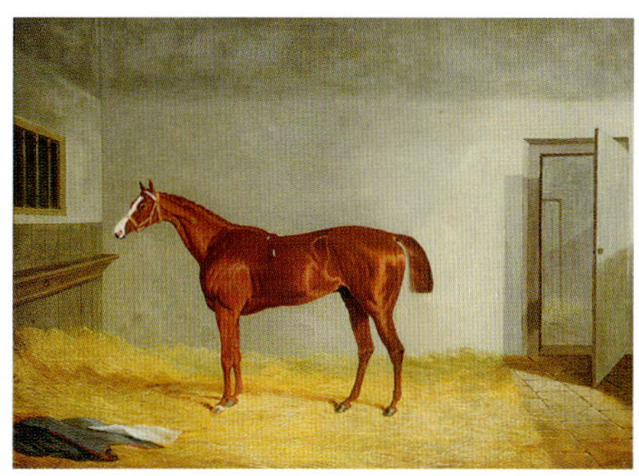

Herring, John Frederick I 1795–1865
'Colonel'
oil on canvas 56 x 76
DONMG : 393.60

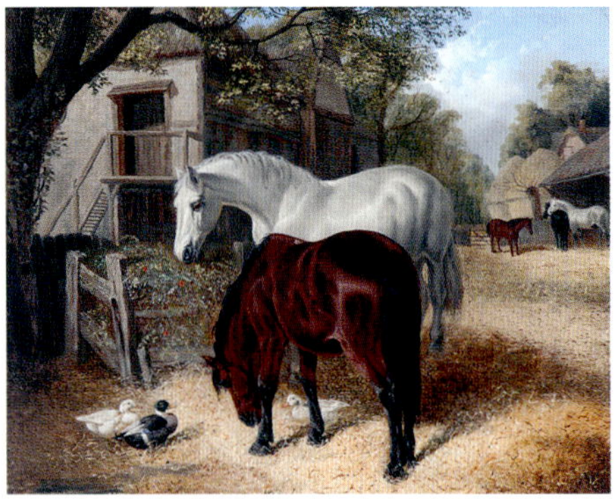

Herring, John Frederick I 1795–1865
Farm Scene with Horses
oil on canvas 34 x 43
DONMG : 446.62

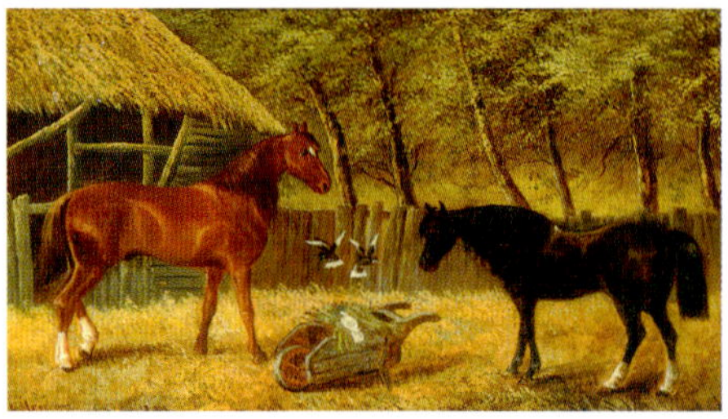

Herring, John Frederick I 1795–1865
Farmyard Scene
oil on canvas 25 x 45
DONMG : 458.63

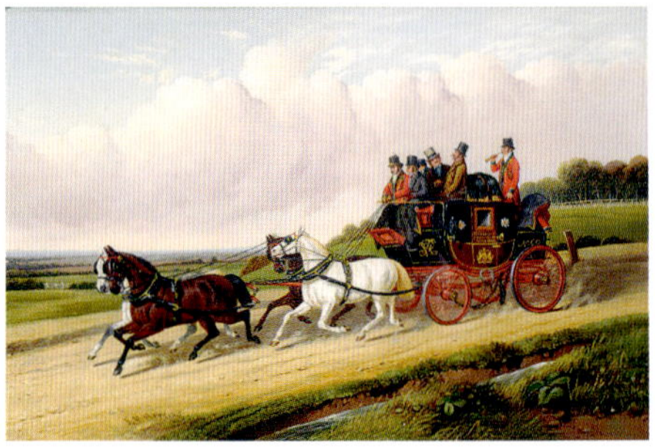

Herring, John Frederick I 1795–1865
Halifax Royal Mail Coach, Doncaster, South Yorkshire
oil on canvas 41 x 61
DONMG : 376.60

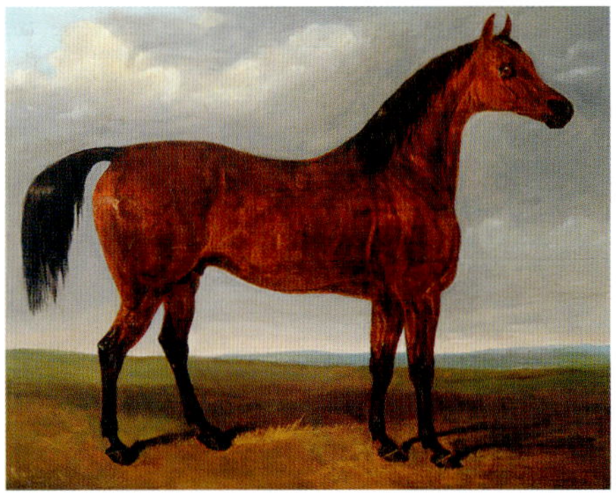

Herring, John Frederick I 1795–1865
Horse
oil on canvas 53 x 66
DONMG : 753.76

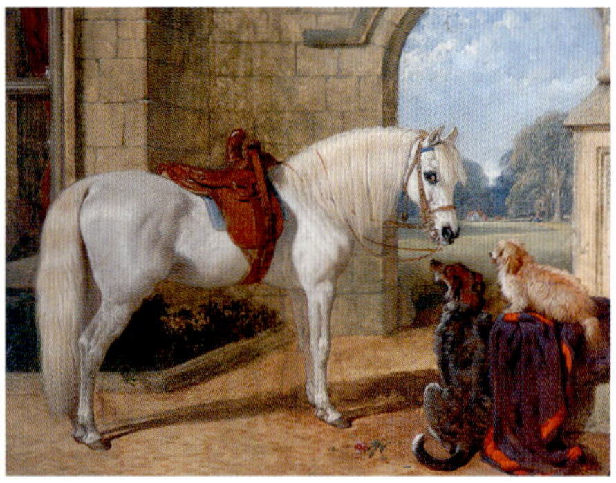

Herring, John Frederick I 1795–1865
'Imaum', a Welsh Arab
oil on canvas 34 x 44
DONMG : 832.80

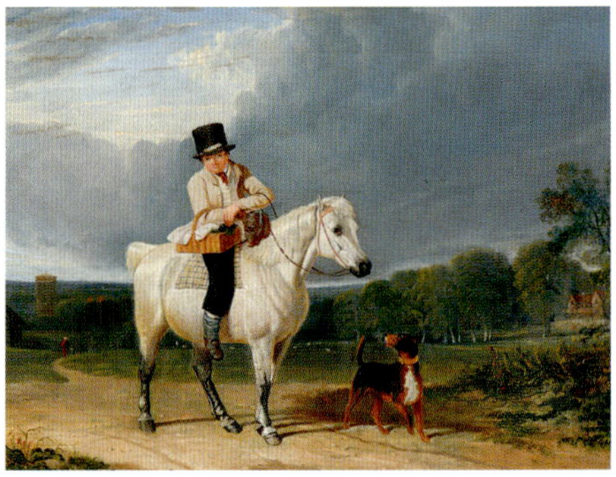

Herring, John Frederick I 1795–1865
Man on a Grey Pony
oil on canvas 33 x 47
DONMG : 833.80

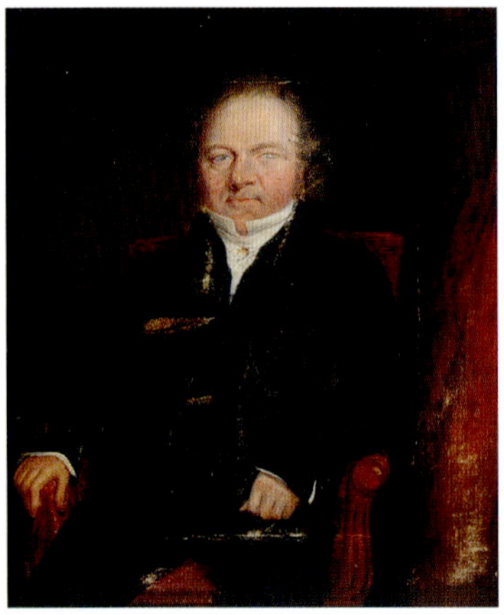

Herring, John Frederick I 1795–1865
Richard Wood
oil on canvas 26.5 x 22.5
DONMG : 3.12

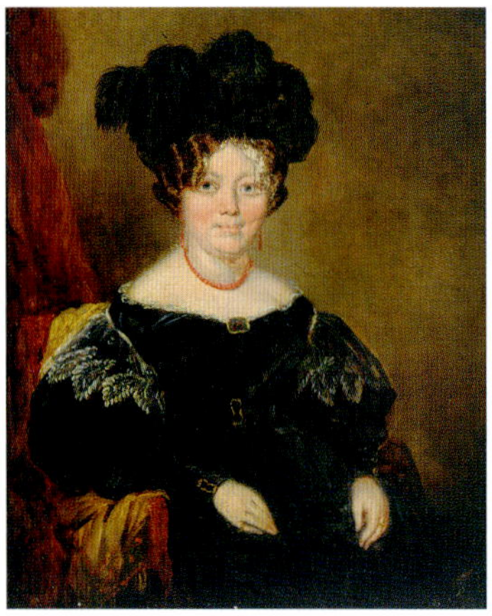

Herring, John Frederick I 1795–1865
Mrs Wood
oil on canvas 26.5 x 22.5
DONMG : 4.12

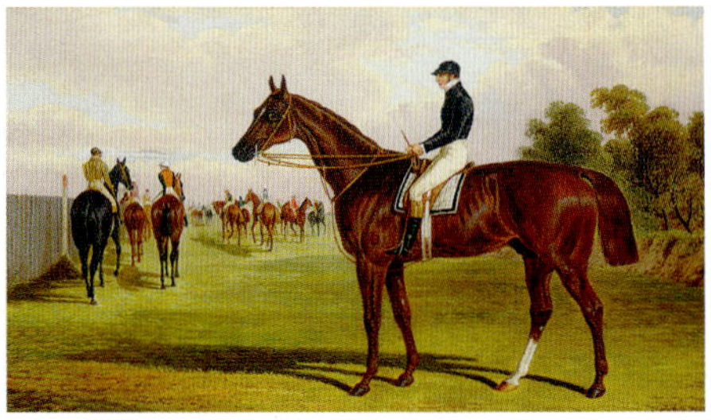

Herring, John Frederick I 1795–1865
'Mundig'
oil on canvas 28 x 49
DONMG : 445.62

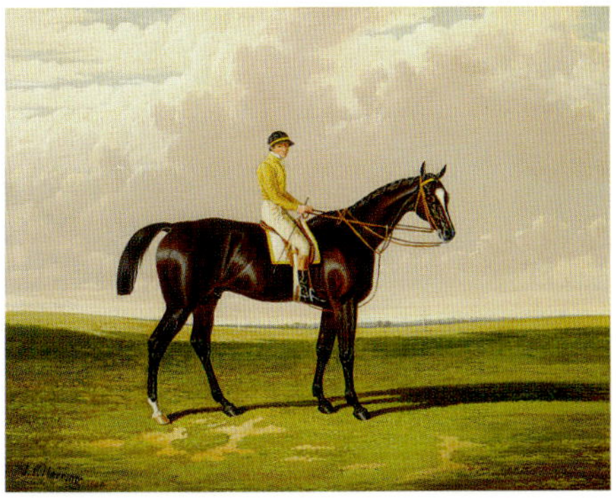

Herring, John Frederick I 1795–1865
'Touchstone'
oil on canvas 40.3 x 50.5
DONMG : 443.62

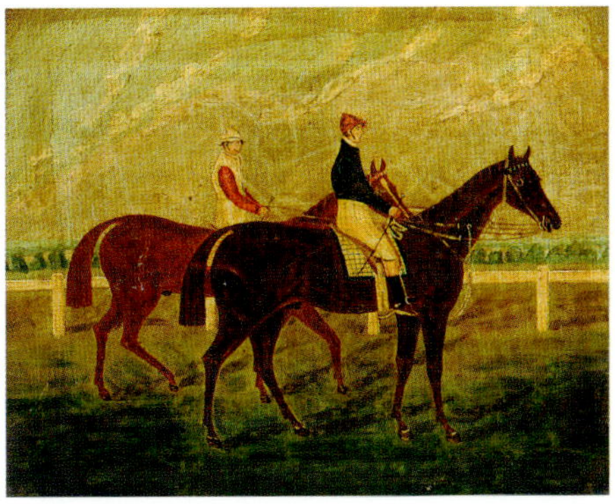

Herring, John Frederick I (after) 1795–1865
'Charles XII' and 'Euclid' 1840
oil on canvas 37 x 44
DONMG : 2008.44

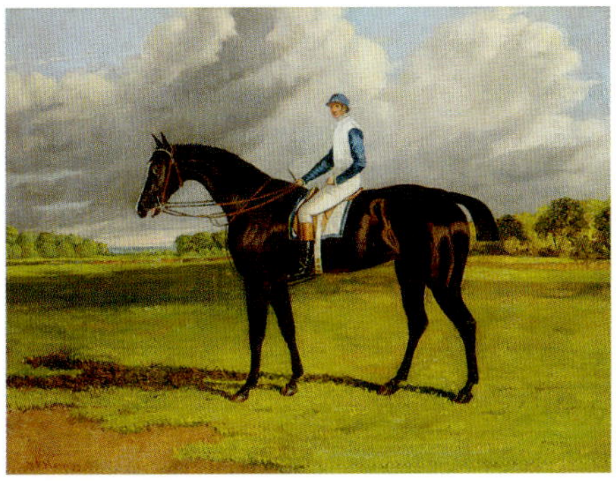

Herring, John Frederick I (style of)
'Filho da puta'
oil on canvas 34.5 x 45
DONMG : 311.58

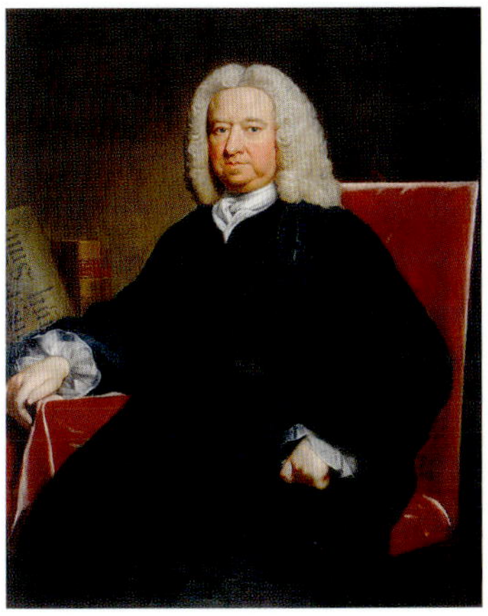

Highmore, Joseph (attributed to)
1692–1780
William Wrightson mid-18th C
oil on canvas 124 x 99
PCF2

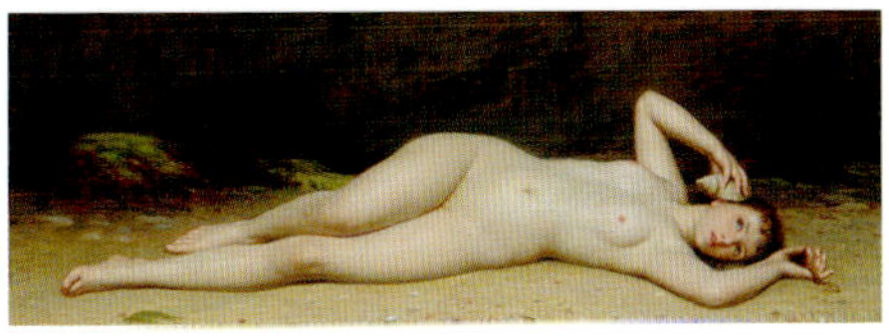

Hill, Arthur c.1829–1894
The Shell 1884
oil on canvas 25 x 65
DONMG : 459.63

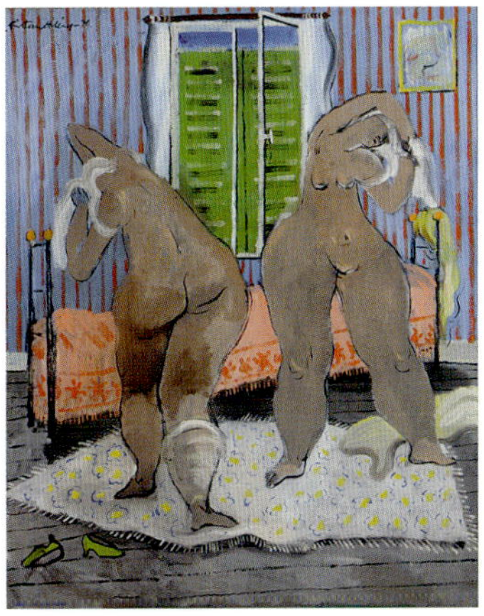

Hillier, Tristram Paul 1905–1983
Nudes in a Bedroom 1979
oil on canvas 90 x 73
DONMG : 519.65

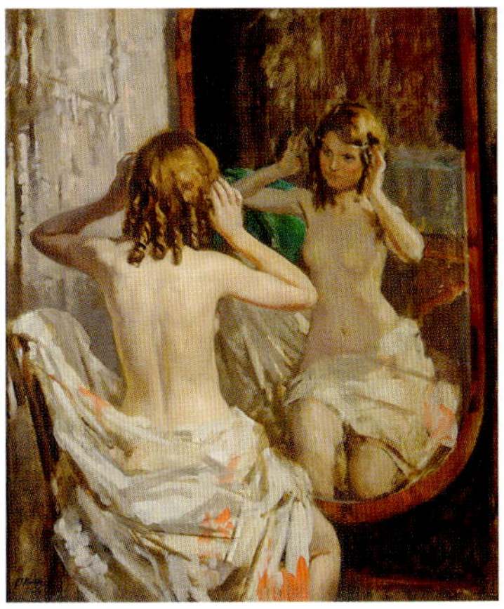

Hodge, Francis Edwin 1883–1949
Vanity
oil on canvas 74 x 62
DONMG : 103.37

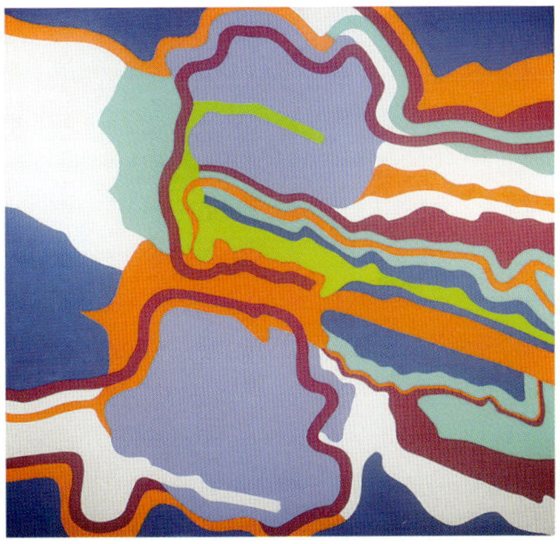

Howlin, John b.1941
Staten, 1962 1962
acrylic on canvas 168 x 168
DONMG : 740.76

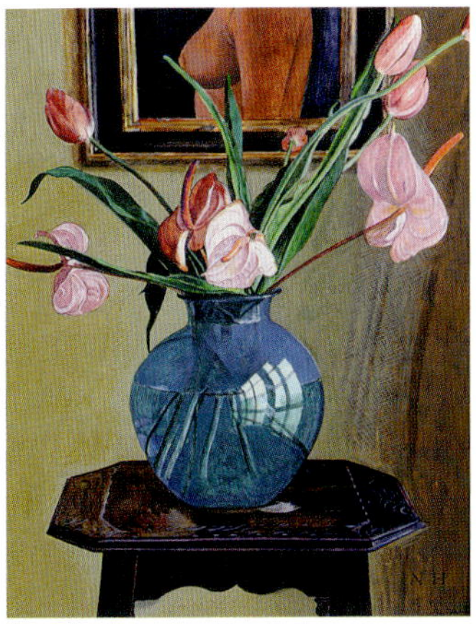

Hutchinson, Norman Douglas 1932–2010
Lilies and Tulips 1989
tempera on paper 61 x 47
DONMG : 1028.92

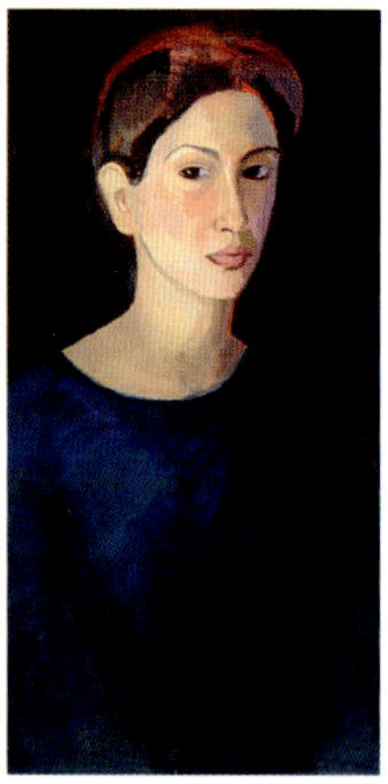

Hutchinson, Rebecca b.1961
Self Portrait with Miss Rebecca Hutchinson 1984
oil on canvas 61 x 30
DONMG : 928.84

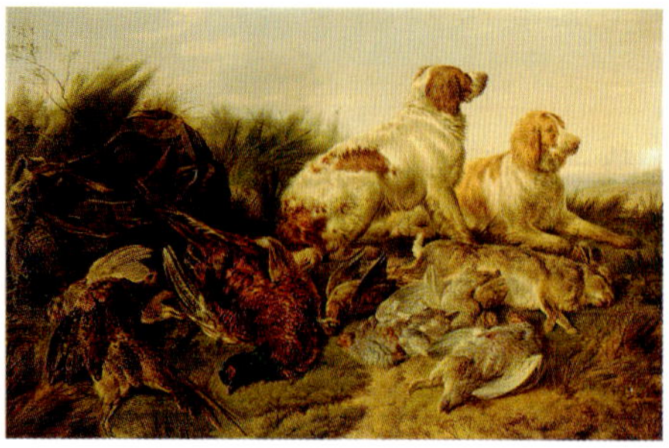

Jones, Charles 1836–1902
Hunting Dogs and Pheasants
oil on canvas 61 x 91.5
PCF9

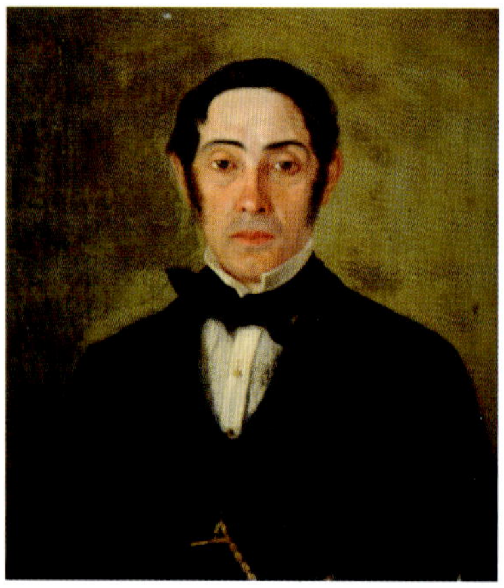

Koutousoff
James Cope
oil on canvas 64 x 54
DONMG : 440.62

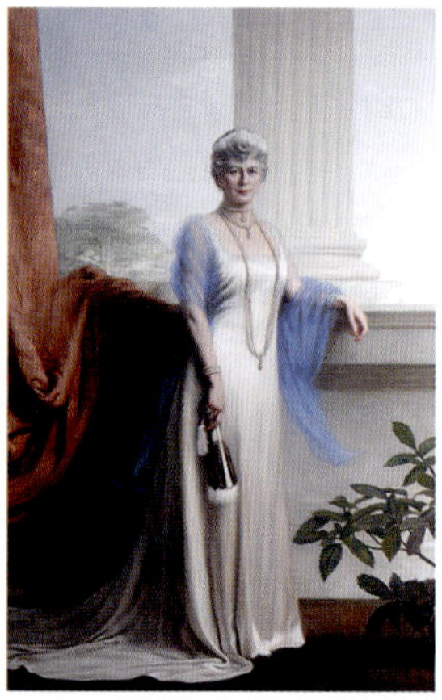

Lander, John Saint-Hélier 1869–1944
Queen Mary (1867–1953) 1936
oil on canvas 240 x 148
DONMG : 113.38

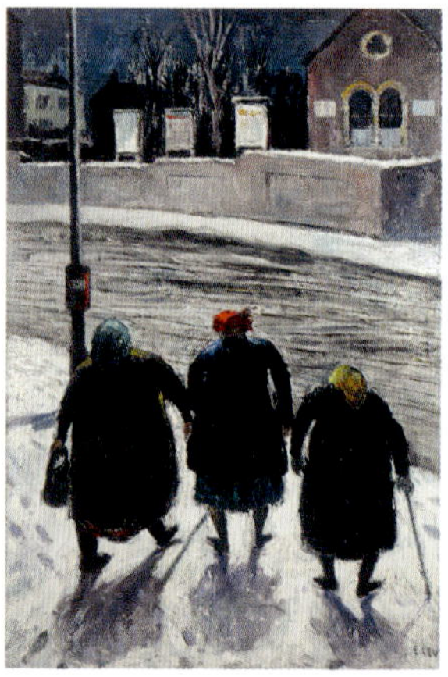

Levy, Emmanuel 1900–1986
Snow in the North
oil on board 122 x 80
DONMG : 918.83

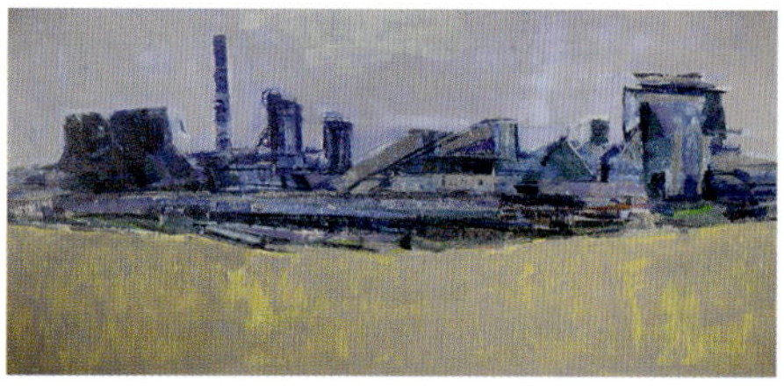

Lillford, Ralph b.1932
Yorkshire Main Pit, Edlington
oil on canvas 90 x 182
DONCH : B982

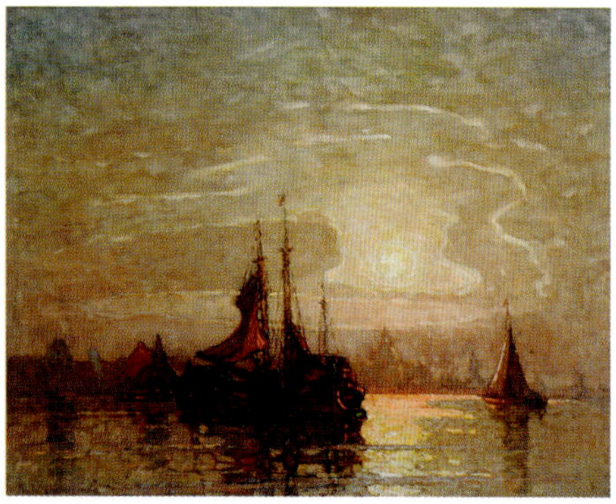

Lindner, Moffat Peter 1852–1949
Golden Afternoon, Dordrecht, The Netherlands
oil on canvas 64.5 x 80
DONMG : 30.24

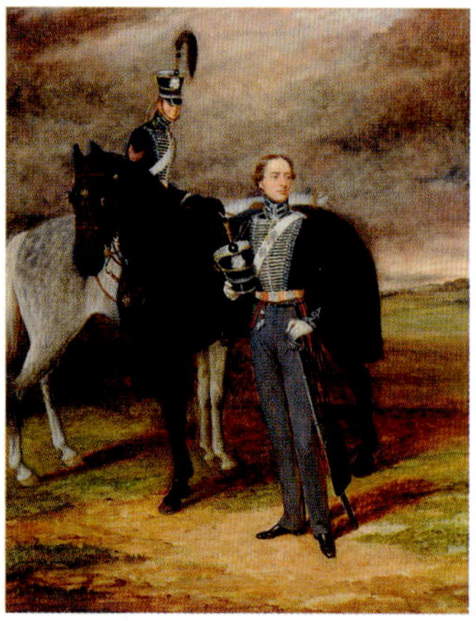

Loader, James active 19th C
Captain H. J. Ellison
oil on canvas 91 x 72
DONMG : 1006.88

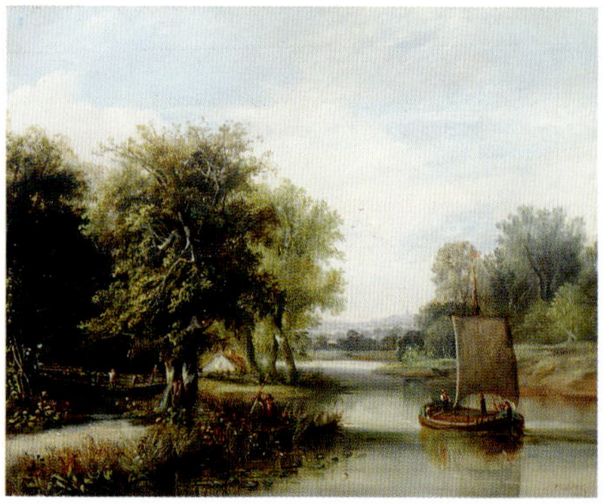

Lowthin, T. A.
On the River Don, near Doncaster, South Yorkshire 1862
oil on board 49 x 60
DONMG : 92.35

Facing page: Barnes, Edward Charles, 1830–1890, *The Flower Girl* (detail), c.1870, Rotherham Museum & Art Gallery, (p. 114)

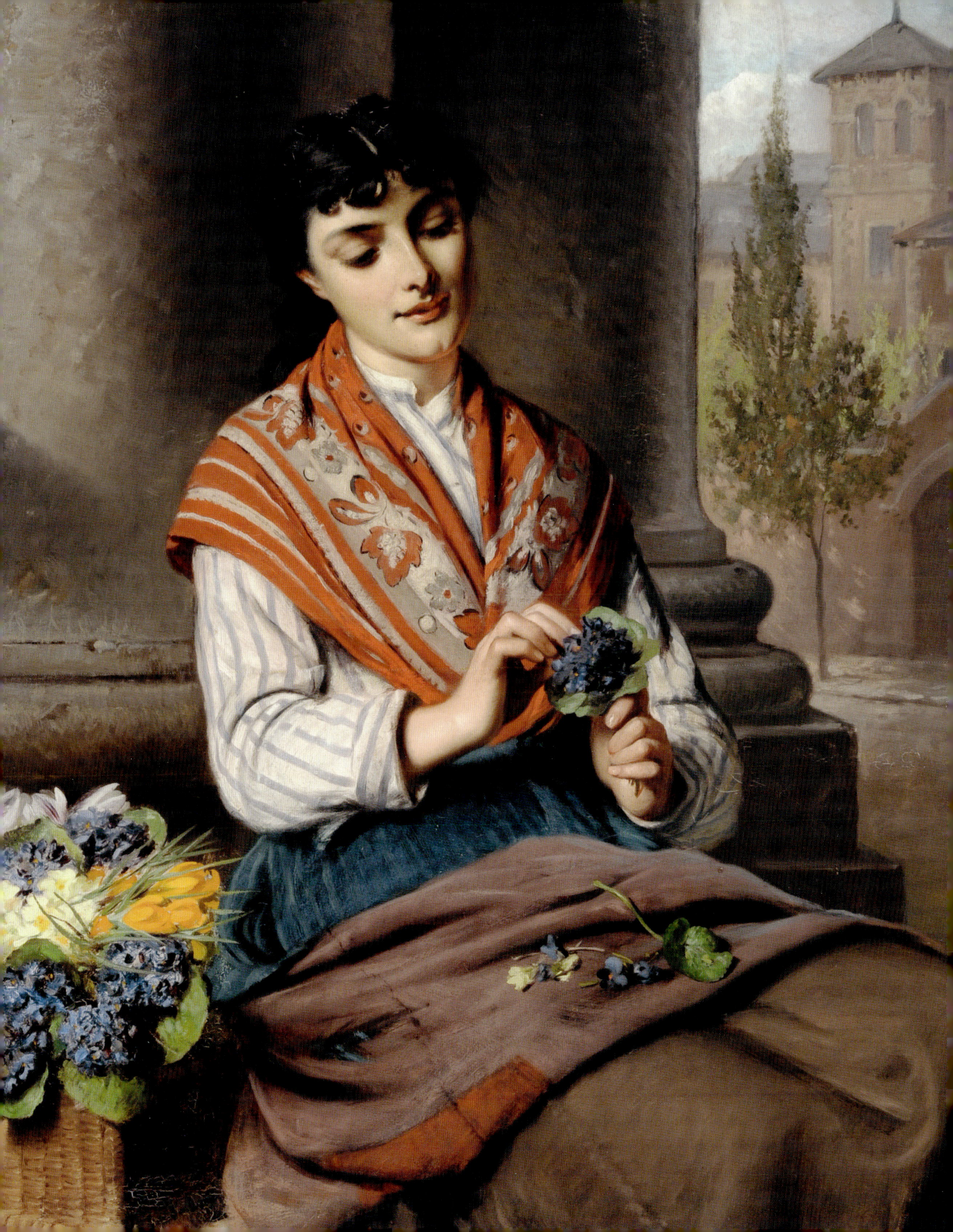

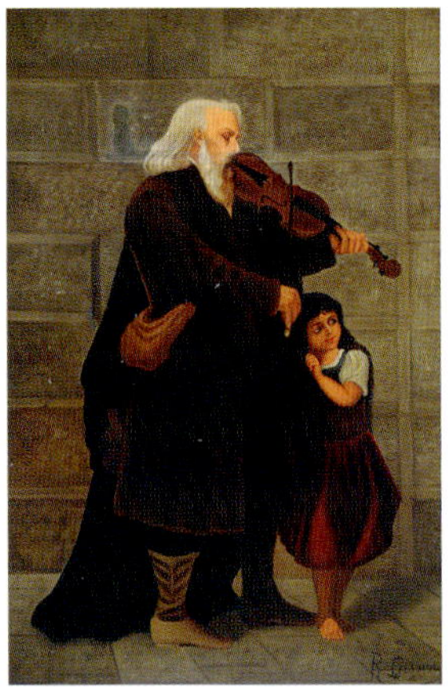

Lussen, R. (attributed to) active 19th C
Blind Violinist
oil on canvas 105 x 69
PCF7

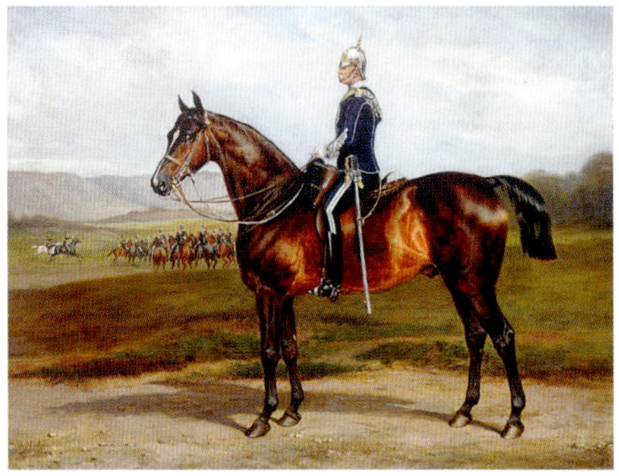

Matthews, John Chester active 1884–1912
A Senior Officer, Queen's Own Yorkshire Dragoons
oil on canvas 32 x 63
DONMG : 929.84

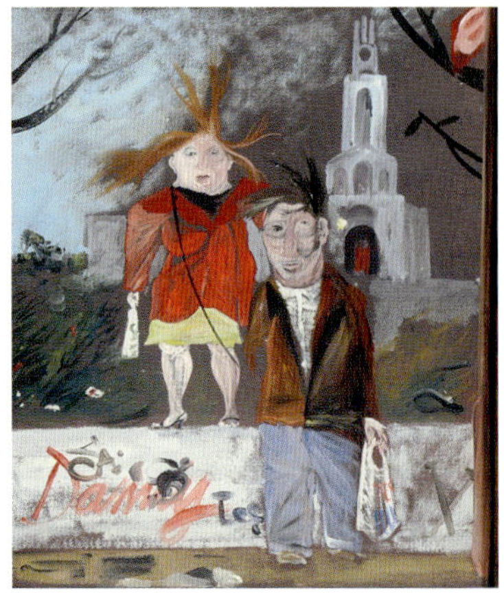

McFadyen, Jock b.1950
Untitled (Hawksmoore Series No.3) c.1988
oil on panel 30.5 x 25.3
PCF6

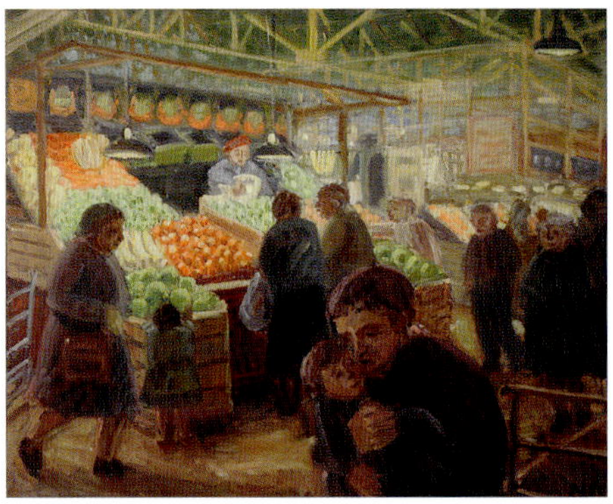

McGregor, Neil b.1963
Miss Harris' Vegetable Stall 1986
oil on board 115.5 x 137.5
DONMG : 1997.2

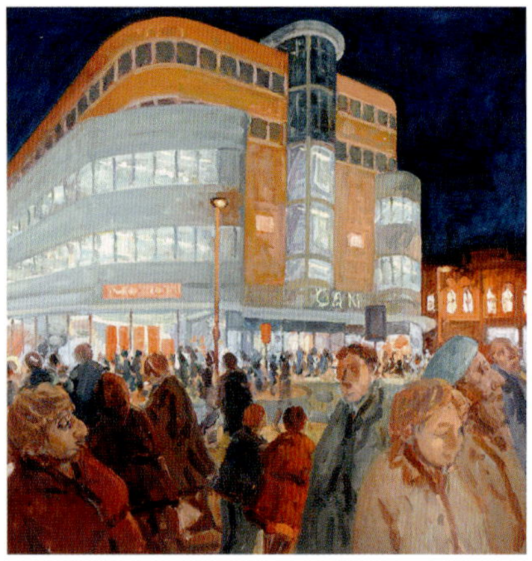

McGregor, Neil b.1963
The Co-Op at Night 1990
oil on board 129.5 x 122.5
DONMG : 1023.91

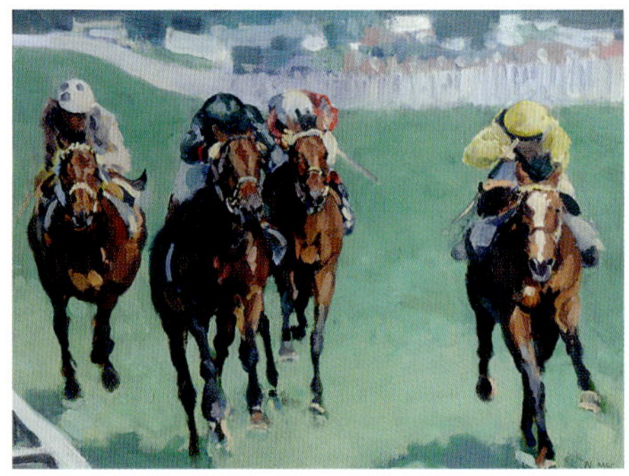

McGregor, Neil b.1963
Final Furlong 1995
oil on board 45.5 x 61
DONMG : 2002.45

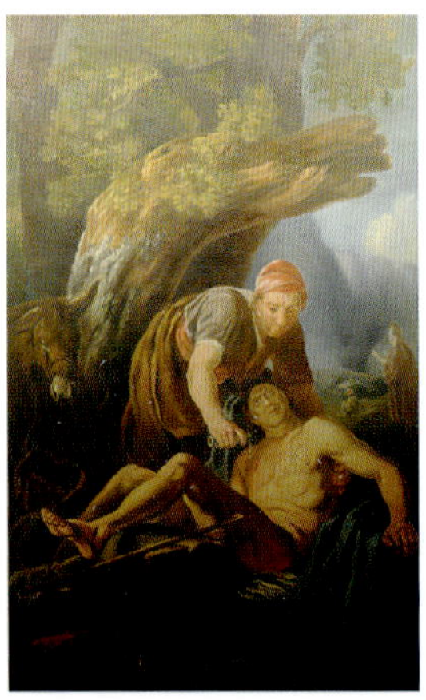

McGregor, Neil b.1963
The Good Samaritan (copy after Francis Hayman) 2006
oil on canvas 199 x 121
PCF5

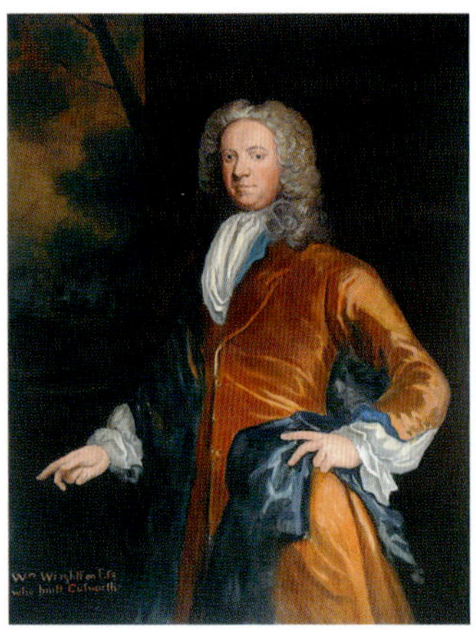

McGregor, Neil b.1963
William Wrightson (copy after Francis Hayman)
oil on canvas 126 x 95
PCF1

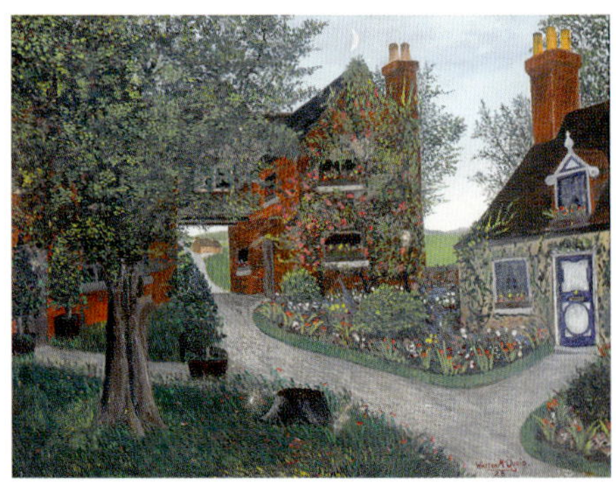

McQuoid, Winston 1909–1984
Back of the Old Inn 1928
oil on canvas 71 x 92
DONMG : 495.63

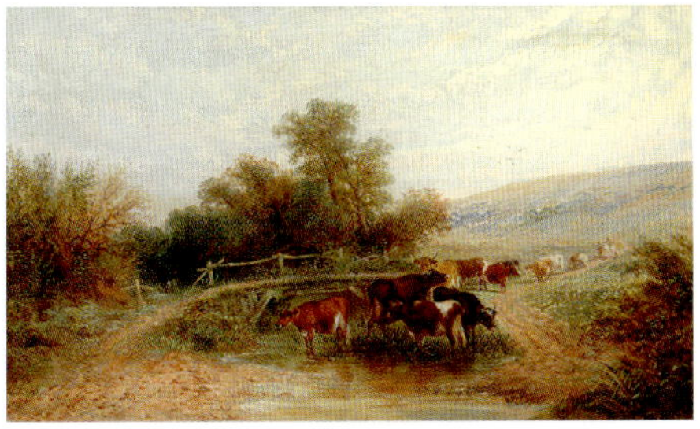

Meadows, William George c.1825–1907
Eller's Bridge, Kent 1889
oil on canvas 76 x 127 (E)
DONMG : 10.13

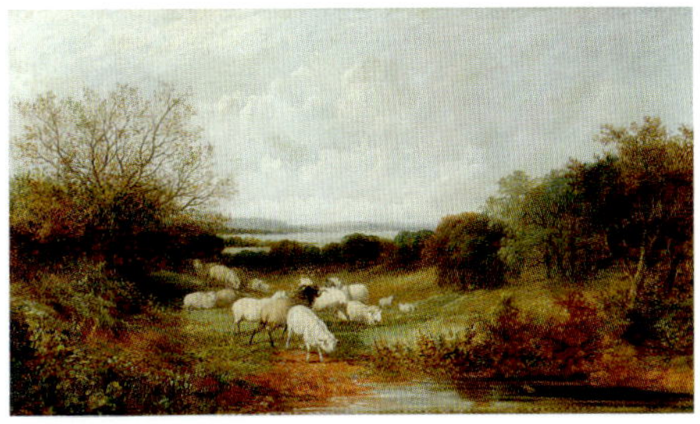

Meadows, William George c.1825–1907
Shoreham Abbey, Kent 1890
oil on canvas 76 x 127 (E)
DONMG : 9.13

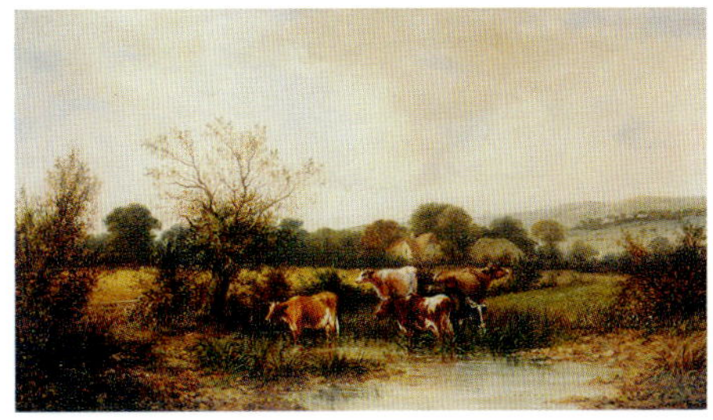

Meadows, William George c.1825–1907
Rural Scenery
oil on canvas 75 x 126
DONMG : 57.30

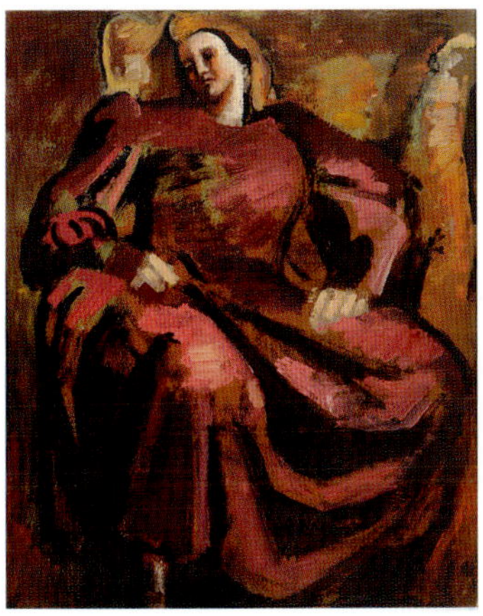

Meninsky, Bernard 1891–1950
The Purple Dress
oil on canvas 49.5 x 39.5
DONMG : 269.56

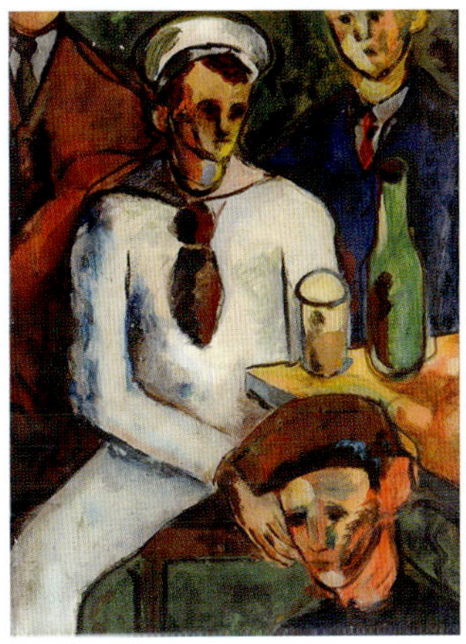

Meria, Oscar
Sailor c.1949
oil on canvas 68 x 48.5
DONMG : 230.49

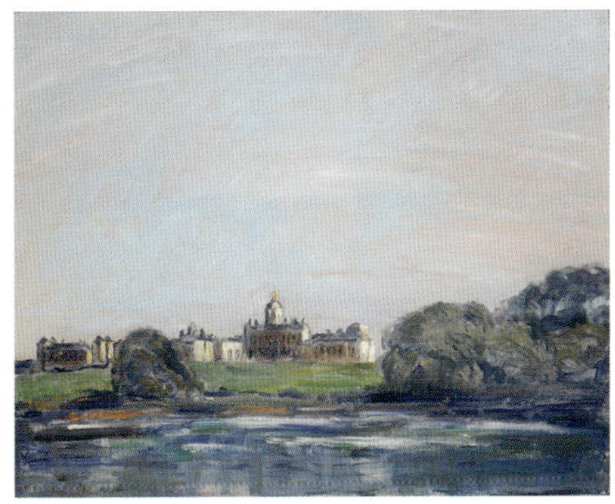

Methuen, Paul Ayshford 1886–1974
Castle Howard, Yorkshire
oil on canvas 51 x 61
DONMG : 821.79

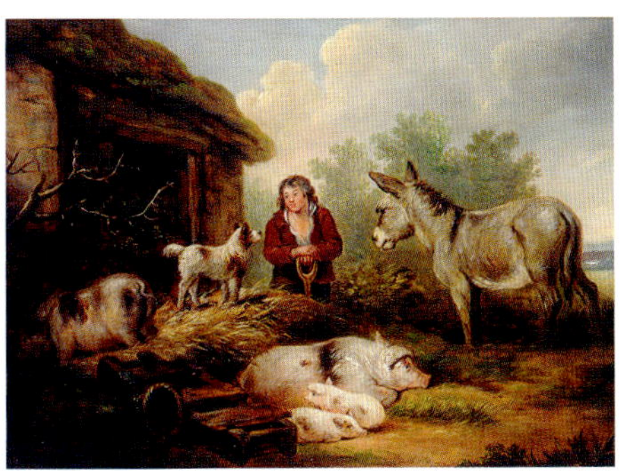

Morland, George 1763–1804
Farmyard Scene
oil on canvas 42 x 59
DONMG : 924.83

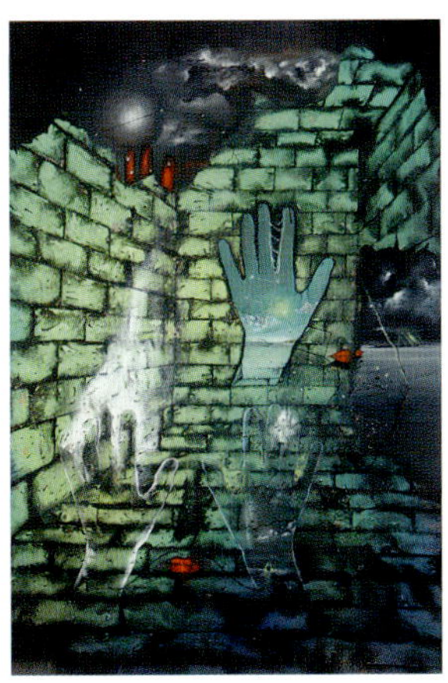

Morley, Michael active c.1965–1970s
The Far Reality c.1965
oil on board 90 x 60
DONMG : 526.65

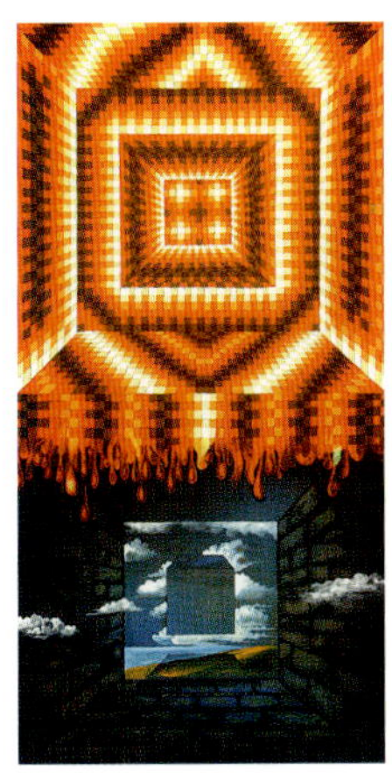

Morley, Michael active c.1965–1970s
Untitled 1970s
oil on board 91.5 x 46.5
DONMG : 856.81

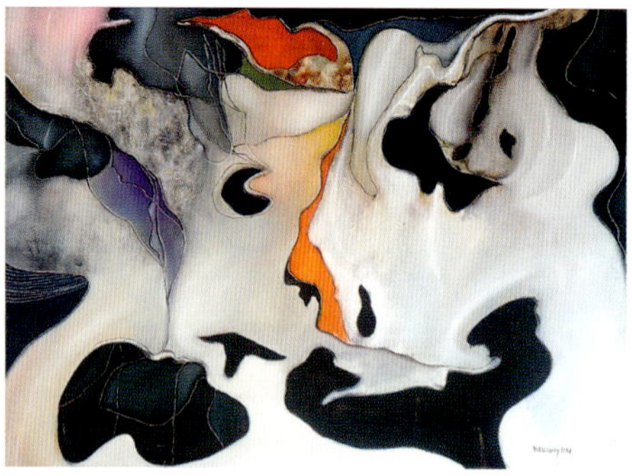

Mowzeshy
Untitled 1987
oil on canvas 60 x 79.5
PCF12

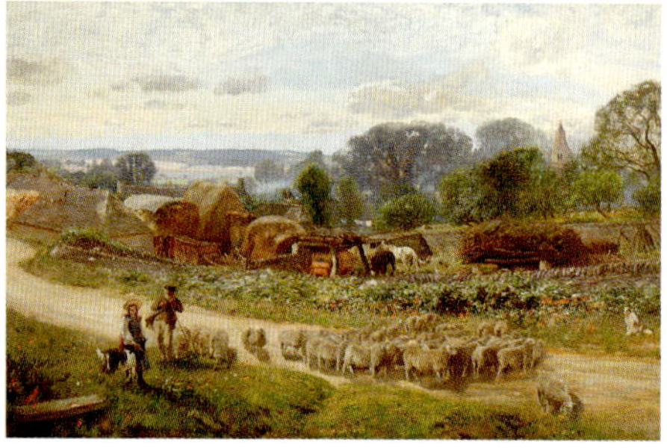

Murray, David 1849–1933
A Roadside Farm 1901
oil on canvas 119 x 160 (E)
DONMG : 121.39

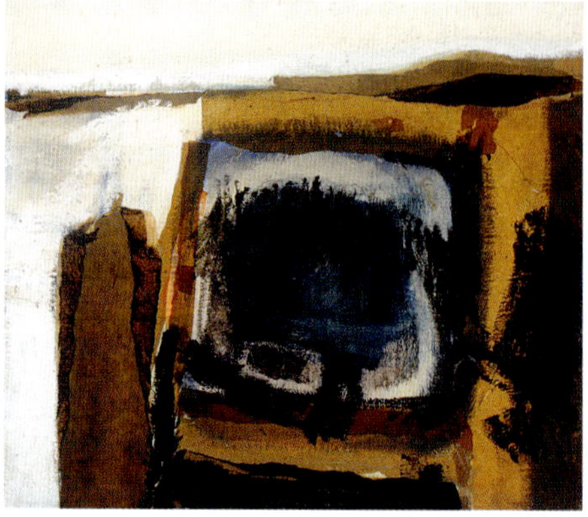

Naylor, Albert b.1932
Untitled Abstract
oil on canvas laid on board 81 x 91.5
PCF13

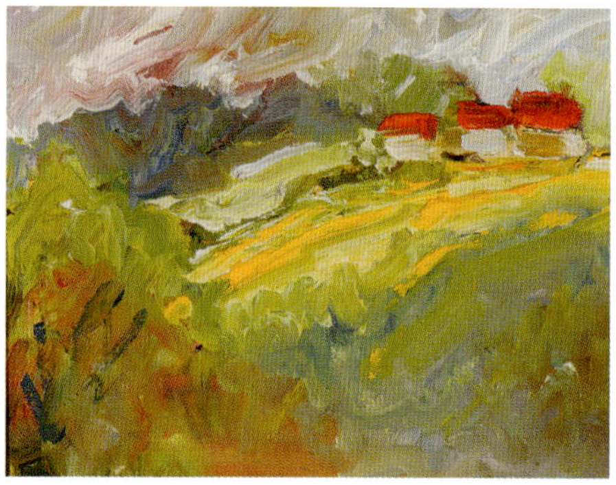

Nettleship, Patrick 1941–1998
Cottages near Percuil, Cornwall
oil on board 9 x 14
PCF18

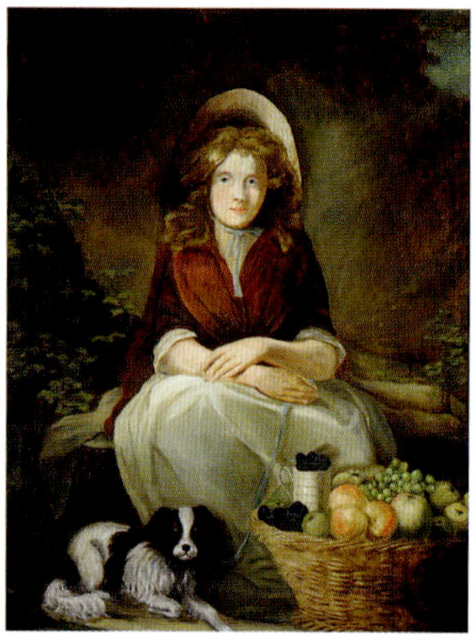

Northcote, James 1746–1831
Fruit Girl
oil on canvas 122 x 92
DONMG : 139.43

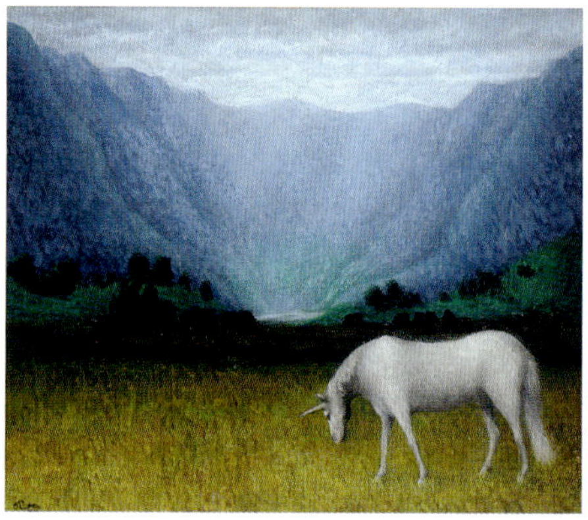

O'Dea, Eric active 1934–1938
The Unicorn 1938
oil on canvas 70 x 79.5
DONMG : 494.63

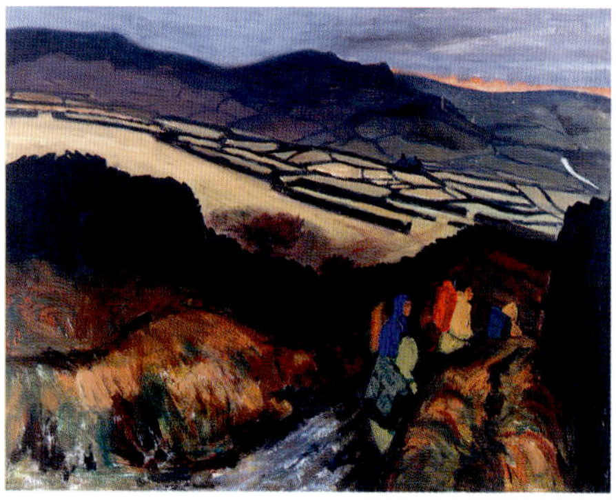

Ogden, Geoff 1929–1977
Pennine Landscape
oil on board 98 x 122
DONMG : 838.80

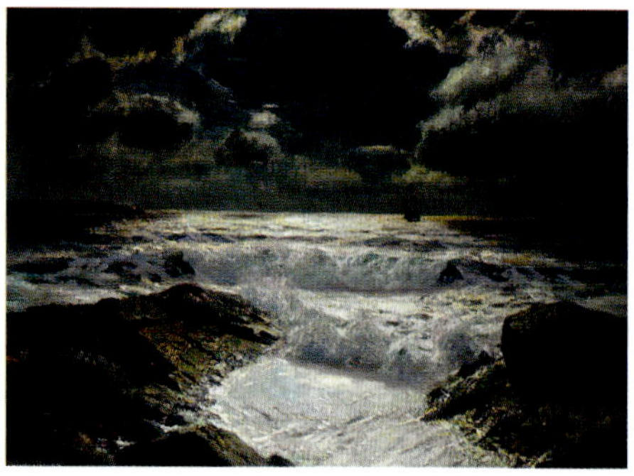

Olsson, Albert Julius 1864–1942
Cloudy Moonlight c.1900
oil on canvas 75 x 100.5
DONMG : 45.28

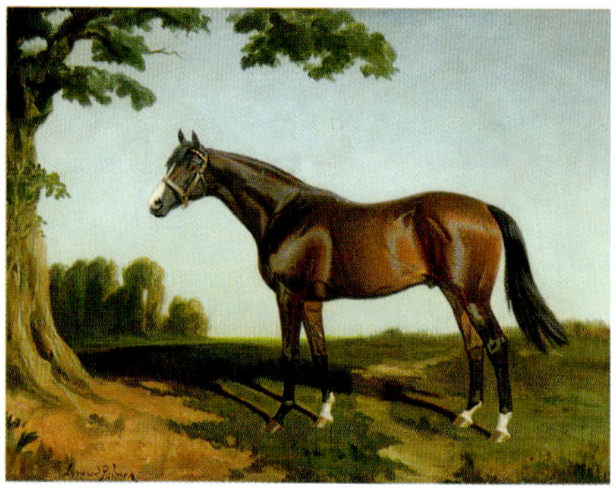

Palmer, James Lynwood 1867/1868–1941
'Royal Lancer', Winner of 1922 St Leger Stakes 1922
oil on canvas 83 x 107
DONMG : 515.64

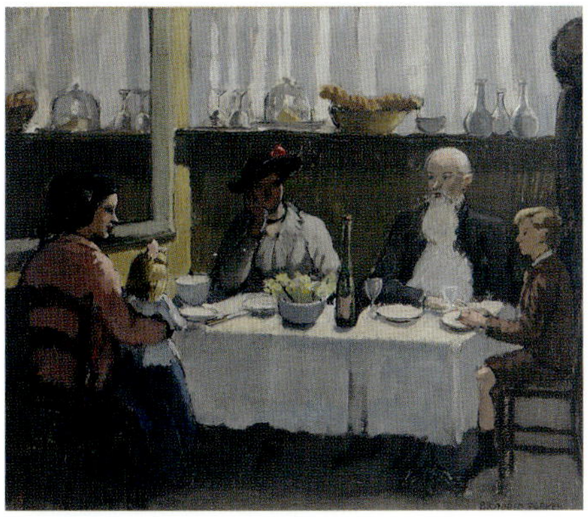

Parker, Brynhild 1907–1987
Conversation Piece c.1930
oil on canvas 45 x 54
DONMG : 489.63

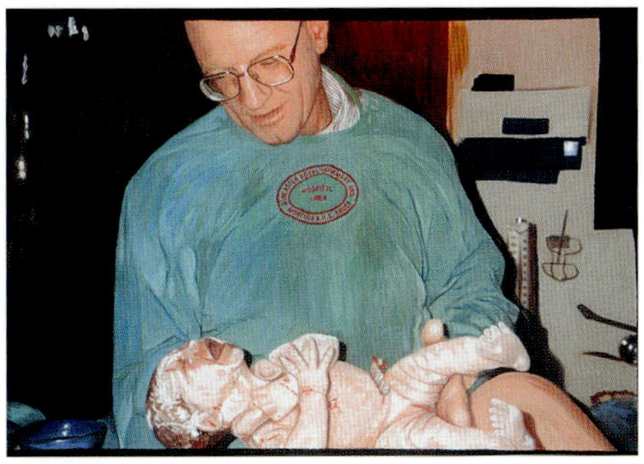

Parkhurst, Wendy b.1966
First Breath 2004
acrylic on paper 99 x 138
DONMG : 2008.32

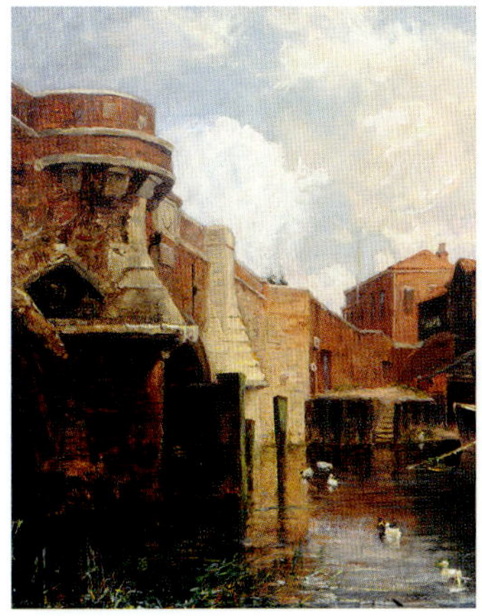

Pickering, James Langsdale 1845–1912
Bishop's Bridge, Norwich, Norfolk
oil on canvas 44 x 34
DONMG : 6.12

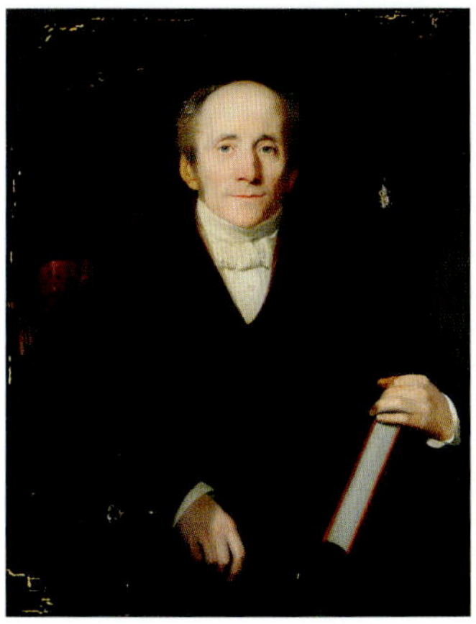

Pickersgill, Henry William 1782–1875
Henry Bower
oil on canvas 91.5 x 71
DONMG : 71.32

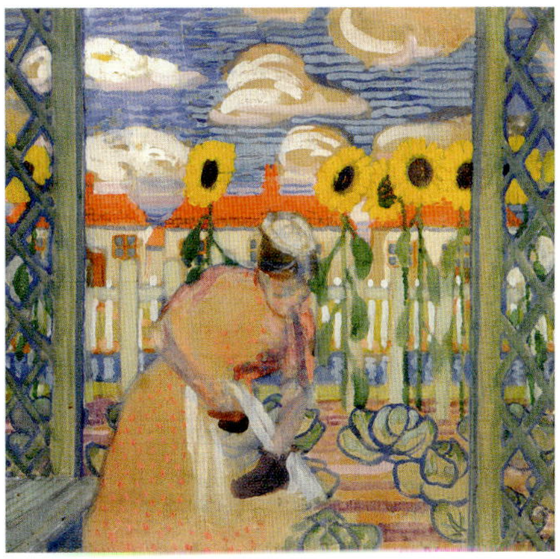

Polunin, Elizabeth Violet 1878–1950
Clean Boots
oil on canvas 54.7 x 55.5
DONMG : 485.63

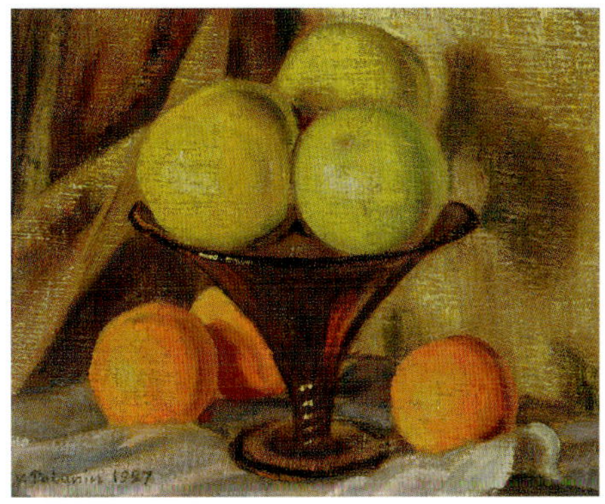

Polunin, Vladimir 1880–1957
Grapefruit 1927
oil on canvas 31 x 37
DONMG : 486.63

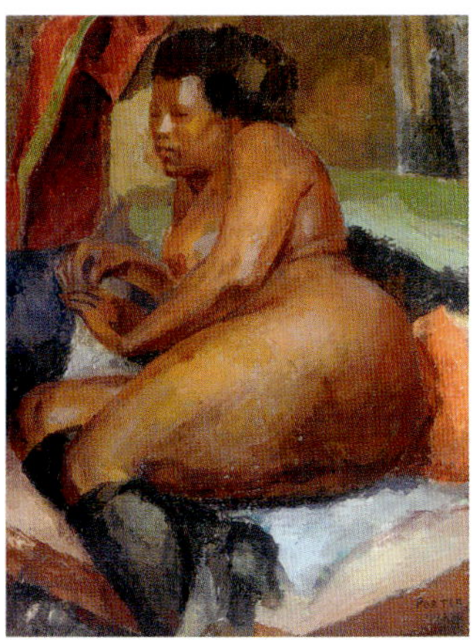

Porter, Frederick James 1883–1944
Negress
oil on canvas 73 x 53
DONMG : 491.63

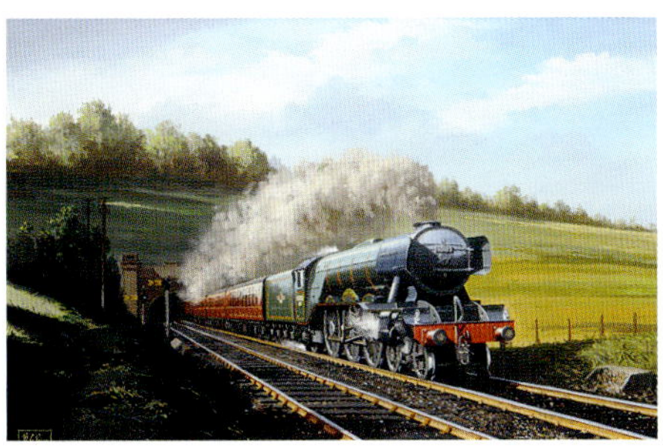

Price, Barry Graham b.1938
'Flying Scotsman'
oil on canvas 50 x 76
DONMG : ZP274

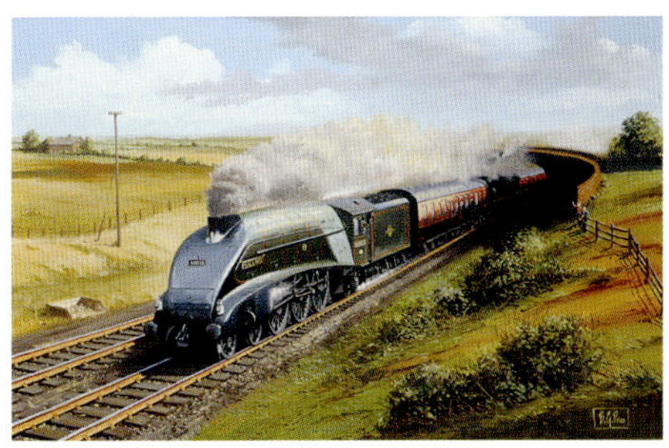

Price, Barry Graham b.1938
'Mallard'
oil on canvas 50 x 76
PCF14

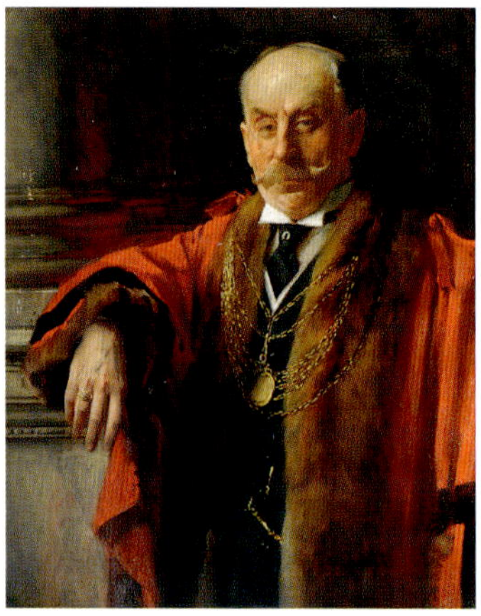

Priest, Alfred 1874–1929
George Thomas Tuby (1857–1932) c.1900
oil on canvas 90 x 69.5
DONMG : 620.75

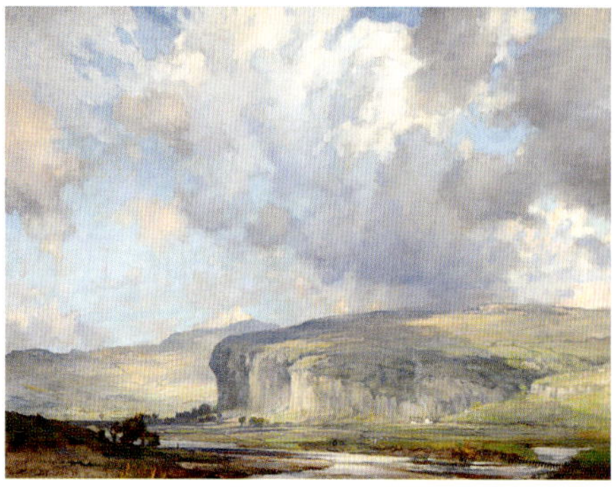

Priestman, Bertram 1868–1951
Kilnsey Crag, Wharfedale, Yorkshire 1929
oil on canvas 115 x 146
DONMG : 59.30

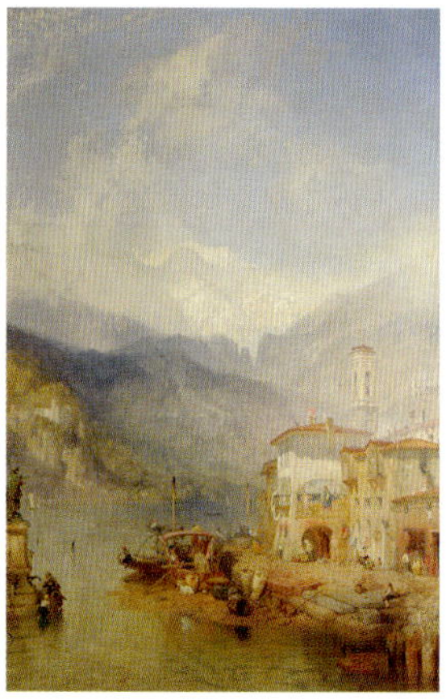

Pyne, James Baker 1800–1870
Lake Maggiore, Italy
oil on canvas 144 x 94
DONMG : 528.66

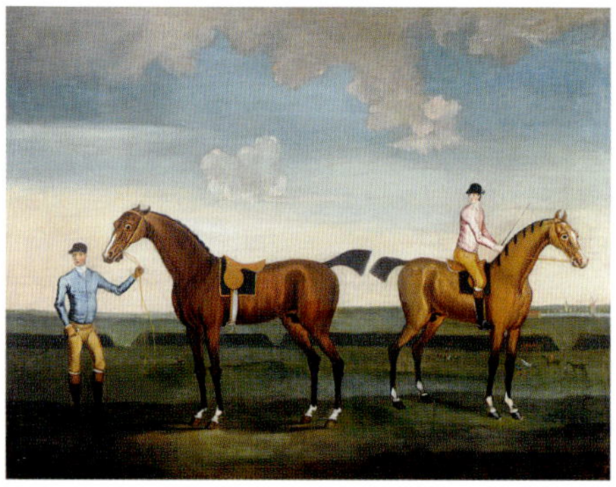

Quigley, Daniel active 1750–1780
'Flying Childers' and 'Dimple' on a Racecourse, Other Racehorses Beyond
oil on canvas 96.5 x 122
DONMG : 1996.64

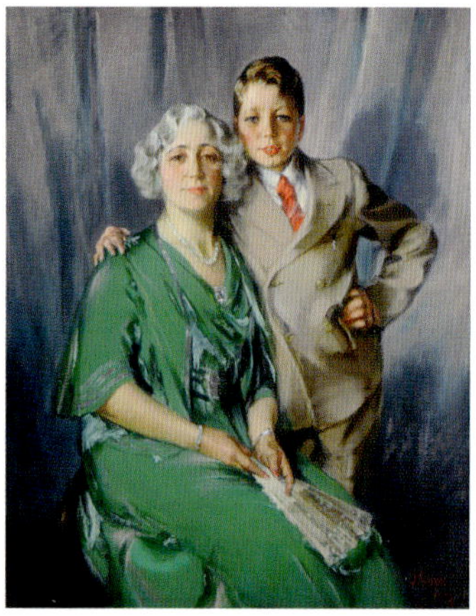

Quin, G.
Mrs Philys Jackson and Philip Clovis Jackson
oil on canvas 126 x 100
DONMG : 920.83

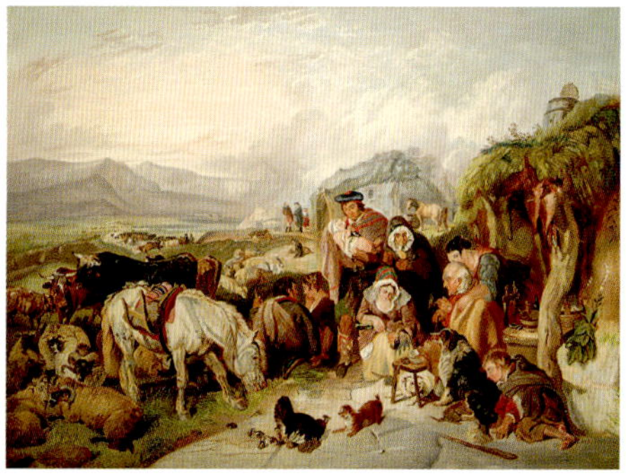

Radley, Rosa
The Highlanders' Home 1847
oil on canvas 98 x 128 (E)
DONMG : 303.57

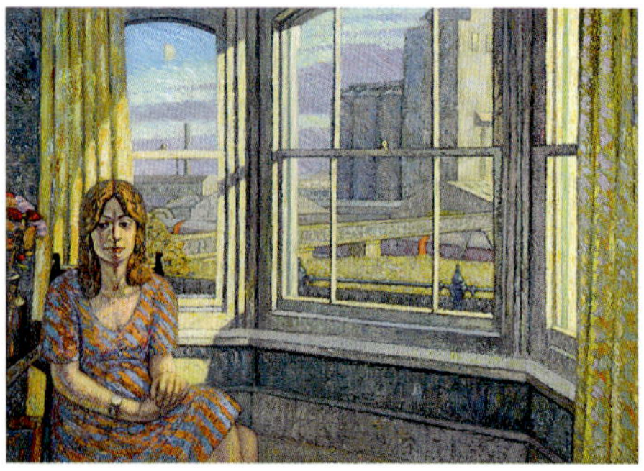

Reay, John 1947–2011
Portrait of Joan, Autumn Sunset c.1979
oil on board 122 x 167.5
DONMG : ZP275

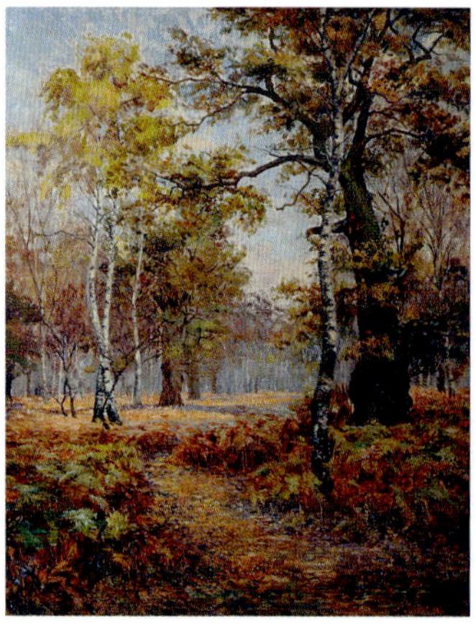

Reekie, William Maxwell 1869–1948
Sherwood Forest, Nottinghamshire 1903
oil on canvas 90 x 70
DONMG : 538.68

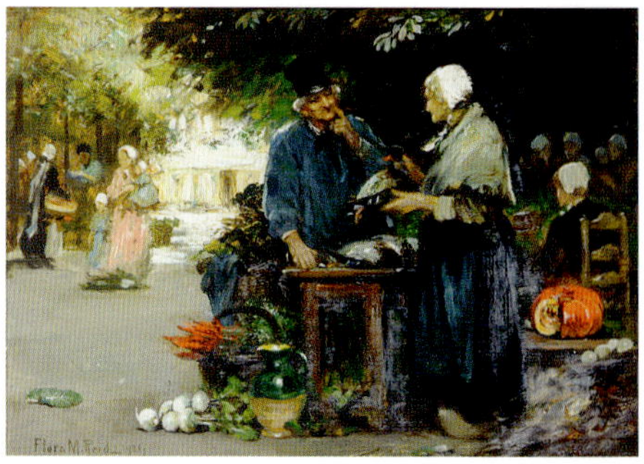

Reid, Flora Macdonald 1860–c.1940
A Great Bargain 1921
oil on canvas 27 x 36
DONMG : 26.22

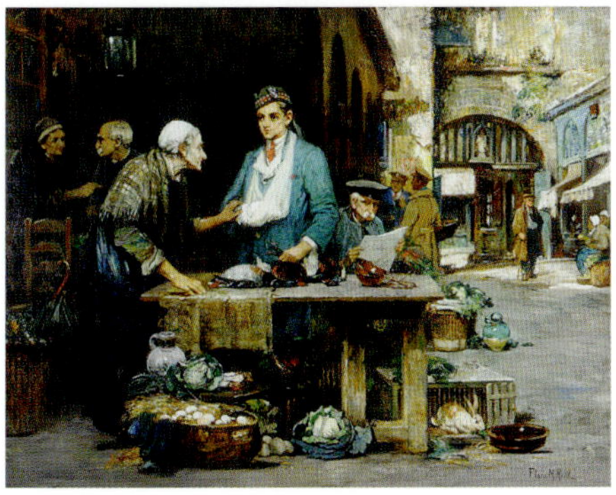

Reid, Flora Macdonald 1860–c.1940
Youth
oil on canvas 101 x 126
DONMG : 35.26

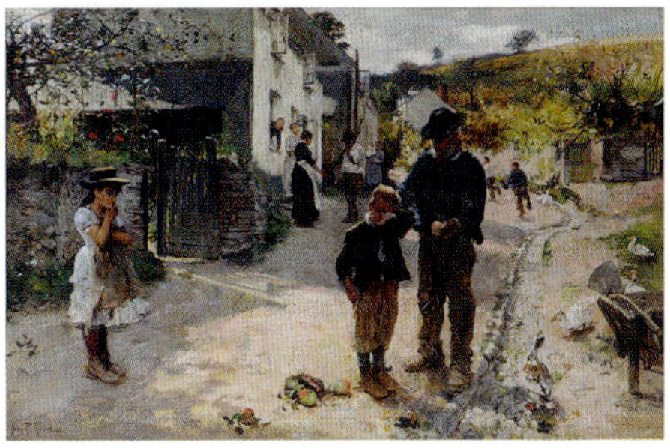

Reid, John Robertson 1851–1926
The Plagues of His Village
oil on canvas 59 x 99
DONMG : 50.29

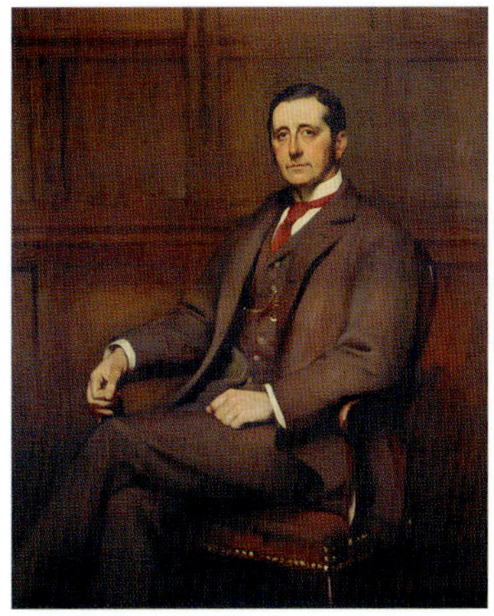

Reilly, John Lewis c.1835–after 1901
Portrait of an Unknown Gentleman (after James Jebusa Shannon) 1899
oil on canvas 143 x 102
PCF19

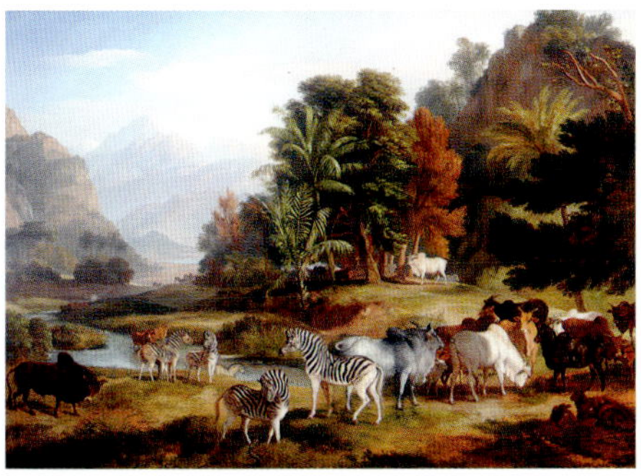

Reinagle, Ramsay Richard 1775–1862
Landscape with Animals 1828
oil on canvas 129 x 180
DONMG : 38.26

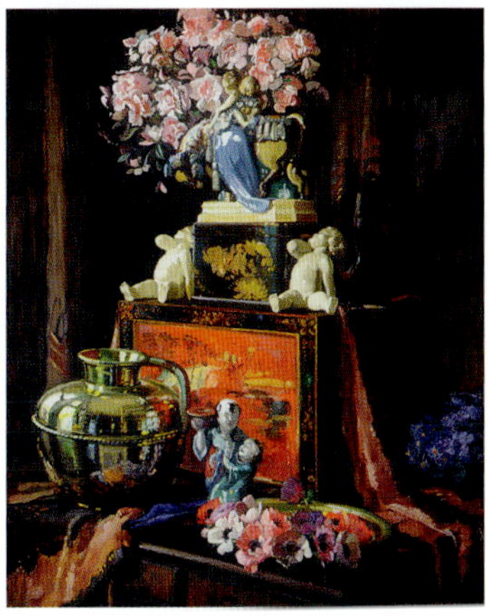

Richter, Herbert Davis 1874–1955
A Festival
oil on canvas 127 x 101
DONMG : 28.23

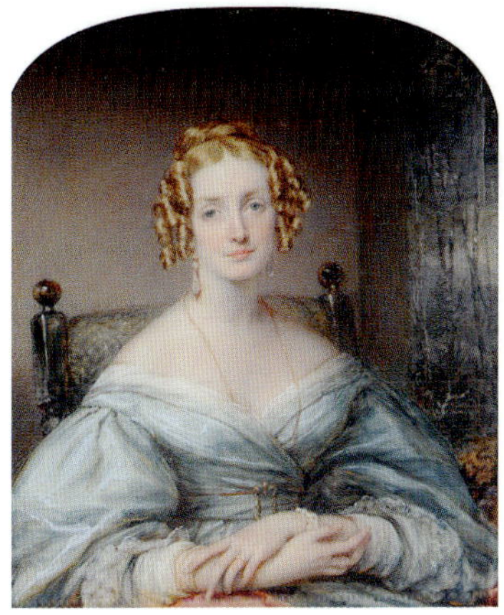

Robertson, Andrew (Mrs)
Georgiana Battie-Wrightson (1813–1878)
oil on canvas 14 x 11
DONCH : C528

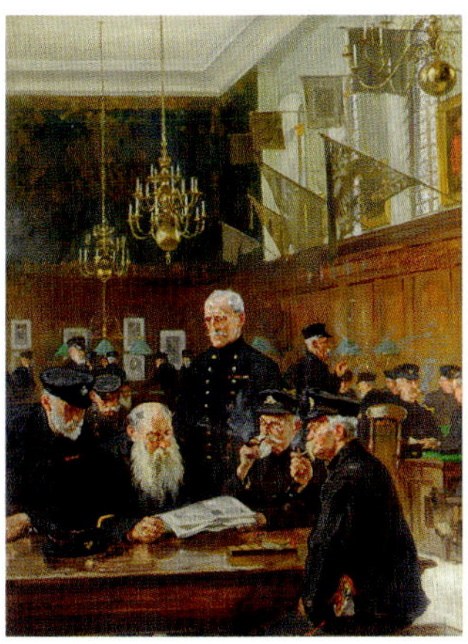

Roe, Fred 1864–1947
The News, Chelsea Pensioners
oil on canvas 102 x 74.5
DONMG : 64.31

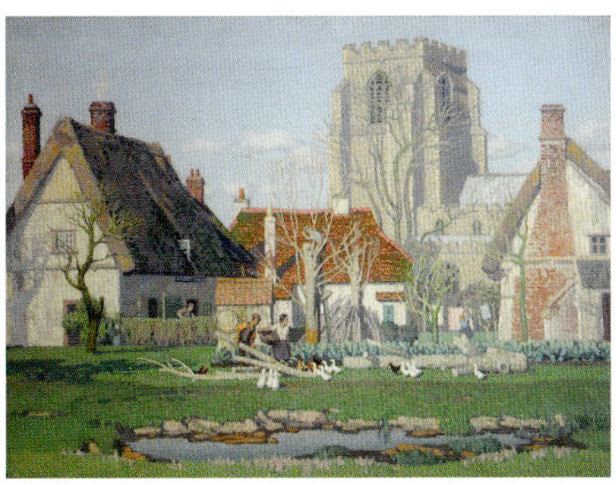

Royle, Stanley 1888–1961
Harthill, South Yorkshire 1949
oil on canvas 69.5 x 90
DONMG : 407.61

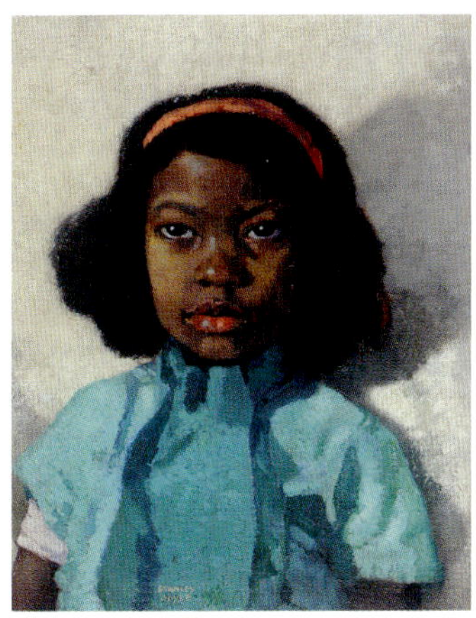

Royle, Stanley 1888–1961
Portrait of a West Indian Girl
oil on canvas 49 x 38
DONMG : 408.61

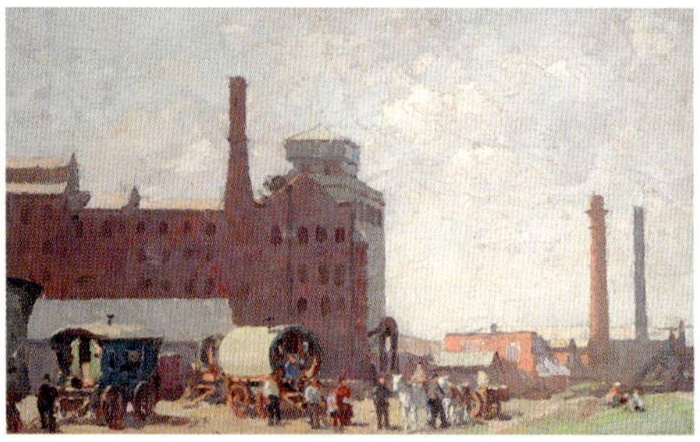

Russell, Gyrth 1892–1970
Doncaster Gypsy Encampment
oil on board 35 x 53
DONMG : 913.83

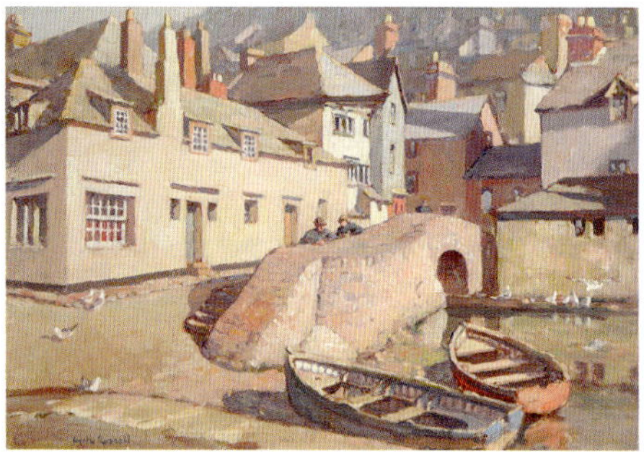

Russell, Gyrth 1892–1970
Polperro, Cornwall
oil on canvas 54 x 77
DONMG : 453.63

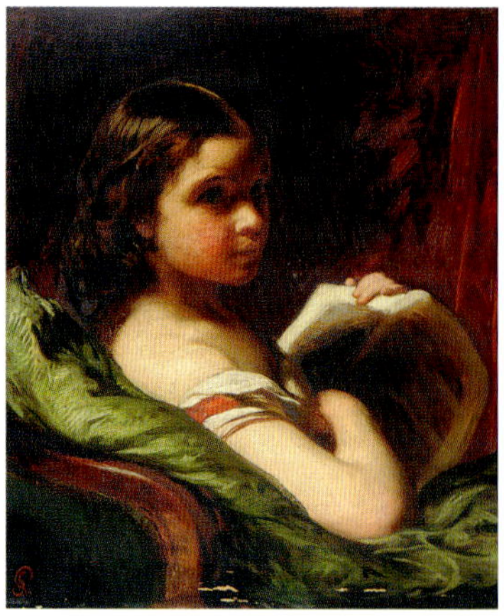

Sant, James 1820–1916
Portrait of a Young Girl Holding a Book
oil on canvas 61 x 51
DONMG : 775.77

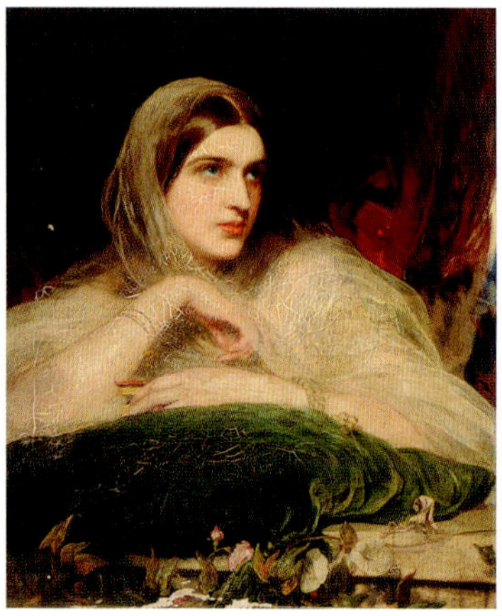

Sant, James 1820–1916
Thought Folded Over
oil on canvas 76.5 x 63.5
DONMG : 774.77

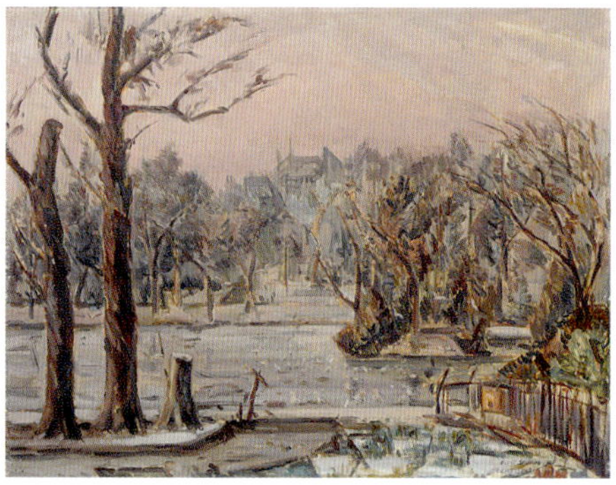

Seabrooke, Elliott 1886–1950
Regent's Park, London, Winter 1940
oil on canvas 68.5 x 89.5
DONMG : 497.63

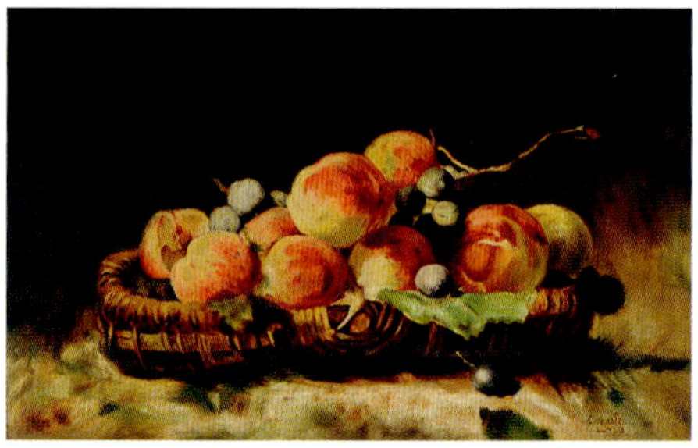

Searle, G.
Fruit in a Basket 1903
oil on canvas 32 x 48.5
DONMG : 460.63

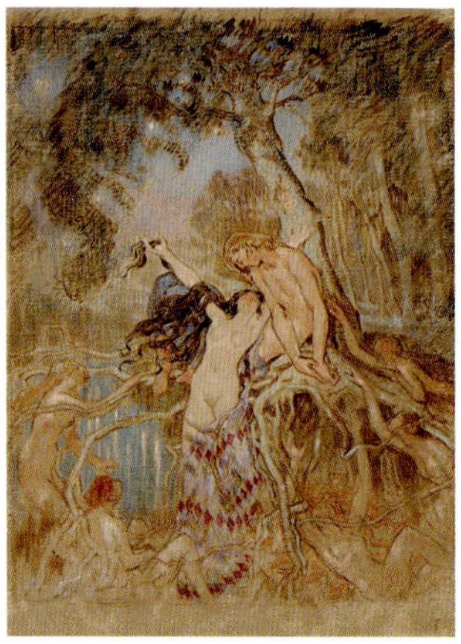

Shackleton, William 1872–1933
Study for 'The Eternal Dream' c.1924
oil on canvas 55.5 x 38
DONMG : 110.38

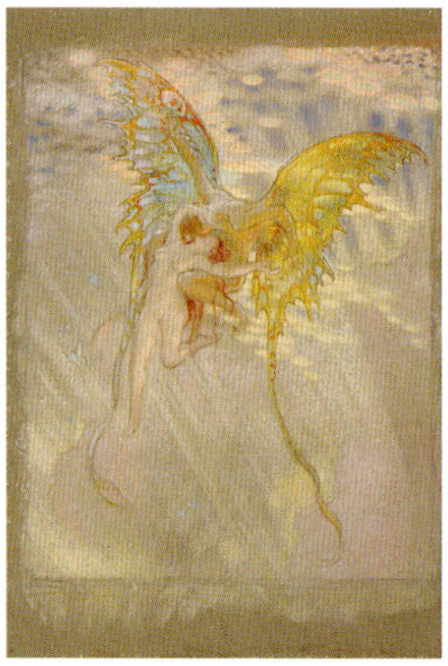

Shackleton, William 1872–1933
Study for 'The Eternal Dream' c.1924
oil on canvas 56 x 37.5
DONMG 111.38

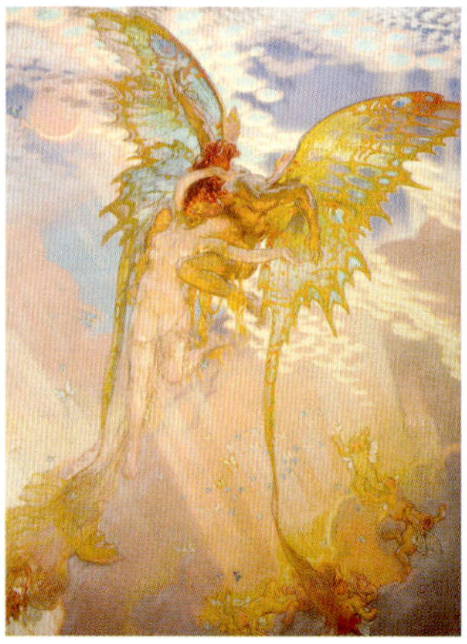

Shackleton, William 1872–1933
The Eternal Dream c.1924
oil on canvas 105 x 79
DONMG : 109.38

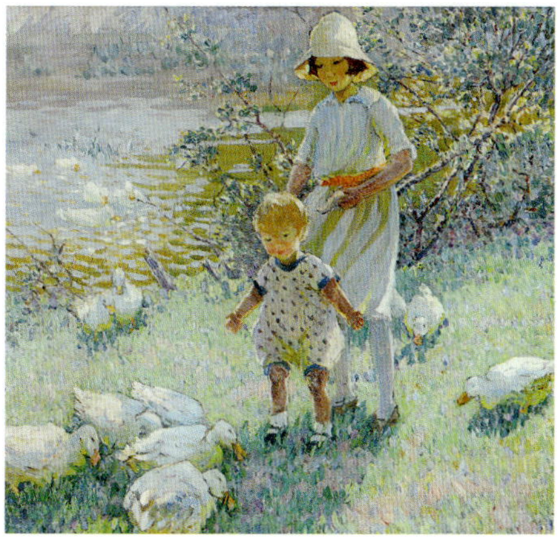

Sharp, Dorothea 1874–1955
White Ducks
oil on canvas 79.5 x 82
DONMG : 42.27

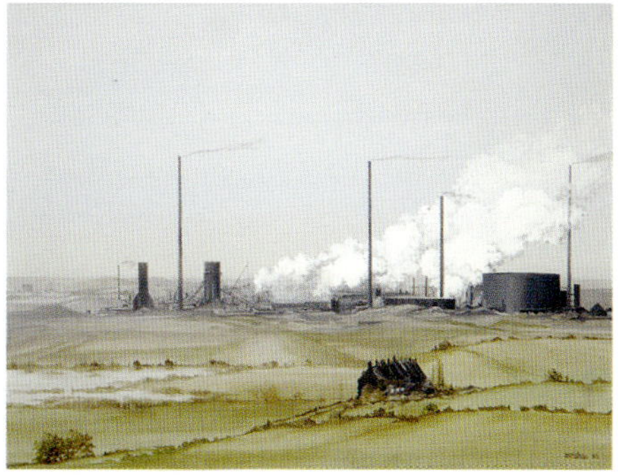

Shaw, Mike b.1946
Catcliffe, South Yorkshire
oil on canvas 35 x 45
DONMG : 2002.40

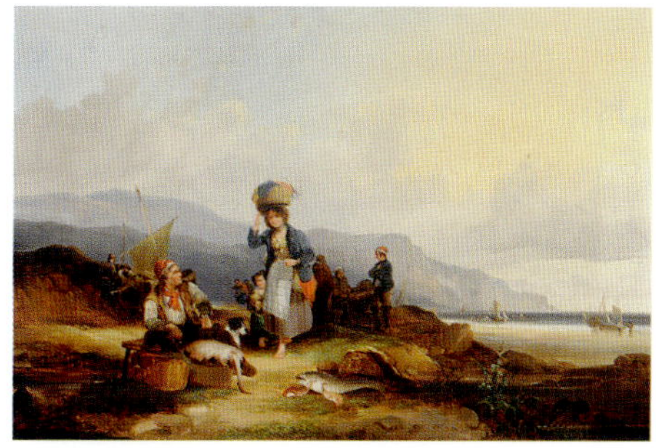

Shayer, William 1788–1879
Fisher Folk
oil on canvas 65 x 93
PCF15

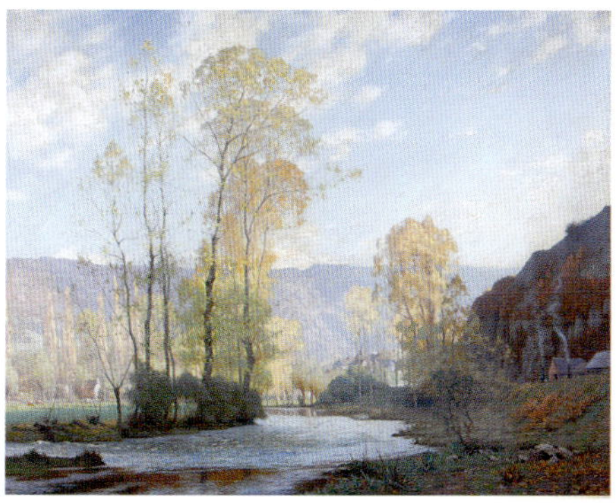

Sheard, Thomas Frederick Mason
1866–1921
The Pride of Autumn
oil on canvas 126 x 160
DONMG : 31.24

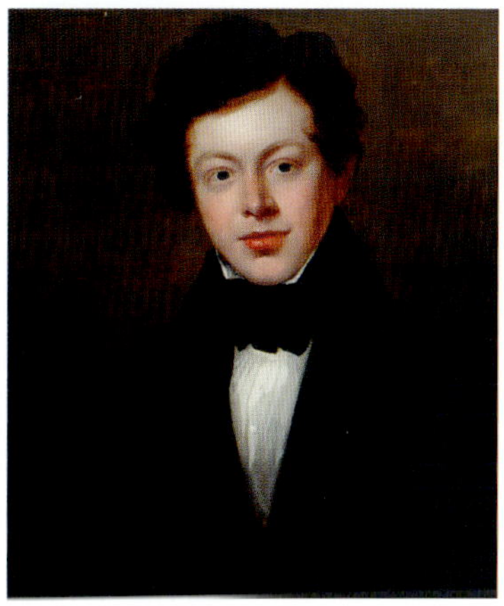

Sibley, Charles c.1801–1866
Josiah Cowell
oil on canvas 59 x 49
DONMG : 266.55

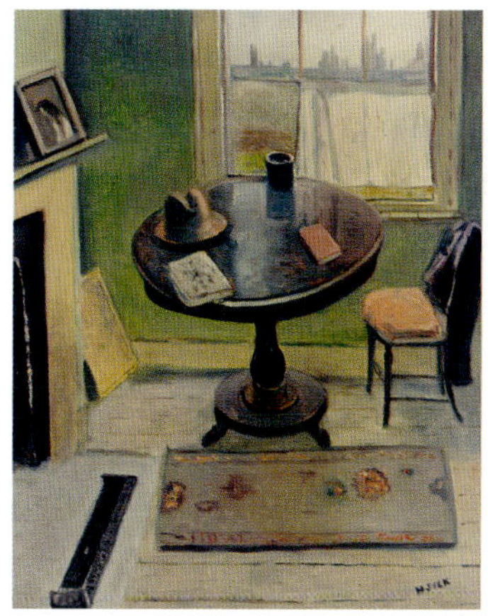

Silk, Henry 1883–1947
Hat on a Table 1932
oil on canvas 51 x 39.5
DONMG : 487.63

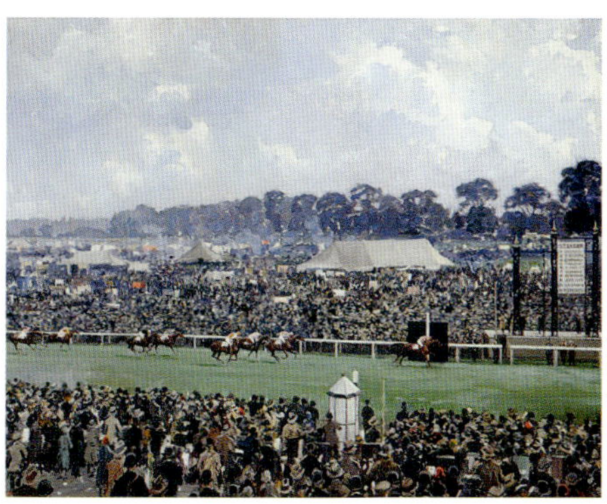

Simpson, Charles Walter 1885–1971
Finish of the 1931 St Leger 1931
oil on canvas 100 x 126
DONMG : 65.31

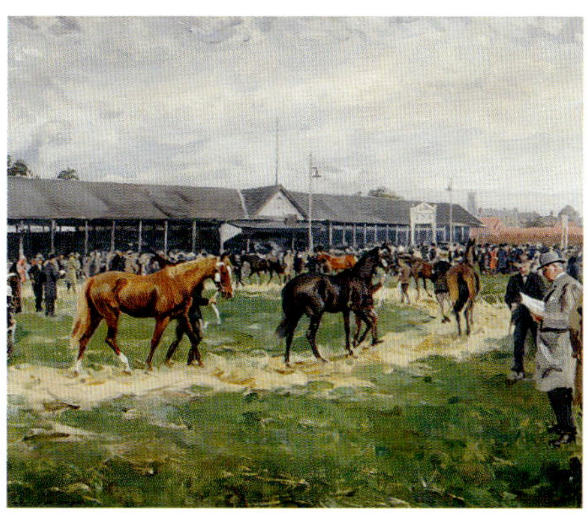

Simpson, Charles Walter 1885–1971
Tattersalls' Sale Ring 1931
oil on canvas 79 x 94
DONMG : 66.31

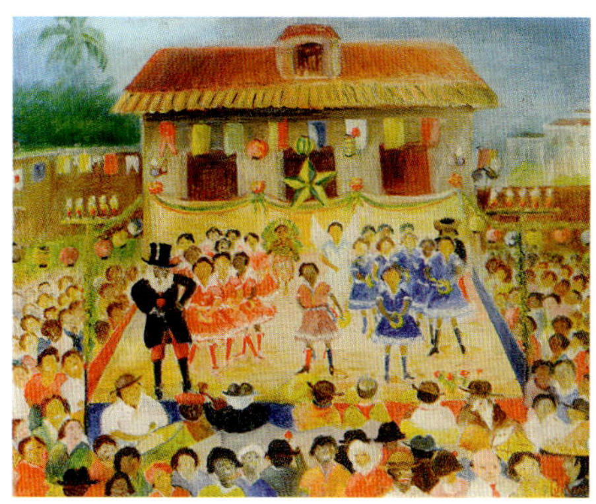

Soares, Luís
Pastoral c.1949
oil on canvas 49 x 59
DONMG : 229.49

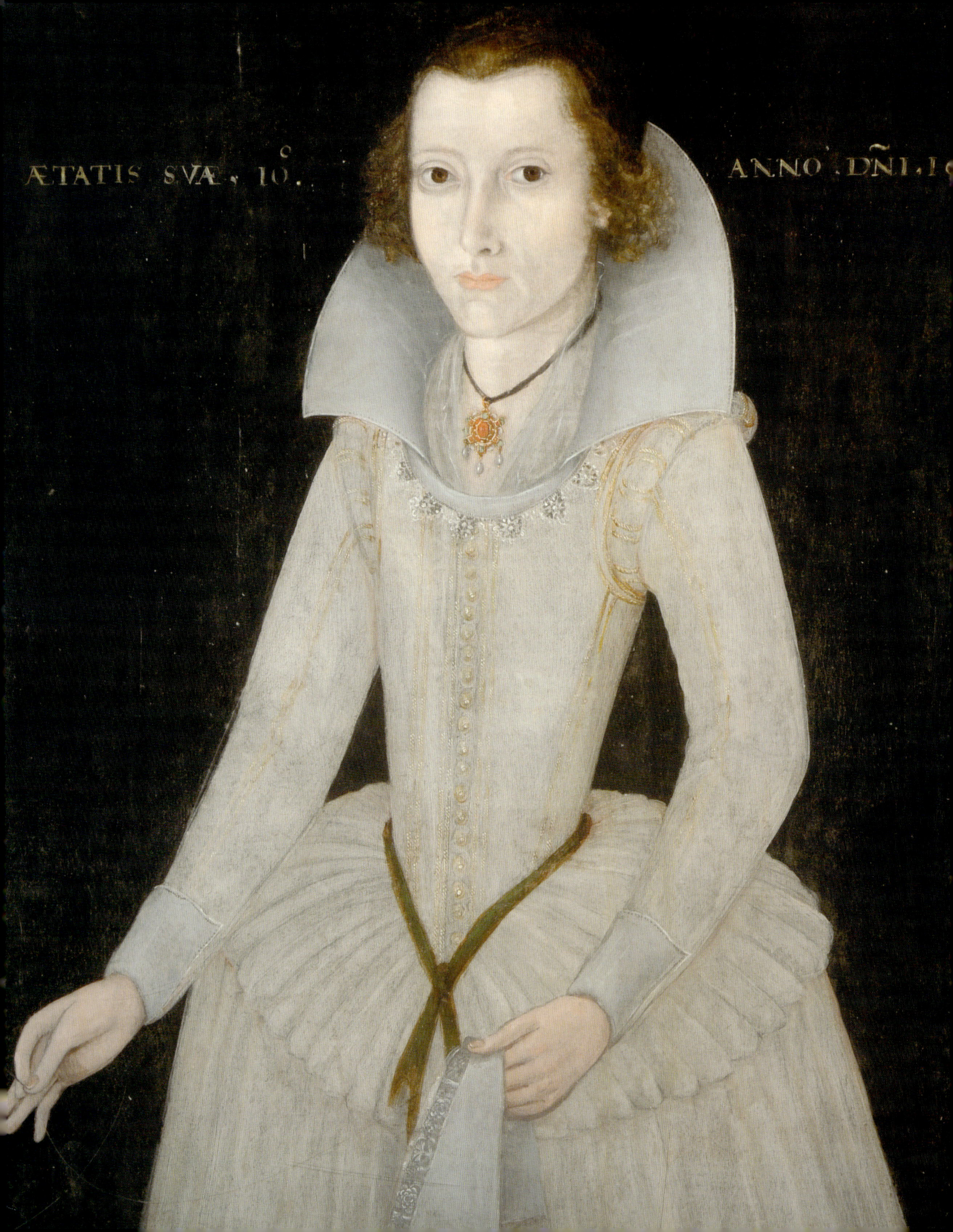
ÆTATIS SVÆ, 10.
ANNO DÑI 1

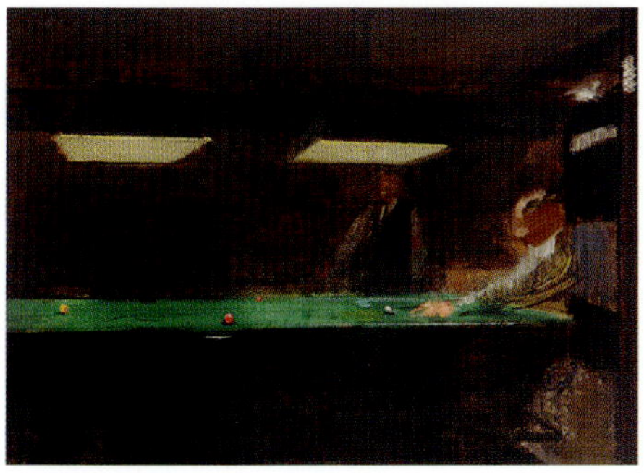

Spear, Ruskin 1911–1990
Snooker
oil on canvas 40 x 53
DONMG : 770.77

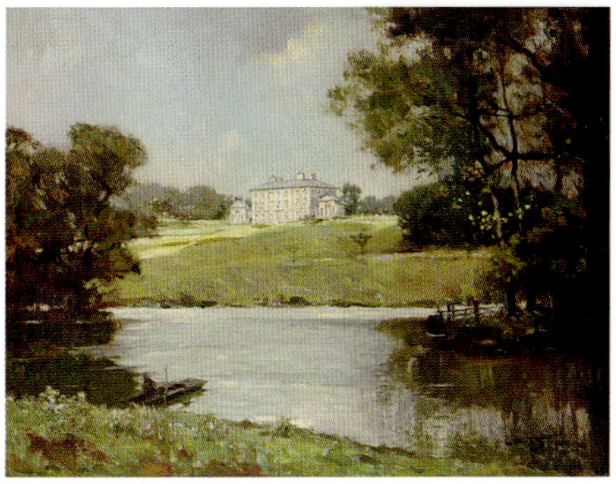

Spooner, Arthur 1873–1962
Cusworth Hall, South Yorkshire
oil on canvas 52 x 68
DONMG : 1996.9

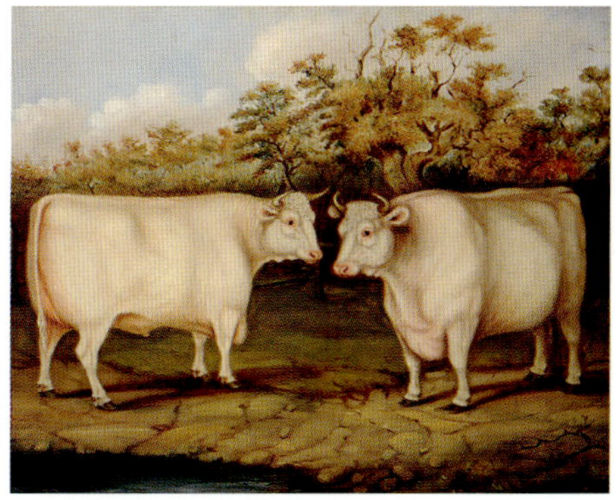

Stafford, Henry 1830–1873
Castle Howard Shorthorns
oil on canvas 63 x 76.2
DONMG : 961.85

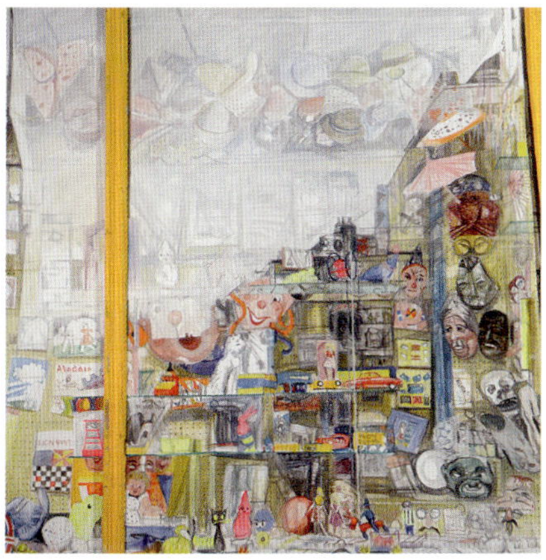

Stanley, Jacqueline b.1928
The Fun Shop c.1969
acrylic & wood on canvas 122 x 119
DONMG : 556.69

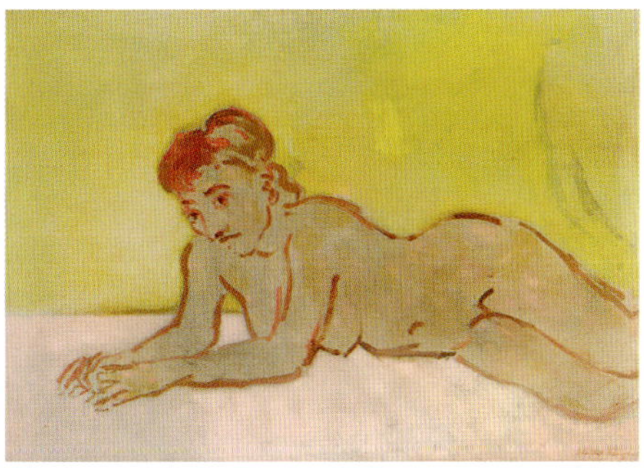

Steyn, Stella 1907–1987
Reclining Nude 1953
oil on canvas 70 x 99.5
DONMG : 496.63

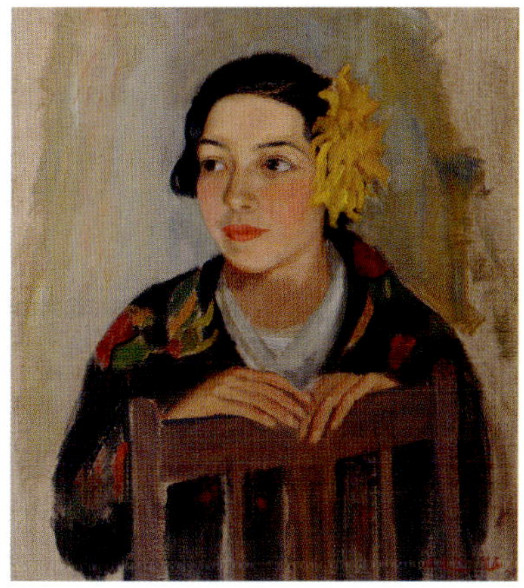

Stocks, Ernest Decimus 1840–1918
Portrait of Vera Way, née Wong
oil on canvas 48.5 x 44
DONMG 2007.9

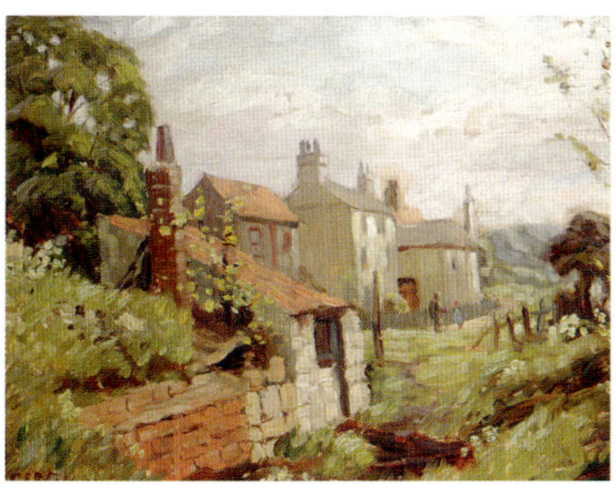

Stubbs, C. E. active c.1960–1962
Farm in a Rural Setting c.1960
oil on canvas 28 x 35.5
DONMG : 1997.22

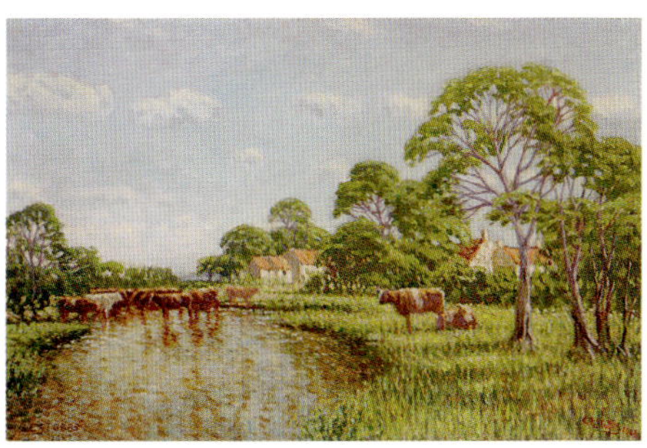

Stubbs, C. E. active c.1960–1962
Landscape with a River and Cows 1962
oil on canvas 61 x 92
DONMG : ZP272

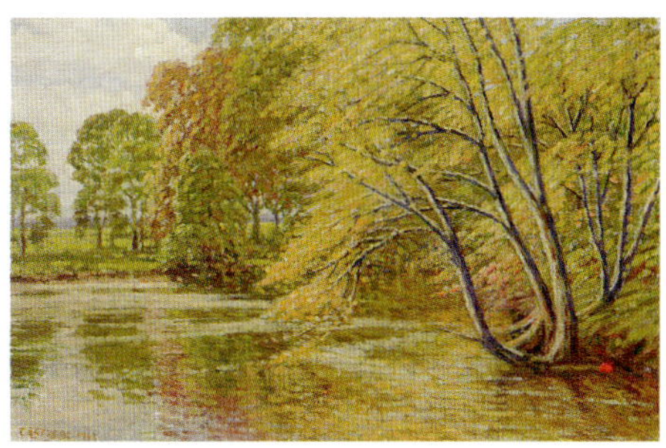

Stubbs, C. E. active c.1960–1962
Landscape with Trees 1962
oil on canvas 54 x 82
DONMG : ZP273

Facing page: unknown artist, *Frances Wansford* (detail), 1608, Doncaster Museum Service, (p. 103)

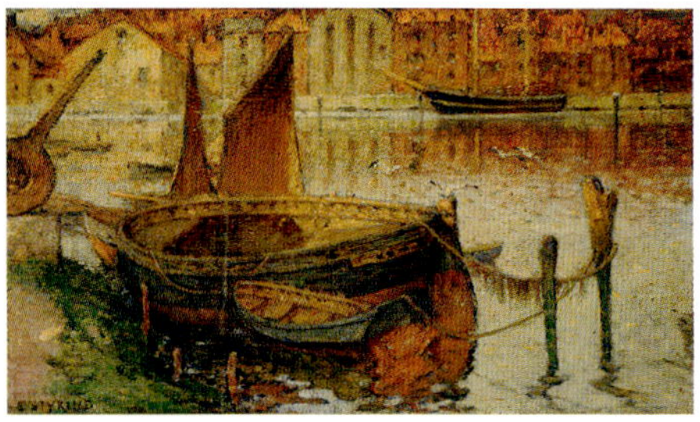

Styring, Elizabeth 1854–1940
The 'Derelict', High Tide, Whitby, North Yorkshire
oil on canvas 56 x 92
DONMG : 135.41

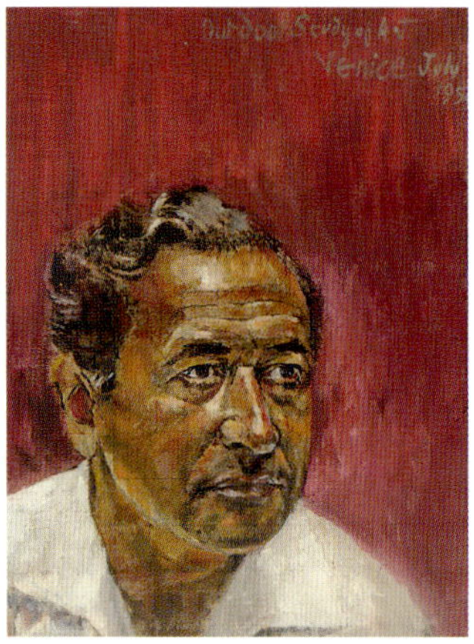

Sutherland, Graham Vivian 1903–1980
Arthur Jeffress (1904–1961) 1953
oil on canvas 38 x 29
DONMG : 962.85

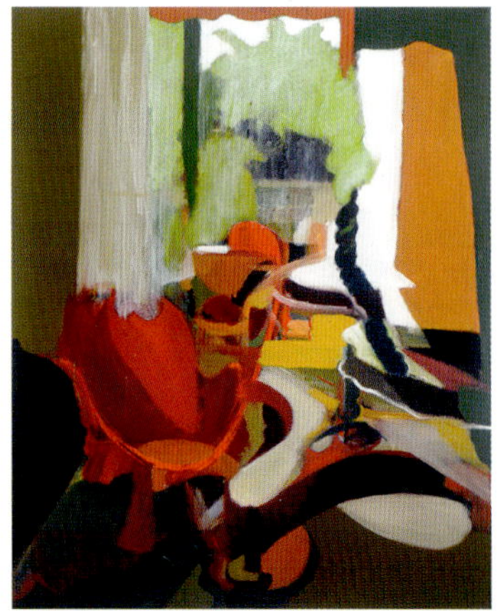

Taylor, Louise
Interior c.1969
oil on canvas 128 x 100.5
DONMG : 557.69

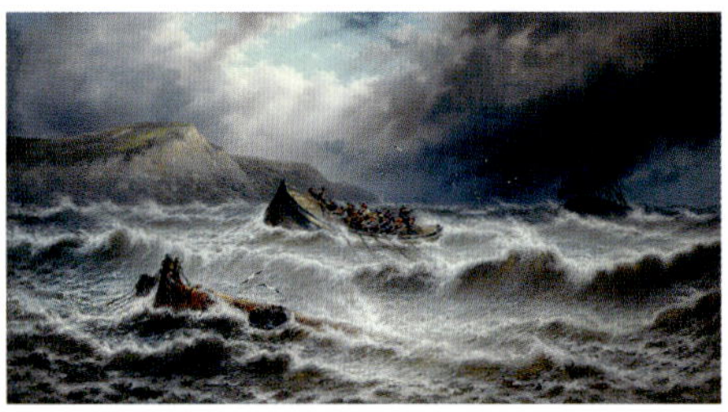

Timmermans, Louis Étienne 1846–1910
Wreck at Whitby, North Yorkshire
oil on canvas 59 x 106
DONMG : 323.58

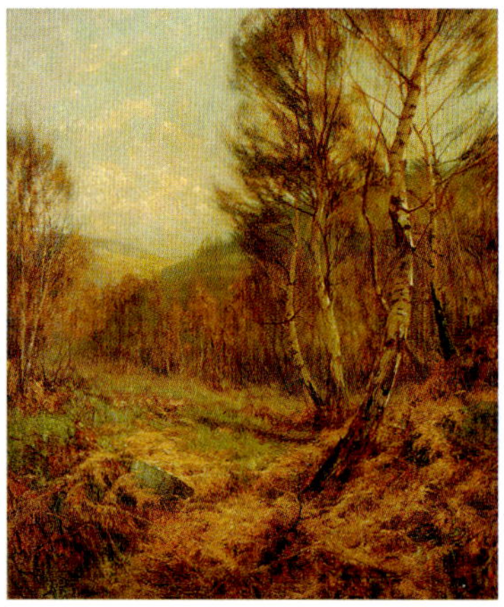

Tindall, William Edwin 1863–1938
A Late Autumn Evening before 1912
oil on canvas 100 x 83
DONMG : 8.12

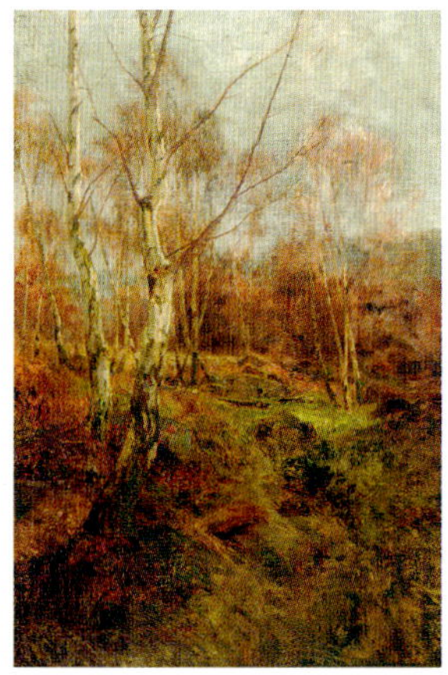

Tindall, William Edwin 1863–1938
Birch and Bracken, Adel Moor, Leeds
oil on canvas 76 x 51
DONMG : 234.51

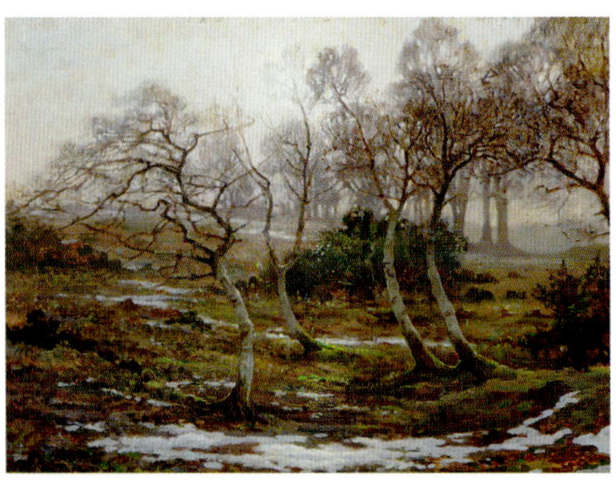

Tindall, William Edwin 1863–1938
Birch Trees and Snow
oil on canvas 31 x 42
PCF21

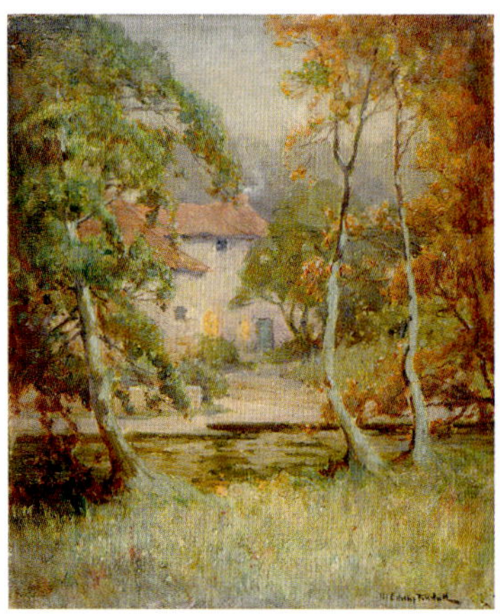

Tindall, William Edwin 1863–1938
The Wharfe
oil on canvas 37 x 31
DONMG : 120.39

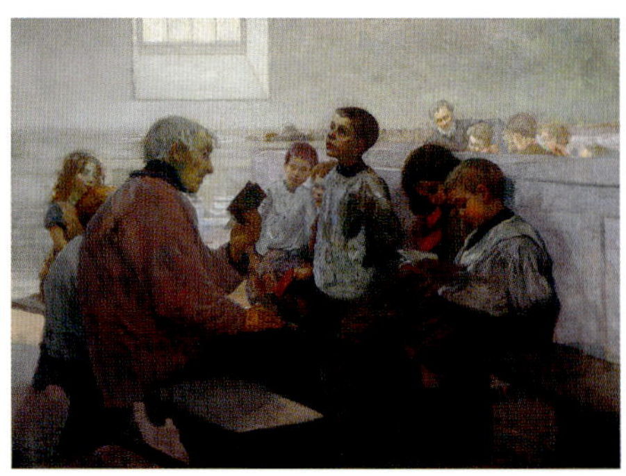

Titcomb, William Holt Yates 1858–1930
The Mariner's Sunday School 1897
oil on canvas 112 x 151
DONMG : 68.31

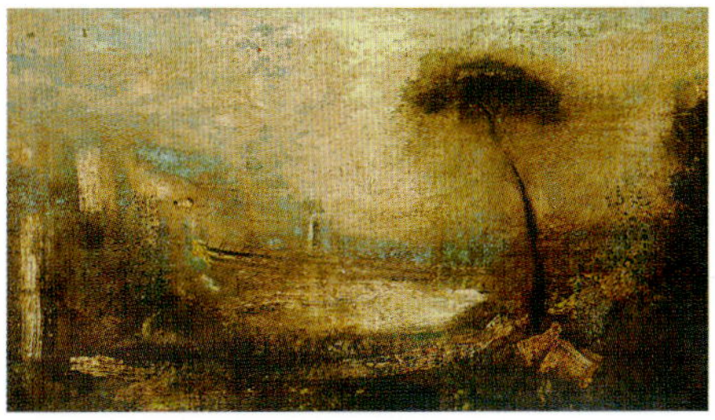

Turner, Joseph Mallord William 1775–1851
The Golden Bough c.1820
oil on canvas 40 x 66
DONMG : 140.43

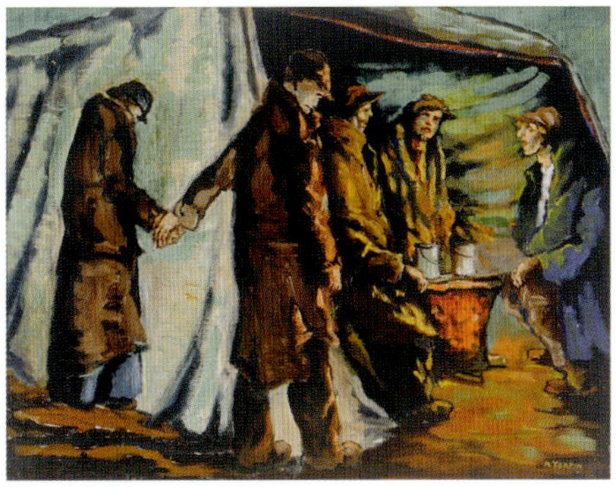

Turpin, Albert 1900–1964
Watchman's Fire (Night Shelter) 1938
oil on canvas 39 x 50
DONMG : 475.63

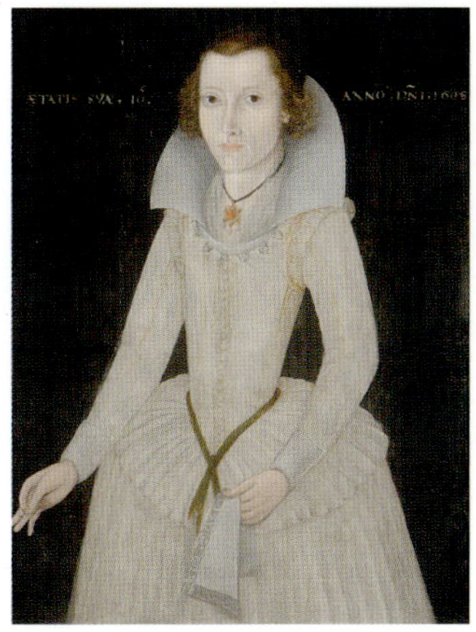

unknown artist
Frances Wansford 1608
oil on panel 89 x 66
DONMG : 999.87

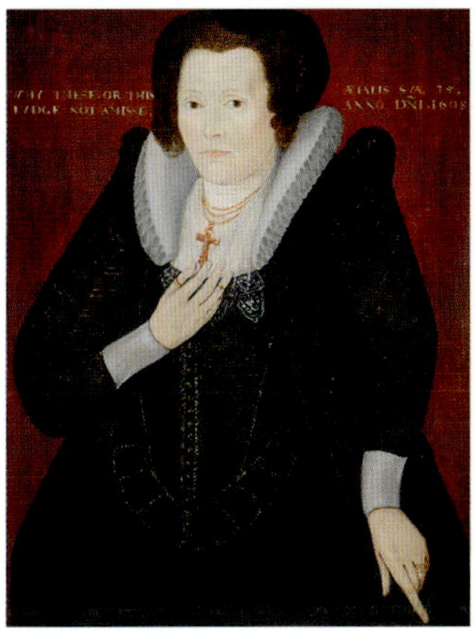

unknown artist
Muriel Wansford 1608
oil on panel 89 x 66
DONMG : 998.87

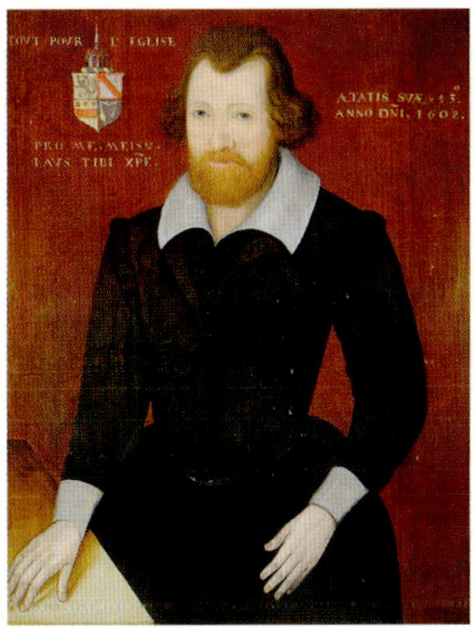

unknown artist
Richard Wansford 1608
oil on panel 89 x 66
DONMG : 997.87

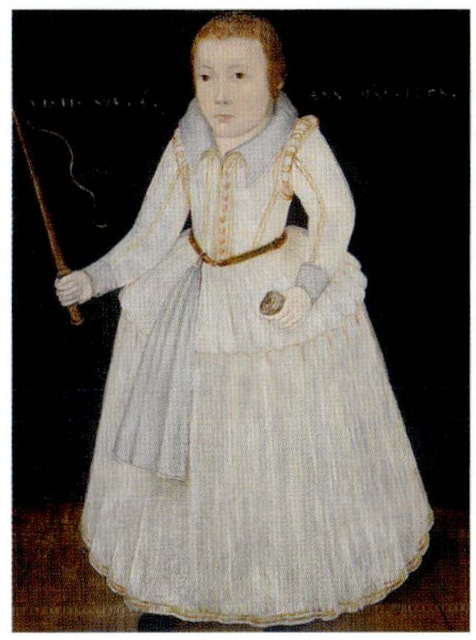

unknown artist
Rowland Wansford 1608
oil on panel 89 x 66
DONMG : 1000.87

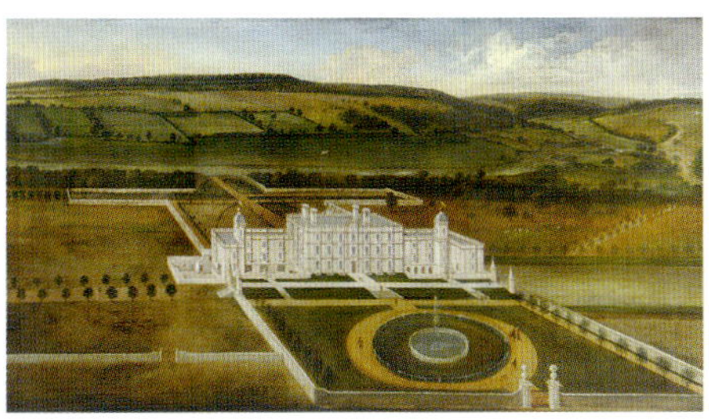

unknown artist
Sprotbrough Hall, South Yorkshire c.1700
oil on canvas 82 x 148
DONMG : 983.86

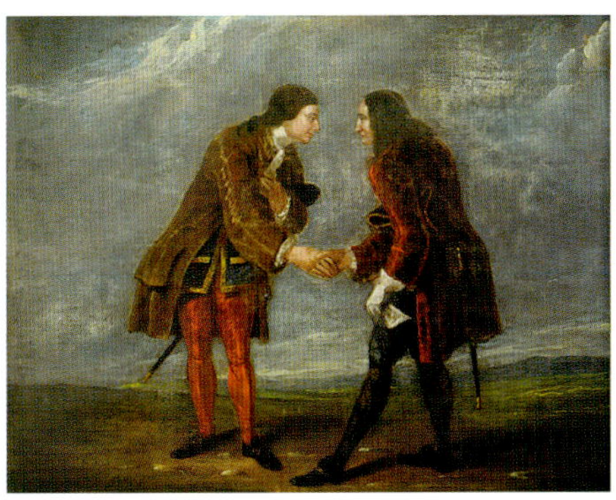

unknown artist
Sign for the 'Salutation Inn' c.1766
oil on board 80 x 100
DONMG : 1996.14

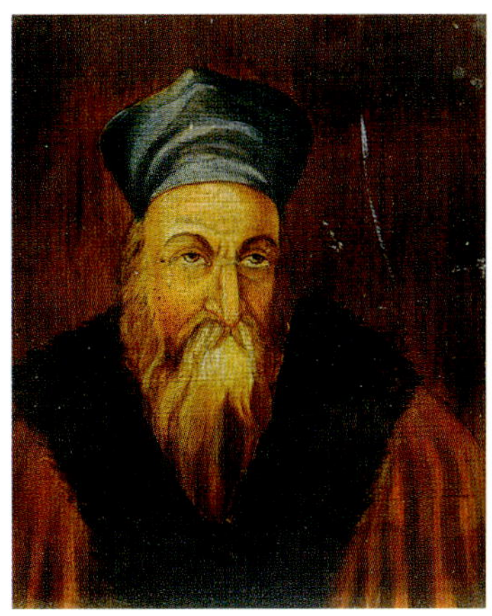

unknown artist
Leonardo da Vinci (1452–1519) 1785
oil on panel 15.5 x 12.5
DONMG : 1967.142

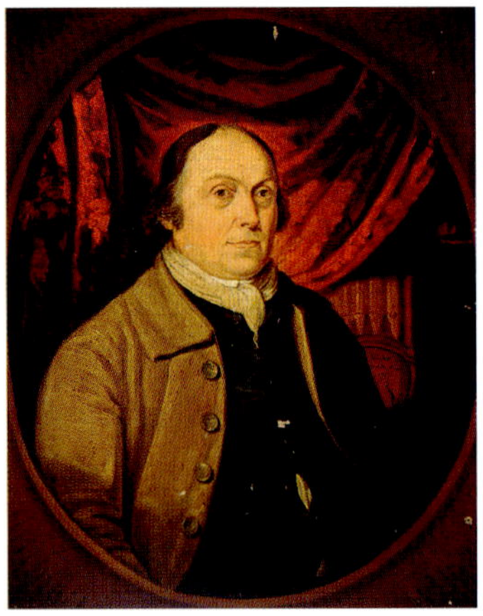

unknown artist
Portrait of a Gentleman 1797
oil on canvas 86 x 68
DONMG : 2008.46

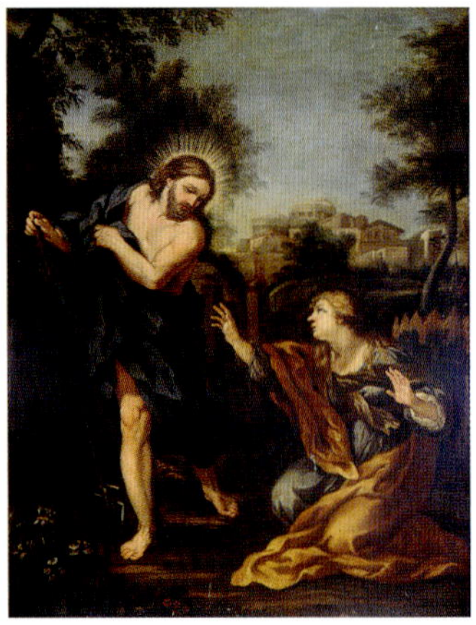

unknown artist 18th C
Noli me tangere
oil on canvas 76 x 59
DONMG : 653.75

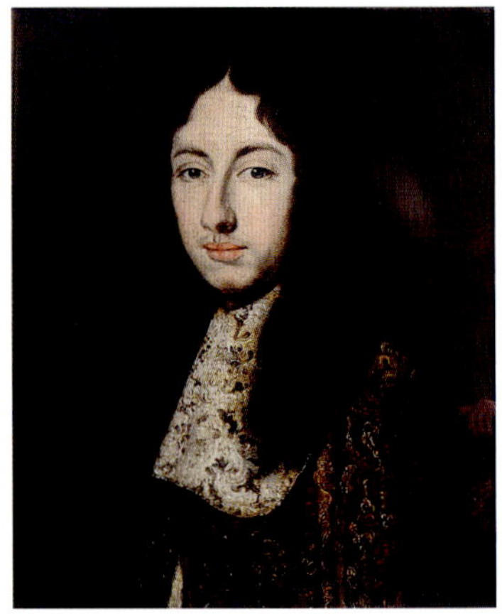

unknown artist 18th C
Thomas Wentworth (1693–1741), Earl of Strafford
oil on canvas 64 x 55
DONMG : 235.51

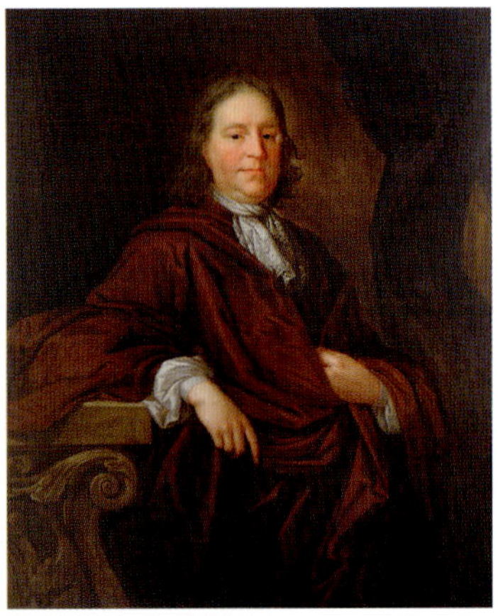

unknown artist mid-18th C
Thomas Fountayne (1639–1709)
oil on canvas 120 x 95
DONMG : 1999.28

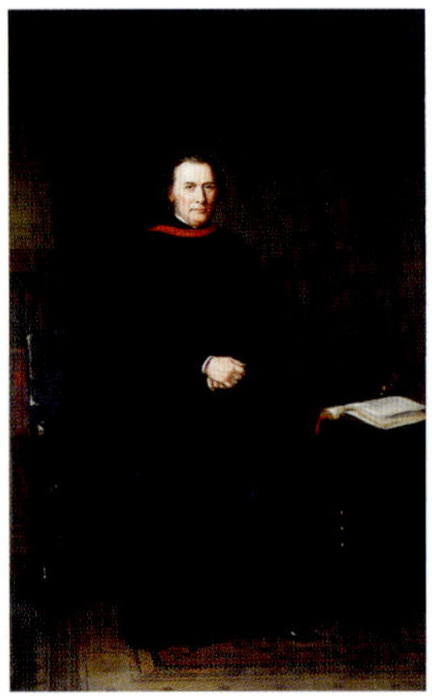

unknown artist
Charles John Vaughan (1816–1897), DD, Vicar of Doncaster 1879
oil on canvas 240 x 146
B

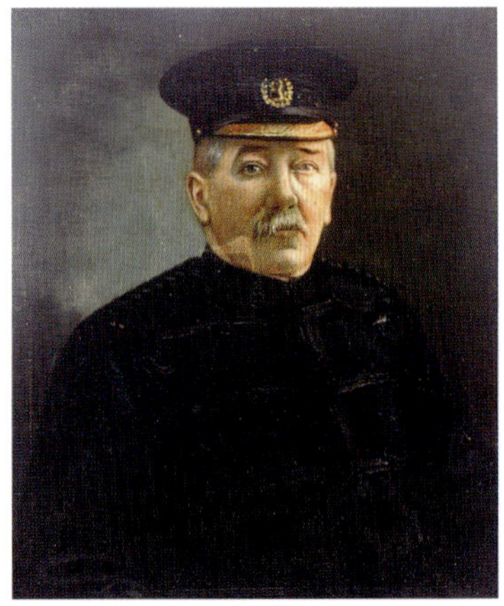

unknown artist 19th C
Mr George Lister, Chief Constable of Doncaster (recto)
oil on canvas 50 x 40
PCF10

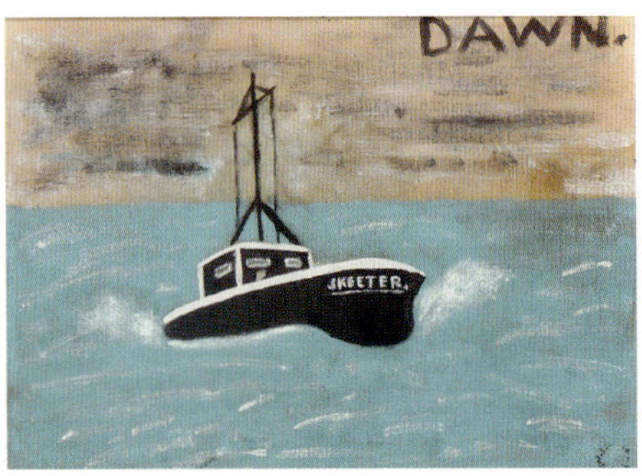

unknown artist 19th C
Fishing Boat (verso)
oil on canvas 40 x 50
PCF10

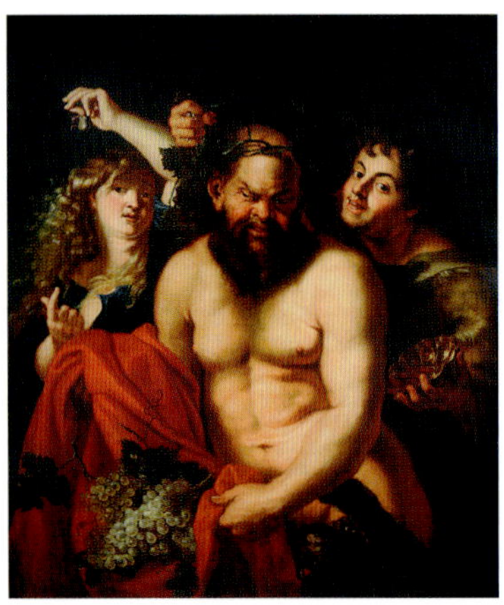

unknown artist 19th C
The Triumph of Bacchus
oil on canvas 134.5 x 114
DONMG : 96.36

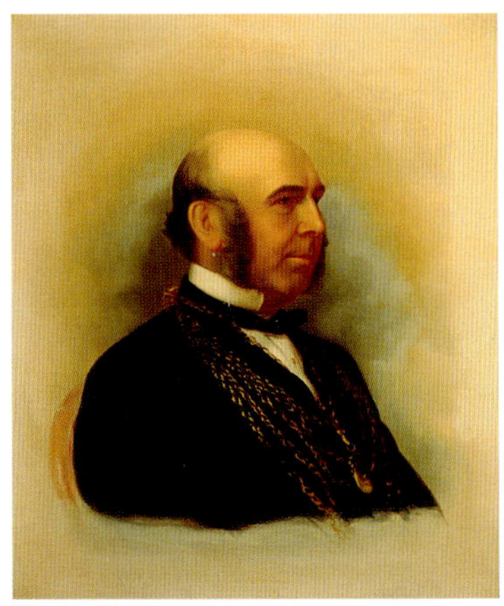

unknown artist late 19th C
Alderman Charles Stockil (1824–1899), JP, Mayor
oil on canvas 77 x 65
DONMG : 2008.45

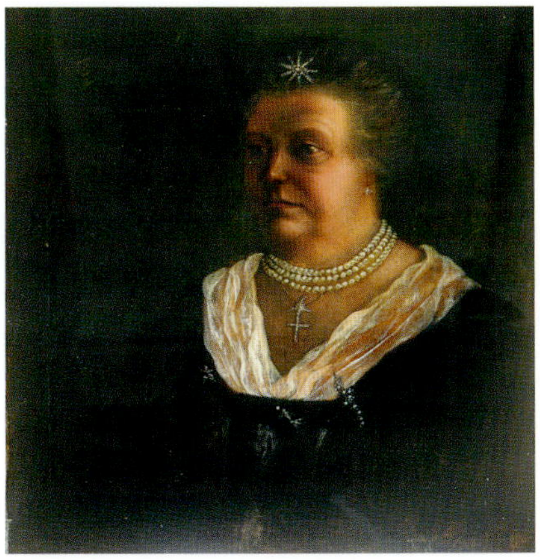

unknown artist late 19th C
Lady Isabella Wrightson (1853–1917)
oil on canvas 61 x 50
DONCH : B387

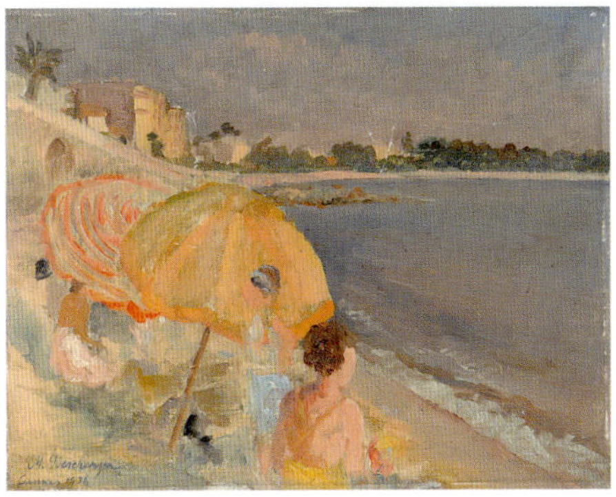

unknown artist
Cannes, France 1936
oil on panel 33 x 41
PCF22

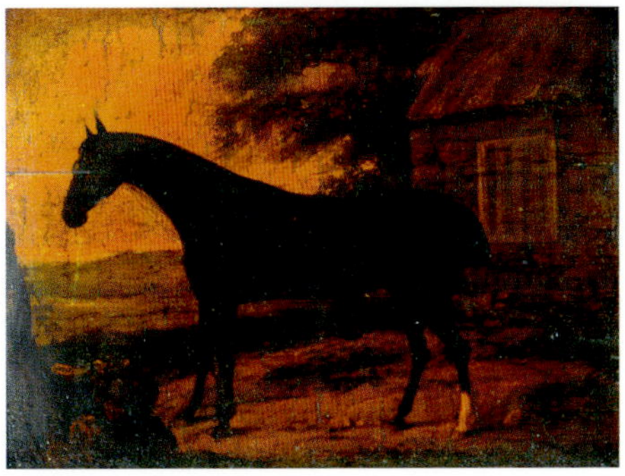

unknown artist
Horse
oil on canvas 36 x 47
DONMG : 743.76

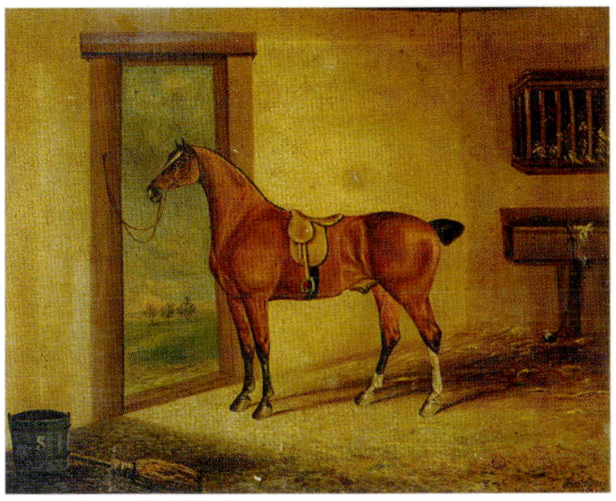

unknown artist
Horse in a Stable
oil on canvas 41.5 x 51
DONMG : 746.76

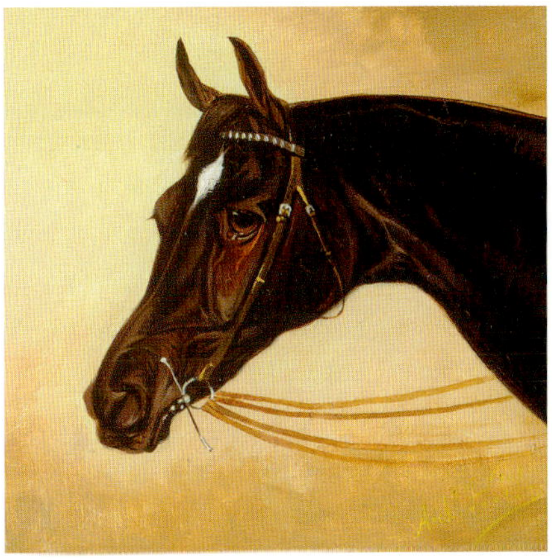

unknown artist
Horses Head, 'Bendigo'
oil on canvas 21 x 21
DONMG : 428.61

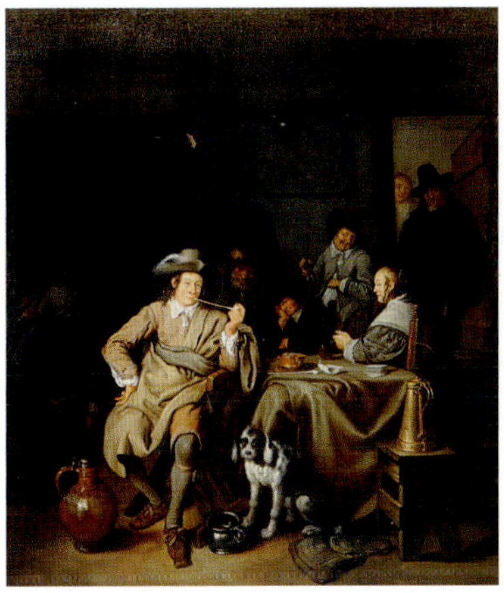

unknown artist
Interior with Figures
oil on canvas 91 x 77
DONMG : 74.33

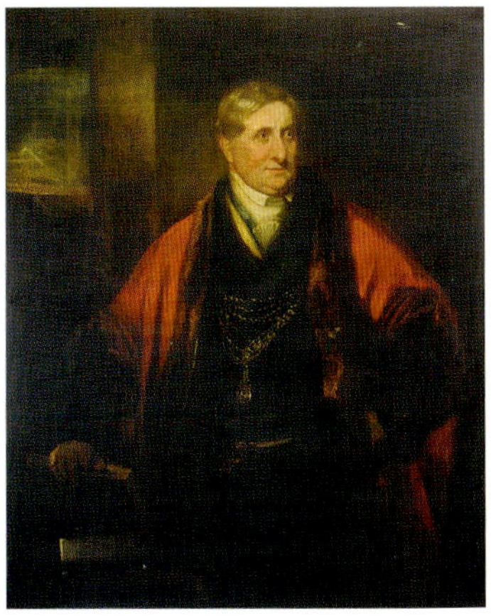

unknown artist
Mayor of Doncaster
oil on canvas 142 x 114
PCF20

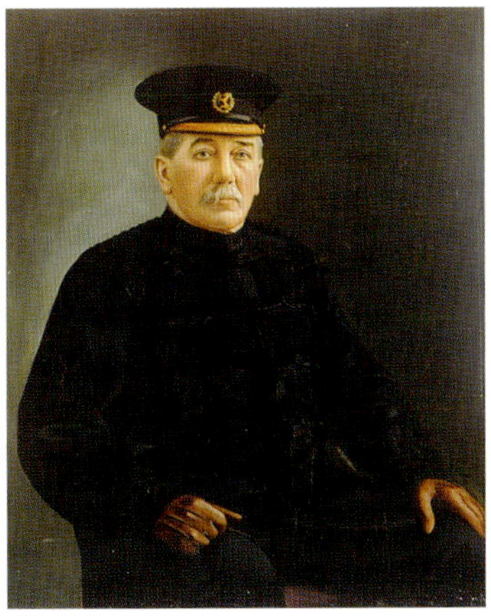

unknown artist
Mr George Lister, Chief Constable of Doncaster
oil on canvas 76 x 61
DONMG : 1957.289

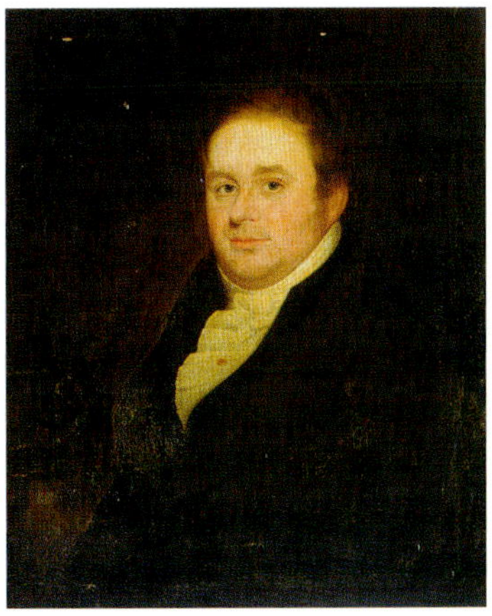

unknown artist
Portrait of a Man
oil on canvas 74 x 59
DONMG : 795.77

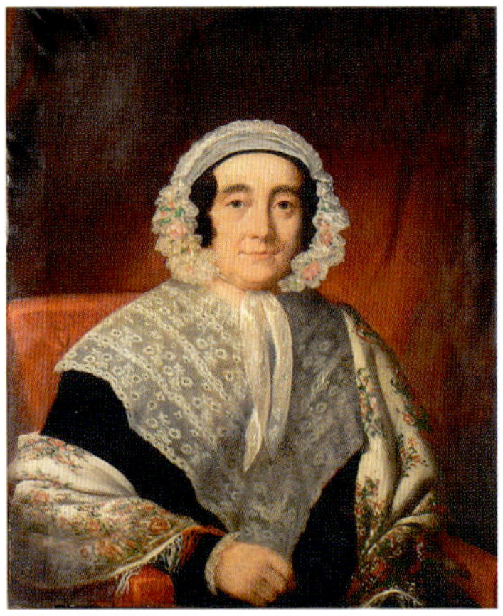

unknown artist
Portrait of a Woman
oil on canvas 76 x 63
DONMG : 2008.43

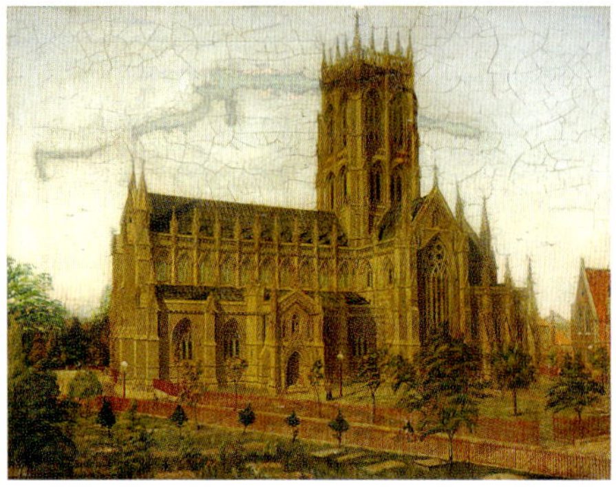

unknown artist
St George's Church, Doncaster, South Yorkshire
oil on canvas 100 x 125
PCF17

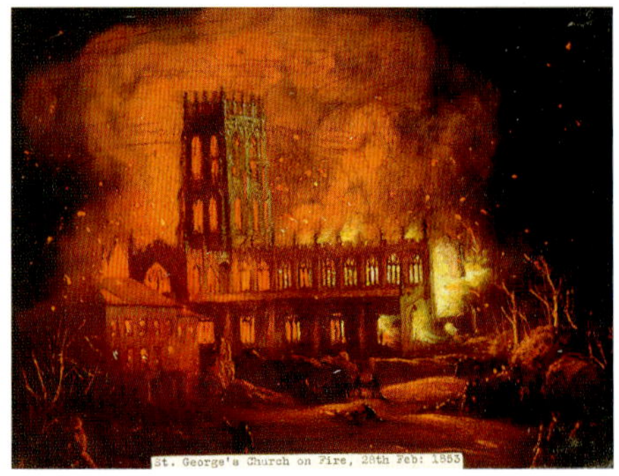

unknown artist
St George's Church on Fire, 1953, Doncaster, South Yorkshire
oil on board 17 x 21.5
DONMG : 672.75

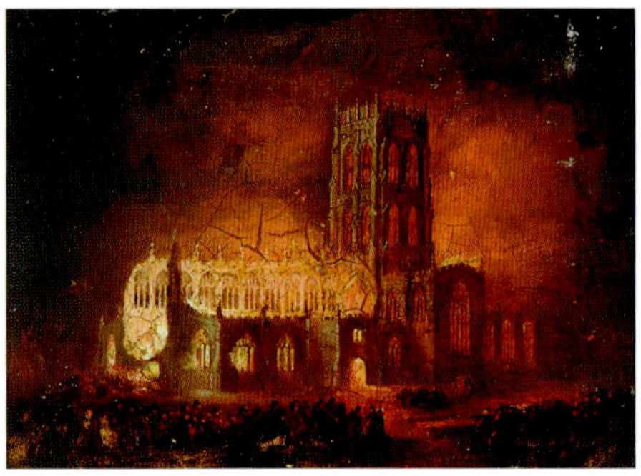

unknown artist
St George's Church on Fire, 1953, Doncaster, South Yorkshire
oil on board 17 x 21.5
DONMG : 673.75

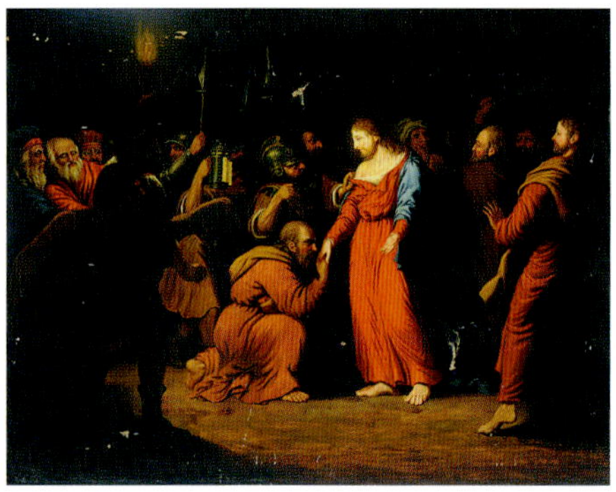

unknown artist
The Taking of Christ
oil on canvas 88 x 110.5
DONMG : 654.75

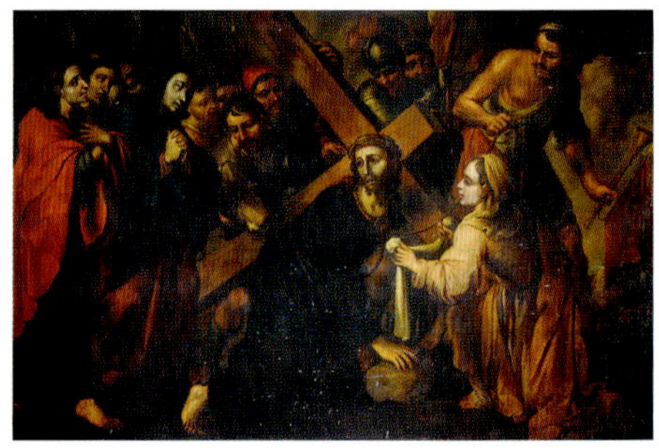

unknown artist
The Way of the Cross
oil on canvas 149 x 220
DONMG : 116.38

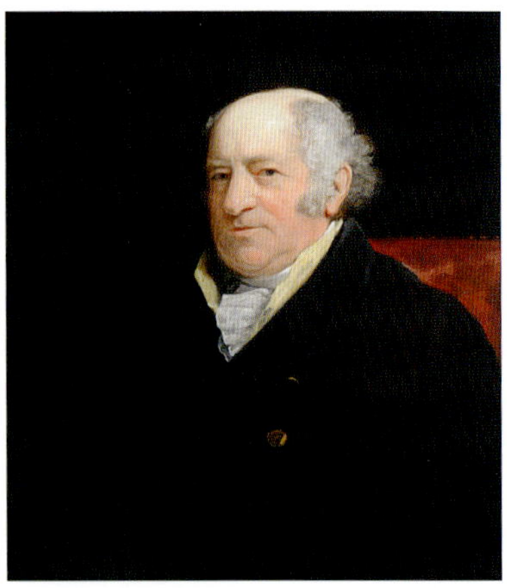

unknown artist
William Battie-Wrightson (1789–1879), MP for Retford and North Allerton
oil on canvas 75 x 62
PCF4

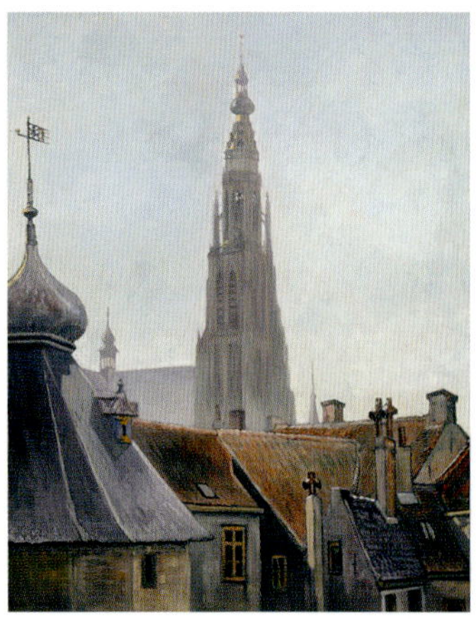

Van der Heyden, Gerard 1864–1939
The Cathedral, Breda, The Netherlands
oil on canvas 62 x 49
DONMG : 606.73

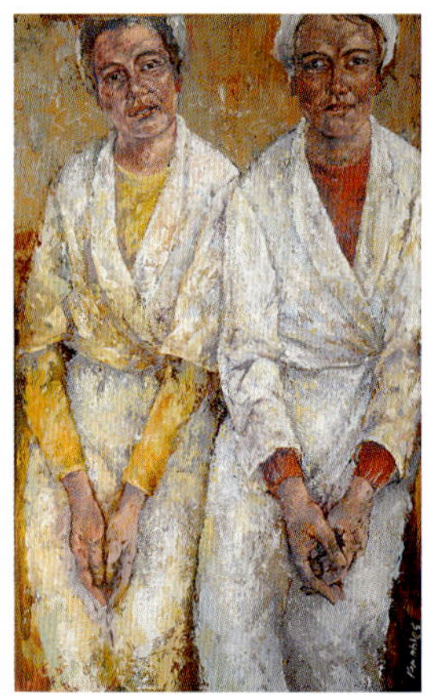

Venables, David b.1943
The Toffee Girls 2002
acrylic on canvas 135 x 80
DONMG : 2008.31

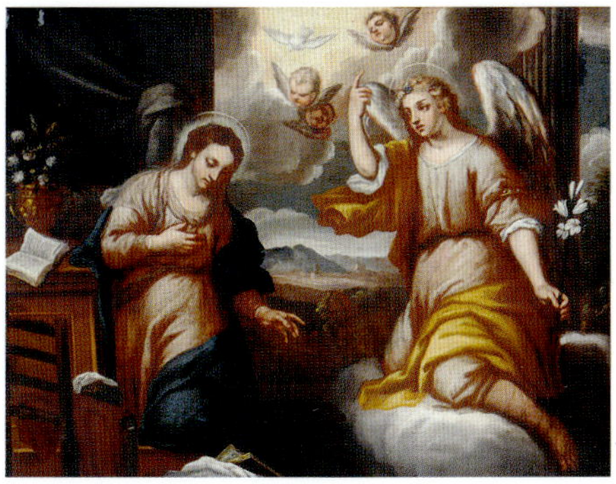

Veronese, Paolo (attributed to) 1528–1588
The Annunciation
oil on canvas 75 x 95
DONMG : 218.48

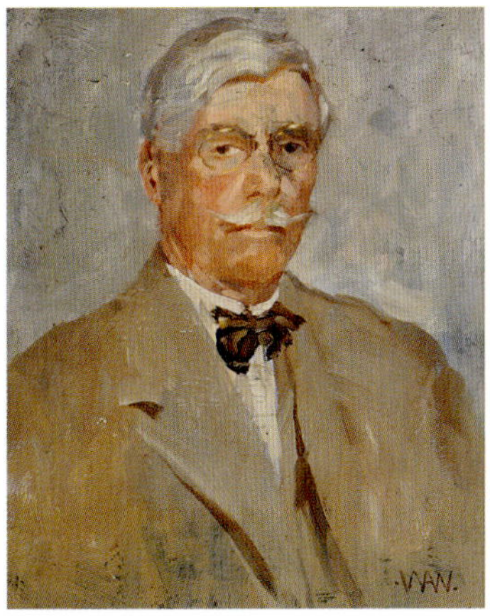

W. A. W.
William Edwin Tindall (1863–1938) c.1930
oil on board 35 x 28
DONMG : 963.85 (P)

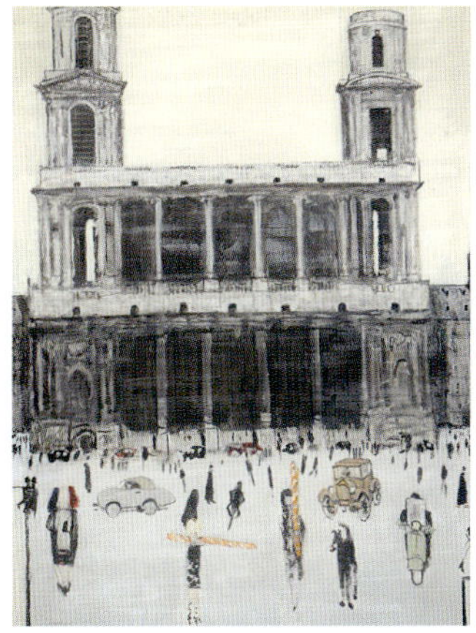

Wakeford, Edward 1914–1973
St Sulpice, Paris c.1950
oil on canvas 124 x 93.5
DONMG : 2001.13.2

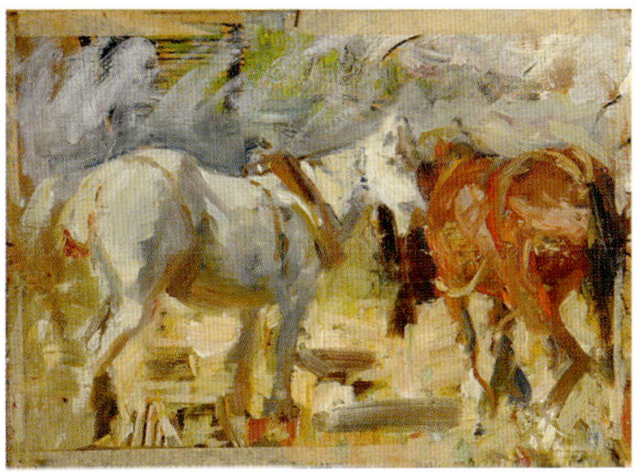

Wakeford, Edward 1914–1973
Two Horses (recto)
oil on canvas 24.5 x 34.5
DONMG : 488.63

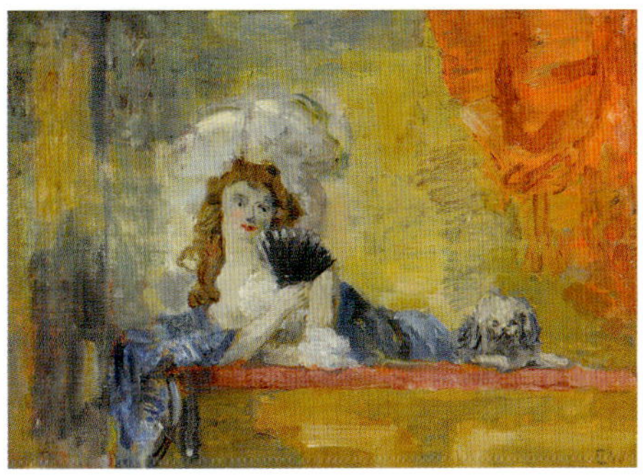

Wakeford, Edward 1914–1973
Temptation (verso)
oil on canvas 24.5 x 34.5
DONMG : 488.63

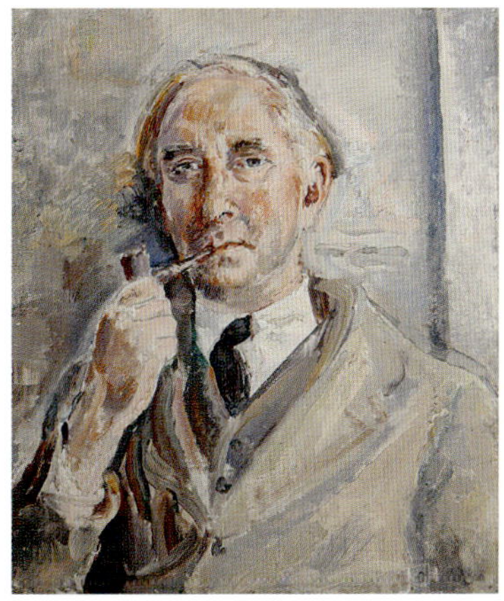

Walker, Ethel 1861–1951
Man with a Pipe
oil on canvas 61 x 49
DONMG : 349.59

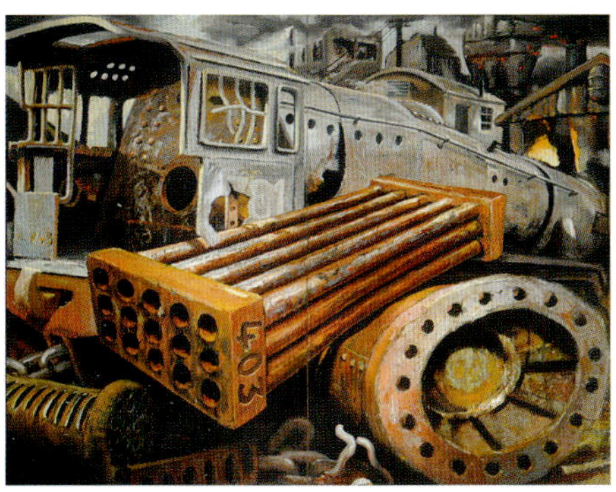

Waller, Jonathan b.1956
Breakdown 1986
oil on canvas 243 x 304
DONMG : 1007.88

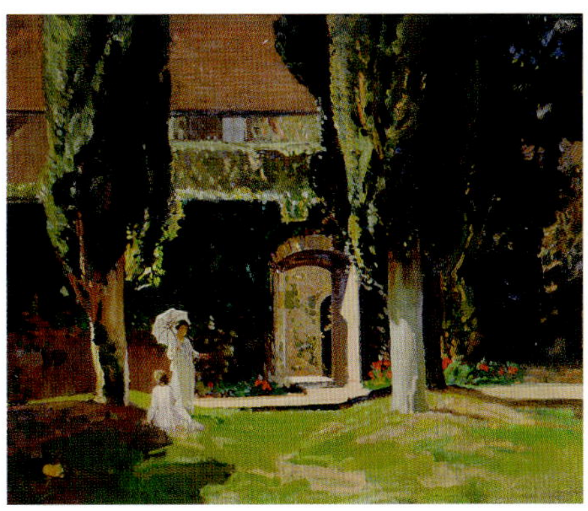

Watson, Harry 1871–1936
The Gateway, Beaulieu Abbey, Hampshire
oil on canvas 70.5 x 91.5
DONMG : 33.25

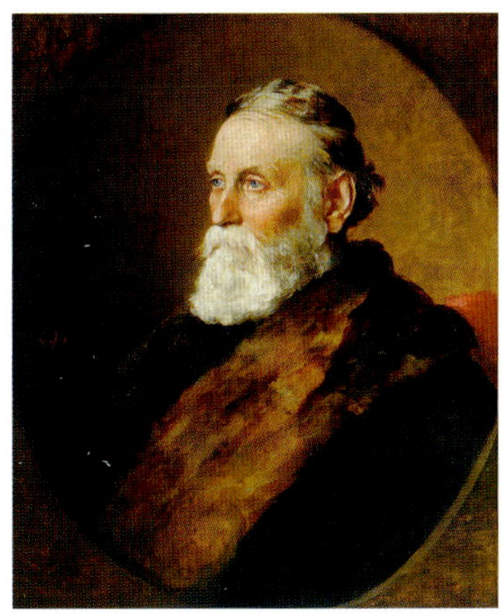

Weigall, Henry 1829–1925
Reverend Charles Edward Thomas (1823–1901)
oil on canvas 75 x 62
PCF3

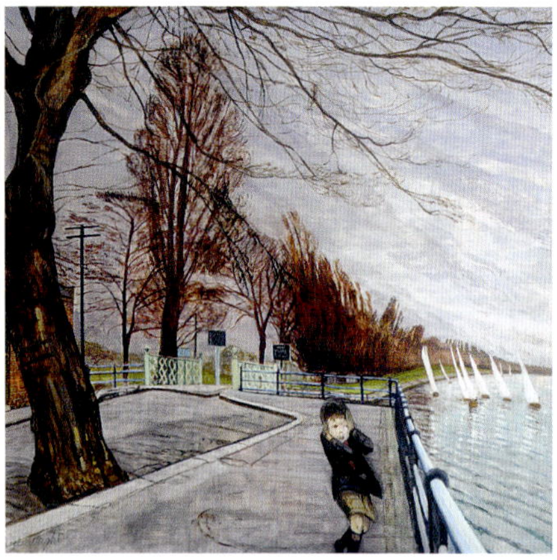

Weight, Carel Victor Morlais 1908–1997
Child's Wonderment c.1975
oil on canvas 121 x 121
DONMG : 742.76

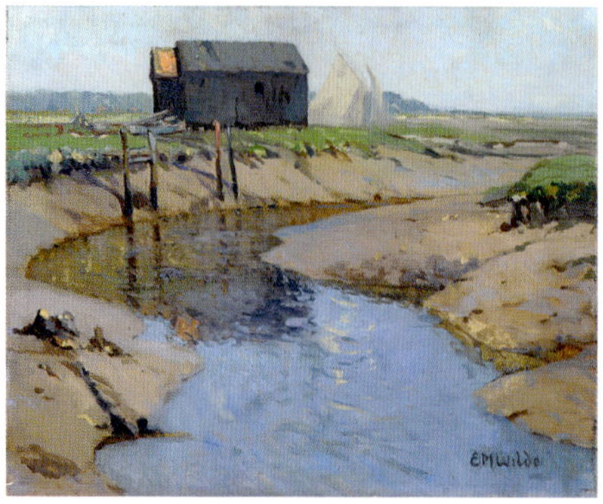

Wilde, Elizabeth M. active 1897–1938
Low Tide c.1912
oil on canvas 49 x 59
DONMG : 7.12

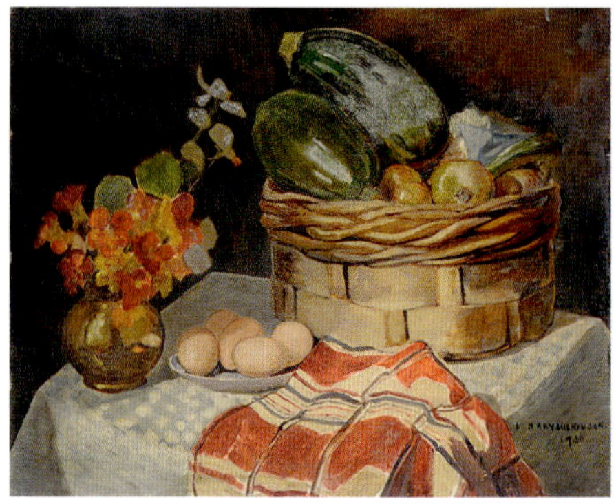

Wilkinson, Emma Mary b.1864
Country Produce 1930
oil on canvas 48 x 58.5
DONMG : 107.38

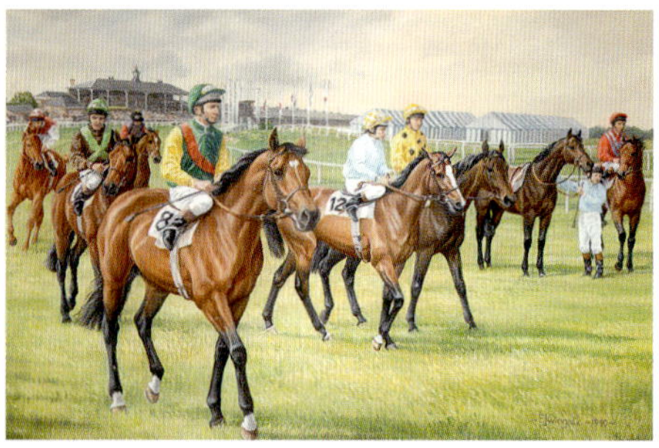

Wingate, Sue active since 1980
Spirit of the St Leger 1990
oil on canvas 57 x 85
DONMG : 1019.90

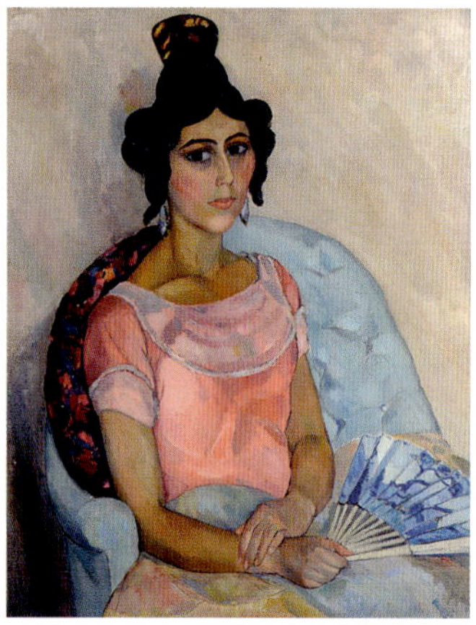

Wolfe, Edward 1897–1982
Spanish Girl 1922
oil on canvas 104 x 80
DONMG : 981.86

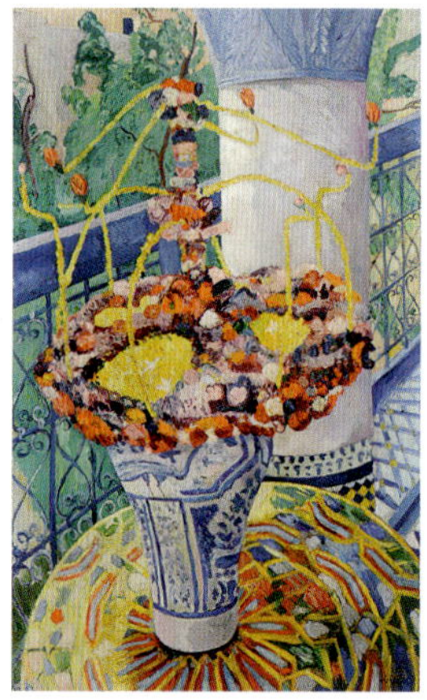

Wolfe, Edward 1897–1982
Vase of Flowers 1936
oil on canvas 120 x 73
DONMG : 492.63

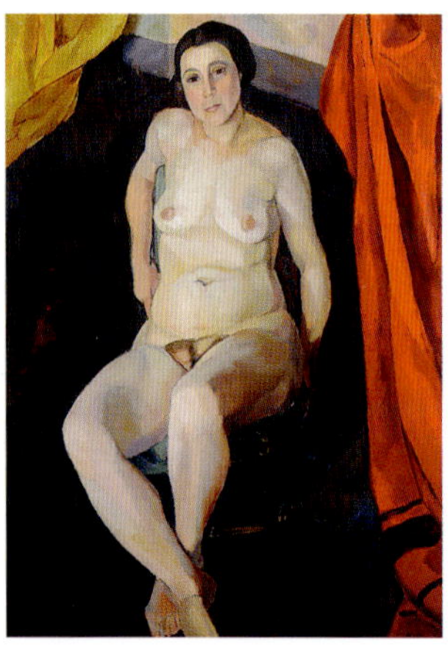

Wolfe, Edward 1897–1982
Florentine Model
oil on canvas 142 x 102
DONMG : 859.81

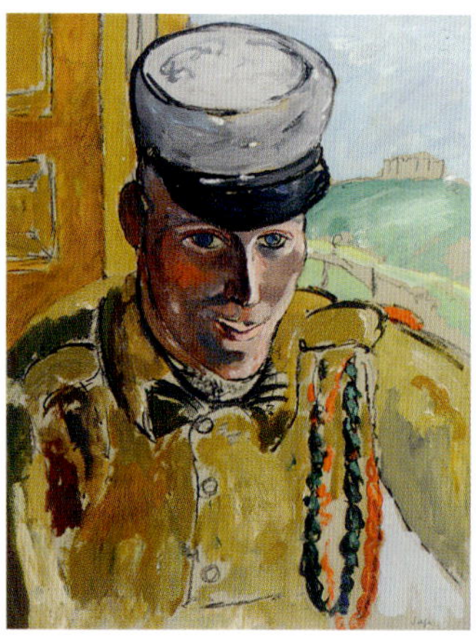

Wolfe, Edward 1897–1982
Unknown Warrior
oil on canvas 62.5 x 49
DONMG : 493.63

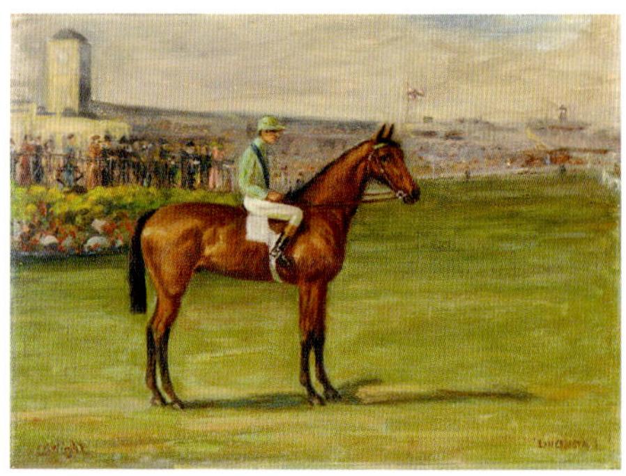

Wright, C. H.
'Linchister'
oil on canvas 33 x 44.5
DONMG : 745.76

Facing page: Backhuysen, Ludolf I, 1630–1708, *Shipping: A Fresh Breeze* (detail), Barnsley Museum and Heritage Service, (p. 48)

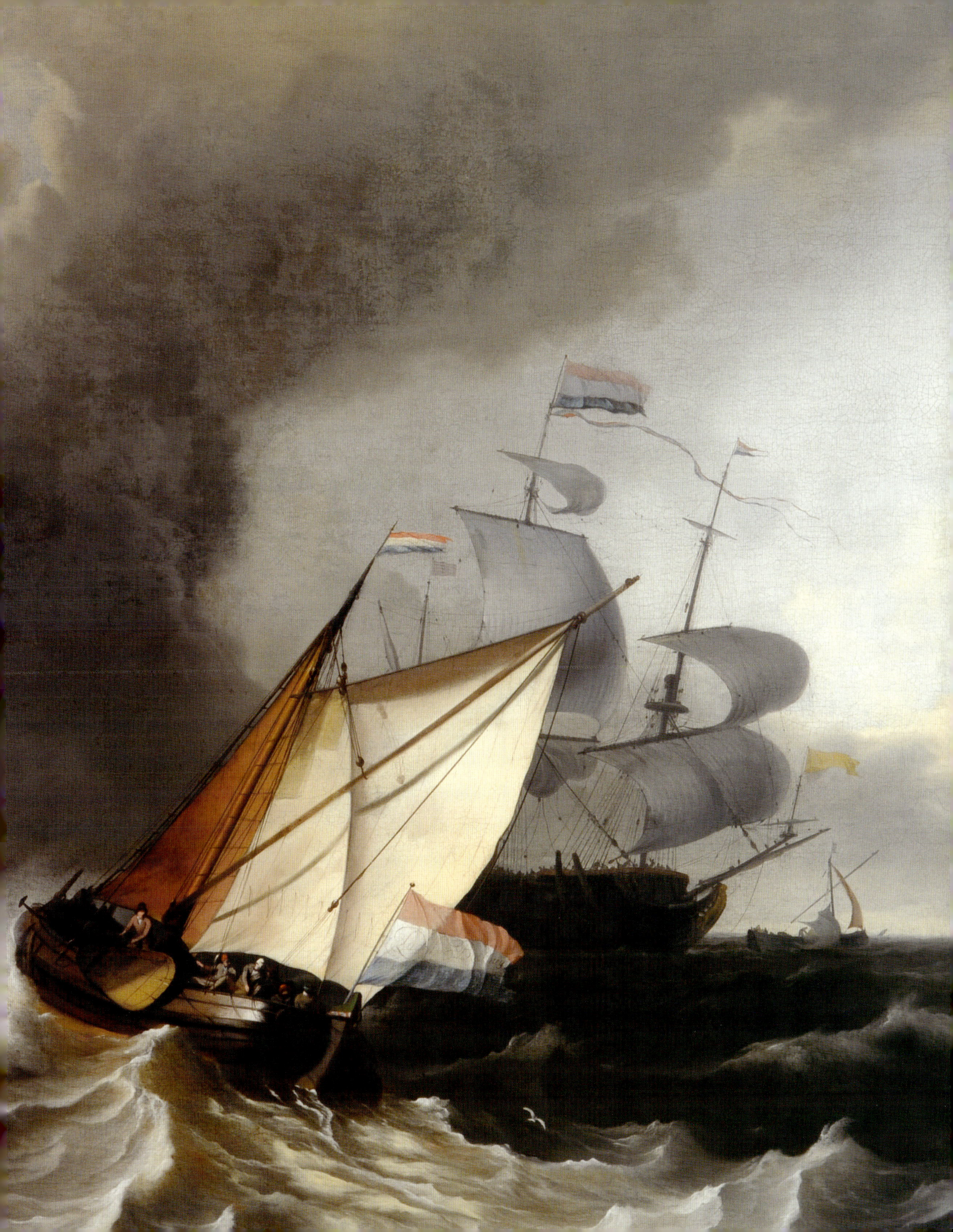

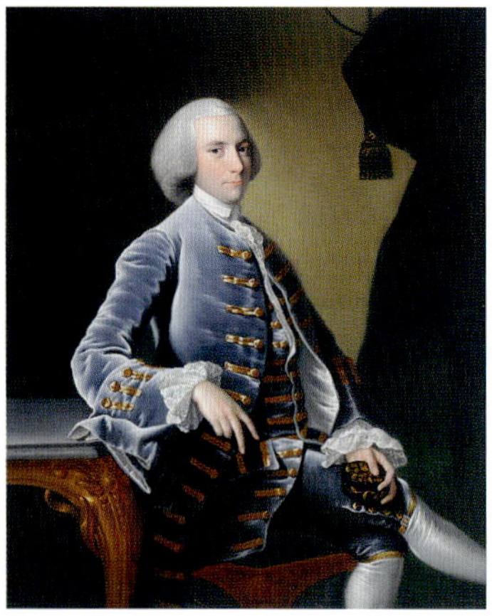

Wright, Joseph of Derby 1734–1797
William Pigot (1729–1782) 1760
oil on canvas 127 x 102
DONMG : 1999.8

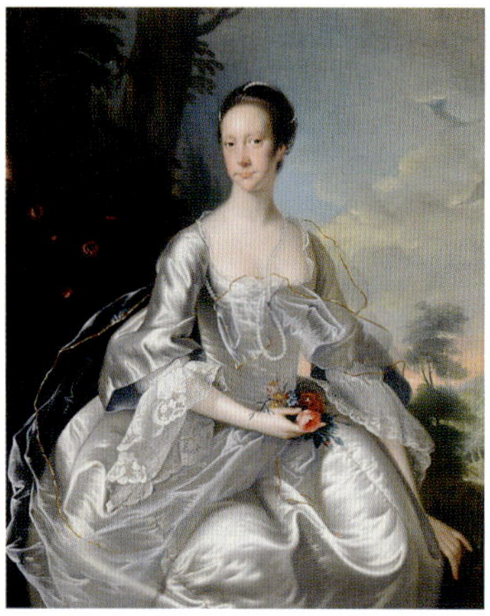

Wright, Joseph of Derby 1734–1797
Elizabeth Pigot (1726–1766) 1760
oil on canvas 127 x 102
DONMG : 1999.7

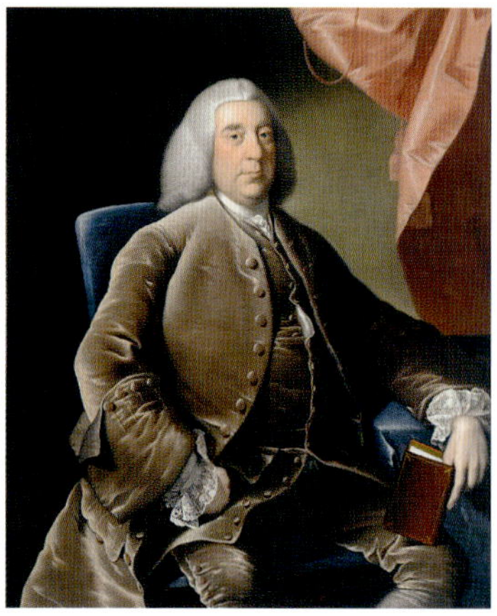

Wright, Joseph of Derby 1734–1797
William Brooke (1694–1763) 1760
oil on canvas 127 x 102
DONMG : 1999.6

The Regimental Museum of the King's Own Yorkshire Light Infantry

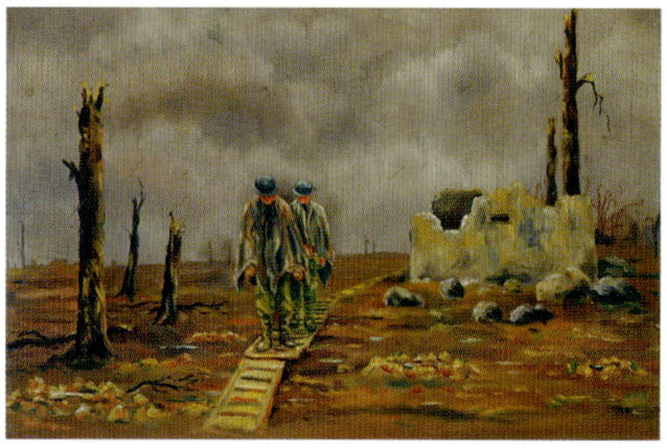

Headlam, Hugo
Scene in the Trenches
oil on canvas 35 x 52
P262

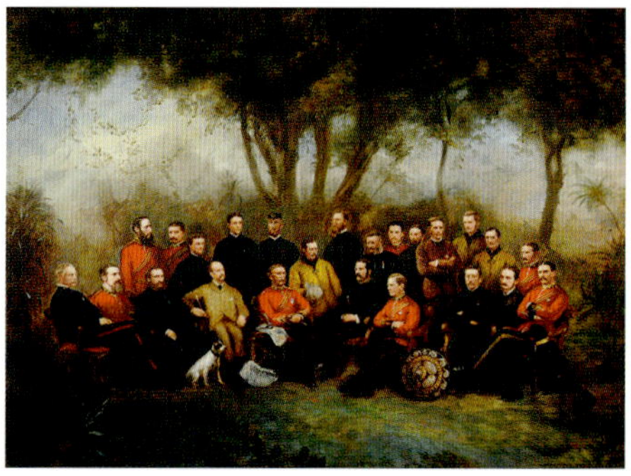

Horsborough, Victor active 1881–1935
Colonel S. A. Madden and Officers (51st Light Infantry) 1881
oil on canvas 70 x 90
P159

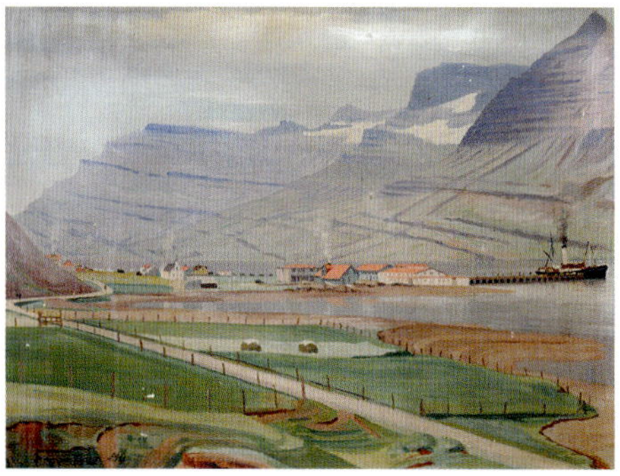

Johannsson, Freydomur (attributed to) b.1895
Budareyri, Iceland 1940
oil on canvas 47 x 62
PCF1

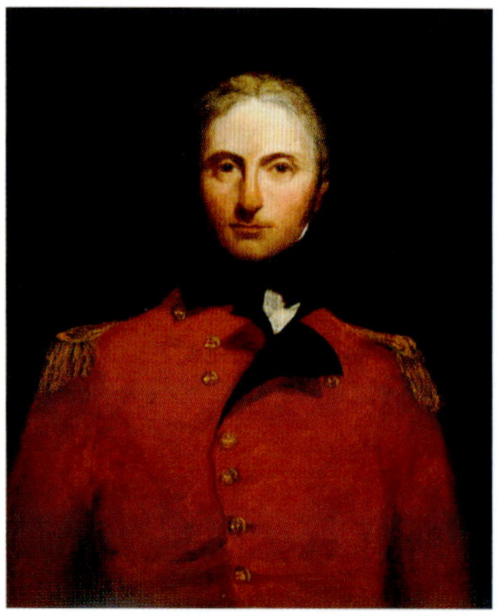

Lawrence, Thomas (after) 1769–1830
Sir John Moore (1761–1809)
oil on canvas 74 x 60
P181

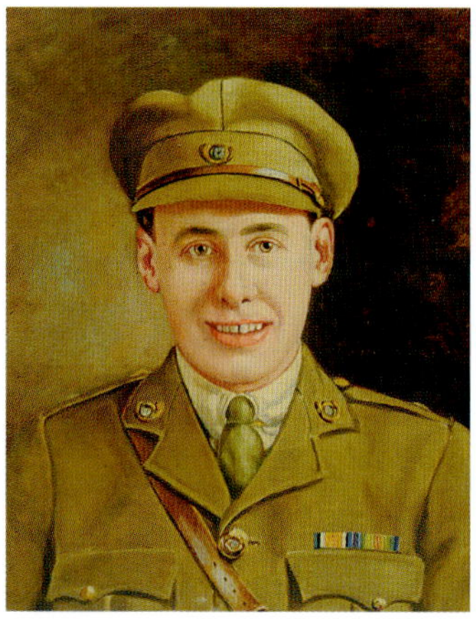

Marston, T.
Harold Hutson
oil on canvas 50 x 39
2008.31

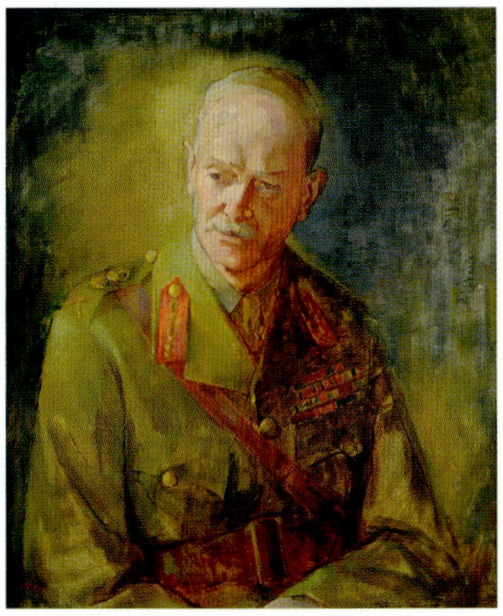

Napper, John 1916–2001
General Sir C. P. Deedes (1879–1969) 1947
oil on canvas 75 x 62
P154

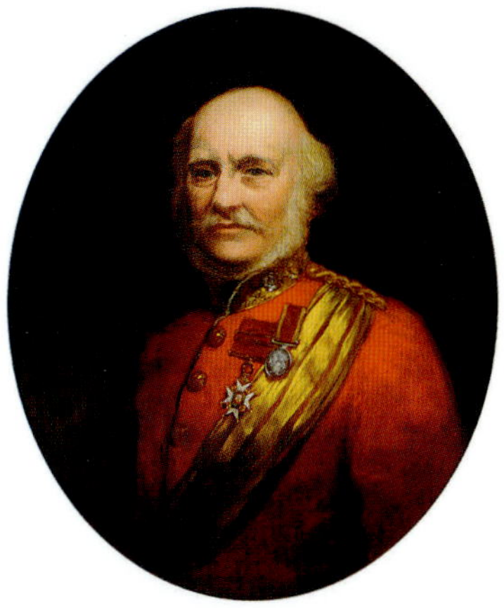

unknown artist 20th C
General G. A. Malcolm (d.1888)
oil on canvas 74 x 62
P180

Rawmarsh Community Library

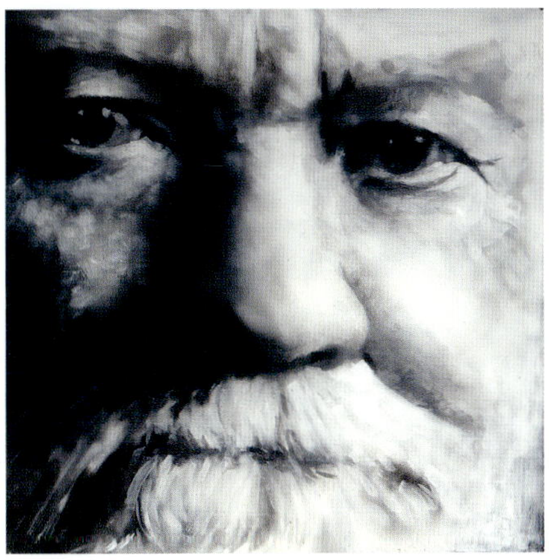

Padfield, Philip
Andrew Carnegie (1835–1919) 2005
acrylic spray paint on wood panel 124 x 120
PCF1

Rotherham Museum & Art Gallery

Rotherham Museum & Art Gallery's Collection has been acquired since the opening of Clifton Park Museum in 1893. The fine art collection consists of oil paintings, watercolours, drawings, prints and sculpture totalling some 3,000 items, around half of which are prints. The fine art is complemented by a good collection of decorative arts (mainly ceramics and glass) of around 5,500 items with a particular focus on local makers.

Within the oil paintings the largest group of 46 was donated (with an additional 35 watercolours) by local benefactor Edward Nightingale in 1908 and 1913 (some had been on loan to the Museum from 1893). He did this specifically 'to form the nucleus of a really good and instructive series of art productions, which a town of such importance as Rotherham should possess'. Of this group are a number of significant artworks including *Bay of Biscay* by Henry Redmore, *Interior of a Church* by David Roberts, *Mary, Queen of Scots and David Rizzio* by John Rogers Herbert, and *La zingarella* after Correggio.

Nightingale's donation formed the start of the fine art collection, and the Museum continued to collect work, much of which has a particular local significance. Clifton Park Museum was originally the home of the Walker family (an important local family of iron founders), who built Clifton House (as it was then) in 1784. The Collection includes a number of oil paintings related to the Walker Family, which fall broadly into three groups: those donated by Mrs Winifred Causton, descendant of the Walker family (including the large full-length portraits of Joshua and Susannah Walker of Clifton House); those donated by Michael Walker, descendent of the Walker family (including a portrait of Susannah Walker in later life); and those painted by Dame Ethel Walker, descendant of the Walker family, including her *Self Portrait* and *Decoration for an Ivory Room: Invocation to the Dance*. Many of the Walker-related paintings are on display at Clifton Park Museum because of their direct connection to the building.

The portrait collection extends beyond the Walkers and includes the widely exhibited *Ann Verelst (1751–1823)* by George Romney. Anne was the younger daughter of Josiah Wordsworth of Wadworth. She married Henry Verelst and lived at Aston Hall, near Rotherham. Ann is depicted in a pose adapted from an antique prototype – the statue of Ceres in the Mattei Collection in Rome. Other portraits include *Portrait of an Unknown Lady* after Godfrey Kneller, *William Pitt the Younger (1759–1806)* after Thomas Gainsborough, and a pair of portraits by Jonathan Singleton Copley after David Morier of *George II (1683–1760)* and *Frederick Louis (1707–1751), Prince of Wales*.

The Collection then extends into those inspired by religious belief or mythology and allegory. *The Adoration of the Shepherds*, by the circle of Scarsellino is probably the best of those inspired by religion, although with conservation some of the remaining items might rival this work. The best of the mythological or allegorical paintings are two by well-known artists: *Diana, Returning from the Chase* by William Etty and *The Adventure* by William Shackleton.

Beyond these are the townscapes, seascapes, landscapes and rural scenes. The seascapes form a particularly good collection with paintings by John Callow, George Chambers and William Brooker. Many of these paintings were exhibited at Rotherham Art Gallery in the exhibition 'Rotherham by the Sea' in 2006. The landscapes and townscapes include some paintings of national or international interest such as *Landscape Study* by Henry Herbert La Thangue, although the majority are of local scenes. The Collection is especially strong in its paintings of cattle, with around 15 images, including three by Louis Bosworth Hurt.

The majority of the Collection focuses on paintings with a local connection. In some cases this means having a local scene or sitter, and a well-known local artist. Examples of this are the portrait of *Thomas Newbould (1845–1933)* (a local colliery manager) by David Jagger (this painting is complemented by sculptures by his more famous brother Charles Sargeant Jagger in the sculpture collection), and the William Cowen painting *View of Rotherham, South Yorkshire*, which is complemented by two other oil works by Cowen in the Collection.

Rotherham Museum & Art Gallery also cares for the paintings at other Rotherham Metropolitan Borough Council locations including Rotherham Town Hall. Most of these represent past mayors, although some of the more recent works have been presented to the town from our overseas partners.

The Museum & Art Gallery continues to collect items of fine art, particularly those with a local connection, which extend our existing collection.

Frances Yeo, Senior Curator and Collections Manager

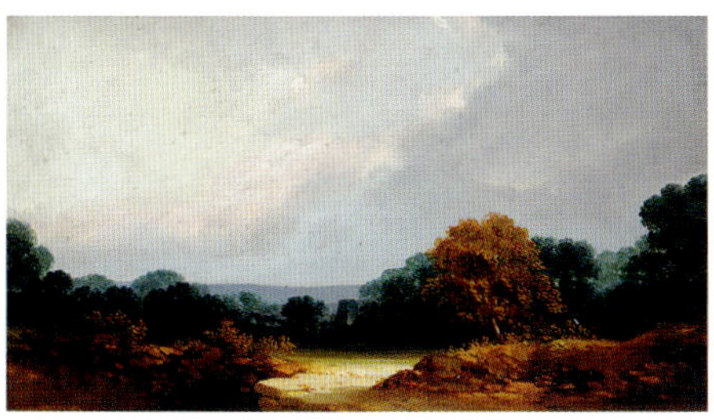

Allport, Thomas 1804–1879
Landscape 1827
oil on board 17.5 x 31.5
ROTMG : OP.1977.60

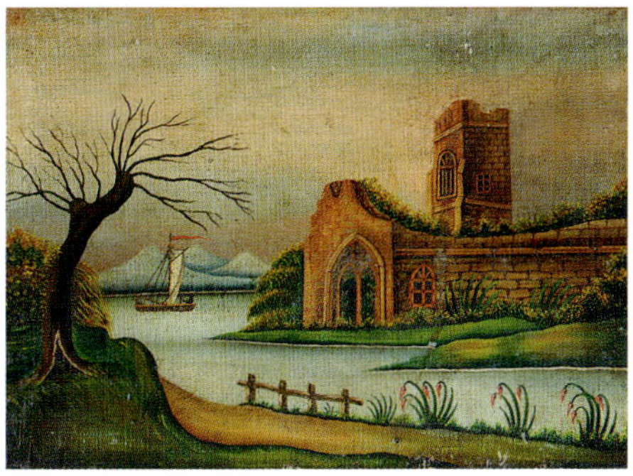

Andrews, J. B.
Priory in Cumberland 1848
oil on canvas 38 x 50.5
ROTMG : OP.1977.131

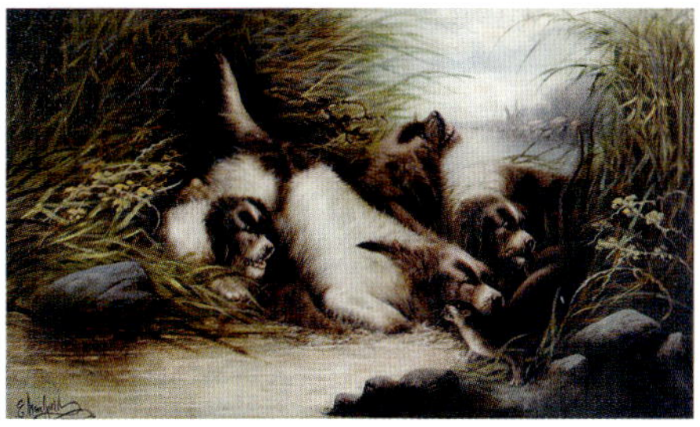

Armfield, George 1810–1893
Terriers c.1840
oil on canvas 76 x 127
ROTMG : OP.1977.35

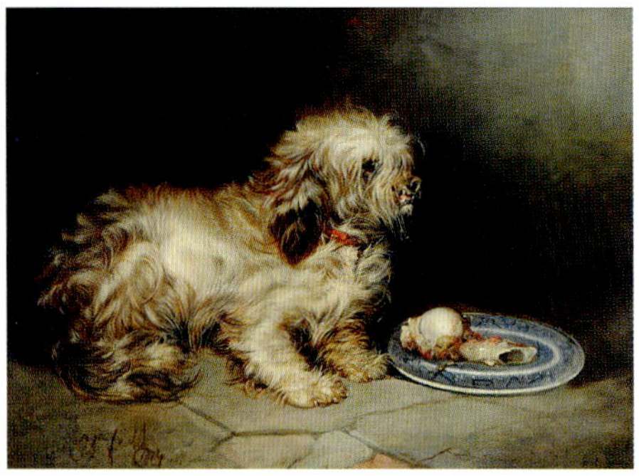

Armfield, George 1810–1893
Terrier c.1850
oil on canvas 46 x 62
ROTMG : OP.1977.143

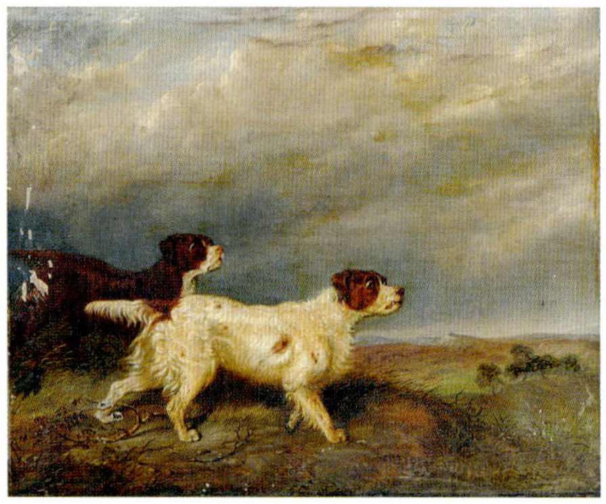

Armfield, George 1810–1893
Two Hunting Dogs c.1850
oil on canvas 40.5 x 48
ROTMG : OP.1977.127

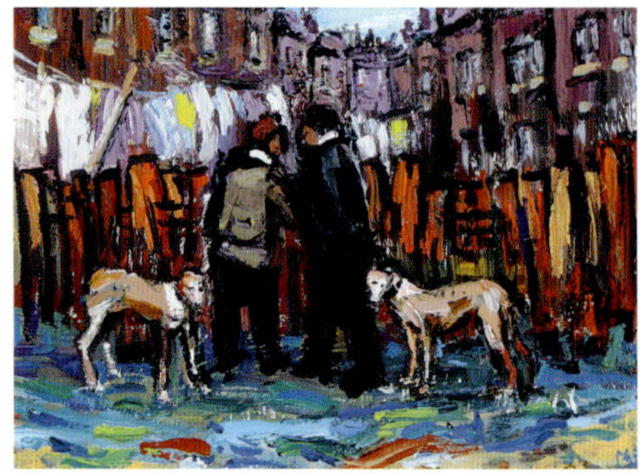

Arnfield, Marjorie 1930–2001
Miners and Dogs c.1995
oil on board 19.5 x 31 (E)
ROTMG : 1998.69

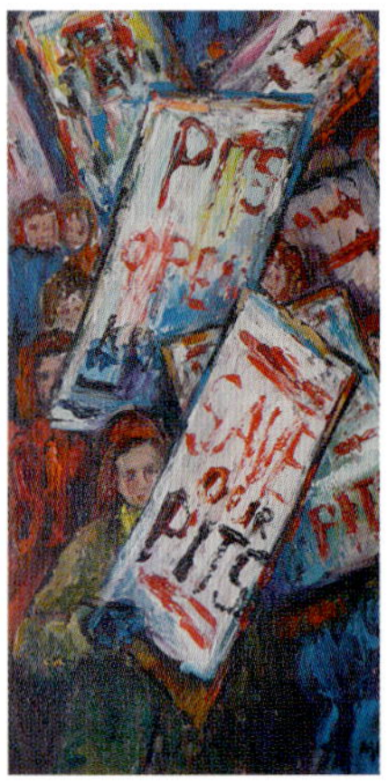

Arnfield, Marjorie 1930–2001
Save Our Pits c.1995
oil on board 61.5 x 30.5
ROTMG : 1998.70

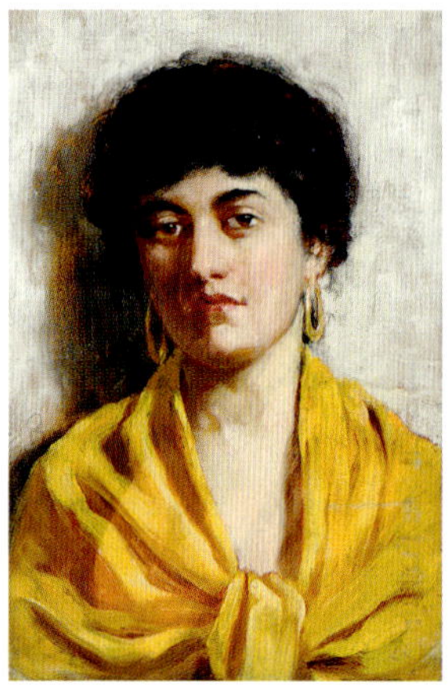

Bache, Edward active 1874–1893
Portrait of a Girl c.1880
oil on canvas 30.5 x 20.5
ROTMG : OP.1977.77

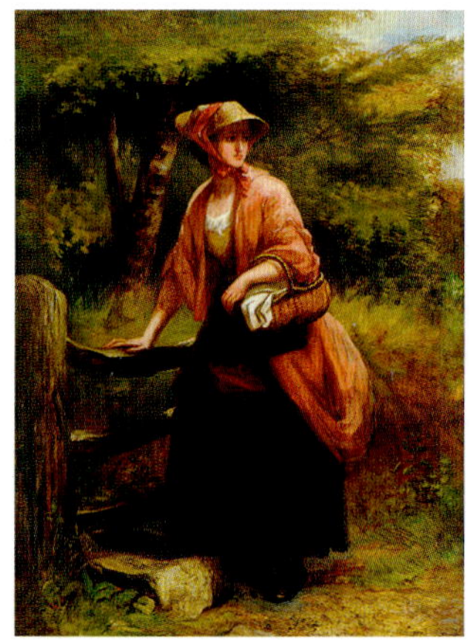

Barnes, Edward Charles 1830–1890
At the Stile c.1870
oil on canvas 62 x 43
ROTMG : OP.1977.16

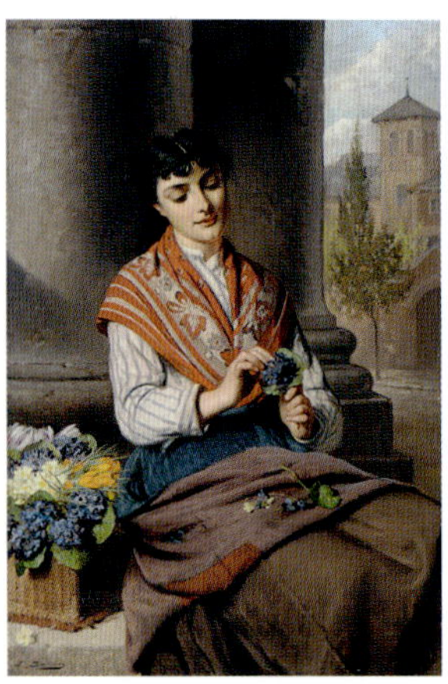

Barnes, Edward Charles 1830–1890
The Flower Girl c.1870
oil on canvas 88.5 x 59 (E)
ROTMG : OP.1977.43

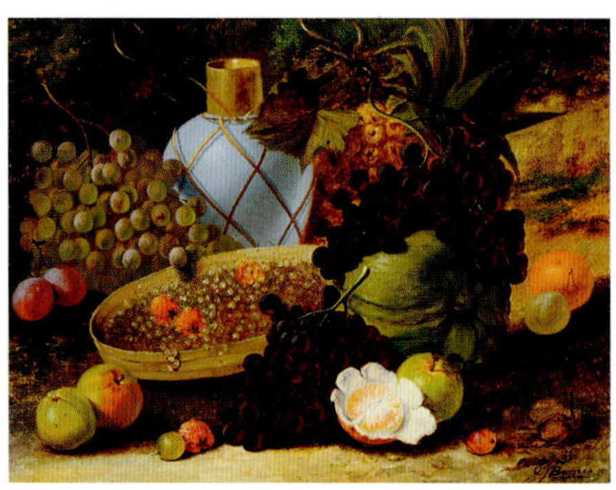

Barnes, J. T.
Still Life c.1890
oil on canvas 54 x 69.5
ROTMG : OP.1977.57

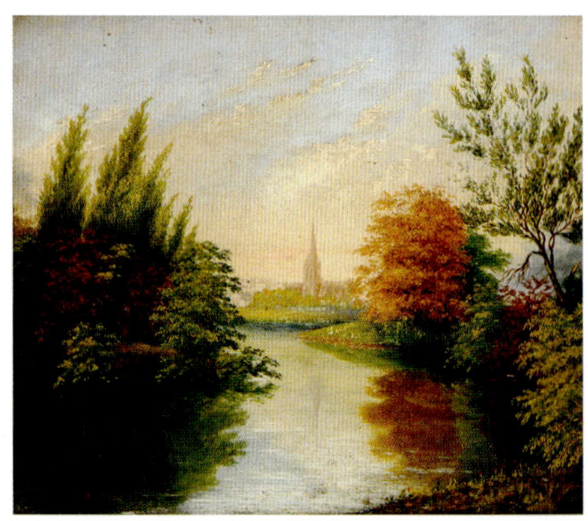

Barras, Thomas c.1790–1870
Rotherham from Rawmarsh Lane, South Yorkshire 1851
oil on canvas 31.5 x 36
ROTMG : OP.1978.214

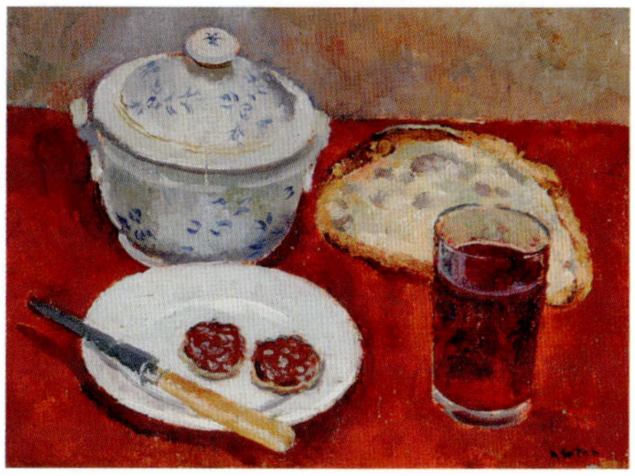

Barton, M.
Still Life c.1955
oil on panel 25 x 34
ROTMG : OP.1977.178

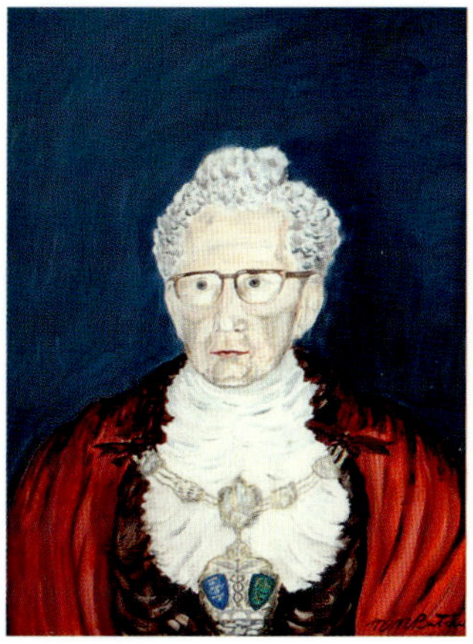

Batchel, M. M.
Percy Clarence Wright (1900–1991) c.1968
oil on board 60 x 44
ROTMG : OP.1989.7

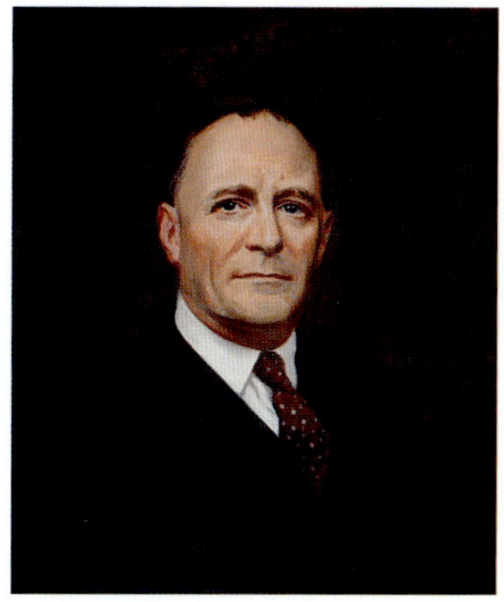

Bateman, James 1893–1959
Gerald Steel (1894–1957) c.1949
oil on board 60 x 50
ROTMG : E1651.2 (P)

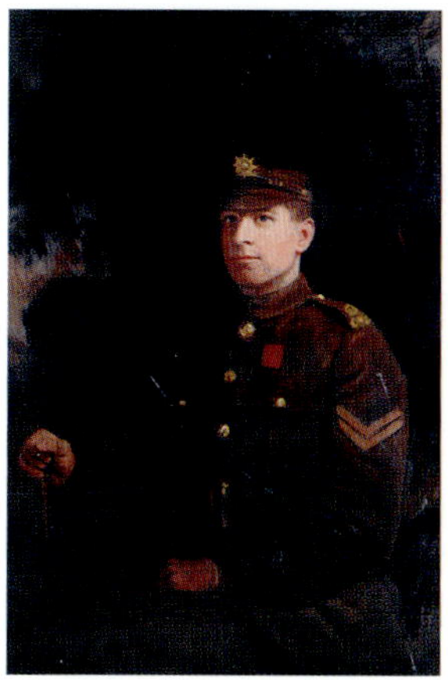

Bentley, Joseph Herbert 1866–1934
Corporal Thomas Norman Jackson (1897–1918), VC 1919
oil on canvas 121 x 80
ROTMG : OP.1978.219

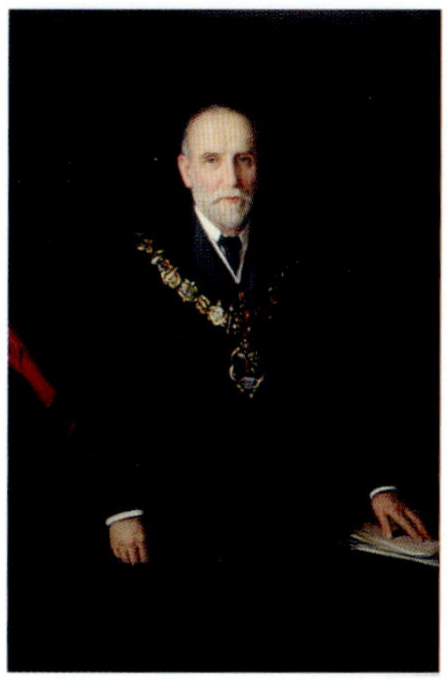

Beulley, J. M. active 1911–1914
Alderman Peter Bancroft Coward (1855–1931), JP, Mayor of Rotherham (1910–1915) 1914
oil on canvas 150 x 100
ROTMG : TUF0546

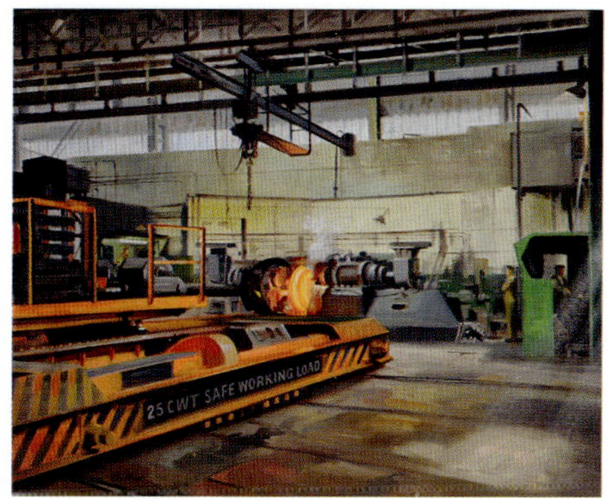

Billin, Edward Stanley 1911–1994
Vertical Wheel Mill c.1946
oil on canvas 62 x 75
ROTMG : OP.1987.1

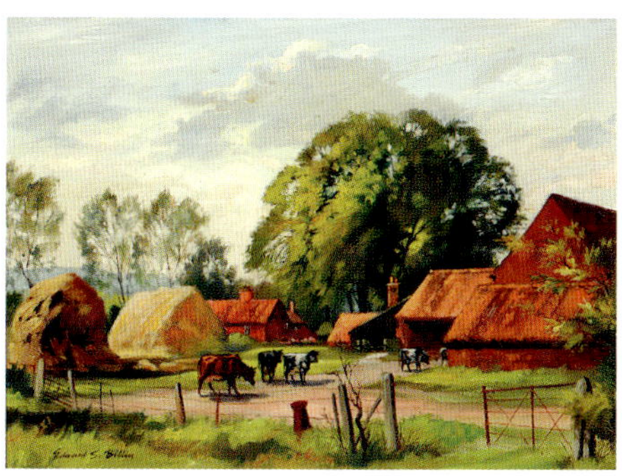

Billin, Edward Stanley 1911–1994
Lodge Farm, Wellow, Nottinghamshire c.1975
oil on canvas 44.5 x 59
ROTMG : OP.1977.194

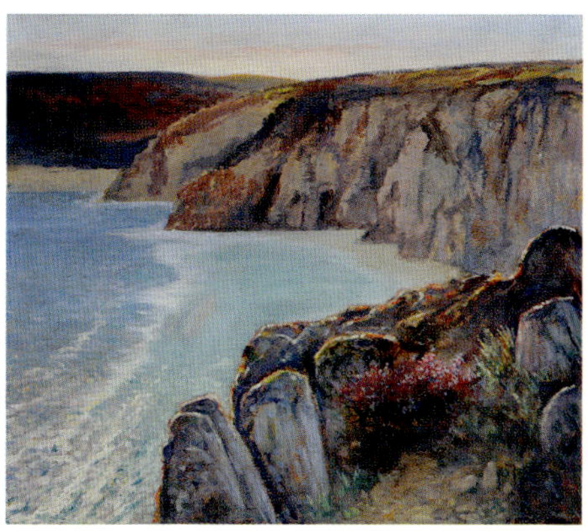

Binns, Harry Etchel 1869–c.1947
The Cornish Coast near Porthcurno c.1925
oil on canvas 59 x 67
ROTMG : OP.1977.69

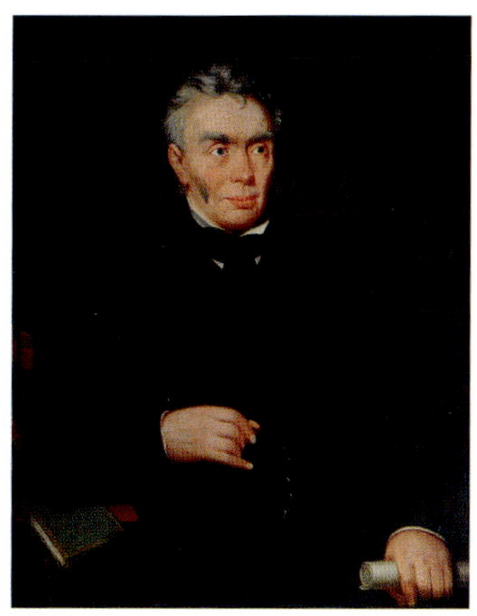

Birch, John (attributed to) 1807–1857
Ebenezer Elliott (1781–1849), the Anti-Corn Law Rhymer c.1840
oil on canvas 91.5 x 71.5
ROTMG : OP.1977.15 (P)

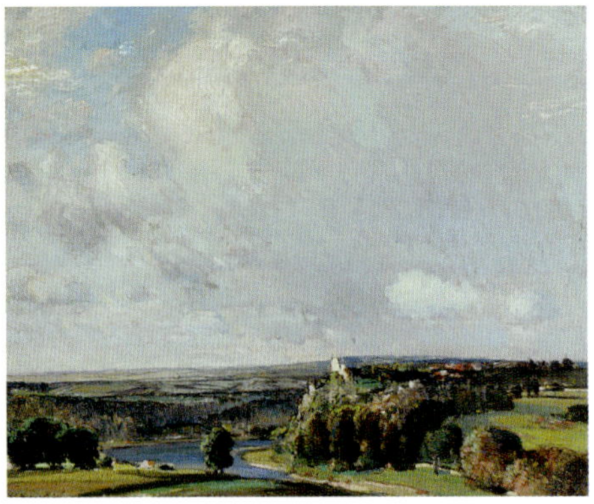

Birch, Samuel John Lamorna 1869–1955
Loe Pool, Helston, Cornwall c.1910
oil on canvas 50 x 59.5
ROTMG : OP.1977.72

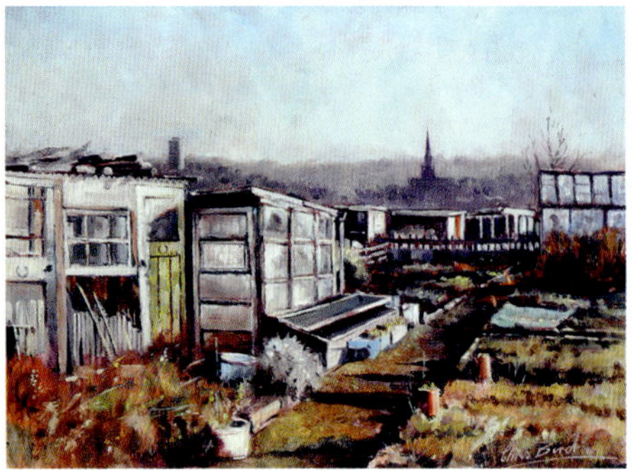

Bird, Chris b.1949
Rotherham, South Yorkshire, over the Allotments c.1995
oil on board 29 x 39.5
ROTMG : 1998.44

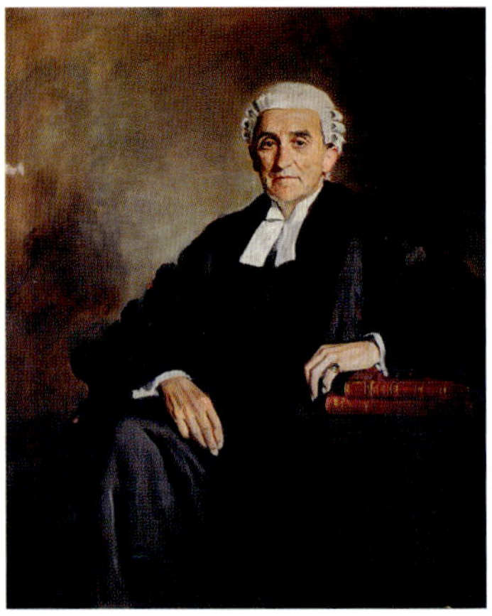

Birley, Oswald Hornby Joseph 1880–1952
Sir Charles Lee des Forges (1879–1972) 1946
oil on canvas 124 x 99
ROTMG : TUF0584

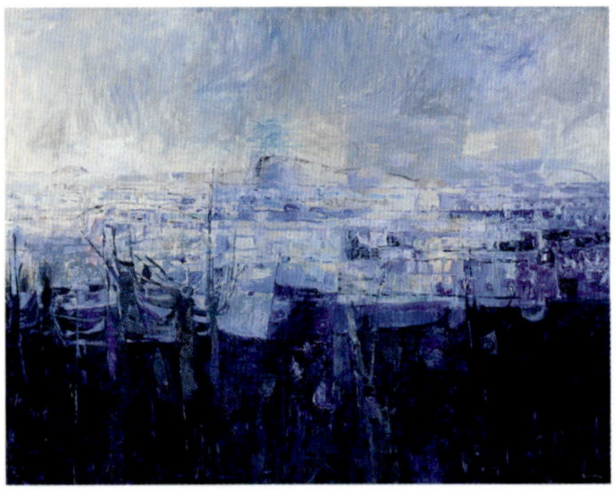

Blackshaw, Basil b.1932
Blue Landscape 1962
oil on canvas 101 x 127.5
ROTMG : OP.1977.135

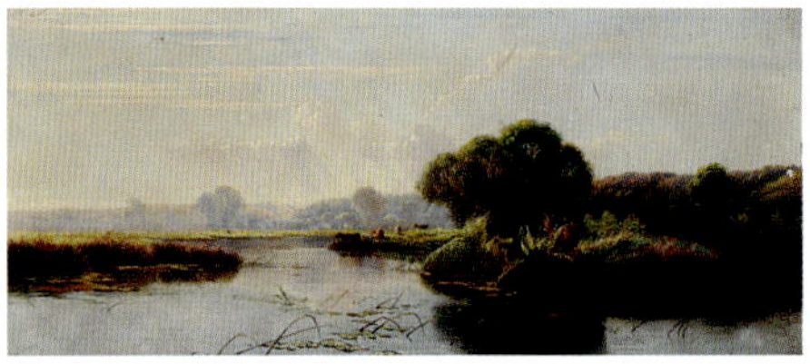

Boddington, Edwin Henry 1836–1905
A Bright Day (Sketch on the Thames) c.1875
oil on canvas 26 x 58
ROTMG : OP.1977.144

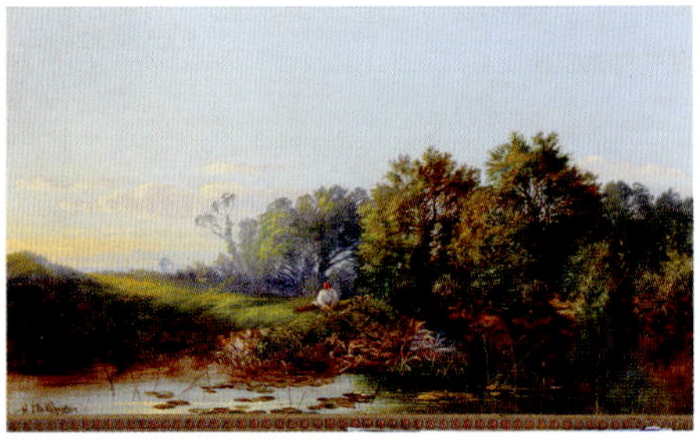

Boddington, Henry John 1811–1865
On the Thames c.1850
oil on canvas 26.5 x 44.5
ROTMG : OP.1984.20

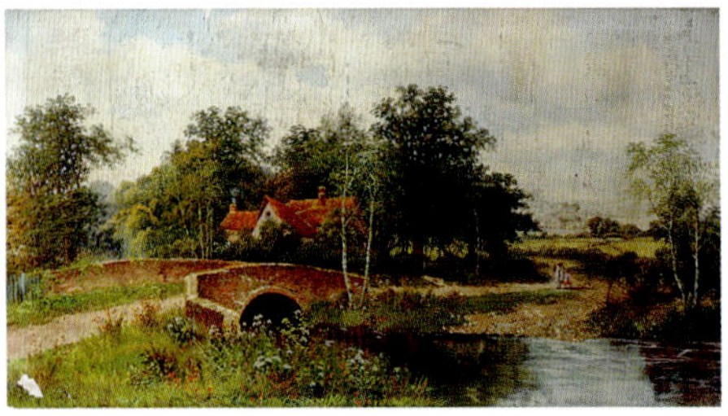

Boel, John Henry active 1875–1922
Landscape 1898
oil on canvas 60 x 108
ROTMG : OP.1977.87

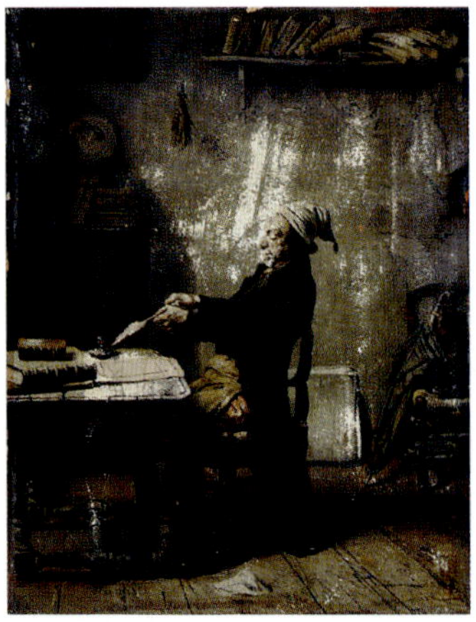

Bogaerts (attributed to)
Figure Sitting Writing c.1850
oil on canvas 40 x 31
ROTMG : OP.1978.228

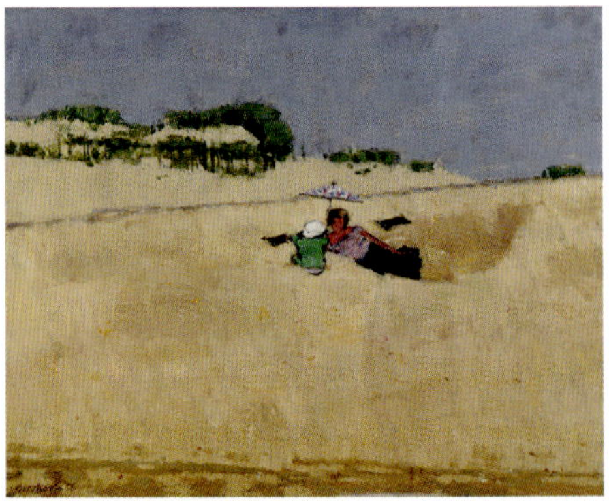

Brooker, William 1918–1983
Dunes, Littlehampton, West Sussex 1956
oil on canvas 50 x 60
ROTMG : OP.1977.169

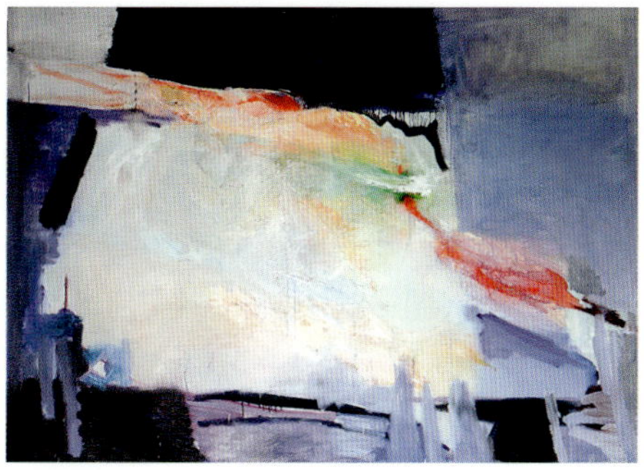

Brown, Jo b.1945
Natal Day c.1995
oil & PVA on canvas 152.5 x 215
ROTMG : OP.1996.4

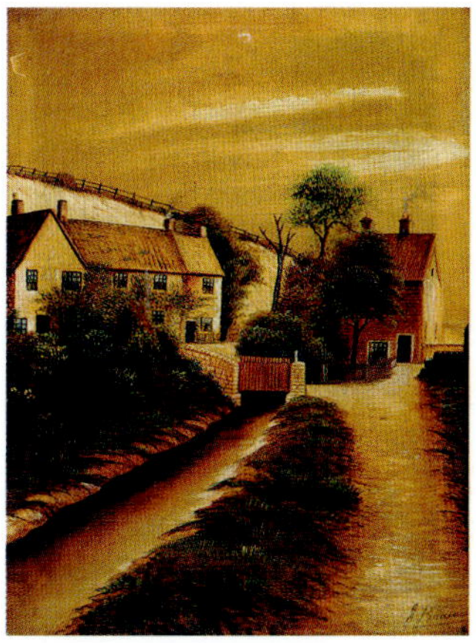

Bruce, Joseph active c.1900–1951
Mill Bridge c.1900
oil on canvas 61 x 46
ROTMG : TUF0552

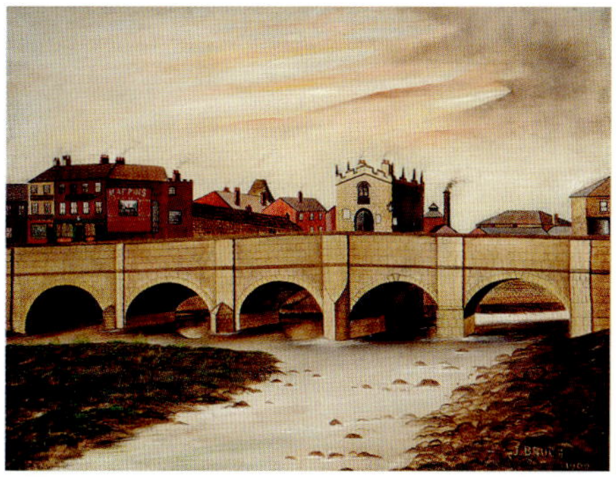

Bruce, Joseph active c.1900–1951
Rotherham Bridge (Gaol Bridge), South Yorkshire 1902
oil on canvas 22 x 30
ROTMG : OP.1977.62

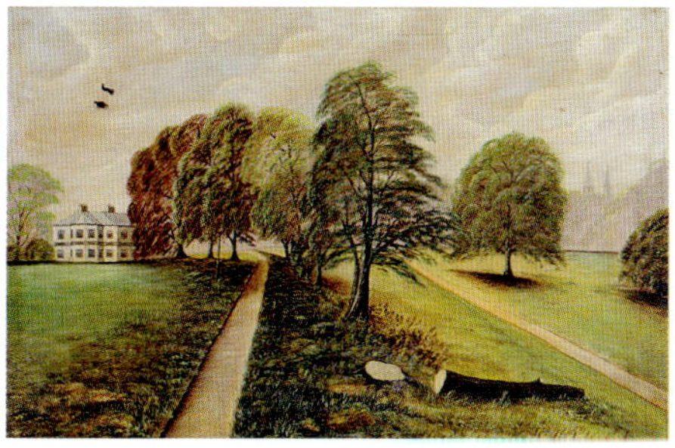

Bruce, Joseph active c.1900–1951
Landscape, Clifton Park, South Yorkshire 1906
oil on canvas 70 x 90
ROTMG : OP.1977.74

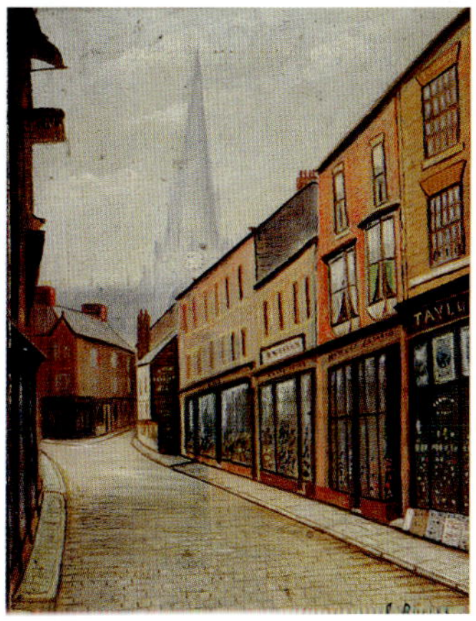

Bruce, Joseph active c.1900–1951
Rotherham Church, South Yorkshire 1951
oil on canvas 91.5 x 61
ROTMG : OP.1977.158

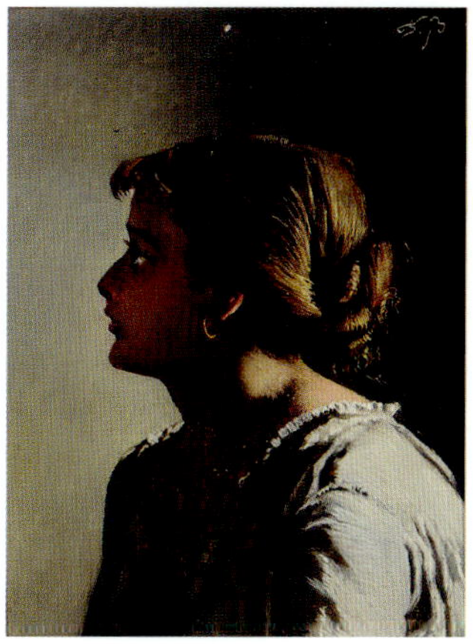

Buchser, Frank 1828–1890
Adoration c.1870
oil on board 26.5 x 20.5
ROTMG : OP.1977.70

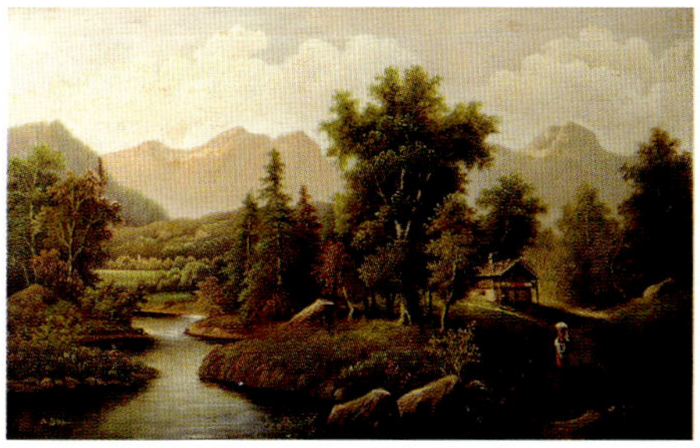

Buhn, A.
Landscape c.1860
oil on canvas 67 x 103
ROTMG : OP.1989.11

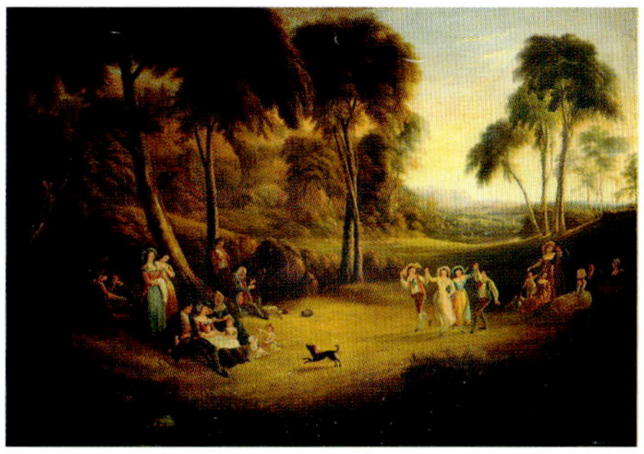

Bulkley, J.
Pastoral Scene with Dancing Figures 1831
oil on canvas 147.3 x 212.3
ROTMG : OP.1984.6

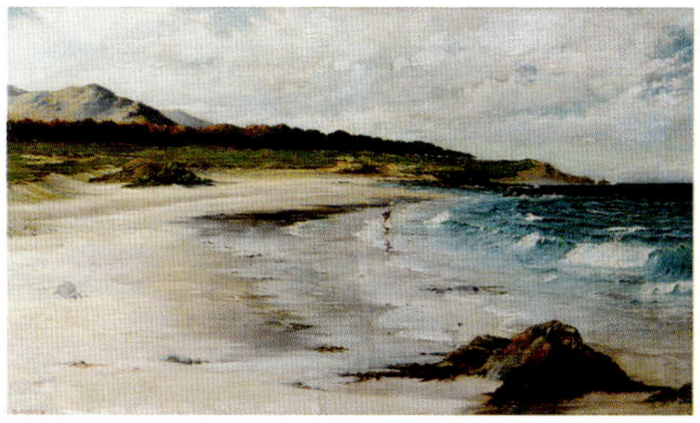

Burden, George c.1895–c.1930
Seascape c.1930
oil on canvas 68 x 113.5
ROTMG : OP.1977.110

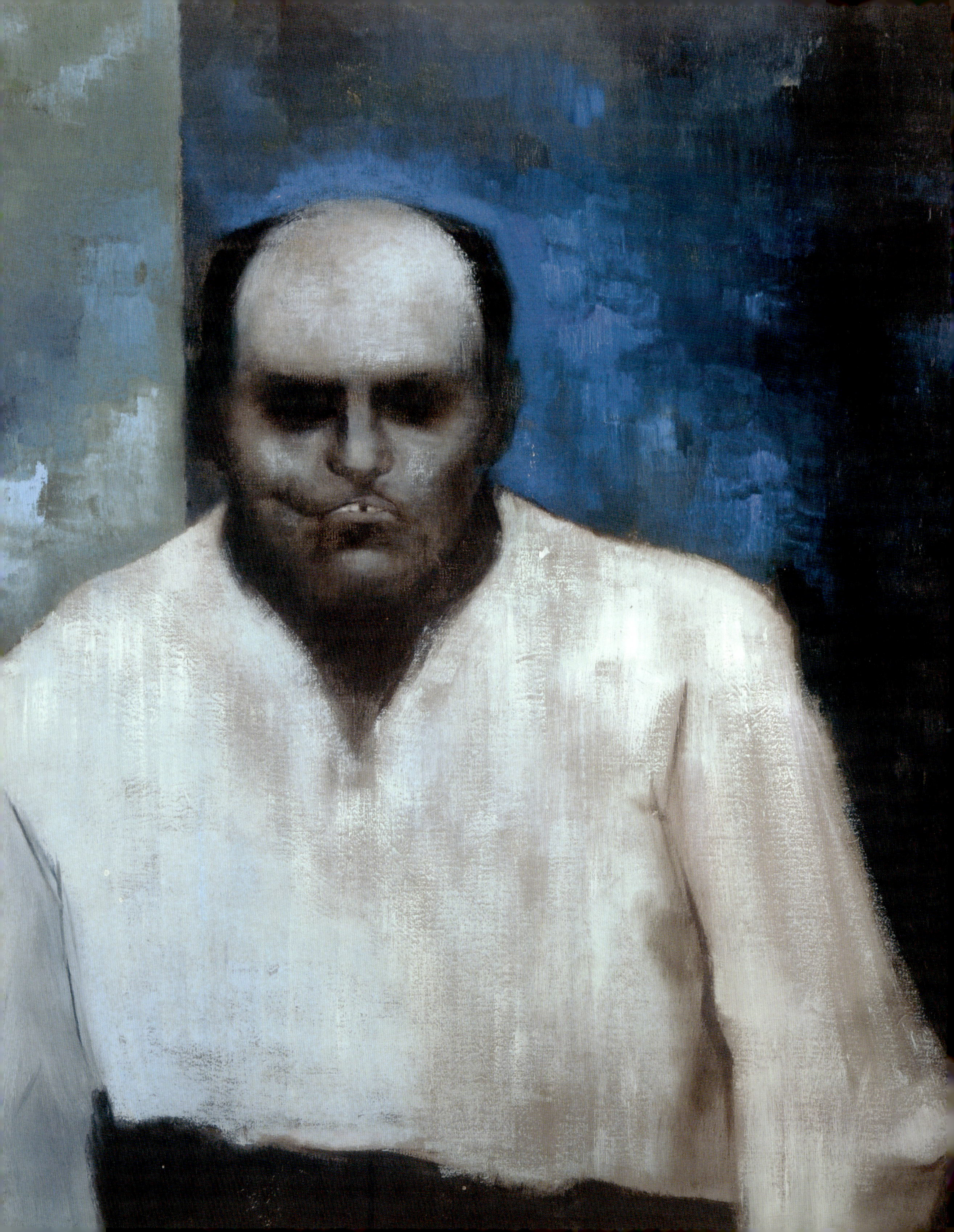

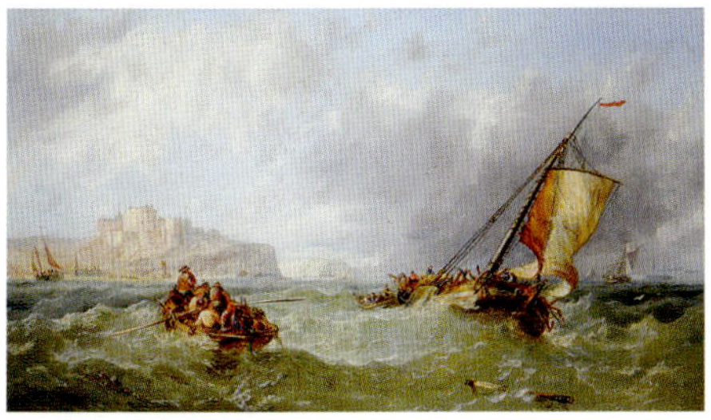

Callow, John 1822–1878
Seascape off Brittany, France c.1860
oil on canvas 78 x 130
ROTMG : OP.1978.216

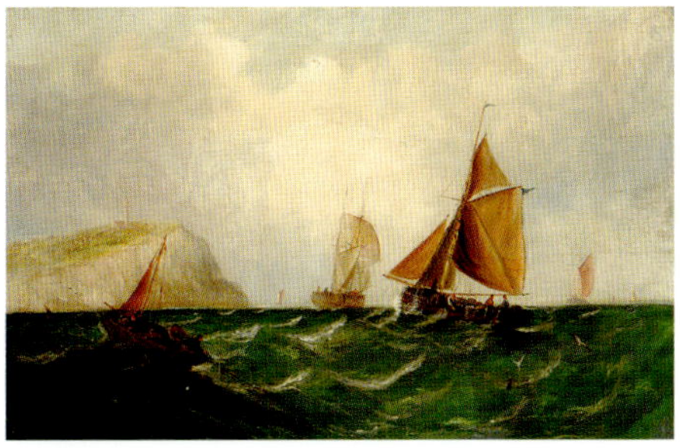

Callow, John (attributed to) 1822–1878
A Fresh Breeze c.1860
oil on canvas 50.5 x 76.5
ROTMG : OP.1977.84

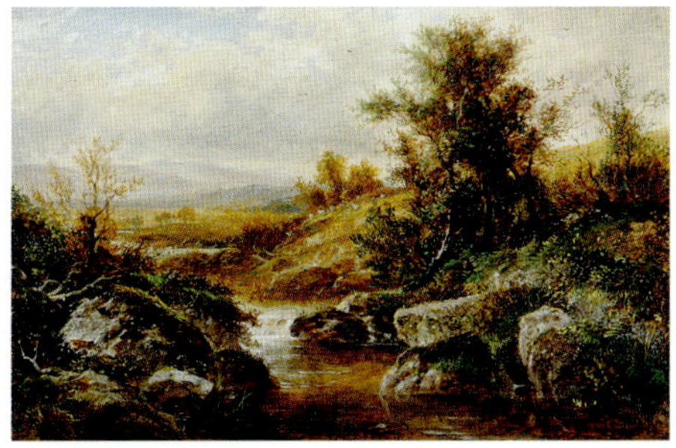

Callowhill, N. W.
Landscape, North Wales c.1880
oil on canvas 49.5 x 75
ROTMG : OP.1977.80

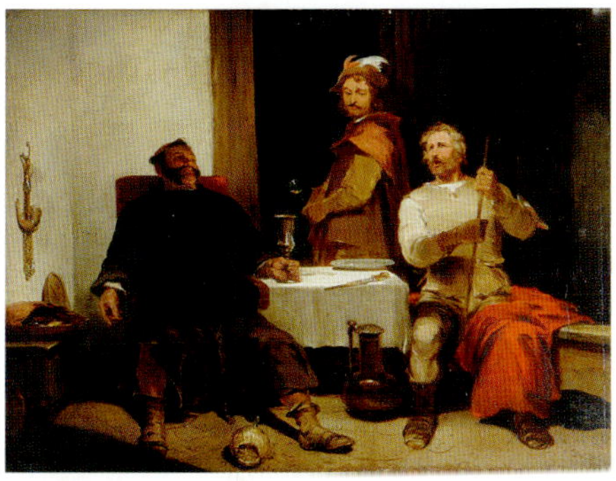

Cattermole, George 1800–1868
Interior (Tales from Robin Hood, Featuring Friar Tuck) c.1850
oil on canvas 58 x 75.5
ROTMG : OP.1977.113

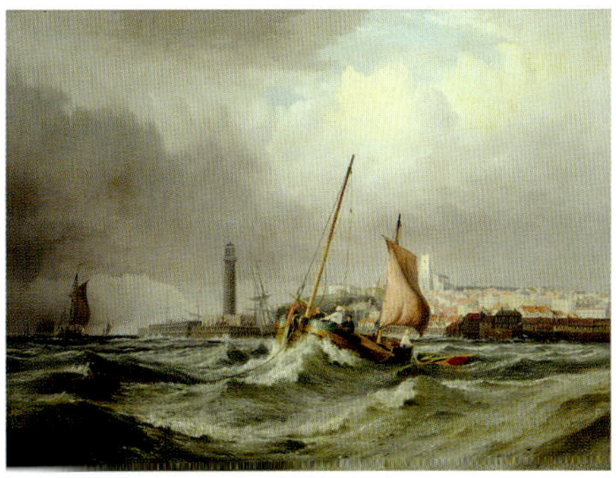

Chambers, George 1803–1840
Off Margate, Kent c.1836
oil on canvas 85.5 x 112
ROTMG : OP.1977.32

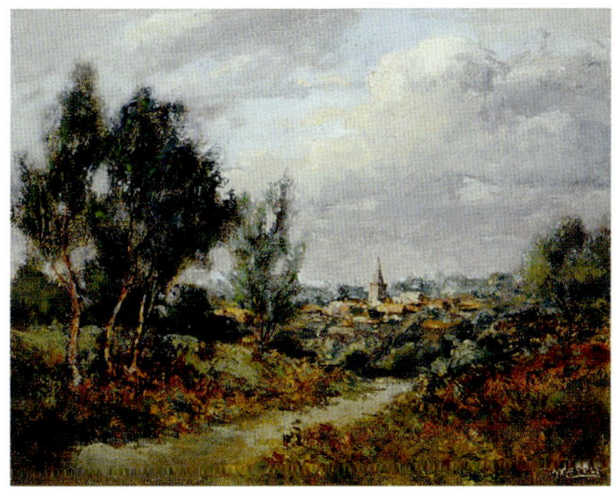

Chapple, T. W. active c.1914–1935
Eckington Church from Masbrough Flats, South Yorkshire c.1914
oil on canvas 28 x 34
ROTMG : OP.1977.177

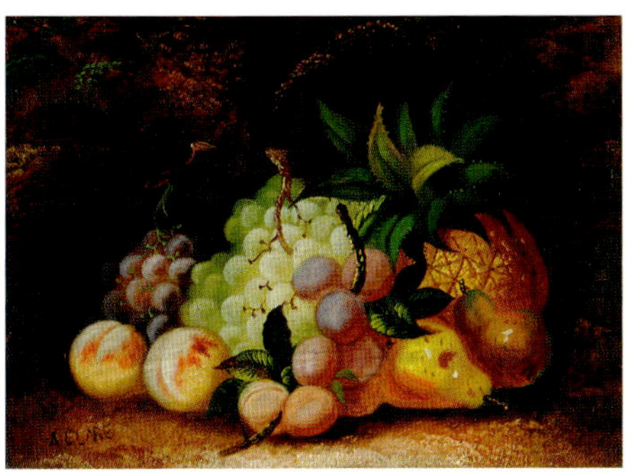

Clare, Oliver 1852–1927
Fruit Piece c.1880
oil on canvas 38 x 51
ROTMG : OP.1977.107

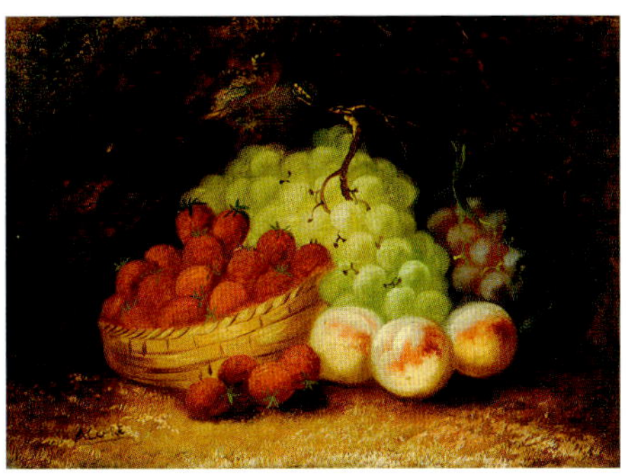

Clare, Oliver 1852–1927
Fruit Piece c.1880
oil on canvas 37 x 49
ROTMG : OP.1977.152

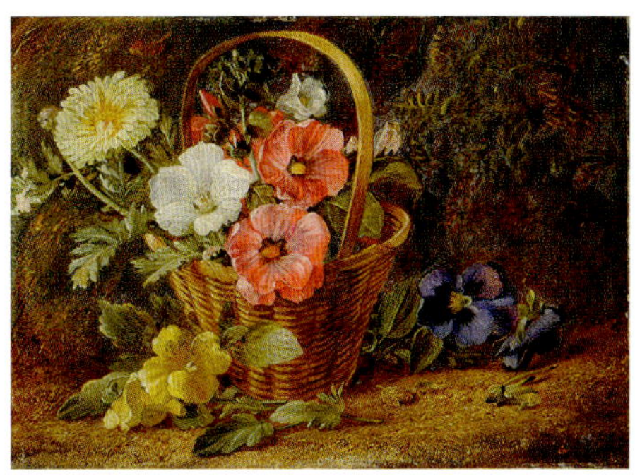

Clare, Vincent 1856–1925
Flower Piece 1896
oil on canvas 22.5 x 30.5
ROTMG : OP.1977.109

Facing page: Drury, Paul, 1903–1987, *Man's Head in Blue* (detail), c.1963, Doncaster Museum Service, (p. 83)

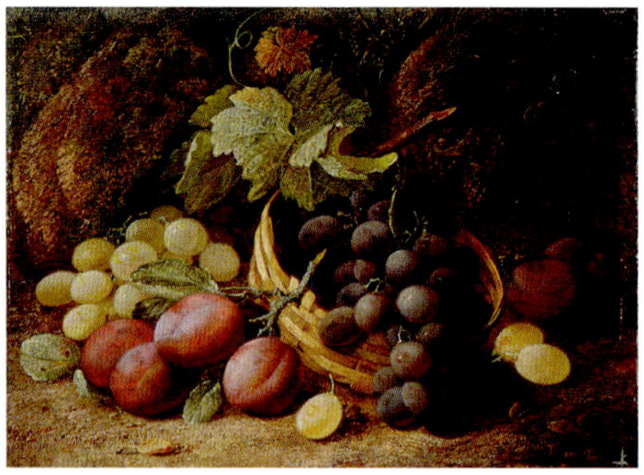

Clare, Vincent 1856–1925
Fruit Piece 1896
oil on canvas 22.8 x 30.5
ROTMG : OP.1977.108

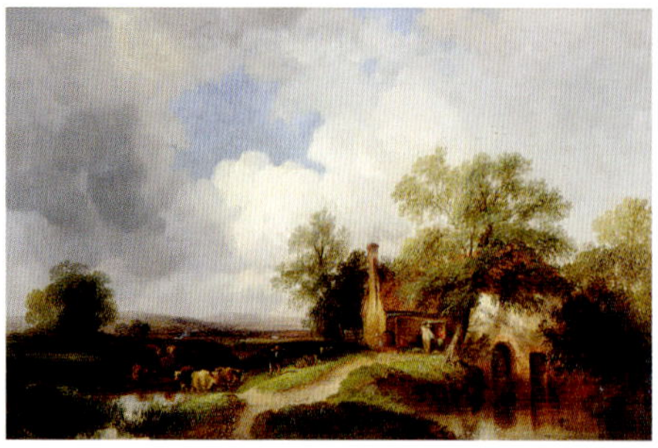

Cole, George Vicat 1833–1893
Homewards 1850
oil on canvas 35 x 54
ROTMG : OP.1984.14

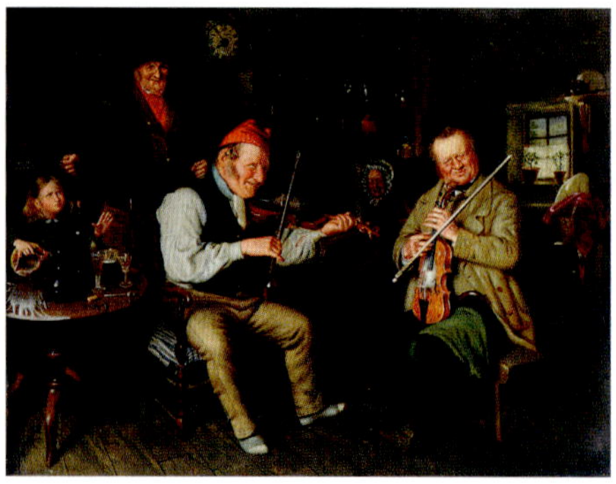

Collins, Hugh c.1834–1896
The Village Musicians 1880
oil on canvas 48 x 61
ROTMG : OP.1977.17

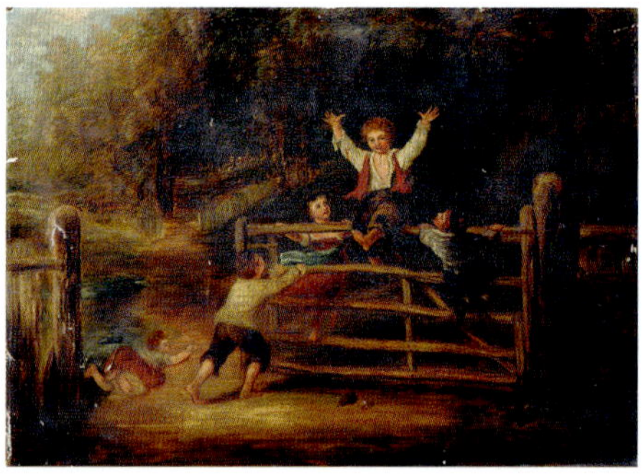

Collins, William (after) 1788–1847
Happy as a King c.1860
oil on canvas 46 x 61
ROTMG : OP.1977.189

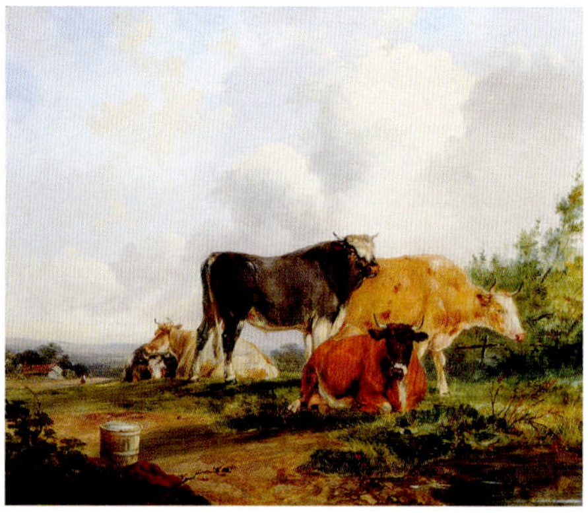

Cooper, Thomas Sidney 1803–1902
Cattle Piece c.1870
oil on canvas 62.5 x 74
ROTMG : OP.1977.112

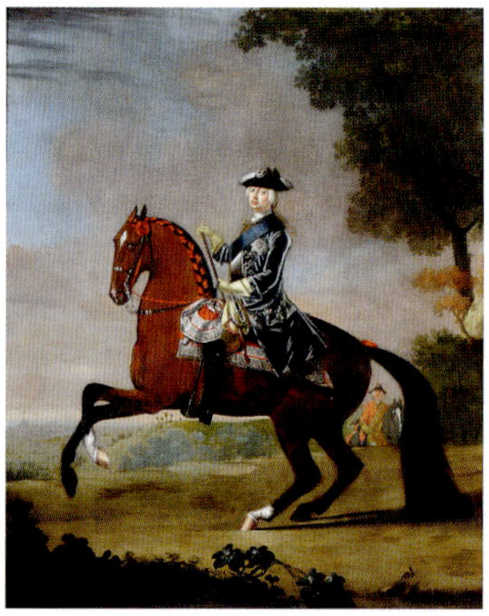

Copley, John Singleton 1738–1815
Frederick Louis (1707–1751), Prince of Wales (after David Morier) 1775–1815
oil on canvas 121 x 100
ROTMG : OP.1984.11

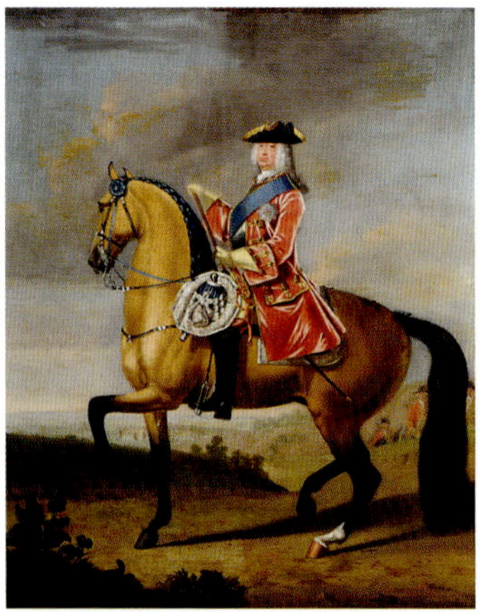

Copley, John Singleton 1738–1815
George II (1683–1760) (after David Morier) 1775–1815
oil on canvas 125 x 99
ROTMG : OP.1984.10

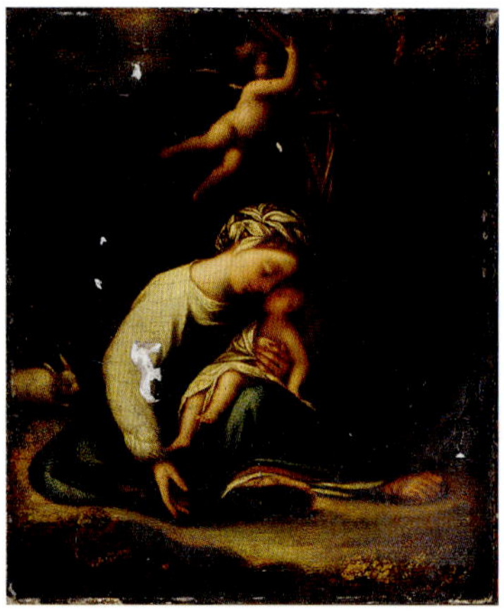

Correggio (after) c.1489–1534
La zingarella c.1615
oil on board 47 x 37.3
ROTMG : OP.1977.31

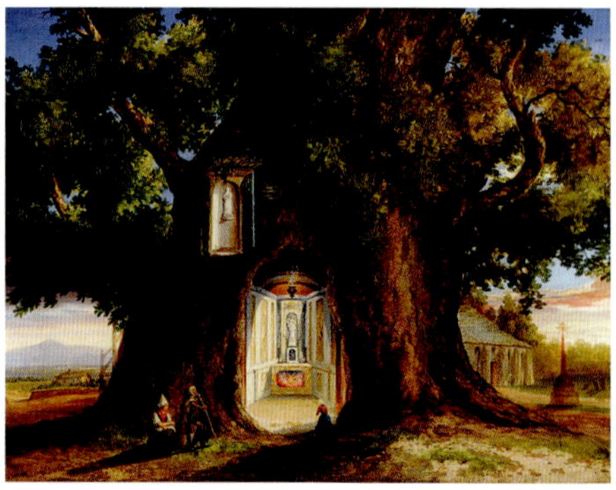

Cowen, William 1791–1864
The Chapel in the Oak c.1830
oil on canvas 111 x 141.5
ROTMG : OP.1977.200

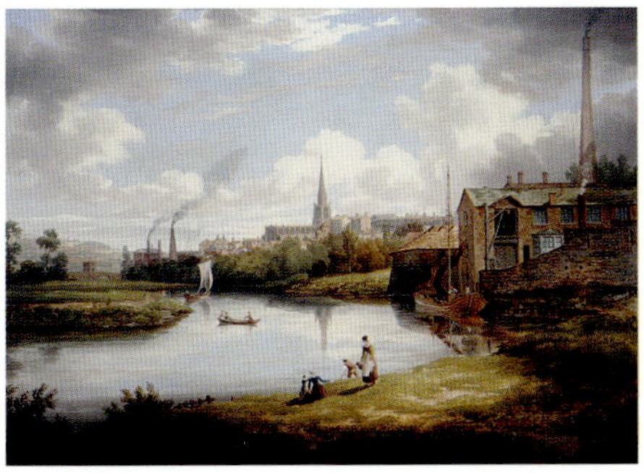

Cowen, William 1791–1864
View of Rotherham, South Yorkshire c.1830
oil on canvas 54 x 74
ROTMG : OP.1982.234

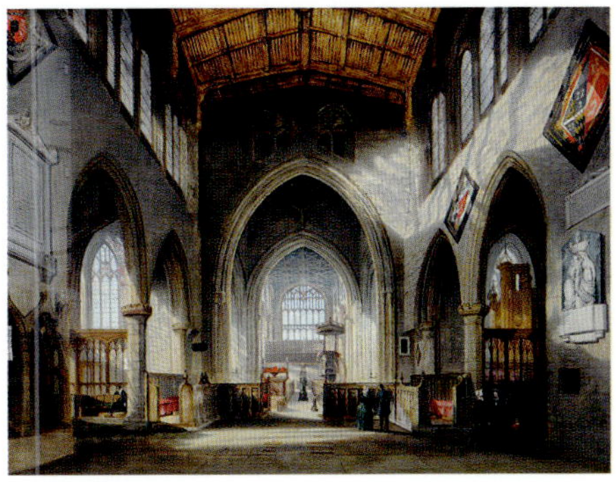

Cowen, William 1791–1864
Interior of Rotherham Parish Church, South Yorkshire 1846
oil on canvas 104 x 138
ROTMG : OP.1977.2

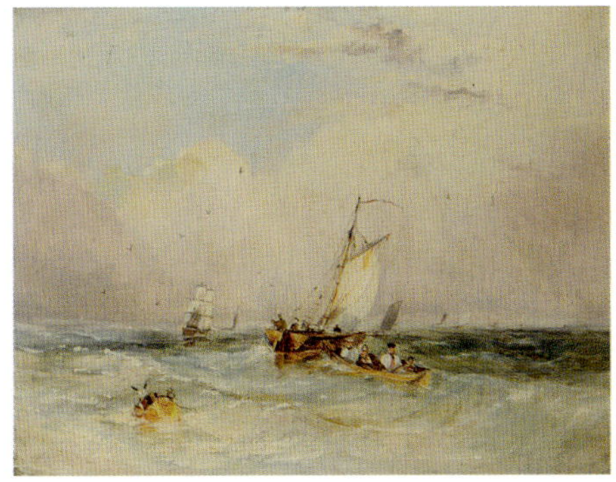

Creswick, Thomas 1811–1869
Seascape c.1850
oil on panel 19 x 24
ROTMG : OP.1978.211

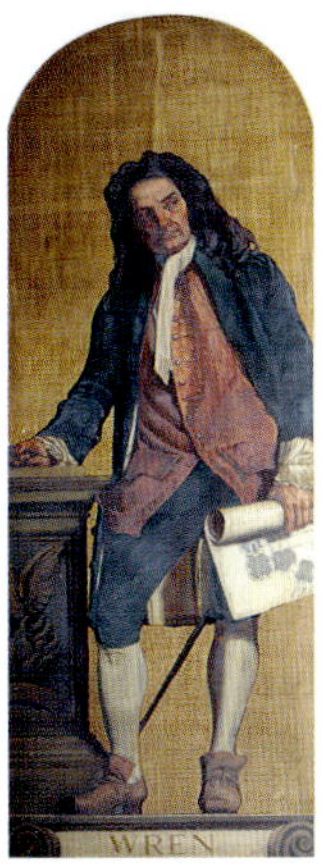

Crowe, Eyre (after) 1824–1910
Sir Christopher Wren (1632–1723) c.1869
oil on canvas panel 239 x 89
ROTMG : TUF1442

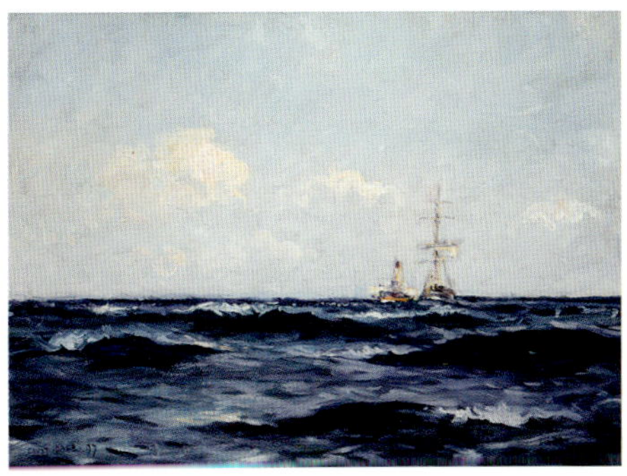

Dade, Ernest 1868–1936
Off Scarbro' 1897
oil on canvas 47 x 61.5
ROTMG : OP.1977.79

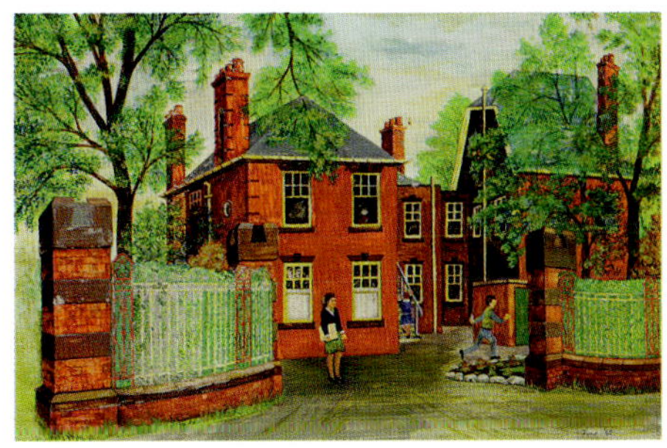

Danks, Albert (attributed to)
Kimberworth Isolation Hospital, South Yorkshire 1965
oil on canvas 50 x 75
ROTMG : OP.1996.3

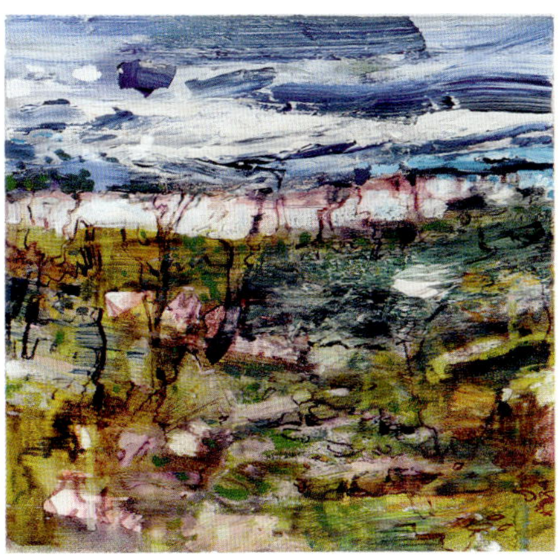

Dearden, Paul
Treescape (Boston Park, Rotherham, South Yorkshire) 2006
oil on canvas 39 x 39
ROTMG : 2006.13

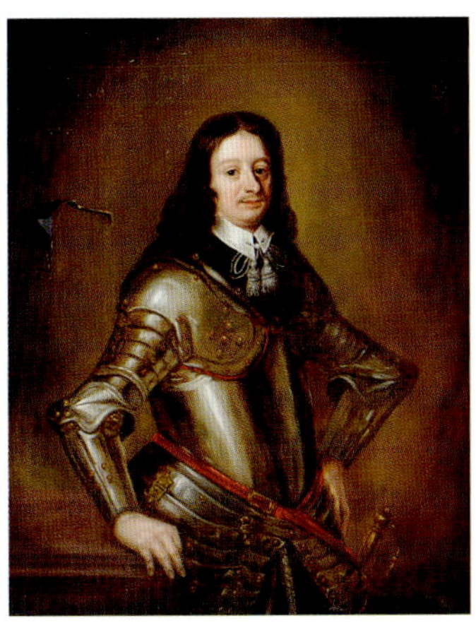

Dyck, Anthony van (after) 1599–1641
Sir Thomas Fairfax (1612–1671)
oil on canvas 118.5 x 95.5
ROTMG : OP.1977.185

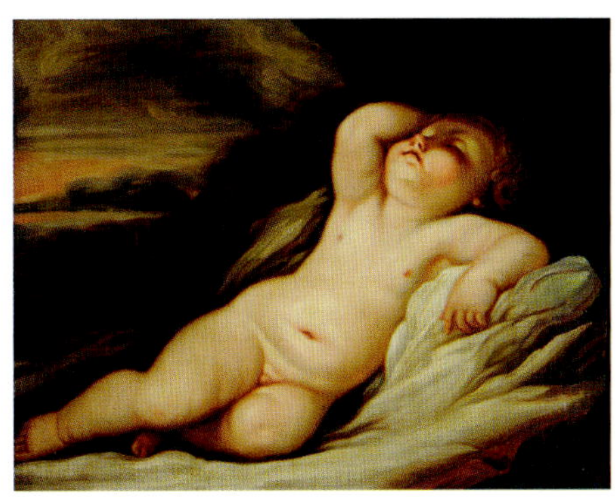

Eckhardt, K. P.
Putto 1832
oil on canvas 54 x 67
ROTMG : OP.1977.20

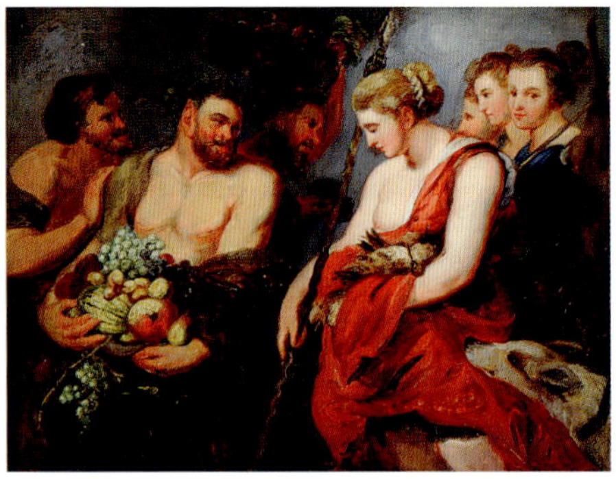

Etty, William 1787–1849
Diana, Returning from the Chase c.1830
oil on canvas 34 x 44
ROTMG : OP.1978.208

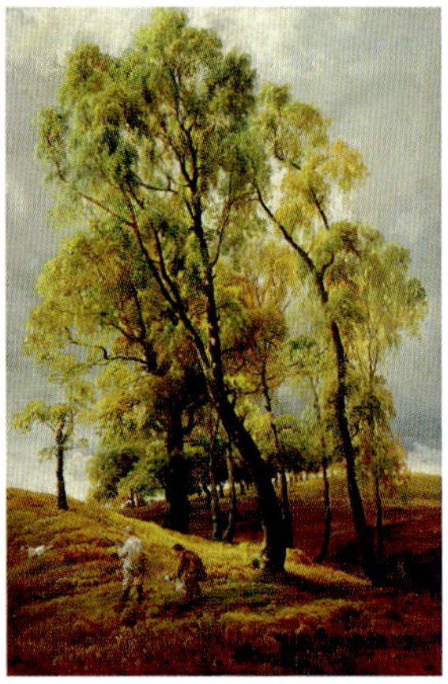

Evans, Bernard Walter 1843–1922
Cannock Chase c.1890
oil on canvas 92 x 61
ROTMG : OP.1977.130

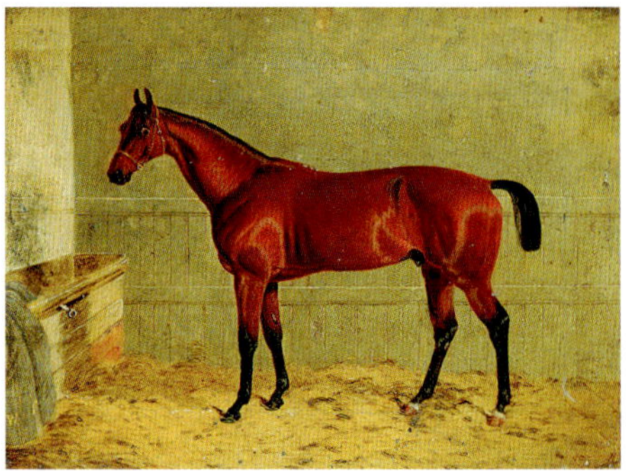

W. F.
Horse in a Stable c.1860
oil on canvas 22 x 29.5
ROTMG : OP.1977.40

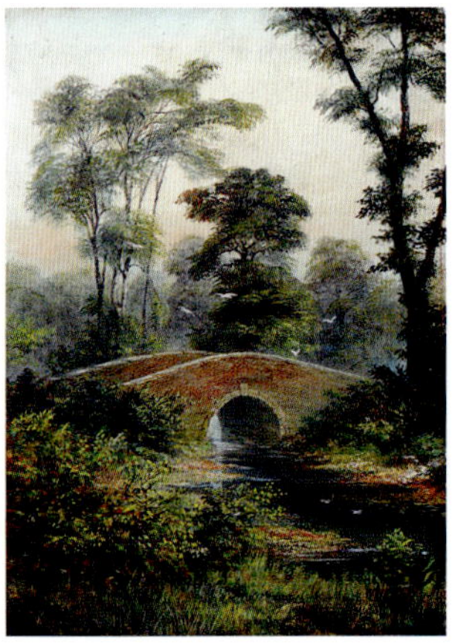

Fann, W.
Soar Brook, Leicestershire 1903
oil on canvas 35.5 x 25
ROTMG : OP.1977.103

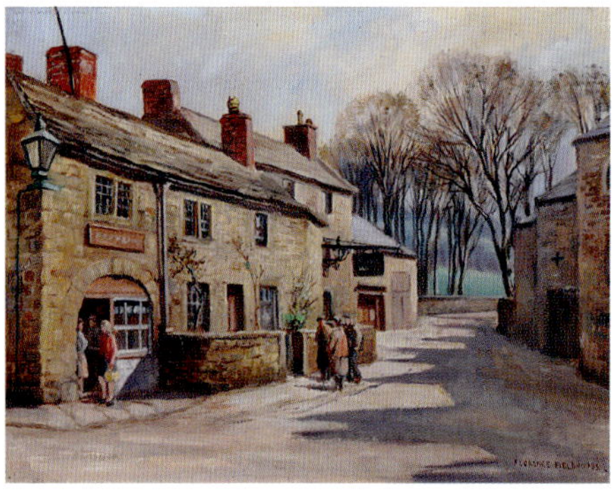

Fieldhouse, Florence 1898–1974
Ashover, Derbyshire c.1940
oil on canvas 40 x 50
ROTMG : OP.1977.187

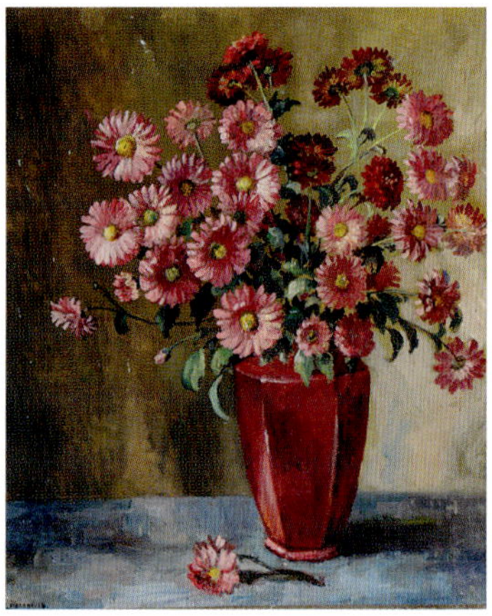

Fieldhouse, Florence 1898–1974
Pink Chrysanthemums c.1950
oil on canvas 59 x 49
ROTMG : OP.1977.168

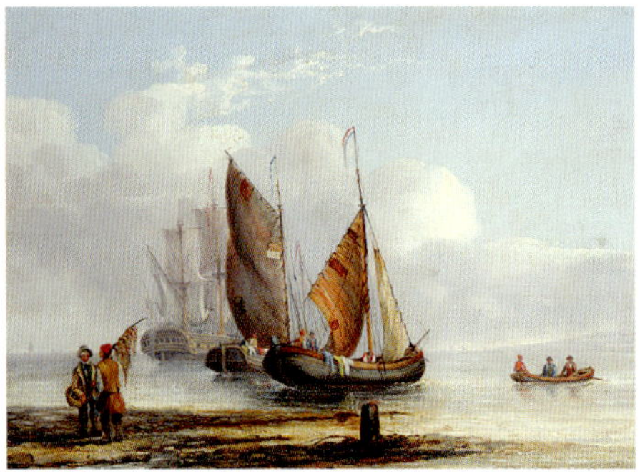

Fielding, Anthony V. C. 1787–1855
Seascape c.1830
oil on canvas 41 x 57
ROTMG : OP.1977.59

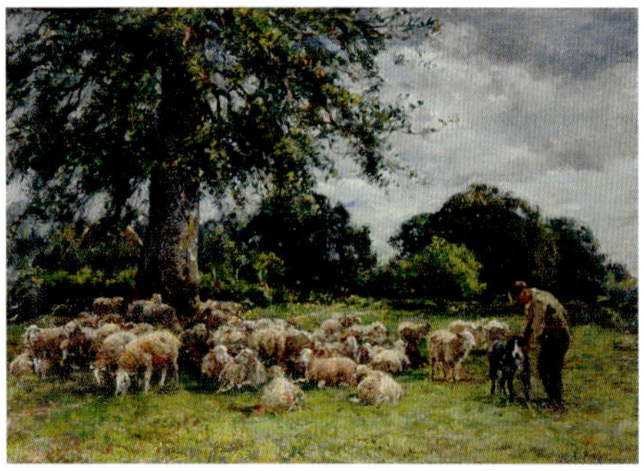

Fisher, Mark 1841–1923
Landscape with Sheep c.1910
oil on canvas 43.5 x 61
ROTMG : OP.1978.227

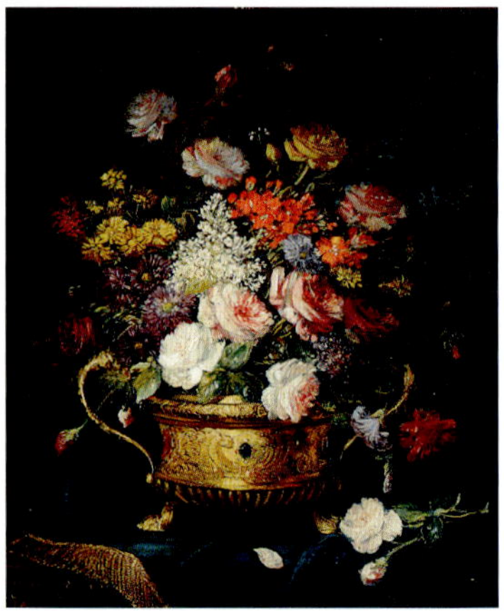

Foret, J.
Flower Study c.1880
oil on canvas 62 x 51
ROTMG : OP.1977.71

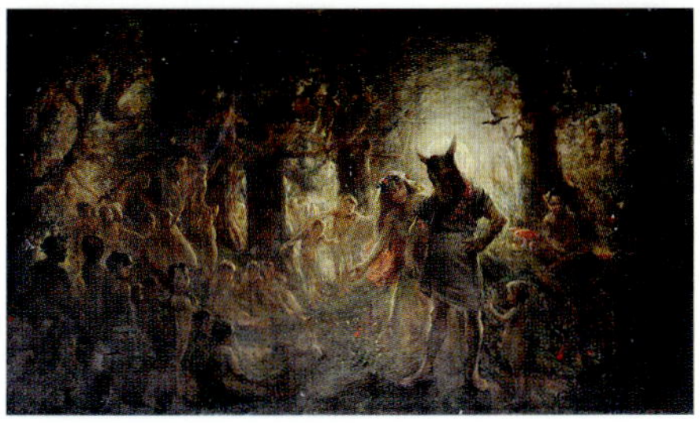

Fowler, Robert 1853–1926
A Midsummer Night's Dream (from the play by William Shakespeare) c.1900
oil on canvas 125 x 212
ROTMG : OP.1977.1

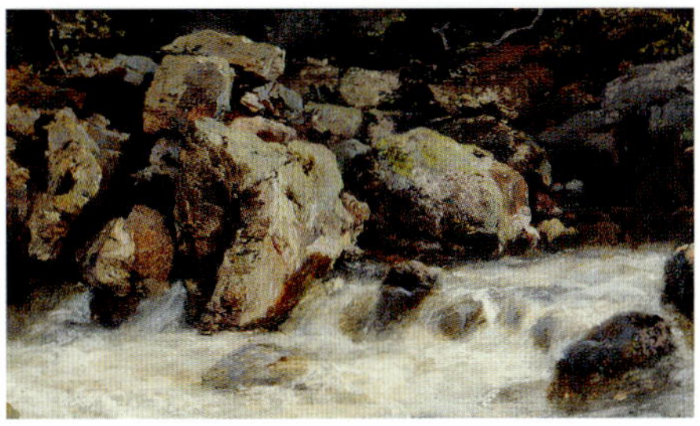

Frisch, John Carl b.c.1845
Rocks and River c.1880
oil on panel 20.5 x 34
ROTMG : OP.1977.55

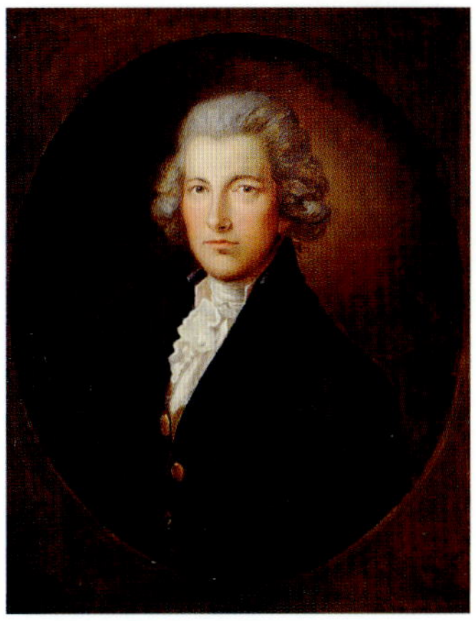

Gainsborough, Thomas (after) 1727–1788
William Pitt the Younger (1759–1806) c.1795
oil on canvas 78 x 60
ROTMG : OP.1977.76

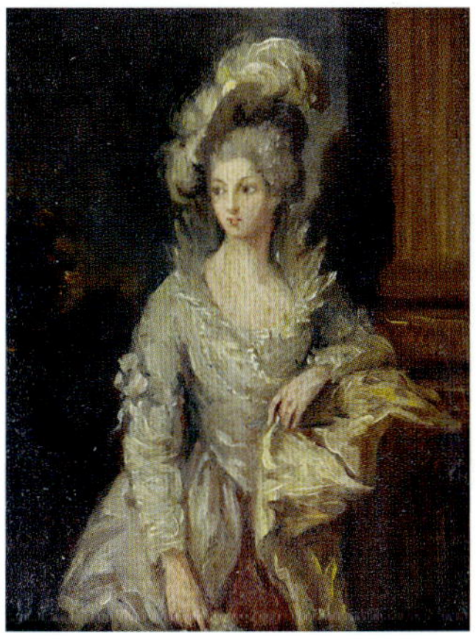

Gainsborough, Thomas (after) 1727–1788
The Honourable Mrs Thomas Graham, née Mary Cathcart (1757–1792) c.1830
oil on canvas 12 x 9.5
ROTMG : OP.1984.12

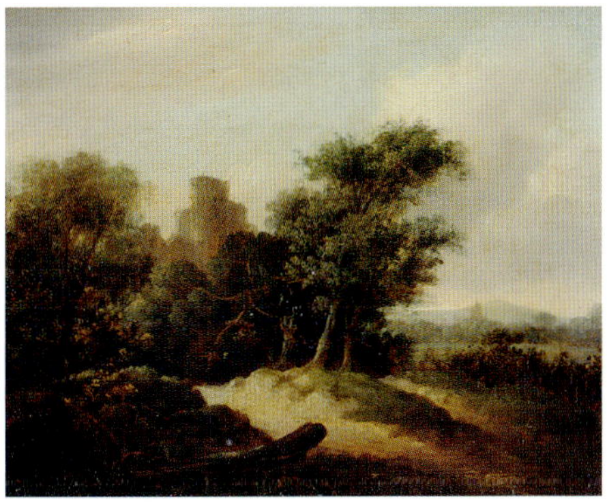

Gainsborough, Thomas (attributed to) 1727–1788
Blaize Castle, Bristol c.1770
oil on canvas on board 17.5 x 21.5
ROTMG : OP.1977.100

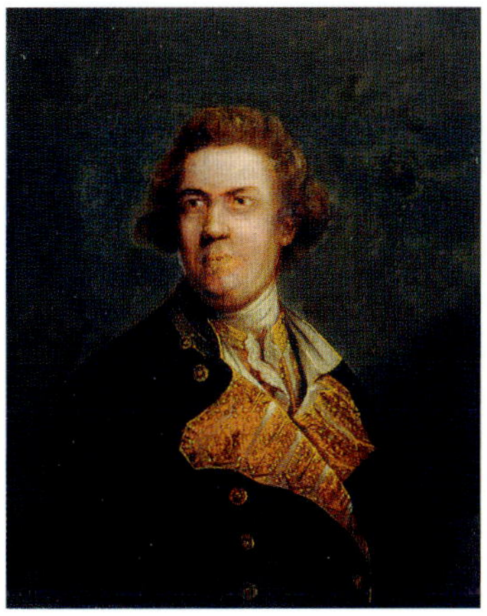

Gainsborough, Thomas (school of) 1727–1788
Admiral Keppel (1725–1786) c.1780
oil on canvas 40.5 x 32
ROTMG : OP.1978.229

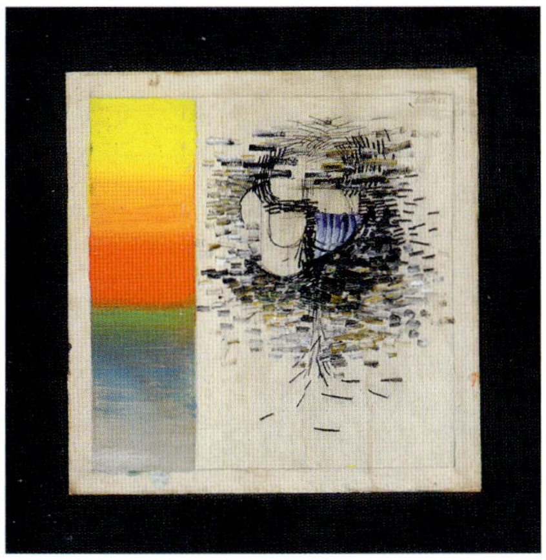

Giobbi, Edward Gioachino b.1926
Landscape 1966
oil & charcoal on board 41 x 39
ROTMG : OP.1978.226

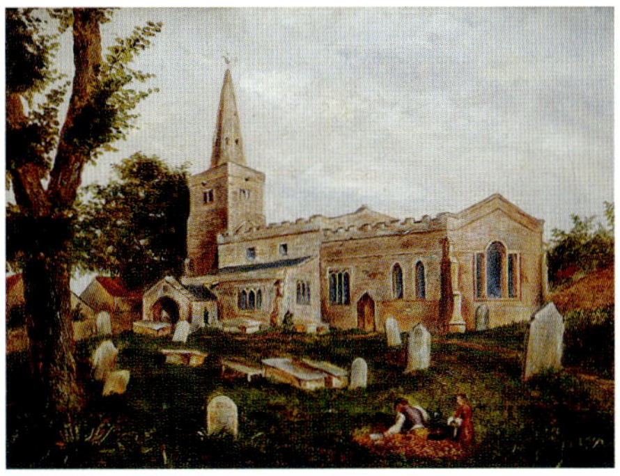

Glassby, Robert 1835–1892
Mexborough Church, South Yorkshire 1860
oil on canvas 22 x 29
ROTMG : OP.1978.232

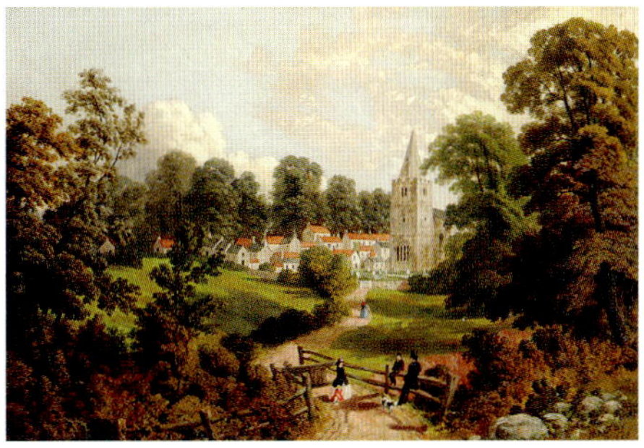

A. W. H.
View of Maltby, South Yorkshire 1863
oil on canvas 43.2 x 61
ROTMG : 1999.63

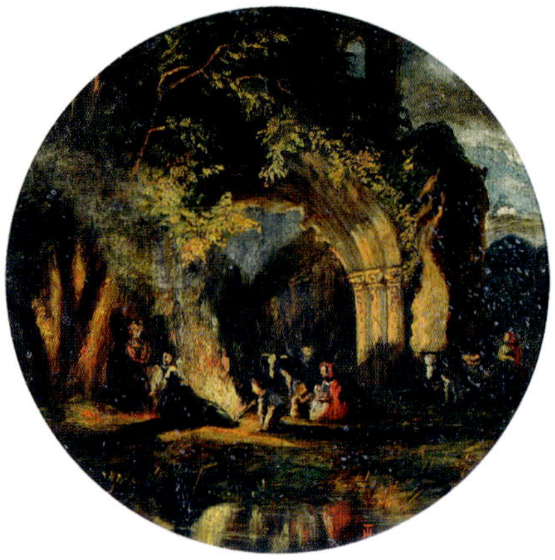

T. H.
Nativity c.1880
oil on canvas 29
ROTMG : OP.1977.96

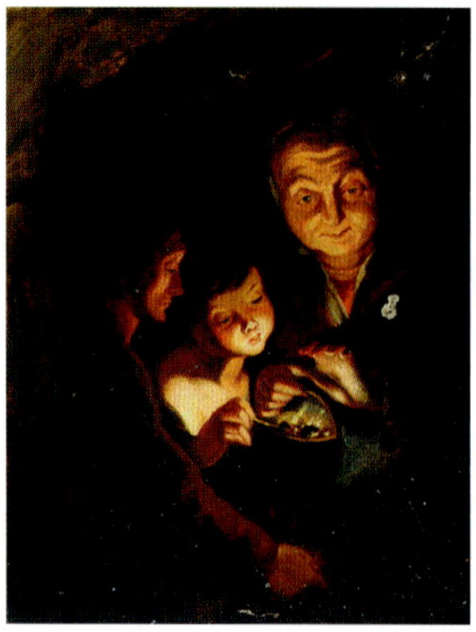

Hammond, J. active c.1870–c.1880
A Family Group c.1870
oil on canvas 41.5 x 31
ROTMG : OP.1977.51

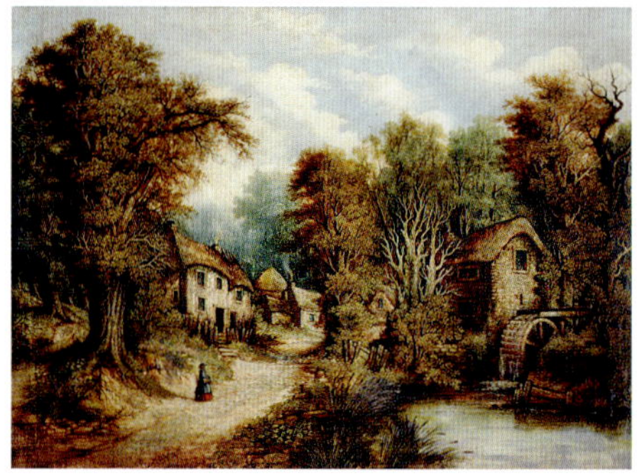

Hammond, J. active c.1870–c.1880
Canklow Wood Bottom, Rotherham, South Yorkshire c.1880
oil on canvas 90 x 120
ROTMG : OP.1977.201

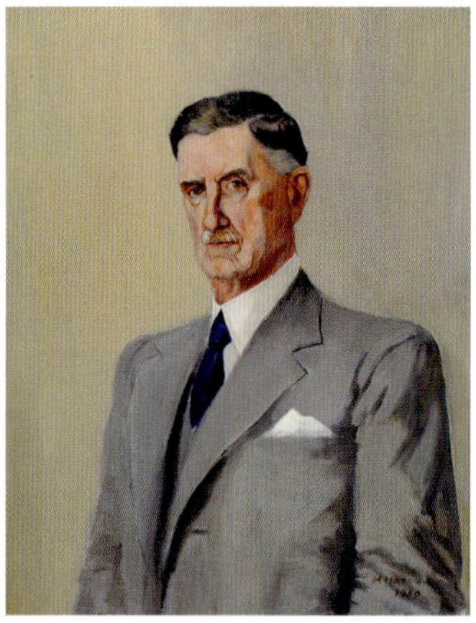

Hardwick, H. active c.1950–c.1952
Fred Turner of Rotherham 1950
oil on board 69 x 53.5
ROTMG : OP.1977.148

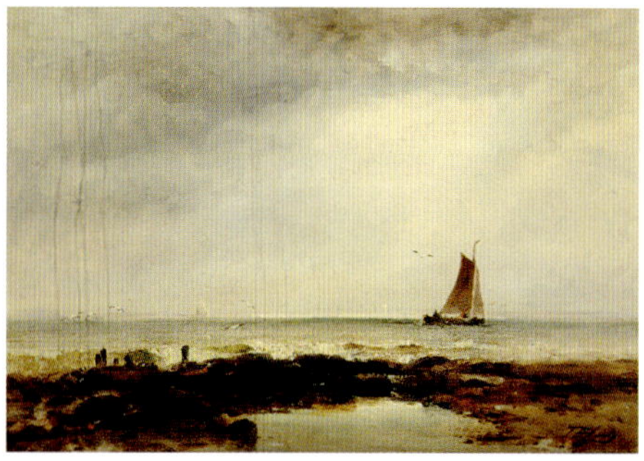

Hardy, Thomas Bush 1842–1897
Seascape c.1880
oil on board 24 x 34
ROTMG : OP.1977.12

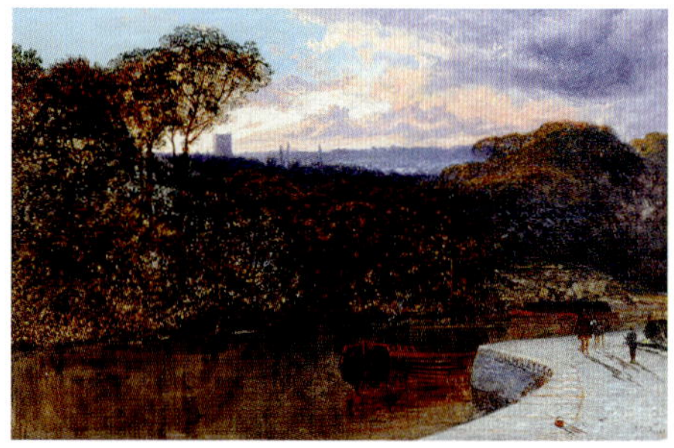

Hargitt, Edward 1835–1895
Canal Scene 1868
oil on panel 21 x 31
ROTMG : OP.1978.209

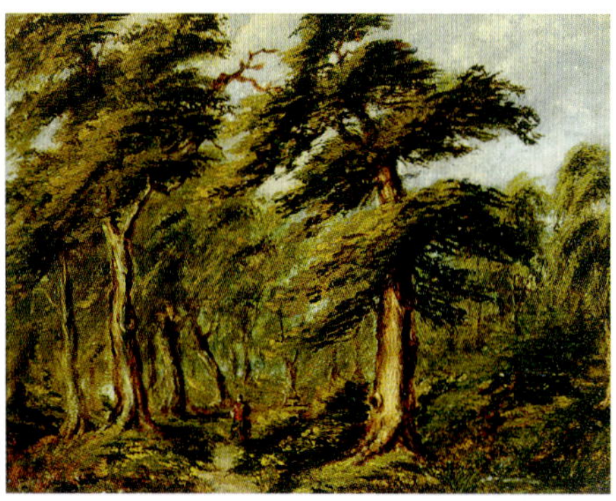

Harrison, J. (attributed to) active 1845–1865
In Wharncliffe Woods, South Yorkshire c.1865
oil on board 22 x 29
ROTMG : OP.1977.23

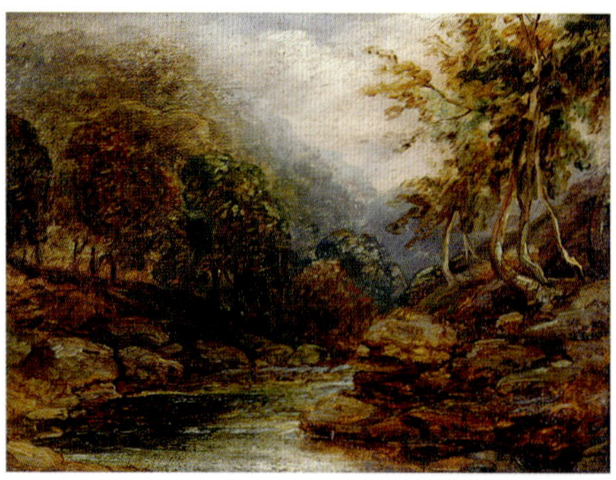

Hawkesworth, Joseph Hallam 1827–1908
On the Don, near Wortley, South Yorkshire 1865
oil on canvas 18.5 x 24
ROTMG : OP.1982.235

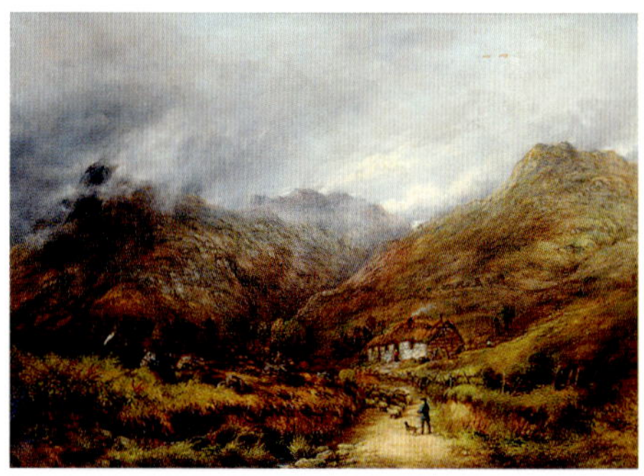

Hawkesworth, Joseph Hallam 1827–1908
Duncraggan, Scotland c.1870
oil on canvas 62.4 x 87.8
ROTMG : OP.1977.26

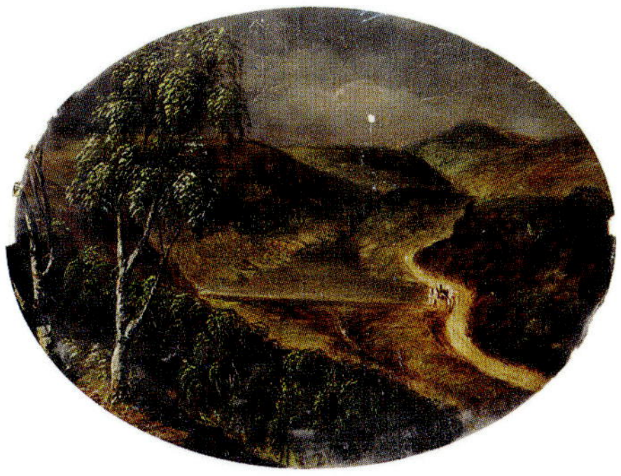

Hawkesworth, Joseph Hallam 1827–1908
Landscape c.1870
oil on board 18.6 x 24.1
ROTMG : OP.1977.61

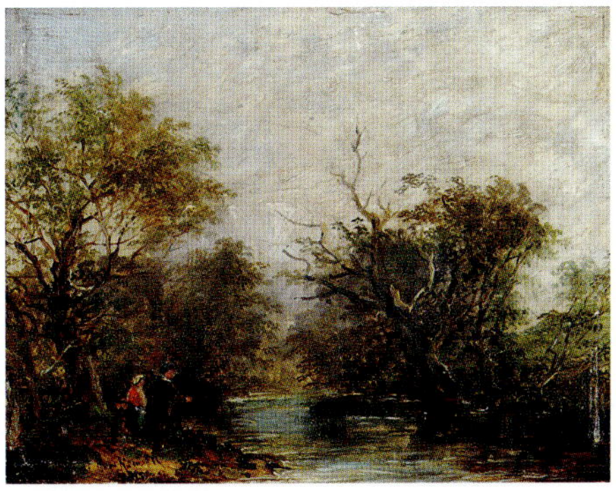

Hawkesworth, Joseph Hallam 1827–1908
Landscape with Fishing Scene c.1870
oil on canvas 20.8 x 26.2
ROTMG : OP.1977.104

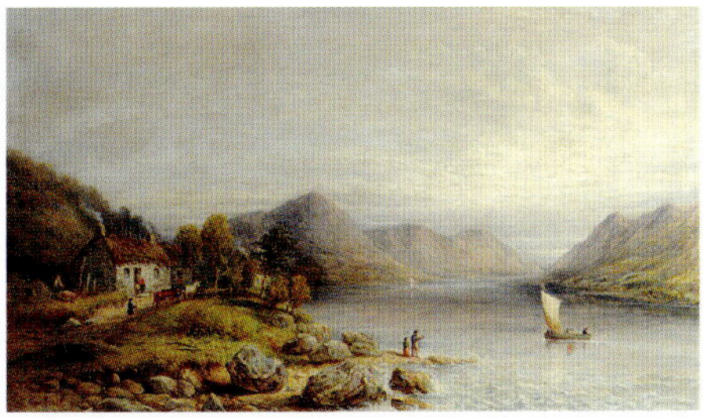

Hawkesworth, Joseph Hallam 1827–1908
Loch Earn, Scotland c.1870
oil on canvas 45.8 x 76.4
ROTMG : OP.1977.63

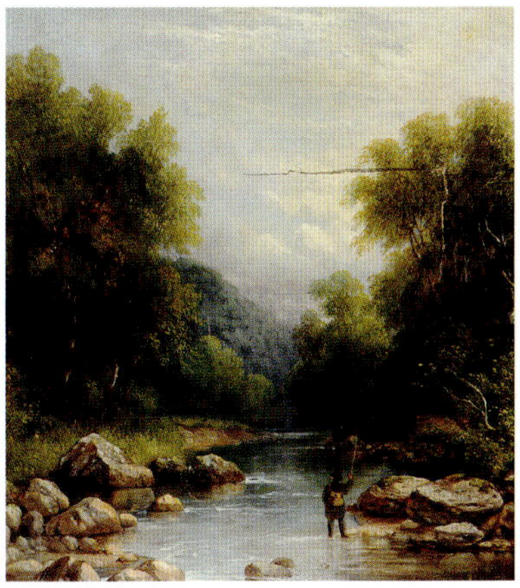

Hawkesworth, Joseph Hallam 1827–1908
On the Don, Wharncliffe, South Yorkshire c.1870
oil on canvas 65 x 54
ROTMG : OP.1977.157

Hawkesworth, Joseph Hallam 1827–1908
On the Rother, near Catcliffe, South Yorkshire c.1870
oil on canvas 30 x 40
ROTMG : OP.1978.233

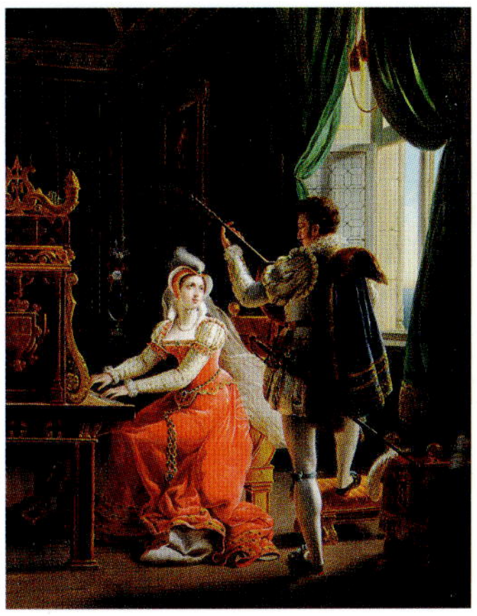

Herbert, John Rogers 1810–1890
Mary, Queen of Scots and David Rizzio c.1870
oil on canvas 109 x 84
ROTMG : OP.1977.202

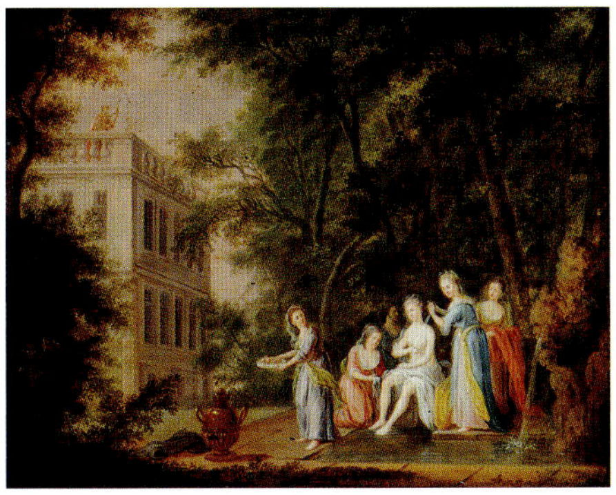

Hergenröder, Georg Heinrich 1736–c.1794
Ladies Bathing c.1775
oil on copper panel 28 x 49
ROTMG : OP.1977.186

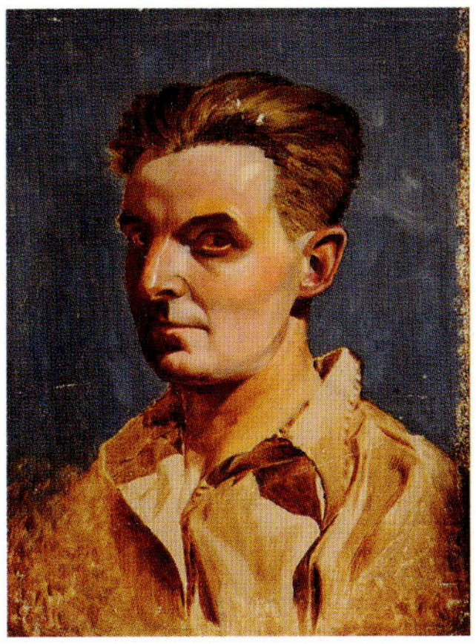

Hickman, Arthur 1902–1987
Self Portrait as a Young Man c.1930
oil on cardboard 50.9 x 38.2
ROTMG : OP.1993.3

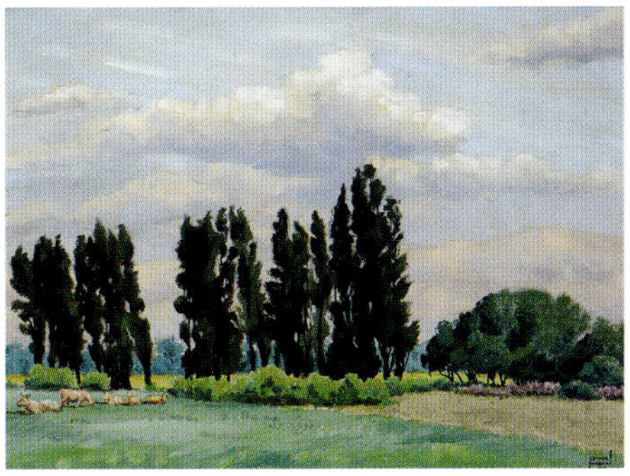

Hickman, Arthur 1902–1987
Landscape 1953
oil on board 29 x 39.5
ROTMG : OP.1991.1

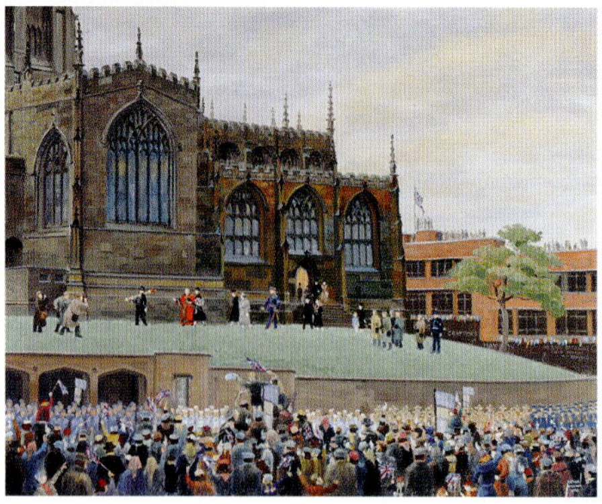

Hickman, Arthur 1902–1987
The Visit of Princess Margaret 1956
oil on board 62 x 74
ROTMG : 1999.25

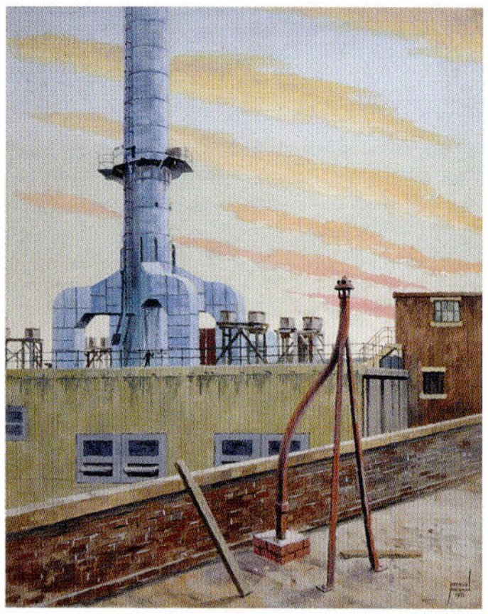

Hickman, Arthur 1902–1987
On the Prince of Wales Power Station Roof, Effingham Street, Rotherham, South Yorkshire 1971
oil on board 50.5 x 40.6
ROTMG : OP.1993.1

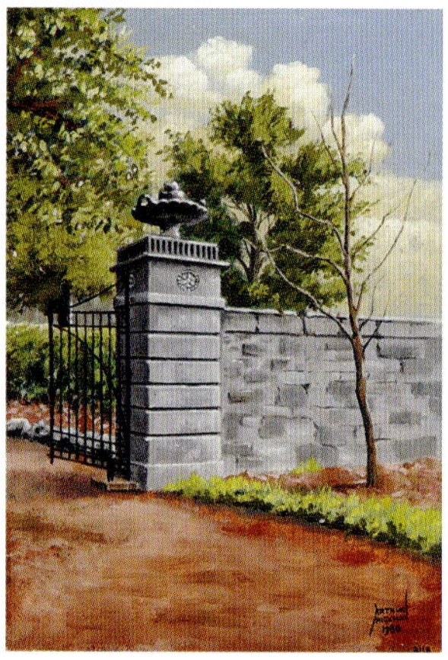

Hickman, Arthur 1902–1987
One Post of Entrance to Colliery Offices, Wash Lane, Rotherham, South Yorkshire 1980
oil on board 27 x 19
ROTMG : OP.1993.2

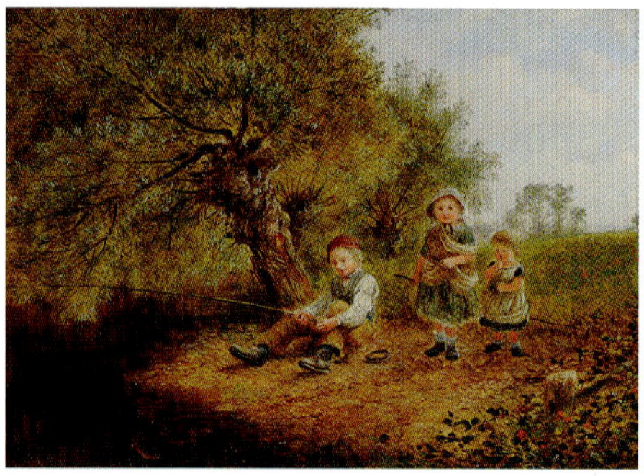

Hill, James John 1811–1882
The Young Anglers c.1840
oil on board 30.5 x 39
ROTMG : OP.1977.24

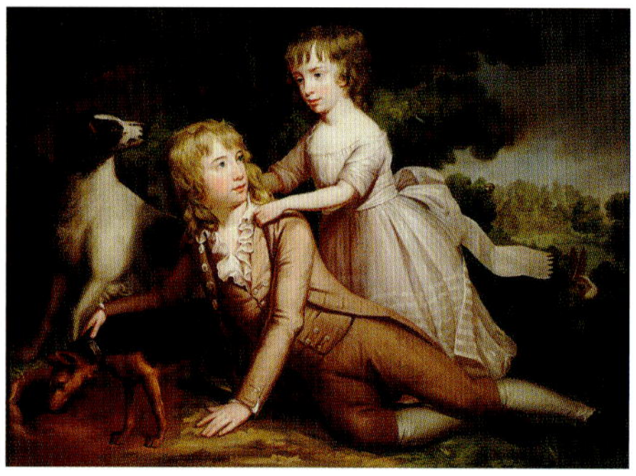

Hilton, William I 1752–1822
Jonathan (1781–1842), and Mary Anne Walker (1783–1855), of Ferham c.1790
oil on canvas 98.5 x 131.5
ROTMG : LOP.1 (NCM 1937-42)

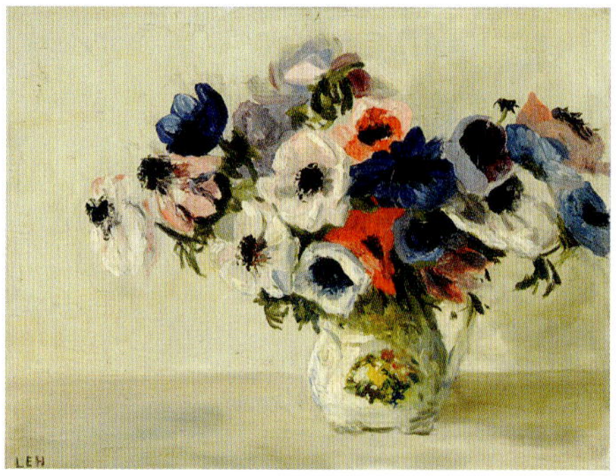

Hogan, Laura E. c.1880–1970
Anemones c.1920
oil on canvas 35.5 x 45.5
ROTMG : OP.1982.237

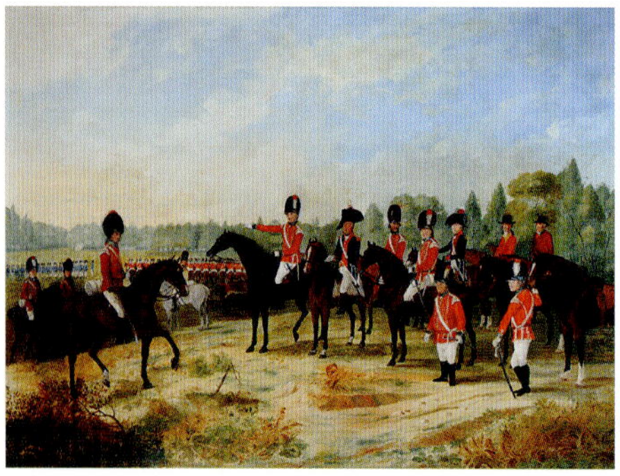

Holden, Richard 1768–1809
Review of Local Volunteers on Brinsworth Common, Rotherham, South Yorkshire 1804
oil on canvas 146 x 192.5
ROTMG : OP.1978.218

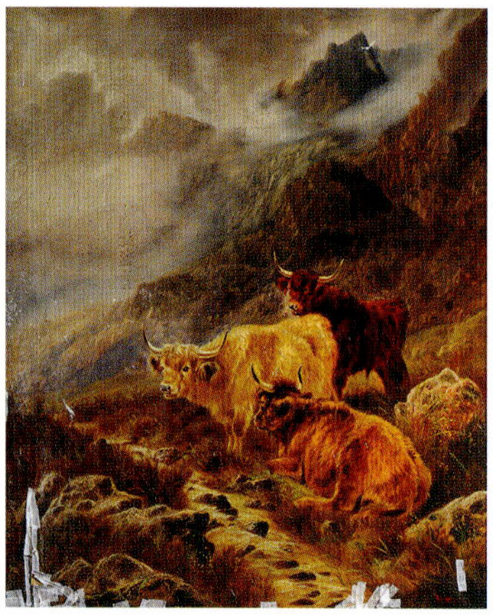

Hollyer, William Perring 1834–1922
Highland Cattle c.1885
oil on canvas 126.5 x 102
ROTMG : OP.1984.13

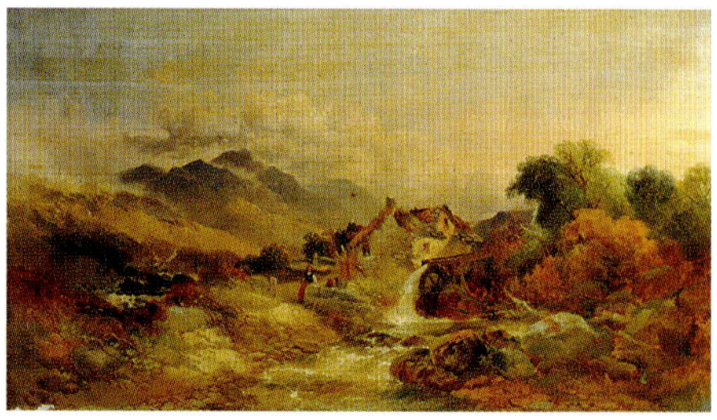

Horton, J.
Mill at Ambleside, Cumbria c.1820
oil on canvas 57 x 99.5
ROTMG : OP.1977.53

Facing page: Cowen, William, 1791–1864, *View of Rotherham, South Yorkshire* (detail), c.1830, Rotherham Museum & Art Gallery, (p. 121)

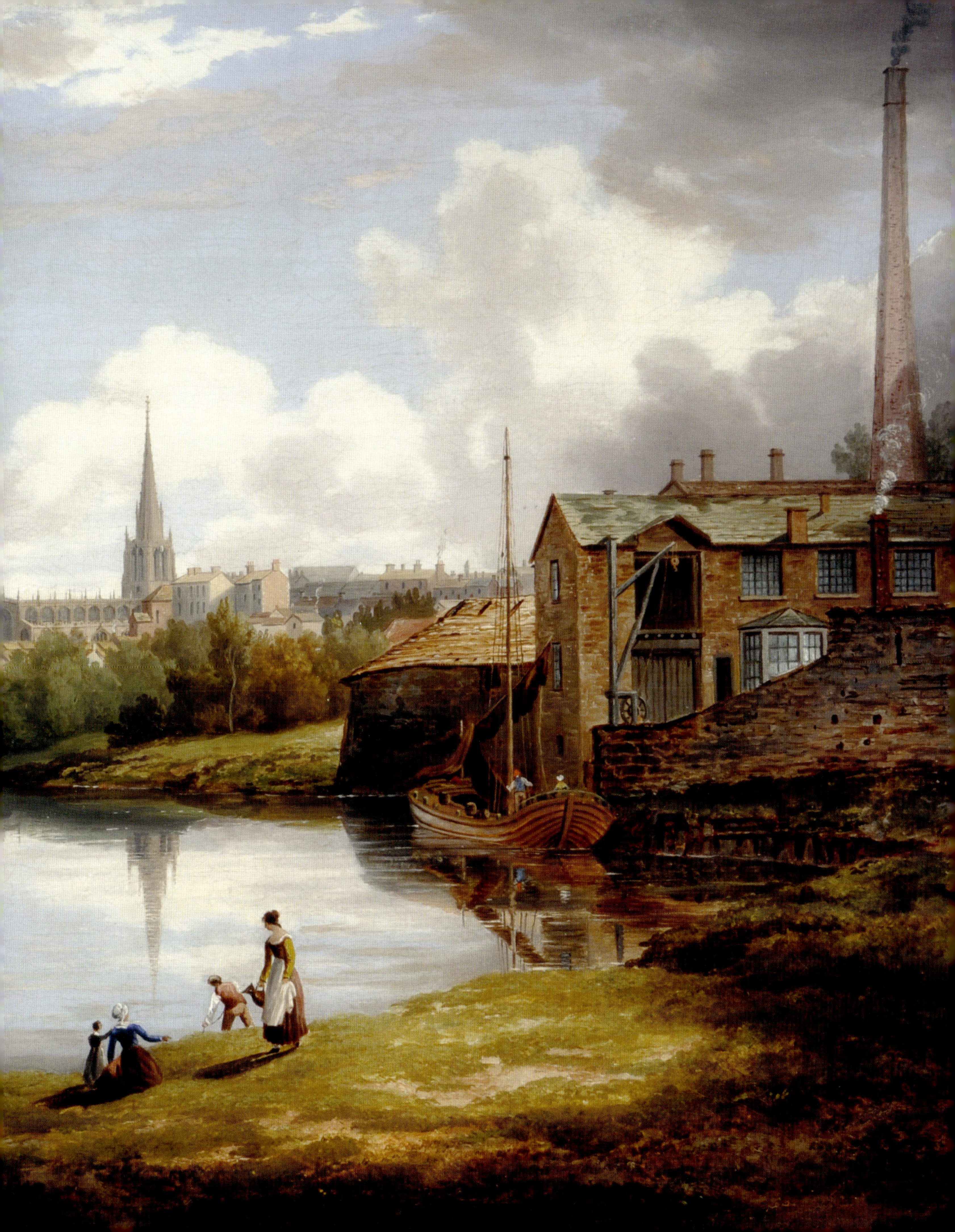

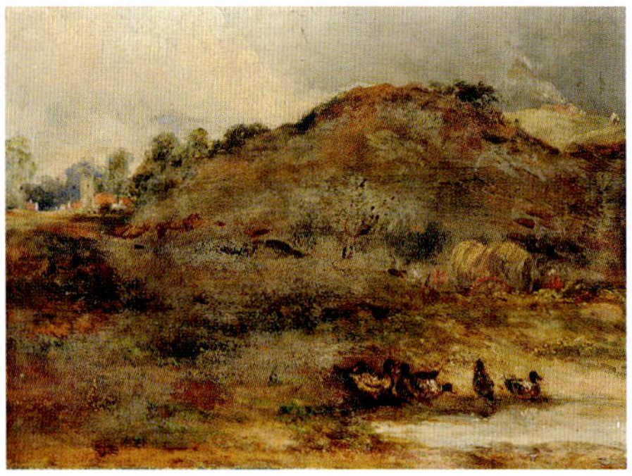

Hudson, Marianne (attributed to)
active 1878
Farmyard c.1878
oil on panel 22.7 x 30.2
ROTMG : OP.1977.124

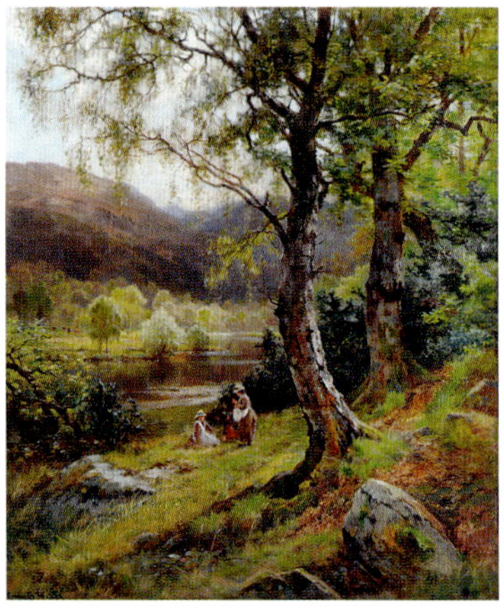

Hurt, Louis Bosworth 1856–1929
A Pleasant Stream in a Quiet Land c.1890
oil on canvas 75 x 62
ROTMG : OP.1977.27

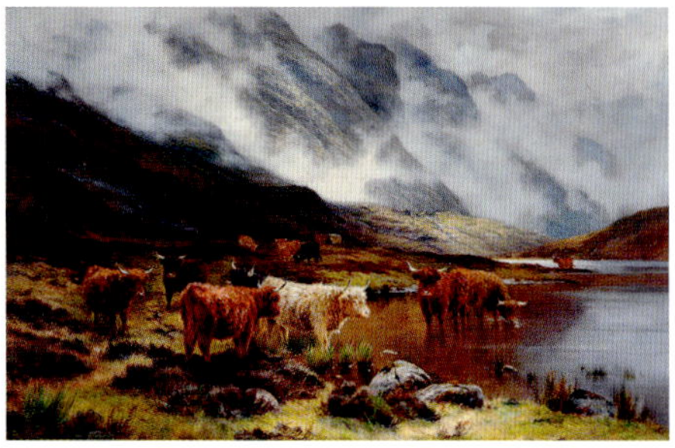

Hurt, Louis Bosworth 1856–1929
Highland Cattle 1892
oil on canvas 60 x 89
ROTMG : OP.1977.111

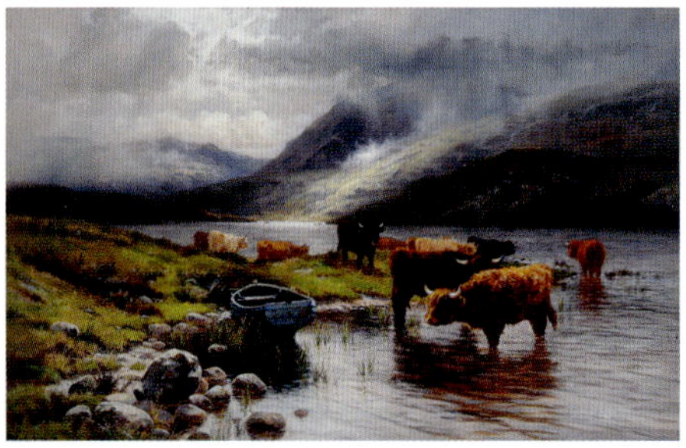

Hurt, Louis Bosworth 1856–1929
Between the Showers c.1895
oil on canvas 59 x 89
ROTMG : OP.1977.154

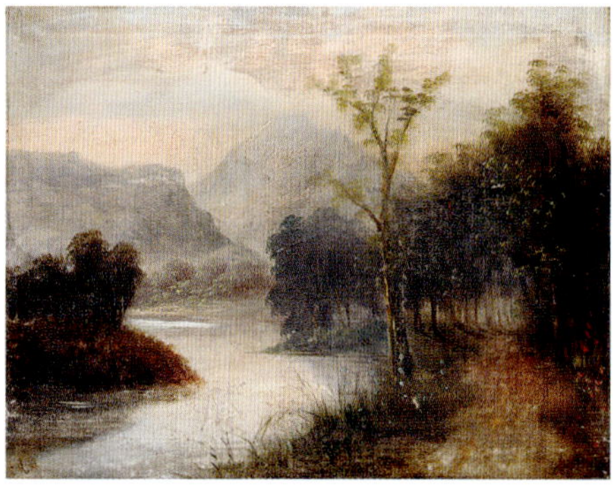

Huur, C. (attributed to)
Landscape c.1900
oil on canvas 40.3 x 50.8
ROTMG : OP.1977.38

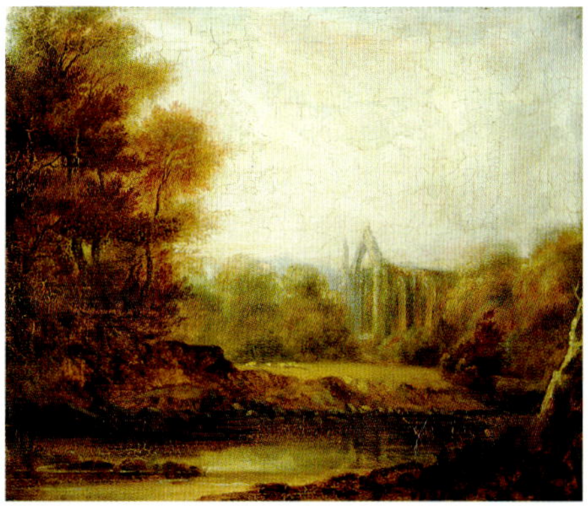

Ibbetson, Julius Caesar 1759–1817
Distant View of Bolton Abbey, North Yorkshire c.1780
oil on canvas 28 x 32
ROTMG : OP.1977.101

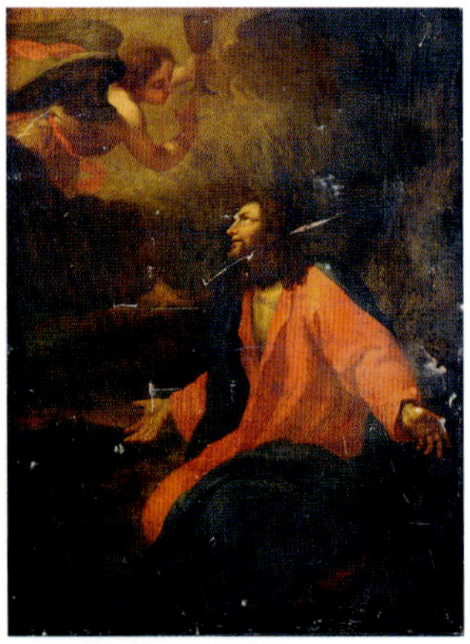

Italian School
Christ in the Garden of Gethsemane c.1640
oil on canvas 134 x 98
ROTMG : OP.1984.9

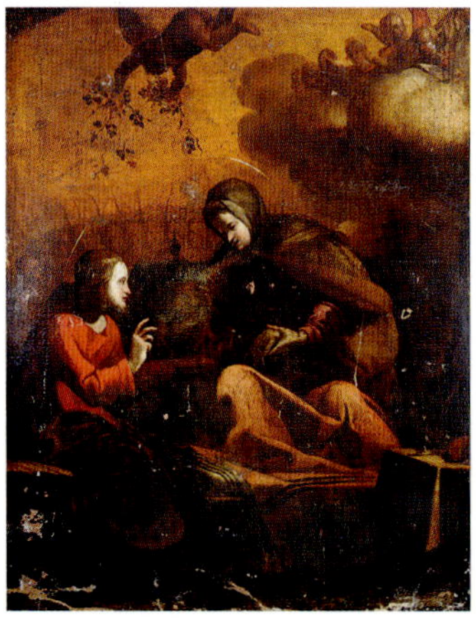

Italian School 17th C
The Death of St Joseph
oil on canvas 142 x 111.2
ROTMG : OP.1984.8

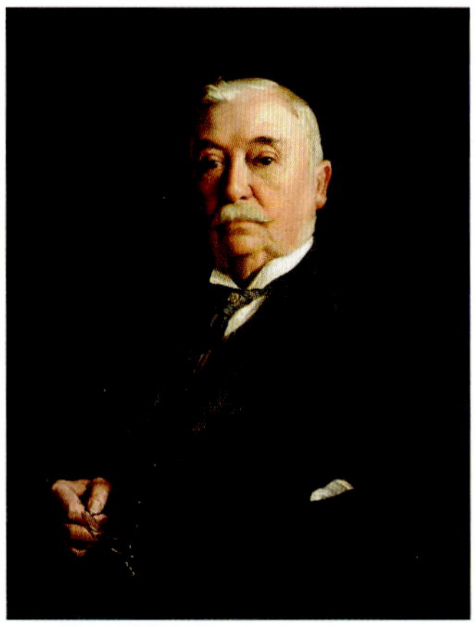

Jagger, David 1891–1958
Thomas Newbould (1845–1933) 1921
oil on canvas 81 x 62
ROTMG : OP.1984.16

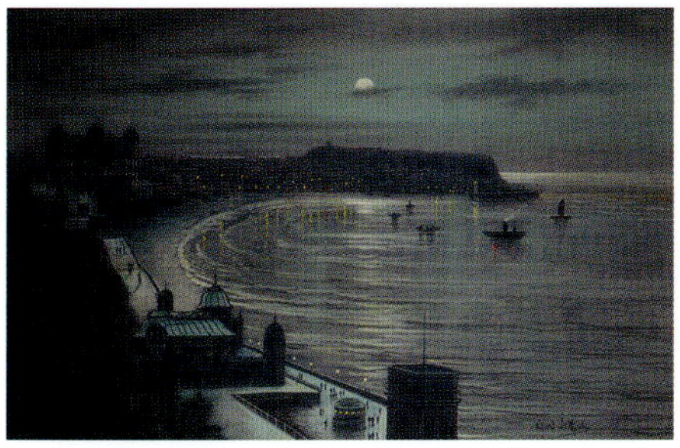

Jenkins, Wilfred 1857–1936
Moonlight Coastal Scene c.1885
oil on canvas 38.5 x 59
ROTMG : OP.1977.162

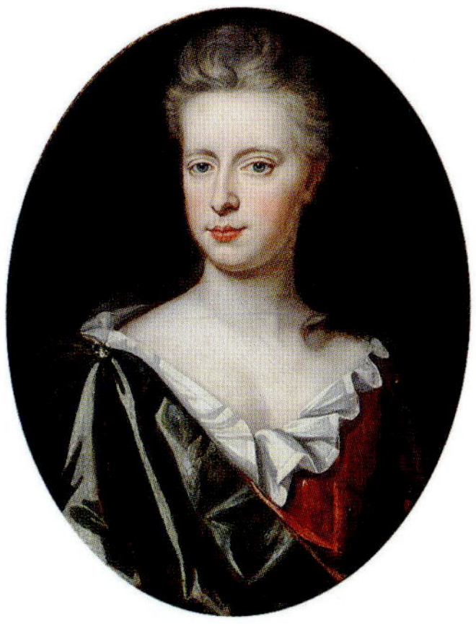

Kneller, Godfrey (after) 1646–1723
Portrait of an Unknown Lady c.1685
oil on canvas 62 x 47
ROTMG : OP.1978.217

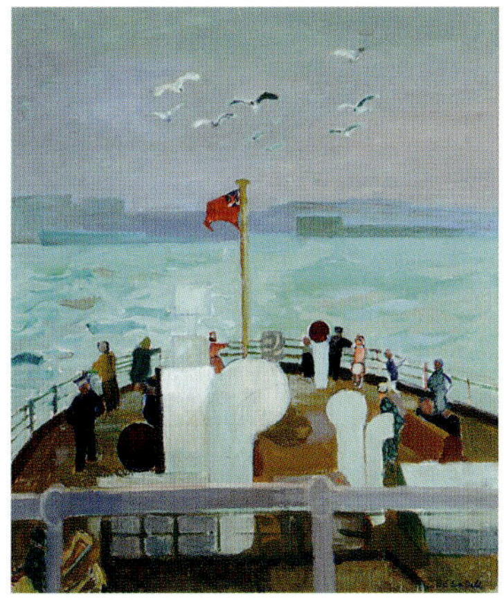

La Dell, Edwin 1914–1970
Leaving Boulogne, France c.1960
oil on canvas 76 x 64
ROTMG : OP.1977.174

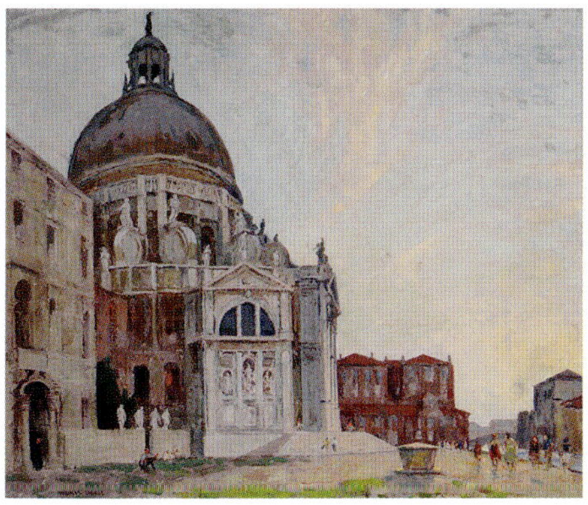

La Dell, Thomas 1883–1971
View of Venice 1883–1971 c.1910
oil on paper on board 41.5 x 49
ROTMG : OP.1979.232

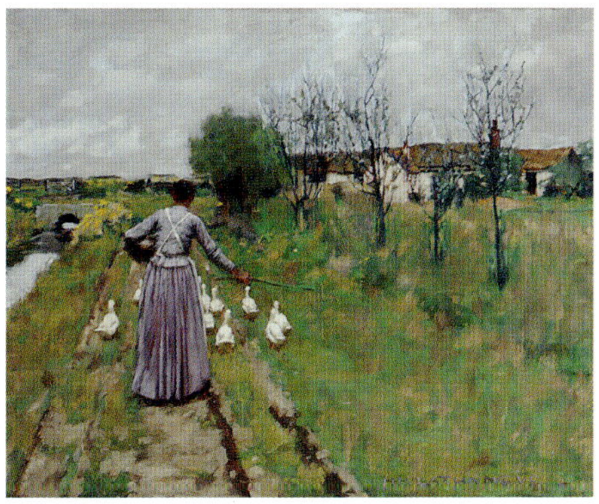

La Thangue, Henry Herbert 1859–1929
Landscape Study c.1889
oil on canvas 50 x 61
ROTMG : OP.1978.215

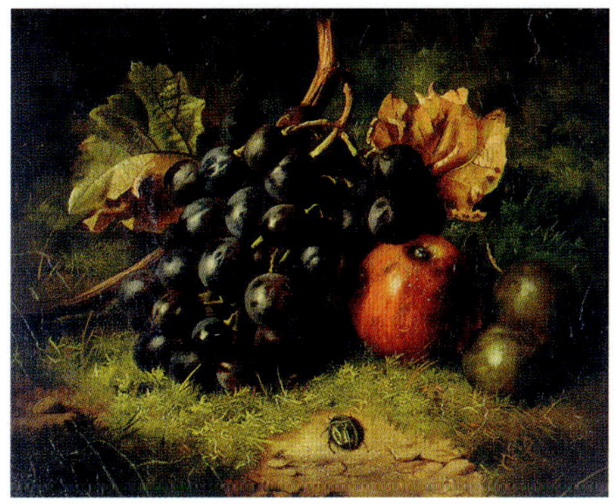

Lance, George 1802–1864
Fruit Piece c.1845
oil on canvas 25 x 30.5
ROTMG : OP.1977.92

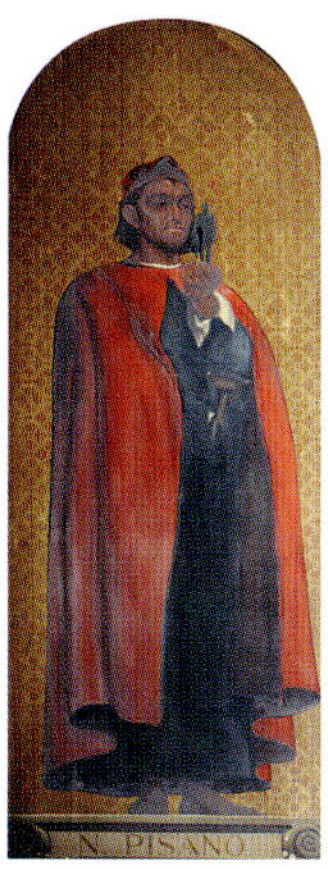

Leighton, Frederic (after) 1830–1896
Niccolò Pisano (c.1220/1225–c.1284) c.1865
oil on canvas panel 239 x 89
ROTMG : TUF1419

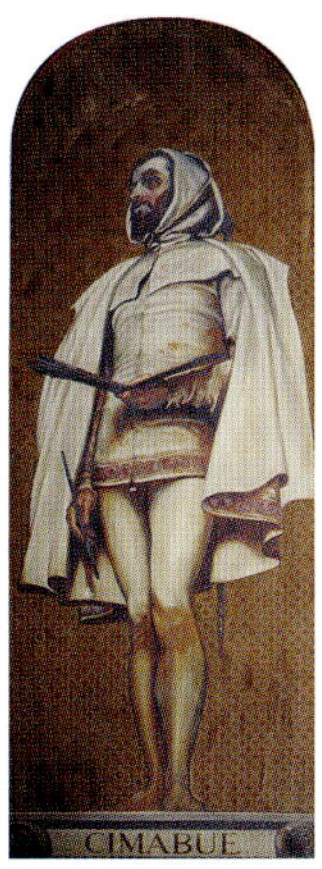

Leighton, Frederic (after) 1830–1896
Giovanni Cimabue (c.1240–c.1302) c.1866
oil on canvas panel 239 x 89
ROTMG : TUF1418

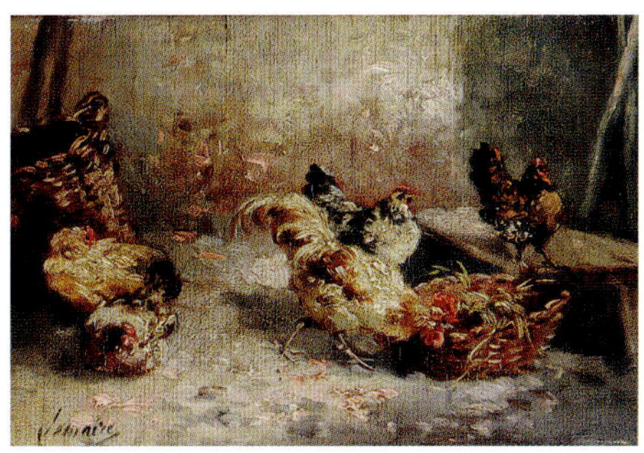

Lemaire, Louis Marie (attributed to)
1824–1910
Poultry c.1860
oil on canvas 15.5 x 23
ROTMG : OP.1977.44

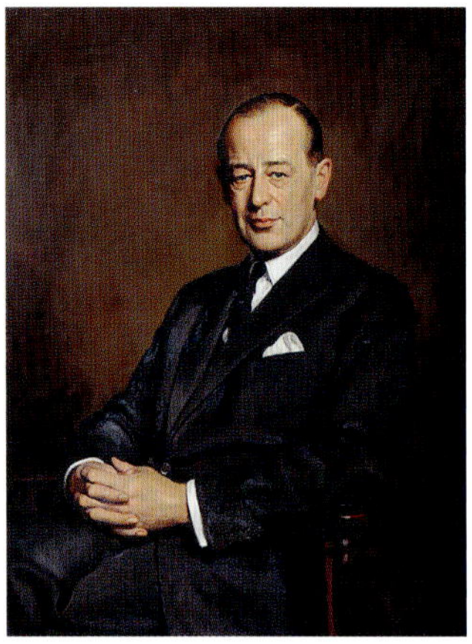

Lewis, Reginald Henry 1894–1973
James Peech (1906–after 1962) (after Edward Irvine Halliday) c.1955
oil on canvas 100 x 75
ROTMG : E1651.1 (P)

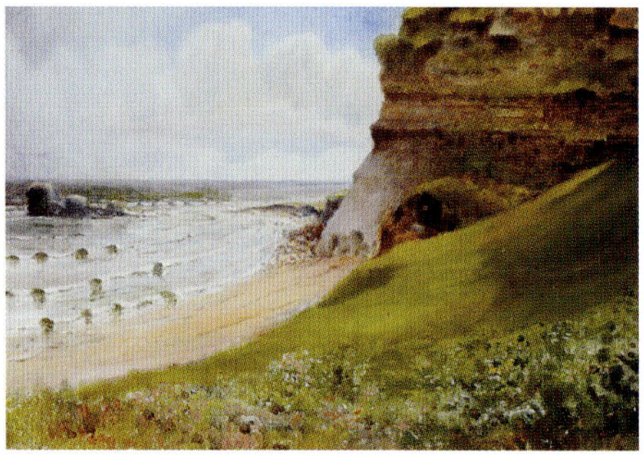

H. M.
Coastal Scene c.1920
oil on paper 32 x 44.5
ROTMG : OP.1977.166

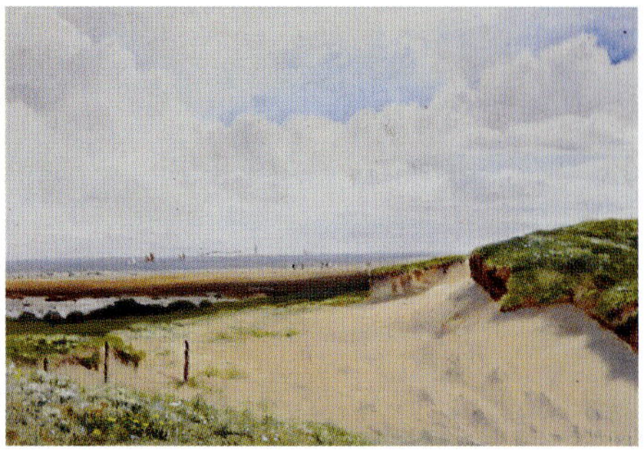

H. M.
Coastal Scene c.1920
oil on paper 17.5 x 24.5
ROTMG : OP.1977.167

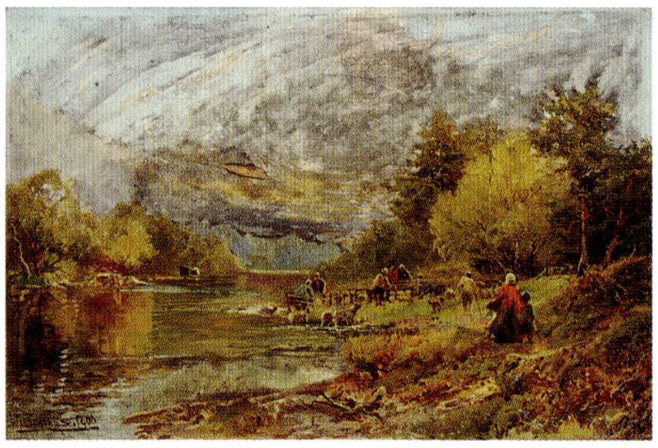

Mahrrs, W.
Animals at a Ford 1906
oil on panel 20.7 x 30.5
ROTMG : OP.1977.121

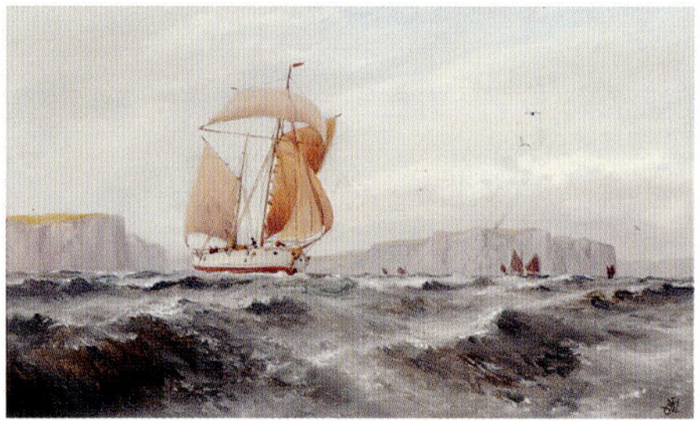

Malender, J.
Sailing Clipper off the Coast c.1890
oil on card 17.4 x 25.7
ROTMG : OP.1977.199

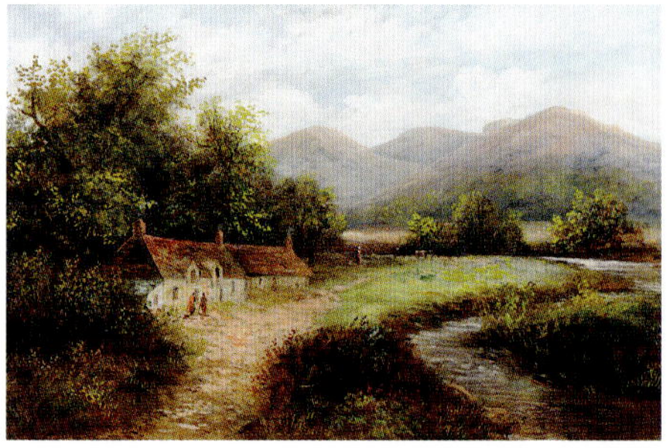

Marshall, W.
Mountain Scene c.1870
oil on canvas 51 x 76.6
ROTMG : OP.1977.164

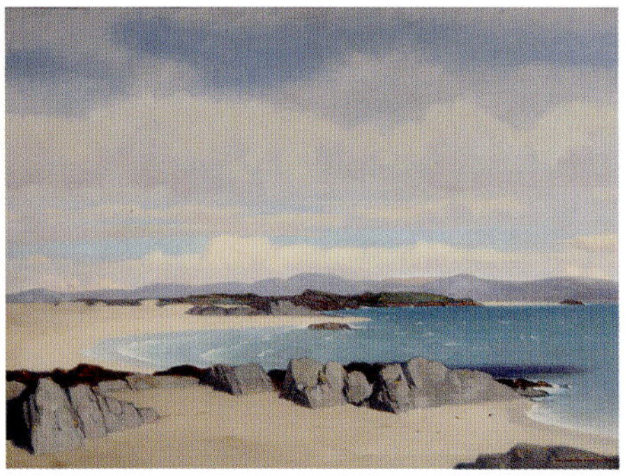

Matthews, William F. 1878–1966
Iona, Scotland 1946
oil on canvas 46 x 61
ROTMG : OP.1977.8

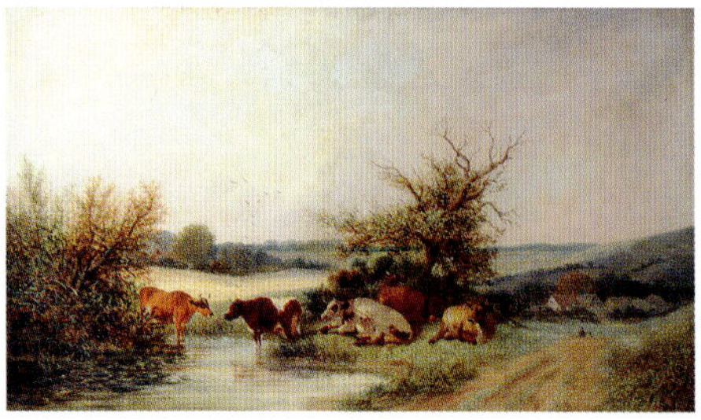

Meadows, William George c.1825–1907
Landscape 1879
oil on canvas 74 x 124.5
ROTMG : OP.1984.2

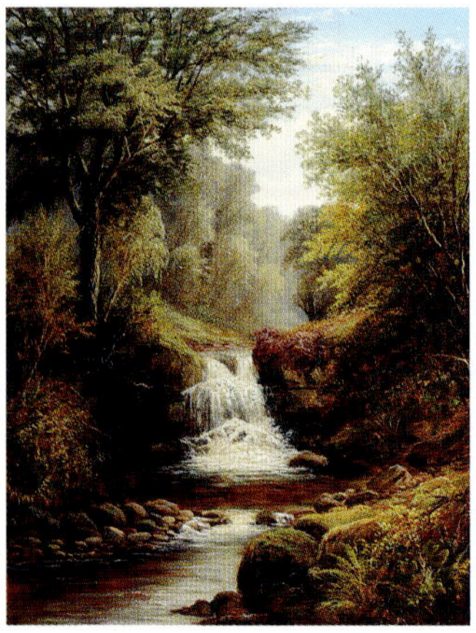

Mellor, William 1851–1931
Landscape c.1890
oil on canvas 91 x 70
ROTMG : OP.1977.97

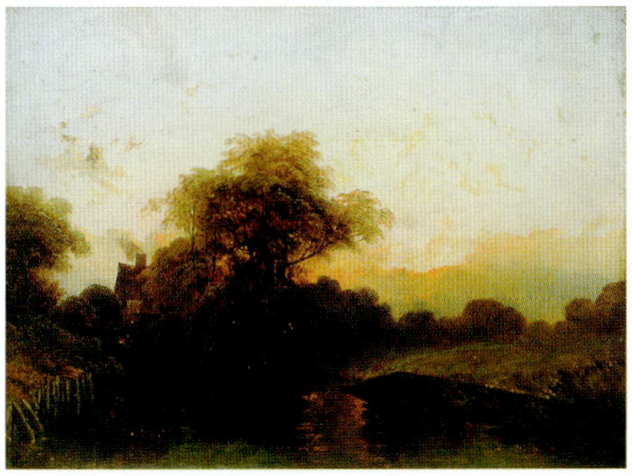

Montague, Alfred 1832–1883
Evening c.1860
oil on canvas 26 x 34.5
ROTMG : OP.1977.54

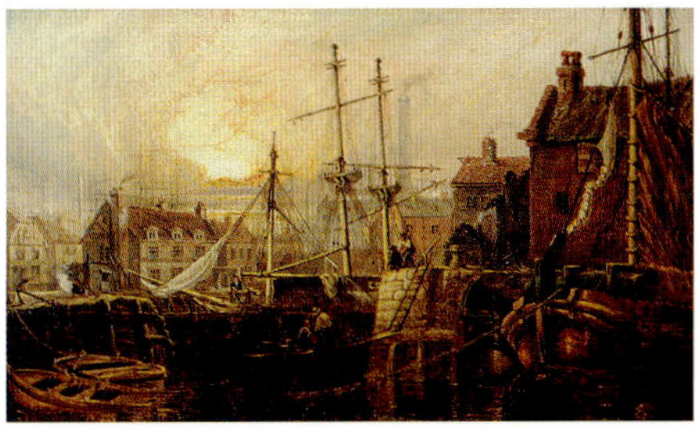

Moore, Claude Thomas Stanfield
1853–1901
Sea Port 1875
oil on canvas 31 x 46
ROTMG : OP.1977.11

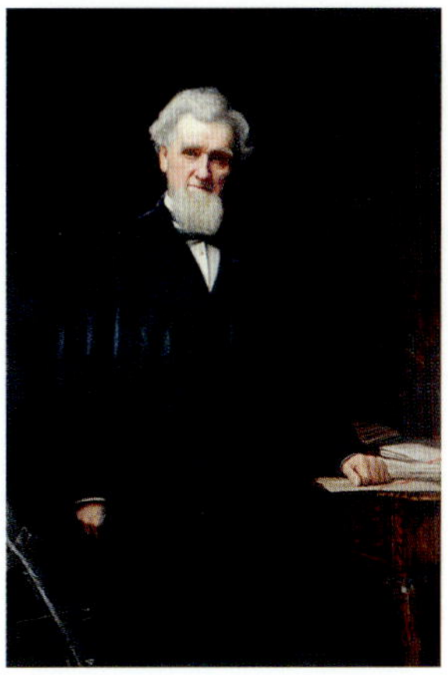

Moore, Ernest 1865–1940
Alderman George E. C. Wragg (1826–1915)
c.1890
oil on canvas 151 x 102
ROTMG : TUF1416

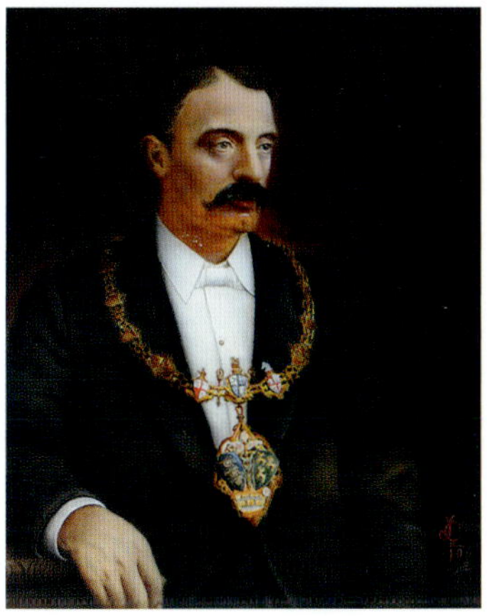

Moore, Ernest 1865–1940
Alderman George Gummer (1855–1934) 1900
oil on canvas 74.5 x 59.5
ROTMG : 2008.29.1

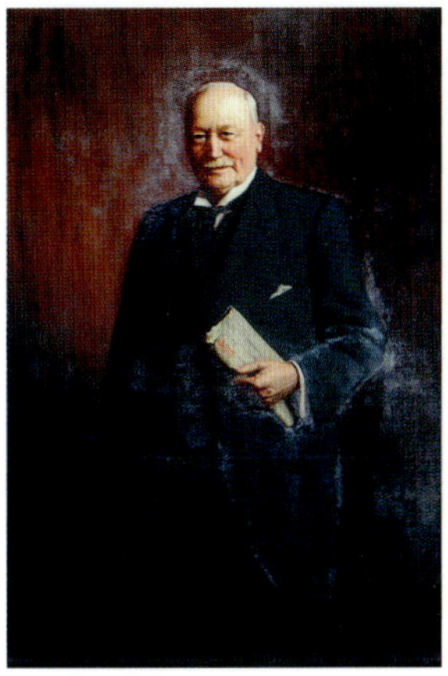

Moore, Ernest 1865–1940
Alderman David Llewellyn Winter (1853–1925), JP, Mayor of Rotherham (1901–1902) 1901
oil on canvas 150 x 100
ROTMG : TUF1414

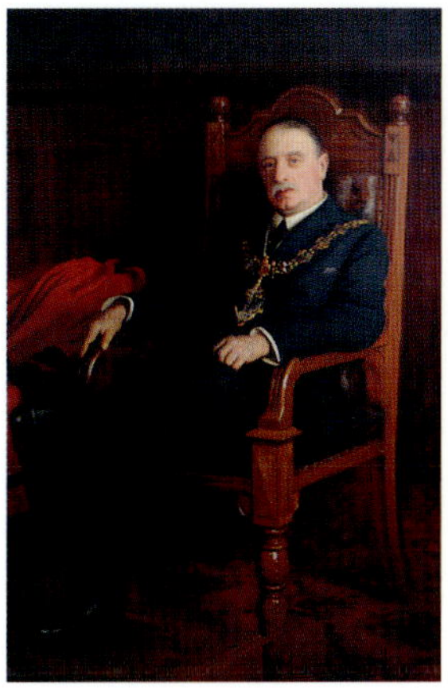

Moore, Ernest 1865–1940
Alderman George Gummer (1855–1934) 1920
oil on canvas 177 x 114
ROTMG : OP.1989.2

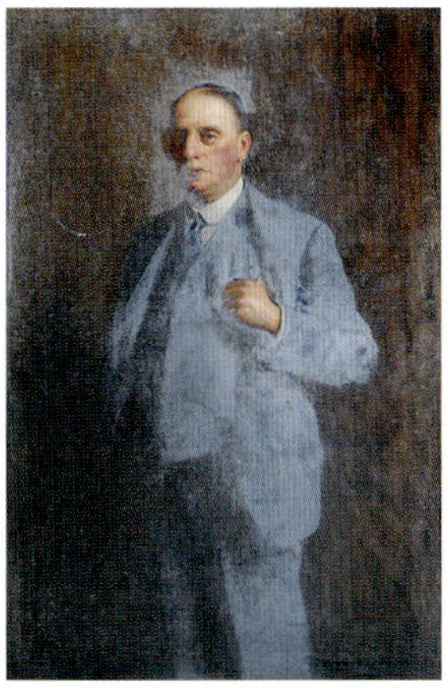

Moore, Ernest 1865–1940
Alderman George Gummer (1855–1934) 1920
oil on canvas 149 x 98
ROTMG : TUF0550

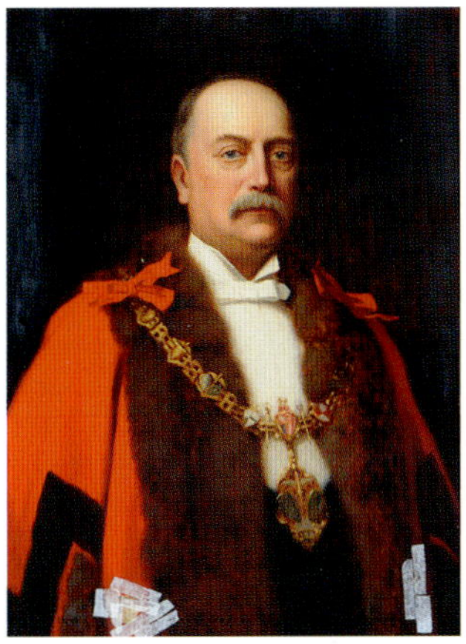

Moore, Ernest 1865–1940
Colonel Sir Charles John Stoddart (1839–1913), VD, JP 1920–1929
oil on canvas 85 x 62
ROTMG : OP.1984.18

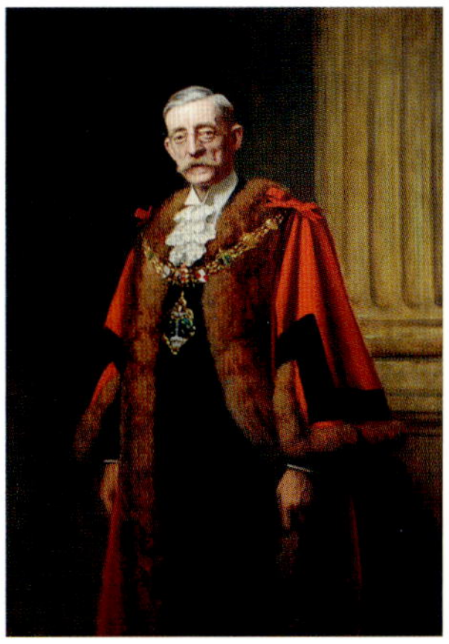

Moore, Ernest 1865–1940
Alderman George E. Caine (1876–1969), JP
c.1931
oil on canvas 152 x 100
ROTMG : THP2

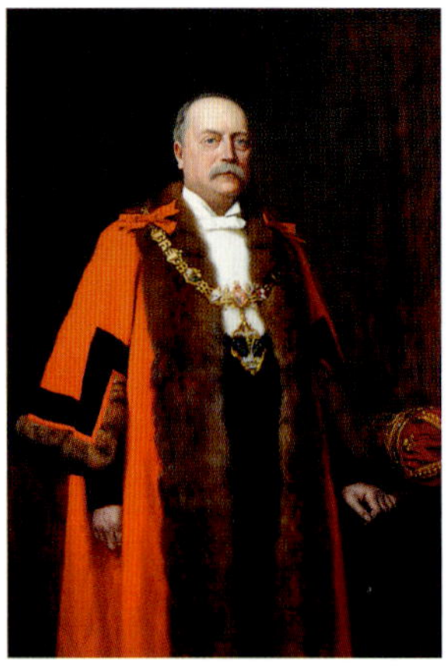

Moore, Ernest (attributed to) 1865–1940
Colonel Sir Charles John Stoddart (1839–1913), VD, JP c.1886
oil on canvas 150.5 x 99.5
ROTMG : THP5

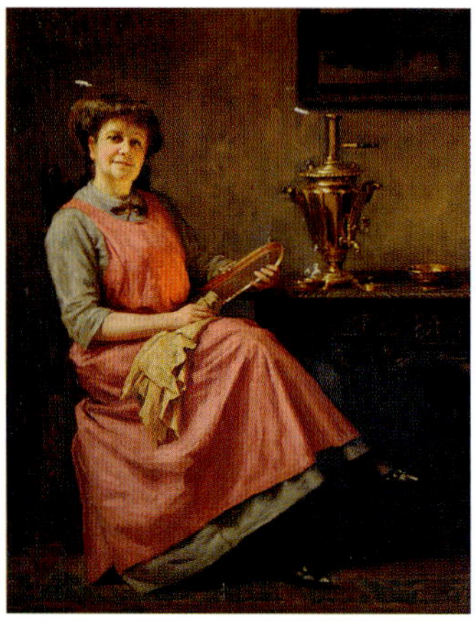

Moore, Ernest (attributed to) 1865–1940
Woman with a Samovar c.1890
oil on canvas 90 x 70
ROTMG : OP.1977.156

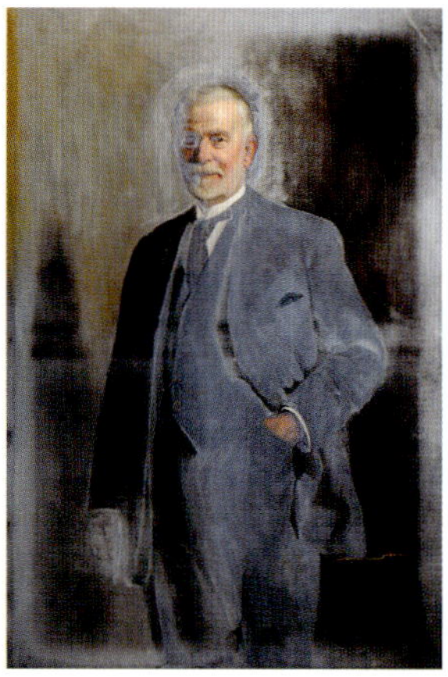

Moore, Ernest (attributed to) 1865–1940
Alderman George Clark (1844–1924) c.1905
oil on canvas 149 x 98
ROTMG : TUF1445

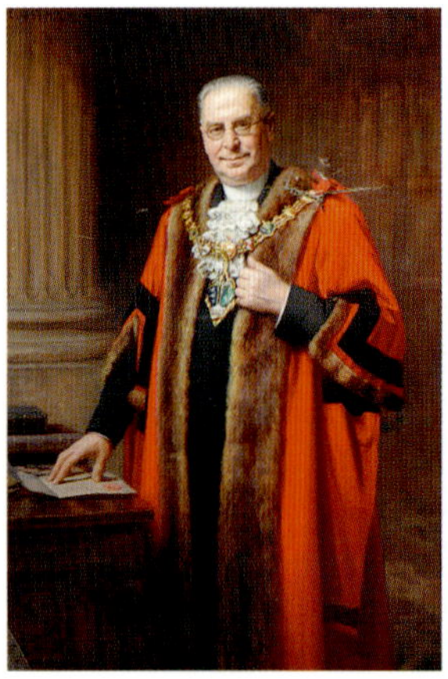

Moore, Ernest (attributed to) 1865–1940
Alderman Albert Percy Aizlewood (1864–1953), JP c.1934
oil on canvas 150.5 x 100
ROTMG : TUF1415

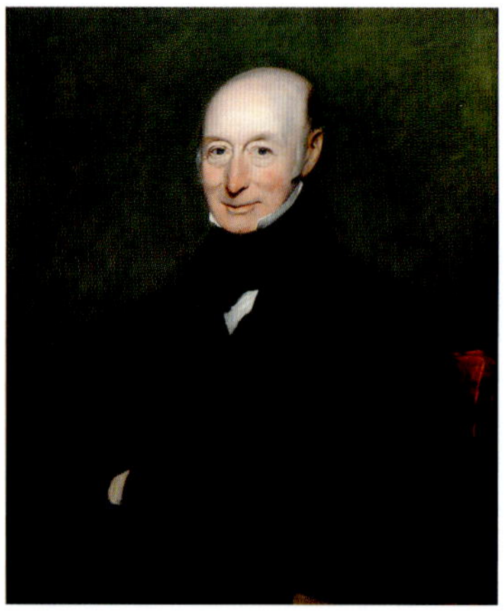

Moore, William I 1790–1851
Samuel Clark (1771–1845), Esquire of Dumfries House c.1830
oil on canvas 76 x 65.5
ROTMG : OP.1977.75

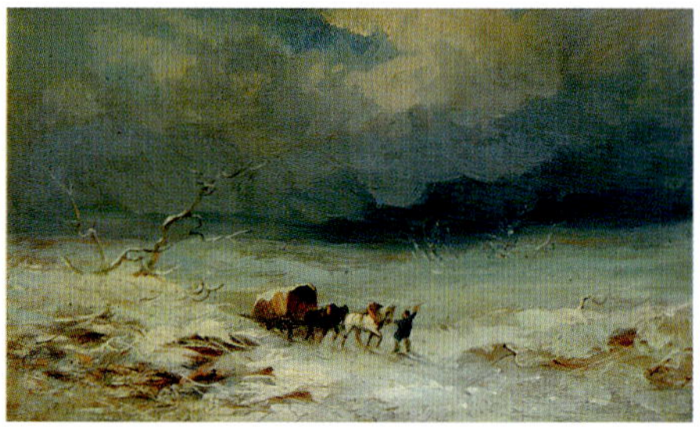

Morland, George 1763–1804
Landscape c.1800
oil on board 25.5 x 37
ROTMG : OP.1977.78

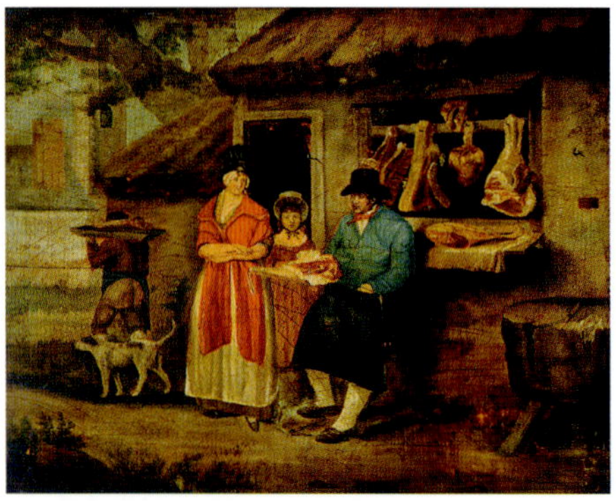

Morland, George 1763–1804
The Village Butcher c.1800
oil on panel 43.5 x 53.5
ROTMG : OP.1977.150

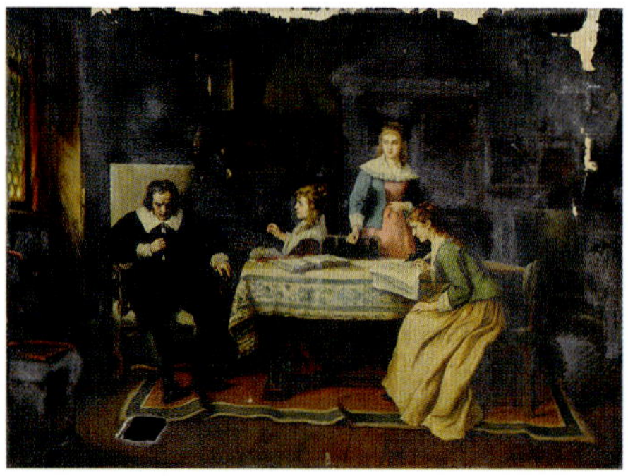

Munkácsy, Mihály (after) 1844–1900
Milton c.1880
oil on canvas 73.5 x 100
ROTMG : OP.1977.195

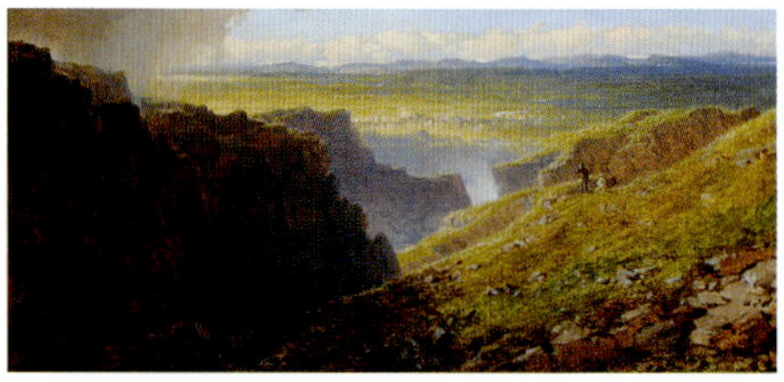

Niemann, Edmund John 1813–1876
Cheddar Cliffs, Somerset c.1855
oil on canvas 21 x 48
ROTMG : OP.1989.4

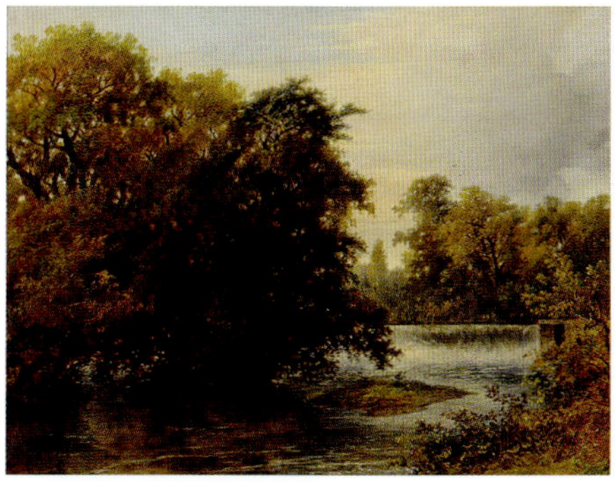

Niemann, Edmund John 1813–1876
Landscape and Waterfall c.1855
oil on canvas 71.5 x 91.2
ROTMG : OP.1989.5

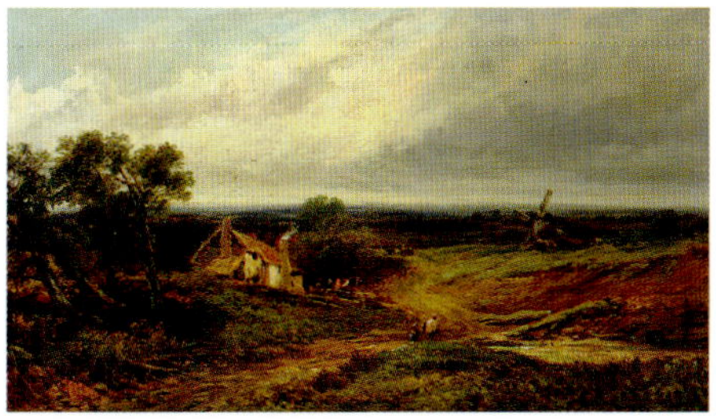

Niemann, Edmund John 1813–1876
Moorland Scene c.1855
oil on canvas 53 x 92
ROTMG : OP.1977.6

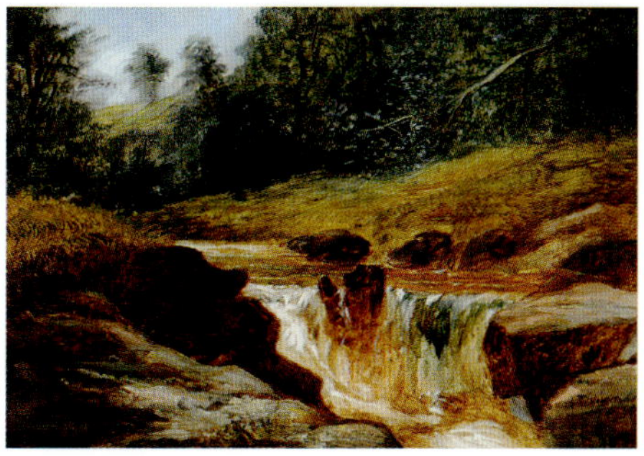

Niemann, Edmund John 1813–1876
Mountain Stream c.1855
oil on canvas 25 x 36
ROTMG : OP.1978.207

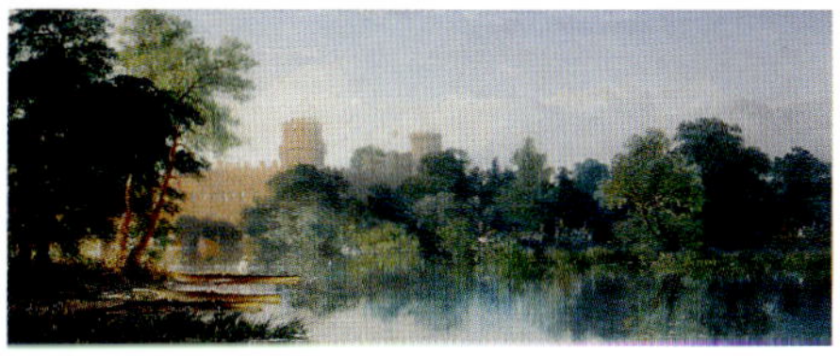

Niemann, Edmund John 1813–1876
Warwick Castle c.1855
oil on canvas 19 x 47
ROTMG : OP.1989.3

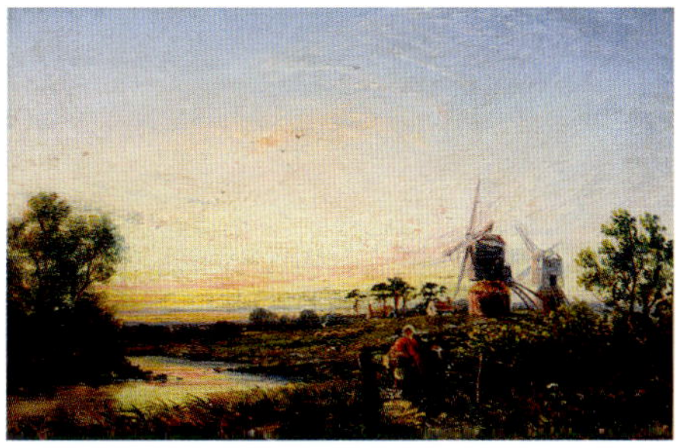

Niemann, Edmund John 1813–1876
Landscape with Windmills c.1860
oil on canvas 19 x 29.5
ROTMG : OP.1982.236

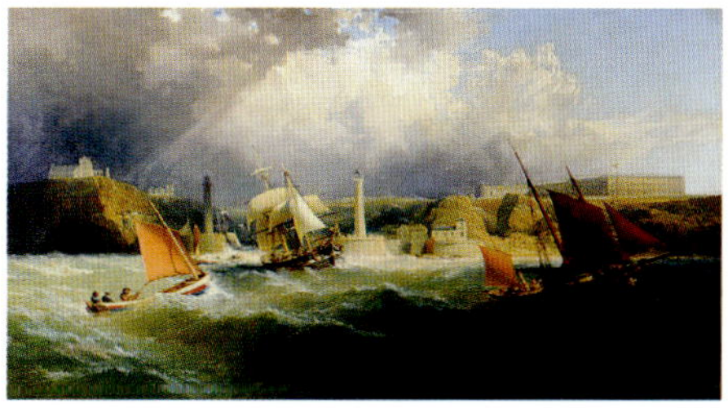

Niemann, Edmund John 1813–1876
Whitby, North Yorkshire, from the Sea 1862
oil on canvas 64 x 115
ROTMG : OP.1977.33

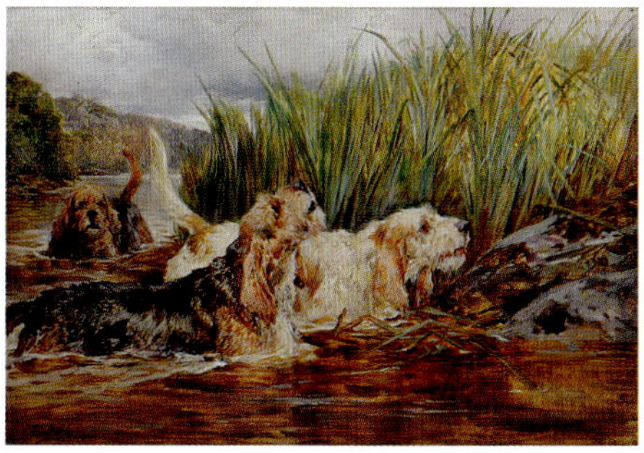

Noble, John Sargeant 1848–1896
Otter Hunting c.1885
oil on mahogany panel 34.5 x 49.5
ROTMG : OP.1977.58

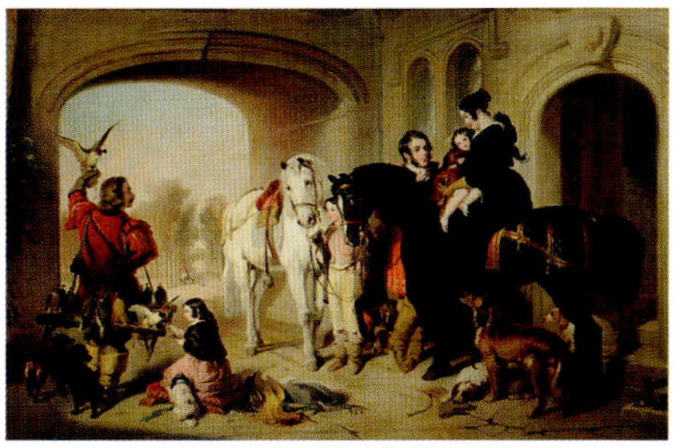

Norman, Edward Glossop Augustus b.c.1816
The Hawking Party (after Edwin Henry Landseer) c.1849
oil on canvas 128.5 x 236.5
ROTMG : OP.1984.3

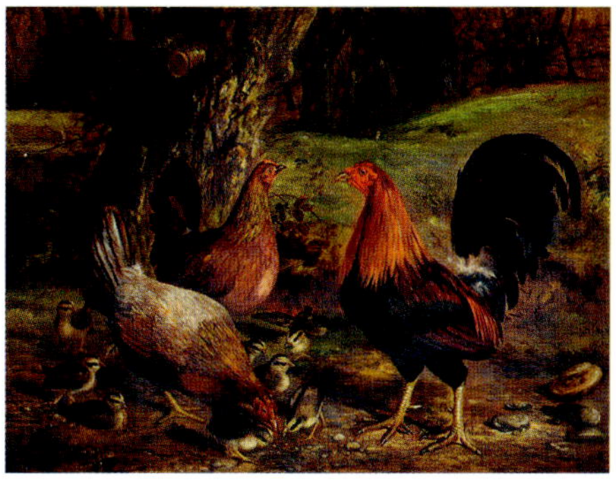

Norton, Benjamin Cam 1835–1900
Hen and Chicks 1886
oil on canvas 71 x 91
ROTMG : OP.1977.39

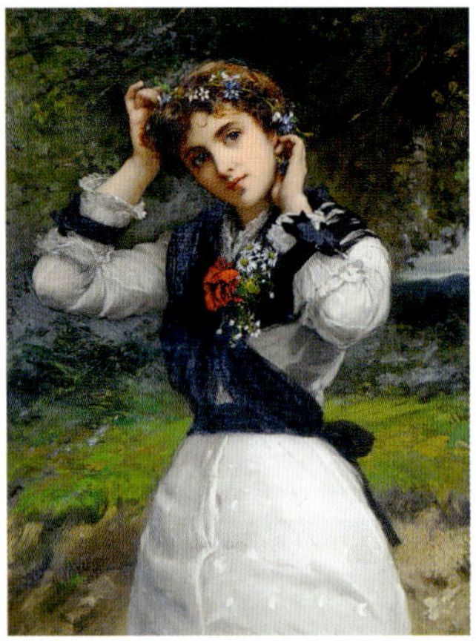

Oliver, William 1804–1853
Olivette c.1845
oil on canvas 61 x 46
ROTMG : OP.1977.52

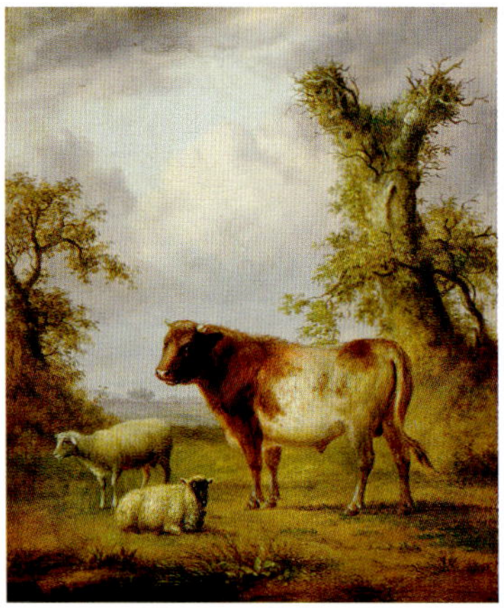

W. P.
Cattle c.1860
oil on board 23.5 x 19
ROTMG : OP.1977.30

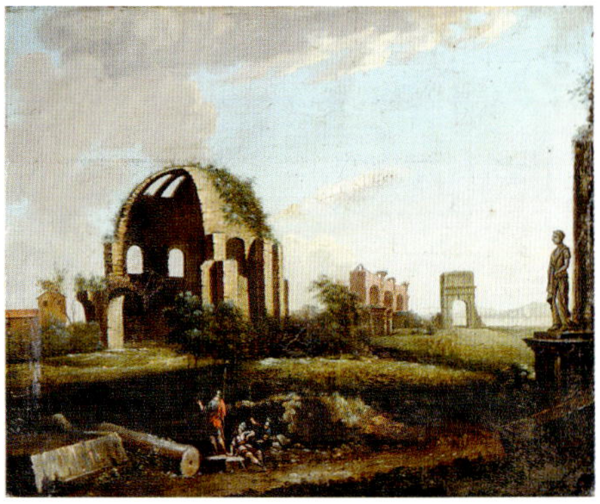

Panini, Giovanni Paolo (after) 1691–1765
Landscape
oil on canvas 46 x 63
ROTMG : OP.1977.102

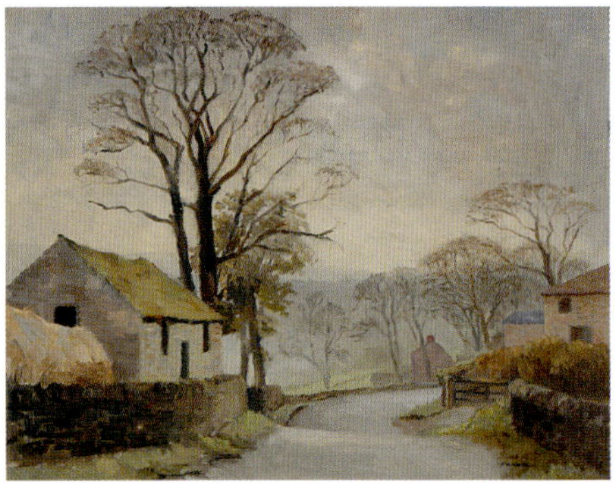

Parker, Vincent active c.1950–1970
November Day, Stannington, South Yorkshire
c.1950
oil on board 29 x 38
ROTMG : OP.1977.160

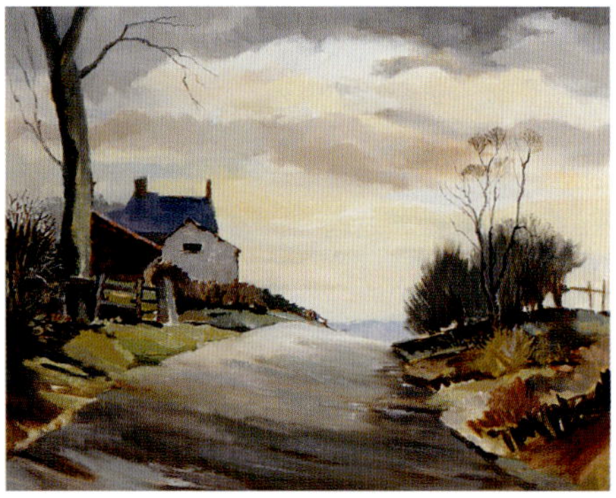

Parker, Vincent active c.1950–1970
After the Shower, near Harthill, South Yorkshire
1970
oil on board 39.5 x 49.5
ROTMG : OP.1977.191

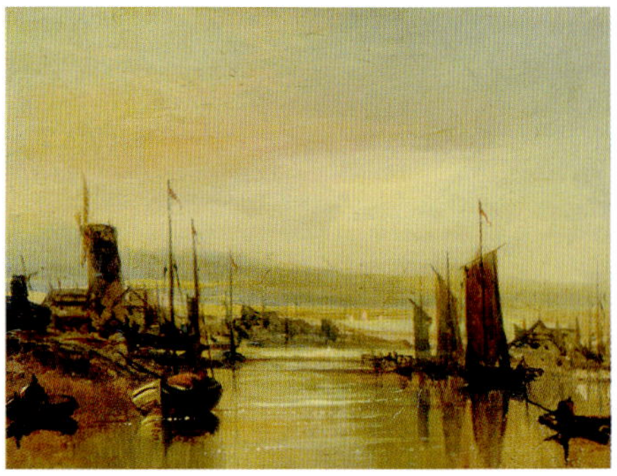

Paul, John Dean 1775–1852
River Yare c.1850
oil on canvas 17 x 22
ROTMG : OP.1977.66

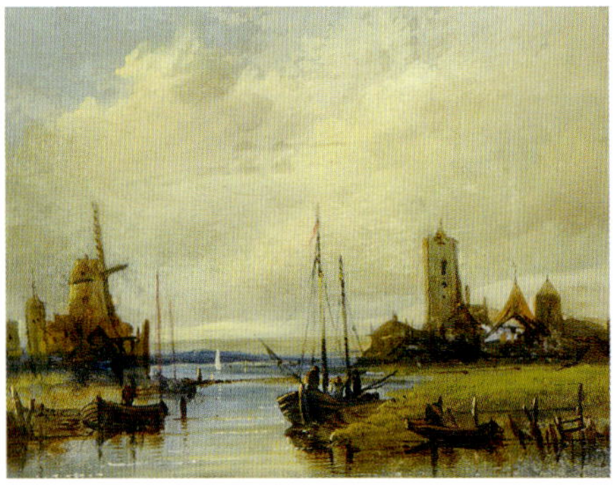

Paul, John Dean 1775–1852
River Yare c.1850
oil on canvas 17 x 22
ROTMG : OP.1977.67

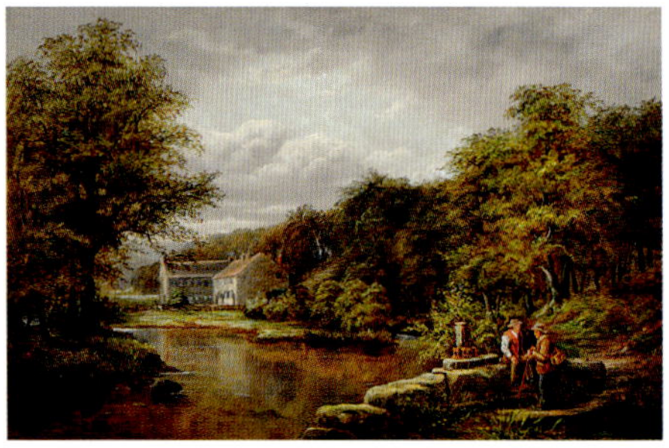

Pearson, G. Hattersley 1858–1937
Roscoe Wheel, Rivelin Valley, South Yorkshire
c.1890
oil on canvas 51 x 76.5
ROTMG : OP.1977.139

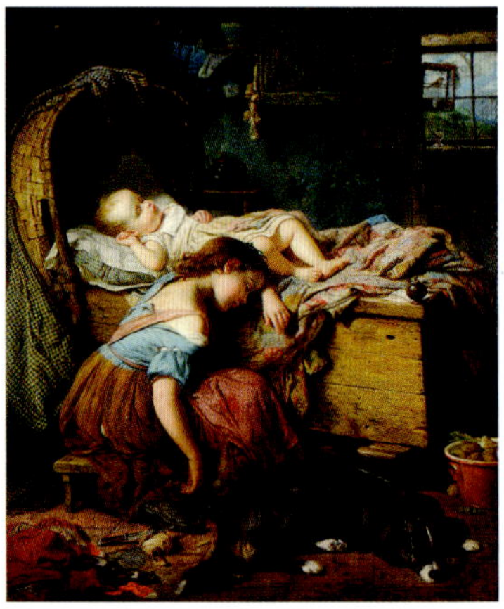

Peele, John Thomas 1822–1897
Asleep on the Watch 1872
oil on canvas 120 x 98
ROTMG : OP.1977.29

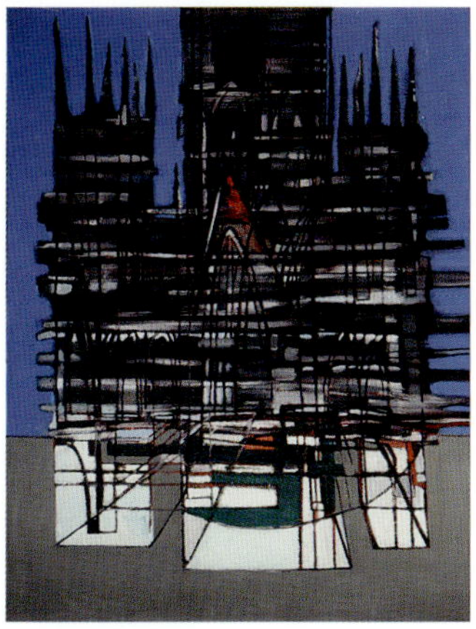

Platt, Russell b.1920
Minster Exterior, West Front c.1970
oil on board 120 x 91
ROTMG : E1524

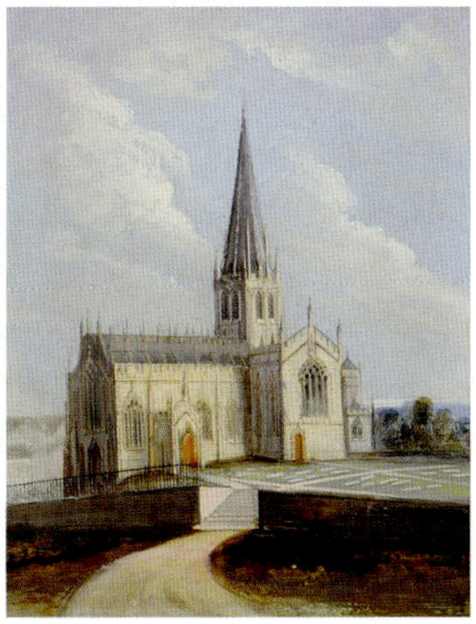

Pontis, Kate 1876–1970
All Saints' Church, Rotherham, South Yorkshire 1938
oil on panel 29 x 21.5
ROTMG : OP.1977.99

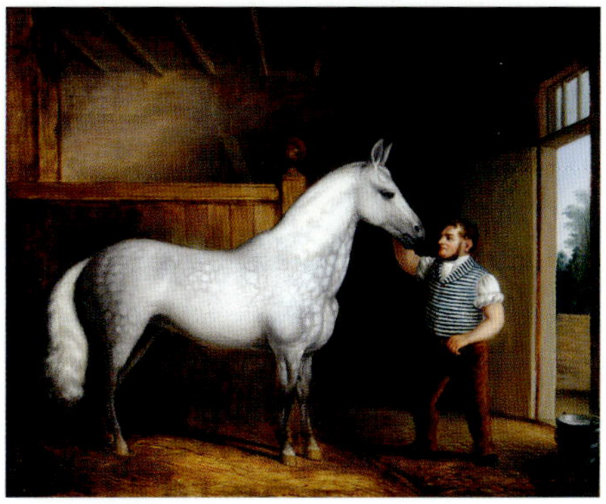

Poole, James 1803–1886
'Cinderella', a Favourite Cob of Mrs Henry Walker's and Her Coachman William Sales c.1840
oil on canvas 62 x 68
ROTMG : OP.1988.11

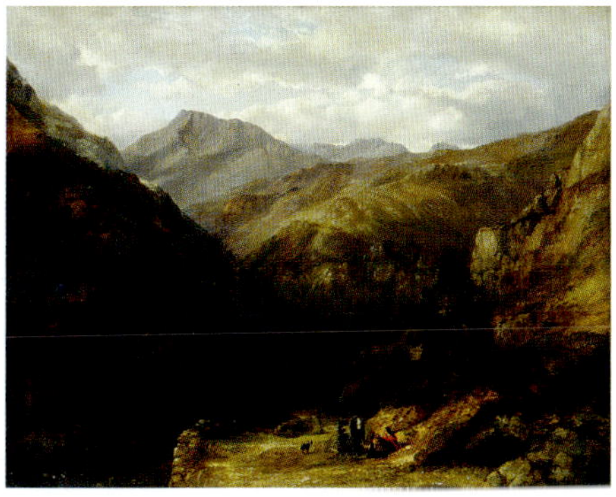

Poole, James 1803–1886
Skiddaw, Cumbria c.1845
oil on canvas 102 x 128
ROTMG : OP.1977.85

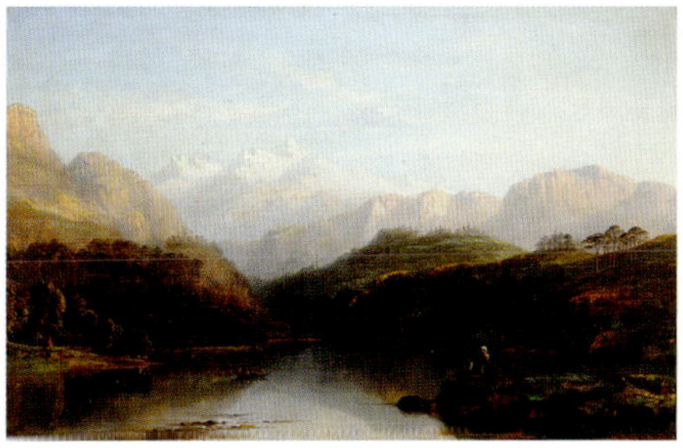

Poole, James 1803–1886
Near Coed Mawr, North Wales c.1850
oil on canvas 38 x 58
ROTMG : OP.1978.206

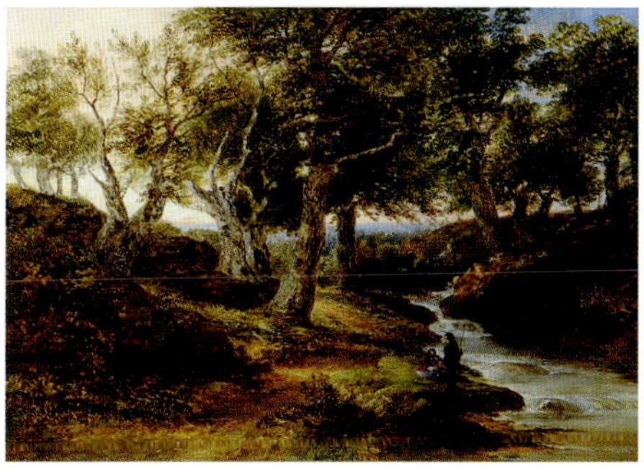

Poole, James 1803–1886
Over the Greta c.1850
oil on canvas 66 x 92
ROTMG : OP.1977.86

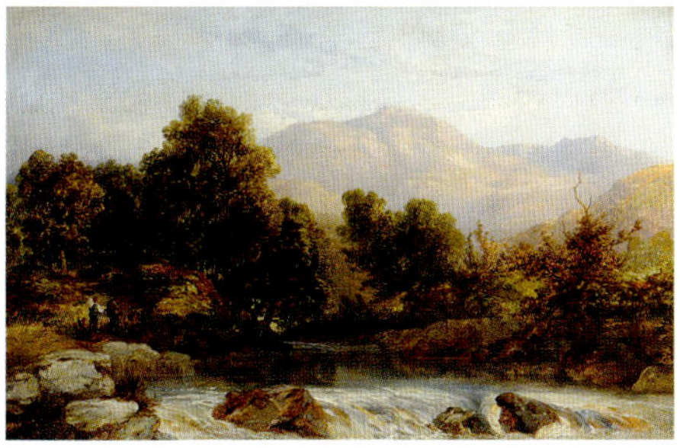

Poole, James 1803–1886
Glen Falloch, Scotland c.1860
oil on canvas 41 x 61
ROTMG : OP.1978.210

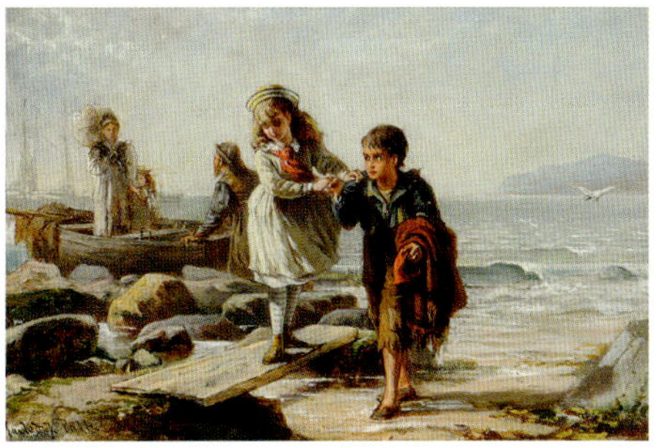

Pott, Laslett John 1837–1898
A Morning Sail c.1870
oil on canvas 53 x 76
ROTMG : OP.1977.19

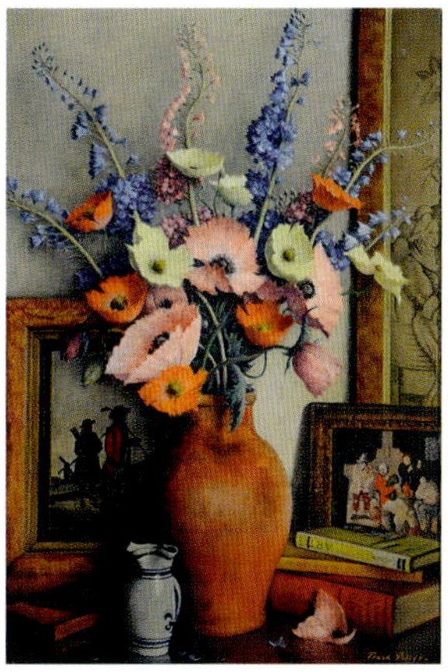

Potter, Frank b.1885
Flower Study c.1930
oil on canvas 90 x 60
ROTMG : OP.1977.153

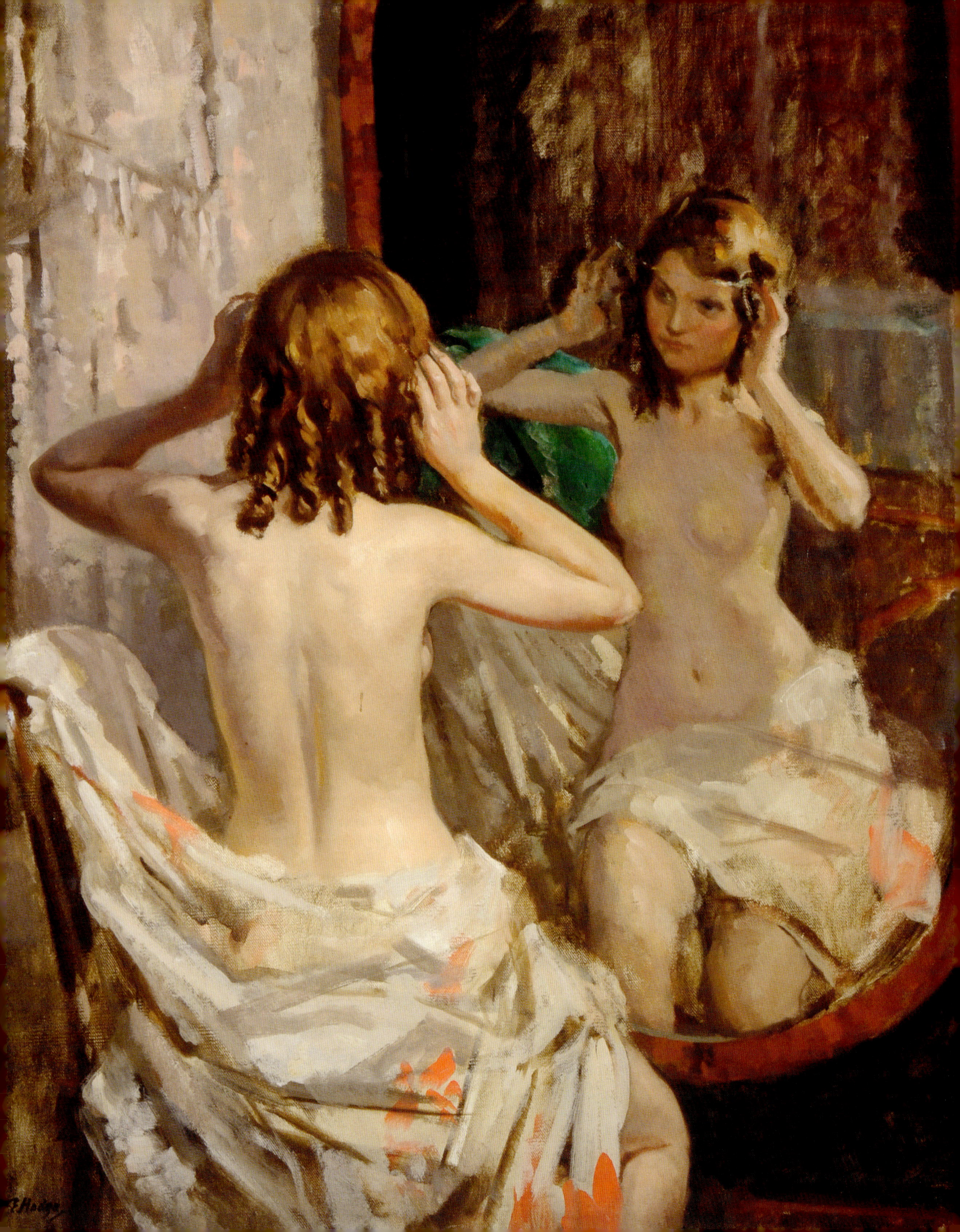

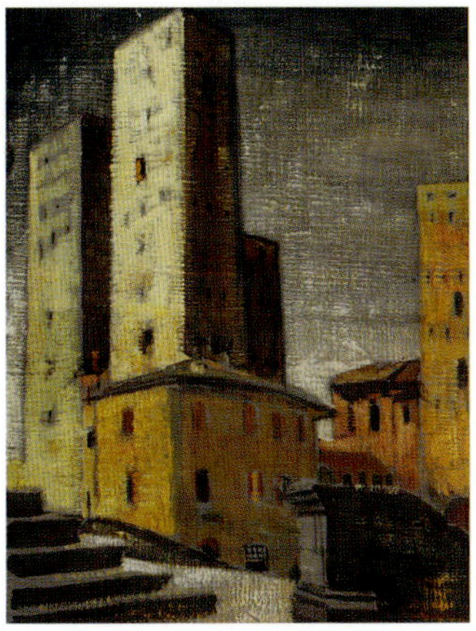

Pryde, James (attributed to) 1866–1941
Townscape
oil on canvas 44 x 34.5
ROTMG : OP.1977.159

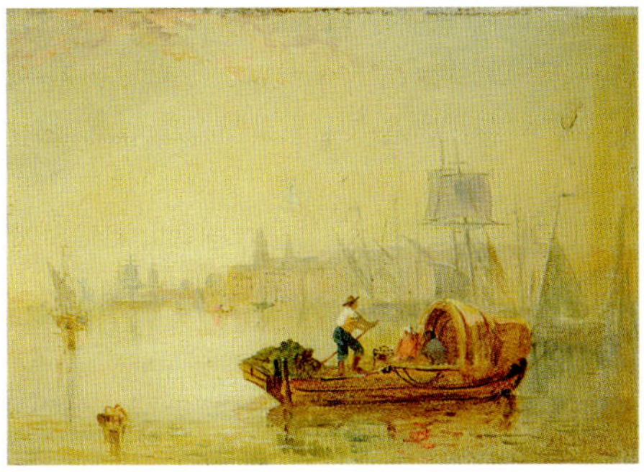

Pyne, James Baker 1800–1870
Venice c.1840
oil on panel 20.5 x 28
ROTMG : OP.1977.68

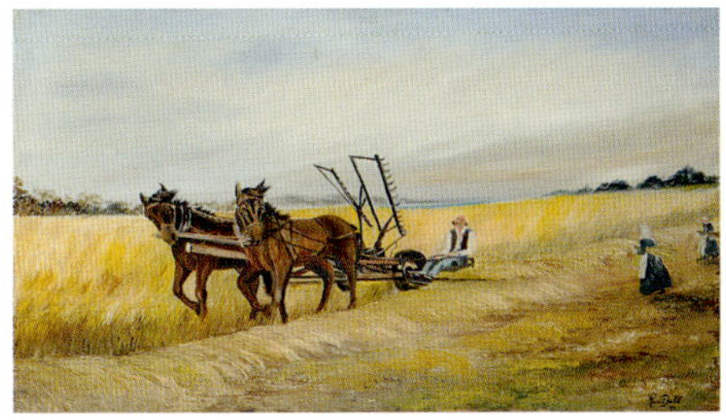

Randell, L.
The Hard Way 1971
oil on canvas 60 x 102
ROTMG : OP.1977.165

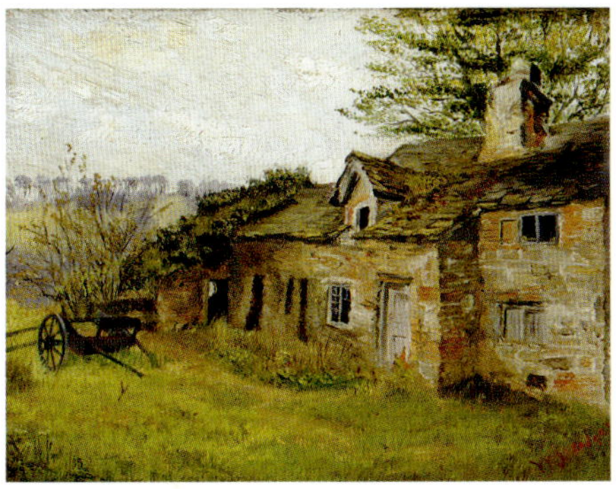

Redgate, W. H.
Old Cottage near Fulwood, Lancashire c.1880
oil on board 22 x 29
ROTMG : OP.1977.173

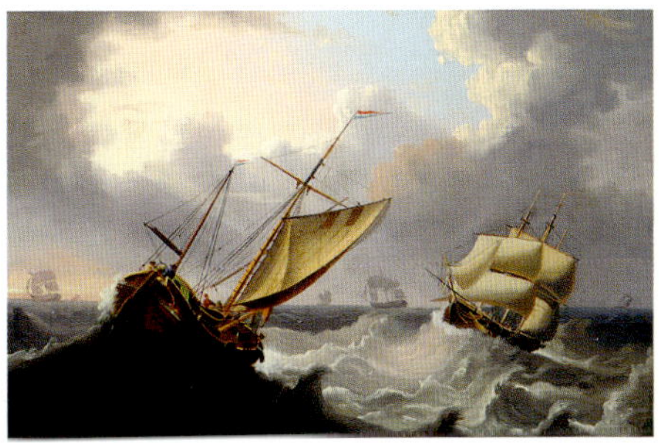

Redmore, Henry 1820–1887
Bay of Biscay c.1860
oil on canvas 62 x 91
ROTMG : OP.1977.21

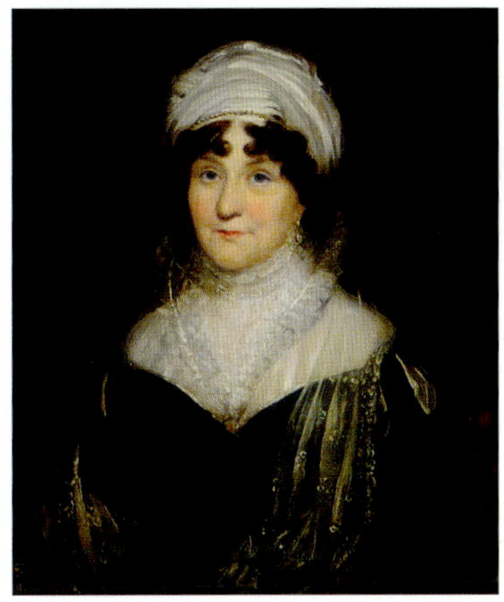

Reinagle, Ramsay Richard (attributed to)
1775–1862
Mary Walker, née Need, Mrs Thomas Walker (1763–1823) c.1820
oil on canvas 74 x 61
ROTMG : OP.1988.6

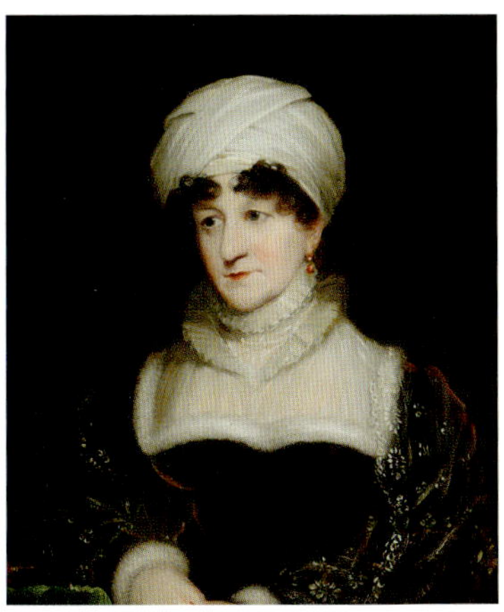

Reinagle, Ramsay Richard (attributed to)
1775–1862
Susannah Walker (1760–1831) c.1820
oil on canvas 81.5 x 74
ROTMG : OP.1988.9

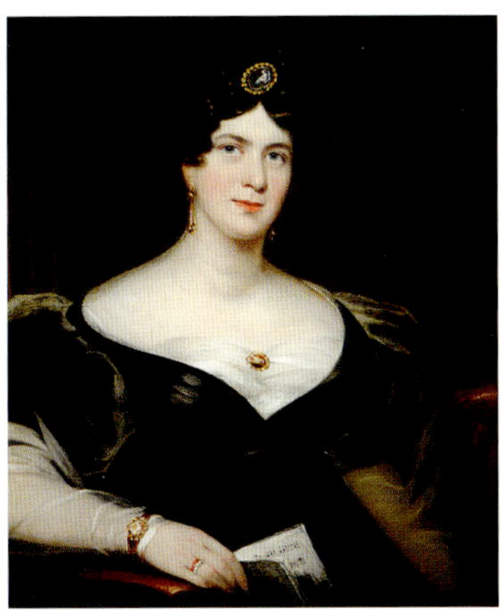

Reinagle, Ramsay Richard (attributed to)
1775–1862
Elizabeth Walker (1786–1850) c.1825
oil on canvas 75 x 62
ROTMG : OP.1988.2

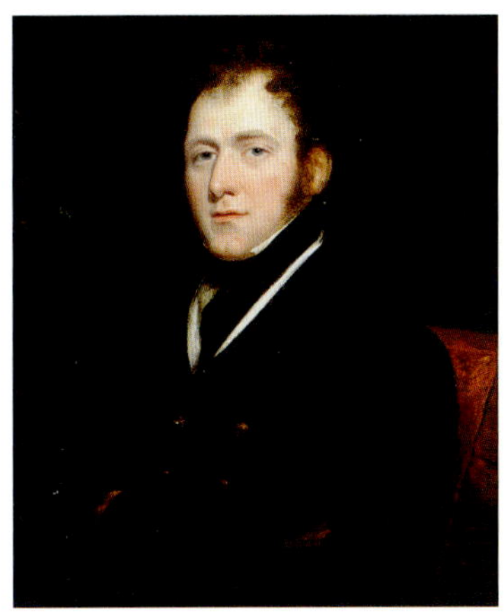

Reinagle, Ramsay Richard (attributed to)
1775–1862
Henry Walker (1785–1860) c.1825
oil on canvas 75 x 62
ROTMG : OP.1988.3

Facing page: Hodge, Francis Edwin, 1883–1949, *Vanity* (detail), Doncaster Museum Service, (p. 89)

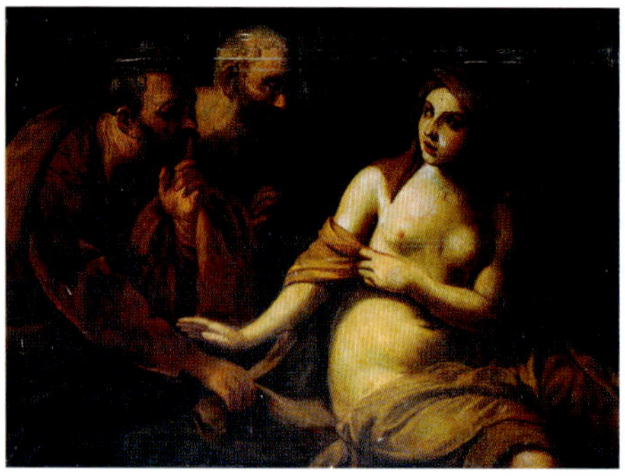

Ricci, Ezio 1885–1968
Susannah and the Elders (after Guido Reni) c.1915
oil on canvas 114 x 148
ROTMG : OP.1977.42

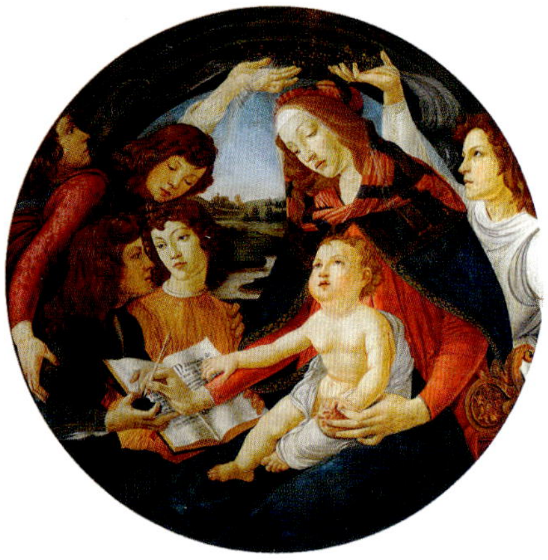

Ricci, Ezio 1885–1968
Virgin and Child (after Sandro Botticelli) c.1915
oil on canvas 109
ROTMG : OP.1989.1

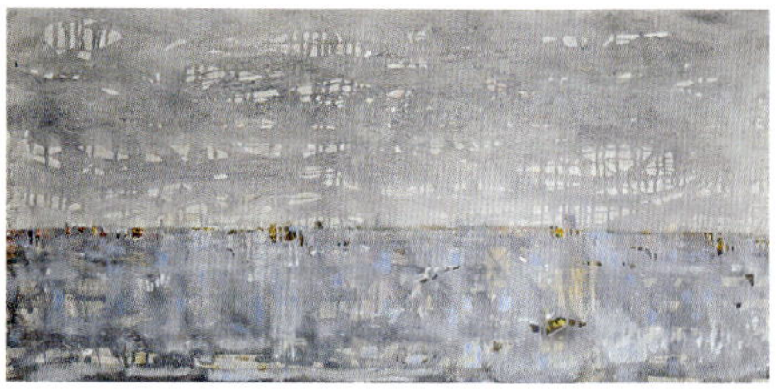

Robb, Brian 1913–1979
Lagoon 1967
oil on canvas 46 x 91.5
ROTMG : OP.1977.184

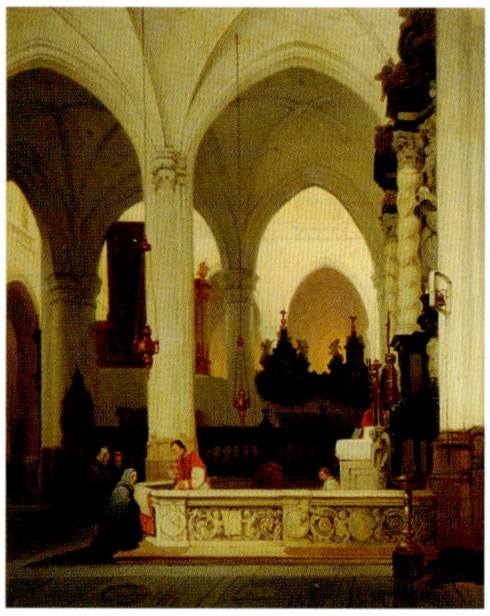

Roberts, David 1796–1864
Interior of a Church c.1836
oil on canvas 58 x 45
ROTMG : OP.1977.28

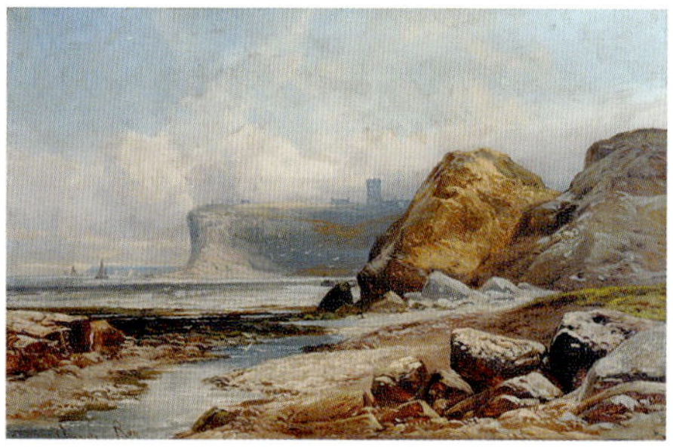

Roe, Clarence 1850–1909
Scarborough, North Yorkshire c.1890
oil on canvas 50.5 x 76
ROTMG : OP.1977.36

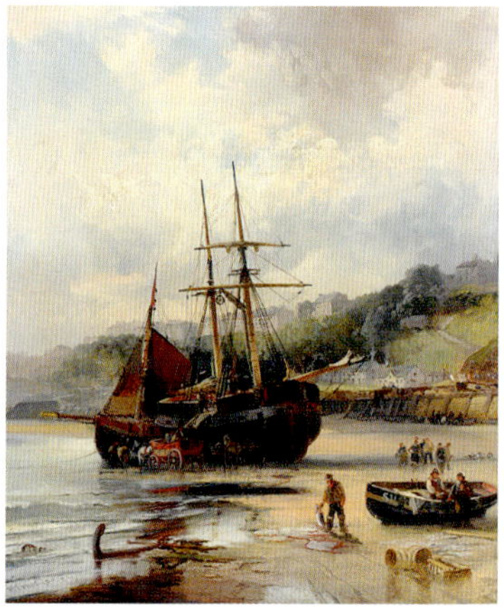

Roe, Robert Ernest 1852–1921
Beached Sailing Vessel 1886
oil on canvas 74 x 62
ROTMG : OP.1977.82

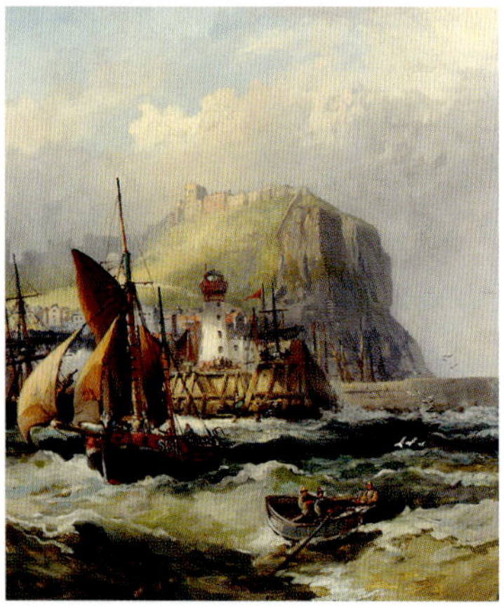

Roe, Robert Ernest 1852–1921
Sailing Vessel 1886
oil on canvas 80.5 x 68
ROTMG : OP.1977.81

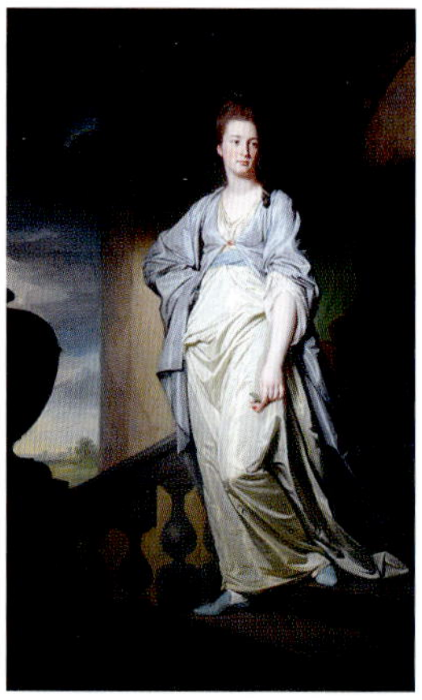

Romney, George 1734–1802
Ann Verelst (1751–1823) 1771–1772
oil on canvas 235 x 143
ROTMG : OP.1987.2

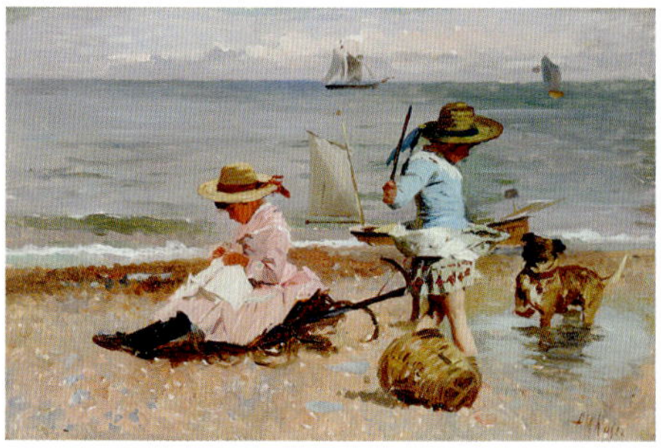

Rossi, Alexander Mark 1840–1916
Children at Play c.1880
oil on canvas 35 x 52
ROTMG : OP.1977.83

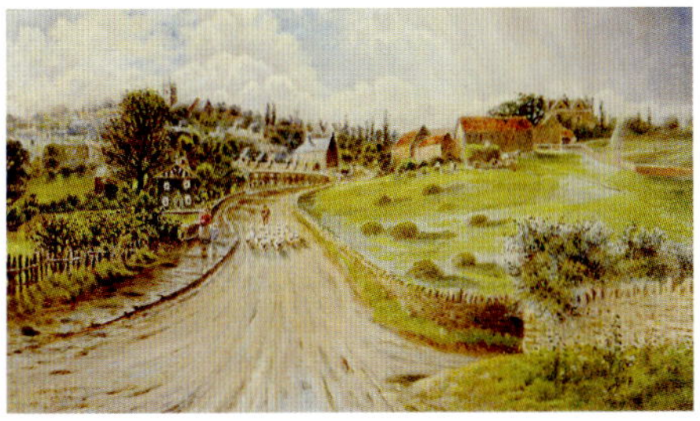

Smitheman, Herbert 1861–1938
Kimberworth, South Yorkshire (from a sketch made in 1902) 1902
oil on canvas 29 x 50
ROTMG : OP.1989.8

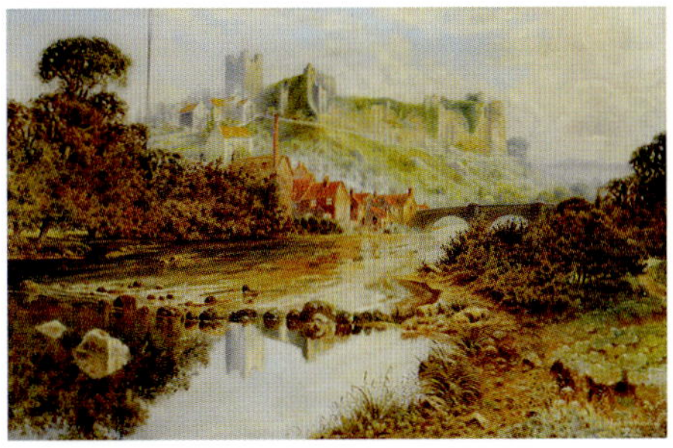

Smitheman, Herbert 1861–1938
Richmond Castle, North Yorkshire from the Swale 1906
oil on canvas 48 x 73
ROTMG : OP.1977.90

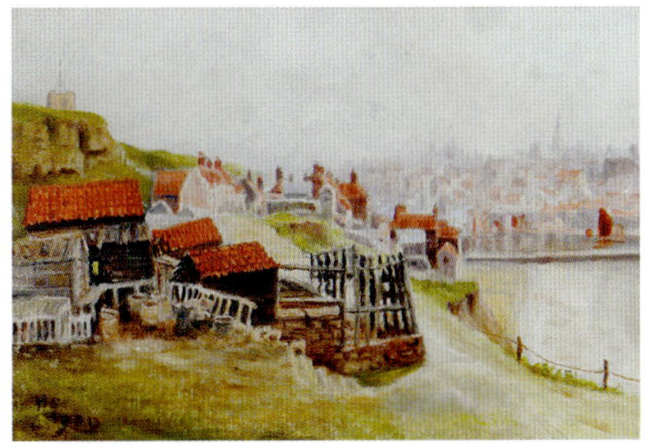

Smitheman, Herbert 1861–1938
Landscape 1909
oil on paper 17 x 24.5
ROTMG : OP.1977.179

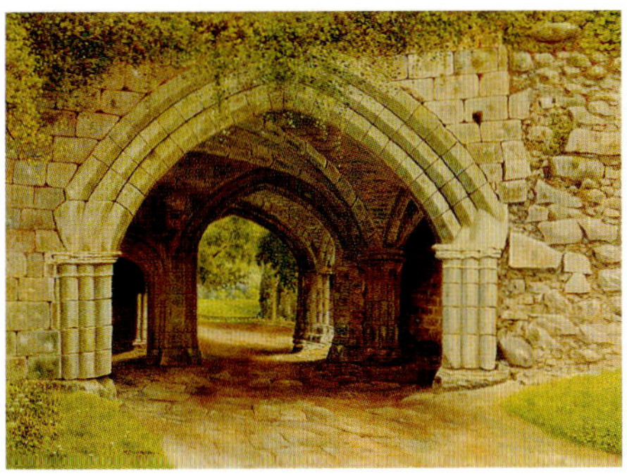

Smitheman, Herbert 1861–1938
Gateway in Roche Abbey, South Yorkshire 1910
oil on canvas 51 x 68.5
ROTMG : OP.1977.142

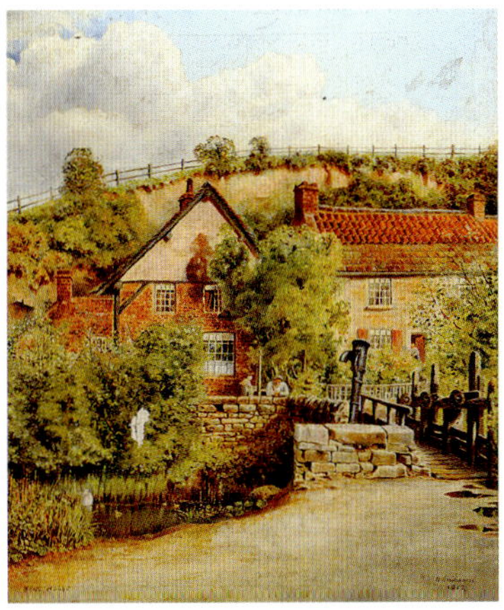

Smitheman, Herbert 1861–1938
Canklow Holes, South Yorkshire 1912
oil on canvas 75 x 62
ROTMG : OP.1977.56

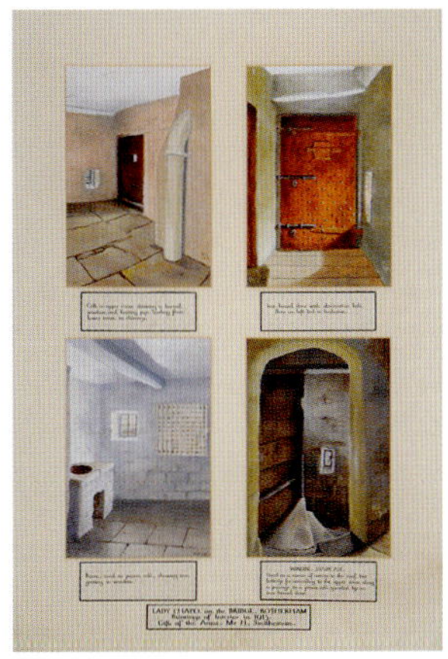

Smitheman, Herbert 1861–1938
Four Interior Views of the Chapel on the Bridge, Rotherham, South Yorkshire 1913
oil on canvas 71 x 48
ROTMG : OP.1984.1

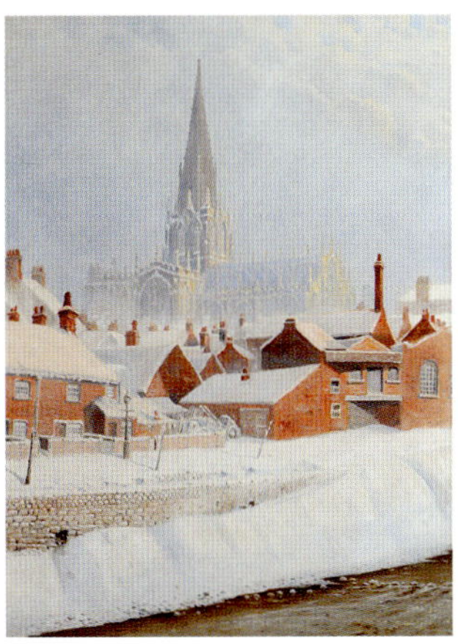

Smitheman, Herbert 1861–1938
Millgate, Rotherham, South Yorkshire 1914
oil on canvas 66.5 x 49
ROTMG : OP.1977.198

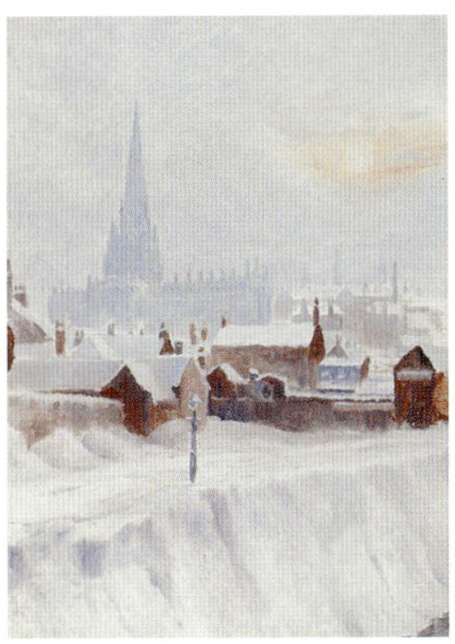

Smitheman, Herbert 1861–1938
Snow Scene, Rotherham Parish Church, South Yorkshire c.1915
oil on card 24 x 17
ROTMG : OP.1977.197

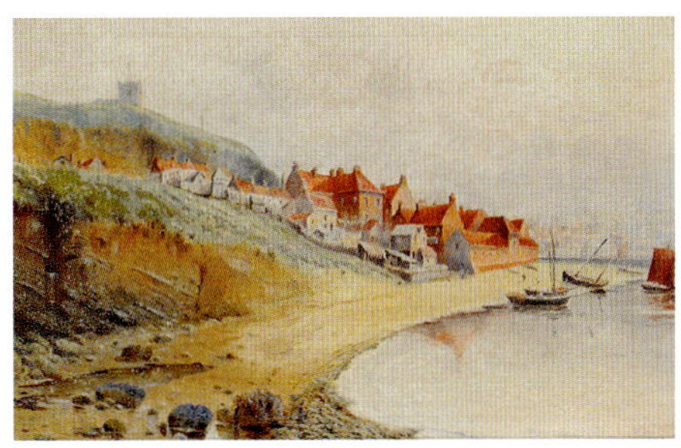

Smitheman, Herbert (attributed to) 1861–1938
Coastal Scene c.1910
oil on canvas 26.5 x 42
ROTMG : OP.1977.7

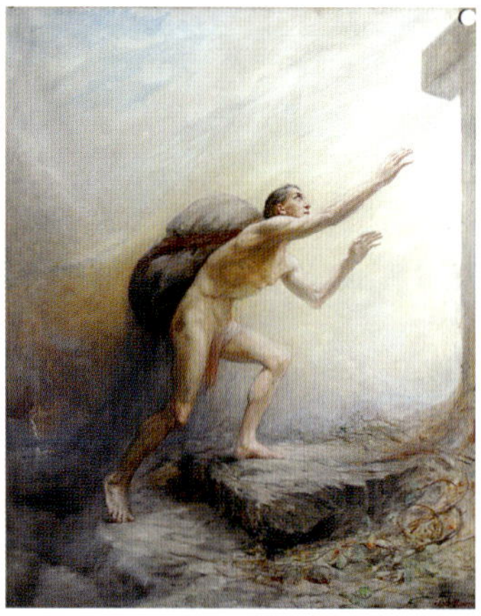

Someren, Edmund Lawrence van
1875–1963
The Pilgrim 1912
oil on canvas 125.5 x 100
ROTMG : OP.1977.3

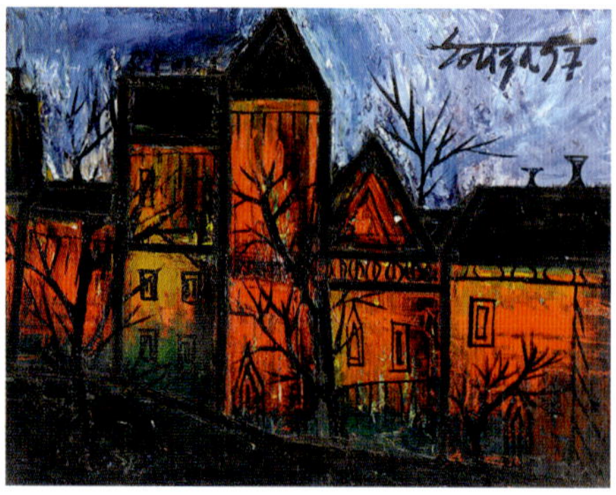

Souza, Francis Newton 1924–2002
Red Houses 1957
oil on board 59 x 74.5
ROTMG : OP.1977.149

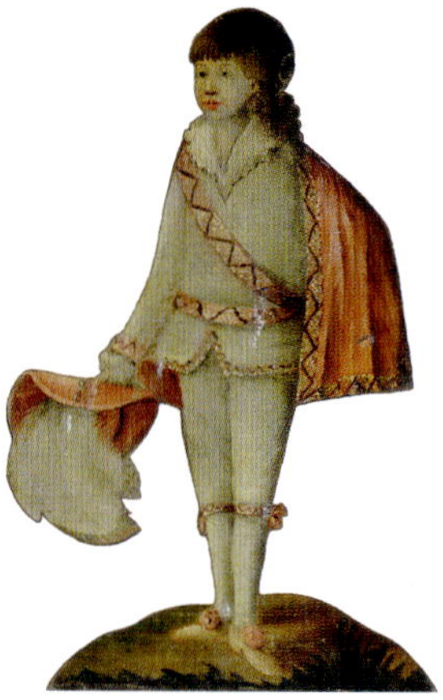

Spanish School 16th C
Spanish Child
oil on canvas on board 38 x 23
ROTMG : OP.1989.10

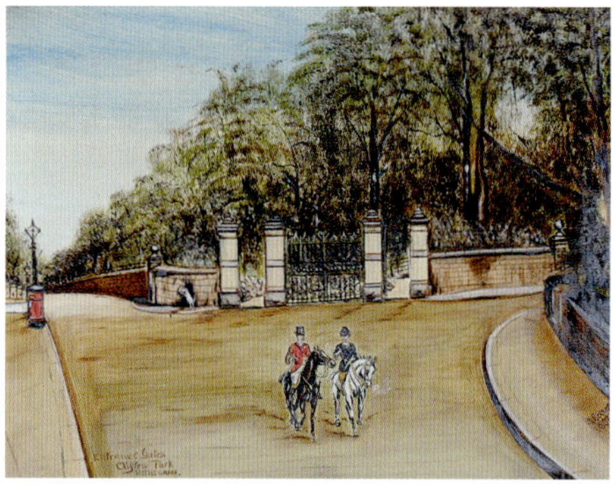

Spence, S.
Entrance Gates, Clifton Park, Rotherham, South Yorkshire 1908
oil on canvas 35.5 x 46
ROTMG : OP.1978.212

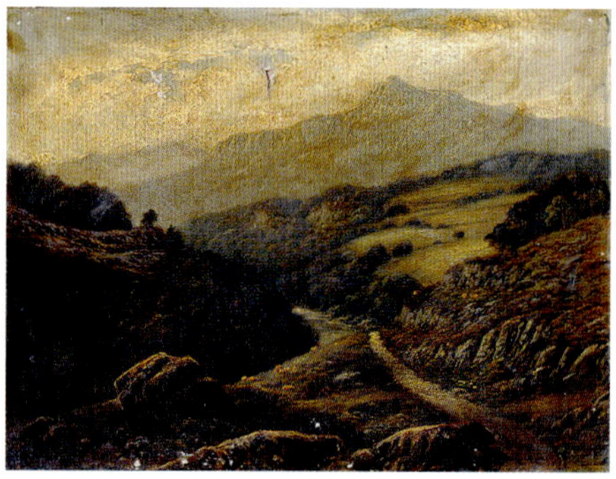

Spinks, Thomas 1847–1927
View in North Wales c.1900
oil on canvas 35 x 45.9
ROTMG : OP.1977.41

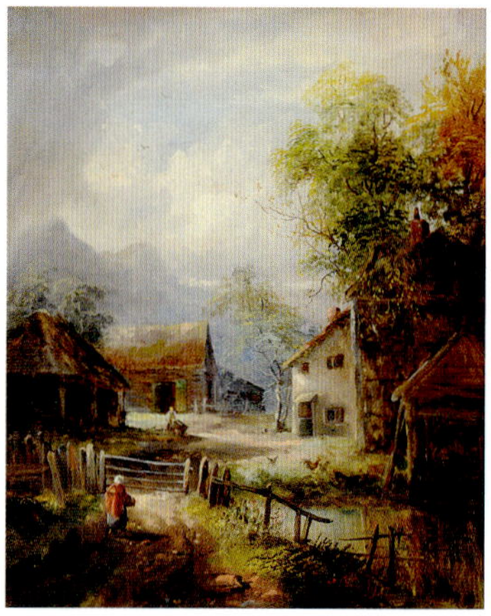

Stanby, A.
Farmyard Scene c.1880
oil on panel 39.5 x 32
ROTMG : OP.1977.132

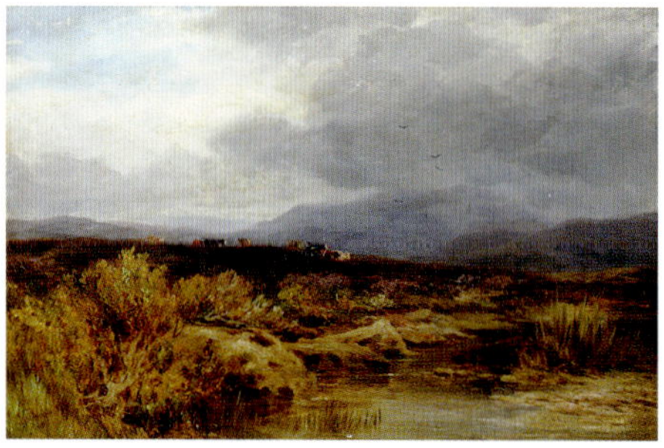

Steeple, John 1823–1887
The Moorland Pool 1876
oil on canvas 33 x 47
ROTMG : OP.1984.19

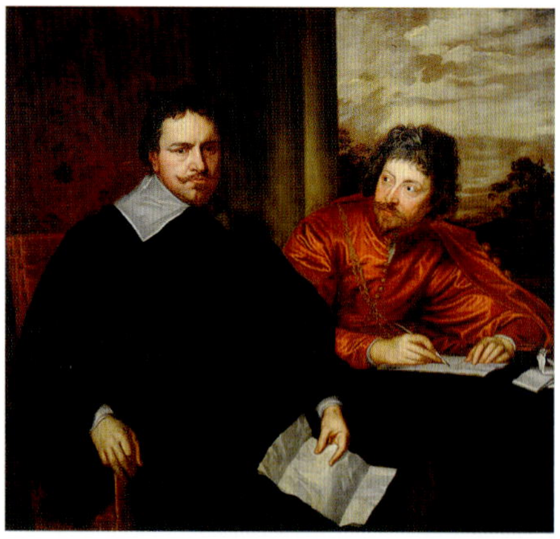

Stone, Henry 1616–1653
Sir Thomas Wentworth (1593–1641), Earl of Strafford and Sir Philip Mainwaring (1589–1661) (after Anthony van Dyck) c.1653
oil on canvas 152 x 161
ROTMG : OP.1984.4

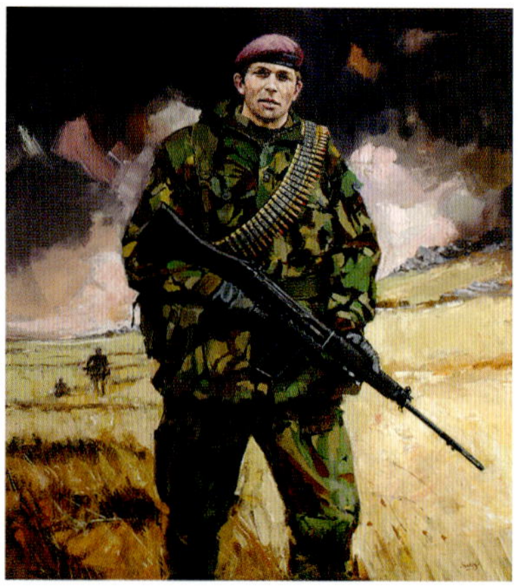

Stubley, Trevor 1932–2010
Sergeant Ian John McKay (1953–1982), VC c.1983
oil on canvas 120.5 x 105.2
ROTMG : THP4

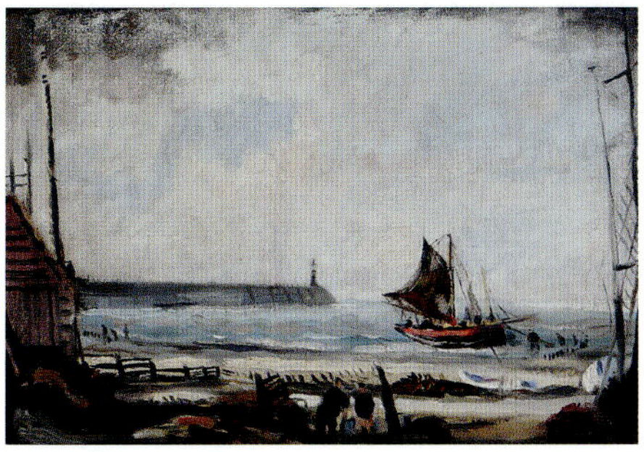

Suddaby, Rowland 1912–1972
Coast Scene near the Stour Estuary, Suffolk
1946
oil on canvas 34.5 x 55
ROTMG : OP.1977.64

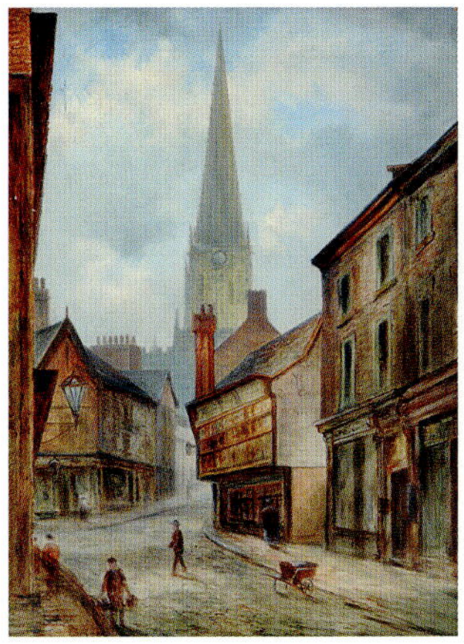

Thomas, A.
Bridgegate, Rotherham, South Yorkshire 1862
oil on board 36.5 x 26.5
ROTMG : OP.1978.230

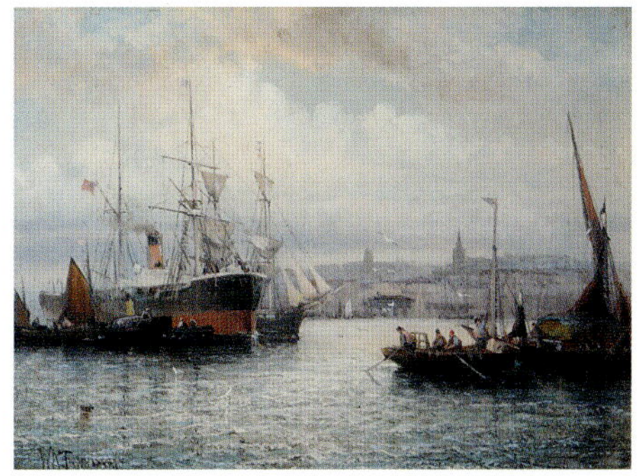

Thompson, Wilfred active 1884–c.1921
Gravesend from Tilbury, Essex, Flood Tide
c.1884
oil on canvas 14.5 x 19
ROTMG : OP.1977.13

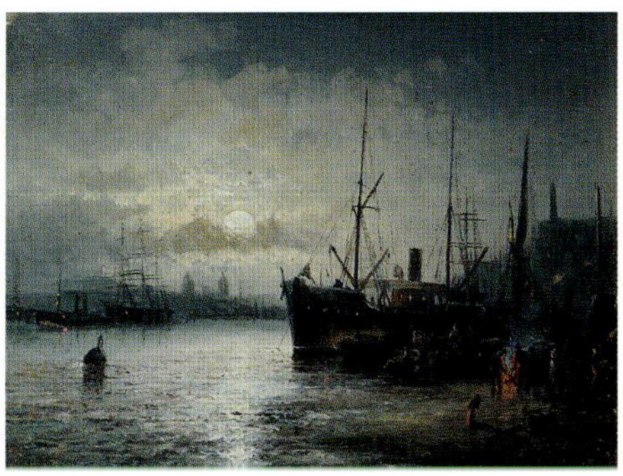

Thompson, Wilfred active 1884–c.1921
Moonlight Greenwich from Blackwall Reach, London c.1884
oil on panel 14.5 x 19
ROTMG : OP.1977.73

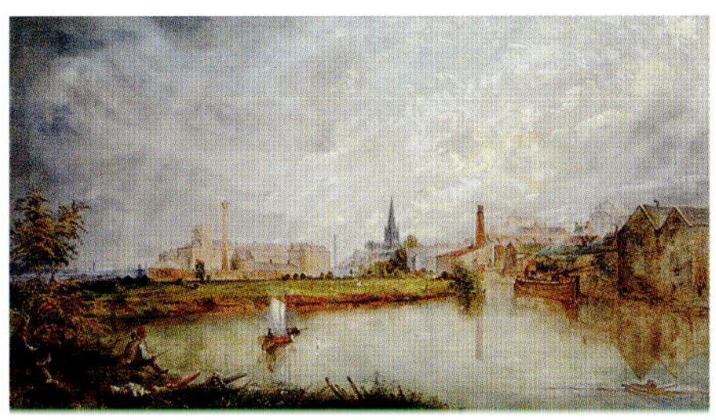

Thomson, Christopher 1799–1871
Rotherham, South Yorkshire c.1860
oil on canvas 59 x 184
ROTMG : OP.1977.170

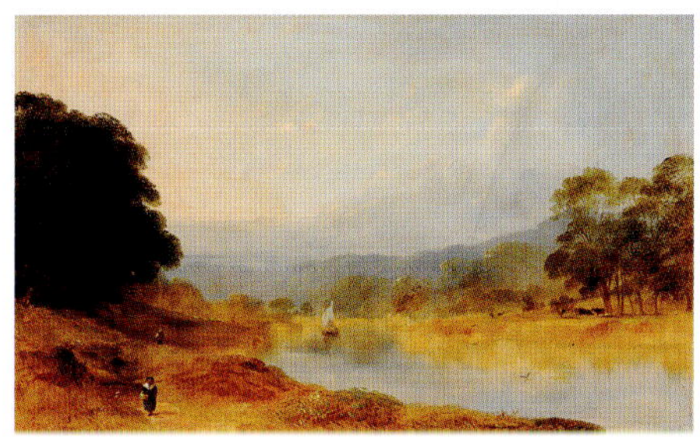

Tilbury, Henry 1815/1820–1866
River Don near Conisbrough, South Yorkshire
c.1835
oil on card 46 x 63
ROTMG : OP.1977.204

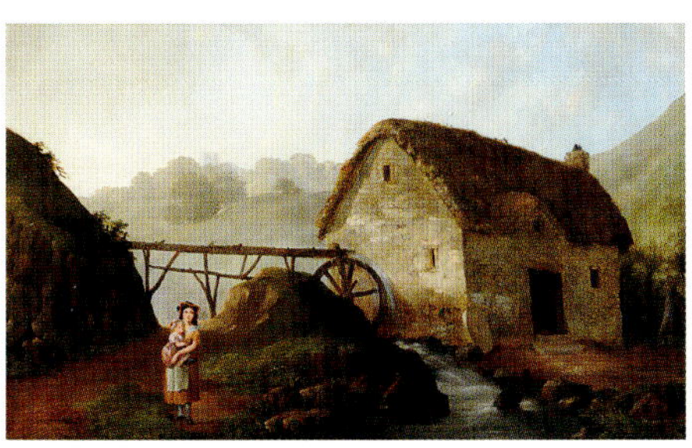

Tilbury, Henry 1815/1820–1866
Conisbrough Old Mill, South Yorkshire c.1838
oil on canvas 76 x 122
ROTMG : OP.1977.37

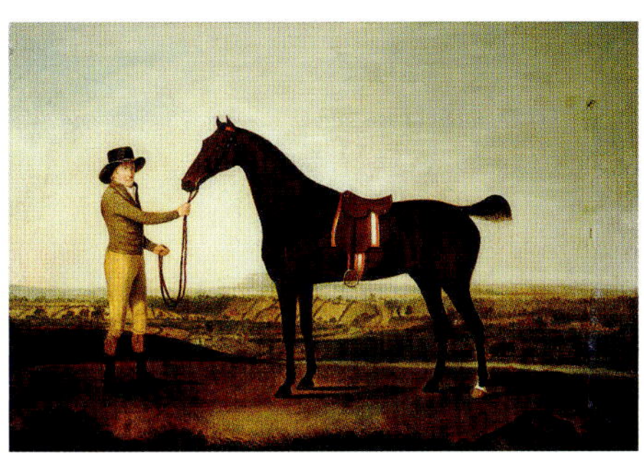

Towne, Charles 1763–1840
'Toxopholite' c.1790
oil on canvas 62 x 90
ROTMG : OP.1977.93

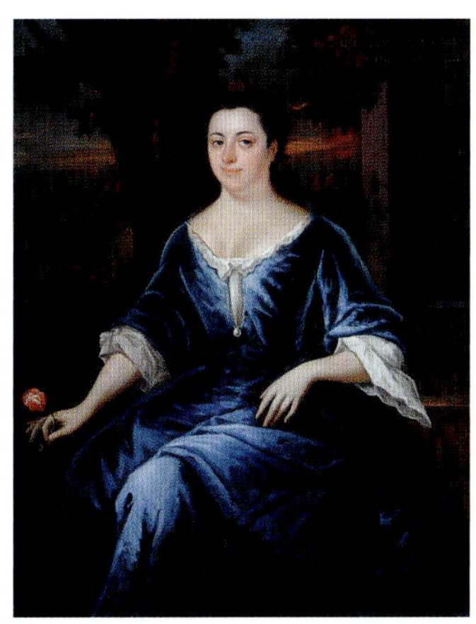

unknown artist
Elizabeth Parkin (1703–1766) c.1750
oil on canvas 125 x 96
ROTMG : 2006.8

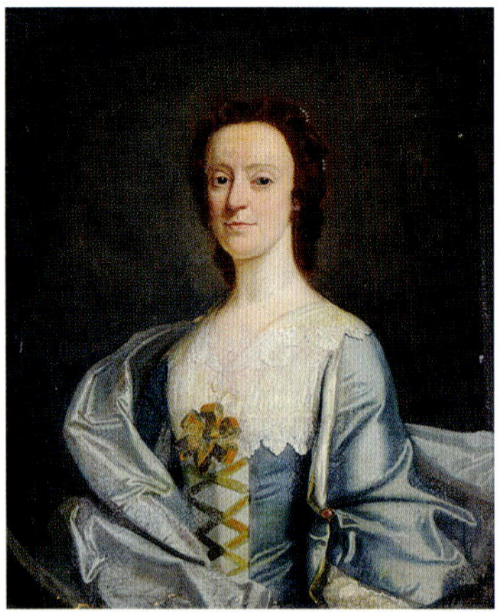

unknown artist
Portrait of a Lady c.1790
oil on canvas 74 x 62
ROTMG : OP.1977.137

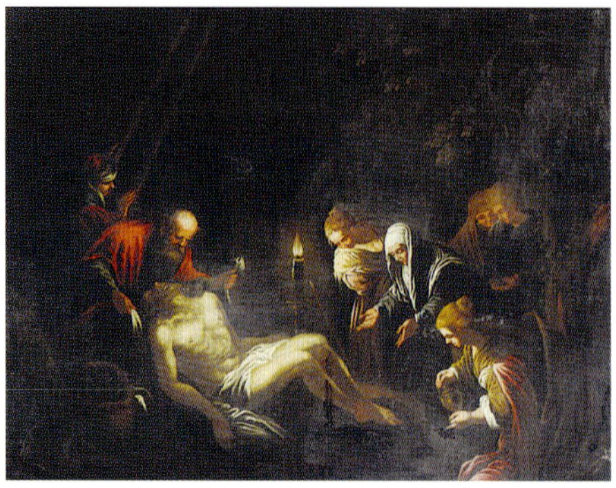

unknown artist
The Descent from the Cross c.1790
oil on canvas 109 x 141
ROTMG : OP.1984.5

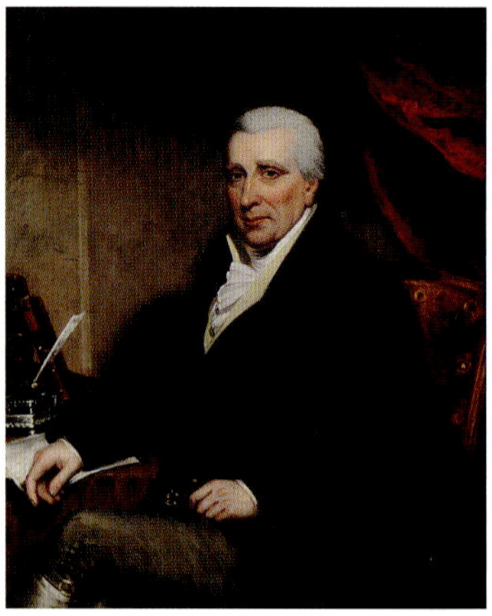

unknown artist
Joshua Walker (1750–1815) c.1795
oil on canvas 109 x 87.5
ROTMG : LOP.6 (P)

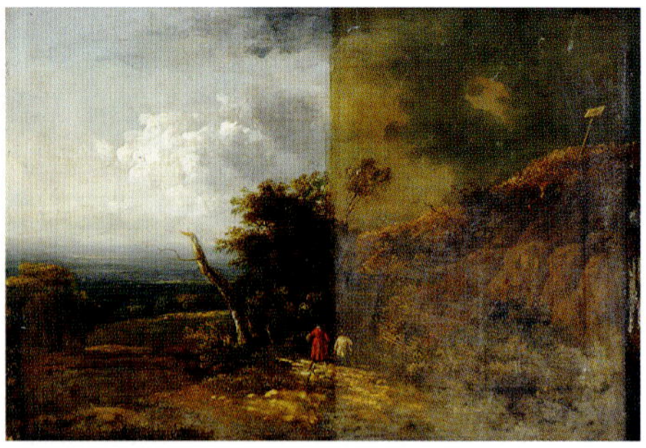

unknown artist
Landscape with Figures 1800–1850
oil on canvas 35.5 x 51.2
ROTMG : OP.1977.48

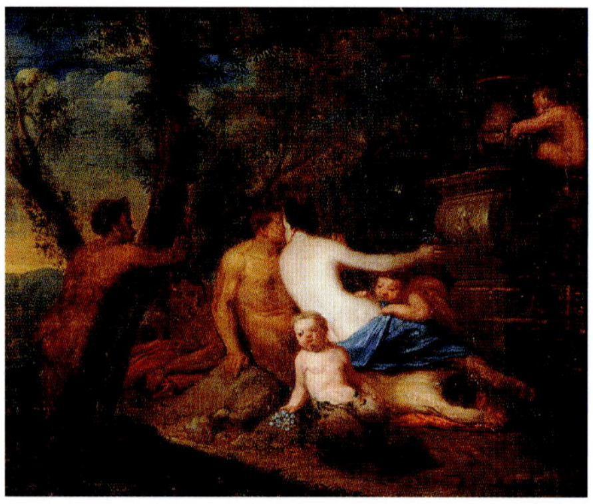

unknown artist
Bacchanalian Feast c.1800
oil on canvas 31 x 38
ROTMG : OP.1977.47

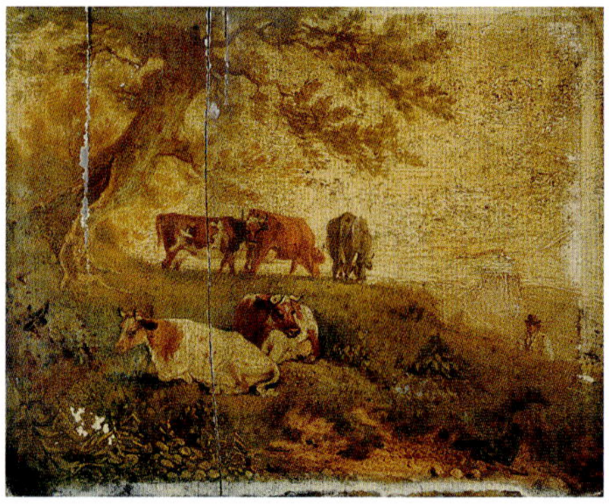

unknown artist
Cows c.1800
oil on panel 21.5 x 27
ROTMG : OP.1977.118

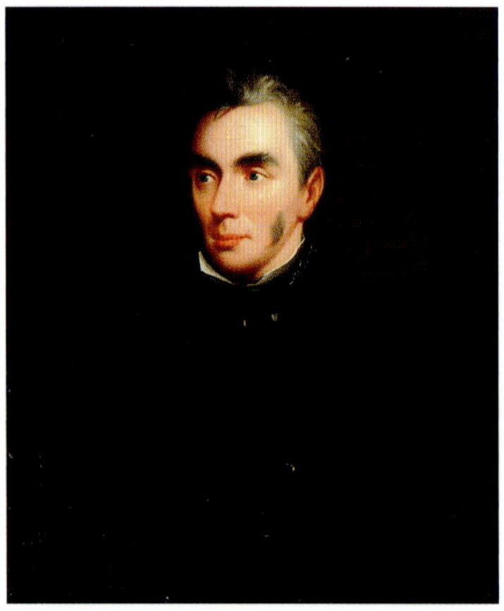

unknown artist
Ebenezer Elliott (1781–1849), as a Young Man c.1800
oil on canvas 75.5 x 63
ROTMG : OP.1977.125

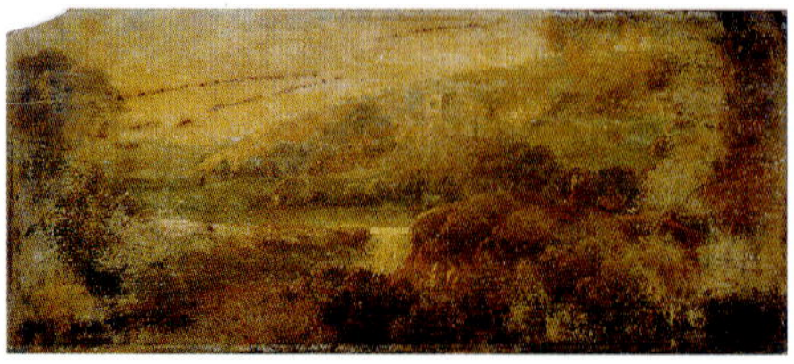

unknown artist
Landscape c.1800
oil on panel 18 x 40.6
ROTMG : OP.1977.117

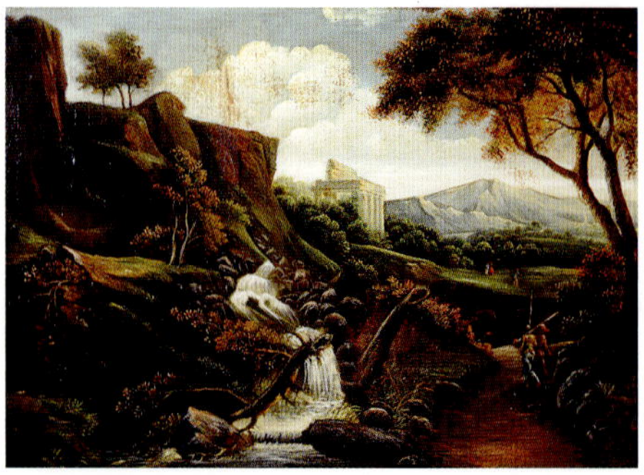

unknown artist
Landscape with a Waterfall and a Temple c.1800
oil on canvas 74 x 100.5
ROTMG : OP.1977.180

Facing page: Sellaer, Vincent, c.1500–c.1589, *The Holy Family with Saints Elizabeth, Catherine and John the Baptist* (detail), 1550–1575, The Cooper Gallery, (p. 27)

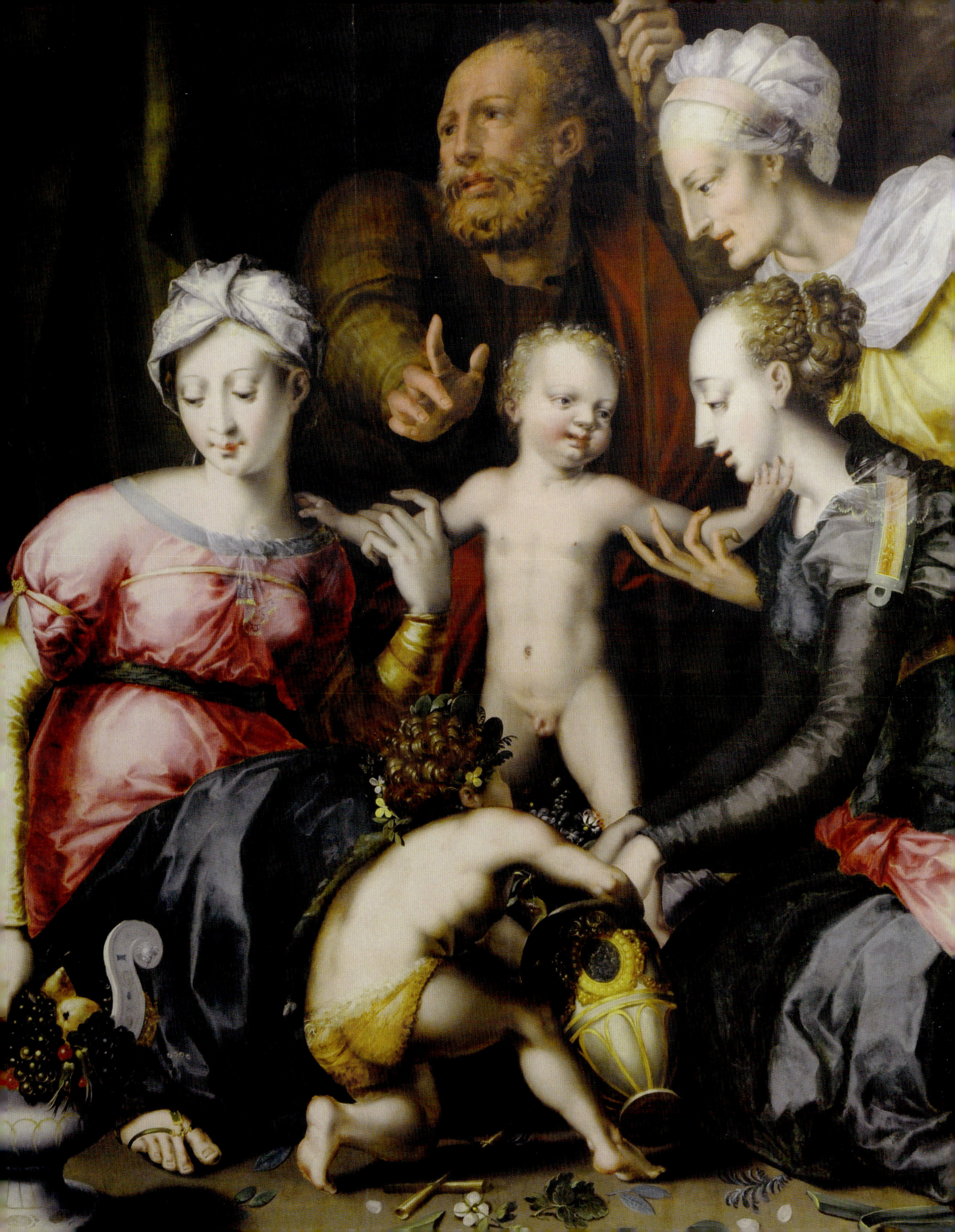

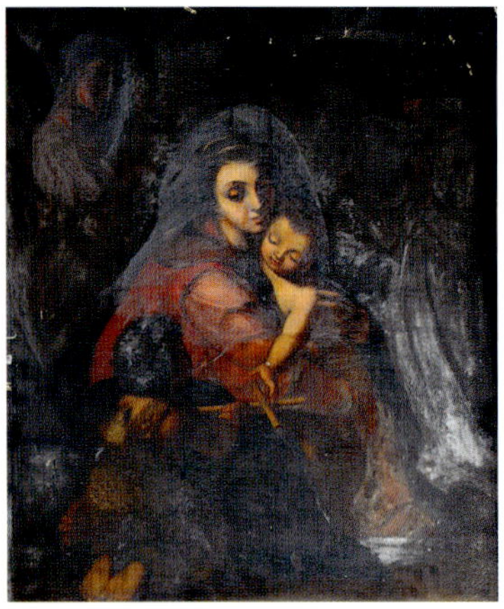

unknown artist
Madonna and Child c.1800
oil on canvas 100 x 81
ROTMG : OP.1977.34

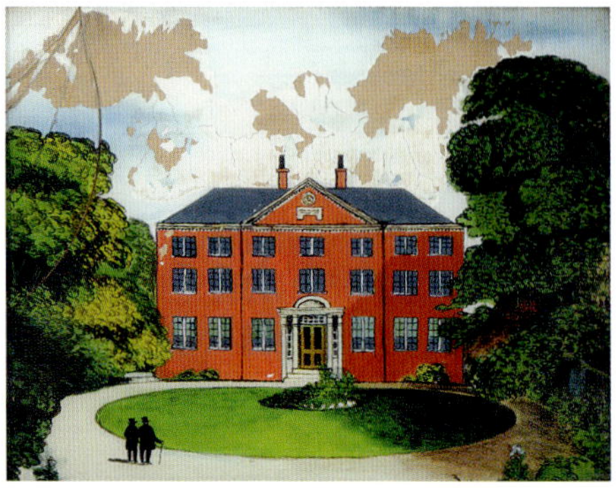

unknown artist
Masbrough Independent Academy, South Yorkshire c.1800
oil & enamel on glass 19 x 24
ROTMG : OP.1978.225

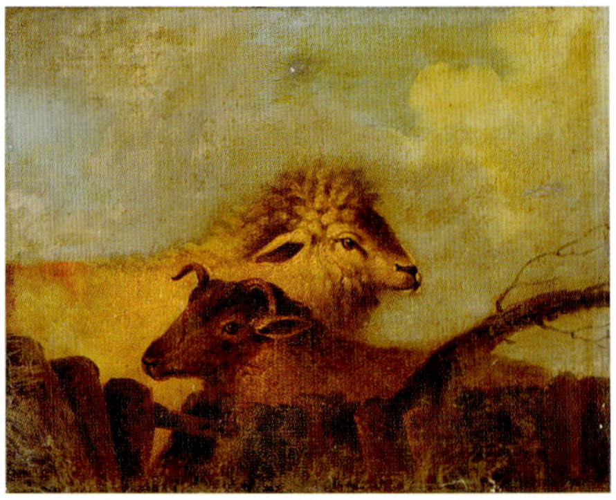

unknown artist
Studies of Two Sheep's Heads c.1800
oil on canvas 25.3 x 31.5
ROTMG : OP.1977.122

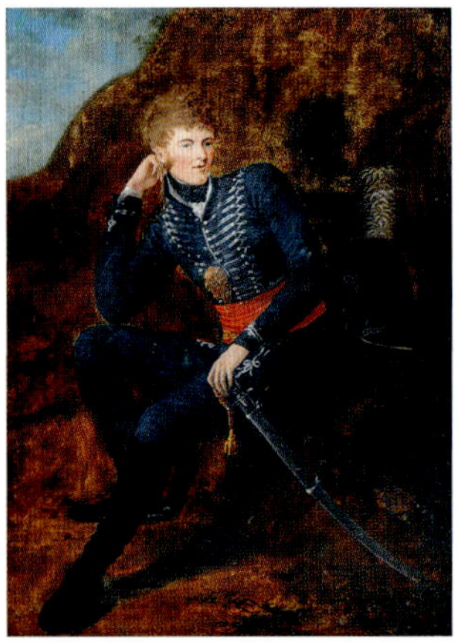

unknown artist
Henry Walker (1785–1860), in the Uniform of the Southern Regiment of West Riding Yeomanry Cavalry c.1808
oil on canvas 72.7 x 51.9
ROTMG : OP.1978.221

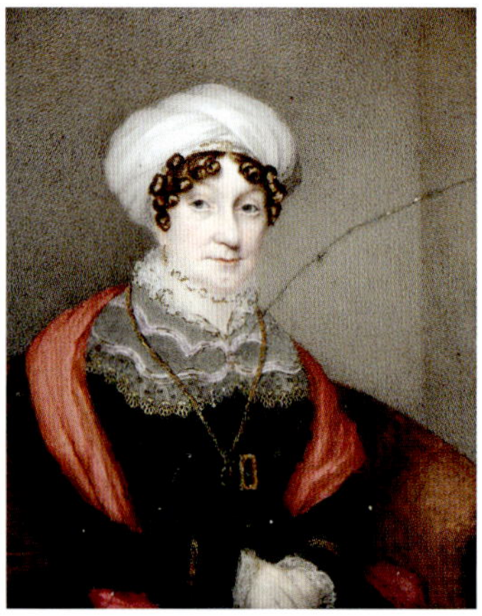

unknown artist
Mrs Joshua Walker (1760–1831) (Susannah Walker of Clifton House) c.1825
oil on porcelain 20 x 15
ROTMG : GC.1994.1

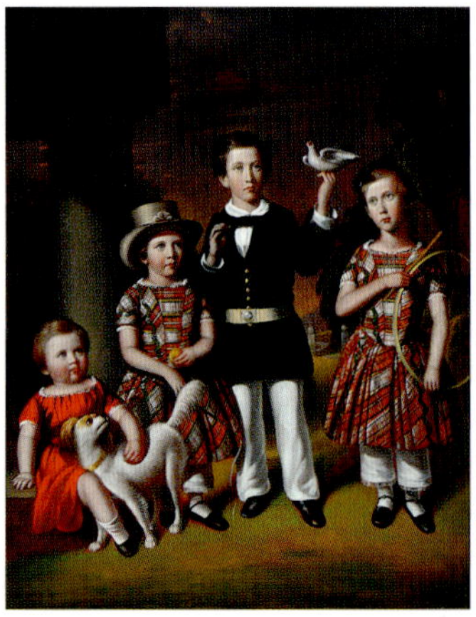

unknown artist
The Oxley Children c.1825
oil on canvas 117 x 92
ROTMG : OP.1977.4

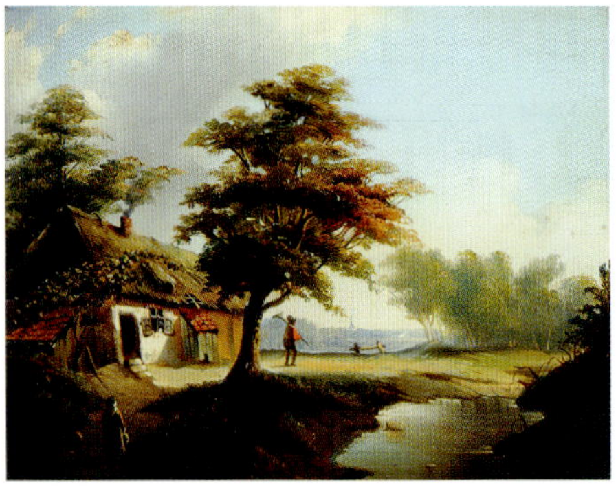

unknown artist
Landscape with a Cottage c.1830
oil on panel 28 x 36
ROTMG : OP.1977.133

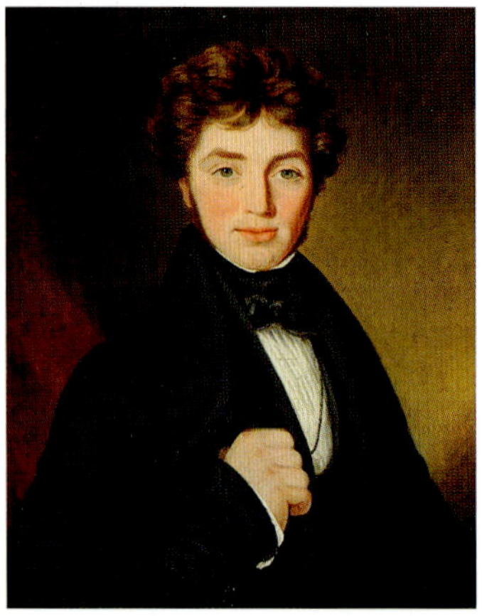

unknown artist
Portrait of a Man c.1830
oil on canvas 45 x 35
ROTMG : OP.1977.106

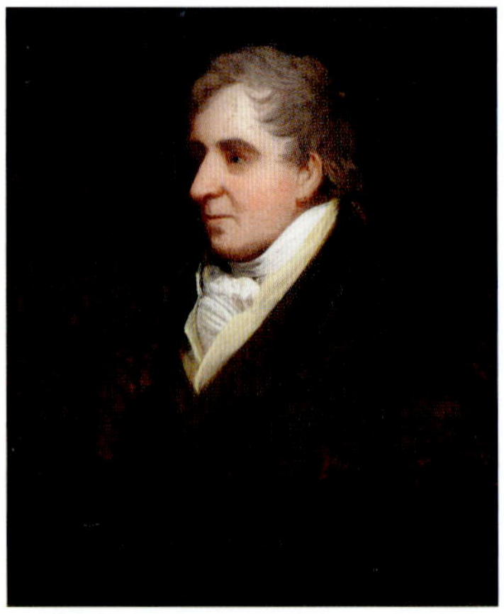

unknown artist
Joshua Walker Junior (1786–1862) c.1840
oil on canvas 75 x 60.5
ROTMG : OP.1988.5

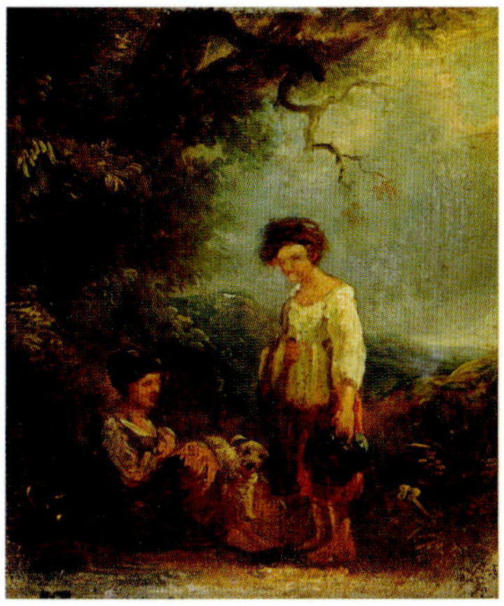

unknown artist
Landscape with Figures c.1840
oil on board 16 x 14
ROTMG : OP.1977.25

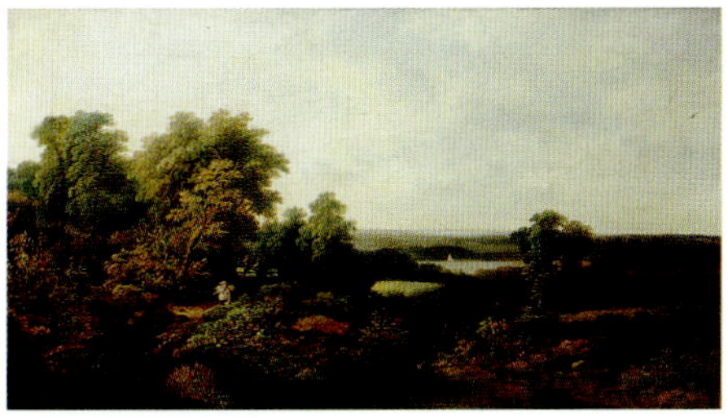

unknown artist
Landscape c.1850
oil on canvas 59.5 x 105.5
ROTMG : OP.1977.155

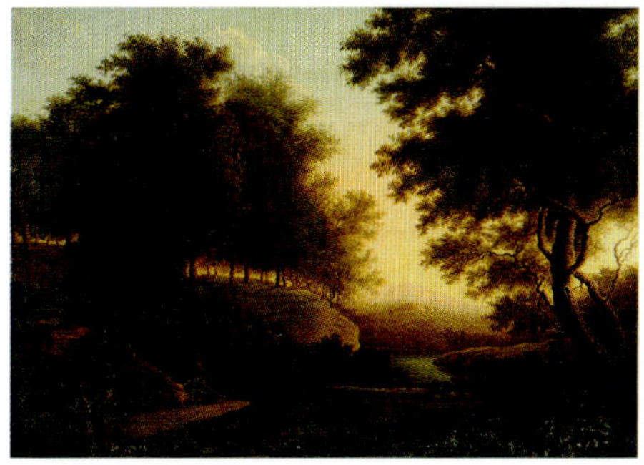

unknown artist
Landscape with Trees c.1850
oil on canvas 44 x 59
ROTMG : OP.1977.182

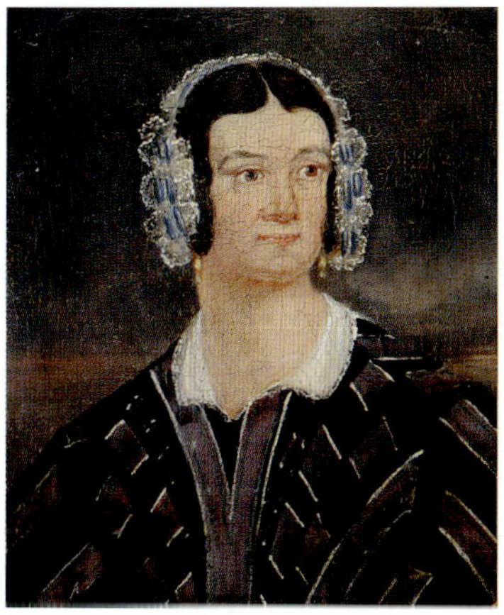

unknown artist
Portrait of a Lady c.1850
oil on canvas 24 x 20
ROTMG : OP.1978.220

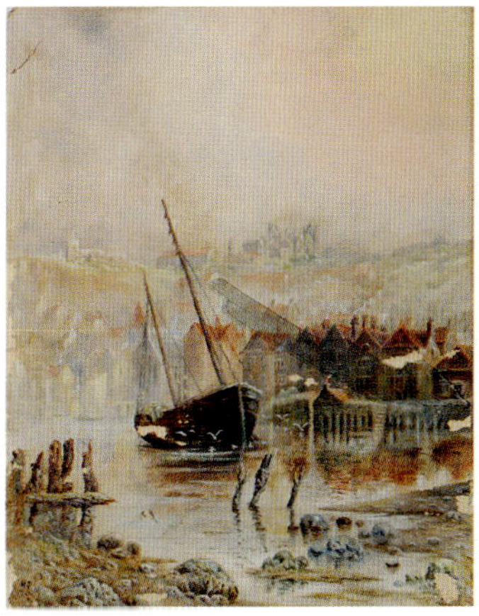

unknown artist
Whitby Harbour, North Yorkshire c.1850
oil on oil card 45.8 x 34.9
ROTMG : OP.1977.203

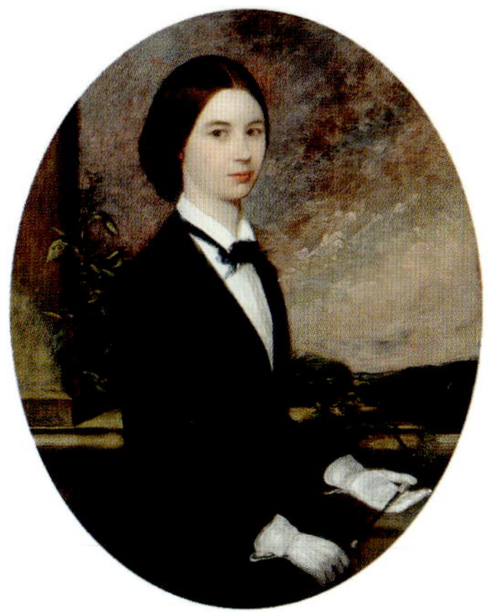

unknown artist
Elizabeth Edith Walker c.1856
oil on canvas 88 x 70
ROTMG : OP.1988.1

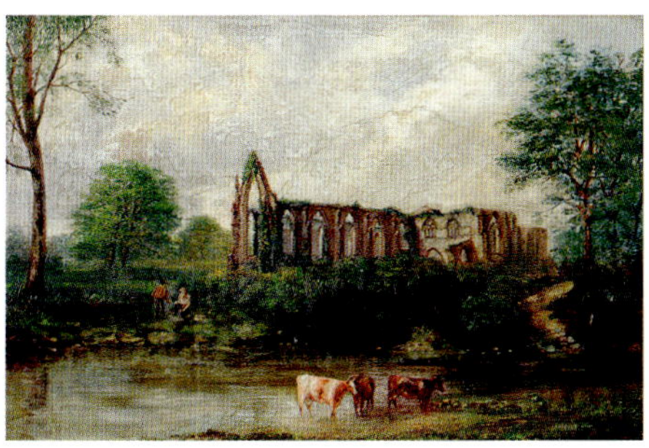

unknown artist
Bolton Abbey, North Yorkshire c.1860
oil on canvas 34.5 x 52
ROTMG : OP.1977.183

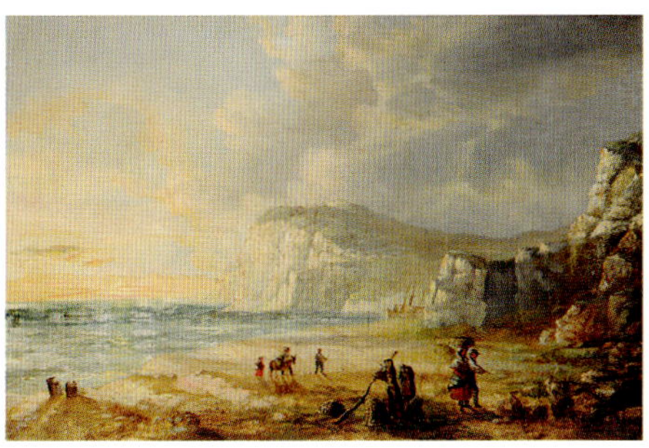

unknown artist
Coastal Scene c.1860
oil on canvas 52 x 77
ROTMG : OP.1977.147

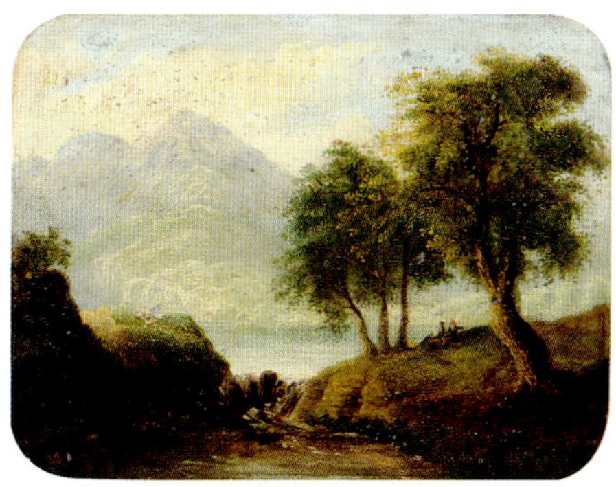

unknown artist
Landscape c.1860
oil on panel 39 x 48.5
ROTMG : OP.1977.114

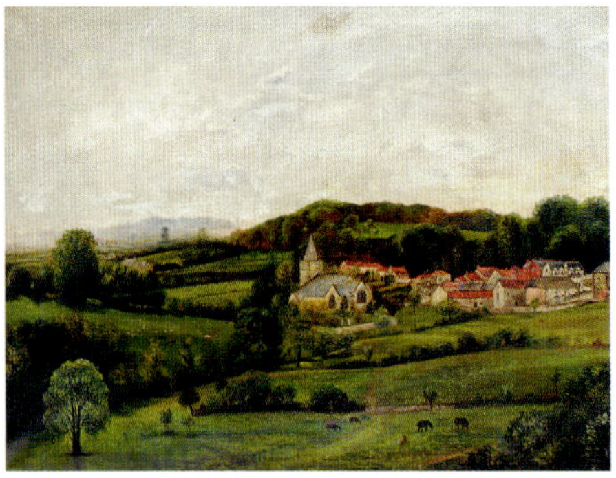

unknown artist
Landscape with a Village Church c.1860
oil on canvas 71 x 91
ROTMG : OP.1977.136

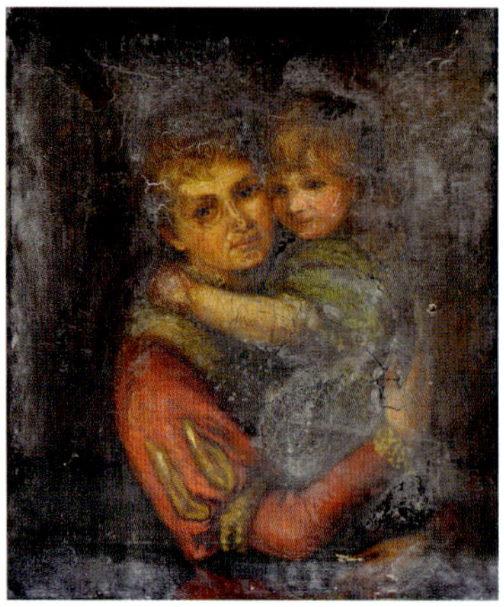

unknown artist
Mother and Child c.1860
oil on canvas 76 x 63.5
ROTMG : OP.1977.46

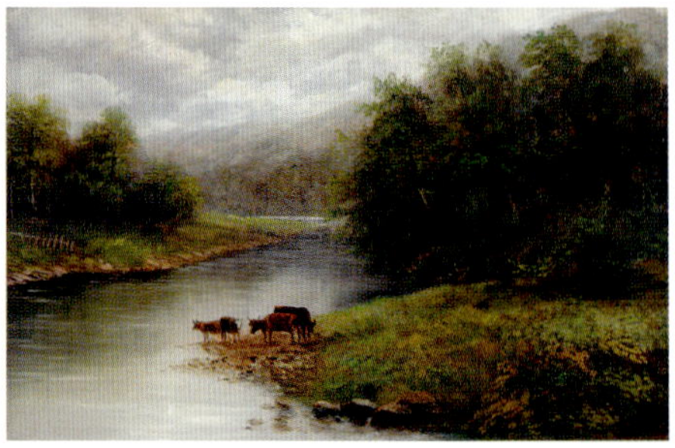

unknown artist
Mountain Scene c.1860
oil on canvas 76 x 101
ROTMG : OP.1977.88

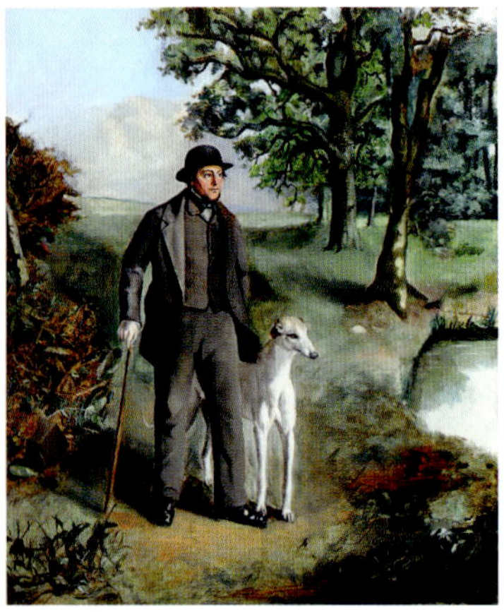

unknown artist
Portrait of a Gentleman and a Greyhound c.1860
oil on canvas 87 x 71.5
ROTMG : OP.1977.146

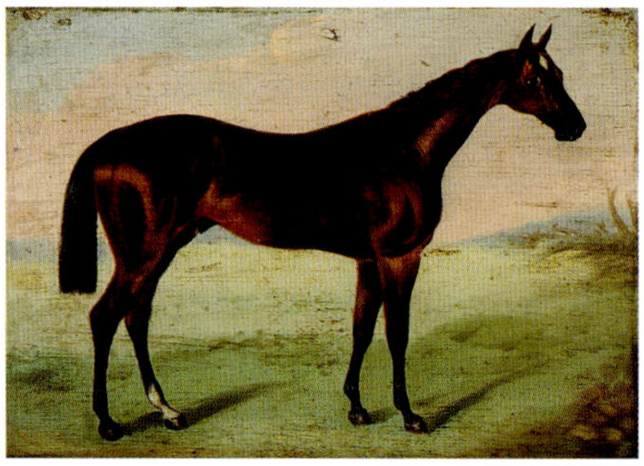

unknown artist
'Gladiator' c.1865
oil on board 37 x 41
ROTMG : OP.1977.45

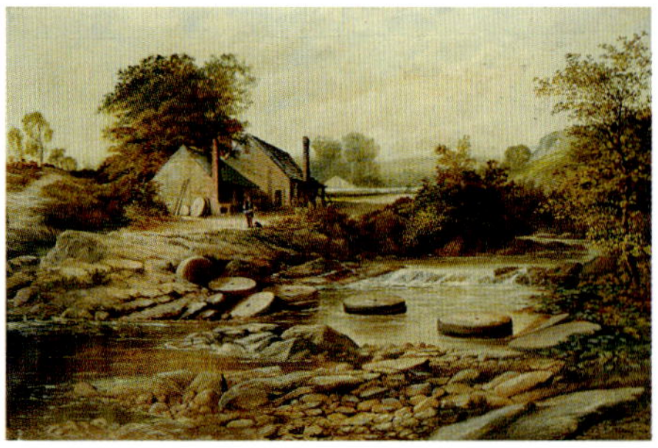

unknown artist
Endcliffe, South Yorkshire c.1870
oil on canvas 43.5 x 64
ROTMG : OP.1977.95

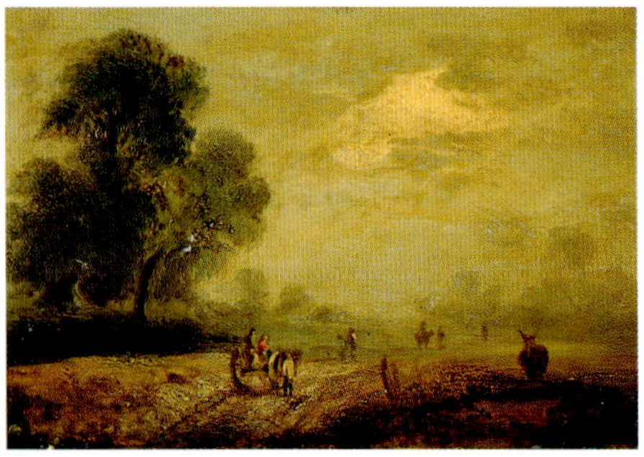

unknown artist
Farming Scene c.1870
oil on panel 17.3 x 25.5
ROTMG : OP.1977.123

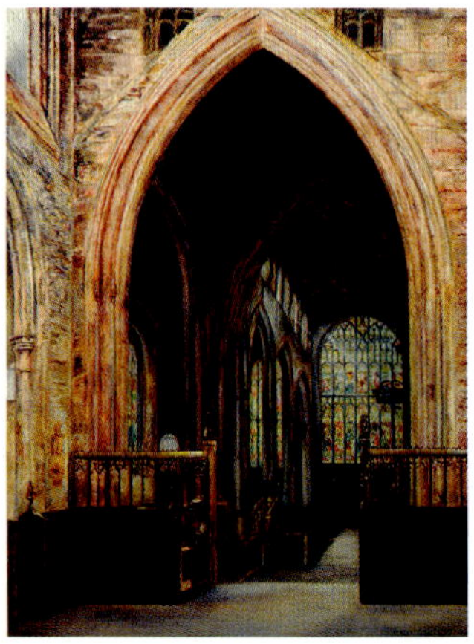

unknown artist
Interior, Rotherham Parish Church, South Yorkshire c.1870
oil on canvas 61 x 46
ROTMG : OP.1977.176

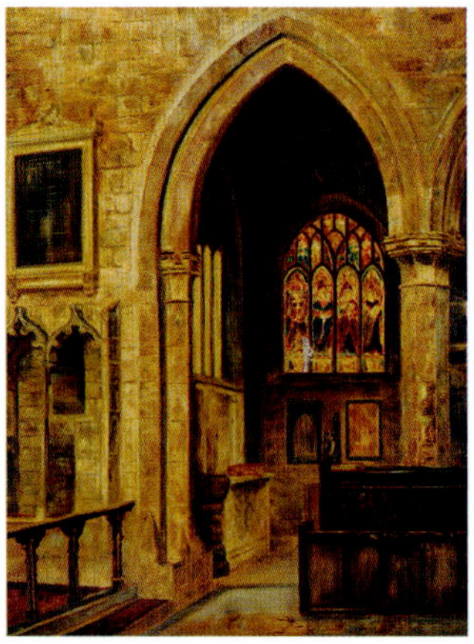

unknown artist
Lady Chapel, Rotherham Parish Church, South Yorkshire c.1870
oil on canvas 60 x 44
ROTMG : OP.1977.175

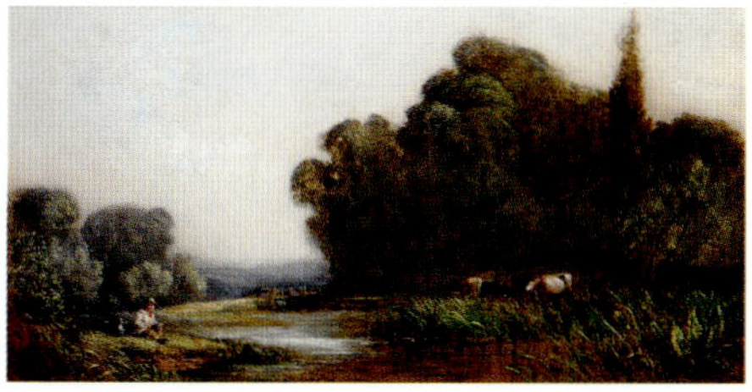

unknown artist
Landscape with a River c.1870
oil on canvas 72 x 107
ROTMG : OP.1977.5

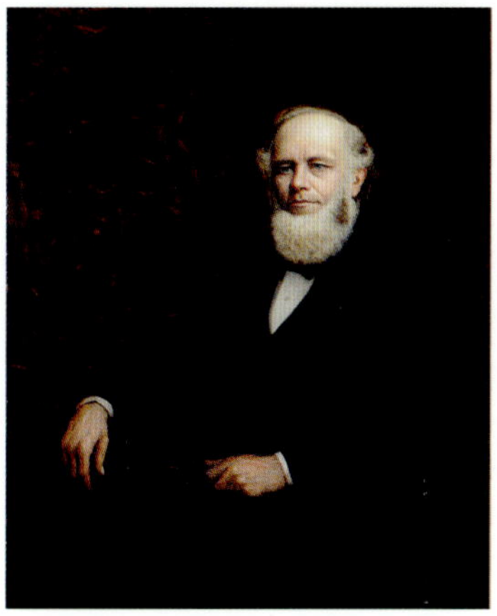

unknown artist
John Matthew Habershon (1824–1894), First Mayor of Rotherham c.1871
oil on canvas 126 x 100
ROTMG : THP1

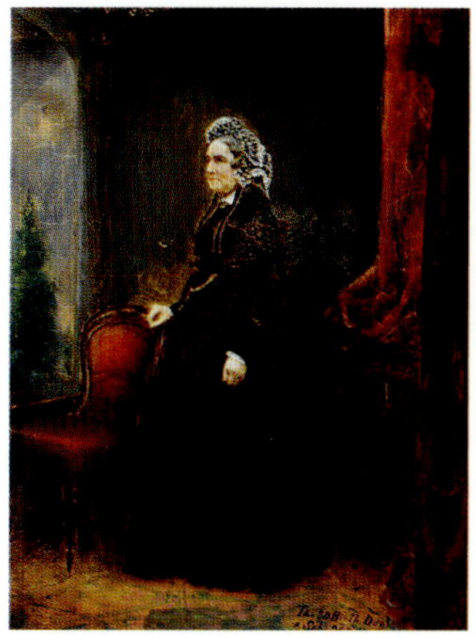

unknown artist
Mrs John Guest, née Hannah Shaw (1797–1882) (The Eightieth Birthday) 1877
oil on panel 45 x 31
ROTMG : OP.1977.163

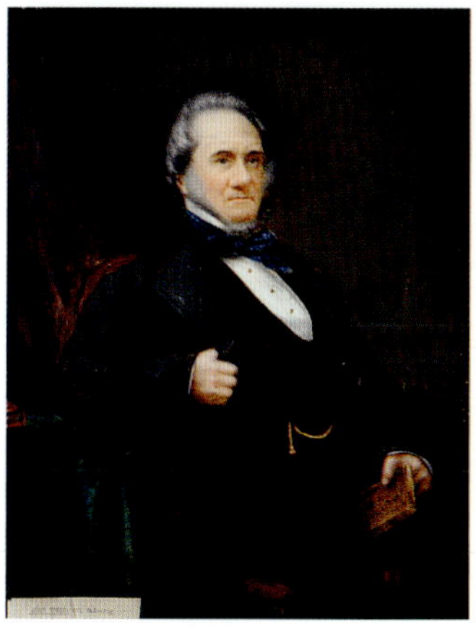

unknown artist
John Guest (1799–1880) c.1880
oil on panel 39 x 29
ROTMG : OP.1978.222

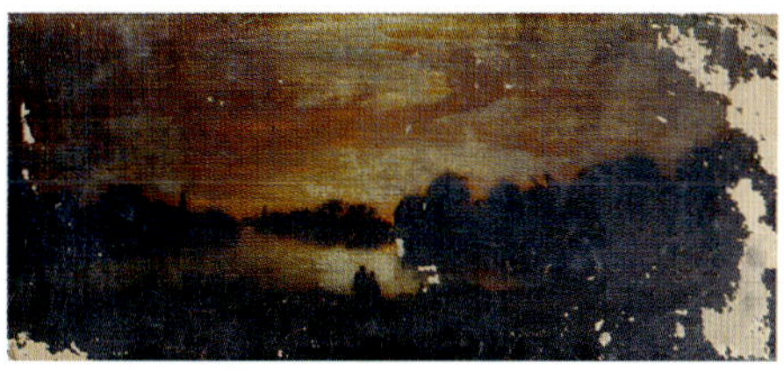

unknown artist
Landscape c.1880
oil on canvas 23.4 x 50.9
ROTMG : OP.1977.134

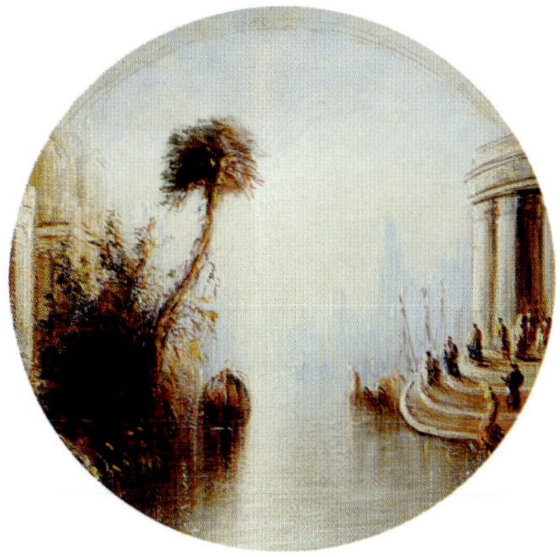

unknown artist
River Scene c.1880
oil on panel 20
ROTMG : OP.1977.126

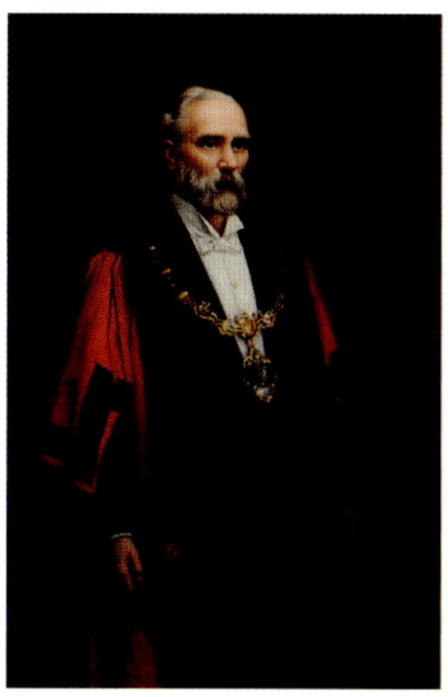

unknown artist
Alderman George Neill (1831–1899), JP c.1881
oil on canvas 152 x 100
ROTMG : THP3

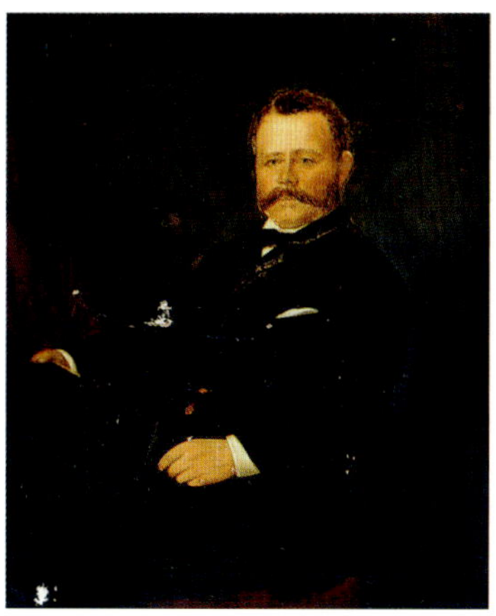

unknown artist
J. A. Bower, Esq., Chairman of Swinton School Board c.1890
oil on canvas 60 x 50
ROTMG : OP.1977.171

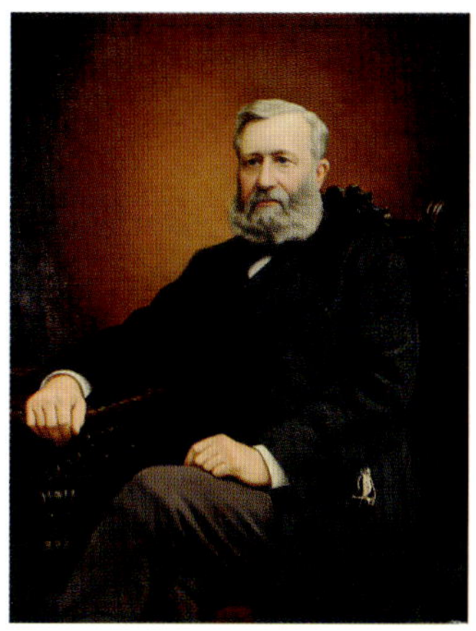

unknown artist
Portrait of an Unknown Gentleman, Seated c.1890
oil on canvas 91 x 71
ROTMG : TUF1446

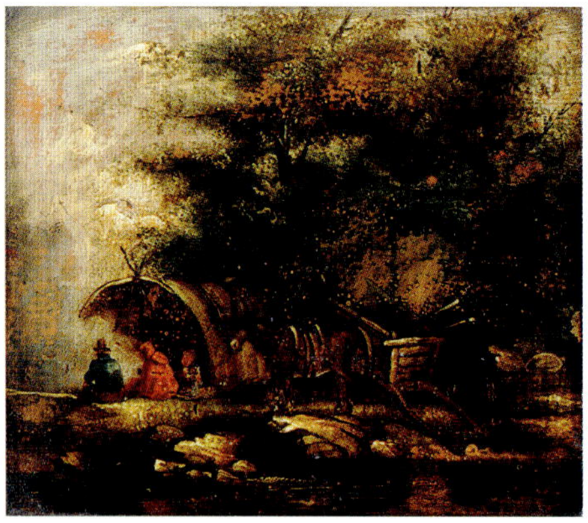

unknown artist
Camping Scene c.1900
oil on panel 17.2 x 19.2
ROTMG : OP.1977.115

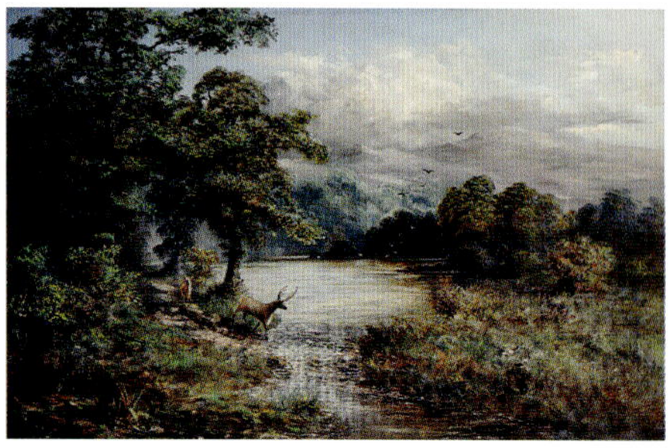

unknown artist
Landscape with a Stag c.1900
oil on canvas 50 x 75
ROTMG : OP.1977.98

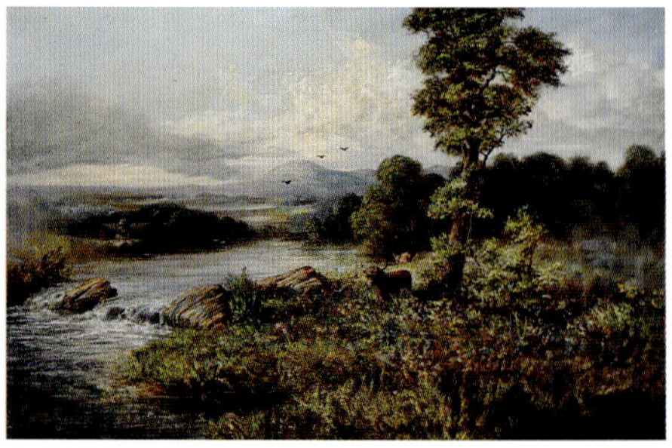

unknown artist
Landscape with Cattle c.1900
oil on canvas 50 x 75
ROTMG : OP.1977.98A

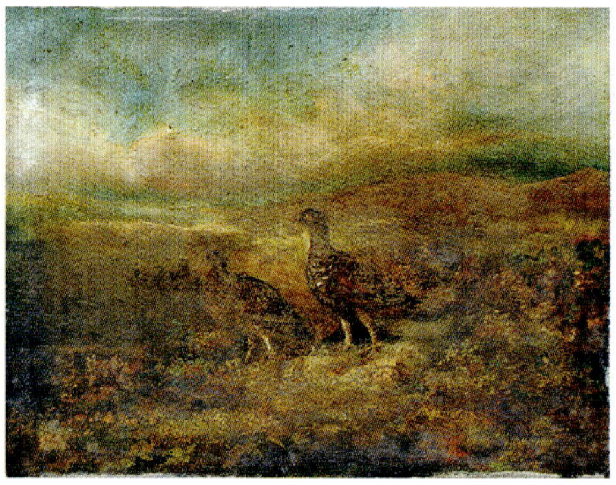

unknown artist
Moorland Scene c.1900
oil on panel 17.7 x 22.4
ROTMG : OP.1977.119

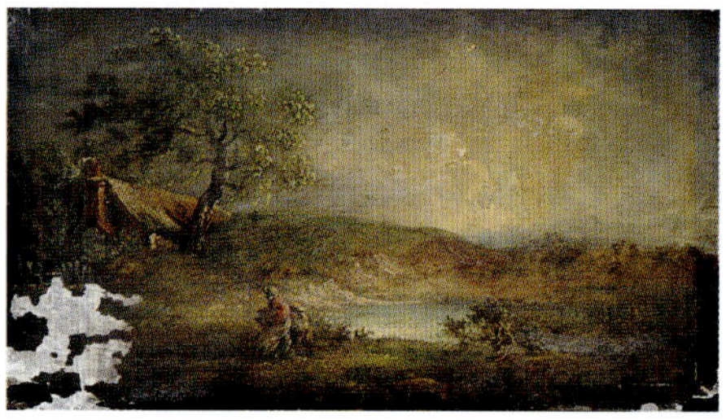

unknown artist
Moorland Scene c.1900
oil on panel 19.5 x 34.4
ROTMG : OP.1977.120

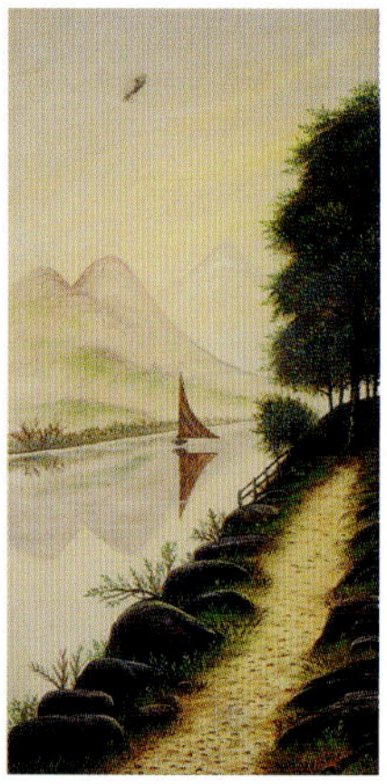

unknown artist
River Scene c.1900
oil on canvas 49.5 x 24
ROTMG : OP.1977.145.1

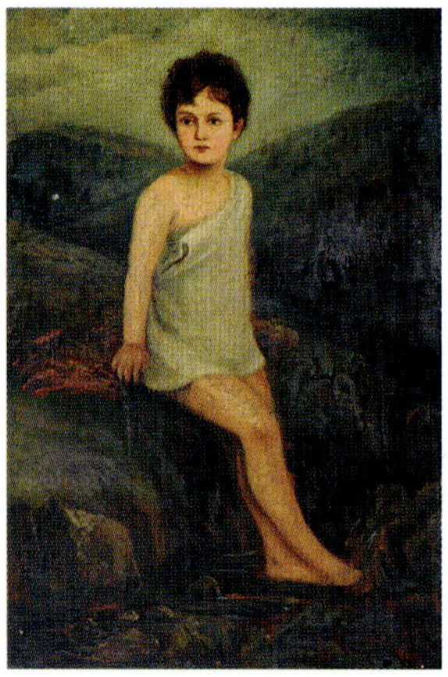

unknown artist
Study of a Child c.1900
oil on canvas 75 x 49.5
ROTMG : OP.1977.151

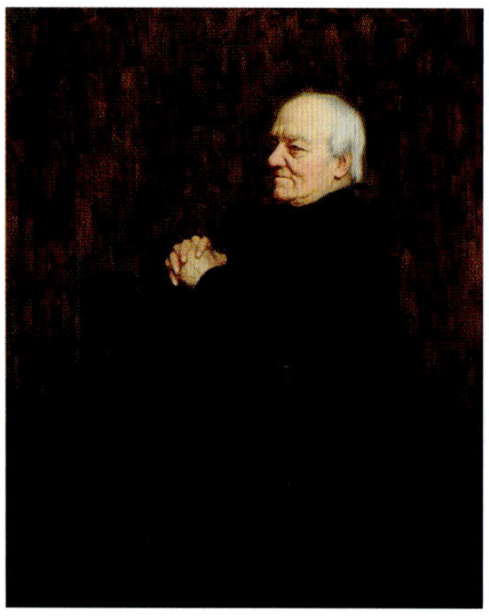

unknown artist
Alderman Robert Marsh (1818–1905) 1905
oil on canvas 125 x 100
ROTMG : TUF1417

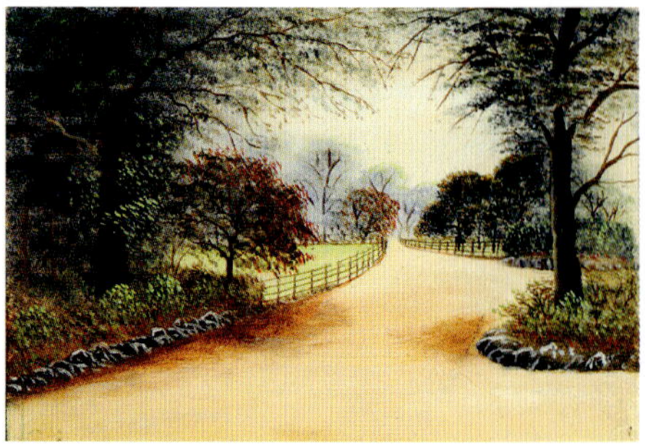

unknown artist
Clifton Park Entrance before the Cenotaph Was Erected, Rotherham, South Yorkshire c.1905
oil on paper 14.5 x 19
ROTMG : TUF1448

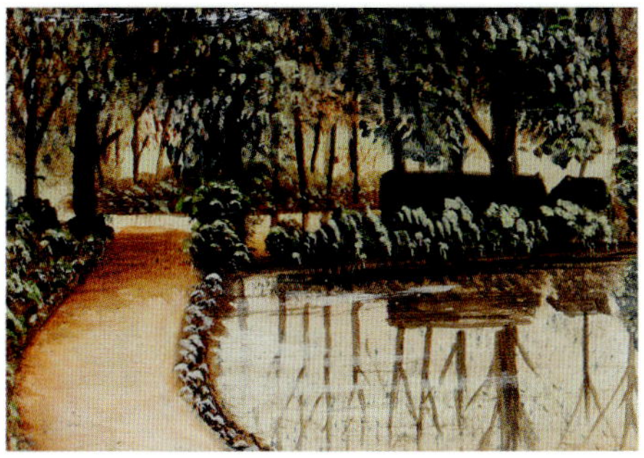

unknown artist
Clifton Park Pond, Rotherham, South Yorkshire c.1905
oil on paper 9.3 x 13.1
ROTMG : TUF1439

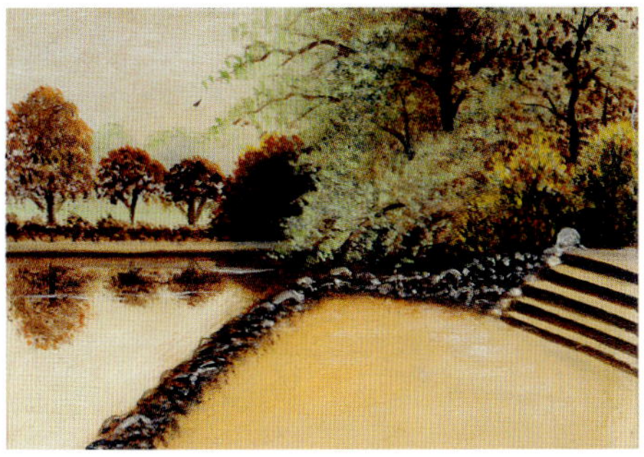

unknown artist
Clifton Park Pond with Steps, Rotherham, South Yorkshire c.1905
oil on paper 9.2 x 13.2
ROTMG : TUF1440

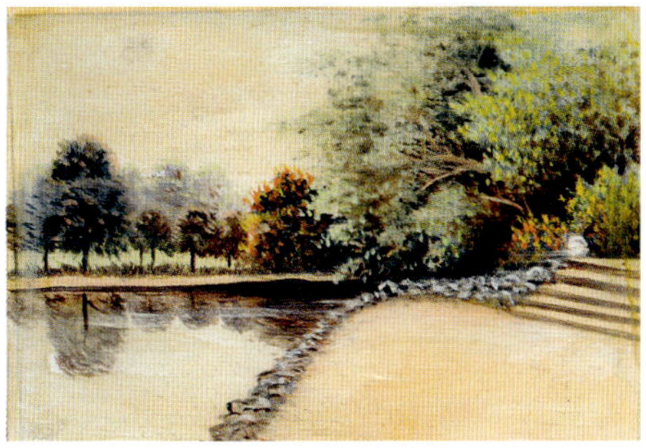

unknown artist
Clifton Park Pond with Steps, Rotherham, South Yorkshire c.1905
oil on paper 14.5 x 19
ROTMG : TUF1447

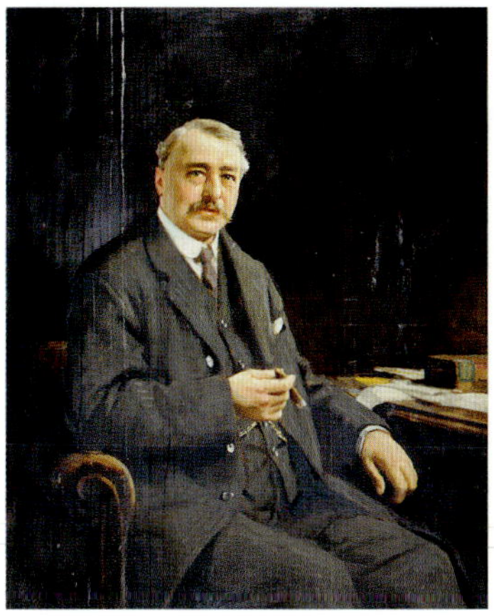

unknown artist
Henry Steel (1831–1915) c.1905
oil on canvas 125 x 100
ROTMG : E1651.4 (P)

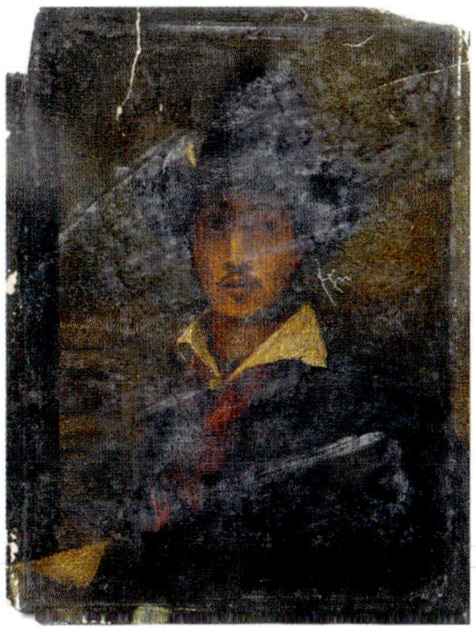

unknown artist
Portrait of an Unknown Man c.1910
oil on paper 28.9 x 21.9
ROTMG : OP.1978.224

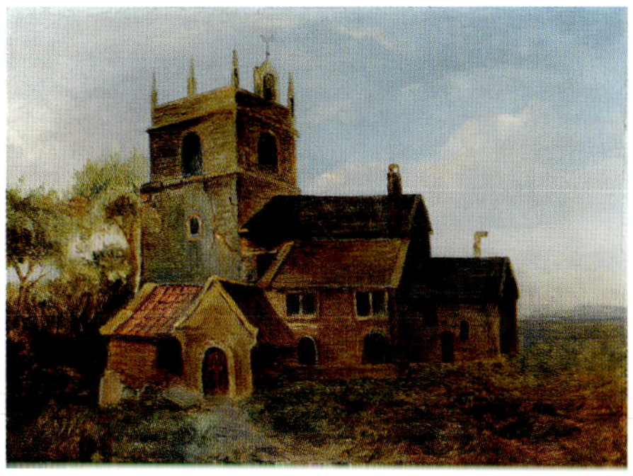

unknown artist
Rawmarsh Church, South Yorkshire c.1910
oil on canvas 30.5 x 41
ROTMG : OP.1984.15

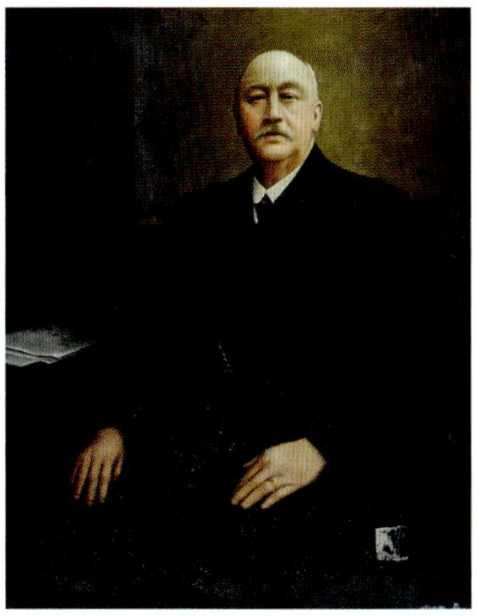

unknown artist
Portrait of an Unknown Gentleman, Seated c.1920
oil on canvas 92 x 72
ROTMG : TUF1444

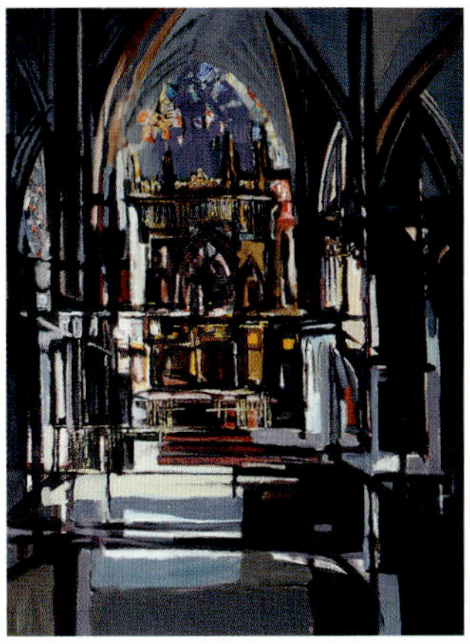

unknown artist
Cathedral Interior c.1965
oil on canvas 151 x 110.5
ROTMG : OP.1977.140

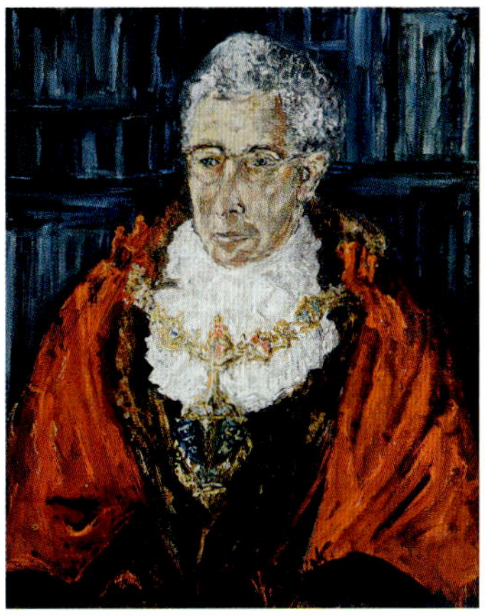

Van Dunk, Ellen
Percy Clarence Wright (1900–1991) 1968
oil on canvas 76 x 61
ROTMG : OP.1989.6

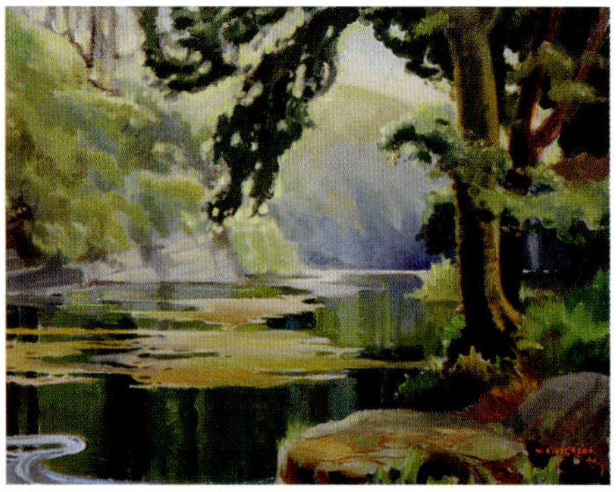

Vickers, W. A.
Lathkill Dale, Cumbria 1944
oil on board 28 x 36
ROTMG : OP.1977.192

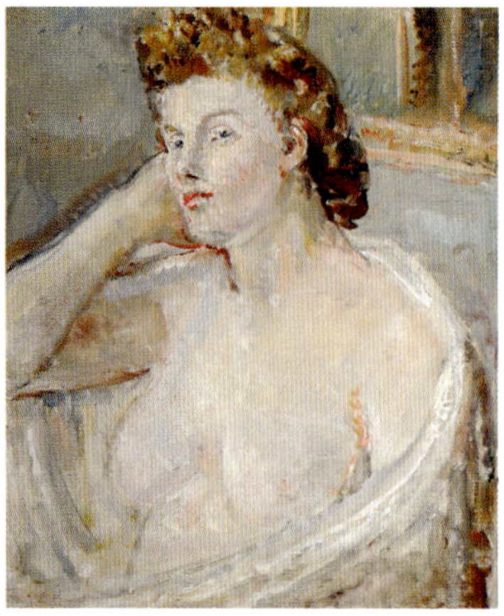

Walker, Ethel 1861–1951
Self Portrait c.1900
oil on canvas 61 x 51
ROTMG : OP.1977.129

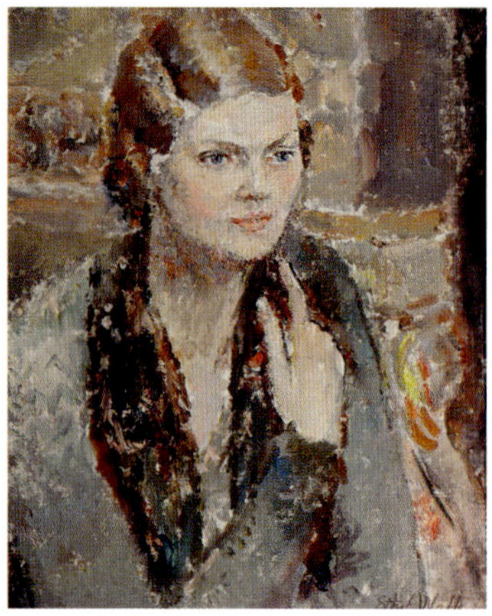

Walker, Ethel 1861–1951
Portrait of a Girl c.1910
oil on canvas 50 x 40
ROTMG : OP.1977.105

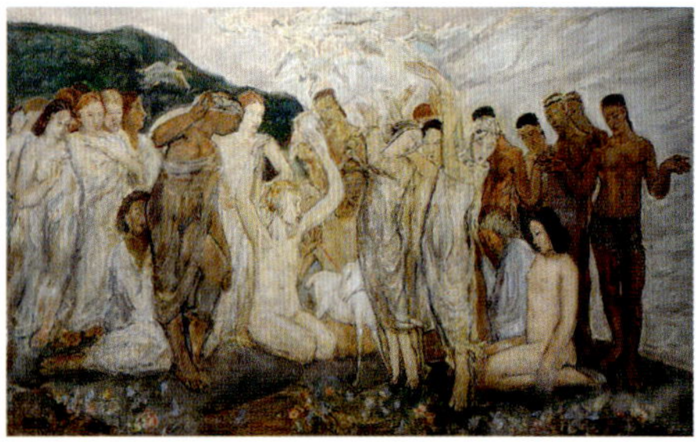

Walker, Ethel 1861–1951
Decoration for an Ivory Room: Invocation to the Dance c.1913
oil on canvas 107 x 168
ROTMG : OP.1996.2

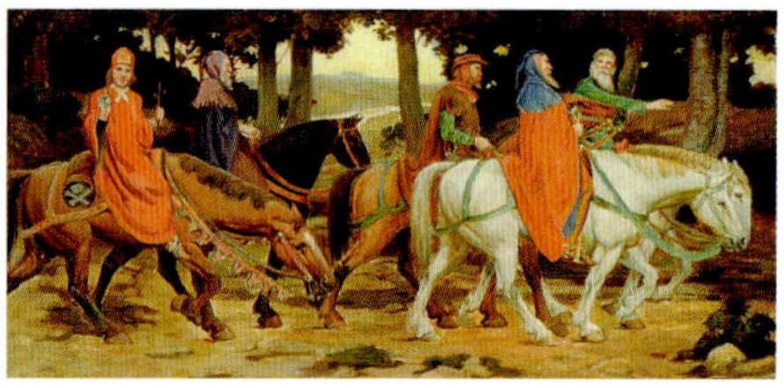

Watson, Thomas J. 1847–1912
Riding thro' the Forest c.1870
oil on canvas 45 x 90
ROTMG : OP.1977.14

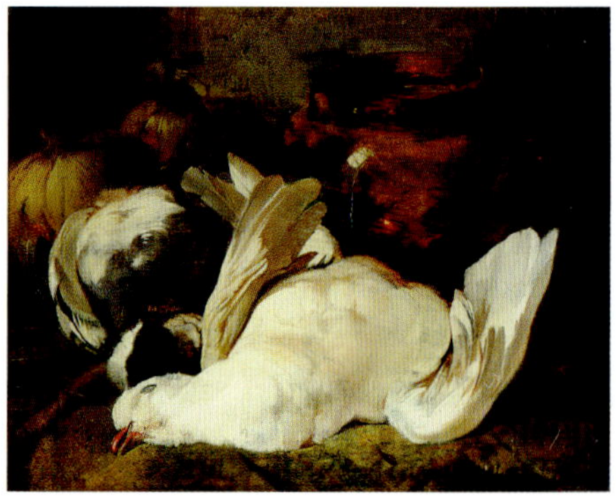

Weekes, Henry II 1849–1888
Wood Pigeons c.1880
oil on board 35 x 42.5
ROTMG : OP.1977.91

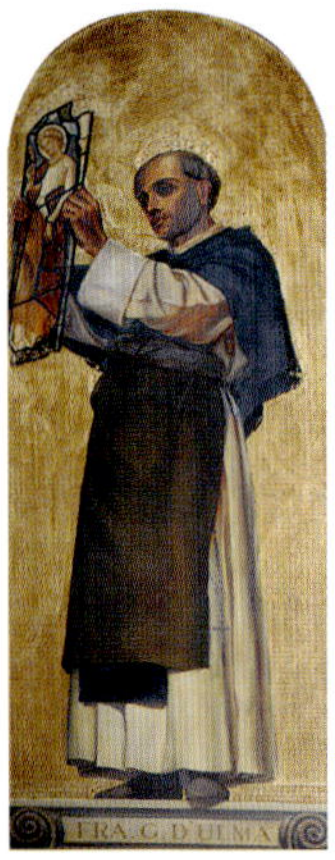

Westlake, Nathaniel Hubert John (after)
1833–1921
Fra Giacomo da Ulma (1407–1491) c.1868
oil on canvas panel 239 x 89
ROTMG : TUF1420

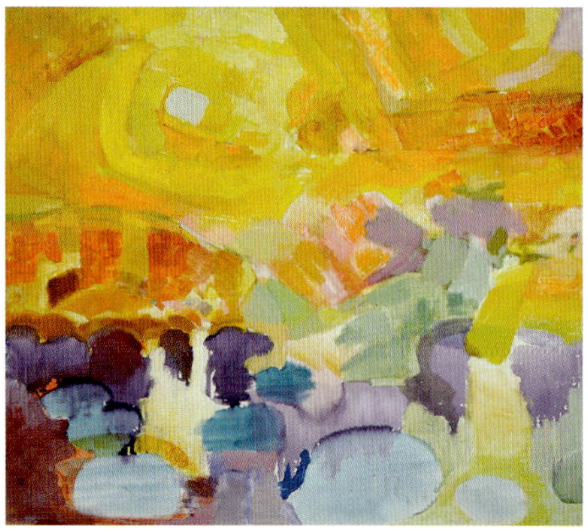

Wey, Peter
Green Coolness 1963
oil on canvas 90.5 x 100
ROTMG : OP.1977.193

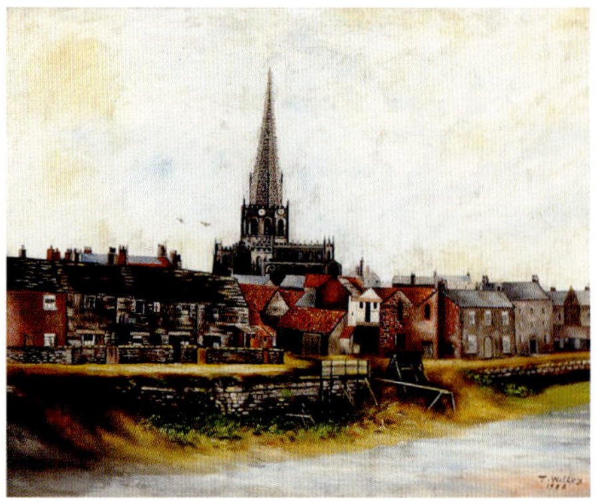

Willey, T.
Millgate, Rotherham, South Yorkshire 1908
oil on canvas 50 x 60
ROTMG : OP.1977.89

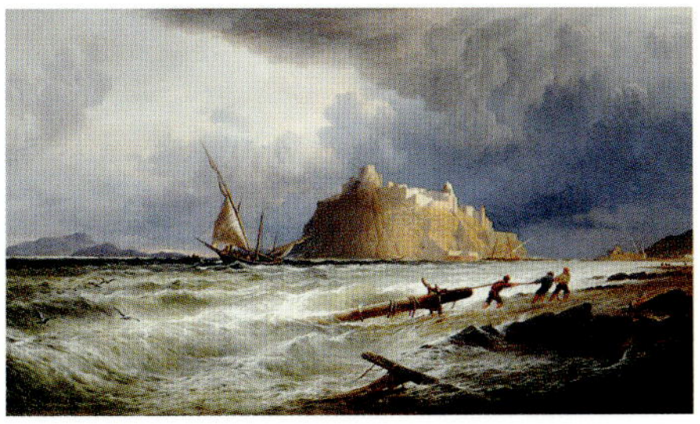

Williams, Alfred Walter 1823–1905
The Castle of Ischia, off the Coast of Naples, Italy 1865
oil on canvas 93 x 153
ROTMG : OP.1977.10

Williams, Alfred Walter 1823–1905
Landscape, Langdale Pikes, Cumbria 1873
oil on canvas 23.5 x 30
ROTMG : OP.1977.65

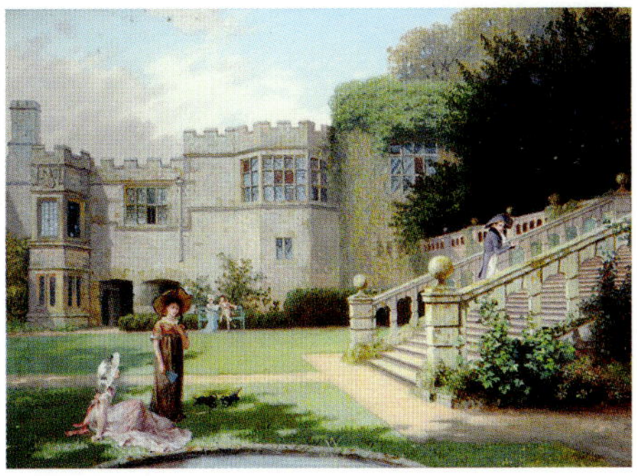

Wilson, Arthur 1838–1914
Haddon Hall, Derbyshire c.1890
oil on canvas 49.5 x 67
ROTMG : OP.1977.94

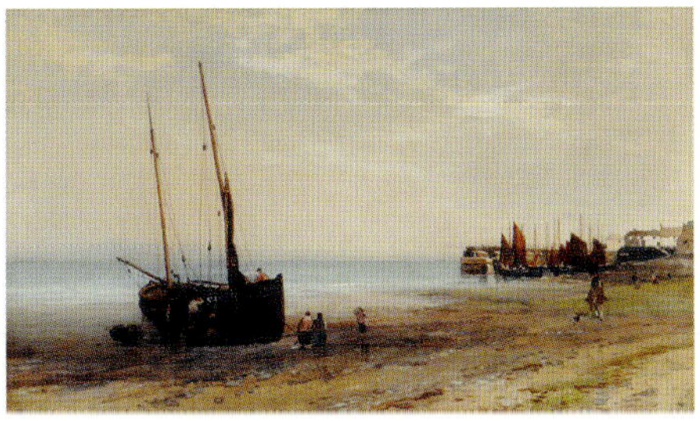

Wimperis, Edmund Morison 1835–1900
Seascape Study c.1875
oil on canvas 29 x 49
ROTMG : OP.1978.231

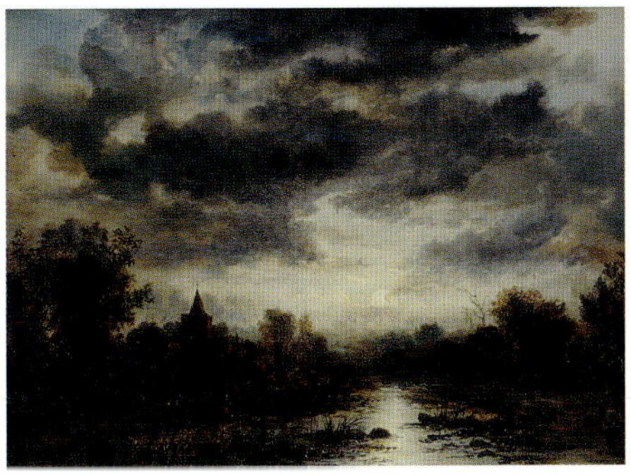

Wood, R. H. active 1865–1889
Shades of Night c.1865
oil on canvas 40 x 54.5
ROTMG : OP.1977.141

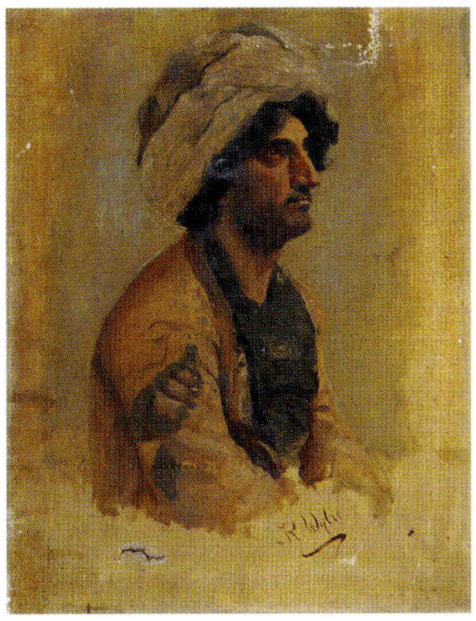

Wylie, Robert 1839–1897
Portrait of a Man in a Turban c.1880
oil on canvas 46 x 35.5
ROTMG : OP.1977.172

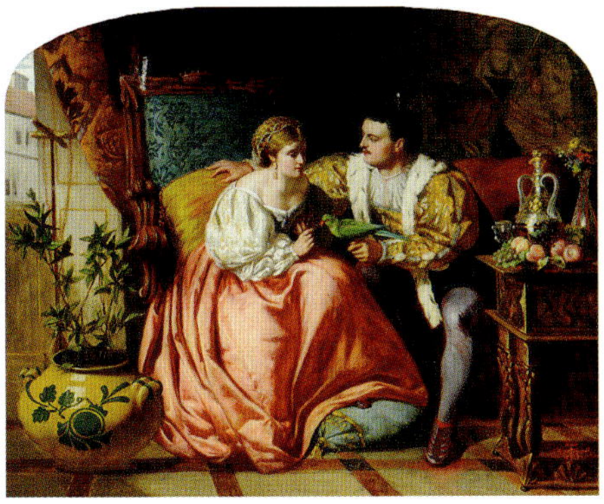

Wynfield, David Wilkie 1837–1887
Henry VIII and Anne Boleyn 1865
oil on canvas 50 x 60
ROTMG : OP.1977.18

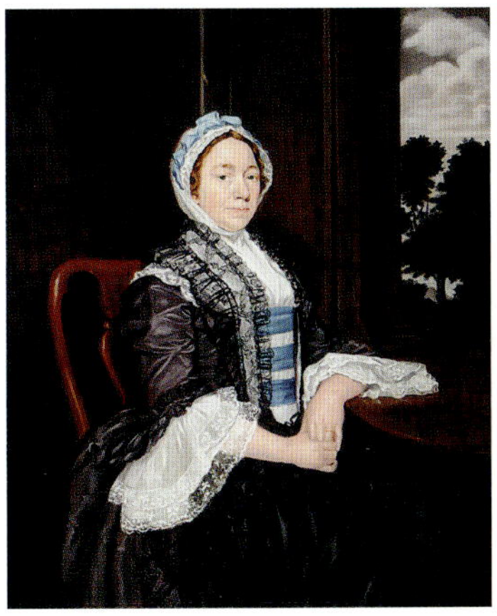

Zoffany, Johann (school of) 1733–1810
Mary Walker (1708–1793) c.1775
oil on canvas 127 x 102.5
ROTMG : OP.1988.7

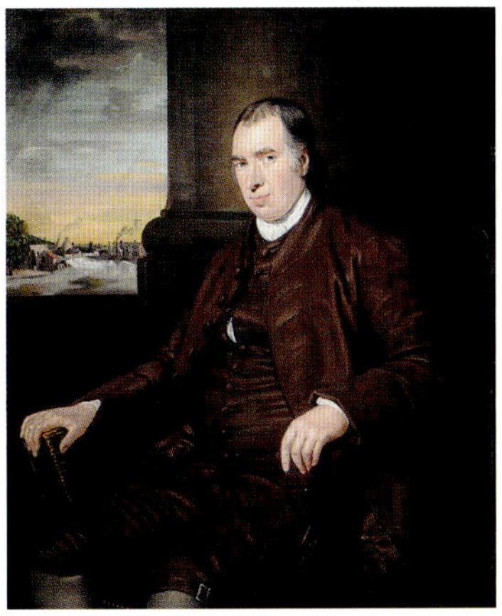

Zoffany, Johann (school of) 1733–1810
Samuel Walker (1715–1782) c.1775
oil on canvas 127 x 102.5
ROTMG : OP.1988.8

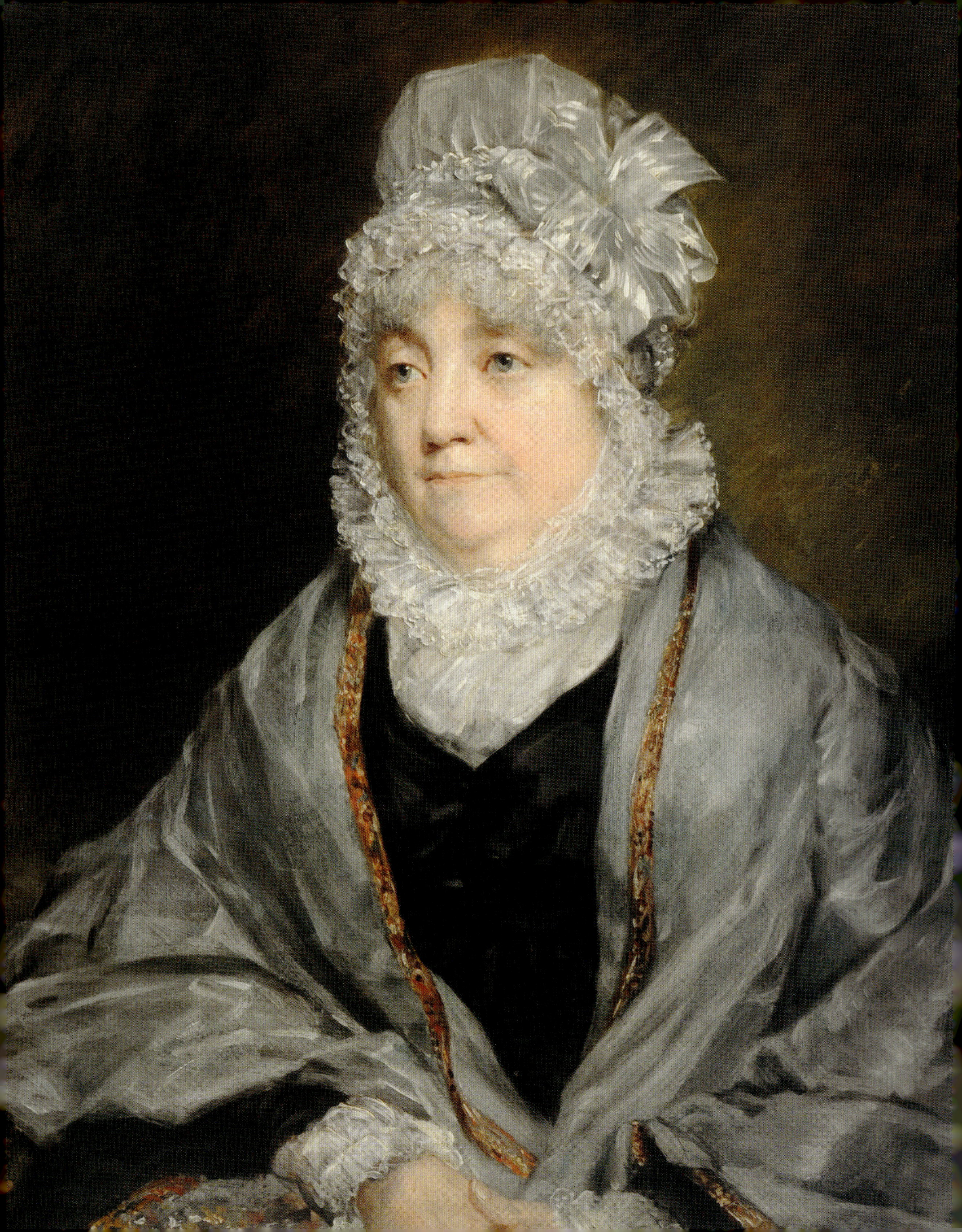

Rotherham Town Hall

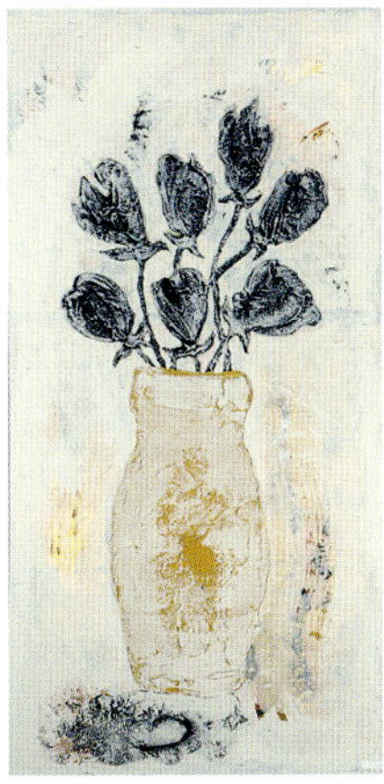

Isseo
Fleures noires c.2008
oil & mixed media on canvas 101 x 50.5
ROTMG : THA2009-0189

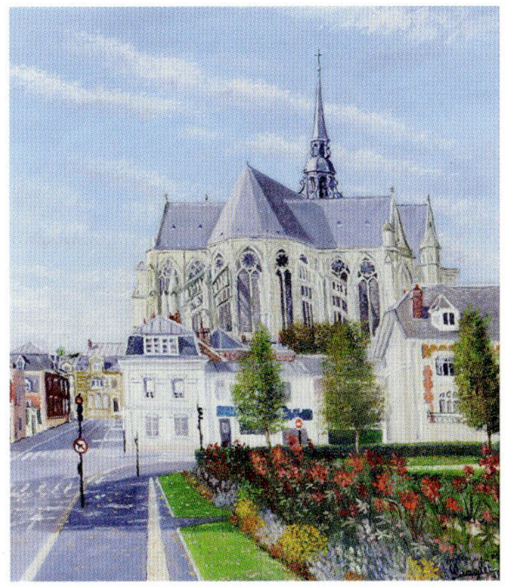

Langlet, Jean-Claude
La basilique vue des Champs Elysées, Saint-Quentin, France 2007
oil on canvas 55.3 x 46
ROTMG : THA2009-0155

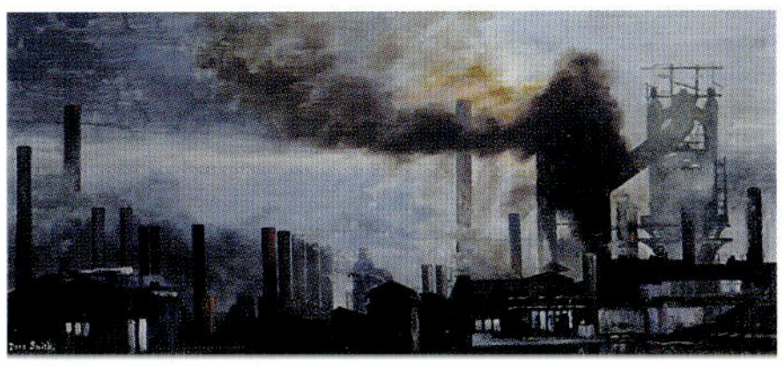

Smith, Dora
Steelworks c.1975
oil on board 34 x 74
ROTMG : THA2009-0141

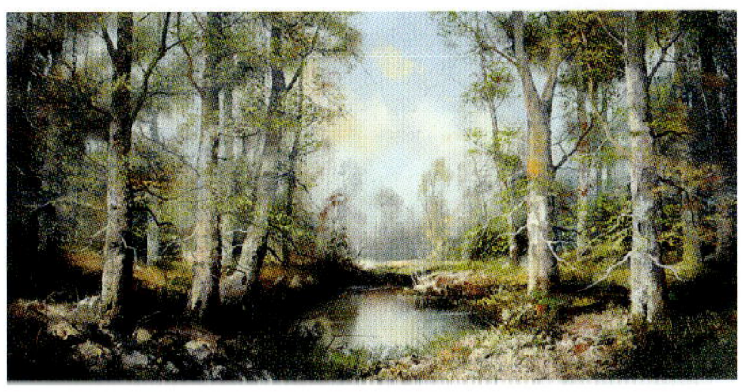

unknown artist
Woodland Scene with a Pond c.1970
oil on canvas 49.5 x 100
ROTMG : THA2009-0191

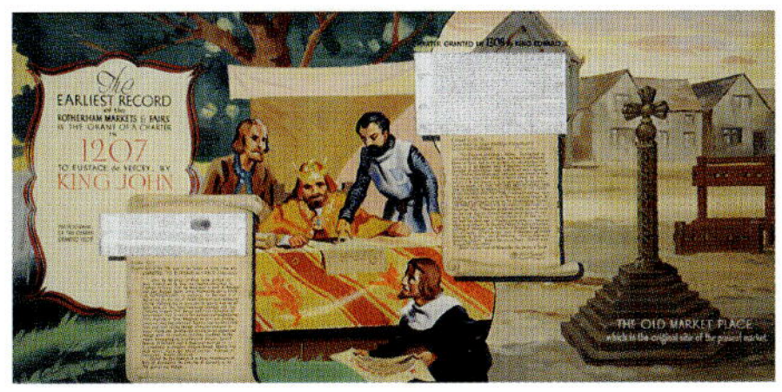

unknown artist
The Old Market Place c.1975
oil on board 70 x 141
ROTMG : THA2009-0262

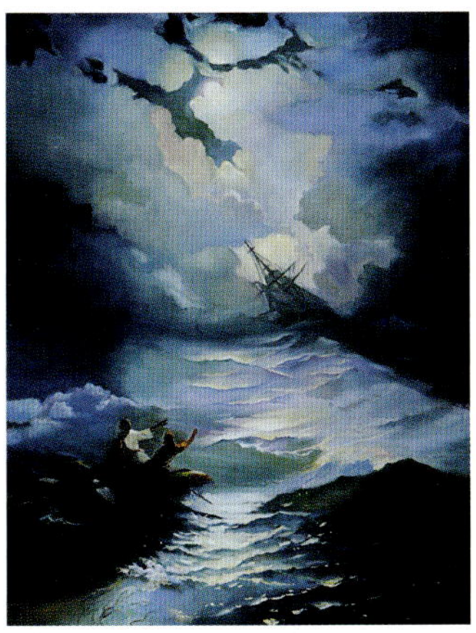

unknown artist
Rescue at Sea c.1994
oil on canvas 74 x 55
ROTMG : THA2009-0154

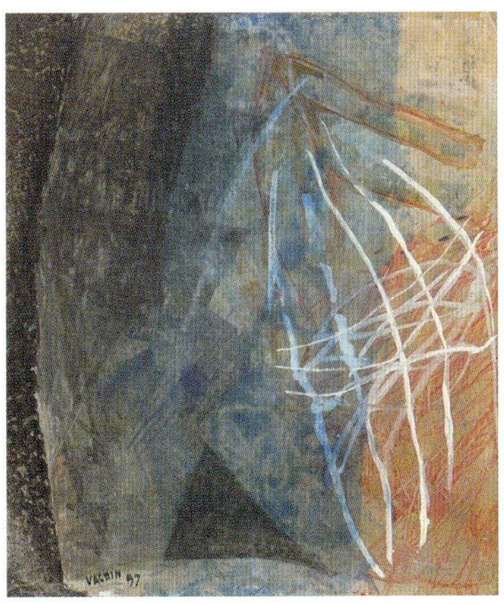

Vachin
Abstract 1997
oil on canvas 55 x 46
ROTMG : THA2009-0268

Facing page: Constable, John, 1776–1837, *Mrs Tuder* (detail), 1818, Barnsley Museum and Heritage Service, (p. 50)

Thomas Rotherham College

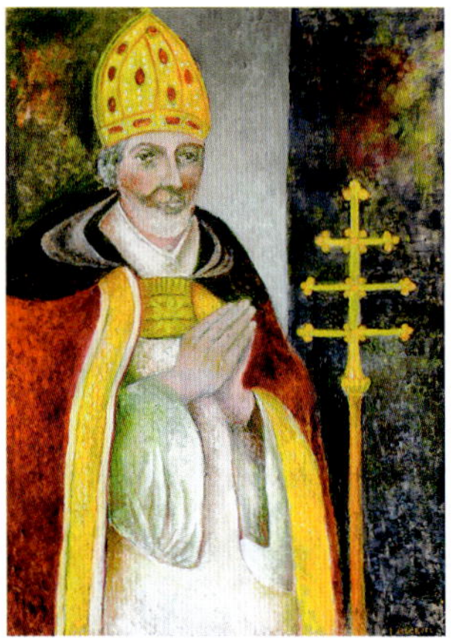

Becket, Leslie b.1913
Thomas Rotherham (1423–1500), Archbishop of York and Founder of the College 2009
oil on canvas 88 x 62
PCF2

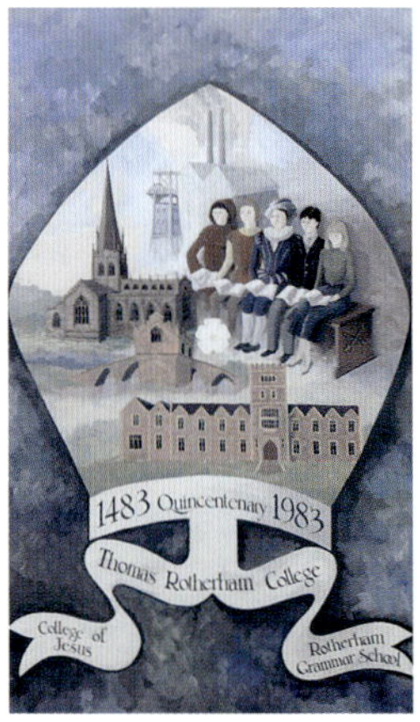

Butler, Helen
Thomas Rotherham College Quincentenary 1983
oil on canvas 180 x 100 (E)
PCF3

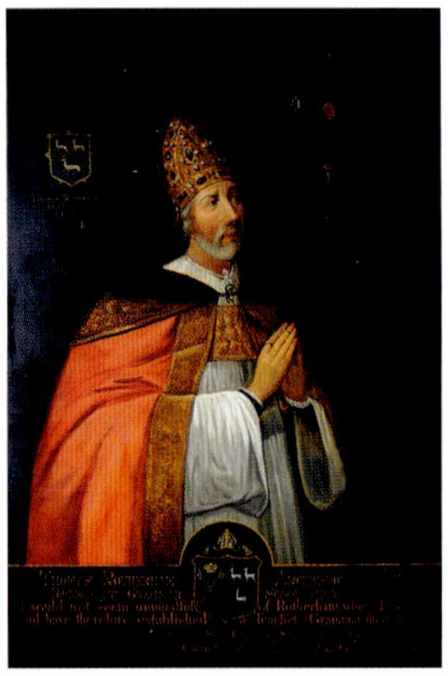

unknown artist early 18th C (?)
Thomas Rotherham (1423–1500), Archbishop of York and Founder of the College
oil on canvas 150 x 100
PCF1

York and Lancaster Regimental Museum

The York and Lancaster Regimental Museum collects objects, photographs and records which originate from or have an association with the York and Lancaster Regiment, or its forbears, the 65th and 84th Regiments of Foot. This includes material from any part of the world in which the Regiment served (principally India, New Zealand, Africa, and Europe) and covers all aspects of Regimental life during the period of 1758–1968.

The Regimental Museum was officially formed in 1985 following the transfer of the collection from the Regiment to Rotherham, and with the opening of the York and Lancaster Regimental Museum.

The Regimental Collection of fine art is relatively small, consisting of around 85 paintings (oil and watercolour), drawings and prints, with prints and drawings forming the majority of the Collection. The majority of the oil paintings were transferred from the Regiment following the formation of the Museum, or transferred from the Regimental Headquarters during the 1990s.

In the main, these paintings were donated by people with family connections to the Regiment.

The paintings themselves show important leaders from the Regiment's history. There are, for instance, two paintings of *Field Marshal Herbert Charles Onslow Plumer (1857–1932), 1st Viscount Plumer* whose collection, including medals and uniform, forms an important part of the wider Regimental Collection. The painting *The Battle of Tamaai, 13 March 1884* is a depiction of one of the 1st Battalion Yorks & Lancs (formerly the 65th of Foot) battles in Egypt in 1884.

The York and Lancaster Regimental Museum continues to collect, and the curators are especially interested in depictions of life in the Regiment, whether modern photographic representations or more traditional artworks.

Frances Yeo, Senior Curator and Collections Manager

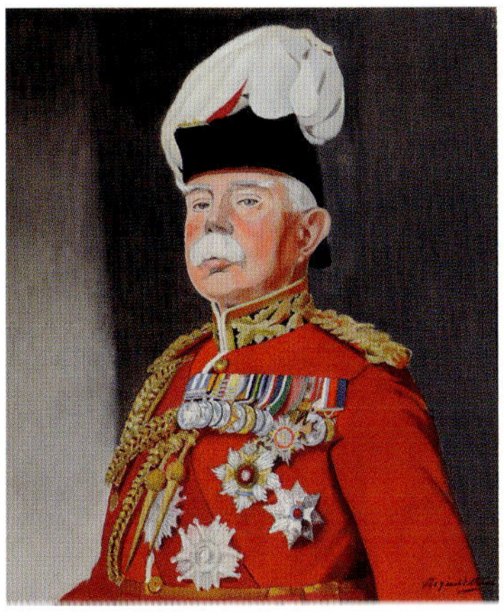

Aird, Reginald b.1890
Field Marshal Herbert Charles Onslow Plumer (1857–1932), 1st Viscount Plumer c.1930
oil on canvas 61 x 52
YLRM : 1979.684

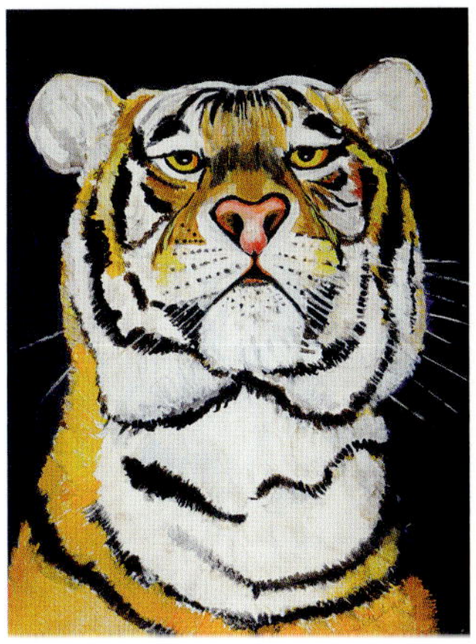

Best, C.
Tiger's Head 1979
oil on board 61 x 45.5
YLRM : 1979.854

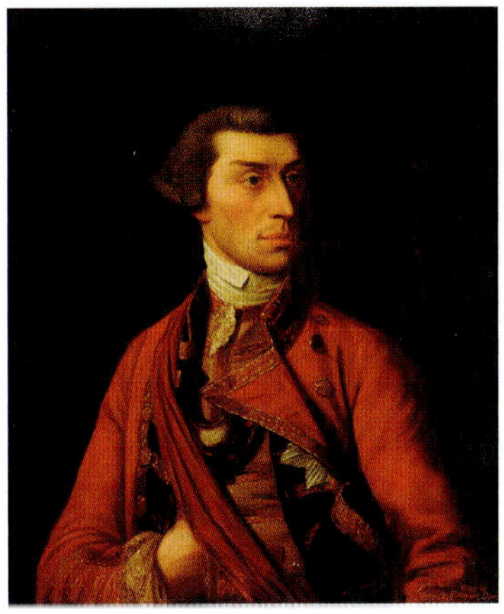

Dyer, Edmund active c.1820–1875
Lieutenant General Sir Eyre Coote (1759–1823) c.1820
oil on canvas 75 x 62
YLRM : 1996.68

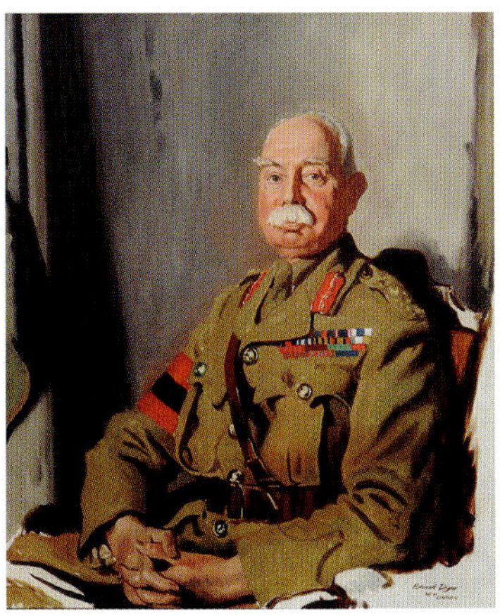

Dyer, Edward active 1919–1938
Field Marshal Herbert Charles Onslow Plumer (1857–1932), 1st Viscount Plumer c.1930
oil on canvas 93.5 x 78
YLRM : 1996.69

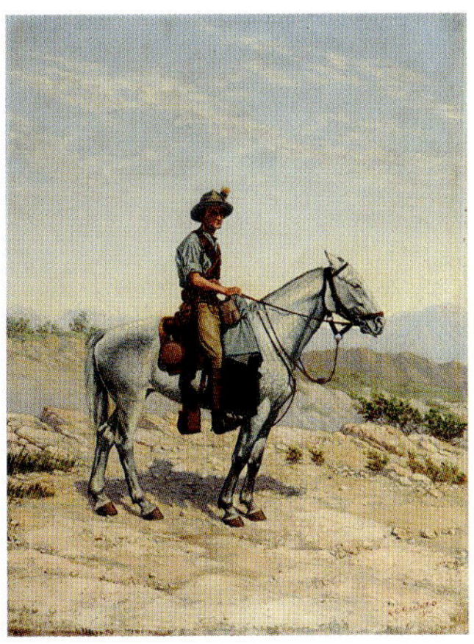

Galindo, Richard Eyles b.c.1847
Mounted Infantryman c.1900
oil on canvas 61 x 46
YLRM : UF 1902

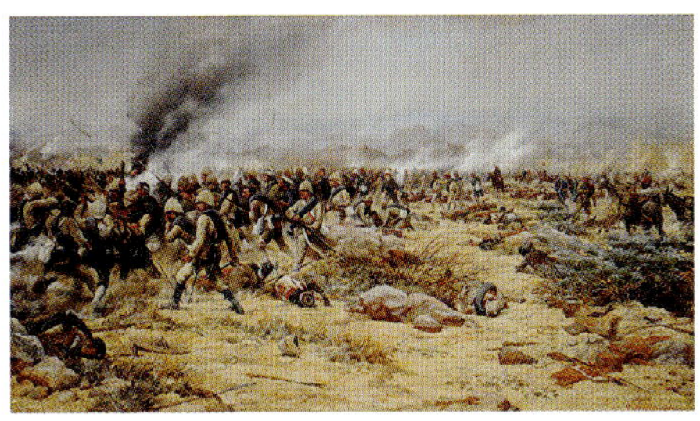

Giles, Godfrey Douglas 1857–1941
The Battle of Tamaai, 13 March 1884 1885
oil on canvas 114 x 190
ROTYL : 2008.11

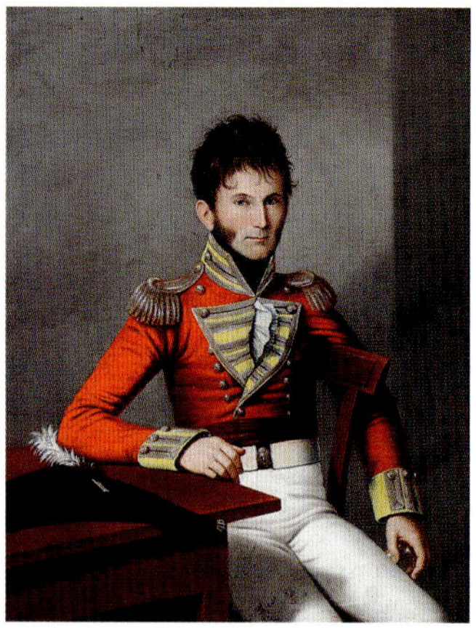

unknown artist
Lieutenant Colonel Richard Lloyd (1777–1813) c.1810
oil on canvas 118 x 90
YLRM : 1996.70

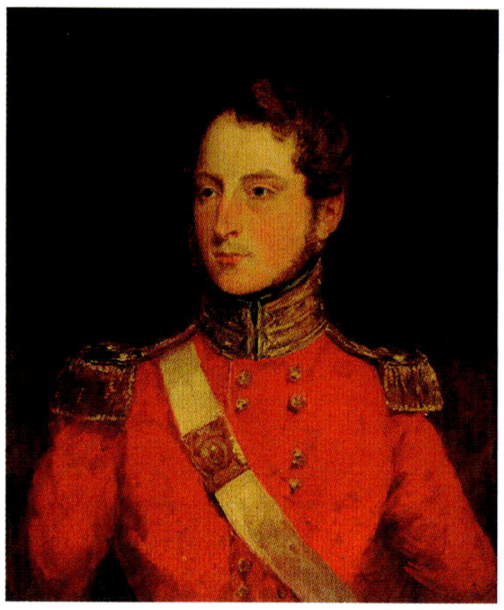

unknown artist
Richard Lovelock Coxe (1813–1844) c.1840
oil on canvas 30.5 x 25.5
YLRM : 1979.697

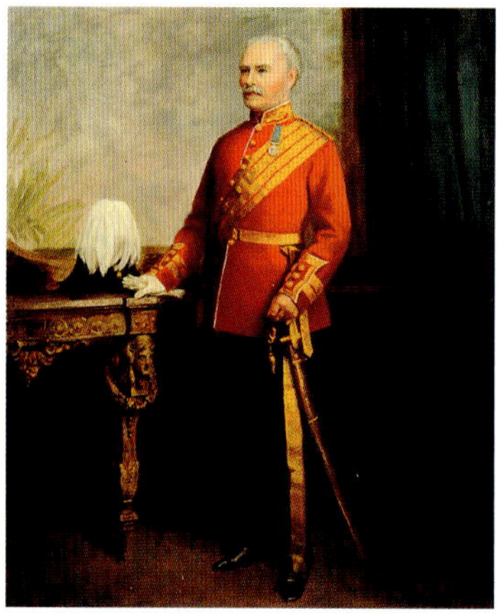

unknown artist
General C. Emilius Gold (1809–1871) c.1860
oil on canvas 60 x 49.5
YLRM : 1982.684A

Swinton Community Library

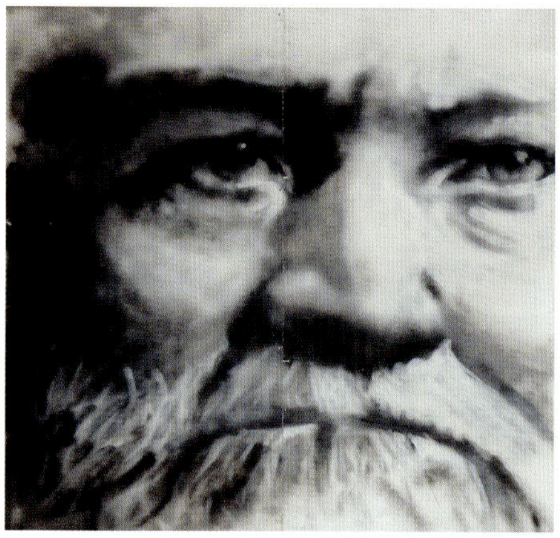

Padfield, Philip
Andrew Carnegie (1835–1919) 2001
acrylic spray paint on wood panel
180 x 200 (E)
PCF1

Dearne Valley College

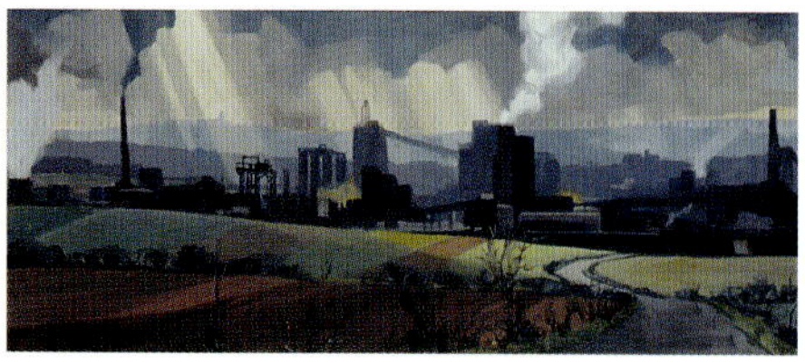

Leadley, W. E. 1903–1973
Manvers Colliery (now the site of Dearne Valley College) 1966
acrylic on canvas board 32 x 74
PCF1

Facing page: McFadyen, Jock, b.1950, *Untitled (Hawksmoore series No.3)* (detail), c.1988, Doncaster Museum Service, (p. 92)

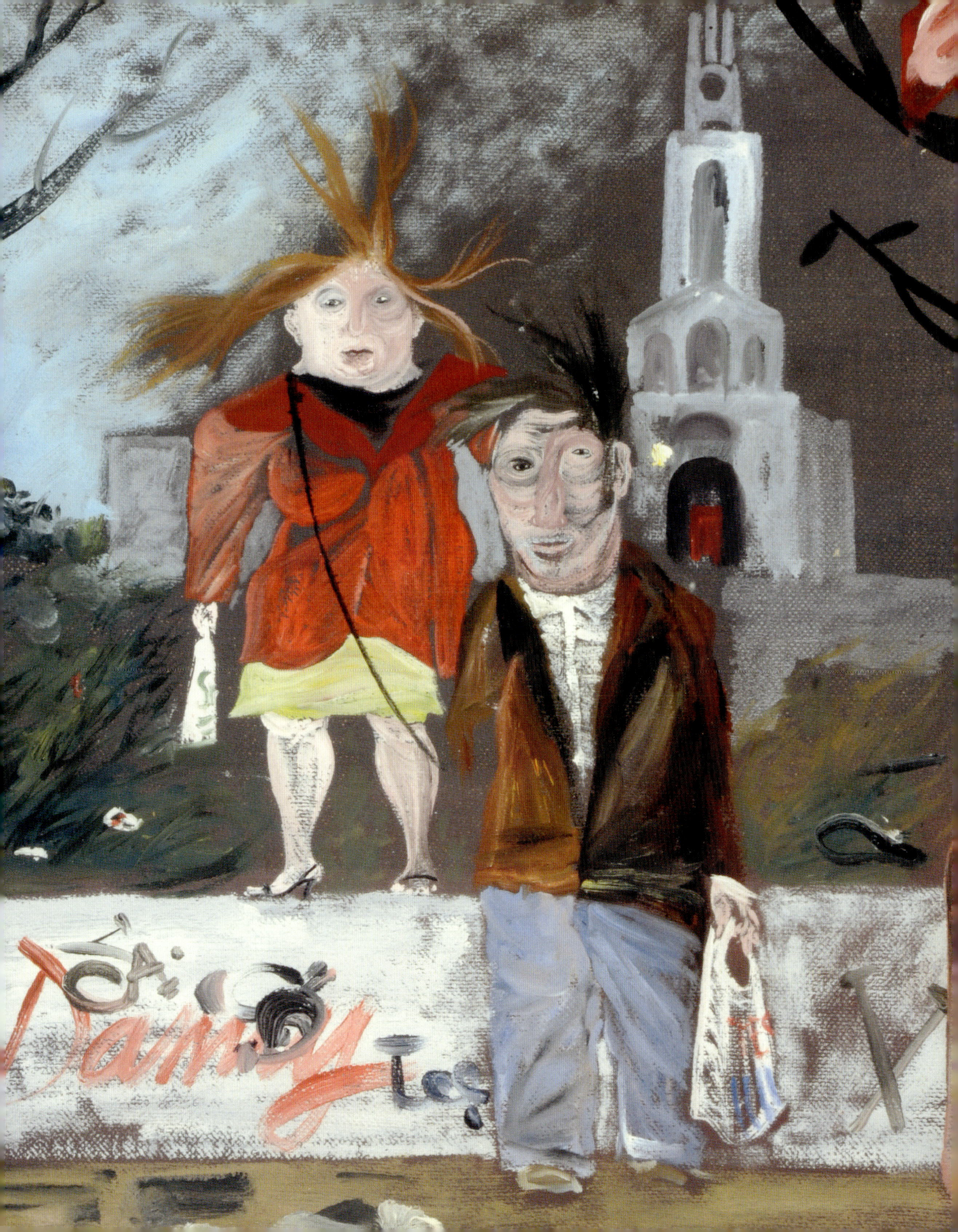

Paintings Without Reproductions

This section lists all the paintings that have not been included in the main pages of the catalogue. They were excluded as it was not possible to photograph them for this project. Additional information relating to acquisition credit lines or loan details is also included. For this reason the information below is not repeated in the Further Information section.

Barnsley College

Mickelthwaite, Don b.1936, *The Pit Head, Barnsley, South Yorkshire*, 1997, 50 x 75, oil on canvas, 9457, gift from the artist, 1997/1998, not available at the time of photography

The Cooper Gallery

Whittaker, Malcolm b.1937, *Partially Reflected Horse*, 2008, 18 x 15.5, oil & wax on board, CP.TR.401, gift from the artist, 2009, not available at the time of photography

Doncaster and Bassetlaw Hospitals NHS Foundation Trust

Bennett, Terence b.1935, *Barge on a Canal*, 1974, 118 x 150, oil on canvas, PCF1, collection refused permission to reproduce images

Bennett, Terence b.1935, *Cottages on the Shore*, 1974, 118 x 150, oil on canvas, PCF2, collection refused permission to reproduce images

Doncaster Museum Service

Shackleton, William 1872–1933, *A Woodland Pool*, 1920s, 24 x 26.5, oil on canvas, DONMG : 112.38, gift from May Shackleton, 1938, not available at the time of photography

Stubbs, C. E. active c.1960–1962, *Scene at Norton, South Yorkshire*, c.1960, 58 x 85, oil on canvas, DONMG : 796.77, purchased from Mrs Holden, 1997, not available at the time of photography

unknown artist *Army Officer, Queen's Own Warwickshire and Worcestershire Yeomanry*, 50 x 40, oil on canvas, ZP316, found in store, not available at the time of photography

unknown artist *Portrait*, oil on canvas, DONMG : 317.6, gift, not available at the time of photography

Rotherham Museum & Art Gallery

unknown artist *River Scene*, c.1900, 49.5 x 24, oil on canvas, ROTMG : OP.1977.145.2, unknown acquisition method, not available at the time of photography

York and Lancaster Regimental Museum

Carr, Henry Marvell 1894–1970, *German Airborn Invasion, Crete, 1941*, c.1945, oil on board, YLRM : 1991.16, gift from the artist, not available at the time of photography

Further Information

The paintings listed in this section have additional information relating to one or more of the five categories outlined below. This extra information is only provided where it is applicable and where it exists. Paintings listed in this section follow the same order as in the illustrated pages of the catalogue.

I	The full name of the artist if this was too long to display in the illustrated pages of the catalogue. Such cases are marked in the catalogue with a (...).
II	The full title of the painting if this was too long to display in the illustrated pages of the catalogue. Such cases are marked in the catalogue with a (...).
III	Acquisition information or acquisition credit lines as well as information about loans, copied from the records of the owner collection.
IV	Artist copyright credit lines where the copyright owner has been traced. Exhaustive efforts have been made to locate the copyright owners of all the images included within this catalogue and to meet their requirements. Any omissions or mistakes brought to our attention will be duly attended to and corrected in future publications.
V	The credit line of the lender of the transparency if the transparency has been borrowed. Bridgeman images are available subject to any relevant copyright approvals from the Bridgeman Art Library at www.bridgemanart.com

Barnsley Central Library

Burden, Samuel b.1932, *Fishermen's Cottages, Polperro, Cornwall*, purchased for the picture loan scheme, 1996, © the artist
Cafieri, Irene *Winter Woodland*, purchased for the picture loan scheme, 1996
Church, M. *Parisian Street Scene*, purchased for the picture loan scheme
Slack, Muriel *Still Life*, purchased for the picture loan scheme

Barnsley College

Evans, Peter *Footprints at Bretton Hall, West Yorkshire*, gift from the artist in memory of Ann Hayward, 1998
Evans, Peter *Footprints at Bretton Hall, West Yorkshire*, gift from the artist, 1998
Mickelthwaite, Don b.1936, *Church Street Site, Barnsley, South Yorkshire*, gift from the artist, 1997/1998, © the artist
Mickelthwaite, Don b.1936, *Fairfield House, Barnsley, South Yorkshire*, gift from the artist, 1997/1998
Mickelthwaite, Don b.1936, *Graham's Orchard, Barnsley, South Yorkshire*, gift from the artist, 1997/1998, © the artist
Mickelthwaite, Don b.1936, *Honeywell Site, Barnsley, South Yorkshire*, gift from the artist, 1997/1998, © the artist
Mickelthwaite, Don b.1936, *Huddersfield Road Site, Barnsley, South Yorkshire*, gift from the artist, 1997/1998, © the artist
Mickelthwaite, Don b.1936, *Old Mill Lane Learning Centre, Barnsley, South Yorkshire*, gift from the artist, 1997/1998, © the artist
Mickelthwaite, Don b.1936, *Old Mill Lane Site, Barnsley, South Yorkshire*, gift from the artist, 1997/1998, © the artist
Mickelthwaite, Don b.1936, *South East Barnsley Landscape, South Yorkshire*, gift from the artist, 1997/1998, © the artist
Mickelthwaite, Don b.1936, *Town Hall, Barnsley, South Yorkshire*, gift from the artist, 1997/1998, © the artist
unknown artist *Swimmer*, probably a gift from the artist (most likely a student of Barnsley College)
Virginio, W. *Parisian Street Scene*, purchased, 2003
Wilkinson *Tour de France*, purchased, 2003

Barnsley Hospital NHS Foundation Trust

Harris, Rolf b.1930, *River Don near Doncaster, South Yorkshire*, painted in Children's Ward and donated by the artist, 1985
Wood, John *Barnsley General Hospital, South Yorkshire*, unknown acquisition method

South Yorkshire Police

Fowler, Michael John b.1957, *Evening Harvest, Sandbeck, South Yorkshire*, gift, 2001, © the artist
Fowler, Michael John b.1957, *Tractor Ploughing a Field*, gift, 2001, © the artist

The Cooper Gallery

Asch, Pieter Jansz. van (attributed to) 1603–1678, *A Mountainous Landscape with Goats*, bequeathed by Samuel Joshua Cooper, 1913
Aznar y García, Francisco 1831–1911, *Guard Room*, bequeathed by Samuel Joshua Cooper, 1913
Baldwin, Samuel 1818–1891, *Village Gossips*, gift from the Fox family, 1934
Balfour, James Lawson 1870–1966, *Portrait of an Elderly Man*, gift from Sir Michael Sadler, 1957
Balfour, James Lawson 1870–1966, *Portrait of an Elderly Woman*, gift from Sir Michael Sadler, 1957
Banks, John Joseph *Yorkshire Moorland, near Whitby*, gift from the Fox family, 1934
Barnes, Edward Charles 1830–1890, *The Flower Girl*, gift from the Fox family, 1934
Barnes, Edward Charles 1830–1890 & **Weekes, Henry I** 1807–1877, *Cattle and Figures*, gift from the Fox family, 1934
Baron, Henri Charles Antoine 1816–1885, *Gathering Fruit*, bequeathed by Samuel Joshua Cooper, 1913
Baron, Henri Charles Antoine 1816–1885, *Girl with a Lamb*, bequeathed by Samuel Joshua Cooper, 1913
Baron, Henri Charles Antoine 1816–1885, *La lecture dans la campagne*, bequeathed by Samuel Joshua Cooper, 1913
Baron, Henri Charles Antoine 1816–1885, *Sancho Panza Recounting His Adventure*, bequeathed by Samuel Joshua Cooper, 1913
Barraud, Henry (circle of) 1811–1874, *A Woman and a Girl Riding in a Mountainous Landscape*, gift from the Fox family, 1934
Beechey, William (studio of) 1753–1839, *The Architect John Carr of York (1723–1807)*, bequeathed by Samuel Joshua Cooper, 1913
Bell, John Christopher 1823–1881, *Patridges in the Snow*, gift from the Fox family, 1934
Bell, John Christopher 1823–1881, *Red Grouse*, gift from the Fox family, 1934
Bompiani, Augusto 1852–1930, *Rocca di Papa, Rome*, bequeathed by Samuel Joshua Cooper, 1913
Bowman, Thomas Stanton 1845–after 1886, *Rustic Grief*, gift from the Fox family, 1934
Bredael, Peeter van (school of) 1629–1719, *The Vintage, Figures Celebrating the Wine Harvest*, bequeathed by Samuel Joshua Cooper, 1913
Breling, Heinrich 1849–1914, *Lady with a Dog*, bequeathed by Samuel Joshua Cooper, 1913
British (English) School 17th C, *Elizabeth I (1533–1603)*, bequeathed by Samuel Joshua Cooper, 1913
British (English) School 19th C, *Portrait of a Gentleman*, unknown acquisition method
British (English) School 19th C, *The Drinker*, bequeathed by Colonel Rowland Addy, 1978
British (English) School mid-20th C, *Colonel Rowland Addy (d.1963)*, bequeathed by the estate of Colonel Rowland Addy, 1978
British School 18th C, *A Naval Engagement*, bequeathed by Samuel Joshua Cooper, 1913
Buchser, Frank (attributed to) 1828–1890, *Charcoal Burners' Hut in the New Forest*, gift from the Fox family, 1934
Callow, John 1822–1878, *On the Mersey*, bequeathed by Samuel Joshua Cooper, 1913
Carmichael, John Wilson 1799–1868, *A German River Scene*, bequeathed by Samuel Joshua Cooper, 1913
Carse, Alexander (attributed to) c.1770–1843, *Tavern Scene with a Soldier*, bequeathed by Samuel Joshua Cooper, 1913
Cartier, Karl (attributed to) 1855–1925, *Cattle*, gift from the Fox family, 1934
Cattermole, George 1800–1868, *The Scribe*, bequeathed by Samuel Joshua Cooper, 1913
Champaigne, Philippe de (style of) 1602–1674, *Anne of Austria (1601–1666)*, bequeathed by Samuel Joshua Cooper, 1913
Chavet, Victor Joseph 1822–1906, *The Blonde*, bequeathed by Samuel Joshua Cooper, 1913
Cicéri, Eugène 1813–1890, *A*

Bavarian Lake with Fishing Boats, bequeathed by Samuel Joshua Cooper, 1913
Clare, George c.1830–c.1900, *Still Life of Various Fruit*, gift from the Fox family, 1934
Clare, George c.1830–c.1900, *Still Life with Fruit*, gift from the Fox family, 1934
Clough, Prunella 1919–1999, *Enclosed Landscape*, bequeathed by Charles Lindsay Sutherland, 2001, © estate of Prunella Clough 2012. All Rights Reserved DACS
Colkett, Samuel David 1806–1863, *A River Landscape with Figures on a Bridge*, gift from the Fox family, 1934
Colkett, Samuel David 1806–1863, *The Old Mill Stream*, gift from the Fox family, 1934
Cook, Charles Henry c.1830–1905, *An Irish Character*, gift from the Fox family, 1934
Cook, Charles Henry c.1830–1905, *Mr James Fox (d.1885)*, gift from the Fox family, 1934
Cook, Charles Henry c.1830–1905, *Mrs James Fox*, gift from the Fox family, 1934
Corot, Jean-Baptiste-Camille (style of) 1796–1875, *Women Fishing*, bequeathed by Samuel Joshua Cooper, 1913
Cot, Pierre Auguste 1837–1883, *The Beggar Girls*, gift from Mr and Mrs W. J. Lawrance, 1927
Cox, David the elder (circle of) 1783–1859, *River Landscape*, bequeathed by Samuel Joshua Cooper, 1913
Cranach, Lucas the elder (after) 1472–1553, *Christian II of Denmark (1481–1559)*, bequeathed by Samuel Joshua Cooper, 1913
Cuylenborch, Abraham van (attributed to) c.1610–1658, *The Raising of Lazarus*, bequeathed by Samuel Joshua Cooper, 1913
De Beaumont, Gustave 1851–1922, *A Sacrifice to Cupid*, bequeathed by Samuel Joshua Cooper, 1913
De Bergue, Tony-François 1820–1893, *Il fait la politesse*, bequeathed by Samuel Joshua Cooper, 1913
De Fleury, James Vivien de 1847–1902, *Coast Scene, Margate, Kent*, gift from the Fox family, 1934
De Fontenay, Léonard Alexis Daligé 1813–1892, *In the Grindelwald, Switzerland*, bequeathed by Samuel Joshua Cooper, 1913
De Léon y Escosura, Ignacio 1834–1901, *The Standard Bearer*, bequeathed by Samuel Joshua Cooper, 1913
de Penne, Charles Olivier 1831–1897, *Hounds with a Boar*, bequeathed by Samuel Joshua Cooper, 1913
Decamps, Alexandre-Gabriel (attributed to) 1803–1860, *Monkey Musicians*, bequeathed by Samuel Joshua Cooper, 1913
Decamps, Alexandre-Gabriel (attributed to) 1803–1860, *Monkey's Music Lesson*, bequeathed by Samuel Joshua Cooper, 1913
Decamps, Alexandre-Gabriel (attributed to) 1803–1860, *An Arab Boy with Donkeys*, bequeathed by Samuel Joshua Cooper, 1913
Decamps, Alexandre-Gabriel (attributed to) 1803–1860, *Le singe au miroir (The Monkey and the Mirror)*, bequeathed by Samuel Joshua Cooper, 1913
Delechaux, Marcelin 1821–1902, *The Meeting*, bequeathed by Samuel Joshua Cooper, 1913
Delort, Charles Edouard 1841–1895, *Girl with Bagpipes*, bequeathed by Samuel Joshua Cooper, 1913
Devedeux, Louis 1820–1874, *The Drawing Lesson*, bequeathed by Samuel Joshua Cooper, 1913
Diaz de la Peña, Narcisse Virgile 1808–1876, *Bas Breau, par le carrefour de Clair-Bois en la forêt de Fontainebleau, France*, bequeathed by Samuel Joshua Cooper, 1913
Dughet, Gaspard 1615–1675, *An Italianate River Landscape*, bequeathed by Colonel Rowland Addy, 1978
Dunlop, Ronald Ossory 1894–1973, *The Weir*, unknown acquisition method
Dupont, William Frederick active 19th C, *River Scene with Cattle*, gift from the Fox family, 1934
Earl, George (attributed to) 1824–1908, *A Terrier by a Rabbit Hole*, bequeathed by Colonel Rowland Addy, 1978
Elwell, Frederick William 1870–1958, *Winter Sunshine*, bequeathed by Colonel Rowland Addy, 1978
Fornara, Sallustro 1852–1922, *The Call to Breakfast*, bequeathed by Samuel Joshua Cooper, 1913
Frère, Charles Théodore 1814–1888, *Café de Galata, Constantinople*, bequeathed by Samuel Joshua Cooper, 1913
Furse, Charles Wellington 1868–1904, *Dr M. T. Sadler, MD*, gift from Sir Michael Sadler, 1957
Gérome, Jean-Léon 1824–1904, *Cardinal Valeane and the Cage of Torture*, bequeathed by Samuel Joshua Cooper, 1913
González, Bartolomé (attributed to) 1564–1627, *Christ Bearing the Cross with the Virgin Mary*, bequeathed by Samuel Joshua Cooper, 1913
Goyen, Jan van 1596–1656, *River Scene with a Tower*, bequeathed by Samuel Joshua Cooper, 1913
Granet, François-Marius 1775–1849, *A Chapel in a Monastery*, bequeathed by Samuel Joshua Cooper, 1913
Granet, François-Marius (attributed to) 1775–1849, *In the Cloisters*, bequeathed by Samuel Joshua Cooper, 1913
Grésely, Gabriel Gaspard 1712–1756, *Gourmandise (Trompe l'Oeil)*, bequeathed by Samuel Joshua Cooper, 1913
Grimshaw, John Atkinson 1836–1893, *A Wooded Valley*, bequeathed by Samuel Joshua Cooper, 1913
Guillemin, Alexandre Marie 1817–1880, *In the Pyrenees*, bequeathed by Samuel Joshua Cooper, 1913
Gysels, Peeter (attributed to) 1621–1691, *A Village Scene*, bequeathed by Samuel Joshua Cooper, 1913
Heath, Adrian 1920–1992, *Composition*, bequeathed by Charles Lindsay Sutherland, 2001, © the estate of Adrian Heath
Herring, John Frederick I 1795–1865, *Horses in a Landscape*, bequeathed by Samuel Joshua Cooper, 1913
Herring, John Frederick I 1795–1865, *The Brood Mare*, gift from the Fox family, 1934
Holbein, Hans the Younger (after) 1497/1498–1543, *Henry VIII (1491–1547)*, bequeathed by Samuel Joshua Cooper, 1913
Hold, Abel 1815–1896, *A Bird's Nest*, gift from the Fox family, 1934
Hold, Abel 1815–1896, *Mrs Tyas*, unknown acquisition method
Hold, Abel 1815–1896, *Peggy Airey (1759–1848)*, gift from the Fox family, 1934
Hold, Abel 1815–1896, *Watter Joe*, gift from the Fox family, 1934
Horemans, Jan Josef the younger 1714–1790, *A Tavern Scene*, bequeathed by Samuel Joshua Cooper, 1913
Huchtenburgh, Jan van 1647–1733, *A Country Skirmish*, bequeathed by Samuel Joshua Cooper, 1913
Huguet, Victor Pierre 1835–1902, *An Eastern Scene with Camels and Figures Resting in the Shade under Trees*, bequeathed by Samuel Joshua Cooper, 1913
Hulk, Abraham I 1813–1897, *Shipping off a Dutch Coast*, gift from the Fox family, 1934
Hunt, Alfred William 1830–1896, *Shadow of the Clouds*, bequeathed by Samuel Joshua Cooper, 1913
Huysmans, Jan Baptist (circle of) 1654–1716, *Italianate Landscape with Classical Ruins*, gift from the Fox family, 1934
Isabey, Eugène 1803–1886, *Hurricane before Saint Malo, France*, bequeathed by Samuel Joshua Cooper, 1913
Isabey, Eugène 1803–1886, *The Wreck*, bequeathed by Samuel Joshua Cooper, 1913
Isabey, Eugène 1803–1886, *Boats Leaving Shore*, bequeathed by Samuel Joshua Cooper, 1913
Isabey, Eugène 1803–1886, *The Entrance into Port*, bequeathed by Samuel Joshua Cooper, 1913
Isabey, Eugène 1803–1886, *Fishing Boats on a Beach*, bequeathed by Samuel Joshua Cooper, 1913
Isabey, Eugène 1803–1886, *Good Friday in the Middle Ages*, bequeathed by Samuel Joshua Cooper, 1913
Isabey, Eugène 1803–1886, *Une visite au château*, bequeathed by Samuel Joshua Cooper, 1913
Isabey, Eugène 1803–1886, *The Duel*, bequeathed by Samuel Joshua Cooper, 1913
Jongkind, Johan Barthold 1819–1891, *Coast Scene with Windmills*, bequeathed by Samuel Joshua Cooper, 1913
Kenning, N. W. active 20th C, *Mandolin*, unknown acquisition method
Ladbrooke, John Berney 1803–1879, *A Passing Storm*, gift from the Fox family, 1934
Ladbrooke, John Berney 1803–1879, *Spring Morning in the Park*, gift from the Fox family, 1934
Ladbrooke, John Berney 1803–1879, *Wooded Landscape with a Farm*, gift from the Fox family, 1934
Lefevre, Adolphe René 1834–1868, *Dans la taverne*, bequeathed by Samuel Joshua Cooper, 1913
Leighton, Frederic 1830–1896, *A Street in Lerici, Italy*, bequeathed by Samuel Joshua Cooper, 1913
Lejin, M. W. active 19th C, *The Performing Monkey*, gift from the Fox family, 1934
Lely, Peter (follower of) 1618–1680, *Louise Renée de Penancoët de Querouaille (1649–1734), Duchess of Portsmouth*, bequeathed by Samuel Joshua Cooper, 1913
Lepoittevin, Eugène Modeste Edmond 1806–1870, *A River Landscape*, bequeathed by Samuel Joshua Cooper, 1913
Leys, Hendrik (attributed to) 1815–1869, *Mary of Burgundy (1457–1482)*, bequeathed by Samuel Joshua Cooper, 1913
Linnell, John 1792–1882, *Evening*, bequeathed by Samuel Joshua Cooper, 1913
Long, John Kenneth 1924–2006, *Fitzwilliam Street, Barnsley, South Yorkshire*, unknown acquisition method, © the artist's estate
Long, John Kenneth 1924–2006, *Pigeon Flying at the Red Lion, Worsbrough, South Yorkshire*, unknown acquisition method, © the artist's estate
Long, John Kenneth 1924–2006, *Winter Market*, unknown acquisition method, © the artist's estate
Luny, Thomas (attributed to) 1759–1837, *Fisherfolk Repairing Boats on a Beach*, bequeathed by Colonel Rowland Addy, 1978
Mander, William Henry (circle of) 1850–1922, *Autumn*, gift from the Fox family, 1934
Martini, Salvatore 1823–1882, *On Guard*, bequeathed by Samuel Joshua Cooper, 1913
Meadows, Arthur Joseph 1843–1907, *Palazzo Rezzonico, Venice*, bequeathed by Samuel Joshua Cooper, 1913
Meadows, Arthur Joseph 1843–1907, *San Nicolò, Venice*, bequeathed by Samuel Joshua Cooper, 1913
Miereveld, Michiel Jansz. van (circle of) 1567–1641, *Portrait of a Gentleman Wearing the Order of the Golden Fleece*, bequeathed by Samuel Joshua Cooper, 1913
Mols, John Henry active 1880–c.1890, *The Descent from the Cross* (copy after Peter Paul Rubens), bequeathed by Samuel Joshua Cooper, 1913
Moltino, Francis (attributed to) 1818–1872, *Oberweisel on the Rhine, Germany*, bequeathed by Colonel Rowland Addy, 1978
Moore, Ernest 1865–1940, *Evening Star*, unknown acquisition method
Moore, Madeline b.1869, *Dancing Children* (after Giacomo Mantegazza), bequeathed by Samuel Joshua Cooper, 1913
Moore, Madeline b.1869, *Doge Loredan (1436–1521)* (after Giovanni Bellini), bequeathed by Samuel Joshua Cooper, 1913
Moore, Madeline b.1869, *Samuel Joshua Cooper (1830–1913)*, bequeathed by the sitter, 1913
Moore, Madeline b.1869, *Mrs Fanny Cooper*, bequeathed by Samuel Joshua Cooper, 1913
Moore, Madeline b.1869, *Samuel Joshua Cooper (1830–1913)*, bequeathed by the sitter, 1913
Morgenstern, Carl Ernst 1847–1928, *Landscape with Peasants by a Pond*, bequeathed by Samuel Joshua Cooper, 1913
Murant, Emanuel 1622–1700, *Woman at a Village Well*, bequeathed by Samuel Joshua Cooper, 1913
Netscher, Caspar (circle of) 1639–1684, *Sarah Jennings (1660–1744), Duchess of Marlborough*, bequeathed by Samuel Joshua Cooper, 1913
Netscher, Caspar (follower of) 1639–1684, *Portrait of a Lady*, bequeathed by Samuel Joshua Cooper, 1913
Netscher, Caspar (follower of) 1639–1684, *Portrait of a Lady*, bequeathed by Samuel Joshua Cooper, 1913
Niemann, Edmund John 1813–1876, *Sandpits near London*, gift from the Fox family, 1934
Parris, Edmund Thomas 1793–1873, *The Young Queen Victoria (1819–1901)*, gift from the Fox family, 1934
Pasini, Alberto 1826–1899, *The Grimani Palace, Venice, Italy*, bequeathed by Samuel Joshua Cooper, 1913
Pasini, Alberto 1826–1899, *The Bridge of the Apostles, Venice, Italy*, bequeathed by Samuel Joshua Cooper, 1913
Pasmore, John Frederick 1820–1881, *The Best of Friends*, gift from the Fox family, 1934
Pearce, Charles Maresco 1874–1964, *A Street in Menton, France*, gift from Sir Michael Sadler, 1957
Peel, James 1811–1906, *Wooded Landscape with Figures and Sheep*,

gift from the Fox family, 1934
Plassan, Antoine Emile 1817–1903, *Child with Fruit*, bequeathed by Samuel Joshua Cooper, 1913
Plassan, Antoine Emile 1817–1903, *The Toilet*, bequeathed by Samuel Joshua Cooper, 1913
Pritchett, Edward active c.1828–1879, *Piazza San Marco, Venice*, bequeathed by Colonel Rowland Addy, 1978
Probst, Carl 1854–1924, *Leaving the Pew*, bequeathed by Samuel Joshua Cooper, 1913
Rhodes, Joseph 1782–1854, *Extensive Landscape with a Viaduct*, bequeathed by Samuel Joshua Cooper, 1913
Rhodes, Joseph 1782–1854, *Richmond Castle, Yorkshire*, bequeathed by Samuel Joshua Cooper, 1913
Ribera, Jusepe de (after) 1591–1652, *Portrait of a Gentleman*, bequeathed by Samuel Joshua Cooper, 1913
Ritchie, John active 1855–1897 & **Mote, George William** 1832–1909, *Greenwich Park, London*, gift from the Fox family, 1934
Roberts, David 1796–1864, *Antwerp Cathedral, Belgium*, gift from F. G. Senior
Roberts, David 1796–1864, *The Château at Chambord, France*, bequeathed by Samuel Joshua Cooper, 1913
Rombouts, Salomon c.1652–c.1702, *A River Scene with Figures*, bequeathed by Samuel Joshua Cooper, 1913
Roybet, Ferdinand 1840–1920, *Man with a Guitar*, bequeathed by Samuel Joshua Cooper, 1913
Roybet, Ferdinand 1840–1920, *Head of a Boy*, bequeathed by Samuel Joshua Cooper, 1913
Rubens, Peter Paul (school of) 1577–1640, *The Reception of St Bavo, the Patron Saint of Ghent*, bequeathed by Samuel Joshua Cooper, 1913
Rumley, Elizabeth active 1851–1876, *Fruit*, gift from the Fox family, 1934
Sabatini, I. active late 19th C–early 20th C, *A Lady Holding a Book*, gift from H. B. Lawrence, before 1935
Santoro, Rubens 1859–1942, *A Canal Scene, Venice*, bequeathed by Samuel Joshua Cooper, 1913
Santoro, Rubens 1859–1942, *Verona*, bequeathed by Samuel Joshua Cooper, 1913
Savery, Roelandt (attributed to) 1576–1639, *Wooded Landscape with a Bridge*, bequeathed by Samuel Joshua Cooper, 1913
Schirmer, Johann Wilhelm 1807–1863, *A Windy Day*, bequeathed by Samuel Joshua Cooper, 1913
Schoenmakers, Johannes Pietersz. 1755–1842, *The Oyster Seller in Town*, bequeathed by Samuel Joshua Cooper, 1913
Schoevaerdts, Mathys (circle of) c.1665–1723, *A Landscape with Peasants on a Bridge*, gift from the Fox family, 1934
Schoevaerdts, Mathys (circle of) c.1665–1723, *River Landscape with Peasants on a Path*, gift from the Fox family, 1934
Schwanfelder, Charles Henry 1774–1837, *Landscape with Figures*, bequeathed by Samuel Joshua Cooper, 1913
Sellaer, Vincent c.1500–c.1589, *The Holy Family with Saints Elizabeth, Catherine and John the Baptist*, bequeathed by Samuel Joshua Cooper, 1913
Serres, Antony 1828–1898, *La procession de la couronne d'épines*, bequeathed by Samuel Joshua Cooper, 1913
Shayer, Charles Waller (circle of) 1826–1914 & **Shayer, Henry Thring (circle of)** 1825–1894, *Landscape with Cattle*, gift from the Fox family, 1934
Somer, Paulus van I (attributed to) 1576–1621, *Portrait of an Unknown Lady*, bequeathed by Samuel Joshua Cooper, 1913
Stademann, Adolf 1824–1895, *A Frozen River Scene*, bequeathed by Samuel Joshua Cooper, 1913
Stubbs, Ralph (attributed to) 1824–1879, *A Winter Landscape*, gift from the Fox family, 1934
Swarbreck, Samuel Dukinfield c.1799–1863, *A Church Interior with a Woman Reading*, bequeathed by Samuel Joshua Cooper, 1913
Swift, Richard b.1918, *Winter*, unknown acquisition method
Thienon, Louis Désireé 1812–after 1884, *The Doge's Palace, Venice*, gift from the Fox family, 1934
Tinkler, W. A. *The Doge's Palace, Venice*, gift from the Fox family, 1934
Tironi, Francesco (follower of) c.1745–1797, *The Colleoni Monument, Venice*, bequeathed by Samuel Joshua Cooper, 1913
Troyon, Constant 1810–1865, *A Flock of Sheep*, bequeathed by Samuel Joshua Cooper, 1913
Turck, Eliza 1832–after 1901, *The Berkshire Boy*, gift from the Fox family, 1934
Uden, Lucas van 1595–1672, *A River Scene*, bequeathed by Samuel Joshua Cooper, 1913
Underhill, William active 1848–1871, *Children in a Hayfield*, bequeathed by Samuel Joshua Cooper, 1913
Velázquez, Diego (after) 1599–1660, *Philip IV of Spain (1605–1665)*, bequeathed by Samuel Joshua Cooper, 1913
Vinea, Francesco 1845–1902, *Page at a Window*, bequeathed by Samuel Joshua Cooper, 1913
Viney, James active 19th C, *Hilly River Landscape with Boys Fishing*, bequeathed by Colonel Rowland Addy, 1978
Watts, Frederick William 1800–1870, *A Village Scene with Figures*, gift from the Fox family, 1934
Watts, Frederick William 1800–1870, *Landscape with Cattle*, bequeathed by Samuel Joshua Cooper, 1913
Whittaker, Malcolm b.1937, *Still Life*, unknown acquisition method, © the artist
Wilson, Richard (after) 1712/1713–1782, *The White Monk*, gift from the Fox family, 1934
Wilson, Richard (attributed to) 1712/1713–1782, *Dolbadern Castle and Llanberis Lake, Wales*, bequeathed by Colonel Rowland Addy, 1978
Wright, John Michael (school of) 1617–1694, *Portrait of a Gentleman*, bequeathed by Samuel Joshua Cooper, 1913
Zeeman, Reinier c.1623–c.1668, *Shipping in an Estuary*, bequeathed by Samuel Joshua Cooper, 1913

English Heritage, Brodsworth Hall

Antonissen, Henricus Josephus 1737–1794, *Landscape with a Cowherd*, purchased, as part of the contents of Brodsworth Hall, from Pamela Williams by the National Heritage Memorial Fund and transferred to English Heritage, 1990
Backhuysen, Ludolf I 1630–1708 & **Dubbels, Hendrik Jacobsz.** 1620/1621–1676, *An Embarkation Scene*, purchased, as part of the contents of Brodsworth Hall, from Pamela Williams by the National Heritage Memorial Fund and transferred to English Heritage, 1990
Balen, Hendrik van I (follower of) 1575–1632, *Bacchus Asleep*, purchased, as part of the contents of Brodsworth Hall, from Pamela Williams by the National Heritage Memorial Fund and transferred to English Heritage, 1990
Barenger, James 1780–after 1831, *Bay Stallion in a Stable*, purchased, as part of the contents of Brodsworth Hall, from Pamela Williams by the National Heritage Memorial Fund and transferred to English Heritage, 1990
Barenger, James 1780–after 1831, *Dark Bay Stallion*, purchased, as part of the contents of Brodsworth Hall, from Pamela Williams by the National Heritage Memorial Fund and transferred to English Heritage, 1990
Barenger, James 1780–after 1831, *Bay Cob*, purchased, as part of the contents of Brodsworth Hall, from Pamela Williams by the National Heritage Memorial Fund and transferred to English Heritage, 1990
Barenger, James 1780–after 1831, *Light Bay Mare*, purchased, as part of the contents of Brodsworth Hall, from Pamela Williams by the National Heritage Memorial Fund and transferred to English Heritage, 1990
Barenger, James 1780–after 1831, *Racehorse with Trainers*, purchased, as part of the contents of Brodsworth Hall, from Pamela Williams by the National Heritage Memorial Fund and transferred to English Heritage, 1990
Barenger, James 1780–after 1831, *Still Life with a Mallard*, purchased, as part of the contents of Brodsworth Hall, from Pamela Williams by the National Heritage Memorial Fund and transferred to English Heritage, 1990
Barenger, James 1780–after 1831, *The Theobald Stud*, purchased, as part of the contents of Brodsworth Hall, from Pamela Williams by the National Heritage Memorial Fund and transferred to English Heritage, 1990
Boucher, François (after) 1703–1770, *Venus and Cupid*, purchased, as part of the contents of Brodsworth Hall, from Pamela Williams by the National Heritage Memorial Fund and transferred to English Heritage, 1990
Camphuysen, Jochem Govertz. (attributed to) 1601–1659, *Travellers in a Landscape*, purchased, as part of the contents of Brodsworth Hall, from Pamela Williams by the National Heritage Memorial Fund and transferred to English Heritage, 1990
Camphuysen, Jochem Govertz. (attributed to) 1601–1659, *Travellers in a Landscape*, purchased, as part of the contents of Brodsworth Hall, from Pamela Williams by the National Heritage Memorial Fund and transferred to English Heritage, 1990
Carpenter, Margaret Sarah 1793–1872, *Miss Theobald* (probably Frances Jane, 1825–1841), purchased, as part of the contents of Brodsworth Hall, from Pamela Williams by the National Heritage Memorial Fund and transferred to English Heritage, 1990
Carpenter, Margaret Sarah 1793–1872, *Mrs Charles Sabine Thellusson (1828–1883), née Georgiana Theobald*, purchased, as part of the contents of Brodsworth Hall, from Pamela Williams by the National Heritage Memorial Fund and transferred to English Heritage, 1990
Cignani, Carlo (after) 1628–1719, *Roman Charity: Cimon and Pero*, purchased, as part of the contents of Brodsworth Hall, from Pamela Williams by the National Heritage Memorial Fund and transferred to English Heritage, 1990
Cooper, Abraham 1787–1868, *The Racehorse, 'Camel'*, purchased, as part of the contents of Brodsworth Hall, from Pamela Williams by the National Heritage Memorial Fund and transferred to English Heritage, 1990
Corbould, Alfred (attributed to) c.1821–1874, *Charles Sabine Augustus Thellusson (1822–1885), as Captain, 12th Royal Lancers*, purchased, as part of the contents of Brodsworth Hall, from Pamela Williams by the National Heritage Memorial Fund and transferred to English Heritage, 1990
Donny, Désiré 1798–1861, *Interior with Figures*, purchased, as part of the contents of Brodsworth Hall, from Pamela Williams by the National Heritage Memorial Fund and transferred to English Heritage, 1990
Elmer, Stephen (style of) c.1714–1796, *Still Life with a Pheasant*, purchased, as part of the contents of Brodsworth Hall, from Pamela Williams by the National Heritage Memorial Fund and transferred to English Heritage, 1990
Flemish School *The Four Seasons: Spring*, purchased at auction, 2001
Flemish School *The Four Seasons: Summer*, purchased at auction, 2001
Flemish School *The Four Seasons: Autumn*, purchased at auction, 2001
Flemish School *The Four Seasons: Winter*, purchased at auction, 2001
Halgate, W. *Fenland, Cambridgeshire*, gift from Pamela Williams with the remaining contents of Brodsworth Hall, 1990
Hall, Harry 1814–1896, *'Rataplan'*, purchased, as part of the contents of Brodsworth Hall, from Pamela Williams by the National Heritage Memorial Fund and transferred to English Heritage, 1990
Hardman, John active 1799–1846, *Horses in a Landscape*, purchased, as part of the contents of Brodsworth Hall, from Pamela Williams by the National Heritage Memorial Fund and transferred to English Heritage, 1990
Herring, John Frederick I 1795–1865, *Bay Stallion*, purchased, as part of the contents of Brodsworth Hall, from Pamela Williams by the National Heritage Memorial Fund and transferred to English Heritage, 1990
Herring, John Frederick I 1795–1865, *'Rockingham'*, purchased, as part of the contents of Brodsworth Hall, from Pamela Williams by the National Heritage Memorial Fund and transferred to English Heritage, 1990
Humphris, William Henry 1850–c.1916, *Bridge and Lakeside*, gift from Pamela Williams with the remaining contents of Brodsworth Hall, 1990
Huysum, Jan van (after) 1682–1749, *Flowers in a Terracotta Vase with Fruit and a Bird's Nest*, purchased, as part of the contents of Brodsworth Hall, from Pamela Williams by the National Heritage Memorial Fund and transferred to English Heritage, 1990
Jacomb-Hood, George Percy 1857–1929, *Peter Thellusson (1850–1899), on Board the Yacht, 'Albion'*, purchased, as part of the contents

of Brodsworth Hall, from Pamela Williams by the National Heritage Memorial Fund and transferred to English Heritage, 1990
Joseph, George Francis 1764–1846, *Head and Shoulders of a Man* (probably William Theobald, 1795–1850), gift from Pamela Williams with the remaining contents of Brodsworth Hall, 1990
Joseph, George Francis 1764–1846, *John Theobald (1766–1849)*, purchased, as part of the contents of Brodsworth Hall, from Pamela Williams by the National Heritage Memorial Fund and transferred to English Heritage, 1990
Largillière, Nicolas de 1656–1746, *Madame Isaac de Thellusson, née Sarah Le Boullenger (1700–1770)*, purchased, as part of the contents of Brodsworth Hall, from Pamela Williams by the National Heritage Memorial Fund and transferred to English Heritage, 1990
Lawrence, Thomas 1769–1830, *Mrs Charles Thellusson, née Sabine Robarts (1775–1814), and Her Son, Charles Thellusson (1797–1856)*, purchased, as part of the contents of Brodsworth Hall, from Pamela Williams by the National Heritage Memorial Fund and transferred to English Heritage, 1990
Loutherbourg, Philip James de (after) 1740–1812, *A Summer's Evening with a View of a Public Road*, purchased, as part of the contents of Brodsworth Hall, from Pamela Williams by the National Heritage Memorial Fund and transferred to English Heritage, 1990
Loutherbourg, Philip James de (after) 1740–1812, *A Winter Morning with a Party Skating*, purchased, as part of the contents of Brodsworth Hall, from Pamela Williams by the National Heritage Memorial Fund and transferred to English Heritage, 1990
Marshall, William active c.1800–1840, *Bay Stallion in a Stable*, purchased, as part of the contents of Brodsworth Hall, from Pamela Williams by the National Heritage Memorial Fund and transferred to English Heritage, 1990
Momper, Frans de (attributed to) 1603–1660, *Travellers Passing through a Village*, purchased from the Trustees of the estate of R. S. Williams, 2004
Neer, Aert van der 1603–1677, *A Canal in a Dutch Town by Moonlight*, purchased, as part of the contents of Brodsworth Hall, from Pamela Williams by the National Heritage Memorial Fund and transferred to English Heritage, 1990
Opie, John (style of) 1761–1807 or **Wheatley, Francis (style of)** 1747–1801, 1761–1807, *Girl Holding a Silver Salver*, purchased, as part of the contents of Brodsworth Hall, from Pamela Williams by the National Heritage Memorial Fund and transferred to English Heritage, 1990
Opie, John (style of) 1761–1807 or **Wheatley, Francis (style of)** 1747–1801, *Girl with a Dog and Fruit*, purchased, as part of the contents of Brodsworth Hall, from Pamela Williams by the National Heritage Memorial Fund and transferred to English Heritage, 1990
Paul, John 1804–1887, *Bay Stallion*, purchased, as part of the contents of Brodsworth Hall, from Pamela Williams by the National Heritage Memorial Fund and transferred to English Heritage, 1990
Perry, William J. active 1861–1871, *Blackberrying*, purchased, as part of the contents of Brodsworth Hall, from Pamela Williams by the National Heritage Memorial Fund and transferred to English Heritage, 1990
Perry, William J. active 1861–1871, *The Bird's Nest*, purchased, as part of the contents of Brodsworth Hall, from Pamela Williams by the National Heritage Memorial Fund and transferred to English Heritage, 1990
Perry, William J. active 1861–1871, *The Old Carthorse*, purchased, as part of the contents of Brodsworth Hall, from Pamela Williams by the National Heritage Memorial Fund and transferred to English Heritage, 1990
Rembrandt van Rijn (after) 1606–1669, *A Seated Man with a Stick*, purchased, as part of the contents of Brodsworth Hall, from Pamela Williams by the National Heritage Memorial Fund and transferred to English Heritage, 1990
Rembrandt van Rijn (after) 1606–1669, *Portrait of a Man*, purchased, as part of the contents of Brodsworth Hall, from Pamela Williams by the National Heritage Memorial Fund and transferred to English Heritage, 1990
Rocca, Michele (attributed to) 1675–1751, *Leda and the Swan*, purchased, as part of the contents of Brodsworth Hall, from Pamela Williams by the National Heritage Memorial Fund and transferred to English Heritage, 1990
Schumann, Wilhelm active 1830–1844, *A Music Party*, purchased, as part of the contents of Brodsworth Hall, from Pamela Williams by the National Heritage Memorial Fund and transferred to English Heritage, 1990
Short, Betty active c.1960–1988, *The Old Cedar Tree at Brodsworth Hall*, gift from Pamela Williams with the remaining contents of Brodsworth Hall, 1990
Solomons, Joel *John Theobald (b.1827), Aged 8 1/2 Years*, purchased, as part of the contents of Brodsworth Hall, from Pamela Williams by the National Heritage Memorial Fund and transferred to English Heritage, 1990
Teniers, David II (after) 1610–1690, *Peasants in an Interior*, purchased, as part of the contents of Brodsworth Hall, from Pamela Williams by the National Heritage Memorial Fund and transferred to English Heritage, 1990
Thellusson, Aline 1856–1880, *St Bernard with Game*, purchased, as part of the contents of Brodsworth Hall, from Pamela Williams by the National Heritage Memorial Fund and transferred to English Heritage, 1990
Thellusson, Aline 1856–1880, *Spaniel with a Pheasant*, purchased, as part of the contents of Brodsworth Hall, from Pamela Williams by the National Heritage Memorial Fund and transferred to English Heritage, 1990
Thellusson, Aline 1856–1880, *Winter Scene with a Shepherd and Sheep*, purchased, as part of the contents of Brodsworth Hall, from Pamela Williams by the National Heritage Memorial Fund and transferred to English Heritage, 1990
Thellusson, Aline 1856–1880, *Cattle Crossing a River with a Drover*, purchased, as part of the contents of Brodsworth Hall, from Pamela Williams by the National Heritage Memorial Fund and transferred to English Heritage, 1990
Thellusson, Aline (attributed to) 1856–1880, *A Music Party* (after Wilhelm Schumann), gift from Pamela Williams with the remaining contents of Brodsworth Hall, 1990
Thellusson, Aline (attributed to) 1856–1880, *Man Playing a Violin* (copy of a detail from 'A Music Party' by Wilhelm Schumann), gift from Pamela Williams with the remaining contents of Brodsworth Hall, 1990
Thellusson, Aline (attributed to) 1856–1880, *A Black Dog*, purchased, as part of the contents of Brodsworth Hall, from Pamela Williams by the National Heritage Memorial Fund and transferred to English Heritage, 1990
Thellusson, Aline (attributed to) 1856–1880, *A Fox in a Kennel with Puppies*, gift from Pamela Williams with the remaining contents of Brodsworth Hall, 1990
Thellusson, Aline (attributed to) 1856–1880, *Charles Sabine Augustus Thellusson (c.1822–1885)*, gift from Pamela Williams with the remaining contents of Brodsworth Hall, 1990
Thellusson, Aline (attributed to) 1856–1880, *Sketch of a Dog's Head*, gift from Pamela Williams with the remaining contents of Brodsworth Hall, 1990
Thellusson, Aline (attributed to) 1856–1880, *Sketch of a Female Head*, purchased, as part of the contents of Brodsworth Hall, from Pamela Williams by the National Heritage Memorial Fund and transferred to English Heritage, 1990
Thellusson, Aline (attributed to) 1856–1880, *Still Life: Flowers* (recto), gift from Pamela Williams with the remaining contents of Brodsworth Hall, 1990
Thellusson, Aline (attributed to) 1856–1880, *Sketch of Cows and Horses* (verso), purchased, as part of the contents of Brodsworth Hall, from Pamela Williams by the National Heritage Memorial Fund and transferred to English Heritage, 1990
Thellusson, Aline (attributed to) 1856–1880, *Two Dogs, 'Juliet' and 'Faust'*, purchased, as part of the contents of Brodsworth Hall, from Pamela Williams by the National Heritage Memorial Fund and transferred to English Heritage, 1990
Thellusson, Aline (attributed to) 1856–1880, *White Dog with Brown Markings*, purchased, as part of the contents of Brodsworth Hall, from Pamela Williams by the National Heritage Memorial Fund and transferred to English Heritage, 1990
Thellusson, Aline (attributed to) 1856–1880, *White Dog with Brown Markings*, purchased, as part of the contents of Brodsworth Hall, from Pamela Williams by the National Heritage Memorial Fund and transferred to English Heritage, 1990
Thellusson, Herbert 1854–1903, *A Dog*, purchased, as part of the contents of Brodsworth Hall, from Pamela Williams by the National Heritage Memorial Fund and transferred to English Heritage, 1990
Thellusson, Aline (attributed to) 1856–1880 or **Thellusson, Herbert (attributed to)** 1854–1903, *A Brown Dog with a Collar*, purchased, as part of the contents of Brodsworth Hall, from Pamela Williams by the National Heritage Memorial Fund and transferred to English Heritage, 1990
Thellusson, Herbert 1854–1903, *A Dog*, purchased, as part of the contents of Brodsworth Hall, from Pamela Williams by the National Heritage Memorial Fund and transferred to English Heritage, 1990
Trood, William Henry Hamilton 1848–1899, *'Coup'*, purchased, as part of the contents of Brodsworth Hall, from Pamela Williams by the National Heritage Memorial Fund and transferred to English Heritage, 1990
Trood, William Henry Hamilton 1848–1899, *St Bernard Dog*, purchased, as part of the contents of Brodsworth Hall, from Pamela Williams by the National Heritage Memorial Fund and transferred to English Heritage, 1990
Trood, William Henry Hamilton 1848–1899, *Sketch of 'Nell'*, purchased, as part of the contents of Brodsworth Hall, from Pamela Williams by the National Heritage Memorial Fund and transferred to English Heritage, 1990
Trood, William Henry Hamilton 1848–1899, *'Prairie Prince'*, purchased, as part of the contents of Brodsworth Hall, from Pamela Williams by the National Heritage Memorial Fund and transferred to English Heritage, 1990
unknown artist *Sir Nicholas Watts (1675–1726), of Shanks House, Cucklington, Somerset*, purchased, as part of the contents of Brodsworth Hall, from Pamela Williams by the National Heritage Memorial Fund and transferred to English Heritage, 1990
unknown artist *Portrait of an Unknown Lady*, purchased, as part of the contents of Brodsworth Hall, from Pamela Williams by the National Heritage Memorial Fund and transferred to English Heritage, 1990
unknown artist *Horse in a Landscape*, purchased, as part of the contents of Brodsworth Hall, from Pamela Williams by the National Heritage Memorial Fund and transferred to English Heritage, 1990
unknown artist *Black Stallion Outside a Stable*, purchased, as part of the contents of Brodsworth Hall, from Pamela Williams by the National Heritage Memorial Fund and transferred to English Heritage, 1990
unknown artist *The Yacht, 'Tartar', in Harbour at Dartmouth, Devon*, purchased, as part of the contents of Brodsworth Hall, from Pamela Williams by the National Heritage Memorial Fund and transferred to English Heritage, 1990
unknown artist *The Yacht, 'Rosalind'*, purchased, as part of the contents of Brodsworth Hall, from Pamela Williams by the National Heritage Memorial Fund and transferred to English Heritage, 1990
unknown artist *The Yacht, 'Tartar'*, purchased, as part of the contents of Brodsworth Hall, from Pamela Williams by the National Heritage Memorial Fund and transferred to English Heritage, 1990
unknown artist *Can-Can Dancers*, gift from Pamela Williams with the remaining contents of Brodsworth Hall, 1990
unknown artist 20th C, *Houses*, gift from Pamela Williams with the remaining contents of Brodsworth Hall, 1990
unknown artist 20th C, *Red and Orange Flowers*, gift from Pamela Williams with the remaining contents of Brodsworth Hall, 1990
unknown artist 20th C, *Sketch of a Male Head*, gift from Pamela Williams with the remaining contents of Brodsworth Hall, 1990

unknown artist 20th C, *Village Scene*, gift from Pamela Williams with the remaining contents of Brodsworth Hall, 1990
unknown artist 20th C, *Watering Can and Objects*, gift from Pamela Williams with the remaining contents of Brodsworth Hall, 1990
unknown artist *Boat on Shore*, gift from Pamela Williams with the remaining contents of Brodsworth Hall, 1990
unknown artist *Coastal Scene*, gift from Pamela Williams with the remaining contents of Brodsworth Hall, 1990
unknown artist *Nymph Bathing*, gift from Pamela Williams with the remaining contents of Brodsworth Hall, 1990
unknown artist *Nymph on a Poppy*, gift from Pamela Williams with the remaining contents of Brodsworth Hall, 1990
unknown artist *Nymph Posing on Daisies*, gift from Pamela Williams with the remaining contents of Brodsworth Hall, 1990
unknown artist *Nymph with Lillies*, gift from Pamela Williams with the remaining contents of Brodsworth Hall, 1990
Walls, Carol Ann *Brodsworth Hall*, gift from Pamela Williams with the remaining contents of Brodsworth Hall, 1990
Ward, James 1769–1859, *'Walton'*, purchased, as part of the contents of Brodsworth Hall, from Pamela Williams by the National Heritage Memorial Fund and transferred to English Heritage, 1990
Ward, James 1769–1859, *'Haphazard'*, purchased, as part of the contents of Brodsworth Hall, from Pamela Williams by the National Heritage Memorial Fund and transferred to English Heritage, 1990
Ward, James 1769–1859, *'Dr Syntax'*, purchased, as part of the contents of Brodsworth Hall, from Pamela Williams by the National Heritage Memorial Fund and transferred to English Heritage, 1990
Ward, James 1769–1859, *Mrs William Theobald, née Sarah Cooke (1795–1867)*, purchased, as part of the contents of Brodsworth Hall, from Pamela Williams by the National Heritage Memorial Fund and transferred to English Heritage, 1990
Ward, James 1769–1859, *'Rockingham', with His Owner, John Theobald, and Jockey, Jem Robinson*, purchased, as part of the contents of Brodsworth Hall, from Pamela Williams by the National Heritage Memorial Fund and transferred to English Heritage, 1990
Webb, William 1780–1846, *Bay Stallion in a Stable*, purchased, as part of the contents of Brodsworth Hall, from Pamela Williams by the National Heritage Memorial Fund and transferred to English Heritage, 1990
West, Reginald Cecil b.1865, *Cornwall*, purchased, as part of the contents of Brodsworth Hall, from Pamela Williams by the National Heritage Memorial Fund and transferred to English Heritage, 1990
Williams, R. active c.1960–1988, *Tawny Owl*, gift from Pamela Williams with the remaining contents of Brodsworth Hall, 1990

Barnsley Museum and Heritage Service

Amos, Glynn *Abstract Landscape*, unknown acquisition method
Asselyn, Jan after 1610–1652, *Landscape with a Bridge in the Italian Countryside*, acquired through the William Harvey Bequest and the National Art Collections Fund, 2003
Backhuysen, Ludolf I 1630–1708, *Shipping: A Fresh Breeze*, acquired through the William Harvey Bequest and the National Art Collections Fund, 2003
Bardwell, Thomas (attributed to) 1704–1767, *Wentworth Castle Estate, Barnsley, South Yorkshire*, on loan from the Wentworth Castle Estate
Bardwell, Thomas (attributed to) 1704–1767, *Wentworth Castle Estate, Barnsley, South Yorkshire*, on loan from the Wentworth Castle Estate
Begeyn, Abraham 1637/1638–1697, *Landscape with Goats*, acquired through the William Harvey Bequest and the National Art Collections Fund, 2003
Berchem, Nicolaes 1620–1683, *Italianate Landscape with Peasants Fording a Brook*, acquired through the William Harvey Bequest and the National Art Collections Fund, 2003
Berchem, Nicolaes 1620–1683, *Studies of a Horse's Head*, acquired through the William Harvey Bequest and the National Art Collections Fund, 2003
Berchem, Nicolaes 1620–1683, *Studies of Cows' Heads*, acquired through the William Harvey Bequest and the National Art Collections Fund, 2003
Blow, Sandra 1925–2006, *Creation*, gift from the Tate Galleries' Allocation of Works, 1961, © the artist's estate
Blyenberch, Abraham van (after) 1575–1624, *Ben Jonson*, acquired through the William Harvey Bequest and the National Art Collections Fund, 2003
Bone, Henry 1755–1834, *Blue Boy* (copy after Thomas Gainsborough), acquired through the William Harvey Bequest and the National Art Collections Fund, 2003
Both, Andries Dirksz. 1611/1612–1641 & **Both, Jan** c.1618–1652, *Landscape with a Tower and Figures by a Lake*, acquired through the William Harvey Bequest and the National Art Collections Fund, 2003
Both, Andries Dirksz. 1611/1612–1641 & **Both, Jan** c.1618–1652, *Landscape with Figures, Evening*, acquired through the William Harvey Bequest and the National Art Collections Fund, 2003
Boursse, Esaias 1631–1672, *Domestic Interior with Still Life*, acquired through the William Harvey Bequest and the National Art Collections Fund, 2003
British (English) School *Philip Stanhope (1673–1726), 3rd Earl of Chesterfield, with His Wife, Lady Elizabeth Savile, Children and Nubian Slave*, purchased from the Beningborough Hall sale, 1958
British (English) School mid-18th C, *Cawthorne Church, South Yorkshire, from the Park*, commissioned
British (English) School, *Mary Winifred Pulleine (1763–after 1787), and Her Son*, on loan from the Fraser Family
Bury, Brenda b.1932, *Alderman A. E. McVie, JP and Mrs McVie*, gift from Alderman McVie, 1955, © the artist, www.brendabury.com
Canaletto 1697–1768, *Capriccio: A Colonnade Opening onto the Courtyard of a Palace*, acquired through the William Harvey Bequest and the National Art Collections Fund, 2003
Cappelle, Jan van de (after) c.1624–1679, *River Scene with Ships Becalmed*, acquired through the William Harvey Bequest and the National Art Collections Fund, 2003
Constable, John 1776–1837, *Mrs Tuder*, purchased from the J. Leger and Sons Galleries, 1959
Coques, Gonzales c.1614–1684, *Portrait of a Lady in a Blue Satin Dress*, acquired through the William Harvey Bequest and the National Art Collections Fund, 2003
Coques, Gonzales c.1614–1684, *Portrait of an Officer in Armour*, acquired through the William Harvey Bequest and the National Art Collections Fund, 2003
Corneille de Lyon, Claude (attributed to) 1510–c.1574, *Sir John Cheke (1514–1557)*, bequeathed by the Alexander Bequest and the National Art Collections Fund, 1994–1995
Cuyp, Aelbert (circle of) 1620–1691, *River Scene with Town and Shipping*, acquired through the William Harvey Bequest and the National Art Collections Fund, 2003
Dubbels, Hendrik Jacobsz. 1620/1621–1676, *Calm*, acquired through the William Harvey Bequest and the National Art Collections Fund, 2003
Dutch School 17th C, *Still Life with Dead Game*, commissioned
Dyck, Anthony van (style of) 1599–1641, *Virgin and Child*, acquired through the William Harvey Bequest and the National Art Collections Fund, 2003
Everdingen, Cesar Boetius van c.1606–1678, *Boy Holding an Apple*, acquired through the William Harvey Bequest and the National Art Collections Fund, 2003
Ferguson, William Gowe c.1632/1633–c.1695, *Still Life*, gift from the National Art Collections Fund, 1959
Ferguson, William Gowe 1632–1695, *Still Life*, gift from the National Art Collections Fund, 1959
Greuze, Jean-Baptiste 1725–1805, *L'écolier*, acquired through the William Harvey Bequest and the National Art Collections Fund, 2003
Greuze, Jean-Baptiste 1725–1805, *La polonaise*, acquired through the William Harvey Bequest and the National Art Collections Fund, 2003
Guardi, Francesco 1712–1793, *Capriccio with a Ruined Archway by the Banks of a Lagoon*, acquired through the William Harvey Bequest and the National Art Collections Fund, 2003
Heyden, Jan van der 1637–1712, *The House in the Wood, The Hague, The Netherlands (Huis ten Bosch)*, acquired through the William Harvey Bequest and the National Art Collections Fund, 2003
Heyden, Jan van der 1637–1712, *View in Amsterdam, The Netherlands*, acquired through the William Harvey Bequest and the National Art Collections Fund, 2003
Heyden, Jan van der 1637–1712, *The House on the Hill*, acquired through the William Harvey Bequest and the National Art Collections Fund, 2003
Highmore, Joseph 1692–1780, *Sir Willoughby Aston and His Wife*, purchased from Thomas Agnew and Sons
Hitchens, Ivon 1893–1979, *Dark West Wood*, purchased with the assistance of the Ministry of Education, 1961–1962, © Ivon Hitchens' estate/Jonathan Clark & Co.
Hogarth, William 1697–1764, *Portrait of a Lady*, acquired through the William Harvey Bequest and the National Art Collections Fund, 2003
Hold, Abel 1815–1896, *Still Life*, transferred from Barnsley Town Hall
Hold, Abel 1815–1896, *Mrs Elizabeth Spencer Stanhope (1795–1873)*, gift from the Friends of Cannon Hall, 2005
Hold, Abel 1815–1896, *Dead Game*, purchased from Elizabeth Bowman
Hold, Abel 1815–1896, *A Wooded River Landscape*, purchased at Bonhams, Leeds, 2007
Hold, Abel 1815–1896, *Still Life*, transferred from Barnsley Town Hall
Hold, Abel 1815–1896, *Still Life*, transferred from Barnsley Town Hall
Hold, Benjamin 1858–1917, *Fish on a Grassy Riverbank*, purchased from Bonhams, Leeds, 2007
Hold, Benjamin 1858–1917, *Still Life*, gift from Mr J. Smallwood
Hold, Benjamin 1858–1917, *Still Life*, gift from Mr J. Smallwood
Hold, Benjamin 1858–1917, *Saw Mill at Cawthorne, South Yorkshire*, gift from John A. G. Lees
Hold, Benjamin 1858–1917, *A Boy Fishing in a Wooded River Landscape*, purchased from Bonhams, Leeds, 2008
Hold, Benjamin 1858–1917, *Fishing in the Highlands*, purchased from Bonhams, Leeds, 2008
Hold, Benjamin 1858–1917, *Landscape of Cawthorne Village, South Yorkshire*, gift from Mr J. Smallwood
Hold, Benjamin 1858–1917, *Landscape of Cawthorne Village, South Yorkshire*, gift from Mr J. Smallwood
Hold, Benjamin 1858–1917, *View of Saw Mill at Cawthorne, South Yorkshire*, gift from Mr J. Smallwood
Hold, Benjamin 1858–1917, *Wooded Scene with Figures*, gift from Miss Jordan, 1987
Hold, Florence 1860–after 1913, *Dead Bird*, gift from Mr Charles Edward Collins, 2008
Hold, Florence 1860–after 1913, *Flowers in a Vase*, gift from Mr Charles Edward Collins, 2008
Hold, Florence (attributed to) 1860–after 1913, *Bird's Nest with Eggs*, gift from Mr Charles Edward Collins, 2008
Hold, Florence (attributed to) 1860–after 1913, *Garden View*, gift from Mr Charles Edward Collins, 2008
Hold, Florence (attributed to) 1860–after 1913, *Landscape with a River*, gift from Mr Charles Edward Collins, 2008
Hold, Florence (attributed to) 1860–after 1913, *Landscape with Birds*, gift from Mr Charles Edward Collins, 2008
Huysmans, Jacob (attributed to) c.1633–1696, *Portrait of a Man* (possibly Sir Thomas Wendy), purchased from Thomas Agnew and Sons, 1960
Huysum, Jan van 1682–1749, *Flower Piece*, acquired through the William Harvey Bequest and the National Art Collections Fund, 2003
Janssens van Ceulen, Cornelis 1593–1661, *Portrait of a Man*, acquired through the William Harvey Bequest and the National Art Collections Fund, 2003
Lely, Peter (attributed to) 1618–1680, *Lady Houblon*, purchased

from Thomas Agnew and Sons, 1956
Lely, Peter (school of) 1618–1680, *Portrait of a Lady*, gift from Wakefield Education Resource, 2004
MacKenzie, Alexander 1923–2001, *Gothic*, purchased from the Waddington Galleries, 1962, © the artist's estate
Marrel, Jacob 1614–1681, *Fruit and Lobster*, acquired through the William Harvey Bequest and the National Art Collections Fund, 2003
Mellor, James *Portrait of a Girl*, gift from Miss Jordan, 1987
Mercier, Philippe 1689–1760, *A Boy Drawing from the Antique*, purchased from Thomas Agnew and Sons, 1961
Metsu, Gabriel (after) 1629–1667, *The Weary Sportsman*, acquired through the William Harvey Bequest and the National Art Collections Fund, 2003
Metsu, Gabriel (studio of) 1629–1667, *The Music Lesson*, acquired through the William Harvey Bequest and the National Art Collections Fund, 2003
Miereveld, Pieter van 1596–1623 & **Miereveld, Michiel Jansz. van (attributed to)** 1567–1641, *Portrait of a Girl, Aged 19*, bequeathed by the Alexander Bequest and the National Art Collections Fund, 1972
Mieris, Frans van the elder (studio of) 1635–1681, *Boy Blowing Bubbles*, acquired through the William Harvey Bequest and the National Art Collections Fund, 2003
Mignon, Abraham (after) 1640–c.1679, *Fruit and Insects*, acquired through the William Harvey Bequest and the National Art Collections Fund, 2003
Moore, Ernest 1865–1940, *Reverend John Sharp Lawson (?), MA, LLD, FRHS, Vicar of St George's, Barnsley, South Yorkshire*, unknown acquisition method
Moore, Ernest 1865–1940, *Henry Horsfield (1879–1912), Town Clerk*, found in store, 2008
Morland, George 1763–1804, *Shipwreck off a Rocky Coast*, purchased from P. and D. Colnaghi and Company Ltd, 1961
Moucheron, Isaac de 1667–1744, *An Italian Landscape in the Region of Tivoli with Classical Figures*, acquired through the William Harvey Bequest and the National Art Collections Fund, 2003
Neer, Aert van der 1603–1677, *Coast Scene with a Fishing Boat*, acquired through the William Harvey Bequest and the National Art Collections Fund, 2003
Neer, Aert van der 1603–1677, *River Landscape in the Evening with Moonlight and a Watermill*, acquired through the William Harvey Bequest and the National Art Collections Fund, 2003
Neer, Aert van der 1603–1677, *Village Landscape at Dusk*, acquired through the William Harvey Bequest and the National Art Collections Fund, 2003
Netscher, Caspar 1639–1684, *Portrait of a Lady*, acquired through the William Harvey Bequest and the National Art Collections Fund, 2003
Nowell, Arthur Trevethin 1862–1940, *Mrs A. Tyne*, gift from Mrs K. W. Eyre, 1978, © the artist's estate
Ostade, Adriaen van 1610–1685, *A Village Fair*, acquired through the William Harvey Bequest and the National Art Collections Fund, 2003
Ostade, Adriaen van 1610–1685, *A Peasant Filling His Pipe*, acquired through the William Harvey Bequest and the National Art Collections Fund, 2003
Ostade, Adriaen van 1610–1685, *A Woman Drinking*, acquired through the William Harvey Bequest and the National Art Collections Fund, 2003
Pynacker, Adam c.1620–1673, *Landscape with Cattle and Figures*, acquired through the William Harvey Bequest and the National Art Collections Fund, 2003
Roberts, David 1796–1864, *The Mausoleum of Plautus Lucanus*, purchased from Thomas Agnew and Sons, 1960
Rubens, Peter Paul (style of) 1577–1640, *Sketch of One of the Artist's Daughters*, acquired through the William Harvey Bequest and the National Art Collections Fund, 2003
Schalcken, Godfried 1643–1706, *Man and Woman with a Wine Glass*, acquired through the William Harvey Bequest and the National Art Collections Fund, 2003
Schalcken, Godfried (after) 1643–1706, *Candlelight: Youth Lighting a Pipe*, acquired through the William Harvey Bequest and the National Art Collections Fund, 2003
Schellinks, Willem 1627–1678, *The Departure for the Chase*, acquired through the William Harvey Bequest and the National Art Collections Fund, 2003
Stott, David Cameron b.1938, *Quarry Pond*, purchased from the artist, 1964
Sutherland, Alan b.1931, *Simon Fraser (1924–2004)*, on loan from the Fraser Family © the artist
Taylor, James Spence b.1921 *Paysage (Landscape)*, purchased from Alex Reid and Lefevre Ltd, 1959
Teniers, David II 1610–1690, *Exterior of an Inn: Peasants Drinking*, acquired through the William Harvey Bequest and the National Art Collections Fund, 2003
Teniers, David II 1610–1690, *Hustle Cap*, acquired through the William Harvey Bequest and the National Art Collections Fund, 2003
unknown artist 17th C, *Portrait of an Unknown Gentleman*, bequeathed by Thomas Whitwell
unknown artist *Sir Willliam Lowther (1663–1729), 1st Bt*, on loan from the Fraser Family
unknown artist *John Spencer*, on loan from the Fraser Family
unknown artist *Adelaide Augusta Wilhelmina Dutton, Wife of Sir Henry Hunloke*, on loan from the Fraser Family
unknown artist *The Coke Sisters*, on loan from the Fraser Family
unknown artist *Walter Spencer Stanhope (1749–1822)*, on loan from the Fraser Family
unknown artist late 18th C/early 19th C, *Portrait of an Unknown Gentleman*, unknown acquisition method
unknown artist *Robert McLintock*, purchased from Mr J. F. Elliot, 1980
unknown artist 19th C, *John S. Beckett, Founder of the Beckett Hospital*, unknown acquisition method
unknown artist 19th C, *Portrait of a Child with a Dog*, unknown acquisition method
unknown artist 19th C, *Rockley Woods, South Yorkshire*, unknown acquisition method
unknown artist *Wooded Landscape*, unknown acquisition method
Vadder, Lodewijk de (style of) 1605–1655, *Landscape with Figures and Haymakers*, acquired through the William Harvey Bequest and the National Art Collections Fund, 2003
Velde, Adriaen van de 1636–1672, *Landscape: Woman Milking a Cow*, acquired through the William Harvey Bequest and the National Art Collections Fund, 2003
Velde, Adriaen van de 1636–1672, *Studies of a Dog*, acquired through the William Harvey Bequest and the National Art Collections Fund, 2003
Velde, Adriaen van de 1636–1672 & **Moucheron, Frederick de** 1633–1686, *Landscape with a Shrine*, acquired through the William Harvey Bequest and the National Art Collections Fund, 2003
Von Tamm, Franz Werner 1658–1724, *Dead Birds*, acquired through the William Harvey Bequest and the National Art Collections Fund, 2003
Wijnants, Jan c.1635–1684, *Landscape: The Mendicant*, acquired through the William Harvey Bequest and the National Art Collections Fund, 2003
Wootton, John c.1682–1764, *Landscape with Cattle*, purchased from P. & D. Colnagi & Co. Ltd
Wright, John Michael 1617–1694, *Henry Howard (1628–1684), 6th Duke of Norfolk*, purchased from Gooden and Fox, 1958

Cawthorne Victoria Jubilee Museum Trust

Billin, Edward Stanley 1911–1994, *Cawthorne Museum*, gift from the artist, 1970
Hold, Abel 1815–1896, *Nest with Three Eggs*, gift
Hold, Abel 1815–1896, *Nest with Four Eggs*, gift
Hold, Abel 1815–1896, *Nest with Four Eggs*, gift
Hold, Abel 1815–1896, *Elkanah Clegg (1803–1872), Woodman for the Spencer Stanhope Family*, gift from Mrs Fraser Spencer Stanhope, c.1950
Hold, Abel 1815–1896, *Four Partridge*, purchased
Hold, Abel 1815–1896, *Jonas Beaumont (1783–1857), Estate Carpenter for the Spencer Stanhope Family*, gift from Mrs Fraser Spencer Stanhope, c.1950
Hold, Abel 1815–1896, *'Lady'*, gift from Mrs Fraser Spencer Stanhope, 1950
Hold, Abel 1815–1896, *Red Cock Grouse*, bequeathed, 1997
Hold, Abel 1815–1896, *Three Red Grouse*, purchased
Hold, Benjamin 1858–1917, *Canon Hall Park River Landscape, South Yorkshire*, gift
Hold, Benjamin 1858–1917, *Canon Hall Park River Meadow with Church, South Yorkshire*, gift
Hold, Tom 1843–1902, *Red Grouse*, bequeathed, 1997
Hold, Tom 1843–1902, *River Landscape with Church*, gift from Mr L. Stirling, c.1950
Hold, Tom 1843–1902, *View of Canon Hall Park, South Yorkshire*, gift
unknown artist *Red Deer Stag*, gift, early 1990s
unknown artist *Young Red Deer Stag*, gift, early 1990s
M. W. *Pansies*, purchased at a local jumble sale

The Regimental Museum of the 13th/18th Royal Hussars (QMO) and the Light Dragoons

Hall, Harry 1814–1896, *18th Hussar Charger 'Hussar'*, gift from Mrs Mieville, 1977
Howard, Ken b.1932, *The Regiment Drives Past Barnsley Town Hall Following the Freedom Parade of 1979*, gift from the Regiment (13th/18th), © the artist/Bridgeman Art Library
Kitodily Williams, J. *Private William Sewell (1830–1910), 13th Light Dragoons*, purchased at auction, 1986
O'Neill, Tessa, *Stuart Tank 'Honey'*, gift from the artist, 2004

Doncaster College: The Hub

Arbones, Nathan *Sumo Sanderson*, commissioned by Doncaster College as part of a project to decorate the new building, 2008, © Doncaster College, 2008
Falding, Jill; Blackhouse, Emma & **Elwood, Paula** *Black and Red Grid*, commissioned by Doncaster College as part of a project to decorate the new building, 2008, © Doncaster College, 2008
Kendal, Victoria; Ogden, Adam & **Wright, Ann** *Five Coal Miners*, commissioned by Doncaster College as part of a project to decorate the new building, 2009, © Doncaster College, 2008
Langton, Adam *Flag*, commissioned by Doncaster College as part of a project to decorate the new building, 2008, © Doncaster College, 2008
Moreman, Wendy *Christ Church Doorway, Doncaster, South Yorkshire*, purchased, 2008
Moreman, Wendy *Minster Walls*, purchased, 2008
Moreman, Wendy *St George's Church Window, Doncaster, South Yorkshire*, purchased, 2008
Smith, Penny & **Pick, Madeleine** *Orange and Lemon Colour Grid*, commissioned by Doncaster College as part of a project to decorate the new building, 2008, © Doncaster College, 2008/the artist
Students of the First Diploma in Art and Design *Famous Faces*, commissioned by Doncaster College as part of a project to decorate the new building, 2008, © Doncaster College, 2008
Students on the Foundation Course at Doncaster College *Beach Abstract*, commissioned by Doncaster College as part of a project to decorate the new building, 2008, © Doncaster College, 2008
Students on the Foundation Course at Doncaster College *Geometric Abstract*, commissioned by Doncaster College as part of a project to decorate the new building, 2008, © Doncaster College, 2008
Ward, Rob; Pollit, Belinda & **Leigh, Jerry** *Town View Abstract*, commissioned by Doncaster College as part of a project to decorate the new building, 2008, © Doncaster College, 2008
Webb, Julie *Australian Abstract*, commissioned by Doncaster College as part of a project to decorate the new building, © Doncaster College, 2008

Doncaster Deaf Trust

Gavin, Robert 1827–1883, *Threading the Needle*
Hughes, John Joseph 1820–1909, *Windsor Castle, Berkshire*
Hulk, Johannes Frederik 1829–1911, *Amsterdam Canal Scene, The Netherlands*
unknown artist mid-19th C, *Reverend William Carr-Fenton (1784–1855)*
unknown artist *Portrait of Unknown Gentleman*

Doncaster Magistrates' Court

Marshall, M. *A Path through the Woodlands, Cleeve near Cheltenham, Gloucestershire*, possibly a gift from a magistrate

Doncaster Mansion House

Bird, John b.1948, *St George's Church, Doncaster, South Yorkshire*, gift, 2006, © the artist
Bird, John b.1948, *White House*, gift, 2006, © the artist
Boden, Leonard 1911–1999, *Elizabeth II (b.1926)*, unknown acquisition method, © the artist's estate
British (English) School *Fredrick Fisher, Mayor of Doncaster*, unknown acquisition method
British (English) School early 19th C, *Sir William Bryan Cooke (1782–1851), Mayor of Doncaster (1835–1836)*, unknown acquisition method
British (English) School 19th C, *Joseph Lockwood, Esq.*, gift
British (English) School 19th C, *Sir Edmund Beckett (1787–1874), MP for The West Riding (1841–1859)*, unknown acquisition method
British (English) School 19th C, *Thomas Blackwell Mason*, gift
British (English) School late 19th C/early 20th C, *Portrait of a Seated Gentleman*, unknown acquisition method
British (English) School late 19th C/early 20th C, *Robert Stockil, Esq., JP*, gift
British (English) School late 19th C/early 20th C, *Sir Frank Lockwood (1846–1897)*, gift
British (English) School late 19th C/early 20th C, *The Right Honourable William Thomas Spencer Wentworth-Fitzwilliam (1815–1902), 6th Earl Fitzwilliam*, gift
British (English) School 20th C, *Queen Alexandra (1844–1925)*, gift
Calkin, Lance 1859–1936, *Edward VII (1841–1910)*, gift
Gainsborough, Thomas (copy of) 1727–1788, *Sarah Siddons*, unknown acquisition method
Jack, Richard 1866–1952, *George Sandford, MA, Archdeacon of Doncaster*, gift, © the artist's estate
Jackson *The Right Honourable William Thomas Spencer Wentworth-Fitzwilliam (1815–1902), 6th Earl Fitzwilliam*, unknown acquisition method
Lavery, John 1856–1941, *The Right Honourable Earl of Lonsdale, KG, GCUO*, unknown acquisition method, © the estate of Sir John Lavery by courtesy of Felix Rosenstiel's Widow & Son Ltd
L'Hôpital, René le Brun Comte de 1877–1929, *Charles Lindley Wood (1839–1934), Viscount Halifax*, gift
Phillips, Thomas 1770–1845, *The Most Honourable Charles Watton-Wentworth (1730–1782), 2nd Marquess of Rockingham*, unknown acquisition method
Priest, Alfred 1874–1929, *Alderman George Thomas Tuby (1857–1932), Mayor of Doncaster (1921–1922)*, gift from the Showman's Guild
Winterhalter, Franz Xaver 1805–1873, *Queen Victoria (1819–1901)*, unknown acquisition method
Woodforde, Samuel 1763–1817, *George III (1738–1820)*, unknown acquisition method
Wootton, Frank 1911–1998, *616 AAE Squadron, Manston, Kent*, unknown acquisition method, © the artist's estate

Doncaster Museum Service

Airy, Anna 1882–1964, *Morning Sunlight*, purchased, 1927
Alken, Samuel Henry 1810–1894, *'Sittingbourne' with S. Rogers II and 'West Australian' with F. Butler, Winner of the 1853 Derby*, gift, 1994
Alma-Tadema, Lawrence 1836–1912, *Reverie: Far Away Thoughts*, purchased from Roy Miles Fine Art, 1986
Anderson, Thomas Alexander active 1929–1973, *Miss Joan Hamilton*, purchased from Mr J. R. Worsdale, 1997
Anderson, Thomas Alexander active 1929–1973, *Portrait of an Unknown Woman*, purchased from Mr J. R. Worsdale, 1997
Anderson, Thomas Alexander active 1929–1973, *The Blue Tarpaulin*, purchased, 1969; since on loan to Doncaster Mansion House
Appleyard, Frederick 1874–1963, *Old Walls*, purchased, 1930, © the artist's estate
Appleyard, Joseph 1908–1960, *The Finish of the 1959 St Leger Stakes*, purchased from the artist, 1960; since on loan to Doncaster Mansion House, © the artist's estate, www.josephappleyard.co.uk
Appleyard, Joseph 1908–1960, *'Airborne'*, purchased, 1960, © the artist's estate, www.josephappleyard.co.uk
Appleyard, Joseph 1908–1960, *'Ballymoss'*, purchased, 1960, © the artist's estate, www.josephappleyard.co.uk
Bailey, George 1796–1822, *'Lavinia'*, purchased from Lane Fine Art, 1981
Beetham, William 1774–1853, *William Sheardown (1797–1877)*, transferred from Doncaster Mansion House, 1977
Belaevsky, Mikhael Nicolaevich active 1893–1930, *A Russian Summer House*, gift from Dr E. K. Graftdyck, 1969
Bennett, Terence b.1935, *Warmsworth Hall, South Yorkshire*, transferred from the Picture Loan Scheme, © the artist
Bingham, Henry 1876–1954, *Hooton Pagnell, Doncaster, South Yorkshire*, gift from E. Bingham, 1961
Bowyer, William b.1926, *Richmond Bridge, Surrey*, purchased from the Fieldbourne Galleries, 1984, © William Bowyer. All rights reserved, DACS 2012
Bowyer, William b.1926, *Ebb Tide, the Thames at Chiswick, London*, purchased from the Fieldbourne Galleries, 1988, © William Bowyer. All rights reserved, DACS 2012
Brangwyn, Frank 1867–1956, *Old Man at Assisi*, purchased from Sir William De-Belleroche, 1962, © the artist's estate/Bridgeman Art Library
Brangwyn, Frank 1867–1956, *Sailing Ships at Sea*, purchased, © the artist's estate/Bridgeman Art Library
Bratby, John Randall 1928–1992, *November Sun from Revolving Studio*, purchased from the Fieldbourne Galleries, 1979, © the artist's estate/Bridgeman Art Library
Bridgehouse, Robert 1818–1881, *River Scene, North Wales*, purchased, 1964
Brieau, P. D. active 19th C, *The Nile*, gift from Lady Matthews, 1933
Bright, Beatrice 1861–1940, *Breakers on the Shore*, gift from Mrs Betrthou, 1940
Bright, Beatrice 1861–1940, *Seascape*, gift from Mrs Betrthou, 1940
Brodzky, Horace 1885–1969, *The Rehearsal*, purchased from the Fieldbourne Galleries, 1982, © the artist's estate
Brumfitt, George Edward 1917–1993, *Hilda Fettling the Kitchen Floor*, gift from the artist, 1984
Brumfitt, George Edward 1917–1993, *Aunty Hilda Washing*, gift from the artist, 1984
Brumfitt, George Edward 1917–1993, *Hilda's Warning: 'Mind you're in by half-past seven, it's bath night'*, gift from the artist, 1984
Brumfitt, George Edward 1917–1993, *Cheeking Hilda*, gift from the artist, 1984
Brumfitt, George Edward 1917–1993, *You were having your way but I was having mine and I always won', Hilda to Me*, gift from the artist, 1984
Brumfitt, George Edward 1917–1993, *Aunty Hilda Waiting for Harry to Come Off Late Turn*, gift from the artist, 1984
Brumfitt, George Edward 1917–1993, *Things Past*, gift from the artist, 1984
Buckle, Janet b.1945, *The Sleeping Giant, Rossington, South Yorkshire*, purchased from the artist, 1997, © the artist
Burn, Rodney Joseph 1899–1984, *Bank Holiday, Hampstead Heath, London*, purchased from the Fieldbourne Galleries, 1978, © the artist's estate
Burn, Rodney Joseph 1899–1984, *King's Road, Chelsea, London*, purchased from the Fieldbourne Galleries, 1985, © the artist's estate
Cadell, Francis Campbell Boileau 1883–1937, *Portrait of a Young Man*, purchased, 1987, © Cadell estate, courtesy of Portland Gallery
Chappell, Reuben 1870–1940, *Humber Keel, 'Helen'*, found in store, 2008, © the artist's estate
Chappell, Reuben 1870–1940, *'William and Mary'*, gift, © the artist's estate
Chowne, Gerard 1875–1917, *Flower Study*, gift from the Contemporary Art Society, 1963
Clark, A. *'Flying Fox'*, purchased from the estate of F. J. Chambers, 1963
Coker, Peter 1926–2004, *Butcher's Shop No.2*, purchased from the Fieldbourne Galleries, 1977, © estate of Peter Coker, RA
Coker, Peter 1926–2004, *Picking Pears at Mouthier, France*, gift from the Royal Academy of Arts (Chantrey Bequest), 2001, © estate of Peter Coker, RA
Craft, Percy Robert 1856–1934, *A Glimpse of the Horseguards*, gift from H. B. Craft, 1935
Crawshaw, Lionel Townsend 1864–1949, *Cattle Market, Doncaster, South Yorkshire*, gift from Mr C. H. Mackie, 1916
Cuneo, Terence Tenison 1907–1996, *Giants Refreshed: Pacifics in the Doncaster Locomotive Works*, purchased with the assistance of the Heritage Lottery Fund and the Museums, Libraries and Archives Council/Victoria and Albert Museum Purchase Grant Fund, 2008, © reproduced with kind permission of the Cuneo estate
Curtis, David Jan b.1948, *Long Grass*, bequeathed by Sally Eunice Glover, 2005, © the artist
Curtis, David Jan b.1948, *Rebecca, Low Tide, Sandsend, Whitby, North Yorkshire*, purchased from the Richard Hagen Gallery, 1990, © the artist
Dalby, David 1794–1836, *'Barefoot'*, purchased from European Fine Arts, 1979
Davis, Joseph Barnard 1861–1943, *Chedworth, Gloucestershire*, gift from Edward Newton, 1944
de Grey, Roger 1918–1995, *From Camer Wood, Scotland*, purchased from the Fieldbourne Galleries, 1978, © the artist's estate
Dickinson, Lowes Cato 1819–1908, *Yearling Sale at Doncaster, South Yorkshire*, transferred from Doncaster Mansion House, 1975
Dobson, William Charles Thomas 1817–1898, *Fairy Tales*, gift, 1977
Donald, Richard Watson Phillip 1865–1937, *The Horseshoe Pond*, unknown acquistion method
Drury, Paul 1903–1987, *Man's Head In Blue*, gift from the Contemporary Art Society, 1963
Dunn, Joseph 1806–1860, *'Sportsman'*, purchased from Lane Fine Art, 1983
Edmondson, Simon b.1955, *The Night*, gift from the Contemporary Art Society, 1986, © the artist
Edwards, J. G. *Evening Scene*, found in store
Etheridge, Peter d.1998, *Pietà*, gift from Gerald Burke, 1997
Etty, William 1787–1849, *Eve at the Fountain*, unknown acquistion method
Etty, William 1787–1849, *Nude*, purchased with the assistance of the Stiles Bequest Fund, 1955
Etty, William 1787–1849, *Nude Study*, gift from Mr Alfred Lockwood, 1914
Etty, William 1787–1849, *Reclining Nude*, found in store
Evans, Nicholas 1907–2004, *Trouble in the Twenties*, gift from the Contemporary Art Society, 1979, © the artist's estate
Fish, Harry 1894–1971, *St George's Gate, Doncaster, South Yorkshire*, purchased
Fish, Harry 1894–1971, *Hooton Pagnell, South Yorkshire*, purchased; since on loan to Doncaster Mansion House
Fish, Harry 1894–1971, *Conisbrough, South Yorkshire*, bequeathed by the artist, 1971
Gilchrist, Philip Thomson 1865–1956, *Tarring the Main Sail*, purchased, 1936, © the artist's estate
Glasgow, Alexander c.1840–1894, *Lady Cooke*, found in store, 2008
Glass, Frederick James 1881–1930, *Stratford Park*, gift from Marcus Outwin, 1977
Gopal-Chowdhury, Paul b.1949, *Preparing a Meal*, purchased from the Fieldbourne Galleries, 1983, © the artist
Gore, Frederick John Pym 1913–2009, *New Year's Day, Paris*, purchased from the Fieldbourne Galleries, 1978, © estate of Frederick Gore. All rights reserved, DACS 2012
Gotlib, Henryk 1890–1966, *Nude*, gift from the Contemporary Art Society (the Harold Widdup Collection), 1965, © the artist's estate
Haberfield, Théa *Paisagem (Landscape)*, gift from the British Council and the Brazilian Government, 1949
Haddock, Edwin Aldridge 1921–1996, *Spartacus*, unknown acquistion method, © the artist's estate
Hall, Harry 1814–1896, *'Hungerford'*, purchased, 1978
Hamnett, Nina 1890–1956, *Rupert Doone (1903–1923), Dancer*, gift from the Contemporary Art Society, 1963, © the artist's estate/Bridgeman Art Library
Haugh, George 1756–1827, *'Rover', the Duke of Kingston's Favourite Setting Dog*, purchased from Lane Fine Art, 1991

Haugh, George 1756–1827, *View up Glen Kinglass, West Highlands, Scotland*, purchased from Lane Fine Art, 1991
Havell, Edmund the younger 1819–1894, *Reverend A. B. Wrightson (1793–1878)*
Hay, Peter Alexander 1866–1952, *Romance*, unknown acquistion method
Hayes, Colin Graham Frederick 1919–2003, *Samos, Greece*, purchased from the Fieldbourne Galleries, 1990, © the artist's estate
Hector, George active 1972–2006, *Miner Working Underground*, transferred, 1999
Hepworth, C. H. *Horse*, unknown acquistion method
Hepworth, John *Christ Church, Doncaster, South Yorkshire, Struck by Lighting*, purchased from H. Green, 1963
Hepworth, John *Christ Church, Doncaster, South Yorkshire, from the West, Showing the Spire Struck by Lightning, 1836*, found in store
Herring, John Frederick I 1795–1865, *'St Patrick'*, purchased, 1962; since on loan to Doncaster Mansion House
Herring, John Frederick I 1795–1865, *Finish of the 1827 Gold Cup*, purchased from W. Hawley, 1963
Herring, John Frederick I 1795–1865, *'Filho da puta'*, purchased from the Leger Galleries, 1960
Herring, John Frederick I 1795–1865, *'Charles XII' and 'Euclid'*, purchased, 1962
Herring, John Frederick I 1795–1865, *'Colonel'*, purchased, 1960
Herring, John Frederick I 1795–1865, *Farm Scene with Horses*, purchased, 1962
Herring, John Frederick I 1795–1865, *Farmyard Scene*, found in store
Herring, John Frederick I 1795–1865, *Halifax Royal Mail Coach, Doncaster, South Yorkshire*, purchased, 1960
Herring, John Frederick I 1795–1865, *Horse*, gift from Doncaster Mansion House, 1976
Herring, John Frederick I 1795–1865, *'Imaum', a Welsh Arab*, gift from Doncaster Mansion House and Doncaster Metropolitan Borough Council, 1980
Herring, John Frederick I 1795–1865, *Man on a Grey Pony*, gift from Doncaster Mansion House and Doncaster Metropolitan Borough Council, 1980
Herring, John Frederick I 1795–1865, *Richard Wood*, gift from Alfred Lockwood, 1912
Herring, John Frederick I 1795–1865, *Mrs Wood*, gift from Alfred Lockwood, 1912
Herring, John Frederick I 1795–1865, *'Mundig'*, purchased, 1962
Herring, John Frederick I 1795–1865, *'Touchstone'*, purchased, 1962
Herring, John Frederick I (after) 1795–1865, *'Charles XII' and 'Euclid'*, found in store
Herring, John Frederick I (style of) *'Filho da puta'*, purchased, 1958
Highmore, Joseph (attributed to) 1692–1780, *William Wrightson*, purchased
Hill, Arthur c.1829–1894, *The Shell*, purchased, 1963
Hillier, Tristram Paul 1905–1983, *Nudes in a Bedroom*, gift from the Contemporary Art Society, 1965, © the artist's estate/Bridgeman Art Library
Hodge, Francis Edwin 1883–1949, *Vanity*, purchased from the artist, 1937
Howlin, John b.1941, *Staten, 1962*, gift from the Contemporary Art Society, 1976
Hutchinson, Norman Douglas 1932–2010, *Lilies and Tulips*, purchased
Hutchinson, Rebecca b.1961, *Self Portrait with Miss Rebecca Hutchinson*, purchased from the Fieldbourne Galleries, 1984, © the artist
Jones, Charles 1836–1902, *Hunting Dogs and Pheasants*, bequeathed by Roger Stockil
Koutousoff *James Cope*, gift from Francis P. Piggott, 1962
Lander, John Saint-Hélier 1869–1944, *Queen Mary (1867–1953)*, purchased, from 1938; since on loan to Doncaster Mansion House
Levy, Emmanuel 1900–1986, *Snow in the North*, purchased from the Fieldbourne Galleries, 1983
Lillford, Ralph b.1932, *Yorkshire Main Pit, Edlington*, purchased, © the artist
Lindner, Moffat Peter 1852–1949, *Golden Afternoon, Dordrecht, The Netherlands*, purchased from Peter Moffat Lindner, 1924, © the artist's estate
Loader, James active 19th C, *Captain H. J. Ellison*, purchased from Lane Fine Arts, 1988
Lowthin, T. A. *On the River Don, near Doncaster, South Yorkshire*, purchased with the assistance of the Stiles Bequest Fund, 1935
Lussen, R. (attributed to) active 19th C, *Blind Violinist*, unknown acquistion method
Matthews, John Chester active 1884–1912, *A Senior Officer, Queen's Own Yorkshire Dragoons*, purchased from the Fieldbourne Galleries, 1984
McFadyen, Jock b.1950, *Untitled (Hawksmoore Series No.3)*, unknown acquistion method, © the artist
McGregor, Neil b.1963, *Miss Harris' Vegetable Stall*, transferred from Doncaster Metropolitan Borough Council's Market Manager's Office, 1997, © the artist
McGregor, Neil b.1963, *The Co-Op at Night*, purchased from the artist, 1991, © the artist
McGregor, Neil b.1963, *Final Furlong*, purchased from Doncaster Library Service, 2002, © the artist
McGregor, Neil b.1963, *The Good Samaritan* (copy after Francis Hayman), purchased, from 2006, © the artist
McGregor, Neil b.1963, *William Wrightson* (copy after Francis Haymen), purchased, © the artist
McQuoid, Winston 1909–1984, *Back of the Old Inn*, gift from the Contemporary Art Society, 1963
Meadows, William George c.1825–1907, *Eller's Bridge, Kent*, gift from Mr W. Jackson Walker; since on loan to Doncaster Mansion House, 1913
Meadows, William George c.1825–1907, *Shoreham Abbey, Kent*, gift from Mr W. Jackson Walker; since on loan to Doncaster Mansion House, 1913
Meadows, William George c.1825–1907, *Rural Scenery*, gift from Mrs Hibbs, 1930
Meninsky, Bernard 1891–1950, *The Purple Dress*, gift from the National Art Collections Fund, 1956, © the artist's estate/ Bridgeman Art Library
Meria, Oscar *Sailor*, gift from the British Council and the Brazilian Government, 1949
Methuen, Paul Ayshford 1886–1974, *Castle Howard, Yorkshire*, purchased from the Fieldbourne Galleries, 1979, © trustees of the Corsham estate
Morland, George 1763–1804, *Farmyard Scene*, bequeathed by Dr Bessie Cook, 1983
Morley, Michael active c.1965–1970s, *The Far Reality*, unknown acquistion method
Morley, Michael active c.1965–1970s, *Untitled*, gift from Colin Howes, 1981
Mowzeshy *Untitled*, found in store, 2008
Murray, David 1849–1933, *A Roadside Farm*, bequeathed by the artist, 1933; since on loan to Doncaster Mansion House
Naylor, Albert b.1932, *Untitled Abstract*, transferred from the Picture Loan Scheme, 2005, © the artist
Nettleship, Patrick 1941–1998, *Cottages near Percuil, Cornwall*, found in store, 2008, © the artist's estate
Northcote, James 1746–1831, *Fruit Girl*, gift from Miss Hilda A. Walker and Walker Hubert Walker, 1943
O'Dea, Eric active 1934–1938, *The Unicorn*, gift from the Contemporary Art Society (the Edward Marsh Collection), 1963
Ogden, Geoff 1929–1977, *Pennine Landscape*, purchased from the Fieldbourne Galleries, 1980, © the artist's estate
Olsson, Albert Julius 1864–1942, *Cloudy Moonlight*, purchased, 1928
Palmer, James Lynwood 1867/1868–1941, *'Royal Lancer', Winner of 1922 St Leger Stakes*, gift; since on loan to Doncaster Mansion House, 1964
Parker, Brynhild 1907–1987, *Conversation Piece*, gift from the Contemporary Art Society (the Edward Marsh Collection), 1963
Parkhurst, Wendy b.1966, *First Breath*, gift from the artist, 2008, © the artist
Pickering, James Langsdale 1845–1912, *Bishop's Bridge, Norwich, Norfolk*, purchased, 1912
Pickersgill, Henry William 1782–1875, *Henry Bower*, found in store, 2008
Polunin, Elizabeth Violet 1878–1950, *Clean Boots*, gift from the Contemporary Art Society (the Edward Marsh Collection), 1963, © the artist's estate
Polunin, Vladimir 1880–1957, *Grapefruit*, gift from the Contemporary Art Society, 1963, © the artist's estate
Porter, Frederick James 1883–1944, *Negress*, gift from the Contemporary Art Society, 1963
Price, Barry Graham b.1938, *'Flying Scotsman'*, unknown acquistion method, © the artist
Price, Barry Graham b.1938, *'Mallard'*, found in store, 2008, © the artist
Priest, Alfred 1874–1929, *George Thomas Tuby (1857–1932)*, found in store
Priestman, Bertram 1868–1951, *Kilnsey Crag, Wharfedale, Yorkshire*, purchased from the artist, 1930
Pyne, James Baker 1800–1870, *Lake Maggiore, Italy*, gift
Quigley, Daniel active 1750–1780, *'Flying Childers' and 'Dimple' on a Racecourse, Other Racehorses Beyond*, purchased at Sotheby's, 1996
Quin, G. *Mrs Philys Jackson and Philip Clovis Jackson*, gift from P. C. Jackson, 1983
Radley, Rosa *The Highlanders' Home*, on loan to Doncaster Mansion House
Reay, John 1947–2011, *Portrait of Joan, Autumn Sunset*, unknown acquistion method, © the artist's estate
Reekie, William Maxwell 1869–1948, *Sherwood Forest, Nottinghamshire*, unknown acquistion method
Reid, Flora Macdonald 1860–c.1940, *A Great Bargain*, purchased from the artist, 1922
Reid, Flora Macdonald 1860–c.1940, *Youth*, purchased from the Summer Exhibition, 1926
Reid, John Robertson 1851–1926, *The Plagues of His Village*, purchased, 1929
Reilly, John Lewis c.1835 after 1901, *Portrait of an Unknown Gentleman* (after James Jebusa Shannon), found in store, 2008
Reinagle, Ramsay Richard 1775–1862, *Landscape with Animals*, purchased
Richter, Herbert Davis 1874–1955, *A Festival*, purchased, 1923
Robertson, Andrew (Mrs) *Georgiana Battie-Wrightson (1813–1878)*, purchased
Roe, Fred 1864–1947, *The News, Chelsea Pensioners*, purchased, 1931, © the artist's estate
Royle, Stanley 1888–1961, *Harthill, South Yorkshire*, purchased from Mrs F. Copleston, 1961, © the artist's estate/Bridgeman Art Library
Royle, Stanley 1888–1961, *Portrait of a West Indian Girl*, purchased, 1961, © the artist's estate/ Bridgeman Art Library
Russell, Gyrth 1892–1970, *Doncaster Gypsy Encampment*, purchased from Manor House Fine Art, 1983, © the artist's estate
Russell, Gyrth 1892–1970, *Polperro, Cornwall*, purchased, 1963, © the artist's estate
Sant, James 1820–1916, *Portrait of a Young Girl Holding a Book*, gift, 1977
Sant, James 1820–1916, *Thought Folded Over*, gift, 1977
Seabrooke, Elliott 1886–1950, *Regent's Park, London, Winter*, gift from the Contemporary Art Society, 1963
Searle, G. *Fruit in a Basket*, gift, 1963
Shackleton, William 1872–1933, *Study for 'The Eternal Dream'*, gift from May Shackleton, 1938
Shackleton, William 1872–1933, *Study for 'The Eternal Dream'*, gift from May Shackleton, 1938
Shackleton, William 1872–1933, *The Eternal Dream*, gift from May Shackleton, 1938
Sharp, Dorothea 1874–1955, *White Ducks*, purchased from the artist, 1927
Shaw, Mike b.1946, *Catcliffe, South Yorkshire*, purchased from Doncaster Library Service, 2002, © the artist
Shayer, William 1788–1879, *Fisher Folk*, bequeathed by Roger Stockil
Sheard, Thomas Frederick Mason 1866–1921, *The Pride of Autumn*, purchased from Mrs Sheard, 1924
Sibley, Charles c.1801–1866, *Josiah Cowell*, gift from Mr W. W. Nicholas, 1955
Silk, Henry 1883–1947, *Hat on Table*, gift from the Contemporary Art Society, 1963
Simpson, Charles Walter 1885–1971, *Finish of the 1931 St Leger*, purchased, 1931, © the artist's estate
Simpson, Charles Walter 1885–1971, *Tattersalls' Sale Ring*, purchased, 1931, © the artist's estate
Soares, Luís *Pastoral*, gift from the British Council and the Brazilian Government, 1949
Spear, Ruskin 1911–1990, *Snooker*, purchased, 1977, © the artist's estate/Bridgeman Art Library
Spooner, Arthur 1873–1962, *Cusworth Hall, South Yorkshire*, purchased, 1966 © the artist's estate/Bridgeman Art Library
Stafford, Henry 1830–1873, *Castle Howard Shorthorns*, purchased from Lane Fine Art, 1985
Stanley, Jacqueline b.1928, *The*

Fun Shop, purchased, 1969, © the artist
Steyn, Stella 1907–1987, *Reclining Nude*, gift from the Contemporary Art Society, 1963
Stocks, Ernest Decimus 1840–1918, *Portrait of Vera Way, née Wong*, gift from Mr and Mrs R. Lindley, 2007
Stubbs, C. E. active c.1960–1962, *Farm in a Rural Setting*, purchased from Mr J. R. Worsdale, 1997
Stubbs, C. E. active c.1960–1962, *Landscape with a River and Cows*, unknown acquistion method
Stubbs, C. E. active c.1960–1962, *Landscape with Trees*, found in store
Styring, Elizabeth 1854–1940, *The 'Derelict', High Tide, Whitby, North Yorkshire*, gift from Mrs L. Longman, 1941
Sutherland, Graham Vivian 1903–1980, *Arthur Jeffress (1904–1961)*, purchased from Roy Miles Fine Art, 1985, © estate of Graham Sutherland
Taylor, Louise *Interior*, gift from the Royal Academy with the assistance of the Annie Hugill bequest, 1969
Timmermans, Louis Étienne 1846–1910, *Wreck at Whitby, North Yorkshire*, gift, 1958
Tindall, William Edwin 1863–1938, *A Late Autumn Evening*, purchased from the artist, 1912
Tindall, William Edwin 1863–1938, *Birch and Bracken, Adel Moor*, gift from Mrs N. O. Arnold, 1951
Tindall, William Edwin 1863–1938, *Birch Trees and Snow*, found in store, 2008
Tindall, William Edwin 1863–1938, *The Wharfe*, gift from Doncaster Art Collections Fund, 1939
Titcomb, William Holt Yates 1858–1930, *The Mariner's Sunday School*, gift from Mrs Titcomb, 1931
Turner, Joseph Mallord William 1775–1851, *The Golden Bough*, gift from Miss Hilda A. Walker and Lieutenant Colonel Hubert Walker, 1943
Turpin, Albert 1900–1964, *Watchman's Fire (Night Shelter)*, gift from the Contemporary Art Society (the Edward Marsh Collection), 1963
unknown artist *Frances Wansford*, purchased from Lane Fine Art, 1987
unknown artist *Muriel Wansford*, purchased from Lane Fine Art, 1987
unknown artist *Richard Wansford*, purchased from Lane Fine Art, 1987
unknown artist *Rowland Wansford*, purchased from Lane Fine Art, 1987
unknown artist *Sprotbrough Hall, South Yorkshire*, purchased from the Rutland Gallery, 1986
unknown artist *Sign for the 'Salutation Inn'*, purchased, 1996
unknown artist *Leonardo da Vinci (1452–1519)*, gift from Mr R. J. Welch, 1967
unknown artist *Portrait of a Gentleman*, found in store
unknown artist 18th C, *Noli me tangere*, found in store
unknown artist 18th C, *Thomas Wentworth (1693–1741), Earl of Strafford*, gift from Mrs W. A. Townend
unknown artist mid-18th C, *Thomas Fountayne (1639–1709)*, purchased from Edward Carrol Fine Arts, 1999
unknown artist *Charles John Vaughan (1816–1897), DD, Vicar of Doncaster*, on loan from Doncaster Mansion House
unknown artist 19th C, *Mr George Lister, Chief Constable of Doncaster* (recto), found in store, 2008
unknown artist 19th C, *Fishing Boat* (verso), found in store, 2008
unknown artist 19th C, *The Triumph of Bacchus*, gift from W. J. Sayles, 1936
unknown artist late 19th C, *Alderman Charles Stockil (1824–1899), JP, Mayor*, found in store
unknown artist late 19th C, *Lady Isabella Wrightson (1853–1917)*, gift
unknown artist early 20th C, *Cannes, France*, unknown acquistion method
unknown artist *Horse*, gift from Dr J. S. Taylor, 1976
unknown artist *Horse in a Stable*, gift from Dr J. S. Taylor, 1976
unknown artist *Horses Head, 'Bendigo'*, found in store
unknown artist *Interior with Figures*, gift from J. G. Nicholson, 1933
unknown artist *Mayor of Doncaster*, found in store, 2008
unknown artist *Mr George Lister, Chief Constable of Doncaster*, found in store
unknown artist *Portrait of a Man*, transferred from Doncaster Mansion House, 1977
unknown artist *Portrait of a Woman*, found in store
unknown artist *St George's Church, Doncaster, South Yorkshire*, found in store, 2008
unknown artist *St George's Church on Fire, Doncaster, South Yorkshire*, found in store, 2008
unknown artist *St George's Church on Fire, Doncaster, South Yorkshire*, found in store, 2008
unknown artist *The Taking of Christ*, found in store
unknown artist *The Way of the Cross*, found in store
unknown artist *William Battie-Wrightson (1789–1879), MP for Retford and North Allerton*, purchased
Van der Heyden, Gerard 1864–1939, *The Cathedral, Breda, The Netherlands*, gift from Dr E. K. Graftdyck, 1973
Venables, David b.1943, *The Toffee Girls*, purchased from the artist, 2008, © the artist
Veronese, Paolo (attributed to) 1528–1588, *The Annunciation*, bequeathed by Mr M. G. Mounsden, 1948
W. A. W. *William Edwin Tindall (1863–1938)*, on loan from Doncaster Art Club
Wakeford, Edward 1914–1973, *St Sulpice, Paris*, gift from the Royal Academy of Arts with the assistance of the Chantrey bequest, 2001
Wakeford, Edward 1914–1973, *Two Horses* (recto), gift from the Contemporary Art Society (the Edward Marsh Collection), 1963
Wakeford, Edward 1914–1973, *Temptation* (verso), gift from the Contemporary Art Society (the Edward Marsh Collection), 1963
Walker, Ethel 1861–1951, *Man with a Pipe*, unknown acquistion method, © the artist's estate/ Bridgeman Art Library
Waller, Jonathan b.1956, *Breakdown*, gift from the Contemporary Art Society, 1988, © the artist
Watson, Harry 1871–1936, *The Gateway, Beaulieu Abbey, Hampshire*, purchased, 1925
Weigall, Henry 1829–1925, *Reverend Charles Edward Thomas (1823–1901)*, purchased
Weight, Carel Victor Morlais 1908–1997, *Child's Wonderment*, purchased from the Fieldbourne Galleries, 1976, © the artist's estate/Bridgeman Art Library
Wilde, Elizabeth M. active 1897–1938, *Low Tide*, purchased, 1912
Wilkinson, Emma Mary b.1864, *Country Produce*, gift from the artist, 1938
Wingate, Sue active since 1980, *Spirit of the St Leger*, purchased from the artist, 1990; since on loan to Doncaster Mansion House, © the artist
Wolfe, Edward 1897–1982, *Spanish Girl*, gift from the Contemporary Art Society, 1986, © the estate of Edward Wolfe
Wolfe, Edward 1897–1982, *Vase of Flowers*, gift, 1963, © the estate of Edward Wolfe
Wolfe, Edward 1897–1982, *Florentine Model*, purchased from the Fieldbourne Galleries, 1981, © the estate of Edward Wolfe
Wolfe, Edward 1897–1982, *Unknown Warrior*, gift from the Contemporary Art Society (the Edward Marsh Collection), 1963, © the estate of Edward Wolfe
Wright, C. H. *'Linchister'*, purchased from Dr J. S. Taylor, 1976
Wright, Joseph of Derby 1734–1797, *William Pigot (1729–1782)*, purchased from Mallett and Son, 1999
Wright, Joseph of Derby 1734–1797, *Elizabeth Pigot (1726–1766)*, purchased from Mallett and Son, 1999
Wright, Joseph of Derby 1734–1797, *William Brooke (1694–1763)*, purchased from Mallett and Son, 1999

The Regimental Museum of the King's Own Yorkshire Light Infantry

Headlam, Hugo *Scene in the Trenches*, unknown acquisiton method
Horsborough, Victor active 1881–1935, *Colonel S. A. Madden and Officers (51st Light Infantry)*, unknown acquisiton method
Johannsson, Freydomur (attributed to) b.1895, *Budareyri, Iceland*, unknown acquisiton method
Lawrence, Thomas (after) 1769–1830, *Sir John Moore (1761–1809)*, unknown acquisiton method
Marston, T. *Harold Hutson*, unknown acquisiton method
Napper, John 1916–2001, *General Sir C. P. Deedes (1879–1969)*, gift from the sitter, © the artist's estate
unknown artist 20th C, *General G. A. Malcolm (d.1888)*, unknown acquisiton method

Rawmarsh Community Library

Padfield, Philip *Andrew Carnegie (1835–1919)*, gift from the artist to celebrate the Library's centenary, 2005

Rotherham Museum & Art Gallery

Allport, Thomas 1804–1879, *Landscape*, gift from Mrs J. Allport, 1931
Andrews, J. B. *Priory in Cumberland*, gift from Mr Andrews, 1977
Armfield, George 1810–1893, *Terriers*, bequeathed by Mr Fletcher, 1946
Armfield, George 1810–1893, *Terrier*, gift from Edward Nightingale, 1908
Armfield, George 1810–1893, *Two Hunting Dogs*, unknown acquisition method
Arnfield, Marjorie 1930–2001, *Miners and Dogs*, purchased, 1998, © the artist's estate, www.marjoriearnfield.co.uk
Arnfield, Marjorie 1930–2001, *Save Our Pits*, purchased, 1998, © the artist's estate, www.marjoriearnfield.co.uk
Bache, Edward active 1874–1893, *Portrait of a Girl*, gift from Edward Nightingale, 1908
Barnes, Edward Charles 1830–1890, *At the Stile*, gift from Edward Nightingale, 1908
Barnes, Edward Charles 1830–1890, *The Flower Girl*, bequeathed by Edward Nightingale, 1913
Barnes, J. T. *Still Life*, unknown acquisition method
Barras, Thomas c.1790–1870, *Rotherham from Rawmarsh Lane, South Yorkshire*, gift from the Mechanics Institute, c.1893
Barton, M. *Still Life*, gift from Contemporary Art Society, 1963
Batchel, M. M. *Percy Clarence Wright (1900–1991)*, unknown acquisition method
Bateman, James 1893–1959, *Gerald Steel (1894–1957)*, on loan from a private collection, since 2005
Bentley, Joseph Herbert 1866–1934, *Corporal Thomas Norman Jackson (1897–1918), VC*, transferred from Swinton Unitary District Council, 1974
Beulley, J. M. (active 1911–1914) *Alderman Peter Bancroft Coward (1855–1931), JP, Mayor of Rotherham (1910–1915)*, transferred from Rotherham Metropolitan Borough Council Town Hall, 1987
Billin, Edward Stanley 1911–1994, *Vertical Wheel Mill*, gift from Railway Ring Rolled Products, 1987
Billin, Edward Stanley 1911–1994, *Lodge Farm, Wellow, Nottinghamshire*, gift from the Rotherham Society of Artists, 1975
Binns, Harry Etchel 1869–c.1947, *The Cornish Coast near Porthcurno*, gift from the Binns family, 1947
Birch, John (attributed to) 1807–1857, *Ebenezer Elliott (1781–1849), the Anti-Corn Law Rhymer*, on loan from a private collection, since 1968
Birch, Samuel John Lamorna 1869–1955, *Loe Pool, Helston, Cornwall*, gift from Sir Harry Williams, 1974, © the artist's estate
Bird, Chris b.1949, *Rotherham, South Yorkshire, over the Allotments*, purchased, 1995, © the artist
Birley, Oswald Hornby Joseph 1880–1952, *Sir Charles Lee des Forges (1879–1972)*, transferred from Rotherham Metropolitan Borough Council Town Hall, 1987, © the artist's estate
Blackshaw, Basil b.1932, *Blue Landscape*, gift from the Contemporary Art Society, 1962, © the artist
Boddington, Edwin Henry 1836–1905, *A Bright Day (Sketch on the Thames)*, purchased, 1938
Boddington, Henry John 1811–1865, *On the Thames*, gift from Edward Nightingale, 1908
Boel, John Henry active 1875–1922, *Landscape*, gift from W. H. Gummer, 1941
Bogaerts (attributed to) *Figure Sitting Writing*, bequeathed by Miss K. Pontis, 1970
Brooker, William 1918–1983, *Dunes, Littlehampton, West Sussex*, gift from the Contemporary Art Society, 1959, © the artist's estate
Brown, Jo b.1945, *Natal Day*, purchased, 1995, © the artist
Bruce, Joseph active c.1900–1951, *Mill Bridge*, unknown acquisition method

Bruce, Joseph active c.1900–1951, *Rotherham Bridge (Gaol Bridge), South Yorkshire*, purchased, 1972
Bruce, Joseph active c.1900–1951, *Landscape, Clifton Park, South Yorkshire*, gift from Mrs J. Skidmore, 1973
Bruce, Joseph active c.1900–1951, *Rotherham Church, South Yorkshire*, unknown acquisition method
Buchser, Frank 1828–1890, *Adoration*, gift from Edward Nightingale, 1908
Buhn, A. *Landscape*, unknown acquisition method
Bulkley, J. *Pastoral Scene with Dancing Figures*, unknown acquisition method
Burden, George c.1895–c.1930, *Seascape*, gift from Mrs S. M. Rack, 1953
Callow, John 1822–1878, *Seascape off Brittany, France*, bequeathed by Edward Nightingale, 1913
Callow, John (attributed to) 1822–1878, *A Fresh Breeze*, gift from Miss Allot, 1959
Callowhill, N. W. *Landscape, North Wales*, gift from Edward Nightingale, 1908
Cattermole, George 1800–1868, *Interior (Tales from Robin Hood, Featuring Friar Tuck)*, unknown acquisition method
Chambers, George 1803–1840, *Off Margate, Kent*, gift from Edward Nightingale, 1908
Chapple, T. W. active c.1914–1935, *Eckington Church from Masbrough Flats, South Yorkshire*, gift from the artist, 1935
Clare, Oliver 1852–1927, *Fruit Piece*, unknown acquisition method
Clare, Oliver 1852–1927, *Fruit Piece*, unknown acquisition method
Clare, Vincent 1856–1925, *Flower Piece*, unknown acquisition method
Clare, Vincent 1856–1925, *Fruit Piece*, unknown acquisition method
Cole, George Vicat 1833–1893, *Homewards*, bequeathed by Edward Nightingale, 1913
Collins, Hugh c.1834–1896, *The Village Musicians*, gift from Edward Nightingale, 1908
Collins, William (after) 1788–1847, *Happy as a King*, unknown acquisition method
Cooper, Thomas Sidney 1803–1902, *Cattle Piece*, bequeathed by Edward Nightingale, 1913
Copley, John Singleton 1738–1815, *Frederick Louis (1707–1751), Prince of Wales* (after David Morier), gift from Mr W. Hafferty, 1923
Copley, John Singleton 1738–1815, *George II (1683–1760)* (after David Morier), gift from Mr W. Hafferty, 1923
Correggio (after) c.1489–1534, *La zingarella*, gift from Edward Nightingale, 1908
Cowen, William 1791–1864, *The Chapel in the Oak*, gift from the Committee of the Mechanics Institute, 1893
Cowen, William 1791–1864, *View of Rotherham, South Yorkshire*, purchased with the assistance of the Victoria and Albert Museum Purchase Grant Fund, 1982
Cowen, William 1791–1864, *Interior of Rotherham Parish Church, South Yorkshire*, gift from Mr W. Booth, 1893
Creswick, Thomas 1811–1869, *Seascape*, purchased, 1937
Crowe, Eyre (after) 1824–1910, *Sir Christopher Wren (1632–1723)*, acquired, before 1929
Dade, Ernest 1868–1936, *Off Scarbro'*, gift from Edward Nightingale, 1908
Danks, Albert (attributed to) *Kimberworth Isolation Hospital, South Yorkshire*, gift from Mrs Knutton, 1993
Dearden, Paul *Treescape (Boston Park, Rotherham, South Yorkshire)*, gift from the artist, 2006
Dyck, Anthony van (after) 1599–1641, *Sir Thomas Fairfax (1612–1671)*, gift from Miss Fellows, 1975
Eckhardt, K. P. *Putto*, gift from Mrs F. R. Anderson, 1948
Etty, William 1787–1849, *Diana, Returning from the Chase*, gift from Mrs F. R. Anderson, 1948
Evans, Bernard Walter 1843–1922, *Cannock Chase*, gift from Edward Nightingale, 1908
W. F. *Horse in a Stable*, unknown acquisition method
Fann, W. *Soar Brook, Leicestershire*, purchased, 1938
Fieldhouse, Florence 1898–1974, *Ashover, Derbyshire*, purchased, 1942
Fieldhouse, Florence 1898–1974, *Pink Chrysanthemums*, unknown acquisition method
Fielding, Anthony V. C. 1787–1855, *Seascape*, purchased, 1951
Fisher, Mark 1841–1923, *Landscape with Sheep*, unknown acquisition method
Foret, J. *Flower Study*, bequeathed by Miss K. Pontis, 1970
Fowler, Robert 1853–1926, *A Midsummer Night's Dream* (from the play by William Shakespeare), gift from Robert Fowler Junior, 1930
Frisch, John Carl b.c.1845, *Rocks and River*, gift from Sir Charles des Forges, 1945
Gainsborough, Thomas (after) 1727–1788, *William Pitt the Younger (1759–1806)*, gift from Mrs S. Williams, 1991
Gainsborough, Thomas (after) 1727–1788, *The Honourable Mrs Thomas Graham, née Hon Mary Cathcart (1757–1792)*, unknown acquisition method
Gainsborough, Thomas (attributed to) 1727–1788, *Blaize Castle, Bristol*, purchased, 1943
Gainsborough, Thomas (school of) 1727–1788, *Admiral Keppel (1725–1786)*, purchased from Wentworth Woodhouse, 1949
Giobbi, Edward Gioachino b.1926, *Landscape*, gift from the Contemporary Art Society, 1972
Glassby, Robert 1835–1892, *Mexborough Church, South Yorkshire*, gift from W. Glassby, 1929
A. W. H. *View of Maltby, South Yorkshire*, purchased, 1999
T. H. *Nativity*, unknown acquisition method
Hammond, J. *A Family Group*, gift from Miss Grace E. Hammond, 1945
Hammond, J. *Canklow Wood Bottom, Rotherham, South Yorkshire*, purchased, 1929
Hardwick, H. active c.1950–c.1952, *Fred Turner of Rotherham*, gift from the sitter, 1958
Hardy, Thomas Bush 1842–1897, *Seascape*, purchased, 1946
Hargitt, Edward 1835–1895, *Canal Scene*, gift from Edward Nightingale, 1908
Harrison, J. (attributed to) active 1845–1865, *In Wharncliffe Woods, South Yorkshire*, gift from Miss Grace E. Hammond, 1945
Hawkesworth, Joseph Hallam 1827–1908, *On the Don, near Wortley, South Yorkshire*, unknown acquisition method
Hawkesworth, Joseph Hallam 1827–1908, *Duncraggan, Scotland*, gift from Edward Nightingale, 1908
Hawkesworth, Joseph Hallam 1827–1908, *Landscape*, unknown acquisition method
Hawkesworth, Joseph Hallam 1827–1908, *Landscape with Fishing Scene*, purchased, 1938
Hawkesworth, Joseph Hallam 1827–1908, *Loch Earn, Scotland*, gift from Edward Nightingale, 1908
Hawkesworth, Joseph Hallam 1827–1908, *On the Don, Wharncliffe, South Yorkshire*, gift from Edward Nightingale, 1908
Hawkesworth, Joseph Hallam 1827–1908, *On the Rother, near Catcliffe, South Yorkshire*, gift from Edward Nightingale, 1908
Herbert, John Rogers 1810–1890, *Mary, Queen of Scots and David Rizzio*, gift from Edward Nightingale, 1908
Hergenröder, Georg Heinrich 1736–c.1794, *Ladies Bathing*, purchased, 1946
Hickman, Arthur 1902–1987, *Self Portrait as a Young Man*, gift from Mrs J. Roberts, 1993
Hickman, Arthur 1902–1987, *Landscape*, gift from W. H. Marriot, 1974 in memory of L. S. Taitt MRCP
Hickman, Arthur 1902–1987, *The Visit of Princess Margaret*, gift from Mrs J. Roberts, 1999
Hickman, Arthur 1902–1987, *On the Prince of Wales Power Station Roof, Effingham Street, Rotherham, South Yorkshire*, gift from Mrs J. Roberts, 1993
Hickman, Arthur 1902–1987, *One Post of Entrance to Colliery Offices, Wash Lane, Rotherham, South Yorkshire*, gift from Mrs J. Roberts, 1993
Hill, James John 1811–1882, *The Young Anglers*, gift from Edward Nightingale, 1908
Hilton, William I 1752–1822, *Jonathan (1781–1842), and Mary Anne Walker (1783–1855), of Ferham*, on loan from Nottingham City Museums and Galleries, since 1972
Hogan, Laura E. c.1880–1970, *Anemones*, gift from Mr J. Richards, 1983
Holden, Richard 1768–1809, *Review of Local Volunteers on Brinsworth Common, Rotherham, South Yorkshire*, gift from the Committee of the Mechanics Institute, 1893
Hollyer, William Perring 1834–1922, *Highland Cattle*, unknown acquisition method
Horton, J. *Mill at Ambleside, Cumbria*, gift from H. Gracie, 1936
Hudson, Marianne (attributed to) active 1878, *Farmyard*, unknown acquisition method
Hurt, Louis Bosworth 1856–1929, *A Pleasant Stream in a Quiet Land*, unknown acquisition method
Hurt, Louis Bosworth 1856–1929, *Highland Cattle*, unknown acquisition method
Hurt, Louis Bosworth 1856–1929, *Between the Showers*, unknown acquisition method
Huur, C. (attributed to) *Landscape*, unknown acquisition method
Ibbetson, Julius Caesar 1759–1817, *Distant View of Bolton Abbey, North Yorkshire*, gift from Sir Charles des Forges, 1945
Italian School *Christ in the Garden of Gethsemane*, gift from Doris Banks, 1978
Italian School 17th C, *The Death of Saint Joseph*, gift from Doris Banks, 1978
Jagger, David 1891–1958, *Thomas Newbould (1845–1933)*, gift from G. T. Newbould, 1971, © the artist's estate
Jenkins, Wilfred 1857–1936, *Moonlight Coastal Scene*, gift from Mrs Pontis, 1959
Kneller, Godfrey (after) 1646–1723, *Portrait of an Unknown Lady*, bequeathed by Rachel Fourmaintraux-Winslow, 1975
La Dell, Edwin 1914–1970, *Leaving Boulogne, France*, gift from the Contemporary Art Society, © the artist's estate
La Dell, Thomas 1883–1971, *View of Venice, Italy*, purchased, 1979
La Thangue, Henry Herbert 1859–1929, *Landscape Study*, unknown acquisition method
Lance, George 1802–1864, *Fruit Piece*, bequeathed by Edward Nightingale, 1913
Leighton, Frederic (after) 1830–1896, *Niccolò Pisano (c.1220/1225–c.1284)*, acquired, before 1929
Leighton, Frederic (after) 1830–1896, *Giovanni Cimabue (c.1240–c.1302)*, acquired, before 1929
Lemaire, Louis Marie (attributed to) 1824–1910, *Poultry*, purchased, 1946
Lewis, Reginald 1894–1973, *James Peech (1906–after 1962)* (after Edward Irvine Halliday), on loan from a private collection, since 2005
H. M. *Coastal Scene*, unknown acquisition method
H. M. *Coastal Scene*, unknown acquisition method
Mahrrs, W. *Animals at a Ford*, unknown acquisition method
Malender, J. *Sailing Clipper off the Coast*, unknown acquisition method
Marshall, W. *Mountain Scene*, gift from Miss Allot, 1959
Matthews, William F. 1878–1966, *Iona, Scotland*, purchased, 1947
Meadows, William George c.1825–1907, *Landscape*, gift from Mr W. H. Gummer, 1941
Mellor, William 1851–1931, *Landscape*, unknown acquisition method
Montague, Alfred 1832–1883, *Evening*, gift from Edward Nightingale, 1908
Moore, Claude Thomas Stanfield 1853–1901, *Sea Port*, gift from Sir Charles des Forges, 1945
Moore, Ernest 1865–1940, *Alderman George E. C. Wragg (1826–1915)*, transferred from Rotherham Metropolitan Borough Council Town Hall, 1987
Moore, Ernest 1865–1940, *Alderman George Gummer (1855–1934)*, gift from George Gummer, 2008
Moore, Ernest 1865–1940, *Alderman David Llewellyn Winter (1853–1925), JP, Mayor of Rotherham (1901–1902)*, transferred from Rotherham Metropolitan Borough Council Town Hall, 1987
Moore, Ernest 1865–1940, *Alderman George Gummer (1855–1934)*, bequeathed by the sitter, 1934
Moore, Ernest 1865–1940, *Alderman George Gummer (1855–1934)*, transferred from Rotherham Metropolitan Borough Council Town Hall, 1987
Moore, Ernest 1865–1940, *Colonel Sir Charles John Stoddart (1839–1913), VD, JP*, transferred from Rotherham Metropolitan Borough Council Town Hall, 1987
Moore, Ernest 1865–1940, *Alderman George E. Caine (1876–1969), JP*, transferred from Rotherham Metropolitan Borough Council Town Hall, 1987
Moore, Ernest (attributed to) 1865–1940, *Colonel Sir Charles John Stoddart (1839–1913), VD, JP*, transferred from Rotherham Metropolitan Borough Council Town Hall, 1987

Moore, Ernest (attributed to) 1865–1940, *Woman with a Samovar*, gift from Mr Moore, son of the artist, 1930

Moore, Ernest (attributed to) 1865–1940, *Alderman George Clark (1844–1924)*, transferred from Rotherham Metropolitan Borough Council Town Hall, 1987

Moore, Ernest (attributed to) 1865–1940, *Alderman Albert Percy Aizlewood (1864–1953), JP*, transferred from Rotherham Metropolitan Borough Council Town Hall, 1987

Moore, William I 1790–1851, *Samuel Clark (1771–1845), Esquire of Dumfries House*, gift from Mr A. Taffinder, before 1929

Morland, George 1763–1804, *Landscape*, purchased, 1949

Morland, George 1763–1804, *The Village Butcher*, purchased, before 1977

Munkácsy, Mihály (after) 1844–1900, *Milton*, gift from a garage in Swinton, 1973

Niemann, Edmund John 1813–1876, *Cheddar Cliffs, Somerset*, gift from Edward Nightingale, 1908

Niemann, Edmund John 1813–1876, *Landscape and Waterfall*, gift from Edward Nightingale, 1908

Niemann, Edmund John 1813–1876, *Moorland Scene*, bequeathed by Edward Nightingale, 1913

Niemann, Edmund John 1813–1876, *Mountain Stream*, gift from Edward Nightingale, 1908

Niemann, Edmund John 1813–1876, *Warwick Castle*, gift from Edward Nightingale, 1908

Niemann, Edmund John 1813–1876, *Landscape with Windmills*, gift from Edward Nightingale, 1908

Niemann, Edmund John 1813–1876, *Whitby, North Yorkshire, from the Sea*, bequeathed by Edward Nightingale, 1913

Noble, John Sargeant 1848–1896, *Otter Hunting*, bequeathed by Edward Nightingale, 1913

Norman, Edward Glossop Augustus b.c.1816, *The Hawking Party* (after Edwin Henry Landseer), unknown acquisition method

Norton, Benjamin Cam 1835–1900, *Hen and Chicks*, gift from Mrs J. Mennie, 1961

Oliver, William 1804–1853, *Olivette*, gift from Edward Nightingale, 1908

W. P. *Cattle*, purchased, 1946

Panini, Giovanni Paolo (after) 1691–1765, *Landscape*, unknown acquisition method

Parker, Vincent active c.1950–1970, *November Day, Stannington, South Yorkshire*, purchased, 1952

Parker, Vincent active c.1950–1970, *After the Shower, near Harthill, South Yorkshire*, purchased, 1975

Paul, John Dean 1775–1852, *River Yare*, gift from Sir Charles des Forges, 1945

Paul, John Dean 1775–1852, *River Yare*, gift from Sir Charles des Forges, 1945

Pearson, G. Hattersley 1858–1937, *Roscoe Wheel, Rivelin Valley, South Yorkshire*, purchased, 1950

Peele, John Thomas 1822–1897, *Asleep on the Watch*, bequeathed by George Gummer, 1941

Platt, Russell b.1920, *Minster Exterior, West Front*, transferred from Rotherham Metropolitan Borough Council's Human Resources Department, 2002, © the artist

Pontis, Kate 1876–1970, *All Saints' Church, Rotherham, South Yorkshire*, bequeathed by the artist, 1970

Poole, James 1803–1886, *'Cinderella', a Favourite Cob of Mrs Henry Walker's and Her Coachman William Sales*, gift from Mr J. Wilcox, 1903

Poole, James 1803–1886, *Skiddaw, Cumbria*, unknown acquisition method

Poole, James 1803–1886, *Near Coed Mawr, North Wales*, unknown acquisition method

Poole, James 1803–1886, *Over the Greta*, gift from Edward Nightingale, 1908

Poole, James 1803–1886, *Glen Falloch, Scotland*, unknown acquisition method

Pott, Laslett John 1837–1898, *A Morning Sail*, gift from Edward Nightingale, 1908

Potter, Frank b.1885, *Flower Study*, purchased from the Art Exhibition Bureau, 1946

Pryde, James (attributed to) 1866–1941, *Townscape*, gift from the Contemporary Art Society, 1963

Pyne, James Baker 1800–1870, *Venice*, gift from Edward Nightingale, 1908

Randell, L. *The Hard Way*, gift from Mrs L. Randell, 1974

Redgate, W. H. *Old Cottage near Fulwood, Lancashire*, gift from Miss Grace E. Hammond, 1945

Redmore, Henry 1820–1887, *Bay of Biscay*, gift from Edward Nightingale, 1908

Reinagle, Ramsay Richard (attributed to) 1775–1862, *Mary Walker, née Need, Mrs Thomas Walker (1763–1823)*, gift from Michael Walker, 1963

Reinagle, Ramsay Richard (attributed to) 1775–1862, *Susannah Walker (1760–1831)*, gift from Michael Walker, 1963

Reinagle, Ramsay Richard (attributed to) 1775–1862, *Elizabeth Walker (1786–1850)*, gift from Mrs Winifred Causton, 1944

Reinagle, Ramsay Richard (attributed to) 1775–1862, *Henry Walker (1785–1860)*, gift from Mrs Winifred Causton, 1944

Ricci, Ezio 1885–1968, *Susannah and the Elders* (after Guido Reni), gift from Mrs E. Davidson, 1943

Ricci, Ezio 1885–1968, *Virgin and Child* (after Sandro Botticelli), gift from Mrs E. Davidson, 1943

Robb, Brian 1913–1979, *Lagoon*, gift from the Contemporary Art Society, 1968, © the artist's estate

Roberts, David 1796–1864, *Interior of a Church*, bequeathed by Edward Nightingale, 1913

Roe, Clarence 1850–1909, *Scarborough, North Yorkshire*, gift from Mr W. H. Gummer, 1943

Roe, Robert Ernest 1852–1921, *Beached Sailing Vessel*, unknown acquisition method

Roe, Robert Ernest 1852–1921, *Sailing Vessel*, unknown acquisition method

Romney, George 1734–1802, *Ann Verelst (1751–1823)*, purchased with the assistance of the Victoria and Albert Museum Purchase Grant Fund and the National Art Collections Fund, 1987

Rossi, Alexander Mark 1840–1916, *Children at Play*, gift from Edward Nightingale, 1908

Royle, Stanley 1888–1961, *Mill Bridge, Stone*, purchased, 1952, © the artist's estate/Bridgeman Art Library

Rubens, Peter Paul (after) 1577–1640, *Susanne Fourment (Le chapeau de paille)*, unknown acquisition method

Russell, Charles 1852–1910, *Martha Russell*, unknown acquisition method

Russell, John 1745–1806, *Joshua Walker (1750–1815), of Clifton House*, gift from Mrs Winifred Causton, 1944

Russell, John 1745–1806, *Susannah Walker (1760–1831)*, gift from Mrs Winifred Causton, 1944

Ryder, J. T. active c.1933–c.1960, *Prize Pigeon*, gift from Mrs J. Mennie, 1961

F. S. *Henry Steel (1831–1915)*, on loan from a private collection, since 2005

Salter, George active c.1870–c.1875, *A Calm Evening*, unknown acquisition method

Salter, George active c.1870–c.1875, *A Mountain Stream in Wales*, unknown acquisition method

Scarsellino (circle of) 1551–1620, *The Adoration of the Shepherds*, gift from Doris Banks, 1978

Scott, William Bell (after) 1811–1890, *Peter Vischer (c.1455–1529)*, acquired, before 1929

Shackleton, William 1872–1933, *The Adventure*, gift from Mrs M. Shackleton, 1938

Shalders, George c.1826–1873, *Landscape with Cattle*, gift from Edward Nightingale, 1908

Shalders, George c.1826–1873, *Sunset with Cattle*, gift from Edward Nightingale, 1908

Sharp, Miles Bamford 1897–1973, *Thorpe in Wharfedale, North Yorkshire*, purchased, 1948

Sharp, Miles Bamford 1897–1973, *Heather and Gorse, Woodbury Common, East Devon*, gift from the artist, 1969

Smith, H. Thomas *Rotherham Public Library, South Yorkshire*, gift from Rotherham Creative Art Club, 1940

Smitheman, Herbert 1861–1938, *Green Lane, Kimberworth, South Yorkshire*, gift from the artist, c.1930

Smitheman, Herbert 1861–1938, *Kimberworth, South Yorkshire* (from a sketch made in 1902), bequeathed by Mrs M. A. Smitheman, 1965

Smitheman, Herbert 1861–1938, *Richmond Castle, North Yorkshire, from the Swale*, bequeathed by Mrs M. A. Smitheman, 1965

Smitheman, Herbert 1861–1938, *Landscape*, bequeathed by Mrs M. A. Smitheman, 1965

Smitheman, Herbert 1861–1938, *Gateway in Roche Abbey, South Yorkshire*, gift from Mrs H. Smitheman, 1947

Smitheman, Herbert 1861–1938, *Canklow Holes, South Yorkshire*, bequeathed by Mrs M. A. Smitheman, 1965

Smitheman, Herbert 1861–1938, *Four Interior Views of the Chapel on the Bridge, Rotherham, South Yorkshire*, gift from the artist, c.1930

Smitheman, Herbert 1861–1938, *Millgate, Rotherham, South Yorkshire*, gift from the artist

Smitheman, Herbert 1861–1938, *Snow Scene, Rotherham Parish Church, South Yorkshire*, bequeathed by Mrs M. A. Smitheman, 1965

Smitheman, Herbert (attributed to) 1861–1938, *Coastal Scene*, unknown acquisition method

Someren, Edmund Lawrence van 1875–1963, *The Pilgrim*, gift from Mrs Elizabeth Garden-Smith, 1964

Souza, Francis Newton 1924–2002, *Red Houses*, gift from the Contemporary Art Society, 1965, © estate of F. N. Souza. All rights reserved, DACS 2012

Spanish School 16th C, *Spanish Child*, unknown acquisition method

Spence, S. *Entrance Gates, Clifton Park, Rotherham, South Yorkshire*, gift from Mrs D. M. Hutton, 1945

Spinks, Thomas 1847–1927, *View in North Wales*, unknown acquisition method

Stanby, A. *Farmyard Scene*, gift from Mrs York, 1961

Steeple, John 1823–1887, *The Moorland Pool*, gift from Edward Nightingale, 1908

Stone, Henry 1616–1653, *Sir Thomas Wentworth (1593–1641), Earl of Strafford and Sir Philip Mainwaring (1589–1661)* (after Anthony van Dyck), purchased from the Cusworth Hall sale, 1952

Stubley, Trevor 1932–2010, *Sergeant Ian John McKay (1953–1982), VC*, transferred from Rotherham Metropolitan Borough Council Town Hall, 1987, © the artist's estate

Suddaby, Rowland 1912–1972, *Coast Scene near the Stour Estuary, Suffolk*, purchased, 1946, © the artist's estate

Thomas, A. *Bridgegate, Rotherham, South Yorkshire*, purchased, 1950

Thompson, Wilfred active 1884–c.1921, *Gravesend from Tilbury, Essex, Flood Tide*, purchased, 1949

Thompson, Wilfred active 1884–c.1921, *Moonlight Greenwich from Blackwall Reach, London*, purchased, 1949

Thomson, Christopher 1799–1871, *Rotherham, South Yorkshire*, purchased, 1946

Tilbury, Henry 1815/1820–1866, *River Don near Conisbrough, South Yorkshire*, gift from Mr D. Holland, 1965

Tilbury, Henry 1815/1820–1866, *Conisbrough Old Mill, South Yorkshire*, gift from Mr D. Holland, 1965

Towne, Charles 1763–1840, *'Toxopholite'*, gift from Mrs F. R. Anderson, 1948

unknown artist *Elizabeth Parkin (1703–1766)*, gift from Mrs Pamela Baldwin with the assistance of the Art Fund, 2006

unknown artist *Portrait of a Lady*, unknown acquisition method

unknown artist *The Descent from the Cross*, purchased from Wentworth Woodhouse, 1949

unknown artist *Joshua Walker (1750–1815)*, on loan from a private collection, since 1961

unknown artist *Landscape with Figures*, unknown acquisition method

unknown artist *Bacchanalian Feast*, unknown acquisition method

unknown artist *Cows*, unknown acquisition method

unknown artist *Ebenezer Elliott (1781–1849), as a Young Man*, unknown acquisition method

unknown artist *Landscape*, bequeathed by Ethert Brand, 1938

unknown artist *Landscape with a Waterfall and a Temple*, unknown acquisition method

unknown artist *Madonna and Child*, unknown acquisition method

unknown artist *Masbrough Independent Academy, South Yorkshire*, unknown acquisition method

unknown artist *Studies of Two Sheep's Heads*, unknown acquisition method

unknown artist *Henry Walker (1785–1860) in the Uniform of the Southern Regiment of West Riding Yeomanry Cavalry*, gift from Mr W. H. Soresby, 1946

unknown artist *Mrs Joshua Walker (1760–1831) (Susannah Walker of Clifton House)*, purchased with the assistance of the National Art Collections Fund, 1994

unknown artist *The Oxley Children*, gift from Herbert John Oxley, 1935

unknown artist *Landscape with a Cottage*, purchased, 1938
unknown artist *Portrait of a Man*, unknown acquisition method
unknown artist *Joshua Walker Junior (1786–1862)*, gift from Michael Walker, 1963
unknown artist *Landscape with Figures*, gift from Edward Nightingale, 1908
unknown artist *Landscape*, gift from Mr W. H. Gummer, 1941
unknown artist *Landscape with Trees*, unknown acquisition method
unknown artist *Portrait of a Lady*, gift from Mr Andrews, 1977
unknown artist *Whitby Harbour, North Yorkshire*, unknown acquisition method
unknown artist *Elizabeth Edith Walker*, purchased, 1972
unknown artist *Bolton Abbey, North Yorkshire*, gift from A. Kitchen, 1946
unknown artist *Coastal Scene*, unknown acquisition method
unknown artist *Landscape*, bequeathed by Ethert Brand, 1938
unknown artist *Landscape with a Village Church*, gift from Mrs A. Nelson, 1959
unknown artist *Mother and Child*, unknown acquisition method
unknown artist *Mountain Scene*, gift from Miss Allott, 1959
unknown artist *Portrait of a Gentleman and a Greyhound*, unknown acquisition method
unknown artist *'Gladiator'*, gift from Mrs A. Cottam, 1941
unknown artist *Interior, Rotherham Parish Church, South Yorkshire*, unknown acquisition method
unknown artist *Endcliffe, South Yorkshire*, purchased, 1945
unknown artist *Farming Scene*, unknown acquisition method
unknown artist *Lady Chapel, Rotherham Parish Church, South Yorkshire*, unknown acquisition method
unknown artist *Landscape with a River*, purchased, 1946
unknown artist *John Matthew Habershon (1824–1894), First Mayor of Rotherham*, transferred from Rotherham Metropolitan Borough Council Town Hall, 1987
unknown artist *Mrs John Guest, née Hannah Shaw (1797–1882) (The Eightieth Birthday)*, unknown acquisition method
unknown artist *John Guest (1799–1880)*, unknown acquisition method
unknown artist *Landscape*, unknown acquisition method
unknown artist *River Scene*, unknown acquisition method
unknown artist *Alderman George Neill (1831–1899), JP*, transferred from Rotherham Metropolitan Borough Council Town Hall, 1987
unknown artist *J. A. Bower, Esq., Chairman of Swinton School Board*, unknown acquisition method
unknown artist *Portrait of an Unknown Gentleman, Seated*, unknown acquisition method
unknown artist *Camping Scene*, unknown acquisition method
unknown artist *Landscape with a Stag*, purchased, 1938
unknown artist *Landscape with Cattle*, purchased, 1938
unknown artist *Moorland Scene*, unknown acquisition method
unknown artist *Moorland Scene*, unknown acquisition method
unknown artist *River Scene*, unknown acquisition method
unknown artist *Study of a Child*, unknown acquisition method
unknown artist *Alderman Robert Marsh (1818–1905)*, transferred from Rotherham Metropolitan Borough Council Town Hall, 1987
unknown artist *Clifton Park Entrance before the Cenotaph Was Erected, Rotherham, South Yorkshire*, unknown acquisition method
unknown artist *Clifton Park Pond, Rotherham, South Yorkshire*, unknown acquisition method
unknown artist *Clifton Park Pond with Steps, Rotherham, South Yorkshire*, unknown acquisition method
unknown artist *Clifton Park Pond with Steps, Rotherham, South Yorkshire*, unknown acquisition method
unknown artist *Henry Steel (1831–1915)*, on loan from a private collection, since 2005
unknown artist *Portrait of an Unknown Man*, unknown acquisition method
unknown artist *Rawmarsh Church, South Yorkshire*, unknown acquisition method
unknown artist *Portrait of an Unknown Gentleman, Seated*, unknown acquisition method
unknown artist *Cathedral Interior*, transferred from Maltby Urban District Council, 1978
Van Dunk, Ellen *Percy Clarence Wright (1900–1991)*, purchased, 1968
Vickers, W. A. *Lathkill Dale, Cumbria*, purchased, 1944
Walker, Ethel 1861–1951, *Self Portrait*, purchased, 1959, © the artist's estate/Bridgeman Art Library
Walker, Ethel 1861–1951, *Portrait of a Girl*, gift from the Contemporary Art Society, 1965, © the artist's estate/Bridgeman Art Library
Walker, Ethel 1861–1951, *Decoration for an Ivory Room: Invocation to the Dance*, purchased with the assistance of the Victoria and Albert Museum Purchase Grant Fund and the National Art Collections Fund, 1996, © the artist's estate/Bridgeman Art Library
Watson, Thomas J. 1847–1912, *Riding thro' the Forest*, gift from Mrs Mennie, 1961
Weekes, Henry II 1849–1888, *Wood Pigeons*, gift from Edward Nightingale, 1908
Westlake, Nathaniel Hubert John (after) 1833–1921, *Fra Giacomo da Ulma (1407–1491)*, acquired, before 1929
Wey, Peter *Green Coolness*, gift from the Contemporary Art Society
Willey, T. *Millgate, Rotherham, South Yorkshire*, purchased, 1954
Williams, Alfred Walter 1823–1905, *The Castle of Ischia, off the Coast of Naples, Italy*, bequeathed by J. Dickinson, 1960
Williams, Alfred Walter 1823–1905, *Landscape, Langdale Pikes, Cumbria*, gift from Edward Nightingale, 1908
Wilson, Arthur 1838–1914, *Haddon Hall, Derbyshire*, gift from Mrs York, 1961
Wimperis, Edmund Morison 1835–1900, *Seascape Study*, unknown acquisition method
Wood, R. H. active 1865–1889, *Shades of Night*, gift from Sir Charles des Forges, 1945
Wylie, Robert 1839–1897, *Portrait of a Man in a Turban*, unknown acquisition method
Wynfield, David Wilkie 1837–1887, *Henry VIII and Anne Boleyn*, gift from Edward Nightingale, 1908
Zoffany, Johann (school of) 1733–1810, *Mary Walker (1708–1793)*, gift from Mrs Winifred Causton, 1944
Zoffany, Johann (school of) 1733–1810, *Samuel Walker (1715–1782)*, gift from Mrs Winifred Causton, 1944

Rotherham Town Hall

Isseo *Fleures noires*, gift from the artist, 2009
Langlet, Jean-Claude *La basilique vue des Champs Elysées, Saint-Quentin, France*, gift from Saint-Quentin, Rotherham's twin town, 2007
Smith, Dora *Steelworks*, unknown acquisition method
unknown artist *Woodland Scene with a Pond*, unknown acquisition method
unknown artist *The Old Market Place*, gift from Rotherham Markets
unknown artist *Rescue at Sea*, gift from Rotherham's Ukrainian twin town, 1994
Vachin *Abstract*, unknown acquisition method

Thomas Rotherham College

Becket, Leslie b.1913, *Thomas Rotherham (1423–1500), Archbishop of York and Founder of the College*, gift from the artist, 2009, © the artist
Butler, Helen *Thomas Rotherham College Quincentenary*, commissioned to celebrate the 500th anniversary of Rotherham Grammar School and Thomas Rotherham College
unknown artist early 18th C, *Thomas Rotherham (1423–1500), Archbishop of York and Founder of the College*, unknown acquisition method

York and Lancaster Regimental Museum

Aird, Reginald b.1890, *Field Marshal Herbert Charles Onslow Plumer (1857–1932), 1st Viscount Plumer*, transferred from the York and Lancaster Regiment, 1985
Best, C. *Tiger's Head*, transferred from the York and Lancaster Regiment, 1985
Dyer, Edmund active c.1820–1875, *Lieutenant General Sir Eyre Coote (1759–1823)*, transferred from the Regimental Headquarters, Strensall, York, 1996
Dyer, Edward active 1919–1938, *Field Marshal Herbert Charles Onslow Plumer (1857–1932), 1st Viscount Plumer*, transferred from the Regimental Headquarters, Strensall, York, 1996
Galindo, Richard Eyles b.c.1847, *Mounted Infantryman*, gift from Major M. J. Rose, 1994
Giles, Godfrey Douglas 1857–1941, *The Battle of Tamaai, 13 March 1884*, transferred from the York and Lancaster Regiment, 1998
unknown artist *Lieutenant Colonel Richard Lloyd (1777–1813)*, transferred from the Regimental Headquarters, Strensall, York, 1996
unknown artist *Richard Lovelock Coxe (1813–1844)*, transferred from the York and Lancaster Regiment, 1985
unknown artist *General C. Emilius Gold (1809–1871)*, transferred from the York and Lancaster Regiment, 1985

Swinton Community Library

Padfield, Philip *Andrew Carnegie (1835–1919)*, commissioned by Swinton Youth Action Group and transferred to Swinton Community Library, 2001

Dearne Valley College

Leadley, W. E. 1903–1973, *Manvers Colliery* (now the site of Dearne Valley College), gift from the artist's family

Facing page: Walker, Ethel, 1861–1951, *Portrait of a Girl* (detail), c.1910, Rotherham Museum & Art Gallery, (p. 152)

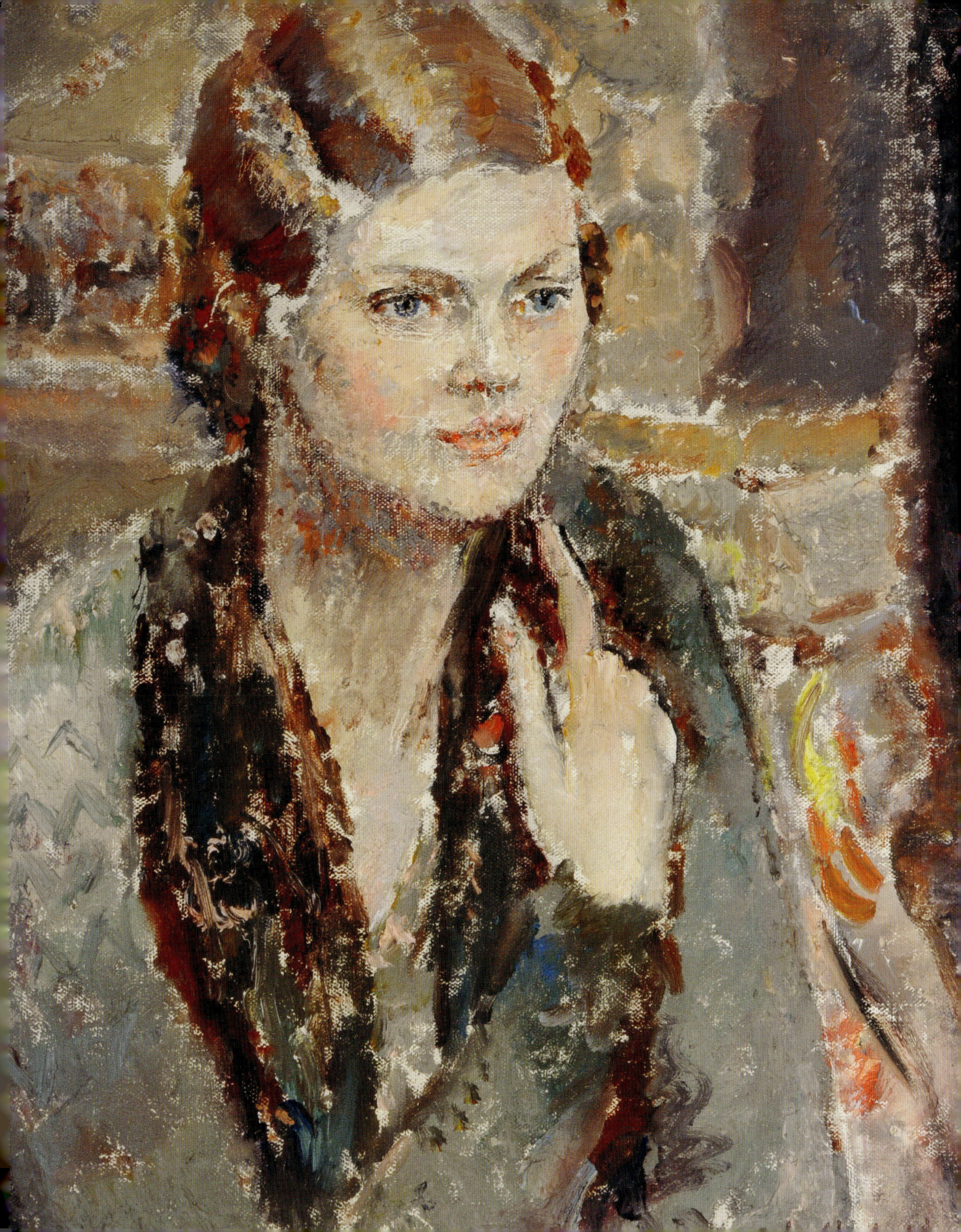

Collection Addresses

Barnsley

Barnsley Central Library
Shambles Street, Barnsley S70 2JF
Telephone 01226 773911

Barnsley College
PO Box 266, Church Street, Barnsley S70 2YW
Telephone 01226 216216

Barnsley Hospital NHS Foundation Trust
Gawber Road, Barnsley S75 2EP
Telephone 01226 432896

South Yorkshire Police
Churchfield, Barnsley S70 2DL
Telephone 01142 202020

The Cooper Gallery
Church Street, Barnsley S70 2AH
Telephone 01226 242905

Brodsworth

English Heritage, Brodsworth Hall
Brodsworth DN5 7XJ
Telephone 01302 722598

Cawthorne

Barnsley Museum and Heritage Service
Cannon Hall Museum, Bark House Lane
Cawthorne S75 4AT
Telephone 01226 790270

Cawthorne Victoria Jubilee Museum Trust
Taylor Hill, Cawthorne S75 4HQ
Telephone 01226 790545

The Regimental Museum of the 13th/18th Royal Hussars (QMO) and the Light Dragoons
Cannon Hall Museum, Bark House Lane
Cawthorne S75 4AT
Telephone 01226 790270

Doncaster

Doncaster and Bassetlaw Hospitals NHS Foundation Trust
Doncaster Royal Infirmary, Armthorpe Road
Doncaster DN2 5LT
Telephone 01302 366666

Doncaster College: The Hub
Chappell Drive, Doncaster DN1 2RF
Telephone 01302 553553

Doncaster Deaf Trust
Leger Way, Doncaster DN2 6AY
Telephone 01302 386722

Doncaster Magistrates' Court
College Road, Doncaster DN1 3HT
Telephone 01302 366711

Doncaster Mansion House
High Street, Doncaster, DN1 1BN
Telephone 01302 734032

Doncaster Museum Service:

Cusworth Hall and Park
Cusworth Lane, Doncaster DN5 7TU
Telephone 01302 782342

Doncaster Mansion House
High Street, Doncaster, DN1 1BN
Telephone 01302 734032

Doncaster Museum & Art Gallery
Chequer Road, Doncaster DN1 2AE
Telephone 01302 734293

The Regimental Museum of the King's Own Yorkshire Light Infantry
Doncaster Museum & Art Gallery, Chequer Road
Doncaster DN1 2AE
Telephone 01302 734293

Rotherham

Rawmarsh Community Library
c/o Clifton Park Museum
Clifton Lane, Rotherham S65 2AA
Telephone 01709 336633

Rotherham Museum & Art Gallery:

Clifton Park Museum
Clifton Lane, Rotherham S65 2AA
Telephone 01709 336633

Rotherham Art Gallery
Clifton Park Museum
Clifton Lane, Rotherham S65 2AA
Telephone 01709 336633

Rotherham Town Hall
Clifton Park Museum
Clifton Lane, Rotherham S65 2AA
Telephone 01709 336633

Thomas Rotherham College
Moorgate Road, Rotherham, S60 2BE
Telephone 01709 300600

York and Lancaster Regimental Museum
Clifton Park Museum
Clifton Lane, Rotherham S65 2AA
Telephone 01709 336633

Swinton

Swinton Community Library
c/o Clifton Park Museum
Clifton Lane, Rotherham S65 2AA
Telephone 01709 336633

Wath-upon-Dearne

Dearne Valley College
Manvers Park, Wath-upon-Dearne S63 7EW
Telephone 01709 513333

Index of Artists

In this catalogue, artists' names and the spelling of their names follow the preferred presentation of the name in the Getty Union List of Artist Names (ULAN) as of February 2004, if the artist is listed in ULAN.

The page numbers next to each artist's name below direct readers to paintings that are by the artist; are attributed to the artist; or, in a few cases, are more loosely related to the artist being, for example, 'after', 'the circle of' or copies of a painting by the artist. The precise relationship between the artist and the painting is listed in the catalogue.

Acknowledgements

The Public Catalogue Foundation would like to thank the individual artists and copyright holders for their permission to reproduce for free the paintings in this catalogue. Exhaustive efforts have been made to locate the copyright owners of all the images included within this catalogue and to meet their requirements. Copyright credit lines for copyright owners who have been traced are listed in the Further Information section.

The Public Catalogue Foundation would like to express its great appreciation to the following organisations for their kind assistance in the preparation of this catalogue:

Bridgeman Art Library
Flowers East
Marlborough Fine Art
National Association of Decorative & Fine Arts Societies (NADFAS)
National Gallery, London
National Portrait Gallery, London
Royal Academy of Arts, London
Tate

The participating collections included in this catalogue would like to express their thanks to the following organisations and individuals who have so generously enabled them to acquire paintings featured in this catalogue:

The Contemporary Art Society
Friends of Cannon Hall Museum, Park and Gardens
Friends of Doncaster Museums
Friends of The Cooper Gallery
Richard Green (for research into attributions at Brodsworth Hall)
The Heritage Lottery Fund
The Museums Libraries and Archives Council
The National Art Collections Fund (The Art Fund)
The National Heritage Memorial Fund
The Victoria and Albert Museum Purchase Grant Fund

The Public Catalogue Foundation

The Public Catalogue Foundation is a registered charity. It was launched in 2003 to create a photographic record of the entire national collection of oil, tempera and acrylic paintings in public ownership in the United Kingdom.

Whilst our public galleries and civic buildings hold arguably the greatest collection of oil paintings in the world, over 80 per cent of these are not on view. Few collections have a complete photographic record of their paintings let alone a comprehensive illustrated catalogue. What is publicly owned is not publicly accessible.

The Foundation is publishing a series of fully illustrated, county-by-county catalogues that will cover, eventually, the entire national UK collection. To date, it has published over 30 volumes, presenting over 72,000 paintings.

In partnership with the BBC, the Foundation will make its database of the entire UK collection of 200,000 oil paintings available online through a new website called *Your Paintings*. The website was launched in the summer of 2011.

Your Paintings (*www.bbc.co.uk/arts/yourpaintings*) offers a variety of ways of searching for paintings as well as further information about the paintings and artists, including links to the participating collections' websites. For those interested in paintings and the subjects they portray *Your Paintings* is an unparalleled learning resource.

Collections benefit substantially from the work of the Foundation, not least from the digital images that are given to them for free following photography, and from the increased recognition that the project brings. These substantial benefits come at no financial cost to the collections.

The Foundation is funded by a combination of support from individuals, charitable trusts, companies and the public sector although the latter provides less than 20 per cent of the Foundation's financial support.

Supporters

Master Patrons

The Public Catalogue Foundation is greatly indebted to the following Master Patrons who have helped it in the past or are currently working with it to raise funds for the publication of their county catalogues. All of them have given freely of their time and have made an enormous contribution to the work of the Foundation.

Peter Andreae *(Hampshire)*
Sir Henry Aubrey-Fletcher, Bt, Lord Lieutenant of Buckinghamshire *(Buckinghamshire)*
Sir Nicholas Bacon, DL, High Sheriff of Norfolk *(Norfolk)*
Sir John Bather, Lord Lieutenant of Derbyshire *(Derbyshire)*
The Hon. Mrs Bayliss, JP, Lord Lieutenant of Berkshire *(Berkshire)*
Ian Bonas *(County Durham)*
Peter Bretherton *(West Yorkshire: Leeds)*
Michael Brinton, Lord Lieutenant of Worcestershire *(Worcestershire)*
Sir Hugo Brunner, KCVO, JP *(Oxfordshire)*
Mr John Bush, OBE, Lord-Lieutenant of Wiltshire *(Wiltshire)*
Lady Butler *(Warwickshire)*
Richard Compton *(North Yorkshire)*
George Courtauld, DL, Vice Lord Lieutenant of Essex *(Essex)*

The Countess of Darnley, Lord Lieutenant of Herefordshire *(Herefordshire)*
The Marquess of Downshire *(North Yorkshire)*
Martin Dunne, Lord Lieutenant of Warwickshire *(Warwickshire)*
Sir Henry Elwes, KCVO, Lord-Lieutenant of Gloucestershire *(Gloucestershire)*
Jenny Farr, MBE, DL *(Nottinghamshire)*
John Fenwick *(Tyne & Wear Museums)*
Mark Fisher, MP *(Staffordshire)*
Patricia Grayburn, MBE, DL *(Surrey)*
The Earl of Halifax, KStJ, JP, DL *(East Riding of Yorkshire)*
Lord Roy Hattersley, PC *(South Yorkshire: Sheffield)*
Algy Heber-Percy, Lord Lieutenant of Shropshire *(Shropshire)*
The Lady Mary Holborow, Lord Lieutenant of Cornwall *(Cornwall)*
Sarah Holman *(Warwickshire)*
Tommy Jowitt *(West Yorkshire)*
Alderman Sir David Lewis, The Rt Hon. The Lord Mayor of London, 2007–2008 *(The City of London)*
Sir Michael Lickiss *(Cornwall)*
Magnus Linklater *(Scotland)*
Lord Marlesford, DL *(Suffolk)*
Dr Bridget McConnell *(Glasgow)*
Lady Sarah Nicholson *(County Durham)*
Malcolm V. L. Pearce, MP *(Somerset)*
Sir John Riddell, Lord Lieutenant of Northumberland *(Northumberland)*
Venetia Ross Skinner *(Dorset)*
The Most Hon. The Marquess of Salisbury, PC, DL *(Hertfordshire)*
Julia Somerville *(Government Art Collection)*
Tim Stevenson, OBE, Lord Lieutenant of Oxfordshire *(Oxfordshire)*
Phyllida Stewart-Roberts, OBE *(East Sussex)*
Lady Juliet Townsend, Lord Lieutenant of Northamptonshire *(Northamptonshire)*
Leslie Weller, DL *(West Sussex)*
Sir Samuel C. Whitbread, KCVO, Lord Lieutenant of Bedfordshire *(Bedfordshire)*

Financial support

The Public Catalogue Foundation is particularly grateful to the following organisations and individuals who have given it generous financial support since the project started in 2003.

National Sponsor

Christie's

Benefactors (£10,000–£50,000)

The 29th May 1961 Charitable Trust
Arts Council England
The Barbour Trust
Binks Trust
City of Bradford Metropolitan District Council
Deborah Loeb Brice Foundation
The Bulldog Trust
A. & S. Burton 1960 Charitable Trust
Christie's
City of London Corporation
The John S. Cohen Foundation
Covent Garden London
Creative Scotland
Department for Culture, Media and Sport
Sir Harry Djanogly, CBE
Mr Lloyd Dorfman
Dunard Fund
The Elmley Foundation
Fenwick Ltd
Fidelity UK Foundation
Marc Fitch Fund
The Foyle Foundation
J. Paul Getty Jr Trust
Hampshire County Council
The Charles Hayward Foundation
Peter Harrison Foundation
Mr Robert Hiscox
Hiscox plc
David Hockney, CH, RA
ICAP plc

The Jordan Charitable Foundation
Kent County Council
The Linbury Trust
The Manifold Trust
Paul Mellon Centre for Studies in British Art
The Mercers' Company
Robert Warren Miller
Mr & Mrs A. Mittal
The Monument Trust
Miles Morland
Allan and Carol Murray
National Gallery Trust
Stavros Niarchos Foundation
Norfolk County Council
Northern Rock Foundation
Nottingham City Council
Malcolm V. L. Pearce, MP
P. F. Charitable Trust
The Pilgrim Trust
Provident Financial
RAB Capital plc
The Radcliffe Trust
Renaissance East Midlands
Renaissance West Midlands
Renaissance Yorkshire
Saga Group Ltd
Scottish Government
The Bernard Sunley Charitable Foundation
Townsend Family Trust
University College, London
University of Leeds
The Walker Trust
The Wolfson Foundation
Sir Siegmund Warburg's Voluntary Settlement
Garfield Weston Foundation
Mr & Mrs A. H. Wilkinson
The Wixamtree Trust

Series Patrons
(Minimum donation of £2,500)

James & Lindsay Adam
Sir John Bather
Harry Bott
Janey Buchan
Mrs Rhona Callander
Dr Peter Cannon-Brookes
The John S. Cohen Foundation
Bushey Museum in memory of Lavender Watson
Mr Lloyd Dorfman
Lord Douro
Jenny Farr, MBE, DL
Mrs Greta Fenston
The FIRS Trust
Glasgow Museums
Patricia Grayburn, MBE, DL
G. Laurence Harbottle
R. K. Harrison Insurance Services Limited
Paul & Fiona Hart
Paul & Kathrine Haworth
Lord & Lady Heseltine
Patrik Holden & Lin Hinds
Neil Honebon
Michael Jacobson
Grace Jenkins
Dr David Johnson, DL
The Keatley Trust
John Kendall, Esq.
Michael A. Lambert, CBE
David & Amanda Leathers
Miles Morland
Allan & Carol Murray
North East Regional Museums Hub
The University of Northampton
Nottingham Civic Society
Richard & Amika Oldfield
The Roper Family Charitable Trust
Adam Sedgwick
Sir Harry & Lady Soloman
Stuart M. Southall
Simon Still
Chloe Teacher
University of Surrey
David & Cissy Walker
Tony Wilkinson
Mr & Mrs Jo Windsor
Mr & Mrs Charles Wyvill

Catalogue Patrons
(£1,000–£10,000)

The 29th May 1961 Charitable Trust
ACE Study Tours
Adams & Remers
Marcus & Kate Agius
The AIM Foundation
D. C. R. Allen
John Alston, CBE
Amberley Castle
The Astor Foundation
The Aylesford Family Charitable Trust
Chairman of Cornwall County Council, Mrs Doris Anson, OBE, JP
Archant Ltd

G. F. Armitage Family Charitable Trust
Mr Ian Askew
Aurelius Charitable Trust
The Bacon Charitable Trust
Lawrence Banks, CBE, DL
Barlow Robbins LLP
Mr James & Lady Emma Barnard
Basingstoke and Deane Borough Council
Bath & North East Somerset District Council Heritage Services
Robert Baxter, DL
Birmingham Common Good Trust
Sir Christopher Bland
Johnnie Boden
The Charlotte Bonham-Carter Charitable Trust
H. R. Pratt Boorman Family Foundation
A. J. H. du Boulay Charitable Trust
The Bowerman Charitable Trust
Viscountess Boyd Charitable Trust
Lord & Lady Bradbury
Bramdean Asset Management LLP
Peter Bretherton
Brewin Dolphin
J. & M. Britton Charitable Trust
Mrs T. Brotherton-Ratcliffe
Janey Buchan
Mr & Mrs Patrick Burgess
Mr & Mrs Mark Burrell
Arnold J. Burton Charitable Trust
Bushey Museum in Memory of Lavender Watson
Mrs Anne Cadbury, OBE, JP, DL
Roger Cadbury
C. J. R. & Mrs C. L. Calderwood
Sir Ralph Carr-Ellison
Mr & Mrs J. Chambers
Chichester District Council
His Honour Richard Cole, DL & Mrs Sheila Cole
The Timothy Colman Charitable Trust
Mr & Mrs Derek Coombs
The Helen Jean Cope Trust
Mr & Mrs Ian Copesteak
Cornwall County Council
Mr S. J. D. Corsan
Graeme Cottam & Gloriana Marks de Chabris
Coutts Charitable Trust
David Crane Trust
Elaine Craven, Earl Street Employment Consultants Ltd
Harriett Cullen
Culture North East
Rt Hon. Viscount Daventry
N. Davie-Thornhill
Brigadier Mike Dauncey, DSO, DL
De La Rue Charitable Trust
Mr Robert Dean
Deborah Gage (Works of Art) Ltd
Derek Johns Ltd, London
Derby City Council
Derby High School Trust Ltd
Derbyshire Building Society
Derbyshire Community Foundation (The Ashby Fund)
J. N. Derbyshire Trust
The Duke of Devonshire's Charitable Trust
S. Dewhirst Charitable Trust
Sir Harry Djanogly, CBE
Dorset County Council
Lord Douro
Professor Patrick & Dr Grace Dowling
Dunn Family Charitable Trust
East Sussex County Council
Eastbourne Borough Council
EEMLAC, through the Association for Suffolk Museums
Lord & Lady Egremont
Sir John & Lady Elliott
Andrew & Lucy Ellis
Peter & Judy Ellwood
Essex County Council
John & Felicity Fairbairn
Fairfield Charitable Trust
Jenny Farr, MBE, DL
John Feeney Charitable Trust
The Trustees of the Finnis Scott Foundation
The Fishmongers' Company
David & Ann FitzWilliam-Lay
Elizabeth & Val Fleming
The Follett Trust
Richard & Elizabeth Fothergill

Christopher & Catherine Foyle
Freemasons of Derbyshire
The Friends of Historic Essex
The Friends of the Laing Art Gallery
The Friends of the Royal Pavilion, Art Gallery & Museums, Brighton
The Friends of Southampton's Museums, Archives and Galleries
The Friends of Sunderland Museums
The Friends of York Art Gallery (E. J. Swift Bequest)
Philip Gibbs
The Hon. H. M. T. Gibson's Charity Trust
Lewis & Jacqueline Golden
The Goldsmiths' Company
Gorringes
Charles Gregson
The Grocers' Company
The Gulland Family
David Gurney
Philip Gwyn
Sir Ernest Hall
The Earl of Halifax, KStJ, JP, DL
The W. A. Handley Charity Trust
The Hartnett Charitable Trust
Hazlitt, Gooden & Fox Ltd
Heartwood Wealth Management Ltd
The Trustees of the King Henry VIII Endowed Trust, Warwick
The Rt Hon. the Lord Heseltine, CH, PC & Lady Heseltine
The Lady Hind Trust
Hobart Charitable Trust
Edward and Anna Hocknell
David Hockney CH, RA
Patrick Holden & Lin Hinds
Mrs Michael Hollingbery
The Holman Family
Mr & Mrs A. Holman-West
The Honourable Company of Gloucestershire
The Hope Scott Trust
David & Prue Hopkinson
Major & Mrs Bill Hutchinson
His Honour Gabriel Hutton
Isle of Wight Council
The J. and S. B. Charitable Trust
Alan & Penny Jerome
James & Lucilla Joll Charitable Trust
Mr & Mrs Peter Jones
Tommy Jowitt
The Keatley Trust
Kent Messenger Group
Garrett Kirk, Jr
Mr John Kirkland, OBE & Mrs Sheila Kirkland
Robert Kirkland
Kirklees Council
The David Laing Foundation
Landau Foundation
Lord Lea of Crondall, OBE
The Leche Trust
Leeds Art Collections Fund
Leeds City Council
Leeds Philosophical and Literary Society
The Hon. David Legh, DL
Lord Leverhulme's Charitable Trust
Mr & Mrs John Lewis
Mark & Sophie Lewisohn
Tom Lugg & the Lane Family
The Orr Mackintosh Foundation
The MacRobert Trust
Maidstone Borough Council
John Manser
Mr & Mrs Derek Mapp
Walter & Barbara Marais
The Marlay Group
Marshall Charitable Trust
Stephen & Carolyn Martin
Tom & Anne Martin
The Medlock Charitable Trust
The Piet Mendels Foundation
MLA East of England
MLA North East of England
Museums Galleries Scotland
Mr Paul Myners
Rupert Nabarro
Nancie Massey Charitable Trust
Newcastle City Council
Bryan Norman
Lord & Lady Northampton
The University of Northampton
NP Aerospace Ltd
Oakmoor Trust
Jasper & Virginia Olivier
The Orr Mackintosh Foundation
Mr Christopher Oughtred
The Owen Family Trust

Sir Idris Pearce
Roger Neville Russ Peers
The Pennycress Trust
Perkins Family
The Lord & Lady Phillimore
Mrs Margaret Pollett
Simon & Ursula Pomeroy
The Portland Family
Portsmouth City Council
George Pragnell Ltd
The Prince Philip Trust Fund for the Royal Borough of Windsor and Maidenhead
Provident Financial plc
Mr John Rank
Rathbone Investment Management Ltd
The Hans and Märit Rausing Charitable Trust
Roger & Jane Reed
Renaissance North East
Renaissance South East
Renaissance South West
Michael Renshall, CBE, MA, FCA
Sir John Riddell
Sir Miles & Lady Rivett-Carnac
Rockley Charitable Trust
Rolls-Royce plc
The Roper Family Charitable Trust
Rothschild Foundation
Royal Cornwall Museum
Graham & Ann Rudd
Sir Nigel Rudd
Russell New
The J. S. & E. C. Rymer Charitable Trust
The Earl St Aldwyn
The Sammermar Trust
Scarfe Charitable Trust
Andrew & Belinda Scott
The Trustees of the Finnis Scott Foundation
Shaftesbury PLC
Mr W. Sharpe
The Shears Foundation
Robert Shields, DL
Smith & Williamson
South West of England Regional Development Agency
Caroline M. Southall
Stuart M. Southall
Southampton City Council
The Jessie Spencer Trust
Hugh & Catherine Stevenson
Mrs Andrew Stewart-Roberts, OBE
Mr Michael Stone
Mr Peter Stormonth Darling
The Stratford-upon-Avon Town Trust
Strutt and Parker
Suffolk County Council, through the Association for Suffolk Museums
Surrey County Council
The John Swire 1989 Charitable Trust
The Tanner Trust
Tennants Auctioneers
Tesco Charity Trust
The Thistle Trust
Prof. Caroline Tisdall
Trusthouse Charitable Foundation
Gladwyn Turbutt
TWM Business Partners
Tyne & Wear Museums
University College Falmouth
University of Derby
University of Essex
David & Grizelda Vermont
Wakefield Metropolitan District Council
Robert & Felicity Waley-Cohen
The Peggy Walker Charitable Trust
The Walland Trust Fund
John Wates Charitable Trust
Leslie Weller, DL
The Welton Foundation
West Sussex County Council
Mr & Mrs David Wigglesworth
Wilkin & Sons Ltd
Mr & Mrs Jo Windsor
Peter Wolton Charitable Trust
Michael J. Woodhall, FRICS
Sir Philip Wroughton
Mrs Angela Yeoman

First published in 2012 by The Public Catalogue Foundation, Printed Catalogue Division, 8 Frederick's Place, London, EC2R 8AB

ISBN 978-1-904931-53-9

South Yorkshire photography: Norman Taylor

Designed by Sally Jeffery

Printed in Hong Kong by Paramount Printing Company Limited

Cover image:

Shackleton, William 1872–1933
The Eternal Dream (detail), c.1924
Doncaster Museum Service, (p. 98)

Back cover images (from top to bottom):

Heath, Adrian 1920–1992
Composition, 1960
The Cooper Gallery, (see p. 17)

Greuze, Jean-Baptiste 1725–1805
La polonaise, 1760–1765
Barnsley Museum and Heritage Service, (see p. 51)

Herring, John Frederick I 1795–1865
Finish of the 1827 Gold Cup, 1827
Doncaster Museum Service, (see p. 87)